Judicial Process in America

Judicial Process in America

SIXTH EDITION

Robert A. Carp, *University of Houston*

Ronald Stidham, *Appalachian State University*

Kenneth L. Manning, *University of Massachusetts Dartmouth*

CQ PRESS

A Division of Congressional Quarterly Inc.

Washington, D.C.

CQ Press
1255 22nd Street, N.W., Suite 400
Washington, D.C. 20037

(202) 729-1900; toll-free, 1-866-4CQ-PRESS (1-866-427-7737)

www.cqpress.com

Printed and bound in the United States of America

08   07   06   05   04   5   4   3   2   1

Grateful acknowledgment is made to the American Judicature Society for granting permission to reprint Tables 6-1 and 6-2 from *Judicature*, the journal of the American Judicature Society.

Photo credits: 1, 23, 57, 73, 98, 171, 229, 256, 281, 362, 389, AP/Wide World Photos; 325, Library of Congress; 111, 151, Reuters; 198, United Press International.

⊗ The paper used in this publication exceeds the requirements of the American National Standard for Information Sciences—Permanence of Paper for Printed Library Materials, ANSI Z39.48-1992.

LIBRARY OF CONGRESS CATALOGING-IN-PUBLICATION DATA

Carp, Robert A.
   Judicial process in America / Robert A. Carp, Ronald Stidham, Kenneth
L. Manning.— 6th ed.
        p.   cm.
Includes bibliographical references and index.
   ISBN 1-56802-828-8 (alk. paper)
   1. Justice, Administration of—United States.   2. Courts—United
States.   3. Judicial process—United States.   I. Stidham, Ronald
II. Manning, Kenneth L. (Kenneth Luis)   III. Title.
KF8700.C37   2004
347.73'1—dc22   2003026621

To the memory of my cousin David William Muchow
R. A. C.

To my grandson Caton Blair Stidham
R. S.

To my wife, Marcia, and daughter, Katherine
K. L. M.

Contents

Tables and Figures

Preface

Since the publication of the fifth edition of *Judicial Process in America* in 2001, many changes have taken place in the United States' political scene and its federal and state judicial systems. The tragic events of September 11, 2001, were a blow to the country not only in terms of lives and resources lost; they also engendered legislation, such as the USA Patriot Act, that threatens to compromise the very rights and liberties that Americans have prized for so long. In addition, the Supreme Court continues to teeter in its ideological balance between conservatives and moderates. With at least three justices leaning toward retirement, all eyes are on President George W. Bush in anticipation of how any new high court appointments will change the razor-thin ideological balance. Likewise, the nation focuses on the lower levels of the federal judiciary, whose members, about evenly divided between Republicans and Democrats at the beginning of the president's term, are likely to be in Republican control by the end of 2004. We await the policy consequences of this phenomenon.

At the state level, the tort reform movement continues in full throttle as more and more legislatures limit the size and nature of awards that civil litigants may win. Yet this is occurring at a time when civil damage awards against some wrongdoers are at all-time highs. Finally, evidence continues to mount that state courts are playing ever-increasing policy-making roles as more and more state programs and policies come under the scrutiny of state jurists. The Massachusetts Supreme Court's November 2003 ruling that it was illegal for the commonwealth to forbid same-sex couples to wed attracted national attention and stirred the country into debate on the policy implications of the issue.

Several changes, both in substance and in style, have been made in this sixth edition. In addition to comprehensive updating throughout the text on such topics as the roles of the courts in the war on terrorism, affirmative action, gay and lesbian rights, and business regulation, the book contains the first reporting of the voting patterns of the U.S. trial court judges appointed by President Bush. We compare and contrast the decisions of these district court jurists with those appointed by other American presidents to determine the relative ideological balance of the Bush judiciary. Second, we have changed the number and organization of the chapters for better flow and readability. Third, in the chapter "Decision Making in Collegial Courts," we have added a section that illustrates with a concrete example—the recent Supreme Court decisions on affirmative action at the University of Michigan—how the various decision-making models would explain how judges decide cases. The models that we use to describe this phenomenon include cue theory, small-group analysis, attitude theory, and rational choice. Fourth, we have expanded the number of comparative references and examples. Although we make no pretense that this is a true comparative judicial text, we continue to highlight with some frequency those aspects of the U.S. judicial system that are uniquely American and those that may be compared with the judicial practices of other nations. We also included a wide variety of countries as the sources of our comparisons—not just Canada or England, which have judiciaries most similar to the U.S. system. Fifth, we have added a new coauthor, Kenneth L. Manning, a bright and promising young scholar who has already published numerous articles in leading political science journals. Professor Manning is responsible for the analysis of the original data on U.S. trial judge voting patterns that appear in the text.

We have also made several pedagogical changes in this revision to better facilitate the efforts of students mastering new material. We are providing for the first time an annotated copy of the U.S. Constitution as an appendix. These annotations make references to those portions of the document that have generated important Supreme Court decisions and that significantly affect the lives of most Americans. As a second learning aid, we have moved the discussion questions that previously appeared at the beginnings of the chapters to their conclusions and retitled them "Further Thought and Discussion Questions." Our hope is that such hypothetical questions will be more useful to students after they have read the contents of the chapter rather than before. Finally, for easy reference, the important concepts and terms that appear in the glossary are bolded throughout the text.

As an additional learning aid, we encourage students to look up the Cornell University Supreme Court Collection (http://supct.law.cornell.edu/supct/), from which they can obtain summaries of Supreme Court decisions immediately after they are handed down by the justices—and at no cost to the students.

As with all editions of this book, we have taken care to prepare a text that is highly readable for both academic and general audiences. The primary emphasis is to offer full coverage of the federal courts, state judicial systems, the role of the lawyer in American society, the nature of crime, and public policy concerns that color the entire judicial fabric. The book is designed as a primary text for courses in judicial process and behavior; it is also useful as a supplement in political science classes in constitutional law, American government, and law and society. Likewise, it may serve as interesting reading in law-related courses in sociology, history, psychology, and criminology.

We have endeavored to use minimal jargon and theoretical vocabulary of political science and the law without being condescending to the student. We believe it is possible to provide a keen and fundamental understanding of the court systems and their impact on Americans' daily lives without assuming that all readers are budding political scientists or lawyers. At times, it is necessary and useful to employ technical terms and evoke theoretical concepts. Still, we address the basic questions on a level that is meaningful to an educated layperson. For students who may desire more specialized explanations or who wish to explore further some of the issues we discuss, the glossary, notes, and suggested readings contain ample resources.

We have also tried to avoid stressing any one theoretical framework for the study of courts and legal questions, such as a systems model approach or a judicial realist perspective. Instructors partial to the tenets of modern behavioralism will find much here to gladden their hearts, but we have also tried to include some of the insights that more traditional scholarship has provided over the years. The book reflects the contributions not only of political scientists and legal scholars but also of historians, psychologists, court administrators, and journalists.

Throughout the text we are constantly mindful of the interrelation between the courts and public policy. We have worked from the premise that significant portions of citizens' lives—both as individuals and as a nation—are affected by what federal and state judges choose to do and what they refrain from doing. We reject the common assumption that only liberals make public policy and only conservatives practice restraint. We believe that to some degree all judges engage in the inevitable activity of making policy. The question, as we see it, is not whether American judges make policy, but which directions their policy decisions take. In the chapters that follow we will explain why this has come to be, how it happens, and what the consequences are for the United States today.

As readers of previous editions of this text may note, the number of chapters has increased from thirteen to fifteen, and the chapters are now more similar in length than in former editions. In Chapter 1 we set the theoretical stage. We note Americans' great respect for the law, but we also document their traditional willingness to violate the law when it is morally, economically, or politically expedient to do so. We also examine sources of jurisprudence in the United States and several of the major philosophies concerning the role and function of law.

In Chapters 2 and 3, respectively, we examine the organizational structure and workloads of the federal and state judicial systems from a historical perspective. The federal and state judiciaries are the products of two centuries of evolution, trial and error, and a pinch of serendipity. The foreign intelligence surveillance court, which has gained a lot of attention since the September 11 attacks, is discussed in Chapter 2. The distinction between routine norm enforcement and policymaking by judges is first addressed in these two chapters. Chapter 3 also makes a special point of emphasizing the increasing policy-making role of state courts.

In Chapter 4 we outline the jurisdiction of the several levels of U.S. courts and discuss the political and nonjusticiable realms of American life into which judges in principle are not supposed to enter. We believe that a full understanding of how judges affect citizens' lives requires knowledge of those many substantive areas into which federal and state jurists may not roam.

Chapter 5, on state judges, highlights research on diversity on the state benches, new styles of judicial election campaigns, and money that is being spent on judicial elections.

In the sixth chapter, which focuses on the federal courts, we take a close look at the men and women who wear the black robe in the United States. What are their background characteristics and qualifications for office? How are they chosen? How are they socialized into their judicial roles, and under what circumstances can they be removed from office?

Chapter 7 examines the work and decision-making patterns of federal judges. We find a discernible policy link among the values of a majority of the voters in a presidential election, those of the appointing president, and the subsequent policy content of decisions made by judges nominated by the chief executive. Through the results of original research published here for the first time, we also offer an assessment of President Bush's impact on the ideological orientation of the federal judiciary.

Chapter 8 is about the role of lawyers in American society—their training, values, attitudes, and the public policy goals of their professional associations. In this chapter we also explore the importance of judicial lobbying and the impact of interest groups on the judicial process in both federal and state courts. Finally, because the roles of the U.S. attorney general and solicitor general have taken on added significance, we discuss their activities in waging the war on terrorism.

In Chapter 9 we focus on the nature of crime and on the various procedures prior to a criminal trial: the arrest, the appearance before a magistrate, the grand jury process, the arraignment, and the possibility of a plea bargain. We also discuss the adversarial process as it exists in American courtrooms.

Chapter 10 continues this theme by exploring the criminal trial itself and its aftermath. We examine the procedural rights of the criminal defendant, the process of selecting a jury, the roles of judge and jury during the trial, the sentencing process, and the possibility of an appeal.

In Chapter 11 we examine the civil court process. We begin with an analysis of the various types of civil cases and the options available to the complainant and the respondent. We then proceed through the various methods of alternative dispute resolution. Following that is a discussion of pretrial hearings and jury selection. Finally, we discuss the trial and judgment.

Chapter 12 is the first of two on judicial decision making. Here we outline those aspects of the decision-making process that are common to all judges, in the context of the legal subculture (the traditional legal reasoning model for explaining judges' decisions) and the democratic subculture (a number of extralegal factors that appear to be associated with judges' policy decisions).

In Chapter 13 we examine the special case of decision making in collegial appellate courts. We explore the assumptions and contributions of cue theory, small-group analysis, attitude theory, and the rational choice model.

In Chapter 14 we explore the policy impact of decisions made by federal and state courts and analyze the process by which some judicial rulings are implemented and some are not.

Chapter 15 has two general goals: to outline the primary factors that impel judges to engage in policymaking and to suggest the variables that determine the ideological direction of such policymaking.

Many people contributed to the writing of this book, and to all of them we offer sincere thanks. At CQ Press, we would like to thank Charisse Kiino, Michael Kerns, Rita Matyi, and Joan Gossett. Lauren Bell at Randolph-Macon College; Scott A. Camparato at Southern Illinois University, Carbondale; and Karen M. Hult at Virginia Polytechnic Institute and State University offered helpful suggestions for updating and improving the text, and we appreciate their assistance. We also would like to express our gratitude to Janet Wilson for her excellent copyediting of the final version of the text. We assume responsibility for any errors that remain.

Robert A. Carp thanks his research assistant, Cameron Matthews, who helped code the decisions of the federal district judges that served as the basis for Tables 7-1, 12-1, and 12-2 and Figure 7-1.

Ronald Stidham would like to express his gratitude to his colleagues in the Political Science/Criminal Justice Department at Appalachian State University. Their friendship and support greatly facilitated the process of writing this new edition. He also thanks his research assistant, Brooke Heafner, for her help in finding information and checking sources in the library.

Kenneth L. Manning wishes to thank his research assistants Erin Murtagh, Brendan Surpless, Oliver Surpless, and Joelle Sylvia for their efforts in data collection.

Robert A. Carp
Ronald Stidham
Kenneth L. Manning

CHAPTER 1

Foundations of Law in the United States

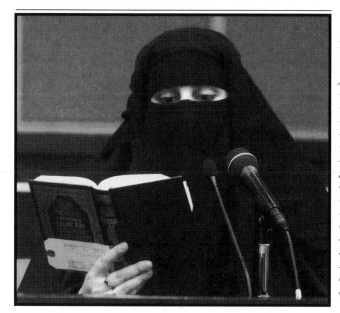

Mrs. Sultaana Freeman, a devout Muslim, refused to remove her full-face veil in order to be photographed for her Florida driver's license. Florida, in turn, denied her a license. Her case epitomizes the conflict between the right of the government to maintain security and the right of individuals to exercise their religion freely. Here, an evidence tag is seen on a Quran that was submitted as part of Mrs. Freeman's pending court case appealing the denial of her license.

I N JANUARY 2002 THE STATE of Florida revoked the driver's license of Mrs. Sultaana Freeman. But what was her offense? Had she killed someone when driving while intoxicated, or had she received an excessive number of reckless-driving citations? Nothing of the sort. Mrs. Freeman, in accordance with her religious tradition, had refused to allow her driver's photo to be taken in a manner that revealed her uncovered face. In so doing she initiated a legal proceeding that encompassed such diverse issues as free exercise of religion; national security in light of the September 11, 2001, terrorist attacks on America; the immediate safety needs of Florida's Department of Highway Safety and Motor Vehicles; and the degree to which this woman might have been singled out for discrimination because of her Muslim faith.

The story began during the winter of 2002—just a few months after the terrorist attacks and during a time when security concerns were at their highest and anger and fear were directed at radical elements within the Muslim community. Mrs. Freeman, a thirty-five-year-old mother of two from Winter Park, would not agree to be photographed without her *niqab*, a full-face veil revealing only the eyes that is worn by many traditional Muslim women. During a three-day nonjury trial held in

1

Orlando in May 2003, Mrs. Freeman argued that it was a violation of her religious beliefs to expose her face to strangers or to men outside her immediate family. The state of Florida counterargued that the government had a compelling interest in promoting public safety, and that this interest was served by providing law enforcement officials with full-face photos on driver's licenses in order to quickly verify a person's identity. The state even offered to allow Mrs. Freeman to lift her veil in a closed room in the presence of a female photographer, but the offer was refused. Religious principles are religious principles.

In a sixteen-page opinion, Florida circuit court judge Janet Thorpe ruled in favor of the state of Florida. After agreeing with the state's arguments about the need for law officers to easily and accurately verify a person's identity, the judge went on to speculate about new safety concerns in light of the post-9/11 world. While conceding that Mrs. Freeman "most likely poses no threat to national security," the jurist speculated about the future possibility of terrorists pretending "to ascribe to religious beliefs in order to carry out activities that would threaten lives." What about the contention that Mrs. Freeman was being singled out for special, egregious treatment that would not be given to individuals who came from America's more traditional, mainstream religions? Not so, contended Judge Thorpe. She stated: "This court would rule the same way for anyone—Christian, Jew, Buddhist, atheist—who wished to have his or her driver's license identification photo taken while wearing anything—ski mask, costume mask, religious veil, hood—which cloaks all facial features except the eyes."

Responding to Judge Thorpe's decision, Howard Simon, executive director of Florida's American Civil Liberties Union (ACLU), said: "Today's ruling runs counter to the most basic principles of religious freedom that give everyone—including members of minority religious communities as well as majority Christian faiths— the right to practice and worship as they choose." [1] The case is currently on appeal.

This factual account reveals much about the United States and the rule of **law,** and it suggests themes that we will articulate not only in this chapter but throughout much of the book: How should individuals respond when obeying the law violates deeply held moral or religious beliefs? Depending on how one views a particular question, can it be at the same time a local issue, a federal question, and a matter that is part of a worldwide clash of interests? How much discretion do law enforcement officials and judges possess and to what degree is the exercise of their discretion a function of their own backgrounds and personal values?

We begin our discussion of the foundations of law in the United States with a look at the law itself. This is appropriate because without law there would be no courts and no judges, no political or judicial system through which disputes could be settled and decisions rendered. In this chapter we examine the sources of law in the United States, that is, the institutions and traditions that establish the rules of the legal game. We discuss the particular types of law that are used and define some of the basic legal terms. Likewise, we will explore the functions of law for society—what it enables citizens to avoid and accomplish as individuals and as a people that would be impossible without the existence of some commonly accepted rules. Finally, we examine America's ambivalent tradition vis-à-vis the law, that is, how a nation founded on an illegal revolution and nurtured with a healthy tradition of civil disobedience can pride itself on being a land where respect for the law is ideally taught at every mother's knee. We also take note of the degree to which American society has become highly litigious and why this is significant for the study of the American judicial system.

Definition of Law

A useful definition of American law postulates that "law is a social norm the infraction of which is sanctioned in threat or in fact by the application of physical force by a party possessing the socially recognized privilege of so acting." [2] This definition suggests that law comprises three basic elements—force, official authority, and regularity—the combination of which differentiates law from mere custom or morals in society.

In an ideal society, force would never have to be exercised; in an imperfect world, the threat of its use is a foundation of any law-abiding society. Although substitutes for physical force may be used, such as confiscation of property or imposition of fines, the possibility of physical punishment must nevertheless remain to deter a potential lawbreaker. The right to apply this force constitutes the official element of the definition of law. The party that exercises this right of physical coercion represents a valid legal authority. Finally, the term *regularity*, as used in the legal sense, can be likened to its use by scientists. While the term does not reflect absolute certainty, it does suggest uniformity and consistency. The law calls for a degree of predictability, of regularity, in the way individuals are expected to behave or to be treated by the state. In American society, this emphasis on regularity is manifested by adherence to prior court decisions and precedents (the **common law** doctrine of **stare decisis**) and also by the mandate of the Fourteenth Amendment to the U.S. Constitution, which forbids the state to "deny to any person within its **jurisdiction** the *equal protection* of the law" (emphasis added).

Sources of Law in the United States

Where does law come from in the United States? At first the question seems a bit simple-minded. A typical response might be: "Law comes from legislatures; that's what Congress and the state legislatures do." This answer is not wrong, but it is far from adequate. Law comes from a large variety of sources.

Constitutions

The U.S. Constitution is the primary source of law in the United States, as it claims to be in Article VI: "This Constitution . . . shall be the supreme Law of the Land; and the Judges in every State shall be bound thereby, any Thing in the Constitution or Laws of any State to the Contrary notwithstanding." Thus none of the other types of law may stand if they are in conflict with the Constitution. Similarly, each state has its own separate constitution, and all local laws must yield to its supremacy.

Acts of Legislative Bodies

Laws passed by Congress and by state legislatures constitute a sizable bulk of law in the United States. Statutes requiring the payment of income tax to Uncle Sam and state laws forbidding the robbing of banks are both examples. But many other types of legislative bodies also enact statutes and ordinances that regulate the lives of U.S. residents. County commissioners (also known as county judges or boards of selectmen), for example, act as legislative bodies for the various counties within the states.

Likewise, city councils serve in a legislative capacity when they pass ordinances, set property tax rates, establish building codes, and so on at the municipal level. Then there are almost fifty thousand "special districts" throughout the country, each of which is headed by an elected or appointed body that acts in a legislative capacity. Examples of these would be school districts, fire prevention districts, water districts, and municipal utility districts.

Decisions of Quasi-Legislative and Quasi-Judicial Bodies

Sprinkled vertically and horizontally throughout the U.S. governmental structure are thousands of boards, agencies, commissions, departments, and so on, whose primary function is not to legislate or to adjudicate but that still may be called on to make rules or to render decisions that are semilegislative or semijudicial in character. The job of the U.S. Postal Service is to deliver the mail, but sometimes it may have to act in a quasi-judicial capacity. For example, a local postmaster may refuse to deliver a piece of mail because he or she believes it to be pornographic. (Congress has mandated that pornography may not be sent through the mail.) The postmaster is acting in a semi- or quasi-judicial capacity in determining that a particular item is pornographic and hence not protected by the First Amendment.

The Securities and Exchange Commission is not basically a lawmaking body either, but when it determines that a particular company has run afoul of the securities laws or when it rules on a firm's qualification to be listed on the New York Stock Exchange, it becomes a source of law in the United States. In effect, it makes rules and decisions that affect a person's or a company's behavior and for which penalties are imposed for noncompliance. Although decisions of such agencies may be appealed to or reviewed by the courts, they are binding unless and until they are overturned by a judicial entity.

A university's board of regents may also be a source of law for the students, faculty, and staff members covered by its jurisdiction. These boards may set rules on such matters as which persons may lawfully enter the campus grounds, procedures to be followed before a staff member may be fired, or definitions of plagiarism. Violations of these rules or procedures carry penalties backed by the full force of the law.

Orders and Rulings of Political Executives

History classes teach that legislatures make the law and executives enforce the law. That is essentially true, but political executives also have some lawmaking capacity. This lawmaking occurs when presidents, governors, mayors, or others fill in the details of legislation passed by legislative bodies and sometimes when they promulgate orders purely in their executive capacity.

When Congress passes reciprocal trade agreement legislation, the goal is to encourage other countries to lower trade and tariff barriers to U.S.-produced goods, in exchange for which the United States will do the same. But there are so many thousands of goods, almost two hundred countries, and countless degrees of setting up or lowering trade barriers. What to do? The customary practice is for Congress not only to set basic guidelines for the reciprocal lowering of trade barriers but also to allow the president to decide how much to regulate a given tariff on any given commodity for a particular country. These executive orders of the president are published regularly in the *Federal Register* and carry the full force of law.

Another current example of an executive order came in November 2001, when America was still in shock from the 9/11 terrorist attacks. President George Bush signed an order that allowed prosecutors to bypass the U.S. criminal justice system and swiftly convict foreigners involved in acts of terror. Under the Bush order, the chief executive would determine who should be tried in the American court system and who should be prosecuted in a military court set up by the secretary of defense in whatever country he would deem appropriate.[3]

Likewise at the state level, when a legislature delegates to the governor the right to "fill in the details of legislation," the state executive uses his or her **ordinance-making power,** which also is a type of lawmaking capacity.

Political executives may promulgate orders that, within certain narrow but important realms, constitute the law of the land. For example, in the wake of a natural disaster such as a flood or tornado, a mayor may declare an official state of emergency that empowers him or her to issue binding rules of behavior for a limited period of time. A curfew ordering persons to be off the streets at a given hour is an example of a law made by a municipal chief executive. Though limited and usually temporary, such orders are law, and violations invoke penalties.

Judicial Decisions

History classes also teach that judges interpret the law. So they do, but judges make law as they interpret it. And judicial decisions themselves constitute a body of law in the United States. All the thousands upon thousands of court decisions that have been handed down by federal and state judges for the past two centuries are part of the **corpus juris**—the body of law—of the United States.

Judicial decisions may be grounded in or surround a variety of entities: any of the above-mentioned sources of law, past decisions of other judges, or legal principles that have evolved over the centuries. (For example, one cannot bring a lawsuit on behalf of another person unless that person is one's minor child or ward.) Judicial decisions may also be grounded in the common law, that is, those written (and sometimes unwritten) legal traditions and principles that have served as the basis of court decisions and accepted human behavior for many centuries. For instance, if a couple lives together as husband and wife for a specified period of years, the common law may be invoked to have their union recognized as a legal marriage.

Types of Law

After examining the wellsprings of American law, it is appropriate to take a brief look at the vessels wherein such laws are contained, that is, to define or explain the formal types of categories of law. (Note that types of law are not necessarily mutually exclusive.)

Codified (or Code) Law

Unlike the United States, most countries (including most of Europe and Latin America) refer to themselves as code law countries. A code is merely a body of laws, but it is one that consists of statutes enacted by a national parliament. These laws address virtually all aspects of the body politic, are often detailed, and are arranged in an orderly, systematic, and comprehensive manner. The U.S. legal system is often seen from abroad as a hodgepodge of legislative acts, judicial decisions, unwritten legal traditions, and so on.

Statutory Law and Common Law

Statutory law is the type of law enacted by a legislative body such as Congress, a state legislature, or a city council, although it could also include the written orders of various quasi-legislative bodies. The key here is that the enactments be in written form and be addressed to the needs of society as a whole. Examples of statutory law would be a congressional act increasing Social Security payments or a statute passed by a state legislature authorizing the death penalty for first-degree murder. Statutory law is often contrasted with the common law, which is a less orderly compilation of traditions, principles, and legal practices that have been handed down from one generation of lawyers and judges to the next. Because much of the common law is not systematically codified and delineated, as is statutory law, it is sometimes referred to as the unwritten law. However, this is not entirely accurate. Much of the common law exists in the form of court decisions and legal precedents that are in written form. The common law is known for its flexibility and capacity to change as it evolves in response to the changing needs and values of society.

Civil Law and Criminal Law

Civil law deals with disagreements between individuals—for example, a dispute over ownership of private property. It also deals with corporations, admiralty matters, and contracts. **Criminal law** pertains to offenses against the state itself—actions that may be directed against a person but that are deemed to be offensive to society as a whole. **Crimes** such as drunken driving, armed robbery, and so on are punishable by fines or imprisonment.

Equity

Equity is best understood when contrasted with law; the primary difference between the two terms is in the remedy involved. At law, the only remedy is financial compensation; in equity, a judge is free to issue a remedy that will either prevent or

of life. As population expands and modern transportation and communication further link people together, every action that each individual takes affects another either directly or indirectly, possibly causing harm. When conflict results, it must be resolved peaceably, using a rule of law. Otherwise, disorder, death, and chaos reign. Some common set of rules must exist that all agree to live by—a rule of law and order.

But what kind of law and order? The anarchist's argument that laws restrict personal freedom is correct. If there are too many rules, laws, and restrictions, totalitarianism results. That may be just about as bad as a state of anarchy. The trick is to strike a balance so that the positive things that law can do are not strangulated by the tyranny of the law and order offered by the totalitarian state.

Assuming, then, that both anarchy and totalitarianism are rejected, what are the positive functions of law when it exists to a reasonable degree? Legal theorists denote several.

Providing Order and Predictability in Society

The world is chaotic and uncertain. People win lotteries while stock markets collapse; more and more persons are living to the age of one hundred while thousands died in the terrorist attacks on the World Trade Center; some ranchers manage to enlarge their herds at the time of a beef shortage while corn farmers suffer from the worst drought in decades. Laws can neither avert most natural disasters nor prevent random episodes of misfortune, but they can create an environment in which people can work, invest, and pursue pleasure with a reasonable expectation that their activity is worth the effort. Without an orderly environment based on and backed by law, the normal activities of life would be lacerated with chaos.

For example, rules must be established that determine which side of the road to drive on, how fast cars can safely go, and when to slow down and stop. Without rules of the road, horrible traffic jams and terrible accidents would result because no driver would know what to expect from the others. Without a climate of law and order, no parent would have the incentive to save for a child's college education. The knowledge that the bank will not close and that one's savings account will not be arbitrarily confiscated by the government or by some powerful party gives the parent an environment in which to save. Law and the predictability it provides cannot guarantee a totally safe and predictable world, but it can create a climate in which people believe it is worthwhile to produce, to venture forth, and to live for the morrow.

Resolving Disputes

No matter how benign and loving people can be at times, altercations and disagreements are inevitable. How disputes are resolved between quarreling individuals, corporations, or governmental entities reveals much about the level and quality of the rule of law in a society. Without an orderly, peaceful process for dispute resolution, there is either chaos or a climate in which the largest gang of thugs or those with the strongest fists prevail.

Suppose a new fraternity house is built next to the home of Mr. Joe Six-Pack, a man who likes his peace and quiet. After Joe's sleep has been disrupted for the umpteenth time by loud music coming from the fraternity house, Joe decides to get even. About sunrise one Sunday, after another sleepless night, Joe angrily runs over to his neighbor's parking lot and systematically begins to let air out of the tires of the students' cars—"just to teach those damn kids a lesson." He is caught in the act by several well-soused fraternity boys marking the end of a raucous night. Angry words are exchanged; "manhood" and "right-and-wrong" are at stake. A brawl ensues, resulting in bloodshed and injury all around. How much better the outcome would have been if Joe had turned this grievance over to the police, the courts, or campus authorities—all empowered by the law to peacefully resolve such matters.

Protecting Individuals and Property

Even libertarians, who take a narrow view of the role of government, will readily acknowledge that the state must protect citizens from the outlaw who would inflict bodily harm or steal or destroy their worldly goods. Because of the importance of the safety of persons and their property, many laws on the books deal with protection and security. Not only are laws in the criminal code intended to punish those who steal and do bodily harm, but civil statutes also permit many crime victims to sue for monetary **damages**. The law has created police and sheriffs' departments, district attorneys' offices, courts, jails, and death chambers to deter and punish the criminal and to help people feel secure. This is not to say that there is no crime; everyone knows otherwise. But without a system of laws, crime would be much more prevalent and the fear of it would be much more paralyzing. Unless everyone could afford to hire his or her own bodyguards and security teams, people would be in constant anxiety about the potential loss of life, limb, and property. However imperfect the system of law, prevention, and enforcement may be, it is certainly better than none.

Providing for the General Welfare

Laws and the institutions and programs they establish enable a society to do corporately what would be impossible, or at least prohibitive, for individuals to do. Providing for the common defense, educating young people, putting out forest fires, controlling pollution, and caring for the sick and aged are all examples of activities that could be done only feebly, if at all, by an individual acting alone but that can be done efficiently and effectively as a society. Citizens may disagree about which endeavors should be undertaken through the government by law. Some may believe, for example, that the aged should be cared for by family members or by private charity; others see such care as a corporate responsibility. Although citizens can disagree about the precise activities that the law should require of government, few would deny that many significant and beneficial results are achieved through corporate endeavors. After all, the foundation of the American legal system, the Constitution, was ordained to "establish Justice, insure domestic Tranquility, provide for the common defence, promote the general Welfare, and secure the Blessings of Liberty to ourselves and our Posterity."

Protecting Individual Liberties

Law should protect the individual's personal and civil rights against those forces that would curtail or restrict them. These basic freedoms might include those provided for in the Bill of Rights, such as freedom of speech, of religion, and of the press, the right to a fair trial, and freedom from cruel and unusual punishment. They might also include some that are not stated in the Bill of Rights but are implied, such as the right to personal privacy, or they might be rights that Congress has provided through legislation, such as the right to be free from job discrimination based on gender or ethnic origin. Potential violators of these freedoms might be the government itself (for example, a law denying American citizens accused of terrorist acts the right to a civilian trial) or one's fellow citizens (for example, a conspiracy among private individuals to discourage certain persons from voting). Although disagreement may arise about which freedoms are basic or about how extensively they should be provided for, it is fair to say that unless the law protects certain basic immutable rights, the nation's citizens are no more than cogs in a machine. It is the meaningful provision for these basic liberties that ensures the dignity and richness of the life of the individual.

The United States and the Rule of Law

Americans pride themselves on being a law-abiding people, and to the casual observer they are. Few would question Abraham Lincoln's admonition that respect for the law should be taught to every child at his or her mother's knee, and most are glad to proclaim that the United States has a government of law, not of individuals. The fact that almost 6.5 million citizens are imprisoned or on parole on any given day is seen not as evidence that society is lawless but as proof that in the United States respect for the law is paramount and disobedience of the law is punished.[5] A careful analysis of U.S. history and traditions reveals, however, that this view of the law has in reality been ambivalent. A few examples will illustrate Americans' love-hate relationship with the rule of law.

An appropriate place to begin is the Revolutionary War. Few Americans can look back on that seven-year struggle and feel anything but pride when certain images come to mind: the bold act of defiance of the Boston Tea Party, the shot fired at Concord that was "heard 'round the world," and George Washington's daring attack on the Hessian troops at Trenton. Despite the goose bumps raised in this patriotic reverie, one bothersome fact is lost—the Revolution was illegal. The wanton destruction of private property wrought by the Boston Tea Party and the killing of British troops sent to America for the colonists' protection were illegal in every sense of the word. The Founders were so keenly aware of this that they prepared a Declaration of Independence to justify to the rest of the world why a bloody and illegal revolt against the lawful government is sometimes permissible:

When in the Course of human events, it becomes necessary for one people to dissolve the political bands which have connected them with another, . . . a decent respect to the opinions of mankind requires that they should declare the causes which impel them to the separation. . . . [W]hen a long train of abuses and usurpations . . . evinces a design to reduce them under absolute Despotism, it is their right, it is their duty, to throw off such Government, and to provide new Guards for their future security.

The irony of America's birth is often overlooked. This citadel of law and order was born under the star of illegality and revolution.

Another example is John Brown's famous raid on the U.S. arsenal at Harpers Ferry, West Virginia, in the fall of 1859. With thirteen white men and five black men, this militant opponent of slavery began his plan to lead a mass insurrection among the slaves and to create an abolitionist republic on the ruins of the South and its plantation economy. After a small but bloody battle that lasted several days, Brown was captured, given a public trial, and duly hanged for murder and other assorted crimes. But were Brown's flagrantly violent and illegal actions justifiable, given the nobility of his vision? Many in the North believed so. Its moral and cultural elite took the line that Brown might have been insane, but his acts and intentions should be excused on the grounds that the compelling motive was divine. Horace Greeley wrote that the Harpers Ferry raid was "the work of a madman," but he had not "one reproachful word." Ralph Waldo Emerson described Brown as a "saint." Henry David Thoreau, Theodore Parker, Henry Wadsworth Longfellow,

William Cullen Bryant, and James Lowell—the whole Northern pantheon—took the position that Brown was an "angel of light," and that it was not Brown but the society that hanged him that was mad. It was also reported that "on the day Brown died, church bells tolled from New England to Chicago; Albany fired off one hundred guns in salute, and a governor of a large Northern state wrote in his diary that men were ready to march to Virginia."[6] Again the ambivalence is evident: One ought always to obey the law—unless one hears a divine call that transcends the law.

The civil rights movement beginning in the 1950s caused many Americans to be torn between their natural desire to obey the law of the land and their call to change the system. As the Reverend Martin Luther King Jr. sat in a Birmingham, Alabama, jail, he wrote a now famous letter to supporters who were disturbed by his having disobeyed the law during his civil rights protests:

You express a great deal of anxiety over our willingness to break laws. This is certainly a legitimate concern. Since we would diligently urge people to obey the Supreme Court's decision in 1954 outlawing segregation in the public schools, at first glance it may seem rather paradoxical for us consciously to break laws. One may well ask: "How can you advocate breaking some laws and obeying others?" The answer lies in the fact that there are two types of laws: just and unjust. I would be first to advocate obeying just laws. One has not only a legal but a moral responsibility to obey just laws. Conversely, one has a moral responsibility to disobey unjust laws. . . . Thus it is that I can urge men to obey the 1954 decision of the Supreme Court, for it is morally right; and I can urge them to disobey segregation ordinances, for they are morally wrong.[7]

Even a member of the Supreme Court of the United States sanctioned civil disobedience during the heady days of the civil rights movement. Justice Abe Fortas said:

If I had been a Negro living in Birmingham or Little Rock or Plaquemines Parish, Louisiana, I hope I would have disobeyed the state laws that said that I might not enter the public waiting room in the bus station reserved for "Whites." I hope I would have insisted upon going into parks and swimming pools and schools which state or city law reserved for "Whites." I hope I would have had the courage to disobey, although the segregation ordinances were presumably law until they were declared unconstitutional.[8]

Those who opposed the civil rights movement and the Supreme Court decisions and congressional statutes that supported it likewise believed that their form of civil disobedience was in response to a higher calling. Quoting Scripture as support for their belief that God created the white race separately from the colored races, segregationists argued that it was the divine will to keep the races apart. Thus defiance of integration orders was seen by many traditionalists as keeping in touch with the natural order of the universe as God had established it. That black and white should not mix with one another was believed to be "a self-evident truth," not to be overturned by the courts' desegregation orders.

The pro-life offensive conducted during the past two decades by opponents of abortion is another example of how basically law-abiding persons may be ready and willing to break the law in response to what they believe is a higher calling. For example, after former preacher Paul Hill was sentenced to death for having murdered a doctor and his unarmed escort at an abortion clinic in Pensacola, Florida, he said: "I know for a fact that I'm going to go to heaven when I die. I am certainly guilty of no crimes. . . . My actions are honorable." Deeds less drastic than Hill's include "rescue actions" at abortion clinics all across the country conducted by protesters who have blocked access to these facilities and harassed doctors and nurses. Arrests of abortion protesters now number in the tens of thousands.[9]

Civil disobedience does not need a divine call. Ample illustrations exist of the wholesale avoidance of laws that were thought to be economically harmful and unfair or that were seen as beyond the rightful authority of the state to enact.

American farmers are probably as law abiding a segment of the population as any, but they, too, can thwart the law when their economic livelihood is at stake. During George Washington's administration, state militias were activated and sent out to quash what came to be known as the Whiskey Rebellion, a series of lawless acts by the tillers of the soil who objected to the federal tax on their homemade elixirs. And during the terrible Great Depression days of the 1930s, when, for example, one-third of the state of Iowa was being sold into bankruptcy, farmers often revolted. Thousands with shotguns held at bay local sheriffs who tried to serve papers on fellow farmers about to be dispossessed.

During the Prohibition era, from 1919 to 1933, many Americans refused to obey a law they regarded as unfair and in excess of the legitimate bounds of state authority. Not only did the laws prohibiting the production and sale of alcohol prove to be ineffective and unenforceable, but Americans also seemed to relish flouting the law. The statistics on Prohibition enforcement reveal how the laws were honored in the breach. In 1921 the government seized a total of 95,933 illicit distilleries, stills, still worms, and fermenters; this number went to 172,537 by 1925 and jumped to 282,122 by 1930.[10] By 1932 President Herbert Hoover, who had originally supported Prohibition, began to talk about "the futility of the whole business."

In many states it is against the law to engage in certain sexual activities, such as fornication and adultery. Indeed at the present time it is illegal in seven states for even straight couples to live together without being married.[11] That these laws are seldom obeyed or enforced is a secret to no one. Although most Americans still approve of forbidding sexual practices and acts that they find personally distasteful, few have much enthusiasm for putting police officers in every bedroom or for strictly enforcing laws that touch on very personal issues. There is some indication that the days may be numbered for laws dictating the nature of intimate relations between consenting adults. For example, on June 26, 2003, the Supreme Court struck down the Texas law that outlawed homosexual sex.[12]

So, are Americans a law-abiding people or not? Is respect for the law only superficial and the belief that everyone ought to obey the law mere cant? The truth, it would appear, is that Americans do honestly have great respect for the law and that their abhorrence of lawbreakers is genuine. But it is also fair to say that mixed with this tradition and orientation is a long-standing belief that sometimes people are called to respond to values higher than the ordinary law and thereby to engage in illegal behavior. However, one person's command to disobey the law and follow the dictates of conscience will appear to another as mere foolishness. Furthermore, Americans have a hefty pragmatic tradition vis-à-vis the law. Laws that drive citizens to the wall economically (such as farm foreclosures during the 1930s) and laws that are seen to needlessly impinge upon personal matters (such as Prohibition and laws forbidding couples to live together without being married) are just not taken as seriously as those that forbid bank robbery and rape.

Like the law, judges are viewed ambivalently by Americans. In general, judges are held in inordinately high esteem, and most Americans would be proud if a son or daughter achieved this position. Yet Americans can be quick to condemn judges whose rulings go against deeply held values or whose decisions are not in the best interests of their pocketbooks.[13] Whether this is hypocrisy or merely the complex and ambivalent nature of humankind is perhaps in the eye of the beholder.

A Litigious Society

The raw statistics reveal that Americans readily look to the courts to redress their grievances. The quarter of a million suits that are filed in the federal courts each year are dwarfed by the 100 million suits filed in the courts of the fifty states and the District of Columbia. That works out to about one for every two people in the United States. Although many of these deal with relatively minor matters, about 12 million are filed in the major state and federal trial courts. As one contemporary expert has noted:

Ours is a law-drenched age. Because we are constantly inventing new and better ways of bumping into one another, we seek an orderly means of dulling the blows and repairing the damage. Of all the known methods of redressing grievances and settling disputes—pitched battle, rioting, dueling, mediating, flipping a coin, suing—only the latter has steadily won the day in these United States.

Though litigation has not routed all other forms of fight, it is gaining public favor as the legitimate and most effective means of seeking and winning one's just deserts.

The impulse to sue is so widespread that "litigation has become the nation's secular religion," and a growing array of procedural rules and substantive provisions is daily gaining its adherents.[14]

It is useful to see Americans' love affair with lawsuits in some type of comparative perspective. Cross-national comparisons reveal that while the United States is a litigious society, citizens in many other industrialized nations institute about an equal amount of civil litigation. Americans file about 44 cases per 1,000 population, which was similar to that of Denmark (41), England (41), Ontario, Canada (47), New Zealand (53), and Australia (62). But the American rate was higher than that of Germany (23) and Sweden (35) and much higher than that of Spain (3), Italy (10), and Japan (12).[15]

This virtual explosion of primarily civil litigation in the United States has led the courts to consider cases that in years past were settled privately between citizens or were issues that often went unresolved. Some deal with momentous subjects, such as the right of the states to curtail abortion and efforts by the Environmental Protection Agency to enjoin polluters of the environment. But many suits stagger the imagination by their audacity or triviality:

A San Diego, California, man sued the city and its stadium beer vendors for emotional distress that he suffered when several women entered the men's restroom and embarrassed him while he was using the facilities. The **plaintiff** contended that the vendors were liable for selling so much beer and causing the women to eschew the long lines in their own restrooms and enter the men's facilities.[16]

A middle-aged Bronx man sued several fast-food chains, accusing them of being responsible for his girth and two prior heart attacks. "I thought when they said 100 percent beef, they meant it," the 272-pound gentleman complained. "I thought the food was OK. . . . Those people in the advertisements don't really tell you what's in the food. . . . It's all fat, fat and more fat. Now I'm obese." [17]

A longtime employee of the Los Alamos Scientific Laboratory sued for occupational disability benefits, claiming that although he had never suffered any physical injury, he had become mentally disabled "by a neurotic fear that radiation would kill him." [18]

While such suits are frivolous, they still require the time and efforts of the jurists who must at least consider their merits in the seventeen thousand courthouses throughout the United States. For example, a federal judge in West Virginia took several printed pages of the *Federal Supplement* to explain why the punishment of a state prisoner for his refusal to bury a dead skunk was not a violation of the prisoner's civil rights. A federal judge in Pennsylvania agonized at length in print as to whether the First Amendment protected *Time* magazine from a **tort** action after the publication had printed a photograph of a man whose fly had become unzipped.[19]

Despite this plethora of less than monumental lawsuits, the judicial system appears to be fighting those who attempt to use the courts to advance frivolous causes. Rule 11 of the Federal Rules of Civil Procedure forbids the filing of worthless petitions, and this was made stronger in 1983 when U.S. trial judges were given the authority to impose sanctions for the filing of frivolous suits. (Critics of the rule have charged that it has had a chilling effect on civil rights suits, but law school studies have largely refuted that claim.)[20] And in 1991 the U.S. Supreme Court handed down two key decisions that reaffirmed the imposition of large fines on those filing specious lawsuits—sending a strong message to the legal community that violations of Rule 11 will be taken seriously.[21] By the end of 2001, thirty-five states had laws on the books (many recently strengthened) to combat those who inundate their legal tribunals with worthless petitions.[22] But as with many things in the judiciary, the matter of human judgment is all important: What is frivolous to one person might be deadly serious to another.

Although a burst of litigation has been evident in the United States during the past several decades, Americans have always been litigious people. As early as 1835, the highly perceptive French observer Alexis de Tocqueville noted that "there is hardly a **political question** in the United States which does not sooner or later turn into a judicial one." [23] As one contemporary scholar has said: "To express amazement at American litigiousness is akin to professing astonishment at learning that the roots of most Americans lie in other lands. We have been a litigious nation as we have been an immigrant one. Indeed, the two are related." [24] This scholar goes on to argue that U.S. history was made by diverse groups who wanted to live according to their own customs but found themselves drawn haphazardly into a larger political community. As these groups bumped into one another and the edges became frayed, disputes resulted. But given a fairly strong common law legal tradition, such disputes were for the most part channeled into the courtroom rather than onto the battlefield. Many reasons can be cited why Americans have been and continue to be a highly litigious people, and it is beyond the scope of this chapter to examine them all systematically. Suffice it to say that in the United States the courthouse has been and is the anvil on which a significant portion of personal, societal, and political problems are hammered out.

And while America is a litigious society, this trend may be part of a worldwide phenomenon. Even countries that historically made little use of public law courts are seeing increasing use of these tribunals as their citizens gradually deem it appropriate and useful to bring grievances before the courts that in earlier times would have been borne in silence or at least viewed as unsuitable for a judicial tribunal. A case in point is China, which is seeing an explosion of lawsuits on an issue that a generation ago would have been considered unthinkable: parents suing their children to provide for them in their old age. A recent article in the *Wall Street Journal* noted: "For more than two millennia, the dictates of the sage Confucius governed Chinese family life. Parents sacrificed for their children, and children cared for parents when they got old. . . . Under Maoist rule, the Communist Party did not stamp out the role of family so much as supplant it. State-run collectives supported the old and the infirm. . . . But that support network is breaking down, while quaint concepts such as duty and sacrifice are being overrun by a fastchanging society. . . . The result: a yawning generation gap, and rising conflicts that force courts into the ticklish task of legislating virtue." The article further noted that such lawsuits were not "confined to rural areas. In Shanghai's Changning district, more than 10% of civil cases involve old people, many in conflicts with their children, judges say there."[25] Additional evidence that a changing, modernizing China is making it a more litigious society is seen in the number of lawyers per capita. In 1992 China had only one attorney for every 35,700 persons; in 2000, one for every 12,000 persons—almost a 300 percent increase in just eight years.[26] Those numbers are small, considering the one attorney for every 250 people in the United States, but it still suggests that modern life and the increasing use of law courts may go hand in glove.

Because America's judicial caseload is so enormous and far ranging, the courts must be examined to understand fully how the nation is governed and how its resources are allocated. Given the significance of courts in formulating and implementing public policy in the United States, it is important to know who the judges are, what their values are, and what powers and prerogatives they possess. And it is essential to study how decisions are made and how they are implemented if the judicial game is to be understood.

Summary

In this chapter we looked briefly at law in the United States—the wells from which it springs, its basic types, and its functions in society. We also examined the ambivalent attitude that Americans have about the rule of law; this is a nation birthed in an illegal revolution, yet proud of its respect for law and order. Finally, we noted that Americans' contentiousness as a people has been channeled largely through the legal and court systems. As a consequence, the high priests of the judicial temples, the judges, play a significant role in Americans' personal lives and in their evolution as a society and political entity.

Further Thought and Discussion Questions

1. In the story introducing this chapter we discussed the refusal of Mrs. Sultaana Freeman, a devout Muslim, to remove the veil covering her face so that she might be properly photographed for a driver's license. Many Americans would believe that she should remove her veil, allowing the interests of national security to prevail over her religious tradition. But would we feel the same way if the petitioner were a Catholic nun whose religious order required her to wear a habit that partially obscured her face?

2. In the United States today almost 6.5 million people, about one of every thirty-two, are either incarcerated or on **probation** or parole. Is this a sign of the inherent lawlessness of the American people, or is it evidence that the United States is a nation that believes in strict law enforcement?

3. Americans are known internationally for their high rate of filing lawsuits, but many other nations, particularly the developing countries, are beginning to close the gap. Is this a sign of progress or regression on their part?

4. How many U.S. citizens would be willing to break the law and risk imprisonment if their economic survival depended on it? If they believed the law was illegal and unjustified? If they felt the law violated a higher moral or religious belief? If they felt the law unfairly violated their individual liberties? Never?

NOTES

1. The factual account and the quotations were taken from the following article: "Her Veil Has To Go for Photo," *Houston Chronicle*, June 7, 2003, A3.

2. Stephen D. Ford, *The American Legal System: Its Dynamics and Limits* (St. Paul, Minn.: West, 1974), 13. Our elaborations on this definition of *law* are borrowed from Chapter 1 of Ford's text.

3. Patty Reinert, "Bush Defends Military Tribunals," *Houston Chronicle*, November 27, 2001, A13.

4. *Youngstown Sheet & Tube Co. v. Sawyer*, 343 U.S. 579 (1952).

5. "Corrections Population Tops Record," *Houston Chronicle*, August 27, 2001, A3. The United States is second only to Russia among all the countries in the world in terms of the percentage of its population that is incarcerated.

6. T. R. Fehrenbach, *Lone Star: A History of Texas and the Texans* (New York: American Legacy Press, 1968), 336.

7. Martin Luther King Jr., "Letter from Birmingham Jail, April 16, 1963." The full text of the letter may be found in Martin Luther King Jr., *Why We Can't Wait* (New York: Harper and Row, 1963).

8. Abe Fortas, *Concerning Dissent and Civil Disobedience* (New York: Signet, 1970), 18.

9. William Booth, "Abortion Doctor's Killer Receives Death Penalty," *Houston Chronicle*, December 7, 1994, A1.

10. Andrew Sinclair, "Prohibition: The Era of Excess," in *Law and the Behavioral Sciences*, ed. Lawrence M. Friedman and Stewart Macaulay (New York: Bobbs-Merrill, 1977), 353.

11. These states include Florida, Michigan, Mississippi, North Carolina, North Dakota, Virginia, and West Virginia. "Cohabitation Still Illegal in 7 States," *Houston Chronicle*, August 22, 2001, A12.

12. *Lawrence v. Texas*, 02–102 (2003). By a 6–3 vote, the justices overturned their previous ruling to the contrary, *Bowers v. Hardwick*, 478 U.S. 186 (1986), decided some seventeen years earlier.

13. See, for example, Jack W. Peltason, *Fifty-Eight Lonely Men* (New York: Harcourt, Brace and World, 1961); and Jack Bass, *Unlikely Heroes* (New York: Simon and Schuster, 1981).

14. Jethro K. Lieberman, *The Litigious Society* (New York: Basic Books, 1983), viii.

15. Christopher E. Smith, *Courts, Politics, and the Judicial Process*, 2d ed. (Chicago: Nelson Hall, 1997), 330.

16. "Highfalutin Lawsuits Validate California's Nickname," *Houston Chronicle*, February 21, 2000, D2.

17. Peter Bailey, "Man's Lawsuit Claims Fast-Food Chains Super-Sized Him," *Houston Chronicle*, July 28, 2002, A 19.

18. Lieberman, *The Litigious Society*, 4.

19. Robert A. Carp and C. K. Rowland, *Policymaking and Politics in the Federal District Courts* (Knoxville: University of Tennessee Press, 1983), 18.

20. Stephen Wermiel, "High Court Agrees to Hear Case on Segregation at State Colleges," *Wall Street Journal*, April 16, 1991, B10.

21. *Chambers v. U.S. Department of the Army*, 499 U.S. 645 (1991); and *Kunstler v. Britt*, 499 U.S. 969 (1991).

22. This number was taken from the Web site of the American Tort Reform Association (http:www.atra.org/wrap/files.cgi/7437_tort-record.html), downloaded June 10, 2003. The states have recently innovated the practice of requiring losing plaintiffs in civil suits to pay the attorney's fee of the defendant. This would supposedly make a potential plaintiff think twice before filing a frivolous lawsuit.

23. Alexis de Tocqueville, *Democracy in America*, ed. J. P. Mayer and Max Lerner, trans. George Lawrence (New York: Harper and Row, 1966), 248.

24. Lieberman, *The Litigious Society*, 13.

25. Leslie Chang, "Confucius Said: Sons, Care for Your Elders; Elders Say: We Sue," *Wall Street Journal*, April 3, 2000, A1.

26. Steven Vago, *Law and Society*, 5th ed. (Upper Saddle River, N.J.: Prentice Hall, 1997), 329. Data for 2000 provided to Robert A. Carp by representatives of Zhejiang Province Lawyers Association in Houston, Texas, on February 11, 2000.

SUGGESTED READINGS

Calvi, James V., and Susan Coleman. *American Law and Legal Systems*, 4th ed. Upper Saddle River, N.J.: Prentice Hall, 2003. A systematic discussion of all the major types of law in the United States.

Hall, Kermit L. *The Magic Mirror: Law in American History*. New York: Oxford University Press, 1989. A discussion of the historical interactions of law with events in the social and political realms.

although possessing the power of constitutional review, rarely exercises it. Judicial review in England is basically of administrative actions.[14]

The Supreme Court as a Policymaker

The Supreme Court's role as a policymaker derives from the fact that it interprets the law. Public policy issues come before the Court in the form of legal disputes that must be resolved.

Courts in any political system participate to some degree in the policy-making process because it is their job. Any judge faced with a choice between two or more interpretations and applications of a legislative act, executive order, or constitutional provision must choose among them because the controversy must be decided. And when the judge chooses, his or her interpretation becomes policy for the specific litigants. If the interpretation is accepted by the other judges, the judge has made policy for all jurisdictions in which that view prevails.[15]

In a recent article about the European Court of Justice, which serves the fifteen member states of the European Union, Sally J. Kenney said that this court, like the U.S. Supreme Court, "is grappling with the most important policy matters of our time—separation of powers, the environment, communications, labor policy, affirmative action, sex discrimination, and human rights issues."[16] Fundamental human rights issues in the European Court of Justice are typically raised in the context of trade, however.[17]

An excellent example of U.S. Supreme Court policymaking may be found in the area of racial equality. In the late 1880s many states enacted laws requiring the separation of blacks and whites in public facilities. In 1890, for instance, Louisiana enacted a law requiring separate but equal railroad accommodations for blacks and whites. A challenge came two years later. Homer Plessy, who was one-eighth black, protested against the Louisiana law by refusing to move from a seat in the white car of a train traveling from New Orleans to Covington, Louisiana. Arrested and charged with violating the statute, Plessy contended that the law was unconstitutional. The U.S. Supreme Court, in *Plessy v. Ferguson* (1896), upheld the Louisiana statute.[18] Thus the Court established the separate-but-equal policy that was to reign for about sixty years. During this period many states required that the races sit in different areas of buses, trains, terminals, and theaters; use different restrooms; and drink from different water fountains. Blacks were sometimes excluded from restaurants and public libraries. Perhaps most important, black students often had to attend inferior schools. This body of laws and extralegal practices was unofficially referred to as Jim Crow.

Separation of the races in public schools was contested in the famous *Brown v. Board of Education* case of 1954.[19] Parents of black schoolchildren claimed that state laws requiring or permitting segregation deprived them of equal protection of the laws under the Fourteenth Amendment. The Supreme Court ruled that separate educational facilities are inherently unequal and, therefore, segregation constitutes a denial of equal protection. In the *Brown* decision the Court laid to rest the separate-but-equal doctrine and established a policy of desegregated public schools.

In an average year the Court decides, with signed opinions, between eighty and ninety cases. Thousands of other cases are disposed of with less than the full treatment. Thus the Court deals at length with a very select set of policy issues that have varied throughout the Court's history.

In a democracy broad matters of public policy are, in theory at least, presumed to be left to the elected representatives of the people—not to judicial appointees with life terms. In principle, U.S. judges are not supposed to make policy, but in practice judges cannot help but do so to some extent.

The Supreme Court, however, differs from legislative and executive policymakers. Especially important is the fact that the Court has no self-starting device. The justices must wait for problems to be brought to them; there can be no judicial policymaking if there is no litigation. The president and members of Congress have no such constraints. Moreover, even the most assertive Supreme Court is limited to some extent by the actions of other policymakers, such as lower-court judges, Congress, and the president. The Court depends upon others to implement or carry out its decisions.

The Supreme Court as Final Arbiter

The Supreme Court has both original and **appellate jurisdiction**. Original jurisdiction means that a court has the power to hear a case for the first time. Appellate jurisdiction means that a higher court has the authority to review cases originally decided by a lower court.

The Supreme Court is overwhelmingly an appellate court because most of its time is devoted to reviewing decisions of lower courts. Regardless of whether its decisions are seen as correct, it is the highest appellate tribunal in the country. As such, it has the final word in the interpretation of the Constitution, acts of legislative bodies, and treaties—unless the Court's decision is altered by a constitutional amendment or, in some instances, by an act of Congress.

Since 1925 a device known as certiorari has allowed the high court to exercise discretion in deciding which cases it should review. Under this method a person may request Supreme Court review of a lower-court decision; then the justices determine whether the request should be granted. In the October 2001 term the Court handed down decisions with full opinions in eighty-five cases.[20] If review is granted, the Court issues a **writ of certiorari,** which is an order to the lower court to send up a complete record of the case. When certiorari is denied, the decision of the lower court stands.

The Supreme Court at Work

The formal session of the Supreme Court lasts from the first Monday in October until the business of the term is completed, usually in late June or July. Since 1935 the Supreme Court has had its own building in Washington, D.C. The imposing five-story marble building, which stands across from the Capitol, has the words "Equal Justice Under Law" carved above the entrance. Formal sessions are held in a large courtroom that seats three hundred people. At the front of the courtroom is the bench where the justices are seated. When the Court is in session, the chief justice, followed by the eight associate justices in order of seniority (length of continuous service on the Court), enters through the purple draperies behind the bench and takes a seat. Seats are arranged according to seniority, with the chief justice in the center, the senior associate justice on the chief justice's right, the second-ranking associate justice on the left, and continuing alternately in declining order of seniority. Near the courtroom are the conference room, where the justices decide cases, and the chambers that contain offices for the justices and their staffs.

The Court's term is divided into sittings, of approximately two weeks each, during which the justices meet in open session and hold internal conferences, and recesses, during which the justices work behind closed doors to consider cases and write opinions. The eighty to ninety cases per term that receive the Court's full treatment follow a fairly routine pattern, which is described below.

Oral Argument. Oral arguments are generally scheduled on Monday through Wednesday during the sittings. The sessions run from 10:00 a.m. until noon and from 1:00 until 3:00 p.m. Because the procedure is not a trial or the original hearing of a case, no jury is assembled and no witnesses are called. Instead, the two opposing attorneys present their arguments to the justices. The general practice is to allow thirty minutes for each side, although the Court may decide that additional time is necessary. The Court can normally hear four cases in one day. Attorneys presenting oral arguments are frequently interrupted with probing questions from the justices. The oral argument is considered very important by both attorneys and justices because it is the only stage in the process that allows such personal exchanges.

The Conference. On Fridays preceding the two-week sittings the Court holds conferences; during sittings it holds conferences on Wednesday afternoon and all day Friday. At the Wednesday meeting the justices discuss the cases argued on Monday. At the longer conference on Friday they discuss the cases that were argued on Tuesday and Wednesday, plus any other matters that need to be considered. The most important of these other matters are the certiorari petitions.

Prior to the Friday conference each justice is given a list of the cases that will be discussed. The conference begins at about 9:30 or 10:00 a.m. and runs until 5:30 or 6:00 p.m. As the justices enter the conference room, they shake hands with one another and take their seats around a rectangular table. They meet behind locked doors, and no official record is kept of the discussions. The chief justice presides over the conference and offers an opinion first in each case. The other justices follow in descending order of seniority. At one time a formal vote was then taken in reverse order (with the junior justice voting first); today the justices usually indicate their view during the discussion, making a formal vote unnecessary.

A quorum for a decision on a case is six members; obtaining a quorum is seldom difficult. Cases are sometimes decided by fewer than nine justices because of vacancies, illnesses, or nonparticipation resulting from possible conflicts of interest. Supreme Court decisions are made by a majority vote. In the event of a tie, the lower-court decision is upheld.

Opinion Writing. After a tentative decision has been reached in conference, the next step is to assign the Court's opinion to an individual justice to write. The chief justice, if voting with the majority, either writes the opinion or assigns it to another justice who voted with the majority. When the chief justice votes with the minority, the most senior justice in the majority makes the assignment.

After the conference the justice who will write the Court's opinion begins work on an initial draft. Other justices may work on the case by writing alternative opinions. The completed opinion is circulated to justices in both the majority and the minority groups. The writer seeks to persuade justices originally in the minority to change their votes and to keep his or her majority group intact. A bargaining process occurs, and the wording of the opinion may be changed to satisfy other justices or obtain their support. A deep division in the Court makes it difficult to achieve a clear, coherent opinion and may even result in a shift in votes or in another justice's opinion becoming the Court's official ruling.

In most cases a single opinion does obtain majority support, although few rulings are unanimous. Those who disagree with the **opinion of the Court** are said to dissent. A dissent does not have to be accompanied by an opinion, but in recent years it usually has been. Whenever more than one justice dissents, each may write an opinion or all may join in a single opinion.

On occasion a justice will agree with the Court's decision but differ in his or her reason for reaching that conclusion. Such a justice may write what is called a **concurring opinion**. A good recent example is Justice Sandra Day O'Connor's concurring opinion in *Lawrence v. Texas* (2003).[21] In that case the majority relied on the Due Process Clause of the Fourteenth Amendment to declare a Texas statute banning same-sex sodomy unconstitutional. Justice O'Connor agreed with the majority that the statute should be struck down, but based her conclusion on the Fourteenth Amendment's Equal Protection Clause. As sodomy between opposite-sex partners is not a crime in Texas, the state treats the same conduct differently based solely on the sex of the participants. According to Justice O'Connor, that violates the Equal Protection Clause.

An opinion labeled "concurring and dissenting" agrees with part of a Court ruling but disagrees with other parts. Finally, the Court occasionally issues a **per curiam opinion**—an unsigned opinion that is usually brief. Such opinions are often used when the Court accepts the case for review but gives it less than full treatment. For example, it may decide the case without benefit of oral argument and issue a per curiam opinion to explain the disposition of the case.

The procedures followed in the U.S. Supreme Court are not common to high courts everywhere. For example, the European Court of Justice differs from the U.S. Supreme Court in two important respects. First, it has no mechanism for denying certiorari; it must hear all cases referred to it regardless of their importance. Second, it issues only one judgment; there are no concurring or **dissenting opinions**.[22]

The U.S. Courts of Appeals

The **courts of appeals** have been described as "perhaps the least noticed of the regular constitutional courts."[23] They receive less media coverage than the Supreme Court, in part because their activities are simply not as dramatic. However, one should not assume that the courts of appeals are unimportant to the judicial system. Recall that in its 2001 term the Supreme Court handed down decisions with full opinions in only eighty-five cases, which means that the courts of appeals are the courts of last resort for most appeals in the federal court system.

Circuit Courts: 1789–1801

The Judiciary Act of 1789 created three circuit courts—the southern, middle, and eastern circuits—each composed of two justices of the Supreme Court and a district judge. The circuit court was to hold two sessions each year in each district within the circuit.

The district judge became primarily responsible for establishing the circuit court's workload. The two Supreme Court justices then came into the local area and participated in the cases. This practice tended to give a local rather than a national focus to the circuit courts.

The circuit court system was regarded from the beginning as unsatisfactory, especially by Supreme Court justices, who objected to the traveling imposed upon them. As early as September 1790, Chief Justice Jay wrote to the president urging changes in the circuit-riding duties prescribed by the Judiciary Act of 1789. Justice Iredell, who resided in North Carolina, was particularly hard-pressed. In addition to traveling some one thousand miles between his home and Philadelphia (where Supreme Court sessions were held), he was required to tour the states of Georgia, North Carolina, and South Carolina twice annually. It is no wonder Iredell referred to his life as that of a "travelling postboy." [24]

Supreme Court justices were not the only ones who objected to the circuit-riding duties. Attorney General Edmund Randolph and President Washington also urged relief for the Supreme Court justices. Congress made a slight change in 1793 by altering the circuit court organization to include only one Supreme Court justice and one district judge. The Randolph proposal for separate circuit court judgeships to replace Supreme Court participation was not implemented, however. The circuit courts had become the center of a political controversy. The Federalists urged passage of Randolph's proposal for separate circuit judges; the Anti-Federalist leaders saw the Randolph proposal as an attempt to enlarge the federal judiciary and remove it from state surveillance.

Circuit Courts: 1801–1891

In the closing days of President John Adams's administration in 1801, Congress passed the "midnight judges" act, which eliminated circuit riding by the Supreme Court justices, authorized the appointment of sixteen new circuit judges, and greatly extended the jurisdiction of the lower courts.

Some saw the Judiciary Act of 1801 as the Federalists' last-ditch effort to prolong their domination of government, whereas others viewed it as an extension of federal jurisdiction to suits that previously had been tried only in state courts. Certainly the Federalists were interested in federal judgeships, and they wanted to protect the judiciary from Anti-Federalists. The act of 1801, however, was not a last-minute effort. Efforts to change the circuit courts had been ongoing for more than ten years.

The new administration of Thomas Jefferson strongly opposed the "midnight judges" act, and Congress wasted little time in repealing it. The Circuit Court Act of 1802 restored circuit riding by Supreme Court justices and expanded the number of circuits. However, the 1802 legislation allowed the circuit court to be presided over by a single district judge. At first glance, such a change may seem slight, but it proved to be of great importance. Increasingly, the district judges began to assume responsibility for both district and circuit courts. In practice, original and appellate jurisdictions were both in the hands of the district judges.

The next major step in the development of the courts of appeals did not come until 1869, although there had been a growing recognition that some form of judicial reorganization was necessary. The pro-state and pro-nationalist interests disagreed on the exact form of judicial relief that should be enacted. The pro-nationalists did not want a plan that would transfer power from the national government to the states. They favored shifting many conflicts to the lower federal courts under the supervision of the Supreme Court. Thus "reorganization of the circuit courts continued to be the key to the nationalists' strategy." [25]

Expansion of the circuit courts, allowing them greater control over appeals, would free the Supreme Court to concentrate on the key cases as well as to formulate policy. The pro-state interests also wanted to lessen the high court's burden, but by reducing its power. Unable to do so, they were willing to accept only minor changes in the basic judicial structure established in 1789.

The political stalemate prevented any major reorganization between 1802 and 1869. Consequently, the courts were unable to handle the flood of litigation. Then, in 1869, Congress approved a measure that authorized the appointment of nine new circuit judges and reduced the Supreme Court justices' circuit court duty to one term every two years. Still, the high court was flooded with cases because no limitations were placed on the right of appeal to the Supreme Court. Six years later Congress broadened the jurisdiction of the circuit courts. The workload of the Supreme Court was not significantly decreased, however, because an automatic right of appeal to the high court still existed. A more drastic revision of the federal judicial system was to come in 1891.

The Courts of Appeals: 1891 to the Present

On March 3, 1891, the Evarts Act was signed into law, creating new courts known as circuit courts of appeals. These new tribunals were to hear most of the appeals from district courts. The old circuit courts, which had existed since 1789, also remained—a situation surely confusing to all but the most serious students of the judicial system. The new circuit court of appeals was to consist of one circuit judge, one circuit court of appeals judge, one district judge, and a Supreme Court justice. Two judges constituted a quorum in these new courts.

Following passage of the Evarts Act, the federal judiciary had two trial tribunals: district courts and circuit courts. It also had two appellate tribunals: circuit courts of appeals and the Supreme Court. Most appeals of trial decisions were to go to the circuit court of appeals, although the act also allowed direct review in some instances by the Supreme Court. In short, creation of the circuit courts of appeals released the Supreme Court from many petty types of cases. Appeals could still be made, but the high court would now have much greater control over its own workload. Much of its former caseload was thus shifted to the two lower levels of the federal judiciary.

The next step in the evolution of the courts of appeals came in 1911. In that year Congress passed legislation abolishing the old circuit courts, which had no appellate jurisdiction and frequently duplicated the functions of district courts.

Today, as a result of a name change implemented in the 1948 Judicial Code, the intermediate appellate tribunals are officially known as courts of appeals. Despite their official name, they continue to be referred to colloquially as circuit courts. Although these intermediate appellate courts have been manned at one time or another by circuit judges, courts of appeals judges, district judges, and Supreme Court justices, they now are staffed by 179 authorized courts of appeals judges.

Nine regional courts of appeals, each covering several states, were created in 1891. Another, covering the District of Columbia, was absorbed into the system after 1893. Next came the Court of Appeals for the Tenth Circuit, which was carved from the Eighth Circuit in 1929. In 1981, following a long battle during which many civil rights activists expressed the fear that a split might negate gains they had made acting through the courts, the Court of Appeals for the Eleventh Circuit was carved from the Fifth Circuit.[26]

For several years the heavy caseload and geographical expanse of the Ninth Circuit have prompted discussions of a split in that circuit. A number of bills to accomplish that purpose have been introduced in Congress since 1990, but none have passed.

The courts of appeals in each of the twelve regional circuits are responsible for reviewing cases appealed from federal district courts (and in some cases from administrative agencies) within the boundaries of the circuit. Figure 2-1 depicts the appellate and district court boundaries and indicates the states contained in each.

FIGURE 2-1 District and Appellate Court Boundaries

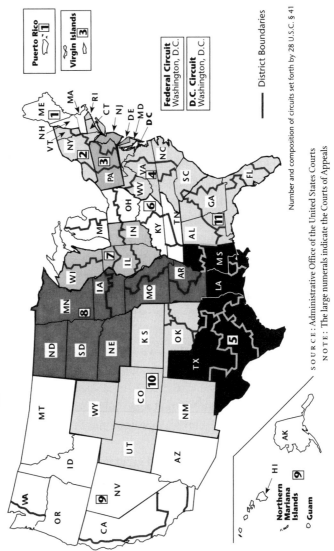

SOURCE: Administrative Office of the United States Courts
NOTE: The large numerals indicate the Courts of Appeals

A specialized appellate court came into existence in 1982, when Congress established the Federal Circuit, a jurisdictional instead of a geographic circuit. The United States Court of Appeals for the Federal Circuit was created by consolidating the Court of Claims and the Court of Customs and Patent Appeals.

The Review Function of the Courts of Appeals

As one modern-day student of the judiciary has noted:

The distribution of labor among the Supreme Court and the Courts of Appeals, implicit in the Judiciary Act of 1925, has matured into fully differentiated functions for federal appellate courts. Substantively, the Supreme Court has become more and more a constitutional tribunal. Courts of Appeals concentrate on statutory interpretation, administrative review, and error correction in masses of routine adjudications.[27]

Although the Supreme Court has had discretionary control of its docket since 1925, the courts of appeals still have no such luxury. Instead, their docket depends on how many and what types of cases are appealed to them.

Most of the cases reviewed by the courts of appeals originate in the federal district courts. Litigants disappointed with the lower-court decision may appeal the case to the court of appeals of the circuit in which the federal district court is located. The appellate courts have also been given authority to review the decisions of certain administrative agencies. This type of case enters the federal judicial system at the court of appeals level instead of at the federal district court level.

Because the courts of appeals have no control over which cases are brought to them, they deal with both routine and highly important matters. At one end of the spectrum are frivolous appeals or claims that have no substance and little or no chance for success. Such appeals are no doubt encouraged by the fact that the Supreme Court has ruled that assistance of counsel for first appeals should be granted to all indigents who have been convicted of a crime.[28] Occasionally a claim is successful, which then motivates other prisoners to appeal.

At the other end of the spectrum are the cases that raise major questions of public policy and evoke strong disagreement. Decisions by the courts of appeals in such cases are likely to establish policy for society as a whole, not just for the specific litigants. Civil liberties, reapportionment, religion, and education cases provide good examples of the kinds of disputes that may affect all citizens.

There are two purposes of review in the courts of appeals. The first is error correction. Judges in the various circuits are called upon to monitor the performance of federal district courts and federal agencies and to supervise their application and interpretation of national and state laws. In doing so, the courts of appeals do not seek out new factual evidence but instead examine the record of the lower court for errors. In the process of correcting errors, the courts of appeals also settle disputes and enforce national law.

The second function is sorting out and developing those few cases worthy of Supreme Court review. The circuit judges tackle the legal issues earlier than the Supreme Court justices do and may help shape what they consider review-worthy claims. Judicial scholars have found that the second hearing of appealed cases sometimes differs from the first.

The Courts of Appeals as Policymakers

The Supreme Court's role as a policymaker derives from the fact that it interprets the law; the same holds true for the courts of appeals. The scope of the courts of appeals' policy-making role takes on added importance given that they are the courts of last resort in the vast majority of cases. A study of three circuits, for example, found that the U.S. Supreme Court reviewed only nineteen of the nearly four thousand decisions of those tribunals.[29]

As an illustration of the impact of circuit court judges, consider the recent decision in a case involving the Fifth Circuit. For several years the University of Texas Law School had been granting preference to black and Mexican American applicants to increase the enrollment of these classes of minority students. This practice was challenged in a federal district court on the ground that it discriminated against white and nonpreferred minority applicants in violation of the Fourteenth Amendment. On March 18, 1996, a panel of Fifth Circuit judges ruled in *Hopwood v. Texas* that the Fourteenth Amendment does not permit the school to discriminate in this way and that the law school may not use race as a factor in law school admissions.[30] The U.S. Supreme Court denied a petition for a writ of certiorari in the case, thus leaving it the law of the land in Texas, Louisiana, and Mississippi, the states constituting the Fifth Circuit.[31] However, the Supreme Court did tackle the use of race as a factor in law school and undergraduate admissions in two cases decided during its 2002–2003 term. The cases, *Gratz v. Bollinger* and *Grutter v. Bollinger*, are discussed more fully in Chapter 13.

A major difference in policymaking by the Supreme Court and by the courts of appeals should be noted. Whereas there is one high court for the entire country, each court of appeals covers only a specific region. Thus the courts of appeals are more likely to make policy on a regional basis. Still, as evidenced by the *Hopwood* case, they are a part of the federal judicial system and "participate in both national and local policy networks, their decisions becoming regional law unless intolerable to the Justices."[32]

The Courts of Appeals at Work

The courts of appeals do not have the same degree of discretion as the Supreme Court to decide whether to accept a case for review. Nevertheless, circuit judges have developed methods for using their time as efficiently as possible.

Screening. During the screening stage the judges decide whether to give an appeal a full review or to dispose of it in some other way. The docket may be reduced to some extent by consolidating similar claims into single cases, a process that also results in a uniform decision. In deciding which cases can be disposed of without oral argument, the courts of appeals increasingly rely on law clerks or staff attorneys. These court personnel read petitions and briefs and then submit recommendations to the judges. As a result, many cases are disposed of without reaching the oral argument stage. In the twelve-month period ending September 30, 2002, for example, a full 67 percent of the appeals were terminated without oral argument.[33]

Three-Judge Panels. Those cases given the full treatment are normally considered by panels of three judges rather than by all the judges in the circuit. This means that several cases can be heard at the same time by different **three-judge panels,** often sitting in different cities throughout the circuit.

Panel assignments are typically made by the circuit executive or someone else, and then a clerk assigns cases blindly to the panels. Because all the circuits now contain more than three judges, the panels change frequently so that the same three judges do not sit together permanently. Regardless of the method used to determine panel assignments, one fact remains clear: A decision reached by a majority of a three-judge panel does not necessarily reflect the views of a majority of the judges in the circuit.

En Banc Proceedings. Occasionally, different three-judge panels within the same circuit may reach conflicting decisions in similar cases. To resolve such conflicts and to promote circuit unanimity, federal statutes provide for an **en banc** procedure, in which all the circuit's judges sit together on a panel and decide a case. The exception to this general rule occurs in the large Ninth Circuit, where assembling all the judges becomes too cumbersome. There, en banc panels normally consist of eleven judges. The en banc procedure may also be used when the case concerns an issue of extraordinary importance, as in the famous *Tinker v. Des Moines Independent Community School District* decision.[34] That case raised the question of whether high school students wearing black armbands in the classroom to protest the Vietnam War should be protected by the First Amendment. When the Court of Appeals for the Eighth Circuit heard that case in 1967, the en banc procedure was used.

The en banc procedure may be requested by the litigants or by the judges of the court. The circuits themselves have discretion to decide if and how the procedure will be used. Clearly, its use is the exception, not the rule.

Oral Argument. Cases that have survived the screening process and have not been settled by the litigants are scheduled for oral argument. Attorneys for each side are given a short amount of time (in some cases no more than ten minutes) to discuss the points made in their written briefs and to answer questions from the judges.

The Decision. Following the oral argument, the judges may confer briefly and, if they are in agreement, may announce their decision immediately. Otherwise, a decision will be announced only after the judges confer at greater length. Following the conference, some decisions will be announced with a brief order or per curiam opinion of the court. A small portion of decisions will be accompanied by a longer, signed opinion and perhaps even dissenting and concurring opinions. Recent years have seen a general decrease in the number of published opinions, although circuits vary in their practices.

U.S. District Courts

The U.S. district courts represent the basic point of input for the federal judicial system. Although some cases are later taken to a court of appeals or perhaps even to the Supreme Court, most federal cases never move beyond the U.S. trial courts. In terms of sheer numbers of cases handled, the district courts are the workhorses of the federal judiciary. However, their importance extends beyond simply disposing of a large number of cases.

The First District Courts

Congress made the decision to create a national network of federal trial courts when it passed the Judiciary Act of 1789. Section 2 of the act established thirteen district courts by (1) making each of the eleven states then in the Union a district and (2) making the parts of Massachusetts and Virginia that were to become Maine and Kentucky into separate districts. That organizational scheme established the practice, which still exists, of honoring state boundary lines in drawing districts. From the very beginning "the federal judiciary was state-contained, with the administrative and political structure of the states becoming the organizational structure of the federal courts." [35]

The First District Judges

Each federal district court was to be presided over by a single judge who resided in the district. As soon as this became known, President Washington began receiving letters from individuals desiring appointment to the various judgeships. Many asked members of Congress or Vice President Adams to recommend them to President Washington. Personal applications were not necessarily successful and were not the only way in which names came to the president's attention. Harry Innes, for example, was not an applicant for the Kentucky judgeship but received it after being recommended by a member of Congress from his state.[36]

Not everyone nominated was willing to serve as a district judge. Three of the thirteen whose names were originally submitted to the Senate for confirmation declined the appointment—perhaps because the nominating process "did not permit consultation either with the individuals concerned or representatives of the 'neighborhood' who might know if the office would be accepted." [37] The rejections were somewhat embarrassing, and Washington resorted to careful preliminary screening of future appointments and relied more heavily on his secretary of state for recommendations.

Many of the early prospective Supreme Court nominees preferred state-level appointments. The same held true for district court appointments. Some declined federal district judgeships to pursue other federal or state positions. Still others simply held a district judgeship and a state office simultaneously.[38] Eventually, states began to pass laws prohibiting state officeholders from accepting federal positions.

As new states came into the Union, additional district courts were created. The additions, along with resignations, gave Washington an opportunity to offer judgeships to thirty-three people, twenty-eight of whom accepted. A student of the early courts offers a profile of the judges Washington appointed. Their average age at appointment was forty-six. All but three were born in the United States, and sixteen had received college educations. All were members of the bar, and all but seven had state or local legal experience as judges, prosecutors, or attorneys general.[39] Presidents have continued to appoint lawyers with public service backgrounds to the federal bench.

Present Organization of the District Courts

The practice of respecting state boundaries in establishing district court jurisdictions began in 1789 and has been periodically reaffirmed by statutes ever since. As the country grew, new district courts were created. Eventually, Congress began to divide some states into more than one district. California, New York, and Texas have the most, with four each. Other than consistently honoring state lines, the organization of district constituencies appears to follow no rational plan. Size and population vary widely from district to district. Over the years, a court was added for the District of Columbia, and several territories have been served by district courts. U.S. district courts now serve the fifty states, the District of Columbia, Guam, Puerto Rico, the Virgin Islands, and the Northern Mariana Islands.

Congress often provides further organizational detail by creating divisions within a district. In doing this, the national legislature precisely lists the counties included in a particular division as well as the cities in which court will be held.

As indicated, the original district courts were each assigned one judge. With the growth in population and litigation, Congress has periodically added judgeships to the districts, bringing the current total to 667. Today all districts have more than one judge; the Southern District of New York, which includes Manhattan and the Bronx, currently has twenty-eight judges and is thus the largest. Because each federal district court is normally presided over by a single judge, several trials may be in session at various cities within the district at any given time.

The District Courts as Trial Courts

Congress established the district courts as the trial courts of the federal judicial system and gave them original jurisdiction over virtually all cases. They are the only federal courts in which attorneys examine and cross-examine witnesses. The factual record is thus established at this level. Subsequent appeals of the trial court decision will focus on correcting errors, not on reconstructing the facts. The task of determining the facts in a case often falls to a jury, a group of citizens from the community who serve as impartial arbiters of the facts and apply the law to the facts.

The Constitution guarantees the right to a jury trial in criminal cases in the Sixth Amendment and the same right in civil cases in the Seventh Amendment. The right can be waived, however, in which case the judge becomes the arbiter of questions of fact as well as matters of law. Such trials are referred to as **bench trials.** Two types of juries are associated with federal district courts. The **grand jury** is a group of men and women convened to determine whether probable cause exists to believe that a person has committed the federal crime of which he or she has been accused. Grand jurors meet periodically to hear charges brought by the U.S. attorney. Petit jurors are chosen at random from the community to hear evidence and determine whether a defendant in a civil trial has liability or whether a **defendant** in a criminal trial is guilty or not guilty. Federal rules call for twelve jurors in criminal cases but permit fewer in civil cases. The federal district courts generally use six-person juries in civil cases.

Norm Enforcement by the District Courts

Some students of the judiciary make a distinction between norm enforcement and policymaking by the courts.[40] Trial courts are viewed as engaging primarily in norm enforcement, whereas appellate courts are seen as having greater opportunity to make policy.

Norm enforcement is closely tied to the administration of justice, because all nations develop standards considered essential to a just and orderly society. Societal norms are embodied in statutes, administrative regulations, prior court decisions, and community traditions. Criminal statutes, for example, incorporate concepts of acceptable and unacceptable behavior into law. A judge deciding a case concerning an alleged violation of that law is basically practicing norm enforcement. Because cases of this type rarely allow the judge to escape the strict restraints of legal and procedural requirements, he or she has little chance to make new law or develop new policy. In civil cases, too, judges are often confined to norm enforcement; opportunities for policymaking are infrequent. Rather, such litigation generally arises from a private dispute whose outcome is of interest only to the parties in the suit.

Policymaking by the District Courts

The district courts also play a policy-making role. One leading judicial scholar explains how this function differs from norm enforcement:

When they make policy, the courts do not exercise more discretion than when they enforce community norms. The difference lies in the intended impact of the decision. Policy decisions are intended to be guideposts for future actions; norm-enforcement decisions are aimed at the particular case at hand.[41]

The discretion that a federal trial judge exercises should not be overlooked, however. As Americans have become more litigation-conscious, disputes that were once resolved informally are now more likely to be decided in a court of law. The courts find themselves increasingly involved in domains once considered private. What does this mean for the federal district courts? According to one study, "These new areas of judicial involvement tend to be relatively free of clear, precise appellate court and legislative guidelines; and as a consequence the opportunity for trial court jurists to write on a clean slate, that is, to make policy, is formidable." [42] In other words, when the guidelines are not well established, district judges have a great deal of discretion to set policy.

Three-Judge District Courts

In 1903 Congress passed legislation providing for the use of special **three-judge district courts** in certain types of cases. Such courts are created on an ad hoc basis; the panels are disbanded when a case has been decided. Each panel must include at least one judge from the federal district court and at least one judge from the court of appeals. Normally, two district judges and one appellate judge constitute the panel. Appeals of decisions of three-judge district courts go directly to the Supreme Court.

The earliest types of cases heard by three-judge district courts were suits filed by the attorney general under the Sherman Antitrust Act or the Interstate Commerce Act. Congress later provided that these special courts could decide suits brought by private citizens challenging the constitutionality of state or federal statutes and seeking injunctions to prevent enforcement of the challenged statutes.

An example of the use of a three-judge district court is provided by the abortion case of *Roe v. Wade*.[43] Jane Roe (a pseudonym), a single, pregnant woman, challenged the constitutionality of the Texas anti-abortion statute and sought an injunction to prohibit further enforcement of the law. The case was initially heard by a three-judge court consisting of district judges Sarah T. Hughes and W. N. Taylor and Fifth Circuit Court of Appeals Judge Irving L. Goldberg. The three-judge district court held the Texas abortion statute invalid but declined to issue an injunction against its enforcement on the ground that a federal intrusion into the state's affairs was not warranted. Roe then appealed the denial of the injunction directly to the Supreme Court.

Over the years congressional statutes, such as the Civil Rights Act of 1964, the Voting Rights Act of 1965, and the Presidential Election Campaign Fund Act of 1974, have specified the use of three-judge district courts. However, the increasing number of cases decided by such courts led to complaints about caseload problems, because appeals from the three-judge panels go directly to the Supreme Court. Thus in 1976 Congress virtually eliminated three-judge district courts except in cases concerning reapportionment of state legislatures and congressional redistricting and in some cases under the civil rights acts.

Constitutional Courts, Legislative Courts, and Courts of Specialized Jurisdiction

The Judiciary Act of 1789 established the three levels of the federal court system in existence today. Periodically, however, Congress has exercised its power, based on Article III and Article I of the Constitution, to create other federal courts. Courts established under Article III are known as constitutional courts, and those created under Article I are called legislative courts. The former handles the bulk of litigation in the system and, for this reason, will remain the focus of discussion here. The Supreme Court, courts of appeals, and federal district courts are constitutional courts. The trial and appellate military courts, created under authority found in Article I, Section 8 of the Constitution, "To constitute Tribunals inferior to the supreme Court," and "To make Rules for the Government and Regulation of the land and naval Forces," are good examples of legislative courts.

The two types of courts may be further distinguished by their functions. Legislative courts, unlike their constitutional counterparts, often have administrative and quasi-legislative as well as judicial duties. Another difference is that legislative courts are often created to help administer a specific congressional statute. For example, bankruptcy courts have been established as adjuncts of the federal district courts, with jurisdiction over civil proceedings arising under the bankruptcy code. Constitutional courts are tribunals established to handle litigation.

Finally, the constitutional and legislative courts vary in their degree of independence from the other two branches of government. Article III (constitutional court) judges serve during a period of good behavior, or what amounts to life tenure. Because Article I (legislative court) judges have no constitutional guarantee of good-behavior tenure, Congress may set specific terms of office for them. Judges of Article III courts are also constitutionally protected against salary reductions while in office. Those who serve as judges of legislative courts have no such protection. Again, bankruptcy courts provide a good example. The bankruptcy judges are appointed for fourteen-year terms by the court of appeals for the circuit in which the district is located and have their salaries set by Congress.

A court of specialized jurisdiction that has garnered much attention since September 11, 2001, is the foreign intelligence surveillance court. Created in 1978 by passage of the Foreign Intelligence Surveillance Act, this court has had its powers expanded since the USA Patriot Act which was passed in October 2001. The court consists of eleven federal district judges appointed by the chief justice of the United States, with no fewer than three of the judges residing within twenty miles of the District of Columbia. It was created for the purpose of passing on requests for surveillance and physical searches aimed at foreign powers and their agents.[44] Some have referred to it as a secret court because the records of its proceedings are not made public but instead are kept confidential under procedures developed by the chief justice, the attorney general, and the CIA director. There is also an appeals panel consisting of three district or court of appeals judges appointed by the chief justice. Their task is to hear appeals from denials of applications for surveillance and physical searches.

Administrative and Staff Support in the Federal Judiciary

The daily operation of federal courts requires a myriad of personnel. Although judges are the most visible actors in the judicial system, a large supporting cast is also needed to perform the tasks for which judges are unskilled or unsuited, or for which they simply do not have adequate time. Some members of the support team, such as law clerks, may work specifically for one judge. Others—for example, U.S. **magistrate** judges—are assigned to a particular court. Still others may be employees of an agency serving the entire judicial system, such as the Administrative Office of the United States Courts.

United States Magistrate Judges

In an effort to help federal district judges deal with increased workloads, Congress passed the Federal Magistrates Act in 1968. This legislation created the office of U.S. magistrate to replace the U.S. commissioners, who had performed limited duties for the federal trial courts for a number of years. In 1990, with passage of the Judicial Improvements Act, their title was changed to U.S. magistrate judge. Magistrate judges are formally appointed by the judges of the district court for eight-year terms of office, although they can be removed for "good cause" before the term expires.

The magistrate judge system constitutes a structure that responds to each district court's specific needs and circumstances. Within guidelines set by the Federal Magistrates Acts of 1968, 1976, and 1979, the judges in each district court establish the duties and responsibilities of their magistrate judges. Most significantly, the 1979 legislation permits a magistrate judge, with the consent of the involved parties, to conduct all proceedings in a jury or nonjury civil matter and enter a judgment in the case and to conduct a trial of persons accused of **misdemeanors** (less serious offenses than felonies) committed within the district, provided the defendants consent.

In other words, Congress has given federal district judges the authority to expand the scope of magistrate judges' participation in the judicial process. Because each district has its own particular needs, a magistrate judge's specific duties may vary from one district to the next and from one judge to another. The decision to delegate responsibilities to a magistrate judge is still made by the district judge, so that a magistrate judge's participation in the processing of cases may be narrower than that permitted by statute.

Law Clerks

The first use of law clerks by an American judge is generally traced to Horace Gray of Massachusetts. In the summer of 1875, while serving as chief justice of the Massachusetts Supreme Court, he employed, at his own expense, a highly ranked new graduate of the Harvard Law School.[45] Each year he would employ a new clerk from Harvard. When Gray was appointed to the U.S. Supreme Court in 1882, he brought a law clerk with him to the nation's highest court.

Justice Gray's successor on the high court was Oliver Wendell Holmes, like Gray a former chief justice of the Massachusetts Supreme Court. Holmes also adopted the practice of annually hiring honor graduates of Harvard Law School as his clerks.

When William Howard Taft, a former law professor at Yale, became chief justice, he secured a new law clerk annually from the dean of the Yale Law School. Harlan Fiske Stone, former dean of the Columbia Law School, joined the Court in 1925 and made it his practice to hire a Columbia graduate each year. Over time, the short-term law professor protégé became the typical Supreme Court law clerk.

Since these early beginnings, the use of law clerks by all federal courts has grown steadily. More than two thousand law clerks now work for federal judges, and more than six hundred serve bankruptcy judges and U.S. magistrate judges.[46] In addition to the law clerks hired by individual judges, all appellate courts and some district courts hire staff law clerks who serve the entire court.

A law clerk's duties vary according to the preferences of the judge for whom he or she works. They also vary according to the type of court. Law clerks for federal district judges often serve primarily as research assistants, spending a good deal of time examining the various motions filed in civil and criminal cases. They review each motion, noting the issues and the positions of the parties involved, then research important points raised in the motions and prepare written memorandums for the judges. Because their work is devoted to the earliest stages of the litigation process, they may have a substantial amount of contact with attorneys and witnesses. Law clerks at this level may also be involved in the initial drafting of opinions. As one federal district judge said, "I even allow my law clerks to write memorandum opinions. I first tell him what I want and then he writes it up. Sometimes I sign it without changing a word."[47]

At the appellate level, the law clerk becomes involved in a case first by researching the issues of law and fact presented by an appeal. Saving the judge's time is important. Consider the courts of appeals. These courts do not have the same discretion to accept or reject a case that the Supreme Court has. Nevertheless, the courts of appeals now use certain screening devices to differentiate between cases that can be handled quickly and those that require more time and effort. Law clerks are an integral part of this screening process.

Beginning around 1960 some courts of appeals began to utilize a new concept: the staff law clerk. The staff clerk, who works for the entire court as opposed to a particular justice, began to be used primarily because of the rapid increase in the number of pro se matters (generally speaking, those involving indigents) coming before the courts of appeals. Today some district courts also have pro se law clerks for handling prisoner petitions. In some circuits the staff law clerks deal only with pro se matters; in others they review nearly all cases on the court's docket. As a result of their review, a truncated process may be followed, that is, no oral argument or full briefing is made.

A number of cases are scheduled for oral argument, and the clerk may be called upon to assist the judge in preparing for it. Intensive analysis of the record by judges prior to oral argument is not always possible. They seldom have time to do more than scan pertinent portions of the record called to their attention by law clerks. As one judicial scholar aptly noted, "To prepare for oral argument, all but a handful of circuit judges rely upon bench memoranda prepared by their law clerks, plus their own notes from reading briefs." [48]

Once a decision has been reached by an appellate court, the law clerk frequently participates in writing the order that accompanies the decision. The clerk's participation generally consists of drafting a preliminary opinion or order pursuant to the judge's directions. A law clerk may also be asked to edit or check citations in an opinion written by the judge.

Because the work of the law clerk for a Supreme Court justice roughly parallels that of a clerk in the other appellate courts, all aspects of their responsibility do not need to be restated here. However, a few important points about Supreme Court law clerks deserve mention. Clerks play an indispensable role in helping justices decide which cases should be heard. At the suggestion of Justice Lewis Powell in 1972, a majority of the Court's members began to participate in a "cert-pool"; the justices pool their clerks, divide up all filings, and circulate a single clerk's certiorari memo to all those participating in the pool. [49] The memo summarizes the facts of the case, the questions of law presented, and the recommended course of action—whether the case should be granted a full hearing, denied, or dismissed. Justice John Paul Stevens, who does not participate in the certpool, nonetheless finds this initial reading of certiorari petitions by the law clerks invaluable. "They examine them all and select a small minority that they believe I should read myself. As a result, I do not even look at the papers in over 80 percent of the cases that are filed."[50]

Once the justices have voted to hear a case, the law clerks, like their counterparts in the courts of appeals, prepare bench memorandums that the justices may use during oral argument. Finally, law clerks for Supreme Court justices, like those who serve courts of appeals judges, help to draft opinions.

Administrative Office of the U.S. Courts

The administration of the federal judicial system as a whole is managed by the Administrative Office of the U.S. Courts, which essentially functions as "the judiciary's housekeeping agency."[51] Since its creation in 1939 it has handled everything from distributing supplies to negotiating with other government agencies for court accommodations in federal buildings to maintaining judicial personnel records to collecting data on cases in the federal courts.

The Administrative Office also serves a staff function for the Judicial Conference of the United States, the central administrative policy-making organization of the federal judicial system. In addition to providing statistical information to the conference's many committees, the Administrative Office acts as a reception center and clearinghouse for information and proposals directed to the Judicial Conference.

Closely related to this staff function is the Administrative Office's role as liaison for both the federal judicial system and the Judicial Conference. The Administrative Office serves as advocate for the judiciary in its dealings with Congress, the executive branch, professional groups, and the general public. Especially important is its representative role before Congress, where, along with concerned judges, it presents the judiciary's budget proposals, requests for additional judgeships, suggestions for changes in court rules, and other key measures.

The Federal Judicial Center

The Federal Judicial Center, created in 1967, is the federal courts' agency for continuing education and research. Its duties fall generally into three categories: (1) conducting research on the federal courts, (2) making recommendations to improve the administration and management of the federal courts, and

(3) developing educational and training programs for personnel of the judicial branch.

Since its inception, judges have benefited from orientation sessions and other educational programs organized by the Federal Judicial Center. In recent years, magistrate judges, bankruptcy judges, and administrative personnel have also been the recipients of educational programs. The Federal Judicial Center's extensive use of videos and satellite technology allows it to reach large numbers of people.

Federal Court Workload

The workload of the courts is heavy for all three levels of the federal judiciary—U.S. district courts, courts of appeal, and the Supreme Court.

For the period ending September 30, 2002, over 341,000 cases were commenced in the federal district courts. This figure has fluctuated somewhat over the past five years, ranging from a previous high of 321,669 cases in 2000 to a low of 313,041 cases in 2001 (see Table 2-1).

Criminal cases accounted for nearly 19 percent of the district courts' docket in 2002. As with the total docket, the number of criminal cases has increased steadily over the past five years, from 57,023 cases in 1998 to 66,452 cases in 2002. Criminal cases, while fewer in number than civil cases, are often very time consuming for the courts. Drug cases, which abound in some of the federal district courts in states bordering international boundaries, are especially complex and often involve multiple defendants.

Civil cases far outnumber criminal cases in the federal trial courts, making up 81 percent of the docket in 2002. Civil case filings have fluctuated over the years. From

TABLE 2-1   Cases Commenced in U.S. District Courts, 1998–2002

Cases	1998	1999	2000	2001	2002
Civil cases	256,787	260,271	259,517	250,907	274,841
Criminal cases	57,023	59,251	62,152	62,134	66,452
Total	313,810	319,522	321,669	313,041	341,293

SOURCE: Compiled from data in *Judicial Business of the United States Courts 2002*, Table D-2, Table S-7, available online at http://www.uscourts.gov/judbus2002/contents.html.

NOTE: Data is for 12-month periods ending September 30 of each year.

TABLE 2-2   Appeals Commenced in U.S. Courts of Appeals, 1998–2002

	1998	1999	2000	2001	2002
Number	53,805	54,693	54,697	57,464	57,555

SOURCE: Compiled from data in *Judicial Business of the United States Courts 2002*, Table B-3, available online at http://www.uscourts.gov/judbus2002/contents.html.

NOTE: Data is for 12-month periods ending September 30 of each year.

a high of 260,271 in 1999, they decreased to a low of 250,907 in 2001 before rising again to 274,841 in 2002.

In 1998, 53,805 appeals were commenced in one of the regional circuit courts (see Table 2-2). This figure increased every year, to a high of 57,555 in 2002.

The total number of cases on the Supreme Court's docket has increased steadily over the past five years (see Table 2-3). The total number of paid cases, pauper cases, and original jurisdiction cases on the high court's docket for the 2001 term stood at 9,176 cases.

Perhaps the key point to remember about the workload of the Supreme Court is that it has discretion to decide which cases merit its full attention. As a result, the number of cases argued before the Court has declined rather dramatically over the years. In the 2001 term only 88 cases were argued and 85 were disposed of by full opinions.

TABLE 2-3   Cases on the Docket, Argued, and Disposed of by Full Opinions in the U.S. Supreme Court, October Terms 1997–2001

Cases	1997	1998	1999	2000	2001
Paid cases	2,432	2,387	2,413	2,305	2,210
Pauper cases	5,253	5,689	6,024	6,651	6,958
Original cases	7	7	8	9	8
Total	7,692	8,083	8,445	8,965	9,176
Cases argued	96	90	83	86	88
Cases disposed of by full opinions	93	84	79	83	85

SOURCE: Compiled from data in *Judicial Business of the United States Courts 2002*, Table A-1, available online at http://www.uscourts.gov/judbus2002/contents.html.

Summary

In this chapter we offered a brief historical review of the development of the federal judiciary. A perennial concern has existed since preconstitutional times for independent court systems.

We focused on the three basic levels created by the Judiciary Act of 1789, noting, however, that Congress has periodically created both constitutional and legislative courts. The bulk of federal litigation is handled by U.S. district courts, courts of appeals, and the Supreme Court. We also briefly examined the role of magistrate judges and law clerks associated with the federal judiciary.

In terms of administrative assistance for the federal courts, our discussion centered on the Administrative Office of the U.S. Courts and the Federal Judicial Center. A brief look at the workload of each of the three levels of the federal judiciary concluded the chapter.

Further Thought and Discussion Questions

1. Under the Articles of Confederation, there was no national judiciary, a situation that was remedied when a national court system was established in Article III of the U.S. Constitution. But if Article III established a national court system, why did Congress pass the massive Judiciary Act of 1789 within months after the Constitution was adopted?

2. Why is the U.S. Supreme Court described as "distinctly American in conception and function"?

3. How can a democracy justify the fact that federal judges appointed for life possess the power to nullify federal and state laws that were enacted by elected representatives?

4. Since Article III judges are appointed for life and are independent of one another, what guarantees exist that justice is consistently and equitably dispensed?

NOTES

1. Charles Evans Hughes, *The Supreme Court of the United States* (New York: Columbia University Press, 1966), 1.

2. Ibid., 2.

3. Charles Warren, *The Supreme Court in United States History*, vol. 1 (Boston: Little, Brown, 1924), 4.

4. Fred Rodell, *Nine Men* (New York: Random House, 1955), 47.

5. See Warren, *The Supreme Court in United States History*, 44.

6. John P. Frank, *Marble Palace* (New York: Knopf, 1958), 9.

7. Warren, *The Supreme Court in United States History*, 51.

8. *Chisholm v. Georgia*, 2 Dallas 419 (1793).

9. Frank, *Marble Palace*, 79.

10. See Sheldon Goldman, *Constitutional Law and Supreme Court Decision-Making* (New York: Harper and Row, 1982), 41.

11. *Marbury v. Madison*, 1 Cranch 137 (1803).

12. See Lawrence Baum, *The Supreme Court*, 5th ed. (Washington, D.C.: CQ Press, 1995), 22.

13. Herbert Jacob, "Conclusion," in Herbert Jacob, Herbert M. Kritzer, Doris Marie Provine, Erhard Blankenburg, and Joseph Sanders, *Courts, Law, and Politics in Comparative Perspective* (New Haven, Conn.: Yale University Press, 1996), 394.

14. Ibid.

15. Robert H. Birkby, *The Court and Public Policy* (Washington, D.C.: CQ Press, 1983), 1.

16. Sally J. Kenney, "The European Court of Justice: Integrating Europe through Law," *Judicature* 81 (1998): 250.

17. Ibid., 251.

18. *Plessy v. Ferguson*, 163 U.S. 537 (1896).

19. *Brown v. Board of Education*, 347 US 483 (1954).

20. *Judicial Business of the United States Courts 2002*, Table A-1, available online at http://www.uscourts.gov/judbus2002/contents.html.

21. *Lawrence v. Texas*, No. 02-102 (2003).

22. See Kenney, "The European Court of Justice," 252, 255.

23. Stephen T. Early Jr., *Constitutional Courts of the United States* (Totowa, N.J.: Littlefield, Adams, 1977), 100.

24. See Warren, *The Supreme Court in United States History*, 85, 86.

25. Richard J. Richardson and Kenneth N. Vines, *The Politics of Federal Courts* (Boston: Little, Brown, 1970), 27.

26. For a thorough account of the Fifth Circuit split, see Deborah J. Barrow and Thomas G. Walker, *A Court Divided: The Fifth Circuit Court of Appeals and the Politics of Judicial Reform* (New Haven, Conn.: Yale University Press, 1988).

27. J. Woodford Howard Jr., *Courts of Appeals in the Federal Judicial System: A Study of the Second, Fifth, and District of Columbia Circuits* (Princeton, N.J.: Princeton University Press, 1981), 75–76.

28. See *Douglas v. California*, 372 U.S. 353 (1963).

29. See Donald R. Songer, "The Circuit Courts of Appeals," in *The American Courts: A Critical Assessment*, ed. John B. Gates and Charles A. Johnson (Washington, D.C.: CQ Press, 1991), 47.

30. *Hopwood v. Texas*, No. 94-50664, Fifth Circuit, March 18, 1996.

31. *Hopwood v. Texas*, 116 S. Ct. 2581 (1996).

32. Howard, *Courts of Appeals in the Federal Judicial System*, 79.

33. *Judicial Business of the United States Courts 2002*, Table S-1, available online at http://www.uscourts.gov/judbus2002/contents.html.

34. *Tinker v. Des Moines Independent Community School District*, 393 U.S. 503 (1969).

35. Richardson and Vines, *The Politics of Federal Courts*, 21.

36. Dwight F. Henderson, *Courts for a New Nation* (Washington, D.C.: Public Affairs Press, 1971), 27.

37. Ibid., 28.

38. Ibid., 29–30.

39. Ibid., 30–31.

40. See Herbert Jacob, *Justice in America*, 4th ed. (Boston: Little, Brown, 1984), chap. 2.

41. Ibid., 37.

42. Robert A. Carp and C. K. Rowland, *Policymaking and Politics in the Federal District Courts* (Knoxville: University of Tennessee Press, 1983), 3.

43. The decision of the three-judge district court may be found in *Roe v. Wade*, 314 F. Supp. 1217 (1970), and the Supreme Court decision in *Roe v. Wade*, 410 U.S. 113 (1973).

44. See "The Secret Court"; available online at http://www.courts.net/secret.htm.

45. Our discussion of the historical evolution of law clerks is drawn from John Bilyeu Oakley and Robert S. Thompson, *Law Clerks and the Judicial Process* (Berkeley: University of California Press, 1980), 10–22.

46. Frank M. Coffin, *On Appeal: Courts, Lawyering, and Judging* (New York: W. W. Norton, 1994), 72.

47. Quoted in Robert A. Carp and Russell R. Wheeler, "Sink or Swim: The Socialization of a Federal District Judge," *Journal of Public Law* 21 (1972): 379.

48. Howard, *Courts of Appeals in the Federal Judicial System*, 198.

49. See David M. O'Brien, *Storm Center: The Supreme Court in American Politics*, 2d ed. (New York: W. W. Norton, 1990), 165.

50. J. P. Stevens, "Some Thoughts on Judicial Restraint," *Judicature* 66 (1982): 179.

51. Peter G. Fish, *The Politics of Federal Judicial Administration* (Princeton, N.J.: Princeton University Press, 1973), 124, 166.

SUGGESTED READINGS

Barrow, Deborah J., and Thomas G. Walker. *A Court Divided: The Fifth Circuit Court of Appeals and the Politics of Judicial Reform.* New Haven, Conn.: Yale University Press, 1988. An excellent study of the politics involved in the splitting of the Fifth Circuit Court of Appeals.

Baum, Lawrence. *The Supreme Court,* 8th ed. Washington, D.C.: CQ Press, 2004. A brief look at all aspects of the U.S. Supreme Court.

Federal Judiciary Homepage. Available online at http://www.uscourts.gov. An excellent source of information about all aspects of the federal judiciary. Also provides links to other useful Internet sites.

Gates, John B., and Charles A. Johnson, eds. *The American Courts: A Critical Assessment.* Washington, D.C.: CQ Press, 1991. A collection of readings about state and federal trial and appellate courts, judicial selection, and judicial decision making.

Richardson, Richard J., and Kenneth N. Vines. *The Politics of Federal Courts.* Boston: Little, Brown, 1970. An excellent study of the politics involved in the creation of the federal judicial system.

Rowland, C. K., and Robert A. Carp. *Politics and Judgment in Federal District Courts.* Lawrence: University Press of Kansas, 1996. A thorough study of the various factors that influence the decisions of federal district judges.

Songer, Donald R., Reginald S. Sheehan, and Susan B. Haire. *Continuity and Change on the United States Courts of Appeals.* Ann Arbor: University of Michigan Press, 2000. The most thorough study to date of the U.S. courts of appeals.

CHAPTER 3

History and Organization
of State Judicial Systems

Lois Farnham, left, and Holly Puterbaugh celebrate the Vermont House of Representatives passing of the Civil Union bill. The women were one of three couples who sued the state of Vermont to attain legal rights for gay and lesbian couples. In response to the suit, the Vermont Supreme Court ruled in 1999 that the state must guarantee committed gay and lesbian couples the same protections and benefits that heterosexual couples receive. Subsequently, the state legislature enacted the Vermont Civil Union law, which does not legalize same-sex marriages, but does provide gay and lesbian couples many of the advantages afforded to heterosexual couples.

E VEN PRIOR TO THE ARTICLES of Confederation and the writing of the U.S. Constitution in 1787, the colonies, as sovereign entities, already had written constitutions. The development of state court systems can therefore be traced from the colonial period to the present in terms of organization and procedures.

Historical Development of State Courts

No two states are exactly alike when it comes to the organization of courts. Each state is entirely free to adopt any organizational scheme it chooses, create as many courts as it wishes, name those courts whatever it pleases, and establish their jurisdiction as it sees fit. Thus the organization of state courts does not necessarily resemble the clear-cut three-tier system found at the federal level. For instance, in the federal system the trial courts are called district courts, and the appellate tribunals are known as circuit courts. However, in well over a dozen states the circuit courts are trial courts. Several other states use the term *superior court* for their major trial courts. Perhaps the most bewildering situation is found in New York, where the major trial courts are known as supreme courts.

A similar situation exists in Canada, where constitutional authority for the judicial system is divided between the federal and provincial governments. The names of the courts are not identical in each province, even though the court system is roughly the same throughout Canada. The provinces divide their court system into two levels: provincial courts and superior courts. However, some provinces, such as Alberta, call their superior court the Court of Queen's Bench.[1]

Although a great deal of confusion surrounds the organization of state courts, no doubt exists about their importance. Because statutory law is more extensive in the states than at the federal level, covering everything from the most basic personal relationships to the state's most important public policies, the state courts handle a wide variety of cases. One study of state supreme courts says that the main categories of cases include

appeals in major felonies; state regulation of business and professions; a wide range of private economic disputes, including business contracts and real estate; wills, trusts, and estates; divorce, child custody, and child support; and personal injury suits involving automobile accidents, medical malpractice, job-related injuries, and the like.[2]

State courts also interpret their own state constitutions, which sometimes have broader protections for their citizens than are found in the federal constitution. In fact, "since the 1970s, state courts (particularly the highest courts of the states) have issued hundreds of opinions interpreting their constitutions to protect rights beyond the federal minima."[3] U.S. Supreme Court Justice William Brennan, in an influential law review article published in 1977, is generally credited with encouraging state courts to interpret their own constitutions in order to provide greater protection of citizens' rights.[4] One recent study of this development, known as "new judicial federalism," indicates that there has been a "dramatic upsurge in state courts' reliance on state declarations of rights in civil-liberties cases over the past twenty-five years."[5] Not surprisingly, then, the number of cases litigated annually in the state courts far exceeds those decided in the federal tribunals.

As colonists moved from England to settle in America, they naturally brought with them the various customs and traditions with which they were familiar. For this reason, American law borrowed heavily from English common law. Likewise, common law traditions became important factors in shaping the state court systems. Ohio and Pennsylvania, for example, still call their major trial courts the courts of common pleas, a title whose origin may be traced to England. Some traditions die hard; nonetheless, state courts have undergone major changes over the years.

The Colonial Period

During the colonial period, political power was concentrated in the hands of the governor, who was appointed by the king of England. Because the governors performed executive, legislative, and judicial functions, an elaborate court system was not necessary. The courts of this period were simple institutions that borrowed their form from the English judiciary. However, the colonists greatly simplified the English procedures to suit their own needs.

The lowest level of the colonial judiciary consisted of local judges called justices of the peace or magistrates, who were appointed by the colony's governor. At the next level in the system were the county courts, the general trial courts for the colonies. These courts "were at the heart of colonial government." [6] In addition to deciding cases, they performed some administrative functions. Appeals from all courts were taken to the highest level—the governor and his council. Grand and **petit juries** were also introduced during this period and remain prominent features of the state judicial systems.

By the early eighteenth century the legal profession had begun to change. Lawyers trained in the English Inns of Court became more numerous, and as a consequence colonial court procedures were slowly replaced by more sophisticated English common law. In addition, common commercial needs and a common language helped to make colonial and English legal practices more similar. As one judicial scholar notes, "In a relatively short time—between 1760 and 1820—a rather backward colonial legal framework was transformed into a very English common law system." [7]

Early State Courts

Following the Revolution, the powers of the government were not only taken over by legislative bodies but also greatly reduced. The former colonists were not eager to see the development of a large independent judiciary, given that many of them harbored a distrust of lawyers and the common law. The state legislatures carefully watched the courts and in some instances removed judges or abolished specific courts because of unpopular decisions. However, the basic structure of the state judiciaries was not greatly altered.

Increasingly, a distrust of the judiciary developed as courts declared legislative actions unconstitutional. Conflicts between legislatures and judges, often stemming from opposing interests, became more prevalent. Legislators seemed more responsive to policies that favored debtors, whereas courts generally reflected the views of creditors. These differences were important, because "out of this conflict over legislative and judicial power . . . the courts gradually emerged as an independent political institution."[8]

Modern State Courts

From the Civil War to the early twentieth century, the state courts were beset by still other problems. Increasing industrialization and the rapid growth of urban areas created new types of legal disputes and resulted in longer and more complex court cases. The state court systems, largely fashioned to handle the problems of a rural agrarian society, were now faced with a crisis of backlogs as they struggled to adjust.

One typical response was to create new courts to handle the increased volume of cases. Courts were often simply piled on top of one another. Another strategy was the addition of new courts, coupled with a careful specification of their jurisdiction in terms of geographic area. Still another response was to create specialized courts to handle one particular type of case. Small-claims courts, juvenile courts, and domestic relations courts, for example, became increasingly prominent.

The result of all this activity was a confusing array of courts, especially in the major urban areas. Additional problems were created as well. One observer noted that

each court was a separate entity; each had a judge and a staff. Such an organizational structure meant there was no way to shift cases from an overloaded court to one with little to do. In addition, each court produced political patronage jobs for the city political machines.[9]

The largely unplanned expansion of state and local courts to meet specific needs led to a situation many have referred to as fragmentation. A multiplicity of trial courts was only one aspect of fragmentation. Many of these courts had very narrow jurisdictions. Furthermore, the jurisdictions of the various courts often overlapped. This meant that a case could be tried in a number of courts depending on the advantages each one offered. Court costs, court procedures, court delays, and, last but certainly not least, the reputation of the judge all entered into the decision. For example, a strict law-and-order district attorney prosecuting a criminal case might choose a court with a reputation for handing out stiff sentences. An attorney filing a civil suit on behalf of a client might seek a court known for its complex procedures to draw the other side into a confusing web of legal technicalities. Political considerations were also involved in the choice of a court. The justice of the peace courts were especially political because many of them operated on a fee basis. Justices of the peace (J.P.s) were often willing to trade favorable decisions for court business. The initials J.P. were often said to stand for "Justice for the Plaintiff." [10]

Early in the twentieth century, people began to speak out against the fragmentation in the state court systems. The program of reforms that emerged in response is generally known as the court unification movement. The first well-known legal scholar to speak out in favor of court unification was Roscoe Pound, dean of the Harvard Law School.[11] Pound and others called for the consolidation of trial courts into a single set of courts or two sets of courts, one to hear major cases and one to hear minor cases.

A good deal of opposition to court unification has arisen. Many trial lawyers who are in court almost daily become accustomed to existing court organization and therefore are opposed to change. Knowledge of the local courts is the key to their success, so they naturally are not eager to try cases in strange new courts.

Also, judges and other personnel associated with the courts are sometimes opposed to reform. Their opposition often grows out of fear—of being transferred to new courts, having to learn new procedures, or having to decide cases outside their area of specialization. Nonlawyer judges, such as justices of the peace, often oppose court reform because they view it as a threat to their jobs.

The court unification movement, then, has not been as successful as many would like, although proponents of court reform have secured victories in some states.

State Court Organization

Some states have moved in the direction of a unified court system, whereas others still operate with a bewildering complex of courts with overlapping jurisdiction. The state courts may be divided into four general categories or levels: trial courts of limited jurisdiction, trial courts of general jurisdiction, intermediate appellate courts, and courts of last resort.

Trial Courts of Limited Jurisdiction

Trial courts of limited jurisdiction handle the bulk of litigation in this country each year and constitute about 85 percent of all courts in the United States.[12] They have a variety of names: justice of the peace courts, magistrate courts, municipal courts, city courts, county courts, juvenile courts, domestic relations courts, and metropolitan courts, to name the more common ones.

The jurisdiction of these courts is limited to minor cases. In criminal matters, for example, state courts deal with three levels of violations: infractions (the least serious), misdemeanors (more serious), and felonies (the most serious). Trial courts of limited jurisdiction handle infractions and misdemeanors. They may impose only limited fines (usually no more than $1,000) and jail sentences (generally no more than one year). In civil cases these courts are usually limited to disputes under a certain amount, such as $500. In addition, these types of courts are often limited to certain kinds of matters: traffic violations, domestic relations, or cases involving juveniles, for example. Another difference from trial courts of general jurisdiction is that in many instances these limited courts are not courts of record. Because their proceedings are not recorded, appeals of their decisions usually go to a trial court of general jurisdiction for what is known as a **trial de novo** (new trial).

Yet another distinguishing characteristic of trial courts of limited jurisdiction is that their presiding judges are often not required to have any formal legal training. Many are only part-time judges who are sometimes unfamiliar with basic legal concepts.[13]

Many of these courts suffer from a lack of resources. They often have no permanent courtroom, meeting instead in grocery stores, restaurants, or private homes. Clerks are frequently not available to keep adequate records. Consequently, the proceedings are informal, and cases are processed on a mass basis. Full-fledged trials are rare, and cases are disposed of quickly.

Finally, trial courts of limited jurisdiction are used in some states to handle preliminary matters in **felony** criminal cases. They often hold **arraignments,** set **bail,** appoint attorneys for indigent defendants, and conduct preliminary examinations. The case is then transferred to a trial court of general jurisdiction for such matters as hearing pleas, holding trials, and sentencing.

Trial Courts of General Jurisdiction

Most states have one set of major trial courts that handle the more serious criminal and civil cases. In addition, in many states, special categories—such as juvenile criminal offenses, domestic relations cases, and probate cases—are under the jurisdiction of the general trial courts.

In the majority of states these courts also have an appellate function. They hear appeals in certain types of cases that originate in trial courts of limited jurisdiction. These appeals are often heard in a trial de novo or tried again in the court of general jurisdiction.

General trial courts are usually divided into judicial districts or circuits. Although the practice varies from state to state, the general rule is to use existing political boundaries such as a county or a group of counties in establishing the district or circuit. In rural areas the judge may ride circuit and hold court in different parts of the territory according to a fixed schedule. In urban areas judges hold court in a prescribed place throughout the year. In larger counties the group of judges may be divided into specializations. Some may hear only civil cases; others try criminal cases exclusively.

The courts at this level have a variety of names. The most common are district, circuit, and superior. Ohio and Pennsylvania still cling to the title "court of common pleas" (see Table 3-1). New York is undoubtedly the most confusing of all; its trial

TABLE 3-1 State Trial Courts of General Jurisdiction

Name of court	State(s)
Chancery Court	Tennessee
Chancery/Probate Court	Arkansas
Circuit Court	Alabama, Arkansas, Florida, Illinois, Indiana, Kentucky, Maryland, Michigan, Mississippi, Missouri, Oregon, South Carolina, South Dakota, Tennessee, Virginia, West Virginia, Wisconsin
Circuit/Family Court	Hawaii
County Court	New York
Court of Chancery	Delaware
Court of Claims	Michigan
Court of Common Pleas	Ohio, Pennsylvania
Criminal Court	Tennessee
Criminal District Court	Texas
District Court	Colorado, Idaho, Iowa, Kansas, Louisiana, Minnesota, Montana, Nebraska, Nevada, New Mexico, North Dakota, Oklahoma, Texas, Utah, Vermont, Wyoming
Family Court	Vermont
Juvenile Court	Louisiana
Probate Court	Indiana, Tennessee
Superior Court	Alaska, Arizona, California, Connecticut, Delaware, Georgia, Indiana, Maine, Massachusetts, New Hampshire, New Jersey, North Carolina, Rhode Island, Vermont, Washington
Supreme Court	New York
Tax Court	Arizona, Oregon
Water Court	Colorado, Montana
Worker's Compensation Court	Montana

SOURCE: Compiled from data in "2000 State Court Structure Charts," *State Court Caseload Statistics, 2001* (Williamsburg, Va.: National Center for State Courts, 2002), 8–59.

NOTE: Some states have more than one trial court of general jurisdiction.

court of general jurisdiction is called the supreme court. The judges at this level are required by law in all states to have law degrees. These courts also maintain clerical help because they are courts of record. In other words, a degree of professionalism is evident at this level that is often lacking in the trial courts of limited jurisdiction.

Intermediate Appellate Courts

The intermediate appellate courts are relative newcomers to the state judicial scene. Only thirteen such courts existed in 1911, whereas forty states now have them. Their basic purpose is to relieve the workload of the state's highest court.

In most instances they are called courts of appeals, although other names are occasionally used. Most states have one court of appeals with statewide jurisdiction. Other states, such as Ohio and Texas, have created regional appellate courts to hear appeals from trial courts in a specific area. Alabama and Tennessee have separate intermediate appellate courts for civil and criminal cases.

The names of these intermediate appellate courts vary (see Table 3-2). The size of intermediate courts also varies from state to state. The court of appeals in Alaska,

TABLE 3-2   State Intermediate Appellate Courts

Name of court	State(s)
Appeals Court	Massachusetts
Appellate Court	Connecticut, Illinois
Appellate Division of Superior Court	New Jersey
Appellate Divisions of Supreme Court	New York
Appellate Terms of Supreme Court	New York
Commonwealth Court	Pennsylvania
Court of Appeals	Alaska, Arizona, Arkansas, California, Colorado, Georgia, Idaho, Indiana, Iowa, Kansas, Kentucky, Louisiana, Michigan, Minnesota, Mississippi, Missouri, Nebraska, New Mexico, North Carolina, Ohio, Oregon, South Carolina, Tennessee, Texas, Utah, Virginia, Washington, Wisconsin
Court of Civil Appeals	Alabama, Oklahoma
Court of Criminal Appeals	Alabama, Tennessee
Court of Special Appeals	Maryland
District Court of Appeals	Florida
Intermediate Court of Appeals	Hawaii
Superior Court	Pennsylvania
Tax Court	Indiana

SOURCE: Compiled from data in "State Court Structure Charts," *State Court Caseload Statistics, 2001* (Williamsburg, Va.: National Center for State Courts, 2002), 8–59.

NOTE: Some states have no intermediate appellate court; some states have more than one.

for example, has only three judges. At the other extreme, Texas has eighty courts of appeals judges.[14] In some states the intermediate appeals courts sit en banc, whereas in other states they sit in permanent or rotating panels.

Generally speaking, the jurisdiction of intermediate appellate courts is mandatory because Americans hold to the view that parties in a case are entitled to at least one appeal. In numerous instances, then, these are the courts of last resort for litigants in the state court system.

Courts of Last Resort

Every state has a court of last resort. Oklahoma and Texas have two highest courts. Both states have a supreme court with jurisdiction limited to appeals in civil cases and a court of criminal appeals for criminal cases. Most states call their highest courts supreme courts (see Table 3-3); other designations are the court of appeals (Maryland and New York), the supreme judicial court (Maine and Massachusetts), and the supreme court of appeals (West Virginia).

The courts of last resort range in size from five to nine judges (or justices in some states). They typically sit en banc and usually, although not necessarily, in the state capital.

The highest courts have jurisdiction in matters pertaining to state law and are the final arbiters in such matters. In states that have intermediate appellate courts, the supreme court's cases come primarily from these midlevel courts. In this situation

TABLE 3-3   State Courts of Last Resort

Name of court	State(s)
Court of Appeals	Maryland, New York
Court of Criminal Appeals	Oklahoma, Texas
Supreme Court	Alabama, Alaska, Arizona, Arkansas, California, Colorado, Connecticut, Delaware, Florida, Georgia, Hawaii, Idaho, Illinois, Indiana, Iowa, Kansas, Kentucky, Louisiana, Michigan, Minnesota, Mississippi, Missouri, Montana, Nebraska, Nevada, New Hampshire, New Jersey, New Mexico, North Carolina, North Dakota, Ohio, Oklahoma, Oregon, Pennsylvania, Rhode Island, South Carolina, South Dakota, Tennessee, Texas, Utah, Vermont, Virginia, Washington, Wisconsin, Wyoming
Supreme Court of Appeals	West Virginia
Supreme Judicial Court	Maine, Massachusetts

SOURCE: Compiled from data in "State Court Structure Charts," *State Court Caseload Statistics, 2001* (Williamsburg, Va.: National Center for State Courts, 2002), 8–59.

NOTE: Oklahoma and Texas have two courts of last resort.

the high court typically is allowed to exercise discretion in deciding which cases to review. Thus it is likely to devote more time to cases that deal with the important policy issues of the state. When there is no intermediate court of appeals, cases generally go to the state's highest court on a mandatory review basis. This is likely to create a role of error correction for the court of last resort in routine cases and to reduce its opportunities for policymaking.[15]

In most instances, the state courts of last resort resemble the U.S. Supreme Court in that they have a good deal of discretion in determining which cases will occupy their attention. Most state supreme courts also follow procedures similar to those of the U.S. Supreme Court. That is, when a case is accepted for review, the opposing parties file written briefs and later present oral arguments. **Amicus curiae** briefs are also filed quite frequently in such states as California, Illinois, Michigan, Oklahoma, Pennsylvania, and Wisconsin.[16] After reaching a decision, the judges issue written opinions explaining that decision.

Juvenile Courts

Even the most casual reading of a daily newspaper or viewing of a nightly news broadcast acquaints one with the fact that Americans are increasingly concerned about the handling of cases involving juveniles. Not surprisingly, states have responded to the problem in a variety of ways.[17] Some have established a statewide network of courts specifically to handle matters involving juveniles. They are commonly called juvenile courts or family courts. Georgia, for example, has 159 juvenile courts throughout the state. Rhode Island and South Carolina provide good examples of another approach. These two states have family courts, which handle domestic relations matters as well as those involving juveniles. Still other states have juvenile courts or family courts or both in limited areas. In Colorado, there is a juvenile court for Denver. Louisiana has created four juvenile courts for the state and one family court in East Baton Rouge.

The most common approach is to give one or more of the state's limited or general trial courts jurisdiction to handle situations involving juveniles. In Alabama, for example, the circuit courts (trial courts of general jurisdiction) deal with juvenile matters. In Kentucky, however, exclusive juvenile jurisdiction is lodged in trial courts of limited jurisdiction—the district courts.

Finally, some states apportion juvenile jurisdiction among more than one court. Recall the juvenile court in Denver. No one would believe that problems among juveniles in Colorado are limited to the city of Denver. Instead, the state has given jurisdiction over juveniles to district courts (general trial courts) in areas other than Denver.

As might be expected, the states vary in determining when jurisdiction belongs to an adult court. States set a standard age at which defendants are tried in an adult court. In addition, many states require that younger offenders be tried in an adult court if special circumstances are present. In Illinois, for instance, the standard age at which juvenile jurisdiction transfers to adult courts is seventeen. The age limit drops to fifteen, however, for first-degree murder, aggravated criminal sexual assault, armed robbery, robbery with a firearm, and unlawful use of weapons on school grounds.

Norm Enforcement and Policymaking in the State Courts

As described in Chapter 2, norm enforcement is closely tied to the administration of justice and the maintenance of societal norms embodied in statutes, administrative regulations, and community traditions. Since statutory law is so extensive in the states, it is only natural that much of the work of state courts, especially in trial courts of limited jurisdiction, involves norm enforcement rather than policymaking. According to one recent study, describing the work of state judges,

Some of their workload is administrative (for example, the probating of wills). Another part involves conflict resolution (for example, deciding which party is correct in contested divorce settlements and property disputes). And still another area of responsibility includes the criminal prosecution and appeals process.[18]

State courts do more than simply enforce norms. There are also opportunities to engage in shaping policies in the state. One good example of policymaking by state high courts involves the issue of school districts within a state spending vastly unequal amounts on the education of their students. When the U.S. Supreme Court held that different spending patterns in poor and wealthy school districts within a state do not violate equal protection rights under the U.S. Constitution,[19] a number of legal challenges were mounted in state courts, arguing that unequal educational opportunities violate various clauses in state constitutions. This strategy has proven successful. One observer notes that

state supreme courts in more than half the states have held that reliance on local property-tax revenues to fund public schools violates the right to a free public education contained in their respective state constitutions.[20]

Gay and lesbian rights are another policy issue that seems to have fared better in the hands of state judges than it has in the federal tribunals. For instance, the Georgia Supreme Court overturned the state's anti-sodomy law under the privacy provisions of the Georgia constitution, even though the same law had been upheld in 1986 by the U.S. Supreme Court (in *Bowers v. Hardwick,* 478 U.S. 186).[21]

Still another example involves the Vermont Supreme Court, which ruled in 1999 that the state must guarantee the same protections and benefits to committed gay and lesbian couples that it does to heterosexuals.[22] In response to the court's mandate, the Vermont legislature enacted the Vermont Civil Union law, which went into effect on July 1, 2000. Although the law doesn't legalize same-sex marriages, it does provide gay and lesbian couples with many of the advantages given to heterosexual couples.

These examples clearly illustrate that state court judges may possess important tools that permit them to be quite active in expanding the rights of the state's citizens.[23] Whether they are willing, and politically able to do so, is a different issue. Many state judges are rather **conservative** and simply not inclined to engage in overt policymaking. In addition, the political and legal climate in the state may work against an active policy-making agenda. In short, a combination of ideology, **judicial role** interpretation, and political pressures may dictate that state high court judges not venture far from the status quo.[24]

Administrative and Staff Support in the State Judiciary

The daily operation of the federal courts requires the efforts of many individuals and organizations. This is no less true for the state court systems.

Magistrates

State magistrates, who may also be known in some states as commissioners or referees, are often used to perform some of the work in the early stages of civil and criminal case processing. In this way they are similar to U.S. magistrate judges. In some jurisdictions they hold bond hearings and conduct preliminary investigations in criminal cases. They are also authorized in some states to make decisions in minor cases. In North Carolina, for example, the magistrates who lend support to the state's district courts may accept guilty pleas on certain traffic violations as well as preside over small-claims cases.

Law Clerks

In the state courts, law clerks are likely to be found, if at all, in the intermediate appellate courts and courts of last resort. Most state trial courts do not utilize law clerks, and they are practically unheard of in local trial courts of limited jurisdiction. As at the national level, some law clerks serve individual judges, while others function as staff attorneys for an entire court.

Administrative Office of the Courts

Every state now has an administrative office of the courts or a similarly titled agency that performs a variety of administrative tasks for its court system. The size of the administrative office and its operating budget vary from state to state, so that some of these agencies perform more tasks than others do. Among the duties more commonly associated with administrative offices are budget preparation, data processing, facility management, judicial education, public information, research, and personnel management. A number of administrative offices have total or partial responsibility for one or more of these tasks. In some states still other jobs are assigned to administrative offices. Juvenile and adult probation are the responsibility of administrative offices in a few states, as is **alternative dispute resolution.**

Court Clerks and Court Administrators

The clerk of the court has traditionally handled the day-to-day routines of the court. This includes making courtroom arrangements, keeping records of case proceedings, preparing orders and judgments resulting from court actions, collecting court fines and fees, and disbursing judicial monies. In the majority of states these officials are elected and may be referred to by other titles.

In many areas the traditional clerks of court have been replaced by court administrators. In contrast to the court clerk, who managed the operations of a specific courtroom, the modern court administrator may assist a presiding judge in running the entire courthouse. Even more broadly, in some states the administrator may work for a statewide organization that oversees all the state court systems at the city or county level.

State Court Workload

The lion's share of the nation's judicial business exists at the state, not the national, level. The fact that federal judges adjudicate several hundred thousand cases in a year is impressive; the fact that state courts handle several million in a year is overwhelming. While justice of the peace and magistrate courts at the state level

TABLE 3-4   Reported Filings in State Appellate Courts, 2000

Type of court	Mandatory appeals	Discretionary petitions	Total
Court of last resort	27,700	57,454	85,154
Intermediate appellate court	131,205	30,762	161,967
Total	158,905	88,216	247,121

SOURCE: Compiled from data in "2000 State Court Caseload Tables," *State Court Caseload Statistics, 2001* (Williamsburg, Va.: National Center for State Courts, 2002), 105.

handle relatively minor matters, a number of multi-million dollar judgments in civil cases are annually awarded by ordinary state trial court juries.

The National Center for State Courts has compiled figures on the caseloads of state courts of last resort and intermediate appellate courts in 2000 (see Table 3-4). In all, some 247,121 mandatory appeals and discretionary petitions were filed in the state appellate courts.

Reliable data on cases filed in the state trial courts are harder to come by. Record keeping is much better in some states than in others, and some of the lower-level courts, which often are not courts of record, often greatly vary. Nonetheless, the National Center for State Courts does an excellent job of tracking the figures for the states' trial courts. In 2000, approximately 92 million cases were filed in the general jurisdiction and limited jurisdiction courts (see Table 3-5). Traffic cases constitute the greatest number, followed in descending order by civil, criminal, domestic, and juvenile cases.

TABLE 3-5   Types of Cases Filed in State Trial Courts, 2000 (in millions)

Case type	Jurisdiction General	Limited	Total
Traffic	14.6	41.1	55.7
Civil	7.2	7.8	15.0
Criminal	4.9	9.2	14.1
Domestic	3.7	1.5	5.2
Juvenile	1.3	.7	2.0
Total	31.7	60.3	92.0

SOURCE: "Overview of State Trial Court Caseloads," *Examining the Work of State Courts, 2001* (Williamsburg, Va.: National Center for State Courts, 2002), 10.

Summary

In this chapter we offered a brief historical review of the development of state judicial systems. No two state court systems are alike. However, there are four basic levels within the states: trial courts of limited jurisdiction, trial courts of general jurisdiction, intermediate appellate courts, and courts of last resort. We examined the work done at each of these four levels. Our discussion also included a brief look at the handling of juvenile cases within the states. In addition, we briefly discussed policymaking by state courts in the context of new judicial federalism.

In discussing administrative assistance for the state courts, our review centered on administrative offices of the courts, law clerks, court clerks and court administrators, and magistrates. We concluded with a brief look at the workload of the state trial and appellate courts.

Further Thought and Discussion Questions

1. Does a unified court system provide the best way for state courts to handle their legal issues?

2. Why are state courts not as commonly recognized for their policy-making activities as the federal courts?

3. What conclusions may be drawn from a comparison of state and federal court caseload statistics?

NOTES

1. See Canada Department of Justice, http://www.canada.justice.gc.ca/en/dept/pub/just/CSJ-page19.html; and Alberta Justice, http://www.gov.ab.ca/just/lawu/roles7.html.

2. Henry R. Glick, "Policy Making and State Supreme Courts," in *The American Courts: A Critical Assessment*, ed. John B. Gates and Charles A. Johnson (Washington, D.C.: CQ Press, 1991), 88.

3. Michael E. Solomine and James L. Walker, *Respecting State Courts: The Inevitability of Judicial Federalism* (Westport, Conn.: Greenwood Press, 1999), 89.

4. William J. Brennan Jr., "State Constitutions and the Protection of Individual Rights," *Harvard Law Review* 90 (1977): 489–504.

5. G. Alan Tarr, *Understanding State Constitutions* (Princeton, N.J.: Princeton University Press, 1998), 165.

6. Lawrence M. Friedman, *A History of American Law*, 2d ed. (New York: Simon and Schuster, 1985), 43.

7. Harry P. Stumpf, *American Judicial Politics*, 2d ed. (Upper Saddle River, N.J.: Prentice Hall, 1998), 74.

8. David W. Neubauer, *America's Courts and the Criminal Justice System*, 2d ed. (Monterey, Calif.: Brooks/Cole, 1984), 37.

9. Ibid., 38.

10. Henry J. Abraham, *The Judicial Process*, 6th ed. (New York: Oxford University Press, 1993), 138.

11. See Roscoe Pound, "The Causes of Popular Dissatisfaction with the Administration of Justice," *Journal of the American Judicature Society* 20 (1937): 178–187.

12. Stumpf, *American Judicial Politics*, 2d ed. 75.

13. See Allan Ashman and Pat Chapin, "Is the Bell Tolling for Nonlawyer Judges?" *Judicature* 59 (1976): 417–421.

14. See National Center for State Courts, *State Court Caseload Statistics, 1998* (Williamsburg, Va.: National Center for State Courts, 1999), 5.2.

15. For a study of the roles of state courts of last resort in these structural settings, see Burton M. Atkins and Henry R. Glick, "Environmental and Structural Variables as Determinants of Issues in State Courts of Last Resort," *American Journal of Political Science* 20 (February 1976): 97–115.

16. See Paul Brace and Melinda Gann Hall, "Comparing Courts Using the American States," *Judicature* 83 (March–April 2000): 264–265.

17. Our discussion of the various approaches to handling juvenile matters in the states is based on material found in National Center for State Courts, *State Court Caseload Statistics, 1998*, 8–59.

18. Thad L. Beyle, ed., *State and Local Government, 2002–2003* (Washington, D.C.: CQ Press, 2002), 141.

19. *San Antonio Independent School District v. Rodriguez*, 411 U.S. 1 (1973).

20. Brian L. Porto, *May It Please the Court* (New York: Longman, 2001), 264. A list of some of the better-known cases and an excerpt from one of them may also be found in this book.

21. See Lee Epstein and Thomas G. Walker, *Constitutional Law for a Changing America: Rights, Liberties, and Justice*, 4th ed. (Washington, D.C.: CQ Press, 2001), 463.

22. *Baker v. State;* available online at http://www.state.vt.us/courts/98-032.txt.

23. For a good summary of state supreme court policy-making activities, see Stumpf, *American Judicial Politics*, 2d ed., 367–376.

24. See the discussion in Albert P. Melone and Allan Karnes, *The American Legal System: Foundations, Processes, and Norms* (Los Angeles: Roxbury Publishing Company, 2003), 119–120.

SUGGESTED READINGS

Courts.Net. Available online at http://www.courts.net. Provides Internet links to judicial Web sites of all state court systems.

National Center for State Courts. Available online at http://www.ncsconline.org. An excellent source of information and statistics related to the work of state courts.

Solomine, Michael E., and James L. Walker. *Respecting State Courts: The Inevitability of Judicial Federalism*. Westport, Conn.: Greenwood Press, 1999. A good book about the relationship between the federal and state court systems.

Tarr, G. Alan. *Understanding State Constitutions*. Princeton, N.J.: Princeton University Press, 1998. An informative book about the development and interpretation of state constitutions.

CHAPTER 4

Jurisdiction and Policy-Making Boundaries

Antiwar protesters gather outside the federal courthouse in Boston. In February 2003 a lawsuit was filed by six congressmen and other individuals in which they asked a judge to declare that President Bush had violated the Constitution by launching a military attack on Iraq. They contended that only Congress may authorize such an endeavor by officially declaring war. The judge subsequently dismissed the lawsuit, saying that this was a "political question," that is, a matter to be resolved through the political process—not by the courts.

I N SETTING THE JURISDICTIONS OF courts, Congress and the U.S. Constitution—and their state counterparts—mandate the types of cases each court can hear. Because the role of legislative bodies in setting courts' jurisdictions is an ongoing one, we will consider how Congress in particular can influence judicial behavior by redefining the types of cases judges can hear. We will also provide a detailed discussion of judicial **self-restraint**, examining ten principles, derived from legal tradition and constitutional and statutory law, that govern a judge's decision about whether to review a case.

Federal Courts

The federal court system is divided into three separate levels: the trial courts, the appellate tribunals, and the U.S. Supreme Court.

U.S. District Courts

In the United States Code, Congress has set forth the jurisdiction of the federal district courts. These tribunals have original jurisdiction in federal criminal and civil cases, that is, by law, the cases must be heard first in these courts, no matter who the parties are or how significant the issues.

Criminal Cases. These cases commence when the local U.S. attorneys have reason to believe that a violation of the U.S. Penal Code has occurred. After obtaining an **indictment** from a federal grand jury, the U.S. attorney files charges against the accused in the district court in which he or she serves. Criminal activity as defined by Congress covers a wide range of behavior, including interstate theft of an automobile, involvement in terrorist activities, illegal importation of narcotics, conspiracy to deprive persons of their civil rights, and even the killing of a migratory bird out of season. For the past decade or so the most numerous types of criminal code violations have been embezzlement and fraud, larceny and theft, drunk driving and other traffic offenses, drug-related offenses, and forgery and counterfeiting. Some federal crimes, such as robbery, are comparatively uniform in occurrence in each of the ninety-four U.S. judicial districts, whereas others are endemic to certain geographic areas. For example, those districts next to the Mexican border get an inordinate number of illegal drug and immigration cases. (In Texas for the past several years, drug and illegal entry cases have accounted for almost three-fourths of all criminal filings.)[1]

After charges are filed against an accused, and if no **plea bargain** has been made, a trial is conducted by a U.S. district judge. In court the defendant enjoys all the privileges and immunities granted in the Bill of Rights (such as the right to a speedy and public trial) or by congressional legislation or Supreme Court rulings (for instance, a twelve-person jury must render a unanimous verdict). Defendants may waive the right to a trial by a jury of their peers. A defendant who is found not guilty of the crime is set free and may never be tried again for the same offense (the Fifth Amendment's protection against double jeopardy). If the accused is found guilty, the district judge determines the appropriate sentence within a range set by Congress. The length of a sentence cannot be appealed so long as it is within the range prescribed by Congress. The government may not appeal a verdict of not guilty, but convicted defendants may appeal if they believe that the judge or jury made an improper legal determination.

In the wake of the 9/11 terrorist attacks, the legal safeguards outlined in the above paragraph may be significantly altered for foreign suspects accused of acts of violence against America. For example, the executive order signed by President

George W. Bush in November 2001 empowered the chief executive to determine whether the accused should stand trial before a U.S. district court jury composed of his or her peers or be prosecuted by a military court set up by the secretary of defense. According to this executive order, the secretary of defense would have the authority to select the jury and determine what evidence could be brought against the accused and what level of proof would be required for conviction. A vote of two-thirds would be enough to convict, and a verdict of guilty could not be appealed.[2]

Civil Cases. A majority of the district court caseload is civil in nature, that is, suits between private parties or between the U.S. government, acting in its non-prosecutorial capacity, and a private party. Civil cases that originate in the U.S. district courts may be placed in several categories. The first is litigation concerning the interpretation or application of the Constitution, acts of Congress, or U.S. treaties. Examples of cases in this category include the following: a petitioner claims that one of his or her federally protected civil rights has been violated; a litigant alleges that he or she is being harmed by a congressional statute that is unconstitutional; and a plaintiff argues that he or she is suffering injury from a treaty that is improperly affecting him or her. The key point is that a **federal question** must be raised in order for the U.S. trial courts to have jurisdiction. It is not enough to say that the federal courts should hear a case "because this is an important issue" or "because an awful lot of money is at stake." Unless one is able to invoke the Constitution or a federal law or treaty, the case must be litigated elsewhere (probably in the state courts).

Some minimal dollar amounts traditionally had to be in controversy in some types of cases before the trial courts would hear them, but such amounts have been waived if the case falls into one of several general categories. For example, an alleged violation of a civil rights law, such as the Voting Rights Act of 1965, must be heard by the federal instead of the state judiciary. Other types of cases in this category are patent and copyright claims, passport and naturalization proceedings, admiralty and maritime disputes, and violations of the U.S. postal laws.

Another broad category of cases over which the U.S. trial courts exercise general original jurisdiction includes citizenship disputes involving parties from different states or between an American citizen and a foreign country or citizen. Thus if a citizen of New York were to be injured in an automobile accident in Chicago by a driver from Illinois, the New Yorker could sue in federal court because the parties to the suit were of "diverse citizenship." The requirement that at least $75,000 must be at stake in diversity cases does not appear to be much of a barrier to the gates of the federal judiciary. Even if physical injuries come to less than $75,000, one can always ask for "psychological damages" to push the amount in controversy above the jurisdictional threshold.

Federal district courts also have jurisdiction over petitions from convicted prisoners who contend that their incarceration (or perhaps their denial of parole) is in violation of their federally protected rights. In the vast majority of these cases prisoners ask for a writ of **habeas corpus,** an order issued by a judge to determine whether a person has been lawfully imprisoned or detained. The judge would demand that the prison authorities either justify the detention or release the petitioner. Prisoners convicted in a state court must take care to argue that a federally protected right was violated—for example, the right to be represented by counsel at trial. Otherwise the federal courts would have no jurisdiction. Federal prisoners have a somewhat wider range for their appeals, given that all their rights and options are within the penumbra of the U.S. Constitution.

Finally, the district courts have the authority to hear any other cases that Congress may validly prescribe by law. For example, although the Constitution grants to the U.S. Supreme Court original jurisdiction to hear "Cases affecting Ambassadors, other public Ministers and Consuls," Congress has also authorized the district courts to have concurrent original jurisdiction over cases involving such parties.

U.S. Courts of Appeals

The U.S. appellate courts have no original jurisdiction whatsoever; every case or controversy that comes to one of these intermediate-level panels has been first argued in some other forum. These tribunals, like the district courts, are the creations of Congress, and their structure and functions have varied considerably over time. Basically, Congress has granted the circuit courts appellate jurisdiction over two general categories of cases. The first of these are ordinary civil and criminal appeals from the federal trial courts, including the U.S. territorial courts, the U.S. Tax Court, and some District of Columbia courts. In criminal cases the appellant is the defendant, because the government is not free to appeal a verdict of not guilty. (However, if the question in a criminal case is one of defining the legal right of the defendant, the government may appeal an adverse trial court ruling.) In civil cases the party that lost in the trial court is usually the appellant, although the winning party can appeal if it is not satisfied with the lower-court judgment.

The second broad category of appellate jurisdiction includes appeals from certain federal administrative agencies and departments and also from important independent regulatory commissions, such as the Securities and Exchange

Commission and the National Labor Relations Board. In recent years about 7 percent of the civil docket has consisted of administrative appeals. However, this jumped to over 12 percent beginning in 2002 because of a surge of cases related to Board of Immigration Appeals decisions. In February 2002 Attorney General John Ashcroft ordered the board to clear its backlog of cases. He argued that this was necessary to help prevent terrorist attacks and enforce the nation's immigration laws.[3]

U.S. Supreme Court

The U.S. Supreme Court is the only federal court mentioned by name in the Constitution, which spells out the general contours of the high court's jurisdiction. Although the Supreme Court is usually thought of as an appellate tribunal, it does have some general original jurisdiction. Probably the most important subject of such jurisdiction is a suit between two or more states. For example, every so often Texas and Louisiana spar in the Supreme Court over the proper boundary between them. By law the Sabine River divides the two states, but with great regularity this effluent changes its snaking course, thus requiring the Supreme Court (with considerable help from the U.S. Army Corps of Engineers) to determine where Louisiana ends and the Lone Star State begins.

In addition, the high court shares original jurisdiction (with the U.S. district courts) in certain cases brought by or against foreign ambassadors or consuls, in cases between the United States and a state, and in cases commenced by a state against citizens of another state or against aliens. In situations such as these, where jurisdiction is shared, the courts are said to have **concurrent jurisdiction.** Cases over which the Supreme Court has original jurisdiction are often important, but they do not constitute a sizable proportion of the overall caseload. In recent years less than 1 percent of the high court's docket consisted of cases heard on original jurisdiction.

The U.S. Constitution declares that the Supreme Court "shall have appellate Jurisdiction . . . under such Regulations as the Congress shall make." Over the years Congress has passed much legislation setting forth the "Regulations" determining which cases may appear before the nation's most august judicial body. In essence, appeals may reach the Supreme Court through two main avenues. First, there may be appeals from all lower federal constitutional and territorial courts and also from most, but not all, federal legislative courts. Second, the Supreme Court may hear appeals from the highest court in a state—provided there is a substantial federal question.

Most of the high court's docket consists of cases in which it has agreed to issue a writ of certiorari—a discretionary action. Such a writ (which must be supported by at least four justices, according to the **rule of four**) is an order from the Supreme Court to a lower court demanding that it send up a complete record of a case so that the Supreme Court can review it. Historically, the Supreme Court has agreed to grant the petition for a writ of certiorari in only a tiny proportion of cases—usually less than 10 percent of the time, and in recent years the number has been closer to only 1 percent.

Another method by which the Supreme Court exercises its appellate jurisdiction is **certification**. This procedure is followed when one of the appeals courts asks the Supreme Court for instructions regarding a question of law. The justices may choose to give the appellate judges binding instructions, or they may ask that the entire record be forwarded to the Supreme Court for review and final judgment.

Jurisdiction of State Courts

The jurisdictions of the fifty separate state court systems in the United States are established in virtually the same manner as those within the national court system. Each state has a constitution that sets forth the authority and decision-making powers of its trial and appellate judges. Likewise, each state legislature passes laws that further detail the specific powers and prerogatives of judges and the rights and obligations of those who bring suit in the state courts. Because no two state constitutions or legislative bodies are alike, it is no surprise that the jurisdictions of state courts vary from one state to another. For example, one state constitution may give its supreme court original jurisdiction over all cases in which a state is suing one of its counties, while another state constitution may confer such jurisdiction only on the low-level circuit courts. Similarly, one state legislature might define felony theft as the stealing of $2,000 or more, sending the case automatically to a county criminal court, whereas a case involving less than $2,000 would go to a municipal court authorized to handle only minor crimes. In another state, the legislature might draw the line between felony and petty theft at $1,000. Thus, while court jurisdictions vary from one state to another and from the national model, they are all derived in part from a constitution and in part from enactments of legislative bodies.

Jurisdiction and Legislative Politics

One political reality regarding the jurisdiction of the federal and state courts that cannot be overemphasized is that, for all intents and purposes, Congress and the fifty state legislatures determine what sorts of issues and cases the courts in their separate realms will hear. And equally important, what the omnipotent legislative branches give, they may also take away. Some judges and judicial scholars argue that the U.S. Constitution (in Article III) and the respective state documents confer a certain inherent jurisdiction upon the judiciaries in some key areas, independent of the legislative will. Nevertheless, the jurisdictional boundaries of American courts clearly are a product of legislative judgments—determinations often flavored with the bittersweet spice of politics.

Congress may advance a particular cause by giving courts the authority to hear cases in a public policy realm that previously had been forbidden territory for the judiciary. For example, when Congress passed the Civil Rights Act of 1968, it gave judges the authority to penalize individuals who interfere with "any person because of his race, color, religion or national origin and because he is or has been . . . traveling in . . . interstate commerce" (18 U.S.C.A., Sec. 245). Prior to 1968 the courts had no jurisdiction over incidents that stemmed from interference by one person with another's right to travel. Likewise Congress may discourage a particular social movement by passing legislation to make it virtually impossible for its advocates to have any success in the courts. For example, when the Hawaii Supreme Court approved same-sex marriages in 1993, a conservative and frightened Congress was determined to discourage judges in other states from rendering similar decisions. The result was the Defense of Marriage Act, which President Bill Clinton signed into law on September 20, 1996. The law was designed in part to prevent judges— both state and federal—from reading any meaning into the Fourteenth Amendment to the U.S. Constitution that would condone same-sex marriages. Among other things, the law defined marriage as "only a legal union between one man and one woman," and it permitted state courts to ignore judgments from courts in other states "respecting" marriages between two persons of the same gender. In addition, since the controversial Hawaii Supreme Court ruling in 1993, at least thirty states have passed legislation to specifically ban gay marriages.[4]

Perhaps the most vivid illustration of congressional power over federal court jurisdiction occurred just after the Civil War, and the awesome nature of this legislative prerogative haunts the judiciary to this day. On February 5, 1867, Congress empowered the federal courts to grant habeas corpus to individuals imprisoned in violation of their constitutional rights. The Supreme Court was authorized to hear appeals of such cases. William McCardle was incarcerated by the military government of Mississippi for being in alleged violation of the Reconstruction laws. McCardle was alleged to have published "incendiary and libelous" articles that attacked his "unlawful restraint by military force." He sought relief in the circuit court, but it was denied. He then appealed to the Supreme Court, which agreed to take the case.

After the arguments had been made before the high court (but prior to a decision), Congress got into the act. Its anti-Southern majority feared that the Court would use the *Ex Parte McCardle* case as a vehicle to strike down all or part of the Reconstruction acts—something Congress had no intention of permitting. And so, over President Andrew Johnson's veto, the following statute was enacted: "That so much of the act approved February 5, 1867 [as] authorized an appeal from the judgment of the Circuit Court to the Supreme Court of the United States, or the exercise of any such jurisdiction by said Supreme Court, on appeals which have been, or may hereafter be taken, [is] hereby repealed." Thus, while the Court was in the process of deciding the case, Congress removed the subject matter from the federal docket. And was all of this strictly legal and constitutional? Yes, indeed. Stunned by Congress's action but obedient to the clear strictures of the Constitution, the Court limply ruled that McCardle's appeal must now "be dismissed for want of jurisdiction."[5]

In other words, while discussing what courts do or may do, we must not lose sight of the commanding reality that the jurisdiction of U.S. courts is established by "the United States of America in Congress assembled." Likewise the jurisdictions of the courts in the states are very much governed by—and the political product of—the will of the state legislatures.

Judicial Self-Restraint

The activities that judges are forbidden to engage in, or at least are discouraged from engaging in, deal not so much with technical matters of jurisdiction as with **justiciability**—the question of whether judges in the system ought to hear or refrain from hearing certain types of disputes. It is only by exploring both sides of this issue that insight into the role and function of the federal and state courts can be gained. In the following sections, ten separate aspects of judicial self-restraint, ten principles that serve to check and contain the power of American judges, will be examined.[6] These maxims originate from a variety of sources—the U.S. Constitution and state constitutions, acts of Congress and of state legislatures, the common law tradition—and whenever possible, their roots and the nature of their evolution will be noted. Some apply more to appellate courts than to trial courts, as will be indicated. Although the primary examples provided will be illustrative of the federal judiciary, most apply to state judicial systems as well.

A Definite Controversy Must Exist

The U.S. Constitution states that "the judicial Power shall extend to all Cases, in Law and Equity, arising under this Constitution, the Laws of the United States, and Treaties made . . . under their Authority" (Article III, Section 2). The key word here is *cases*. Since 1789 the federal courts have chosen to interpret the term in its most literal sense; there must be a controversy between legitimate adversaries who have met all the technical legal standards to institute a suit. The dispute must concern the protection of a meaningful, nontrivial right or the prevention or redress of a wrong that directly affects the parties to the suit. Three corollaries to this general principle breathe a little life into its rather abstract-sounding admonitions.

The first is that the federal courts do not render **advisory opinions,** rulings about situations that are hypothetical or that have not caused an authentic clash between adversaries. A dispute must be real and current before a court will agree to accept it for adjudication. For example, in 1902 Congress passed a law allocating certain pieces of land to the Cherokee Indians. Because such disbursements often stimulate many questions about property rights, Congress sought to head off any possible disputes by authorizing certain land recipients to bring suits against the U.S. government in the court of claims, with appeal to the Supreme Court. They were permitted to do so "on their own behalf and on behalf of all other Cherokee citizens" who received land "to determine the validity of any acts of Congress passed since the said act." Stripped of the legalese, the law said: "If you have any hypothetical questions about how the law might affect anyone, just sue the United States, and the courts will answer these questions for you." The Supreme Court politely but pointedly said, "We don't do that sort of thing; we settle only real, actual cases or controversies." The act of Congress was found to be nothing more

than an attempt to provide for judicial determination, final in this court, of the constitutional validity of an act of Congress. [It] is true the United States is made a defendant to this action, but *it has no interest adverse to the claimants.* The object is not to assert a property right as against the government, or to demand compensation for alleged wrongs because of action on its part. . . . In a legal sense the judgment [amounts] to no more than an expression of opinion upon the validity of the [1902 act]. If such actions as are here attempted [are] sustained, the result will be that this court, instead of keeping within the limits of judicial power, and deciding cases or controversies arising between opposing parties, [will] be required to give opinions in the nature of advice concerning legislative action—a function never conferred upon it by the Constitution. [Emphasis added.][7]

A second corollary of the general principle is that the parties to the suit must have proper **standing.** This deals with the matter of who may bring litigation to court. Although there are many aspects of the term *standing*, the most prominent component is that the person bringing suit must have suffered (or be immediately about to suffer) a direct and significant injury. As a general rule, a litigant cannot bring a claim on behalf of others (except for parents of minor children or in special types of suits called **class actions**). In addition, the alleged injury must be personalized and immediate—not part of some generalized **complaint.**

On January 1, 1997, a new law took effect granting the president a line-item veto. A line-item veto permits the chief executive to cancel individual spending and tax items contained in appropriations bills that he has already signed into law. Immediately after the law was passed, six members of Congress who opposed the line-item veto filed suit in federal court to challenge its validity. They claimed that the statute violated the constitutional separation of powers doctrine, which requires that the powers of the chief executive be kept distinct from the powers of Congress. On April 10 a federal district court judge agreed, ruling that the Line Item Veto Act gave the president the unprecedented and "revolutionary" power to repeal part of a statute, a legislative function that no president can exercise and that Congress may not delegate.

When the case reached the Supreme Court, the justices, by a 7–2 vote, overruled the lower-court judge.[8] Refusing to go into the merits of the case at all, the majority noted that as of the date of the Court's decision, President Clinton had not yet used his line-item veto power; therefore, no one could claim any immediate, direct, or personal injury from the statute. Chief Justice William H. Rehnquist, speaking for the majority, said that "we have consistently stressed that a plaintiff's complaint must establish that he has a 'personal stake' in the alleged dispute. . . . The institutional injury [the plaintiffs] . . . allege is wholly abstract and widely dispersed, and their attempt to litigate this dispute at this time and in this form is contrary to historical experience." [9] That temporarily put an end to the matter. The nation had to wait until Clinton first used the veto, and then someone had to come forward who claimed an injury from the president's action and wished to challenge the law in court.

The wait was a short one. Within months President Clinton began energetically using the line-item veto, canceling more than eighty items in taxing and spending bills passed by Congress. One of these was a provision of the Balanced Budget Act of 1997 that provided funds for hospitals in New York City, and another gave tax breaks to potato growers in Idaho. A federal district court determined that this time at least one party in each suit potentially suffered real and significant financial injury from the vetoes: New York stood to lose hundreds of millions of dollars for its Medicaid programs, and the potato growers were about to lose a lucrative tax break that helped to keep them economically competitive. After the suits were consolidated, the court then ruled that the Line Item Veto law violated the Presentment Clause (Article I, Section 7, Clause 2) of the Constitution. The U.S. Supreme Court later affirmed the district court in its now famous 6–3 ruling.[10] The key point, again, is that no judicial rulings are made on the substantive merits of a case unless and until someone is able to convince the court that he or she will suffer or has suffered real injury from the objectionable law.

The third corollary of this general principle is that courts ordinarily will not hear a case that has become **moot**—when the basic facts or the status of the parties has significantly changed in the interim between when the suit was filed and when it comes before the judge(s). The death of a litigant or the fact that the litigants have ceased to be warring parties would render a case moot in most tribunals.

For example, in 1974 the U.S. Supreme Court agreed to hear a petition from Marco DeFunis, who challenged the constitutionality of the admissions policy of the University of Washington Law School. The law school gave preferential treatment to certain minority racial groups, even though such applicants did not rate as high as other, nonminority applicants according to the school's evaluation procedures based on objective tests and grades. DeFunis, a nonminority applicant, charged reverse discrimination in violation of his Fourteenth Amendment rights. During the initial trial of this case at the state court level, DeFunis had been admitted to the law school (on a sort of conditional basis), and when the case eventually reached the Supreme Court, he was in his final quarter of law school. (The law school conceded at oral argument before the Supreme Court that it would permit DeFunis to graduate if he continued to fulfill all requirements.) When the Supreme Court learned of this, a majority determined that the case had become moot. "The controversy between the parties has thus ceased to be 'definite and concrete' and no longer 'touches the legal relations of parties having adverse legal interests,' " said the Court.[11]

However, sometimes judges for their own reasons may decide that a case is still ripe for adjudication, even though the status of the facts and parties would seem to have radically altered. Examples include cases where someone has challenged a state's refusal to permit an abortion or to permit the life-support system of a terminally ill person to be switched off. (In such cases, by the time the suit reaches an appellate court, the woman may already have given birth or the moribund person may have died.) In these cases the judges believed that the issues were so important that they needed to be addressed by the court. To declare such cases moot would, practically speaking, prevent them from ever being heard in time by an appellate body.

A great deal of flexibility and common sense is built into the U.S. legal system—factors that allow for discretion in judges' decision making. The principle of judicial self-restraint offers a counterpoint, guiding judges to what they may not do. They may not decide an issue unless there is an actual case or controversy. From this it follows that they do not consider abstract, hypothetical questions; they do not take a case unless the would-be litigants can demonstrate direct and substantial personal injury; and they (usually) do not take cases that have become moot. This principle is an important one because it means that judges are not free to wander about the countryside like medieval knights slaying all the evil dragons they encounter. They may rule only on concrete issues brought by truly injured parties directly affected by the facts of a case.

Although federal judges do not rule on abstract, hypothetical issues, many state courts are permitted to do so in some form or other (such as those in Colorado, Massachusetts, and South Dakota).[12] Federal legislative courts may give advisory opinions as well. Also, American judges are empowered to render **declaratory judgments,** which define the rights of various parties under a statute, will, or contract. The judgments do not entail any type of coercive relief. As Justice Rehnquist once put it, "A declaratory judgment is simply a statement of rights, not a binding order." [13] The federal courts were given the authority to act in this capacity in the Federal Declaratory Judgment Act of 1934, and about three-fourths of the states grant their courts this power. Although a difference exists between an abstract dispute that the federal courts (at least) must avoid and a situation where a declaratory judgment is in order, in the real world the line between the two is often a difficult one for jurists to draw.

Even though U.S. courts may not rule on abstract questions or on matters for which no significant injury is to be found, this is by no means the pattern throughout the rest of the world. In Norway, for example, its Parliament may ask its Constitutional Court for advice about the constitutionality of a law before it is ever passed. In Ireland the president is permitted to ask the courts for an opinion about a bill's constitutionality before he signs it into law. Likewise in Canada members of its executive cabinet may ask the country's Supreme Court for advisory opinions on almost any topic, including bills pending in or enacted by the provincial legislative bodies. And in Germany its Land (state) governments may petition the Constitutional

Court for abstract opinions about legal matters. Yet even in these countries obtaining advisory opinions from the courts is mainly a prerogative of government officials and agencies—not private citizens.

A Plea Must Be Specific

Another constraint upon the judiciary is that judges will hear no case on the merits unless the petitioner is first able to cite a specific part of the Constitution as the basis of the plea. For example, the First Amendment forbids government to make a law "respecting an establishment of religion," which means, among other things, that the government may not provide direct financial aid to religious entities. In an effort to improve some of its poorly rated public school systems, the state of Ohio enacted its Pilot Project Scholarship Program, which provides financial assistance to families in any Ohio school district that is or has been "under federal court order requiring supervision and operational management of the district by the state superintendent." (Cleveland became the only Ohio school district to fall within that category.) In the 1999–2000 school year, 56 private schools participated in the program, and of these, 46 (or 82 percent) had a religious affiliation. Furthermore, of the 3,700 students who participated in the scholarship program, a whopping 96 percent enrolled in religiously affiliated schools. In 2002 this program was challenged in the Supreme Court by those who argued that this flow of government aid to schools with a religious affiliation violated the First Amendment's ban on governmental "establishment of religion." [14] Ultimately the Supreme Court, in a divided vote, disagreed with the petitioner's argument, arguing that the aid to religion was indirect rather than direct, because the government money went primarily to the parents. But no one could deny that the original petitioners had relied on a specific portion of the Constitution (the Establishment Clause) as part of their plea.

However, if one went into court and contended that a particular law or official action "violated the spirit of the Bill of Rights" or "offended the values of the Founders," a judge would dismiss the proceeding on the spot. If judges were free to give concrete, substantive meaning to vague generalities such as these, there would be little check on what they could do. Who is to say what is the "spirit of the Bill of Rights" or the collective motivation of those who hammered out the Constitution? Judges who were free to roam too far from the specific clauses and strictures of the constitutional document itself would soon become judicial despots.

Despite what has just been said, in the real world this principle is not as simple and clear-cut as it sounds, because the Constitution contains many clauses that are open to a wide variety of interpretations. For example, the Constitution forbids

Congress to pass any law abridging "freedom of speech," but such a term has been virtually impossible for jurists to define with any degree of precision. The Eighth Amendment prohibits "excessive bail" for criminal defendants, but what is excessive? The Fourteenth Amendment, Section 1, forbids states to abridge "the privileges and immunities of citizens of the United States," but who is to say what these privileges and immunities are? The Constitution gives hardly a clue. Although petitioners must cite a particular constitutional clause as the basis for their plea—as opposed to some ambiguous concept—there are nevertheless enough vague clauses in the Constitution to give federal judges plenty of room to maneuver and make policy.

The United States is not the only country with a constitution that contains ambiguous wording and potentially conflicting clauses to which judges have felt free to give new and imaginative meanings. For instance, Article 40 of the Irish Constitution "guarantees liberty for the exercise" of the rights of citizens "to express freely their convictions and opinions" and "to assemble peaceable without arms." But this same article also stipulates that all of these rights are "subject to public order and morality." And it specifically hedges these guarantees by excluding from the protected realm speech that is "blasphemous, seditious, or indecent" and assemblies that serve "to cause a breach of the peace or to be a danger or nuisance to the general public." Or, for example, Section 92 of the Australian Constitution provides that "trade, commerce and intercourse among the States . . . shall be *absolutely free*" [emphasis added]. But Section 51 empowers Parliament "to make laws for the peace, order, and good government of the Commonwealth with respect to (1) Trade and Commerce with other countries, and among the States."

Beneficiaries May Not Sue

A third aspect of judicial self-restraint is that a case will be rejected out of hand if the petitioner has apparently been the beneficiary of a law or an official action that he or she has subsequently chosen to challenge. Suppose that Farmer Brown has long been a member of the Soil Bank Program (designed to cut back on grain surpluses). Under the program, he agreed to take part of his land out of production and periodically was paid a subsidy by the federal government. After years as a participant he learns that his lazy, ne'er-do-well neighbors, the Joneses, are also drawing regular payments for letting their farmland lie fallow. The idea that his neighbors are getting something for nothing starts to offend Farmer Brown, and he begins to harbor grave doubts about the constitutionality of the whole program. Armed with a host of reasons that Congress had acted illegally, Brown challenges the legality of the Soil Bank Act in the local federal district court. As soon as it is brought to the judge's attention that Farmer Brown had himself been a member of the program and had gained financially from it, the suit is dismissed. One may not benefit from a particular governmental endeavor or official action and subsequently attack it in court.

Appellate Courts Rule on Legal—Not Factual—Questions

In the real world, appellate court justices often find it difficult to tell whether a particular legal dispute is a question of who did what to whom (the facts of the case) or of how to weigh and assess a series of events (the legal interpretation of the facts). A working proposition of state and federal appellate court practice is that these courts will generally not hear cases if the grounds for appeal are that the trial judge or jury wrongly amassed and identified the basic factual elements of the case. It is not that trial judges and juries always do a perfect job of making factual determinations. Rather, they are believed to be closer, sensorially and temporally, to the parties and physical evidence of the case. The odds are, so the theory goes, that they will do a much better job of making factual assessments than would an appellate body reading only a stale transcript of the case some months or years after the trial.[15] However, legal matters—which laws to apply to the facts of a case or how to assess the facts in light of the prevailing law—are appropriate for appellate review. On such issues collegial, or multijudge, appellate bodies presumably have a legitimate and better capacity "to say what the law is," as Chief Justice John Marshall put it.

Nevertheless, some qualification must be offered. In most jurisdictions, appellate courts will hear appeals under "the clearly erroneous rule," that is, when the petitioner contends that the trial court's determination of the facts was obviously and utterly wrong. The issue would not be a minor quibble about what the facts were, but a belief that the trial court had made a finding that totally flew in the face of common sense. Likewise appellate courts may be willing to review an administrative agency's factual determinations that were allegedly made "without substantial evidence." Despite these qualifications, it is still fair to say that trial courts are the primary determiners of the facts or evidence in cases, even though such determinations are not always absolutely conclusive.

For example, if X were convicted of a crime and the sole grounds for her appeal were that the judge and jury had mistakenly found her guilty (that is, incorrectly sifted and identified the facts), the appeals court would probably dismiss the case out of hand. However, assume that X provided evidence that she had asked for and been refused counsel during her FBI interrogation and that her confession was therefore illegal. At trial the district judge ruled that the Fifth Amendment's right against self-incrimination did not apply to X's interrogation by the FBI. The defendant argued to the contrary. Such a contention could be appealed because the issue is one of legal, not factual, interpretation.

The fact that U.S. appellate courts are generally restricted to interpreting the law and not to identifying and assembling facts is one additional check on the scope of their decision making.

The Supreme Court Is Not Bound (Technically) by Precedents

If the high court is free to overturn or circumvent past and supposedly controlling precedents when it decides a case, this might appear to be an argument for **judicial activism**—not restraint. However, this practice must be placed in the restraint column. If the Supreme Court were inescapably bound by the dictates of its prior rulings, it would have very little flexibility. It would not be free to back off when discretion advised a cautious approach to a problem; it would not have the liberty to withdraw from a confrontation that might prove detrimental to the nation's or the Court's interests. By occasionally allowing itself the freedom to over-rule a past decision or to ignore a precedent that would seem to be controlling, the Supreme Court establishes a corner of safety to which it can retreat if need be. When wisdom dictates that the Court change direction or at least keep an open mind, this principle of self-restraint is readily plucked from the judicial kit bag.

Other Remedies Must Be Exhausted

Another principle of self-restraint often frustrates the anxious litigant but is essential to the orderly administration of justice: Courts in the United States will not accept a case until all other remedies, legal and administrative, have been exhausted. Although this caveat is often associated with the U.S. Supreme Court, it is a working principle for virtually all American judicial tribunals. In its simplest form this doctrine means that legal petitions must work their way up the ladder. Federal cases must first be heard by the U.S. trial courts, then reviewed by one of the appellate tribunals, and finally heard by the U.S. Supreme Court. This orderly procedure must and will occur despite the importance of the case or of the petitioners who filed it. For instance, in 1952 President Harry S. Truman seized the American steel mills to prevent a pending strike that he believed would imperil the war effort in the Korean conflict. Both labor and management were suddenly told they were now working for Uncle Sam. The mill owners were furious and immediately brought suit, charging that the president had abused the powers of his office. A national legal-political crisis erupted. One might think that the Supreme Court would immediately take a case of this magnitude. Not so. In the traditional and orderly fashion of American federal justice, the controversy first went to the local district court in Washington, D.C., just as if it were the most ordinary dispute. Not until after the district court had ruled did the nation's highest tribunal have the opportunity to sink its teeth into this hearty piece of judicial meat. (The Supreme Court did, however, concede the need for expeditious action by granting certiorari before the court of appeals could rule on the merits of the case, thereby shortening the normal appellate process.)

Exhaustion of remedies refers to possible administrative relief as well as adherence to the principle of a three-tiered judicial hierarchy. Such relief might be in the form of an appeal to an administrative officer, a hearing before a board or committee, or formal consideration of a matter by a legislative body. Consider a hypothetical illustration. Professor Ben Wheatley is denied tenure at a staunchly conservative institution. He is told that tenure was not granted because of his poor teaching record and lack of scholarly publications. He contends that denial of tenure is in retaliation for his having founded the nearby Sunshine Socialist Society, a nudist colony for gay atheists. He has the option of a hearing before the university's Grievance Committee, but he declines it, saying, "It would do no good; it would just be a waste of time." Instead, he takes his case immediately to the local federal district court, claiming that his Fourteenth Amendment rights have been violated. When the case is brought before the trial court, the judge says to Professor Wheatley: "Before I will even look at this matter, you must first take your case before the official, duly established Grievance Committee at your university. It doesn't matter whether you believe that you will win or lose your petition before the committee. You must establish your record there and avail yourself of all the administrative appeals and remedies that your institution has provided. If you are then still dissatisfied with the outcome, you may at that time invoke the power of the federal district courts."

Thus judicial restraint means that judges do not jump immediately into every controversy that appears to be important or that strikes their fancy. The restrained and orderly administration of justice requires that before any court may hear a case, all administrative and inferior legal remedies must first be exhausted.

Courts Do Not Decide "Political Questions"

U.S. judges are often called upon to determine the winner of a contested election, to rule on the legality of a newly drawn electoral district, or to get involved in voting rights cases. How, then, can the argument be made that political questions are out of bounds for the American judiciary? The answer lies in the narrow, singular use of the word *political*. To U.S. judges, the executive and the legislative branches of government are political in that they are elected by the people for the purpose of making public policy. The judiciary, in contrast, was not designed by the Founders to be an instrument manifesting the popular will and is therefore not political. According to this line of reasoning, a political question is one that ought properly to be resolved by one of the other two branches of government (even though it may appear before the courts wrapped in judicial clothing). When judges determine that something is a political question and therefore not appropriate for judicial review, what they are saying in effect is this: "You litigants may have couched your plea in judicial terminology, but under our form of government, issues such as this ought properly to be decided at the ballot box, in the legislative halls, or in the chambers of the executive."

For example, when the state of Oregon gave its citizens the right to vote on popular statewide referendums and initiatives around the end of the nineteenth century, the Pacific States Telephone and Telegraph Company objected.[16] (The company feared that voters would bypass the more business-oriented legislature and pass laws restricting its rates and profits.) The company claimed that by permitting citizens directly to enact legislation, the state has "been reduced to a democracy," whereas Article IV, Section 4, of the Constitution guarantees to each state "a Republican Form of Government"—a term that supposedly means that laws are to be made only by the elected representatives of the people, not by the citizens directly. Pacific States Telephone demanded that the Supreme Court take action. Opting for discretion rather than valor, the high court refused to rule on the merits of the case, declaring the issue to be a political question. The Court reasoned that because Article IV primarily prescribes the duties of Congress, it follows that the Founders wanted Congress—not the courts—to oversee the forms of government in the several states. In other words, the Court was being asked to invade the decision-making domain of one of the other (political) branches of government. And this it refused to do.

In 2003 Americans witnessed a circus-like political scenario in the state of Texas that some wanted the courts to resolve, but the judges would have none of it. In this instance, the Republican-dominated legislature attempted to redraw congressional boundaries in the state in order to give the GOP four to seven additional seats in the Texas delegation to the U.S. House of Representatives. The Democratic minority in the Texas Senate, unable to defeat the redistricting bill in a straight party-line vote, opted to physically leave the state, thereby depriving the Senate of a quorum and preventing the obnoxious bill from being adopted. During the regular session of the legislature the Democratic senators fled to Oklahoma, and when the governor called a special session of the legislature for redistricting purposes, the Democrats hightailed it to the protective confines of New Mexico, where the Texas Rangers were without jurisdiction. The Republican governor and GOP Senate members repeatedly attempted to have the Texas courts order the wayward Democratic senators back to their posts, but even the all-Republican state supreme court unanimously refused to enter the fray. Putting aside the judges' legalese, the courts said that this was basically a political matter, a dispute to be settled within the framework of the political process and/or ultimately by the voters of Texas. The courts do not enter what Justice Felix Frankfurter called "the political thicket."

When President Jimmy Carter acted on his own initiative to end the Mutual Defense Treaty between the United States and Taiwan, this action was challenged in the courts by a number of senators and representatives. The high court, consistent with tradition, refused to involve itself in this political question.[17] More recently, attempts have been made to challenge the legality of the 2003 war in Iraq. None of these cases have yet reached the Supreme Court, and thus far none of the lower courts have shown any interest in blocking what they regard as essentially a political, nonjusticiable, matter.

Whether judges should assume responsibility for doing what the Founders probably wanted only political leaders to do is a question not confined to the United States. In India, for example, the national judiciary has been widely criticized for taking on issues that the writers of the Indian constitution wanted Parliament alone to address, such as matters of air and water pollution. Article 21 of the Indian Constitution provides its people with "a right to life." In 1991 its Supreme Court ruled that this article meant that the people had a right to pollution-free air and water, and later on it ordered the government to initiate a series of measures to educate the public about environmental pollution.[18]

The Burden of Proof Is on the Petitioner

Another weighty principle of self-restraint is the general agreement among the nation's jurists that an individual who would challenge the constitutionality of a statute bears the burden of proof. This is just a different way of saying that laws and official deeds are all presumed to be legal unless and until proven otherwise by a preponderance of evidence. The question of who has the burden of proof is of keen interest to lawyers because, in effect, it means: which side has the bigger job to perform in the courtroom? And which party must assume the lion's share of the burden of convincing the court—or lose the case entirely? Thus if one were attacking a particular statute, one would have to do more than demonstrate that it was "questionable" or "of doubtful constitutionality"; one must persuade the court that the evidence against the law was clear-cut and overwhelming—not often an easy task. In giving the benefit of the doubt to a statute or an executive act, judges have yet another area in which to exercise restraint.

The only exception to this burden of proof principle is in the realm of civil rights and liberties. Some jurists who are strong civil libertarians have long contended that when government attempts to restrict basic human freedoms, the burden of proof should shift to the government. And in several specific areas of civil rights jurisprudence that philosophy now prevails. For example, the U.S. Supreme Court has ruled in a variety of cases that laws that treat persons differently on the basis of their race or gender are automatically subject to "special scrutiny." This means that the burden of proof shifts to the government to demonstrate a compelling or overriding need for this differential treatment. For instance, the government has long argued (successfully) that some major restrictions can be placed on women in the armed forces to prevent them from being assigned to full combat duty.

Laws Are Overturned on the Narrowest Grounds Only

Sometimes during a trial a judge clearly sees that the strictures of the Constitution have been offended by a legislative or executive act. Even here, however, ample opportunity is available to proceed with caution. Judges have two common ways to exercise restraint even when they must reach for the blue pencil.

First, a judge may have the option of invalidating an official action on statutory rather than constitutional grounds. Statutory invalidation means that a judge overturns an official's action because the official acted beyond the authority delegated to him or her by the law. Such a ruling has the function of saving the law itself while nullifying the official's misdeed.

Suppose that Congress continues to authorize postal officials to seize all obscene nude photographs that are shipped through the mail. A photographer attempts to mail pictures taken at his art studio, but the pictures are seized by postal officials. The photographer protests that the statute violates his First Amendment rights, and the case is eventually taken to the federal courts. Assuming that the judges are generally sympathetic to the position of the photographer, they have two basic options. They may declare the statute to be in violation of the Constitution and thus null and void, or they may select another stance that permits them to have it both ways. They may decide that the law itself passed constitutional muster, but that the postal official in question mistakenly decided that the nude photos were obscene. Thus the statute is preserved and a direct confrontation between the courts and Congress is averted, but the courts are able to give the petitioner virtually everything he wants. This is an example of deciding a case on statutory grounds.

Second, judges may, if possible, invalidate only that portion of a law they find constitutionally defective instead of overturning the entire statute. For instance, in 1963 Congress passed the Higher Education Facilities Act, which provided construction grants for college buildings. Part of the law declared that for a twenty-year period, no part of the newly built structures could be used for "sectarian instruction, religious worship, or the programs of a divinity school." Because church-related universities as well as public institutions benefited from the act, the entire law was challenged in court as being in violation of the Establishment of Religion Clause of the First Amendment. The Supreme Court determined that the basic thrust of the law did not violate the Constitution, but it did find the "twenty-year clause" to be objectionable. After all, the Court reasoned, most buildings last a good deal longer than two decades, and a building constructed at public expense could thus house religious activities during most of its lifetime. Instead of striking down the entire act, however, the Court majority merely substituted the word *never* for the phrase twenty years.[19] Thus the baby was not thrown out with the bath water and judicial restraint was maintained.

No Rulings Are Made on the "Wisdom" of Legislation

This final aspect of judicial self-restraint is probably the least understood by the public, the most often violated by the courts, and yet potentially the greatest harness on judicial activism in existence. What this admonition means, if followed strictly, is that the only basis for declaring a law or an official action unconstitutional is that it violates the Constitution on its face. Statutes do not offend the Constitution merely because they are unfair, fiscally wasteful, or bad public policy. Official actions can be struck down only if they step across the boundaries clearly set forth by the Founders. If taken truly to heart, this means that judges and justices are not free to invoke their own personal notions of right and wrong or of good and bad public policy when they examine the constitutionality of legislation.

A keen expression of this phenomenon of judicial self-restraint is found in Justice Potter Stewart's dissenting opinion in the case of *Griswold v. Connecticut*. The

Court majority had struck down the state's law that forbade the use of contraceptive devices or the dissemination of birth control information. Stewart said, in effect, that the law was bad, but that its weaknesses did not make it unconstitutional.

Since 1897 Connecticut has had on its books a law which forbids the use of contraceptives by anyone. I think this is an uncommonly silly law. As a practical matter, the law is obviously unenforceable, except in the oblique context of the present case. . . . But we are not asked in this case to say whether we think this law is unwise, or even asinine. We are asked to hold that it violates the United States Constitution. And that I cannot do.[20]

Another spin-off of this principle is that a law may be passed that all agree is good and wise but that is nevertheless unconstitutional; conversely, a statute may legalize the commission of an official deed that all know to be bad and dangerous but that still does not offend the Constitution. Permitting the police to dispose of known criminals without benefit of trial would probably save taxpayers a good deal of money and also reduce the crime rate, but it would be a clear prima facie violation of the Constitution. However, a congressional tax on every sex act might be constitutionally permissible but would be a very unwise piece of legislation—not to mention difficult to enforce. Thus when laws or official acts are at issue, the adjectives *goodness* and *constitutionality* are no more synonymous than are *badness* and *unconstitutionality.*

Although few legal scholars would disagree with what has just been said, virtually all would point out that the principle of not ruling on the "wisdom" of a law is difficult to follow in the real world and is often honored in the breach. This is so because the Constitution, a rather brief document, is silent on many areas of public life and contains a number of phrases and admonitions that are open to a variety of interpretations. For instance, the Constitution says that Congress may regulate interstate commerce. But what exactly is commerce, and how extensive does it have to be before it is of an "interstate" character? As human beings, judges have differed in the way they have responded to this question. The Constitution guarantees a person accused of a crime the right to a defense attorney. But does this right continue if one appeals a guilty verdict and, if so, for how many appeals? Strict constructionists and loose constructionists have responded differently to these queries.

In all, despite the inevitable intrusion of judges' personal values into their interpretation of many portions of the Constitution, virtually every jurist subscribes to the general principle that laws can be invalidated only if they offend the Constitution—not the personal preferences of the judges.

Summary

In this chapter we have focused on what federal and state courts are supposed to do and on what they must refrain from doing. They adjudicate cases that come within their lawful original or appellate jurisdiction. Federal district courts hear criminal cases and civil suits that deal with federal questions, a **diversity of citizenship** matters, prisoners' petitions, and any other issues authorized by Congress. The appellate courts, having no original jurisdiction whatever, take appeals from the district courts and from numerous administrative and regulatory agencies. The U.S. Supreme Court has original jurisdiction over suits between two or more states and in cases where ambassadors or public ministers are parties to a suit. Its appellate jurisdiction, regulated entirely by Congress, permits it to hear appeals from the circuit courts and from state courts of last resort. Since 1988 Congress has delegated to the high court the right to control its own appellate caseload. As for state courts, the previous chapter summarized the primary contours of their jurisdictions, but in this chapter we emphasized the great importance of the issues that are adjudicated at the state level.

Under the U.S. legal system, federal courts are not to adjudicate questions unless a real case or controversy is at stake, although many state courts may render advisory opinions. All pleas to the courts must be based on a specific portion of the Constitution. Judges are also to dismiss suits in which a petitioner is challenging a law from which he or she has benefited. Federal and state appellate courts may rule only on matters of law—not on factual questions. Not being bound entirely by its precedents, the Supreme Court is free to exercise flexibility and restraint if it wishes to do so. All courts insist that litigants exhaust every legal and administrative remedy before a case will be decided. Courts in the United States are to eschew political questions and insist that the burden of proof rests on those who contend that a law or official action is unconstitutional. If judges must nullify an act of the legislature or the executive, they are to do so on the narrowest grounds possible. Finally, courts ought not rule on the wisdom or desirability of a law but are to strike down legislation only if it clearly violates the letter of the Constitution.

Further Thought and Discussion Questions

1. Have you ever read your own state's Bill of Rights? Chances are that it not only guarantees as many, and as significant, liberties as are found in the U.S. Constitution, but also that its protections may be even more extensive than those found in

the federal constitution. What are the merits of state protections extending beyond the federal Bill of Rights?

2. What would happen if Congress, because it did not like the decisions the federal courts were handing down in a particular policy area, passed a law that removed the subject matter from the courts' jurisdiction? Would the action be constitutional? It has happened in the past. In what realms might Congress act in a similar manner again?

3. Are "activist" state and federal judges as out of control as some say? Are judges limited enough in what they can do? Who or what establishes those boundaries, and should they be changed?

4. Would it be a good idea if the president, Congress, and other governmental agencies could get the courts to rule on the constitutionality of proposed governmental actions before they were put in place? Wouldn't considerable time and trouble be saved if courts were allowed to nip unconstitutional acts in the bud before they did any harm? Courts in other nations have this authority.

NOTES

1. Deborah Tedford, "Focus of Federal Docket Shifts: Immigration, Drugs Now 70 Percent of Texas Cases," *Houston Chronicle*, August 29, 1999, A1.

2. Patty Reinert, "Bush Defends Military Tribunals," *Houston Chronicle*, November 27, 2001, A13.

3. Administrative Office of the United States Courts, *2002 Annual Report of the Director: Judicial Business of the United States Courts* (Washington, D.C.: U.S. Government Printing Office), 2003, 15.

4. "State High Court Strikes Down Effort to Legalize Gay Marriages," *Houston Chronicle*, December 11, 1999, A12.

5. *Ex Parte McCardle*, 74 U.S. (7 Wall.) 506 (1869).

6. For our discussion of the many aspects of judicial self-restraint we acknowledge our debt to Henry J. Abraham, on whose classic analysis of the subject we largely relied. See Henry J. Abraham, *The Judicial Process*, 7th ed. (New York: Oxford University Press, 1998), chap. 9.

7. *Muskrat v. United States*, 219 U.S. 346 (1911).

8. *Raines v. Byrd*, 521 U.S. 811 (1997).

9. Edward Felsenthal, "Justices Clear Way for Line-Item Veto, Ruling Challengers Lack Legal Standing," *Wall Street Journal*, June 27, 1997, A16.

10. *Clinton v. New York*, 524 U.S. 417 (1998).

11. *DeFunis v. Odegaard*, 416 U.S. 317 (1974).

12. Seven state constitutions expressly impose on their state supreme courts a duty to render advisory opinions (Colorado, Florida, Maine, Massachusetts, New Hampshire, Rhode Island, and South Dakota). In Alabama and Delaware, state courts have upheld laws authorizing advisory opinions even in the absence of a constitutional mandate. In North Carolina, the power to issue advisory opinions comes from a series of judicial decisions. For a general discussion of this topic, see "The State Advisory Opinion in Perspective," *Fordham Law Review* 44 (1975): 81–113.

13. *Steffel v. Thompson*, 415 U.S. 452 (1974) at 482.

14. *Zelman v. Simmons-Harris*, 536 U.S. (2002).

15. One innovation in this realm is worth noting. At the present time in five federal courtrooms and in parts of six states, appeals judges are able to view videotapes of trials whose judgments are appealed to them. For an interesting discussion of this practice and conjecture about its future implications, see Junda Woo, "Videotapes Give Appeals Cases New Dimension," *Wall Street Journal*, April 14, 1992, B1.

16. *Pacific States Telephone & Telegraph v. Oregon*, 223 U.S. 118 (1912).

17. *Goldwater v. Carter*, 444 U.S. 996 (1979).

18. For an excellent discussion of this particular case and also of the degree to which the Indian Supreme Court engages in judicial activism, see Robert Moog, "Activism on the Indian Supreme Court," *Judicature* 82 (1998): 124–132.

19. *Tilton v. Richardson*, 403 U.S. 672 (1971).

20. *Griswold v. Connecticut*, 381 U.S. 479 (1965).

SUGGESTED READINGS

Abraham, Henry J. *The Judicial Process*, 7th ed. New York: Oxford University Press, 1998. A traditional but classic discussion of the judicial process—especially Chapter 9, which focuses on judicial self-restraint.

Halpern, Stephen C., and Charles M. Lamb, eds. *Supreme Court Activism and Restraint.* Lexington, Mass.: Lexington Books, 1982. An excellent series of individual essays about the history and the pros and cons of judicial activism and restraint.

Judicature 81 (1998). The entire issue is dedicated to courts and justice abroad, with a special emphasis on matters of jurisdiction and policy-making boundaries.

Murphy, Walter F., C. Herman Pritchett, and Lee Epstein, eds. *Courts, Judges, & Politics: An Introduction to Judicial Process*, 5th ed. New York: McGraw-Hill, 2002. A rich and varied collection of some of the most important historical documents in the realm of judicial process and behavior.

Tarr, G. Alan. *Understanding State Constitutions*. Princeton, N.J.: Princeton University Press, 1998. An important discussion of state courts as affected by changes in their own constitutions and by the effect of the "new judicial federalism."

Tate, C. Neal. *Comparative Judicial Systems*. Washington, D.C.: CQ Press, 2003. An extremely comprehensive and up-to-date text that compares and contrasts the judicial systems of the major nations of the world. It documents the expansion of the power and jurisdiction of courts throughout the modern era.

The Third Branch: Newsletter of the Federal Courts. Published by the Administrative Office of the U.S. Courts. Washington, D.C.: Government Printing Office. A monthly report on activities, problems, and events related to day-to-day operations of the federal judiciary.

CHAPTER 5

State Judges

Massachusetts Supreme Judicial Court Chief Justice Margaret Marshall delivers the keynote address at the Massachusetts Bar Association's annual conference in 2003. Prior to the 1980s, it was almost unheard of for a woman to serve on a state's highest court. However, by May 2000, women were represented on the highest court of every state except South Dakota and even represented a near majority in several. In spite of these steps, women make up only about one-fourth of state supreme court justices.

A S THE BLACK-ROBED DECISION makers at state and federal levels, to whom most Americans still look with reverence, become the focus of analysis in the next two chapters, keep several questions in mind: What characteristics do these people have that distinguish them from the rest of the citizenry? What are the qualifications—both formal and informal—for appointment to the bench? How are the judges selected and who are the participants in the process? How are they socialized into their judicial roles, that is, how do judges learn to be judges? How are judges disciplined, and when are they removed from the bench?

The focus in this chapter will be on those who wear the black robe in the numerous trial and appellate courts throughout the states.

Qualifications and Backgrounds of State Judges

Although the selection process for state and federal judges differs, there are inevitable comparisons between the men and women who are tapped for judicial service at each level. Regardless of the similarities and differences, state judges share with their federal colleagues the distinction of being local people who made good.

Most state laws and constitutions provide few rigid conditions for being a state judge. The vast majority of the states do not require their justices of the peace or magistrates to have law degrees, but such degrees are virtually required (either formally or in practice) for trial and appellate judges.

Unlike several other countries, the United States has neither a career judiciary nor a specifically prescribed training program for would-be judges. In France, for example, all prospective judges are trained for over two years and can become judges only after passing rigorous competitive examinations. Judicial training in Scandinavian countries is acquired during a practical internship after graduating from law school.[1] While filling a vacancy on a higher court by promoting a judge from a lower court is fairly common in the United States, some of the outstanding judges of the nation's highest courts have had no prior judicial experience. Even though the legal profession is not totally unaware of the advantages of a career judiciary, "it is generally thought that they are outweighed by the experience and independence that lawyers bring to the bench."[2]

The informal qualifications for being a state jurist are reflected in the socioeconomic profile that seems to hold throughout the United States. Although women constitute a slight majority of the American population, judicial service is still very much a man's game. Despite the upsurge in recent decades in the number of women in the legal profession and the number of them appointed to the bench, women still constitute only about one-fourth (25.8 percent) of state supreme court justices.[3]

A recent study noted that whereas only ten females served on state courts of last resort during the years 1980–1981, there were eighty-eight serving in 2000.[4] Given the complex network of state courts, especially at the trial level, an exact figure for the number of female judges who have served as intermediate appellate court or trial court judges is more difficult to obtain. As one judicial scholar noted after Ruth Bader Ginsburg became the second woman appointed to the U.S. Supreme Court (thus doubling the number of female justices),

the number of women judges on courts other than the U.S. Supreme Court has also doubled. In fact, the number of women judges has probably tripled, but accurate figures are hard to come by.[5]

For this reason, our discussion will deal primarily with judges serving on the state courts of last resort.

Women were represented on forty-nine of the state high courts (South Dakota was the lone exception) in May 2000 and even approached a majority in California, Colorado, Massachusetts, Michigan, Nevada, New Jersey, Ohio, Virginia, and Wisconsin.[6] Despite these improvements, women are disproportionately more likely to serve at the lower levels of the state judiciary than on the supreme courts, although even this phenomenon varies greatly from one state to the next.

In the same vein, being non-Anglo is clearly not an asset if one yearns to wear a black robe. A recent study noted that, in 2000, about 88 percent of the state high court justices were white, over 7 percent were African American, about 2 percent were Hispanic, nearly 2 percent more were Asian American, and none were Native American.[7] The author concludes that even though racial minorities are still not represented relative to their numbers in the general population, it is obvious that their numbers have risen substantially since the early 1980s and mid-1990s.[8]

Although state judges were at one time very likely to be closely tied to their region, that has begun to change. Only 65.7 percent of the occupants of state high courts in 2000 were born in the state in which they were serving, a decline of over 12 percent in a twenty-year period.[9] Also, fewer state supreme court justices are receiving their law degrees from in-state institutions than was the case in the past.[10]

In terms of political party affiliation, a slight majority (51.8 percent) of the state high court justices sitting in 2000 were Democrats, compared with 64.3 percent in 1994. Of the remainder, 46.2 percent were affiliated with the Republican Party, and only 2 percent were independents or had no political party affiliation.[11] In Canada, by contrast, judges pride themselves on not being chosen on the basis of their politics. In recent interviews with Canadian judges it was reported that

several went out of their way to note that they were appointed to the superior trial courts by one party and then elevated to the provincial court of appeal by another.[12]

Serving as a prosecutor was a career path chosen by about one-third of the justices serving on state courts of last resort in 2000.[13] Also, nearly 72 percent of those making it to their state's highest court in 2000 had previous judicial experience.[14] If this is considered another way, however, it means that about 28 percent of the justices began their judicial career on their state's highest court.

Finally, we look at whether state high court judges have held political office prior to ascending to this position. The most comprehensive study to date of the characteristics of judges on the state courts of last resort indicates that only 15 percent of those sitting in 2000 were former elected officials.[15] Thus, even though political activity may be important to prospective judges, it does not typically lead to holding public office.

The Selection Process for State Judges

At the state level various methods are used to select jurists, and each of them has many permutations. Basically, there are five routes to a judgeship in any one of the fifty states: partisan election, nonpartisan election, **merit selection,** gubernatorial appointment, and appointment by the legislature. Tables 5-1 and 5-2 indicate which states use each of the methods for selecting judges for full terms in the trial courts of general jurisdiction and the courts of last resort.

But as is often the case in the political world, things are not always what they seem. For instance, in states that officially choose their judges for full terms by partisan elections, a good number of judges may receive their initial position through gubernatorial appointment. This occurs because a sitting judge may die or resign or a new judicial vacancy may occur, and the position is filled by the governor in accordance with state law. The newly appointed judge may eventually have to run for another term in a general election, but most incumbent judges are easily reelected. Likewise in states that are officially in the nonpartisan election category—for example, Minnesota—it is often no secret which judicial candidate is the Democrat and which is the Republican, and the voters may respond accordingly.

TABLE 5-1   Methods of Selecting Judges for Full Terms in State Trial Courts of General Jurisdiction

Method	State(s)
Partisan election	Alabama, Arkansas, Illinois, Indiana, New Mexico, New York, Pennsylvania, Tennessee, Texas, West Virginia
Nonpartisan election	Arizona, California, Florida, Georgia, Idaho, Kentucky, Louisiana, Michigan, Minnesota, Mississippi, Montana, Nevada, North Carolina, North Dakota, Ohio, Oklahoma, Oregon, South Dakota, Washington, Wisconsin
Merit selection	Alaska, Colorado, Delaware, Hawaii, Iowa, Kansas, Maryland, Massachusetts, Missouri, Montana, Nebraska, Utah, Vermont, Wyoming
Gubernatorial appointment	Maine, New Hampshire, New Jersey, Rhode Island
Legislative appointment	Connecticut, South Carolina, Virginia

SOURCE: Compiled from data found in "Judicial Selection and Service," *State Court Organization, 1998* (Williamsburg, Va.: National Center for State Courts, 1999), 34–47.

NOTE: Some states use more than one method for various trial courts.

TABLE 5-2   Methods of Selecting Judges for Full Terms in State Courts of Last Resort

Method	State(s)
Partisan election	Alabama, Arkansas, Illinois, New Mexico, North Carolina, Pennsylvania, Texas, West Virginia
Nonpartisan election	Georgia, Idaho, Kentucky, Louisiana, Michigan, Minnesota, Mississippi, Montana, Nevada, North Dakota, Ohio, Oregon, Washington, Wisconsin
Merit selection	Alaska, Arizona, California, Colorado, Delaware, Florida, Hawaii, Indiana, Iowa, Kansas, Maryland, Massachusetts, Missouri, Nebraska, New York, Oklahoma, Rhode Island, South Dakota, Tennessee, Utah, Vermont, Wyoming
Gubernatorial appointment	Maine, New Hampshire, New Jersey
Legislative appointment	Connecticut, South Carolina, Virginia

SOURCE: Compiled from data found in "Judicial Selection and Service," *State Court Organization, 1998* (Williamsburg, Va.: National Center for State Courts, 1999), 21–24.

NOTE: In Rhode Island the justices are initially appointed by the governor from a list of names submitted by a judicial nomination commission. Once appointed, they have life tenure.

Election of Judges

The election of judges, on either a partisan or a nonpartisan ballot, is the norm in the states. Although almost unheard of in colonial days, this method became popular during the time of President Andrew Jackson—an era when Americans sought to democratize the political process.

In practice, things have not always worked this way. Prior to the 1980s, judicial elections "were traditionally uncompetitive, and the major causes of turnover on the bench were retirements and resignations." [16] Furthermore, uncontested races typically involved modest spending and low levels of candidate visibility. Very little information was imparted in judicial campaigns, and voters relied primarily on such cues as party affiliation and name familiarity.

This began to change in the late 1970s, and "the 1980s brought numerous examples of extremely competitive and remarkably expensive judicial elections." [17] The first signs of a new style of judicial elections appeared in California, where deputy district attorneys in Los Angeles advertised in a local legal newspaper to recruit candidates to run against sitting trial court judges. This resulted in an unprecedented number of contested races and defeated incumbents. Subsequent judicial elections in California have been characterized by "preemptive fundraising and hiring political consultants early in the election season." [18] Naturally, they have also become quite a bit more expensive.

Reports from other states indicate a similar pattern. In Texas, for example, supreme court candidates typically spent less than $200,000 before 1984. Since then, the average has been at least $500,000, and in one year as much as $1.5 million.[19] Winning candidates for the Pennsylvania Supreme Court have generally spent at least a million dollars since 1983, and in Wisconsin campaign expenditures increased from an average of $194,643 in 1989 to $656, 202 in 1999.[20]

Another important change in judicial elections involves the source of campaign funds—a subject that raises concerns about the susceptibility of judges to accusations of favoritism. Judicial candidates raise campaign funds from a variety of sources: individuals (including lawyers with business before the court), political parties, and interest groups. In addition, some use their own personal funds. A recent study indicates that about 40 percent comes from personal funds, nearly 49 percent from individuals, 1.5 percent from political parties, and almost 5 percent from interest groups.[21]

Some suggest that lawyers make contributions to judicial candidates in the hope of receiving favorable treatment in the courts. In addition to seeing a friendly face on the other side of the bench, some lawyers may make a contribution in the hope that a judge will reward them with an appointment to provide some sort of compensated legal service.

On the other side of the coin, there is some concern for lawyers who may be asked to contribute to a judicial campaign. Lawyers with business before the court may find it difficult to refuse a solicitation for a contribution, especially if it comes from a sitting judge.

Interest-group giving to judicial campaigns also raises concerns, as some believe that the judiciary should be a nonpartisan branch of government. However, judicial candidates often see labor unions, business organizations, and other advocacy groups as important sources of funds.[22] Interest groups may be willing contributors because they view judicial elections as a way of influencing court decisions by altering the composition of the bench.

Finally, we should note that the method of actually conducting a judicial campaign has changed over the years. Candidates, especially those running for an intermediate appellate court or a court of last resort, now place greater emphasis on broadcast television and less emphasis on traditional methods of contacting voters. Although many candidates for a judgeship still focus primarily on their qualifications and such traits as judicial temperament and fairness, others have begun to speak out more boldly on policy issues. In fact, the U.S. Supreme Court, in a case decided on June 27, 2002, held that the Minnesota Supreme Court's canon of judicial conduct, which prohibited a candidate for judicial office from announcing his or her views on disputed legal or political issues, violates the First Amendment Freedom of Speech Clause.[23]

In summary, state judicial elections no longer simply subject judges to a cursory review by voters. As the authors of one recent study put it,

Now that electoral uncertainty forces candidates to raise money and gain the support of interested groups, they are subject to electoral pressures that are remarkably similar to those experienced by legislators, mayors, and other elected officials.[24]

As part of the Progressive movement at the turn of the twentieth century, reformers sought to take some of the raw partisanship out of judicial elections by having judges run on a nonpartisan basis. In principle they would run on their ideas and qualifications, not on the basis of which party they belonged to. In practice, however, a recent study reveals that candidates in nonpartisan elections also regard political parties and interest groups as important to their campaigns and as sources of campaign funds.[25]

Merit Selection

Undaunted, reformers have come up with a method other than nonpartisan elections to accomplish the goal of obtaining qualified state judges free from the taint of political bias. Merit selection, by whatever name, has been around since the early 1900s as a preferred method of selecting judges. The first state to fully adopt such a method was Missouri, in 1940, and such schemes have since become known as generic variants of "the Missouri Plan."

The states with Missouri-type plans use a combination of elections and appointments. In effect, this type of plan provides for much greater influence from lawyers than any other selection method. The governor appoints a judge from among several candidates recommended by a nominating panel of five or more people, usually including attorneys (often chosen by the local bar association), nonlawyers appointed by the governor, and sometimes a senior local judge. Either by law or by implicit agreement, the governor appoints someone from the recommended list. After serving for a short period of time, often a year, the newly appointed judge must stand for a retention election, at which time he or she, in effect, runs on his or her record. (The voters are asked, "Shall Judge X be retained in office?") If the judge's tenure is supported by the voters, as is virtually always the case, the judge will serve for a regular and fairly long term. Does a Missouri plan take politics out of the judicial selection process? After an exhaustive study of how the plan had operated in Missouri over a quarter century, two observers concluded that "it is naive to suggest . . . that the Plan takes the 'politics' out of judicial selection." [26]

A recent highly publicized judicial retention contest in Tennessee shows what can happen when a judge is asked merely to run on her own record. Justice Penny White, who had been appointed to Tennessee's high court in 1994 after serving as a trial and court of criminal appeals judge, faced a retention election in August 1996. This election became a referendum on the death penalty.[27] Justice White's most vocal opponents included the Tennessee Conservative Union, the Republican Party, and Republican governor Don Sundquist. The Republican Party mailed a brochure to voters that carried the slogan "Vote for Capital Punishment by Voting NO on August 1 for Supreme Court Justice Penny White." The brochure described three cases as evidence that Justice White placed the rights of criminals before the rights of victims.

Supporters of Justice White mounted a counterattack based on the arguments that the entire court had reached the decisions and that Justice White did not write separate opinions in the cases.[28] The arguments in Justice White's behalf were to no avail, however, and she was removed from the bench.

The merit selection scheme still has plenty of room for politics. One student of retention elections notes that special interest groups have discovered that judicial retention elections "are vehicles by which offending judges can be unseated and state judicial policy making can be influenced." [29] However, the long-term picture is not one of spectacular defeats, but of judges being retained in large numbers. A study covering the years 1964 through 1998 indicates that "in only 52 of 4,588 judicial retention elections were judges not retained." [30]

Despite the unhappy anomalies that occasionally accompany this form of judicial selection and retention (à la Justice White), it still has a number of supporters. Nevertheless, since studies fail to document significant differences in the behavior of elected judges as opposed to those selected under merit systems, support for merit selection is more an act of faith than an argument based on well-documented findings.

Gubernatorial Appointment and Legislative Appointment

In the early days of the Republic, judges were chosen either by the governor or the state legislature, but today such methods are used in only a handful of states. When judges are appointed by the governor, politics almost invariably comes into play. In the dozens of appointment opportunities that arise, governors tend to select individuals who have been active in state politics and whose activity has benefited either the governor personally or the governor's political party or allies. Also, in making judicial appointments, the governor often bargains with local political bosses or with state legislators whose support is needed. A governor may also use a judgeship to reward a legislator or local politico who has given faithful political support in the past.

Only a few states still allow their legislators to appoint state judges. Although a variety of criteria may be used in choosing members of the state supreme courts, when it comes to filling the state trial benches, state legislators tend to turn to former members of the legislature.[31] This does not mean that judges appointed in this way are merely political hacks in need of a job, but it is evidence that friends and colleagues do take care of their own when given the opportunity to do so.

Judicial Selection Methods and the Recruitment of Women and Minorities

As noted earlier, in terms of gender and ethnicity, state judiciaries are highly unrepresentative of the country as a whole. We now examine whether one judicial selection method is more likely than another to enhance diversification of the bench. A recent study looking at representation of women and minorities on the state appellate courts in 1999 indicates that a slightly higher percentage of women and minorities attained their positions by judicial election (26.83 percent), as compared with being appointed in a merit selection system (24.86 percent). However, an even higher percentage (28.18 percent) were appointed by the state's governor.[32] The finding that women and minorities fare better in elections than in a merit plan would seem to indicate the importance of the U.S. Supreme Court's 1991 decision that the Voting Rights Act of 1965 fully applies to the election of state judges.[33] Another recent study, focusing specifically on gender diversity in state supreme courts, found that women are significantly more likely to reach the state supreme court by being appointed rather than winning the judgeship in an election. Furthermore, when an appointment system is used, women are much more likely to be appointed to an all-male court.[34]

Most advocates of increased ethnic and gender diversity on the bench have argued that it is essential, at the very least, on the grounds of basic fairness to these groups. Others point to the symbolic importance of having the judiciary better reflect the gender and ethnic makeup of society as a whole. Whether the decision making of women and ethnic minorities is—or should be—different from that of white males is still the subject of much debate. A few preliminary studies have suggested that, with minor exceptions, women judges and judges belonging to racial minorities decide cases about the same way as their Anglo, male colleagues.[35]

The Retirement and Removal of State Judges

Being burdened with judges too old and unfit to serve seems to be less of a problem at the state level than at the federal level. A goodly number of states have mandatory retirement plans. The U.S. Supreme Court in 1991 gave a major boost to such plans by ruling that they do not violate federal law or the Equal Protection Clause of the Fourteenth Amendment.[36] Minimum ages for retirement range from sixty-five to seventy-five, with seventy being the most common. Some states even go so far as to have declining retirement benefit plans for judges who serve beyond the desired tenure, that is, the longer they stay on the bench, the lower their retirement benefits. Observers say that such plans are often effective in getting old, workaholic jurists to start examining travel brochures.

Retirement plans, no matter how effective in getting the older judge to resign, are still of little use against the younger jurist who is incompetent, corrupt, or unethical. Throughout American history the states have used procedures such as **impeachment,** recall elections, and concurrent resolutions of the legislature to rid themselves of the judge gone bad. For example, on July 5, 2000, the House Judiciary Committee in New Hampshire recommended impeachment for the state's supreme court chief justice, David Brock. The committee alleged, among other things, that he lied under oath to impede an investigation into his court. The full House agreed, and he was impeached on four charges. In his trial before the New Hampshire Senate, however, Chief Justice Brock was acquitted on all four counts. Two other justices, Sherman Horton and John Broderick, were also under scrutiny in the investigation, but they managed to avoid punishment when the committee voted not to recommend impeachment or censure for them. The three justices were accused of initially failing to blow the whistle on a fourth justice, Stephen Thayer, who was accused of trying to influence the appointment of judges to hear an appeal in his own divorce case. Justice Thayer resigned after the scandal became public in March 2000.[37] In spite of the New Hampshire example, the evidence suggests that methods for judicial discipline and removal are only minimally effective, either because they prove to be politically difficult to put into operation or because of their time-consuming, cumbersome nature.

More recently, the states have begun to set up special commissions, often made up of the judges themselves, to police their own members. Reformers have given such commissions only fair-to-poor marks, however, because the persons most familiar with the problem—the judges—are often loath to expose a colleague to public censure and discipline. Policing the state judiciaries remains a challenge that beckons champions of good government.

Summary

This chapter began with a collective portrait of the men and women who have served in the state judiciaries. We noted that state jurists generally have had strong ties to the locales in which they have served and have come from a distinct stratum of American society. The result is a core of judges who share similar values and who therefore strive, with minimal coercion, to keep the judicial system functioning in a relatively harmonious manner. Though formal qualifications for a seat on the bench are few, tradition has established several informal criteria, including a reasonable degree of professional competence, the right political affiliation and contacts, at least some desire for the job itself, and a bit of luck thrown in for good measure.

Politics and the judiciary go hand in glove. If the governor appoints the judges, similarity between the values of the governor and those of the judicial nominees is the norm. If judges are elected—even on nonpartisan ballots—the political and judicial processes are still inexorably intertwined. Judicial decisions by state judges reflect both the process by which the judges are chosen and the values of those who choose them.

Retention elections, such as the one involving Justice Penny White in Tennessee, frequently reflect struggles between politically diverse groups in the state. As one student of the courts puts it, "Judicial retention elections thus become another access point by which special interest groups can influence policy making."

We also discussed the effects of different selection processes on ethnic and gender diversity on the bench. Although both categories have been increasingly represented in recent years, using all methods of selection, recent studies suggest that women are most likely to serve as a judge when the appointment method is used.

The disciplining and removal of corrupt or mentally unfit judges remain a problem. However, implementation of mandatory retirement plans and the establishment of peer policing commissions illustrate the states' commitment to addressing this problem.

Further Thought and Discussion Questions

1. How successful have states been in their efforts to remove politics from the judicial selection process? To what extent is it desirable, or possible, to make judicial selection apolitical?

2. Should steps be taken to ensure that state judiciaries are representative of the general population in terms of gender and ethnicity? Why?

3. Are citizens well enough informed to evaluate judges' performances in retention elections?

NOTES

1. See Steven Vago, *Law and Society*, 6th ed. (Upper Saddle River, N.J.: Prentice Hall, 2000), 372.

2. Ibid., 373.

3. Chris W. Bonneau, "The Composition of State Supreme Courts, 2000," *Judicature* 85 (July–August 2001): 28.

4. Ibid.

5. Elaine Martin, "Women on the Bench: A Different Voice?" *Judicature* 77 (1993): 126.

6. Bonneau, "The Composition of State Supreme Courts, 2000," 31.

7. Ibid., 28.

8. Ibid.

9. Ibid., 29.

10. Ibid.

11. Ibid.

12. Mark C. Miller, "Judicial Activism in Canada and the United States," *Judicature* 81 (1998): 264.

13. Bonneau, "The Composition of State Supreme Courts," 29.

14. Ibid.

15. Ibid.

16. Owen G. Abbe and Paul S. Herrnson, "How Judicial Election Campaigns Have Changed," *Judicature* 85 (May–June 2002): 287.

17. Roy Schotland, "Elective Judge's Campaign Financing: Are State Judges' Robes the Emperor's Clothes of American Democracy?" *Journal of Law and Policy* 57 (1985): 2.

18. Abbe and Herrnson, "How Judicial Election Campaigns Have Changed," 287.

19. See Kyle Cheek and Anthony Champagne, "Money in Texas Supreme Court Elections: 1980–1998," *Judicature* 84 (July–August 2000): 20–25.

20. See Abbe and Herrnson, "How Judicial Election Campaigns Have Changed," 287.

21. Ibid., 289–290.

22. Ibid., 294–295.

23. *Republican Party of Minnesota et al. v. White, Chairperson, Minnesota Board of Judicial Standards et al.*, available online at http://supct.law.cornell.edu/supct/html/01-521.ZS.html.

24. Abbe and Herrnson, "How Judicial Election Campaigns Have Changed," 295.

25. Ibid., 289, 294.

26. Richard A. Watson and Rondal G. Downing, *The Politics of the Bench and the Bar* (New York: Wiley, 1969), 331.

27. Our account of Justice Penny White's retention election is drawn from Stephen B. Bright, "Political Attacks on the Judiciary," *Judicature* 80 (1997): 165–173; and Traciel V. Reid, "The Politicization of Retention Elections: Lessons from the Defeat of Justices Lanphier and White," *Judicature* 83 (1999): 68–77.

28. Reid, "The Politicization of Retention Elections," 72.

29. Ibid., 77.

30. Larry Aspin, "Trends in Judicial Retention Elections, 1964–1998," *Judicature* 83 (1999): 79.

31. Herbert Jacob, "The Effect of Institutional Differences in the Recruitment Process: The Case of State Judges," *Journal of Public Law* 13 (1964): 104–119; Bradley C. Canon, "The Impact of Formal Selection Process on the Characteristics of Judges—Reconsidered," *Law and Society Review* 6 (1972): 575–593; and Henry R. Glick and Craig F. Emmert, "Selection Systems and Judicial Characteristics," *Judicature* 70 (1987): 228–235.

32. See Mark S. Hurwitz and Drew Noble Lanier, "Women and Minorities on State and Federal Appellate Benches, 1985 and 1989," *Judicature* 85 (September–October 2001): 89.

33. See *Chisom v. Roemer, Houston Lawyers' Association v. Texas Attorney General*, 499 U.S. 935 (1991).

34. Kathleen A. Bratton and Rorie L. Spill, "Existing Diversity and Judicial Selection: The Role of the Appointment Method in Establishing Gender Diversity in State Supreme Courts," *Social Science Quarterly* 83 (June 2002): 504.

35. See Cassia Spohn, "The Sentencing Decisions of Black and White Judges: Expected and Unexpected Similarities," *Law and Society Review* 24 (1990): 1197–1216; and David W. Allen and Diane E. Wall, "The Behavior of Women State Supreme Court Justices: Are They Tokens or Outsiders?" *Justice System Journal* 12 (1987): 232–245.

36. *Gregory v. Ashcroft*, 498 U.S. 979 (1991).

37. See "New Hampshire Chief Justice Should Be Impeached, Committee Says," CNN.com, http://www.cnn.com/2000/LAW/07/06/court.crisis.02/index.html; "N.H. House Approves First Article in Preliminary Vote against Chief Justice," CNN.com, http://www.cnn.com/2000/LAW/07/12/bc.courtcrisis.ap/; and "New Hampshire Senate Acquits Chief Justice," CNN.com, http://www.cnn.com/2000/LAW/10/10/court.crisis.03/.

SUGGESTED READINGS

Abbe, Owen G., and Paul S. Herrnson. "How Judicial Election Campaigns Have Changed," *Judicature* 85 (May–June 2002): 286–295. An important study of all aspects of judicial elections in the states.

Baum, Lawrence. "Electing Judges." In *Contemplating Courts*, ed. Lee Epstein, 18–43. Washington, D.C.: CQ Press, 1995. Addresses the question of how voters choose between candidates for Ohio Supreme Court judgeships.

Bonneau, Chris W. "The Composition of State Supreme Courts, 2000," *Judicature* 85 (July–August 2001): 26–31. The most current study of the background characteristics of judges of state supreme courts.

Sheldon, Charles H., and Nicholas P. Lovrich Jr. "State Judicial Recruitment." In *The American Courts: A Critical Assessment*, ed. John B. Gates and Charles A. Johnson, 161–188. Washington, D.C.: CQ Press, 1991. A good general review of the major selection methods for judges in the states and their advantages and disadvantages.

Watson, Richard A., and Rondal G. Downing. *The Politics of the Bench and the Bar.* New York: Wiley, 1969. A study of the impact of merit selection in Missouri.

CHAPTER 6

Federal Judges

After a president nominates someone to a federal judgeship, it is not uncommon for lobbying—for and against the candidate—to occur. Here, NAACP chairman Julian Bond and CEO Kweisi Mfume express their opposition to President Bush's nomination of Charles Pickering to a seat on the U.S. Court of Appeals for the Fifth Circuit. Both NAACP leaders contended that Pickering does not have a strong record in support of civil rights.

T HE MAIN ACTORS IN THE federal system are the men and women who serve as judges and justices, and it is to them that we now turn our attention.

Background Characteristics of Federal Judges

Americans cling eagerly to the log cabin-to-White House myth of attaining high public office—the notion that someone born in the humblest of circumstances (such as Abraham Lincoln) may one day grow up to be the president of the United States, or at least a U.S. judge. As with most myths, it has a kernel of truth. In principle, virtually anyone can become a prominent public official, and a few well-known examples can be cited of people who came from poor backgrounds and climbed to the pinnacle of power. One example is Thurgood Marshall, the great-grandson of a slave and the son of a Pullman car steward who became a Supreme Court justice. Another is Warren E. Burger, who served as chief justice; his father earned his daily bread as a traveling salesman and a railroad car inspector. More typical, however, is the most recent Supreme Court appointee, Stephen G. Breyer, a multimillionaire whose wife is from a family of British nobility. The main criticism leveled against Breyer prior to his appointment was that he was overinvested in the major insurance firm Lloyds of London. For a long time, uncontested data have clearly shown that America's federal judges, like other public officials and the captains of commerce and industry, come from a narrow stratum of American society. Although potential judges are not necessarily the sons and daughters of millionaires, it is at least helpful to their careers if they come from a special segment of the nation's middle and upper-middle classes.

District Judges

Background data for all federal district judges for the past 213 years have never been collected, but a good deal is known about judges who have served in recent decades. Table 6-1 profiles some key characteristics of trial jurists appointed by Presidents Jimmy Carter, Ronald Reagan, George H. W. Bush, Bill Clinton, and George W. Bush.

In terms of their primary occupation before assuming the federal bench, a plurality had been judges at the state or local level. About 37 percent of Reagan's judges had extensive prior judicial experience, and over 48 percent of George W. Bush's judicial team had previously worn the black robe. The next largest blocs were employed either in the political or governmental realms or in moderate- to large-sized law firms. Those working in small law firms or as professors of law made up the smallest bloc.

Their educational backgrounds reveal something of their elite nature. All graduated from college; about half attended either the costly Ivy League schools or other private universities to receive their undergraduate and law degrees. Most adult Americans have never gone to college, and of those who have, only a tiny portion could meet the admission requirements—not to mention the expense—of most Ivy League schools or other private universities.

About half of the district judges had some prior experience on the bench, and somewhat more than four out of ten had served at one time as a public prosecutor. This recent phenomenon has caused some court observers to conclude that "we may be evolving toward the European system of a career judiciary."[1]

Judges differ in yet another way from the population as a whole. Among trial judges—and all U.S. judges, for that matter—a strong tendency toward "occupational

TABLE 6-1   Background Characteristics of Presidents' District Court Appointees, 1977–2003

	George W. Bush	Bill Clinton	George H. W. Bush	Ronald Reagan	Jimmy Carter
Occupation					
Politics/government	8.4%	11.5%	10.8%	13.4%	5.0%
Judiciary	48.2	48.2	41.9	36.9	44.6
Large law firm					
100+ members	9.6	6.6	10.8	6.2	2.0
50–99	6.0	5.2	7.4	4.8	6.0
25–49	8.4	4.3	7.4	6.9	6.0
Medium size firm					
10–24 members	4.8	7.2	8.8	10.0	9.4
5–9	4.8	6.2	6.1	9.0	9.9
Small firm					
2–4	2.4	4.6	3.4	7.2	11.4
solo	2.4	3.6	1.4	2.8	2.5
Professor of law	2.4	1.6	0.7	2.1	3.0
Other	2.4	1.0	1.4	0.7	0.5
Experience					
Judicial	53.0	52.1	46.6	46.2	54.0
Prosecutorial	50.6	41.3	39.2	44.1	38.1
Neither	22.9	28.8	31.8	28.6	31.2
Undergraduate education					
Public	42.2	44.3	46.0	37.9	55.9
Private	51.8	42.0	39.9	48.6	34.2
Ivy League	6.0	13.8	14.2	13.4	9.9
Law school education					
Public	53.0	39.7	52.7	44.8	52.0
Private	39.8	40.7	33.1	43.4	31.2
Ivy League	7.2	19.7	14.2	11.7	16.8
Gender					
Male	79.5	71.5	80.4	91.7	85.6
Female	20.5	28.5	19.6	8.3	14.4
Ethnicity/race					
White	85.5	75.1	89.2	92.4	78.7
African American	7.2	17.4	6.8	2.1	13.9
Hispanic	7.2	5.9	4.0	4.8	6.9
Asian	—	1.3	—	0.7	0.5
Native American	—	0.3	—	—	—
Percentage white male	68.7	52.4	73.0	84.8	67.8
ABA rating					
EWQ/WQ	69.9	59.0	57.4	53.5	51.0
Qualified	28.9	40.0	42.6	46.6	47.5
Not Qualified	1.2	1.0	—	—	1.5

Table continues on next page

TABLE 6-1   Background Characteristics of Presidents' District Court Appointees, 1977–2003 *(continued)*

	George W. Bush	Bill Clinton	George H. W. Bush	Ronald Reagan	Jimmy Carter
Political identification					
Democrat	7.2	87.5	6.1	4.8	91.1
Republican	83.1	6.2	88.5	91.7	4.5
Other	—	0.3	—	—	—
None	9.6	5.9	5.4	3.4	4.5
Past party activism	56.6	50.2	64.2	60.3	61.4
Net worth					
Under $200,000	4.8	13.4	10.1	17.9	35.8[a]
$200–499,999	21.7	21.6	31.1	37.6	41.2
$500–999,999	16.9	26.9	26.4	21.7	18.9
$1+ million	56.6	38.0	32.4	22.8	4.0
Average age at nomination	50.3	49.5	48.2	48.6	49.6
Total number of appointees	83	305	148	290	202

SOURCE: Sheldon Goldman, Elliot Slotnick, Gerard Gryski, Gary Zuk, and Sara Schiavoni, "W. Bush Remaking the Judiciary: Like Father Like Son," *Judicature* 86 (2003): 282–309.

[a] These figures are for Carter appointees confirmed by the 96th Congress for all but six district court appointees for whom no data were available.

heredity" exists. That is, judges tend to come from families with a tradition of judicial and public service.[2] One of President Reagan's trial court appointees, Howell Cobb of Beaumont, Texas, is typical of this phenomenon. The nominee's hometown paper said of him:

The appointee is the fourth generation of a family of lawyers and judges. His great-grandfather, a Confederate officer, served as secretary of the Treasury under President James Buchanan and was governor of Georgia and speaker of the U.S. House of Representatives. Cobb's grandfather was a justice on the Georgia Supreme Court, and his father was a circuit judge in Georgia. Cobb's son, a lawyer in El Paso, also follows tradition. "Most trial lawyers aspire to a seat on the bench," Cobb said.[3]

As one would expect, based on the demographics in state courts described in the previous chapter, being a woman or a member of a racial minority or both has not been an asset if one coveted a federal judicial robe. Although the United States is about 51 percent female, judging has been almost exclusively a man's business. Until the Carter presidency, less than 2 percent of the lower judiciary was female, and even with a conscious effort to increase this number, only 14.4 percent of Carter's district judges were women. The same holds true for racial minorities, whose representation on the trial bench has always been small, not only in absolute numbers but also in comparison with figures for the overall population. Until the present time, only Jimmy Carter, who made affirmative action a cornerstone of his presidency, had appointed a significant number of non-Anglos to the federal bench—over 21 percent. Under the Clinton administration, however, a complete about-face occurred. At the end of his two terms in office the official count reveals that a whopping 48 percent of his judicial appointees were either women or minorities. This figure (which represents both district and appeals court judges) is compared with percentages of only 28, 14, 34, and 32 for Presidents George H. W. Bush, Reagan, Carter, and George W. Bush, respectively. Still, it is interesting to note that George W. Bush's 32 percent is the highest for any Republican president and is only two points behind the record of the liberal Jimmy Carter.

The American Bar Association (ABA) ratings reveal that few make it to the federal bench who are not rated as "qualified" by this self-appointed evaluator of judicial fitness. The difference in quality between the Republican and Democratic appointees is trivial. Thus far the 69.9 percent of George W. Bush's judges who have a "well qualified" rating is the highest for any president.

About nine out of ten district judges have been of the same political party as the appointing president, and until the Clinton administration about 60 percent had a record of active partisanship. The Clinton cohort contained fewer active partisans—about 50 percent. Some 57 percent of George W. Bush's jurists have records of active partisan activity.

That district judge nominees constitute an elite group is clearly revealed in the statistics for their net worth at the time of appointment to the bench. Although these figures do not prove that all potential jurists were wealthy, they do suggest that few candidates for the bench had to ponder the source of their next meal. The Carter cohort seems to have been the least wealthy when they were appointed, whereas 57 percent of George W. Bush's judicial nominees were millionaires at the time they took the judicial oath.

The typical judge has been about forty-nine years old at the time of appointment. Age variations from one presidency to another have been small, with no discernible trend over the years.

Appeals Court Judges

Because the statistics and percentages of the appellate court appointees of the five presidents from Carter through George W. Bush are similar to those for the

TABLE 6-2   Background Characteristics of Presidents' Appeals Court Appointees, 1977–2003

	George W. Bush	Bill Clinton	George H. W. Bush	Ronald Reagan	Jimmy Carter
Occupation					
Politics/government	6.2%	6.6%	10.8%	6.4%	5.4%
Judiciary	50.0	52.5	59.5	55.1	46.4
Large law firm					
100+ members	—	11.5	8.1	5.1	1.8
50–99	6.2	3.3	8.1	2.6	5.4
25–49	—	3.3	—	6.4	3.6
Medium size firm					
10–24 members	12.5	9.8	8.1	3.9	14.3
5–9	—	3.3	2.7	5.1	1.8
Small firm					
2–4	—	1.6	—	1.3	3.6
solo	6.2	—	—	—	1.8
Professor of Law	12.5	8.2	2.7	12.8	14.3
Other	6.2	—	—	1.3	1.8
Experience					
Judicial	68.8	59.0	62.2	60.3	53.6
Prosecutorial	25.0	37.7	29.7	28.2	30.4
Neither	25.0	29.5	32.4	34.6	39.3
Undergraduate education					
Public	43.8	44.3	29.7	24.4	30.4
Private	37.5	34.4	59.5	51.3	51.8
Ivy League	18.8	21.3	10.8	24.4	17.9
Law school education					
Public	50.0	39.3	32.4	41.0	39.3
Private	25.0	31.1	37.8	35.9	19.6
Ivy League	25.0	29.5	29.7	23.1	41.1
Gender					
Male	81.2	67.2	81.1	94.9	80.4
Female	18.8	32.8	18.9	5.1	19.6
Ethnicity/race					
White	81.2	73.8	89.2	97.4	78.6
African American	18.8	13.1	5.4	1.3	16.1
Hispanic	—	11.5	5.4	1.3	3.6
Asian	—	1.6	—	—	1.8
Percentage white male	62.5	49.2	70.3	92.3	60.7
ABA rating					
EWQ/WQ	68.8	78.7	64.9	59.0	75.0
Qualified	31.2	21.3	35.1	41.0	25.0

Table continues on next page

TABLE 6-2   Background Characteristics of Presidents' Appeals Court Appointees, 1977–2003 (continued)

	George W. Bush	Bill Clinton	George H. W. Bush	Ronald Reagan	Jimmy Carter
Political identification					
Democrat	12.5	85.2	2.7	—	82.1
Republican	81.2	6.6	89.2	96.2	7.1
Other	—	—	—	1.3	—
None	6.2	8.2	8.1	26.2	10.7
Past party activism	75.0	54.1	70.3	66.7	73.2
Net worth					
Under $200,000	6.2	4.9	5.4	15.6[a]	33.3[b]
$200–499,999	12.5	14.8	29.7	32.5	38.5
$500–999,999	18.8	29.5	21.6	35.1	17.9
$1+ million	62.5	50.8	43.2	16.9	10.3
Average age of nomination	50.6	51.2	48.7	50.0	51.8
Total number of appointees	16	61	37	78	56

SOURCE: Sheldon Goldman, Elliot Slotnick, Gerald Gryski, Gary Zuk, and Sara Schiavoni, "W. Bush Remaking the Judiciary: Like Father Like Son," *Judicature* 86 (2003): 282–309.

[a] Net worth was unavailable for one appointee.

[b] Net worth only for Carter appointees confirmed by the 96th Congress, with the exception of five appointees for whom net worth was unavailable.

trial judges, we will offer some commentary only on those figures that suggest a difference between the two sets of judges (see Table 6-2).

Appeals court judges are much more likely to have previous judicial experience than their counterparts on the trial court bench. Also, Presidents George W. Bush, Reagan, and Carter were more apt to look to the ranks of law school professors for their appeals court appointments than Presidents George H. W. Bush and Clinton did.

If the trend toward seeking out Ivy League and other private school graduates was strong for trial judge appointments, it is even more pronounced for those selected for seats on the appeals courts. Compared with the population at large or even U.S. district judges, appellate court jurists appear to be solid members of America's social and economic elite.

In terms of opposite-party selections, little difference is seen between trial and appellate court appointments. However, appeals judges have a slight tendency to be more active in their respective parties than their colleagues on the trial bench.

The Clinton initiative to make the bench more accurately reflect U.S. gender and racial demographics is evident in the ranks of the appellate judges as well. A third of his jurists were women. This is compared with just 19, 19, 5, and 20 percent of judges appointed by George W. Bush, George H. W. Bush, Reagan, and Carter, respectively. And the Clinton team was composed of more African Americans, Hispanics, and Asians than the cohorts of any other president. When the gender and race variables are combined, the contrast between the Clinton team and other presidential cohorts is even more vivid. Only 49 percent of Clinton's appellate judges were white males. White males constituted 63, 70, 92, and 61 percent of the judges appointed by George W. Bush, George H. W. Bush, Reagan, and Carter, respectively. Clinton's efforts to increase the representation of women and minorities on the bench have not gone unnoticed in other countries, at least by those whose judicial systems bear some resemblance to that of the United States. For example, international judicial scholar Henry Abraham noted that in recent years "there has been mounting criticism [in Britain] of the [judicial] selection process, because of the scarcity of women and minorities among the high judges. . . . Tony Scrivener, QC [Queen's Counsel], Chairman of the Bar, promised to endeavor to alleviate that condition and also to advance the candidacies of more **liberal** members of the profession to judgeships." [4]

Finally, candidates for the appeals courts seem to be as blessed with financial resources as their colleagues selected to preside over the trial courts. For example, about 63 percent of George W. Bush's nominees to the appellate court and 51 percent of Clinton's nominees had a net worth of over $1 million at the time of their appointment.

Supreme Court Justices

Since 1789, 106 men and two women have sat on the bench of America's highest judicial tribunal. If judges of the trial and appeals courts have been culled primarily from America's cultural elite, then members of the U.S. Supreme Court are the crème de la crème.

Although perhaps 10 percent of the justices were of essentially humble origin, the rest "were not only from families in comfortable economic circumstances, but were chosen overwhelmingly from the socially prestigious and politically influential gentry class in the late 18th and early 19th century, or the professionalized upper class thereafter." [5] A majority of the justices came from politically active families, and about a third were related to jurists and closely connected to families with a tradition of judicial service. Thus the justices were reared in far from commonplace American families.

Until the 1960s the high court had been all white and all male, but in 1967 President Lyndon B. Johnson appointed Thurgood Marshall as the first black member of the Court. When Marshall retired in 1991, President Bush nominated Clarence Thomas, a man who shared Marshall's ethnic heritage, though not his liberal views. In 1981 the gender barrier was broken when President Reagan named Sandra Day O'Connor to the Court, and thirteen years later she was joined by Ruth Bader Ginsburg. In terms of religious background, the membership of the Court has been overwhelmingly Protestant, and most of the justices have been affiliated with the more prestigious denominations (such as the Episcopal, Presbyterian, and Unitarian churches). Thus in terms of ethnicity, gender, and religious preference, the Court is by no means a cross-section of American society.

As for the nonpolitical occupations of the justices, all 108 had legal training and all had practiced law at some stage in their careers. An inordinate number had served as corporation attorneys before their appointments. Only 22 percent had state or federal judicial experience immediately prior to being appointed, although more than half had served on the bench at some time before their nomination to the Supreme Court. Like their colleagues in the lower federal judiciary, the justices were much more likely than the average American to have been politically active, and virtually all shared many of the ideological and political orientations of their appointing president.

An Appraisal of the Statistics

Several conclusions are readily apparent from the summary data just presented. First, federal judges in the United States are an elite within an elite. They come from upper- or upper-middle-class families that are politically active and have a tradition of public and, often, judicial service. Is the narrow judicial selection process the result of pure chance? Has there been a sinister conspiracy for the past two centuries to keep women, blacks, Roman Catholics, the poor, and so on out of the U.S. judiciary, or are the causes more subtle and complex? The evidence points to the latter explanation.

Legislation has never been passed that forbade non-Anglos to wear the black robe. But laws, traditions, and unwritten codes have kept them from entering the better law schools, from working in the more prestigious law firms and corporations, and from making the kind of social and political connections that may lead to nomination to judicial office. Likewise, no statutes have excluded the children of the poor from consideration for a seat on the bench. But few youngsters from impoverished homes can afford expensive, high-quality colleges and law schools that would provide the necessary training and contacts. Also, traditionally, many more young men than young women were encouraged to apply to law school. For instance, Supreme Court Justice Ginsburg remembers that while she was at Harvard Law School during the 1950s, the dean held a reception for the nine women in her class of more than five hundred. "After dinner," she recalled, "the dean asked each of us to explain what we were doing at the law school occupying a seat that could have been filled by a man. When my turn came, I wished I could have pushed a button and vanished through a trapdoor." [6] The process of exclusion, then, has not been part of a conscious, organized conspiracy; instead, it has been the inevitable consequence of more subtle social and economic forces in society.

Another observation about the background profile of federal judges is worthy of mention. Because they tend to come from the same kinds of families, go to the same universities and law schools, and belong to churches, clubs, and societies that uphold similar values, federal judges generally are much more alike than they are different. There may be Democrats and Republicans, former defense attorneys and former prosecutors on the bench, but to a significant degree virtually all play the game by the same rules. What one scholar has said about the recruitment process for the appeals courts is true for federal judgeships in general:

Broadly speaking [the recruitment process] tends to reward supporters of the presidential party; weed out incompetents, mavericks, and ideological extremists; and ensure substantial professional and political experience among those who wield federal appellate power. Forged thereby are continuous links between judges and their political and professional surroundings. Restricted thereby are the types of persons inducted into Courts of Appeals. The multiple filters through which recruits must pass put a premium on moderate, middle-class, and political lawyers, successful people advantaged in life.[7]

The fact that the recruitment process produces a corps of jurists who agree on how the judicial game is to be played is the primary reason that the loosely organized judicial hierarchy does not come flying apart. It is a key explanation for the predictability of most judicial decisions. The judicial machinery runs as smoothly and consistently as it does, not because of outside watchdogs or elaborate enforcement mechanisms but because the principal participants largely share the same values and orientations and are working to further similar goals.

Formal and Informal Qualifications of Federal Judges

Despite the absence of formal qualifications for a federal judgeship, there are well-defined informal requirements.

Formal Qualifications

Students often torture one another with horror stories of the hurdles to be overcome to achieve success in a particular profession. Would-be medical students are awed by the high grade-point averages and aptitude scores required for admission to medical schools; potential university professors shrink at the thought of the many years of work necessary to obtain a Ph.D., only to face the publish-or-perish requirements for a tenured position. It would be logical, then, to assume that the formal requirements for becoming a federal judge—and surely a Supreme Court justice—must be formidable indeed. Not so. No constitutional or statutory qualifications are stipulated for serving on the Supreme Court or the lower federal courts. The Constitution merely indicates that "the judicial Power of the United States, shall be vested in one supreme Court" as well as in any lower federal courts that Congress may establish (Article III, Section 1), and that the president "by and with the Advice and Consent of the Senate, shall appoint . . . Judges of the supreme Court" (Article II, Section 2). Congress has applied the same selection procedure to the appeals and the trial courts. There are no exams to pass, no minimum age requirement, no stipulation that judges be native-born citizens or legal residents, and no requirement that judges even have a law degree.

Informal Requirements

At least four vital although informal factors determine who sits on the federal bench in America: professional competence, political qualifications, self-selection, and the element of pure luck.

Professional Competence. Although candidates for U.S. judicial posts do not have to be attorneys—let alone prominent ones—it has been the custom to appoint lawyers who have distinguished themselves professionally (or at least not to appoint those without merit). Merit may mean no more than an association with a prestigious law firm, publication of a few law review articles, or respect among fellow attorneys. A potential judge need not be an outstanding legal scholar. Nevertheless, one of the unwritten rules is that a judicial appointment is different from run-of-the-mill patronage. Although the political rules may allow a president to reward an old ally with a seat on the bench, even here tradition has created an expectation that the would-be judge have some reputation for professional competence, the more so as the judgeship in question goes from the trial court to the appeals court to the Supreme Court level.

A modern-day example of the unwritten rule that potential judges should be more than just warm bodies with a law degree is found in President Richard M. Nixon's nomination of G. Harrold Carswell to the Supreme Court in 1970. After investigations by the press and the Senate Judiciary Committee revealed that Carswell's record was unimpressive at best, his nomination began to stall on the floor of the Senate. To his aid came the well-meaning senator Roman Hruska of Nebraska, who stated in part: "Even if Carswell were mediocre, there are a lot of mediocre judges and people and lawyers. They are entitled to a little representation, aren't they, and a little chance? We can't have all Brandeises, and Frankfurters, and Cardozos and stuff like that there." [8] With such support Carswell must have wondered why he needed any detractors. In any case the acknowledgment by a friendly senator that the Supreme Court nominee was "mediocre" probably did more than anything else to prompt the Senate to reject Carswell. Although tradition may allow judgeships to be political payoffs and may not require eminence in the nominee, candidates for federal judicial posts are expected to meet a reasonable level of professional competence.

Political Qualifications. When at least 90 percent of all federal judicial nominees are of the same political party as the appointing president, even the most casual observer must notice that certain political requirements are likely being fulfilled for a seat on the bench. The fact that well over half of all federal judges were politically active before their appointments—in comparison with a 10 percent figure for the total population—is further evidence of this phenomenon. In this respect the American practice is not unique in the world. Even countries that pride themselves on keeping politics out of the judicial selection, for example, Canada, often see it manifested at some level. As one keen observer of the Canadian political scene noted: "Most judges appointed by both federal and provincial Liberal governments are Liberal, judges appointed by Conservative governments are Conservative." [9] What are the political criteria used for American judicial appointments? In some cases a judgeship may be a reward for major service to the party in power or to the president or a senator. For example, when federal judge Peirson Hall (of the Central District of California) was asked how important politics was to his appointment, he gave this candid reply:

I worked hard for Franklin Roosevelt in the days when California had no Democratic Party to speak of. In 1939 I began running for the Senate, and the party convinced me it would be best if there wasn't a contest for the Democratic nomination. So I withdrew and campaigned for Martin Downey. They gave me this judgeship as sort of a consolation prize—and one, I might add, that I have enjoyed.[10]

Although examples like this are not uncommon, it would be a mistake to think of federal judgeships merely as political plums handed out to the party faithful. As often as not, a seat on the bench goes to a reasonably active or visible member of the party in power but not necessarily to someone who has made party service the central focus of a lifetime. Political activity that might lead to a judgeship includes service as chair of a state or local party organization, an unsuccessful race for public office, or financial backing for partisan causes.

The reason most nominees for judicial office must have some record of political activity is twofold. First, to some degree judgeships are still considered part of the political patronage system; those who have served the party are more likely to be rewarded with a federal post than those who have not paid their dues. Second, even if a judgeship is not given as a direct political payoff, some political activity on the part of a would-be judge is often necessary. Otherwise, the candidate would simply not be visible to the president, senator(s), or local party leaders who submit the names of candidates. If the judicial power brokers have never heard of a particular lawyer because he or she has no political profile, that person's name will not come to mind when a vacancy occurs on the bench.

Self-Selection. For those seeking the presidency or running for Congress, shyness does not pay. It is necessary to declare one's candidacy, meet a formal filing deadline, and spend considerable time and money to advertise one's qualifications. Although Americans profess to admire modesty and humility in their leaders, successful candidates for elected office do well not to overindulge these virtues. With the judiciary, however, the informal rules of the game are different. Many would consider it undignified and lacking in judicial temperament for someone to announce publicly a desire for a federal judgeship—much less to campaign openly for such an appointment.

However, some would-be jurists orchestrate discreet campaigns on their own behalf or at least pass the word that they are available for judicial service. Few will admit to seeking an appointment actively, but credible anecdotes suggest that attorneys often position themselves in such a way that their names will come up when the powers-that-be have a vacant seat to fill. In 1993, for instance, the *Wall Street Journal* carried a story about a vacancy on the U.S. Court of Appeals for the Federal Circuit, a court that deals with an inordinate number of patent appeals and one that is followed closely by business interests. The article noted that "a lively battle" had broken out among business groups over who should occupy the vacant seat and that

> even major corporations have taken the highly unusual step of weighing in for their favored candidates, while some other candidates have taken to fairly aggressive self-promotion. . . . Among those pushing for such a judge [one committed to science and technology] is John B. Pegram. His preferred choice: himself. In the past few months, Mr. Pegram . . . has written to the White House, offering himself up as a candidate, and made contact with a number of members of Congress, trumpeting his credentials.[11]

At judicial swearing-in ceremonies it is often said that "the judgeship sought the man (or woman) rather than vice versa," and surely this does happen. But sometimes the judgeship does its seeking with a little nudge from the would-be jurist.

The Element of Luck. If professional and political criteria were all that was involved in the selection of a Supreme Court justice or a lower-court judge, the appointment process would be much easier to explain and predict. If, for instance, one wanted to know who was going to be appointed to a vacancy on the Sixth Circuit bench, one would need only to identify the person in the Sixth Circuit to whom the party was most indebted and who had a reputation for legal competence. The problem is that the prevailing party owes much to hundreds of capable attorneys in the Sixth Circuit. Why should one of them out of several hundred be selected? Until judicial scholarship becomes more of a science and less of an art, accurate predictions cannot be made about who will wear the black robe; there are just too many variables and too many participants in the selection process. Consider, for example, President Harry S. Truman's appointment of Carroll O. Switzer to fill a vacant judgeship in 1949.

The story begins in 1948 when Truman was seeking a full term as president. The campaign had not gone well from the start. Even the party faithful could barely muster a faint cheer when Truman proclaimed to sparse crowds, "We're gonna win this election and we're gonna make those Republicans like it. Just you wait 'n' see." Almost everyone predicted Truman would lose, and lose badly. Then one morning his campaign train stopped in the little town of Dexter, Iowa. An unexpectedly large number of farmers had put aside their milking chores and the fall corn harvest to see the feisty little man from Missouri "give those Republicans hell." Truman picked up a real sense of enthusiasm among the cheering crowd, and for the first time in the campaign he smelled victory.

On the campaign platform with Truman that morning was Carroll Switzer, a bright young Des Moines attorney who was the (unsuccessful) Democratic candidate for Iowa governor that year. No evidence exists that Truman met Switzer before or after that one propitious occasion. But when a vacancy occurred on the U.S. bench a year later, Truman's mind jumped like a spring to the name of his lucky horseshoe, Carroll Switzer. A longtime administrative assistant to an Iowa senator related the story as follows:

I am sure that this day at Dexter was the first time President Truman and his staff were sure he could win—later proved right. I am sure that he recalled that day favorably when an appointment . . . came up in the Iowa judgeship. . . . Every time the Iowa judgeship came up, Truman would hear of no one but Switzer. Truman would say "That guy Switzer backed me when everyone else was running away, and, by God, I'm going to see that he gets a judgeship." [12]

That morning in Dexter was Switzer's lucky day. Although he had the professional and political credentials for a judicial post, no one could have foreseen that he would happen to appear with Truman the day the national winds of political fortune began to blow in the president's favor. Had it been any other day, Switzer might never have been more than just a bright attorney from Des Moines.

This account illustrates the point that a good measure of happenstance exists in virtually all judicial appointments. Being a member of the right party at the right time or being visible to the power brokers at a lucky moment often has as much to do with becoming a judge as the length and sparkle of one's professional résumé.

The Federal Selection Process and Its Participants

The skeletal framework of judicial selection is the same for all federal judges, although the roles of the participants vary depending upon the level of the U.S. judiciary. All nominations are made by the president after due consultation with the White House staff, the attorney general's office, certain senators, and other politicos. Furthermore, the FBI customarily performs a routine security check. After the nomination is announced to the public, various interest groups that believe they have a stake in the appointment may lobby for or against the candidate. Also, the candidate's qualifications will be evaluated by a committee of the American Bar Association. The candidate's name is then sent to the Senate Judiciary Committee, which conducts an investigation of the nominee's fitness for the post. If the committee's vote is favorable, the nomination is sent to the floor of the Senate, where it is either approved or rejected by a simple majority vote.

The President

Technically, the chief executive nominates all judicial candidates, but history has shown that the president manifests greater personal involvement in appointments to the Supreme Court than to the lower courts. This is so for two major reasons. First, Supreme Court appointments are seen by the president—and by the public at large—as generally more important and politically significant than openings on the lesser tribunals. Presidents often use their few opportunities for high court appointments to make a political statement or to set the tone of their administration. For example, during the period of national stress prior to U.S. entry into World War II, Democratic president Franklin D. Roosevelt elevated Republican Harlan Stone to chief justice as a gesture of national unity. In 1969 President Nixon used his appointment of the conservative Warren Burger to make good on his campaign pledge to restore "law and order." And President Reagan in 1981 hoped to dispel his reputation for being unsympathetic to the women's movement by being the first to name a woman to the high court. Likewise, President Clinton's appointment to the Court of two political moderates, Ruth Bader Ginsburg and Stephen Breyer, was viewed by many as an attempt to demonstrate to the public that he was a "new Democrat" and not a left-wing radical. Because appointments to the lower judiciary are less newsworthy, they are less likely to command the personal involvement of the president, who will probably rely much more heavily on the judgment of the White House staff or the Justice Department in selecting and screening candidates for appeals and trial court benches.

Second, presidents are less likely to devote much attention to lower-court appointments because tradition has enabled individual senators and local party bosses to influence and often dominate such activity. The practice known as **senatorial courtesy** is a major restriction on the president's capacity to appoint district judges. This unwritten rule of the game has the following conditions: Senators of the president's political party who object to a candidate whom the president wishes to appoint to a district judgeship in their home state have a virtual veto over the nomination. They exercise this veto through use of the **blue slip**—the printed form that a senator from the nominee's state is supposed to return to the Senate Judiciary Committee to express his or her views about the particular candidate.[13] (When Republicans controlled the Senate under the Clinton administration, Judiciary Committee chairman Orrin G. Hatch stalled Clinton nominees lacking blue slips from *both* senators from the relevant state.) This restriction on the chief executive's appointing prerogatives is so significant that it caused one former assistant attorney general to quip: "The Constitution is backwards. Article II, Section 2 should read: 'The senators shall nominate, and by and with the consent of the President, shall appoint.'"[14] Many senators regard their prerogatives in this realm to be ordained by the Founders. For example, under the Reagan administration when Texas senator Phil Gramm was asked to defend his key role in the appointment of district judges in his state, he said, "I'm given the power to make the appointment. . . . The people elected me to do that." [15] Senatorial courtesy does not apply to appellate court appointments, although presidents customarily defer to senators of their party from states that make up the appellate court circuit. Thus in lower-court appointments presidents have less incentive to devote effort to a game in which they are not the star player.

The president also has authority "to fill up all Vacancies that may happen during the recess of the Senate, by granting Commissions which shall expire at the End of their next Session" (Article II, Section 2). One reason a chief executive may wish to make a **recess appointment** is to fill a judicial vacancy on a court that has a large backlog of business. The other reason is more political. A president may find it easier to secure confirmation for a sitting judge than for a candidate named while the Senate is in session. That is, the Senate might be less likely to reject a fait accompli. For example, when the Senate in the fall of 1999 rejected the appointment of the African American nominee Ronnie White for a federal judgeship for what many believed were racially biased reasons, the Congressional Black Caucus called on President Clinton to bypass the Senate and use recess appointments for six pending nominations of African Americans. The caucus was aware that of the 309 recess appointments made in the nation's history, the Senate ultimately confirmed 85 percent of them. [16]

The Department of Justice

Assisting the president and the White House staff in the judicial selection process are the two key presidential appointees in the Justice Department—the attorney general of the United States and the deputy attorney general. Their primary job is to seek out candidates who conform to general criteria set by the president. For example, if a vacancy were to occur on the Seventh Circuit appellate bench, the attorney general (or a staff member) might phone the U.S. attorneys in the states of Illinois, Indiana, and Wisconsin and ask, "Are there some attorneys in your district who would make good judges and who are members of our political party or at least share the president's basic philosophy?" Once several names are obtained, the staff of the Justice Department will subject each candidate to further scrutiny. They may order an FBI investigation of the candidate's character and background; they will usually read copies of all articles or speeches the candidate has written or evaluate a sitting judge's written opinions; they might check with local party leaders to determine that the candidate is a party faithful and is in tune with the president's major public policy positions.

In the case of district judge appointments, where names are often submitted by home-state senators, the Justice Department's function is more as a screener than as an initiator. Regardless of who comes up with a basic list of names, the Justice Department's primary duty is to evaluate the candidates' personal, professional, and political qualifications. In performing this role, the department may work closely with the White House staff, with the senators involved in the nomination, and with party leaders who may wish to have some input in the choice of the potential nominee.

The current Bush administration relies heavily on Attorney General John Ashcroft and on White House counsel Alberto Gonzales in screening potential federal judges. Gonzales's staff consists of "aggressive conservative lawyers, a number of whom worked for former independent counsel Kenneth Starr in probing various Clinton scandals." [17]

State and Local Party Leaders

Presidential prerogative is dominant in the appointment of Supreme Court justices, so the role of regional party politicos in the choice of appeals court judges is minimal. However, in the selection of U.S. trial judges their impact is formidable, especially when appointments occur in states where neither senator is of the president's political party. In such cases the president need not fear that senatorial courtesy will be invoked against a district court nominee and thus will be more likely to consult with state party leaders rather than with the state's senators. For example, during the Kennedy and Johnson administrations the Democratic mayor of Chicago, Richard J. Daley, personally approved every federal judge appointed in the Northern District of Illinois.

Interest Groups

A number of pressure groups in the United States, representing the whole political spectrum from left to right, often lobby either for or against judicial nominations. Leaders of these groups—civil liberties, business, organized labor, civil rights—have little hesitation about urging the president to withdraw the nomination of someone whose political and social values are different from their own or about lobbying the Senate to support the nomination of someone who is favorably perceived. As one recent study concluded, "Organized interests, at least in the 1980s and early 1990s, mobilized often, on a variety of nominations, mustered an impressive array of capabilities and resources, and employed a wide range of activities on each." [18] More recently, two well-known students of the subject noted, "The participation of organized interests in judicial nominations in recent years extends well beyond the highly visible cases of [Robert H.] Bork, [David H.] Souter, and [Clarence] Thomas. Although these cases have obvious significance for cases reaching the Supreme Court, nominations for federal district judgeships, circuit judgeships, and other appointed positions in the executive branch that are subject to senatorial confirmation also have important implications for organized interests."[19]

At the present time, interest groups representing a wide range of ideologies and constituencies are lobbying for and against the judges that President George W. Bush has been nominating for the federal bench. In opposition to many of the president's judicial candidates is Kim A Gandy, president of the National Organization for Women. After taking office in 2001, she said her "immediate concern was preventing Bush from appointing Supreme Court justices who would overturn *Roe v. Wade*, the 1973 court decision that legalized abortion throughout the United States."[20] Likewise, Kweise Mfume, president of the NAACP, vowed in 2001 that his organization " 'would not sit idly by,' while federal courts are stacked 'with strange, conservative-thinking individuals.' " [21] And groups such as the Earth Justice Legal Defense Fund, "the Sierra Cub, the National Audubon Society, the Endangered Species Coalition . . . and other [environmentalist groups] have sent letters to every U.S. senator, asking them to carefully screen Bush's court nominees to determine whether they will disregard or try to rewrite environmental protection laws they don't like." [22] However, the president is not without his supporters among judicial lobbying groups. An organization called People for Common Sense Courts, headed by Oklahoma's Republican governor, Frank Keating, "announced plans for a national advertising campaign to shore up public support for Bush's nominees. . . . The group, which includes political, legal and business interests, was formed to defend Bush's nominees from partisan attacks." [23]

The American Bar Association

For more than four decades, the Committee on the Federal Judiciary of the ABA has played a key role in evaluating the credentials of potential nominees for positions on the federal bench. The committee, whose fifteen members represent all the U.S. circuits, evaluates candidates on the basis of numerous criteria, including judicial temperament, age, trial experience, character, and intelligence. A candidate approved by the committee is rated either "qualified" or "well qualified," whereas an unacceptable candidate is stamped with a "not qualified" label. (Traditionally, the committee rated the very best candidates as "exceptionally well qualified," but this category was dropped in 1991.)

The traditional composition of the committee has made it the subject of some controversy. Because it has been made up largely of older, well-to-do, Republican, business-oriented corporation attorneys, some observers have argued that their evaluation of potential judicial candidates has been biased in favor of their peers. A strong suspicion exists that the committee has viewed being wealthy and conservative as positive traits and being liberal and outspoken as uncharacteristic of "a sound judicial temperament." It should come as no surprise, then, that the ABA's committee has generally worked more closely with Republican presidents than with Democratic administrations.

Bucking the recommendations of the committee is a risky business, and presidents are likely to think long and hard before nominating a candidate tagged with the "not qualified" label.[24] President John F. Kennedy in 1962 successfully pushed for the appointment of Sarah T. Hughes (of the Northern District of Texas) despite opposition from the ABA, which argued that she was too old. Lobbying from none other than the vice president (Lyndon Johnson) and the Speaker of the House (Sam Rayburn) was required to ease the nomination through.[25]

Some presidents have gone back and forth in terms of their willingness to be bound by the pronouncements of the ABA committee. For example, when he first took office, President Nixon indicated that he would appoint no one who did not have the blessing of the ABA. However, after Senate defeat of two of Nixon's Supreme Court nominees, Clement Haynsworth and G. Harrold Carswell, the ABA began to cast a more critical eye on Nixon's choices. (The ABA had approved the Haynsworth and Carswell nominations and felt somewhat humiliated when investigations by the press and the Senate turned up a variety of negative factors overlooked by the committee.) Late in 1971, when he was trying to fill two vacancies on the Supreme Court, Nixon brought up the possibility of nominating Sen. Robert C. Byrd of West Virginia. Attorney General John Mitchell told Nixon that securing ABA approval would be a problem because Byrd had attended a "night law school" and had little experience as a practicing attorney. Nixon's reported reply to Mitchell indicates that the president's total confidence in the judgment of the ABA had waned. "Fuck the ABA," said Nixon. And from that time on, the president refused to submit names to the ABA committee until after he had selected and publicized them.

Although the ABA has tried to shake its image as being too intertwined with the conservative white male establishment, a recent study still shows a bias in favor of "traditional" judicial candidates. In an analysis of ABA ratings over a recent two-decade time frame, a prominent researcher concluded: "If increased experience

levels are indicative of a well-worn path to the bench, these findings support the results of earlier studies in which ratings were generally higher for candidates with
'traditional' career paths. . . . More disturbing, however, were the results comparing
'traditional' and 'nontraditional' appointees. Caucasian males were more likely to
receive a higher rating when compared to minorities or females, even after controlling for the length of legal and judicial experiences." [26]

The relationship between the administration of George H. W. Bush and the ABA
from 1988 to 1992 was generally a comfortable one, despite some minor initial conflict over whether the association should consider the nominees' political philosophy and ideology. (Bush's advisers called for less emphasis on such matters.) Under
President Clinton, a similar climate of quiet harmony prevailed. For example, during his eight years in office 59 percent of his district court nominees and 79 percent
of his appellate court nominees received the ABA's "well qualified" label—percentages higher than those of any prior administrations.

Under the administration of President George W. Bush, there has been a marked
cooling in its relationship with the American Bar Association. In March of 2001 the
administration announced an end to the forty-eight-year-old practice of letting the
ABA evaluate judicial candidates *before* they are nominated. In a letter to the ABA,
White House counsel Alberto Gonzales said it wasn't fair to give the organization
such a major role in the judicial selection process, particularly because it takes
stands on issues under litigation. (For example, the ABA favors abortion rights,
which the Bush administration opposes.) [27]

The Senate Judiciary Committee

The rules of the Senate require its Judiciary Committee to pass on all nominations to the federal bench and to make recommendations to the Senate as a whole.
Its role is thus to screen individuals who have already been nominated, not to suggest names of possible candidates. The committee by custom holds hearings on all
nominations, at which time witnesses are heard and deliberations take place behind closed doors. The hearings for district court appointments are largely per-
functory because the norm of senatorial courtesy has, for all intents and purposes,
already determined whether the candidate will pass senatorial muster. However, for
appeals court nominees—and surely for an appointment to the Supreme Court—
the committee hearing is a serious proceeding.

Acting as a sort of watchdog of the Senate, the committee can affect the selection
process in several ways. "First, it can delay Senate action on confirmation in the hope
of embarrassing the president or to test his determination to make a particular

appointment." As a general rule, the longer the delay, the poorer the nominee's chances are of securing approval. The failure of two of Reagan's Supreme Court nominees, Robert H. Bork and Douglas H. Ginsburg, to receive Senate approval was the result, in part, of the protracted committee hearings, which permitted the opposition forces to gather negative data and flex their lobbying muscles. Second, the committee can simply recommend against Senate confirmation. Finally, committee opponents of the nomination might engage in an extensive Senate floor debate, which "affords still another opportunity for senators to seek to embarrass the administration by questioning the wisdom of a particular appointment." [28]

Historically, the Judiciary Committee has had a distinctly southern and conservative flavor. As a result, it often did not look kindly upon appointees to the appeals courts and the Supreme Court who were thought to be too liberal—particularly on civil rights matters. Sen. James O. Eastland of Mississippi, the powerful committee chair for many years, often exacted a terrible toll from presidents who sought to put integrationists on the upper federal courts. For example, when President Kennedy tried to secure the appointment of the black and liberal Thurgood Marshall for a seat on the appellate court, Senator Eastland refused to support the nomination unless he could get his old college chum, William Harold Cox, a seat on the federal district court in Mississippi. Cox, who on the bench referred to blacks as "niggers" and "chimpanzees," is regarded as the worst of several racist judges Kennedy was "forced" to appoint in the South. As one black civil rights leader put it: "The brothers had to pay a lot of dues" to get Thurgood Marshall appointed to the bench.[29]

Perhaps the most vivid reminder of the power of the Senate Judiciary Committee came in the fall of 1991 in its much-publicized (and perhaps overly thorough) hearings on the nomination of Clarence Thomas to the Supreme Court. Even before public hearings began, the committee had requested some thirty thousand pages of documentation from Thomas. During weeks of intense questioning, the committee investigated almost every conceivable aspect of the nominee's background, philosophy, and credentials. The committee concluded its work with a dramatic weekend-long televised hearing concerning sexual harassment charges brought by a former employee of Thomas's, Anita F. Hill. Although the conduct of the committee during these proceedings is still being debated, few Americans came away from the spectacle unacquainted with the Judiciary Committee of the United States Senate.

After the Republican takeover of Congress as a result of the 1994 elections, control of the Judiciary Committee passed into the hands of conservative GOP senator Orrin G. Hatch of Utah. Between 1994 and 1996 the relationship between the Clinton administration and Hatch was relatively good, although Clinton's success rate in getting his nominees approved by the Republican Senate did decline markedly.[30] The unwritten rule said that if Clinton did not send up for consideration the names of any potential jurists who were too overtly liberal, then Hatch would grease the skids for easy committee approval. This arrangement seemed to work well for Clinton, whose main objective was to put more women and minorities on the bench rather than to fill the judiciary with left-of-center judges.

All this changed abruptly during the 1996 presidential election campaign when Republican candidate Robert Dole charged that Clinton was filling the judiciary with highly activist liberal judges.

The acrimony between Clinton and the GOP over judicial appointments continued after the election. By the summer of 1997 the Judiciary Committee had entered a state of virtual paralysis on the matter of confirming Clinton's judicial nominations. In May 1997 about one hundred judicial vacancies were unfilled, and the wait from nomination to confirmation reached a record 183 days.[31] Wrangling between Republicans and Democrats increased, while in the House of Representatives right-wing legislators (such as House Majority Whip Tom DeLay) mounted a drive to impeach activist-liberal judges.[32] By 1998, however, the situation began to improve somewhat, and the administration began to have a little more success in getting its nominations approved. The reasons for this were noted by a leading expert in this area, Professor Sheldon Goldman: "These include improvements in the administration's own handling of judicial selection matters, the role of Chief Justice [William H.] Rehnquist in drawing attention to the untenable state of affairs in appointment processes, and in the final analysis, widespread and hostile reaction to the hubris displayed by the conservative right—in particular, a number of conservative senators who had been largely responsible for the gridlock of 1996–97." [33]

After the election of 2000, President George W. Bush had to face a closely divided Judiciary Committee (ten Democrats and nine Republicans), headed by Democratic senator Patrick Leahy. Although most of Bush's nominees made it over the committee hurdle, Leahy and the other Committee Democrats scrutinized the nominees with great care. "We're not trying to appoint judges, but we also feel the advice and consent does not mean appoint and rubber stamp," declared Leahy.[34] From 2001 to 2003, the committee blocked the nomination of two key Bush nominees to the Fifth Circuit Courts of Appeals: Priscilla Owen of Texas and Charles Pickering of Mississippi. Both nominations generated much national publicity and both engendered acrimonious party-line clashes between members of the Judiciary Committee. In addition, the committee blocked the nomination of conservative Miguel Estrada, whom President Bush had nominated for a seat on the U.S. Court of Appeals for the District of Columbia.[35] When the Republicans regained control of the Senate in the 2002 elections, the chairmanship of the Judiciary Committee went to Senator Orrin Hatch. With the GOP once again controlling the committee, President Bush began the new year of 2003 by renominating Priscilla Owen and thirty other judicial nominees who had not been confirmed in 2002 when Democrats controlled the Senate. Although Democratic senators can no longer block Bush appointees on a party-line vote in the Judiciary Committee, they are currently threatening to filibuster on the floor of the Senate against those Bush nominees whom they deem too ideologically conservative.

The Senate

The final step in the judicial appointment process for federal judges is a majority vote by the Senate. The Constitution states that the Senate must give its "advice and consent" to judicial nominations made by the president. Historically, two general views of the Senate's prescribed role have prevailed. Since the time of George Washington, presidents and a few scholars have taken the position that the Senate should quietly go along with the presidential choices unless overwhelmingly strong reasons exist to the contrary. Other scholars and, not unexpectedly, most senators have held to the views of Sen. Birch Bayh of Indiana and Sen. Robert Griffin of Michigan that the Senate "has the right and the obligation to decide in its own wisdom whether it wishes to confirm or not to confirm a Supreme Court nominee." [36] In practice the role of the Senate in the judicial confirmation process has varied, depending on the level of the federal judgeship being considered.

For district judges, the norm of senatorial courtesy prevails. That is, if the president's nominee is acceptable to the senator(s) of the president's party in the state in which the judge is to sit, the Senate is usually happy to give its advice and consent with a quiet nod. However, a recent study found that "race does affect the length of time the Senate takes to process a nomination to the federal district courts. [When all other relevant variables were controlled for], "nominations of minorities ... still take longer to process than those of nonminorities." [37] For appointments to the appeals courts, senatorial courtesy does not apply, because the vacancy to be filled covers more than just the state of one or possibly two senators. But senators from each state in the circuit in which the vacancy has occurred customarily submit names of possible candidates to the president. An unwritten rule is that each state in the circuit should have at least one judge on that circuit's appellate bench, a practice often followed when the vacancy is that of a state's only representative on the circuit bench. As long as the norms are adhered to and the president's nominee has reasonably good qualifications, the Senate as a whole usually goes along with the recommendations of the chief executive.

The Senate has been inclined traditionally to go toe-to-toe with the president if disagreement arises over a nominee's fitness for the high court. Since 1789, presidents have sent the names of 144 persons to the Senate for its advice and consent. Of this number, thirty were either rejected or "indefinitely postponed" by the Senate, or the names were withdrawn by the president. Thus presidents have been successful about 79 percent of the time, and their batting average seems to be improving, given that as many as one-third of the nominations were rejected by the Senate in the nineteenth century. The record shows that presidents have met with the most success in getting their high court nominations approved when (1) the nominee comes from a noncontroversial background and has middle-of-the-road political leanings, and (2) the president's party also controls the Senate, or at least a majority shares the president's basic attitudes and values. As one study of 2,054 Senate roll-call votes on Supreme Court nominations from Earl Warren to Anthony M. Kennedy concluded: "When a strong president nominates a highly qualified, ideologically moderate candidate, the nominee passes the Senate in a lopsided, consensual vote. Presidents have often nominated this type of candidate and consequently consensual votes have been fairly common. When presidents nominate a less well qualified, ideologically extreme candidate, especially when the president is in a weak position, then a conflictual vote is likely." [38]

The Judicial Socialization Process

When scholars use the term **socialization,** they are referring to the process whereby individuals acquire the values, attitudes, and behavior patterns of the existing social system. Factors that aid the process include family, friends, education, coworkers, religious training, political party affiliation, and the communications media. Social scientists also apply the term *socialization* to the process by which a person is formally trained to perform the specific tasks of a particular profession. It is the second meaning of the term that will be of concern here.

Much significant socialization occurs before the judges first mount the bench. From their parents, teachers, exposure to the news media, and so on, future judges learn the rules of the American political game. That is, by the time they are teenagers they have absorbed key values and attitudes that will circumscribe subsequent judicial behavior: "the majority should rule on general matters of public policy, but minorities have their rights, too"; "judges ought to be fair and impartial";

and "the Constitution is an important document and all political leaders should be bound by it." In college and law school, future judges acquire important analytic and communication skills, in addition to the basic substance of the law. After a couple of decades of legal practice, the preparation for a judgeship is in its final stage. The future judge has learned a good deal about how the courts and the law work and has specialized in several areas of the law. Despite all this preparation, sometimes called "anticipatory socialization," most new judges in America still have much to learn even after donning the black robe.[39]

In many other countries, preparing to be a judge is like preparing to be a physician, an engineer, or a pharmacist—one goes to a particular professional school in which one receives many years of in-depth training and perhaps an on-the-job internship. Since 1959 in France, for example, all would-be judges are intensively trained for a minimum of twenty-eight months at the prestigious École Nationale de la Magistrature. They enter judicial service only after passing rigorous competitive examinations. Not only does the United States lack formalized training procedures for the judicial profession, but there is also the naive assumption that being a lawyer for a decade or so is all the experience one needs to be a judge. After all, don't most lawyers, like judges, work in the courtroom? Isn't it enough for the lawyer-turned-judge just to mount the bench and put on a new hat? To the contrary, becoming a judge in America requires a good deal of freshman socialization (short-term learning and adjustment to the new role) and occupational socialization (on-the-job training over a period of years).

Typical new trial court appointees may be first-rate lawyers and experts in a few areas of the law in which they have specialized. As judges, however, they are suddenly expected to be experts on all legal subjects, are required to engage in judicial duties usually unrelated to any tasks they performed as lawyers (for example, sentencing), and are given a host of administrative assignments for which they have had no prior experience (for example, learning how to docket efficiently several hundred diverse cases).[40] The following statements by U.S. trial judges reveal what it was like for each of them as the new kid on the judicial block. (Virtually all the judges who were interviewed for this book were promised anonymity, and thus no references will appear.)

Before I became a federal judge I had been a trial lawyer dealing mainly with personal injury cases and later on with some divorce cases. Needless to say, I knew almost nothing about criminal law. With labor law I had had only one case in my life on this subject, and that was a case going back to the early days of World War II. In other words when I became a federal judge I really had an awful lot to learn about many important areas of the law.

My legal background and experience really didn't prepare me very well for the kind of major judicial problems I face. For instance, most lawyers don't deal with constitutional issues related to the Bill of Rights and the Fourteenth Amendment; rather they deal with much more routine questions, such as wills and contracts. Civil liberties questions were really new to me as a judge, and I think this is true for most new judges.

A report about one of George H. W. Bush's appointees to the trial bench confirms the persistence of this phenomenon. Before becoming a U.S. district judge, Melinda F. Harmon

was a Houston [Texas] attorney for Exxon for 12 years. She had no experience in criminal litigation or in constitutional law, fields that will make up a significant portion of her case load as a federal judge. Harmon acknowledged at her confirmation hearing that she would have to rely on "on-the-job training" to become prepared for the federal bench. She said she used part of her trip to Washington to stop by the federal judicial training center and check out seven videotapes to help her prepare.[41]

At the appeals court level there is also a period of freshman socialization—despite the circuit judge's possible prior judicial experience—and former trial judges appear to make the transition with fewer scars. As a couple of appeals judges said of their first days on the circuit bench: "I was no blushing violet in fields I knew something about. How effective I was is another question." Even an experienced former trial judge recalled his surprise that "it takes a while to learn the job—and I'm not addressing myself to personal relationships. . . . That's a very different job." Another appeals judge, regarded by his peers as a leader from the beginning, said, "I don't know how I got through my first year." [42] During the transition time (the period of learning the ropes of the appellate court), circuit judges tend to speak for the court less frequently than their more experienced colleagues do. They often take longer to write opinions, defer more often to senior colleagues, or just wallow about in indecision.

The learning process for new Supreme Court justices is even harder—if the personal testimonies of justices as diverse as Benjamin Cardozo, Frank Murphy, Harlan F. Stone, Earl Warren, William Brennan, and Arthur Goldberg are to be believed. As one scholar has noted, "Once on the Court, the freshman Justice, even if he has been a state or lower federal court judge, moves into a strange and shadowy world." [43] Perhaps this is the metaphor that Chief Justice William Howard Taft had in mind when he confided that in joining the Court he felt that he had come "to live in a monastery." As with new appeals court judges, novice Supreme Court justices tend to defer to senior associates, to write fewer majority and dissenting opinions, and to manifest a good deal of uncertainty. New high court appointees may have more judicial experience than their lower-court colleagues, but the fact that the Supreme Court is involved in broad judicial policymaking—as opposed to the error correction of the appeals courts and the norm enforcement of the trial courts—may account for their initial indecisiveness. Still, not all new justices experience what scholars have come to call "the freshman effect," and of those who do, not all manifest it in the same way.[44]

Supreme Court appointee David Souter's first year on the Court provides a good example of "the freshman effect phenomenon." Near the end of his first term on the Court, one observer noted that "Souter has gotten off to a notably slow start and written only one opinion of the 64 released this term, a unanimous ruling on a procedural point about jury selection" (hardly a bombshell case).[45] As *Newsweek* pointed out,

He may be a New Englander, but Justice David Souter hasn't shown much Yankee independence in his first term. . . . So far Souter has voted with the majority in all 40 of the decisions in which he has participated. Each of the other eight justices has written at least one dissenting opinion and joined the dissenting side several other times. Souter also lags behind in writing majority decisions—producing only one while the other justices have averaged six each. In the next few weeks, Souter may catch up; but some blame his anemic output for the court's end-of-term gridlock. "There's just one reason and that's the total breakdown in one chamber," says a former court clerk.[46]

Given the need on the part of all new federal jurists for both freshman and occupational socialization, where do they go for instruction? Although there are many agents of socialization for novice judges, the evidence is strong that the older, more experienced judges have the primary responsibility for this task: The system trains and nurtures its own. As one trial judge said, "My prime sources of help were the two judges here in [this city]. They sent me various things even before I was appointed, and I was glad to get them." Another recalled, "I had the help I needed right down here in the corner of this building on this floor," pointing in the direction of another judge's chambers. One district judge gave a more graphic description of his "schooling":

They [the other trial judges] let me sit next to them in actual courtroom situations, and they explained to me what they were doing at every minute. We both wore our robes and we sat next to each other on the bench. I would frequently ask them questions and they would explain things to me as the trial went along. Other times I would have a few free minutes and I would drop into another judge's courtroom and just sit and watch. I learned a lot that way.

For both the rotating appeals court judges and their trial court peers, then, the lion's share of training comes from their more senior, experienced colleagues on the bench—particularly the chief judge of the circuit or district.[47] For example, when Houston's senior federal trial judge Norman Black passed away in July 1997, one of his junior colleagues, Judge David Hittner, said of him: "Norman taught a lot of us younger federal judges how to do this job." [48] One scholar has noted that "the impact of chief judges was most noticeable on freshmen.... ('If all the judges are new, he'll pack a wallop out of proportion to one vote.')" [49] Likewise on the Supreme Court, older associates, often the chief justice, play a primary part in passing on to novice justices the essential rules and values on which their very serious game is based.[50] For example, Justice Ruth Bader Ginsburg recalled that when she was first appointed to the Court, Justice Byron R. White had given her a manual outlining her work. "A new justice could not have had a clearer, more sensible introduction to the ways of the court," she said, adding that she has kept the manual up-to-date and will pass it on to her successor.[51]

The training seminars provided by the Federal Judicial Center for newly appointed judges should also be mentioned again in this regard, because over the years the center has played an ever-increasing role in the training and socialization of new jurists. Although some of these seminars are conducted by outside specialists—law school experts on particular subjects—the key instructors still tend to be seasoned judges whose real-life experience on the bench commands the respect of the new members of the federal judiciary.

The fact that judges in America require socialization even after their appointments is interesting in and of itself, but the question arises: What is the significance of all this for the operation of the judicial-legal system? First, the agents of socialization that are readily available to the novice jurists allow the system to operate more smoothly, with a minimum of down time. If new judges were isolated from their more experienced associates, geographically or otherwise, they would require much more time to learn the fine points of their profession, and a greater number of errors would presumably be foisted upon hapless litigants.

Second, the judicial system is a loose hierarchy that is constantly subjected to centrifugal and centripetal forces from within and without. The fact that the system is able to provide its own socialization—that the older, experienced jurists train the novices—serves as a sort of glue that helps to bond the fragmented system It allows the judicial values, practices, and orientations of one generation of judges to be passed on to another. It gives continuity and a sense of permanence to a system that operates in a world where chaos and random behavior appear to be the order of the day.

The Retirement and Removal of Judges

Judges cease to perform their judicial duties either by choice, because of ill health or death, or because of the disciplinary actions of others.

Disciplinary Action against Federal Judges

All federal judges appointed under the provisions of Article III of the Constitution hold office "during good Behavior," which means, in effect, for life or until they choose to step down. The only way they can be removed from the bench is by impeachment (indictment by the House of Representatives) and conviction by the Senate. In accordance with constitutional requirements (for Supreme Court justices) and legislative standards (for appeals and trial court judges), impeachment may occur for "Treason, Bribery, or other high Crimes and Misdemeanors." An impeached jurist would face trial in the Senate, which could convict by a vote of two-thirds of the members present.[52]

The impeachment of a federal judge is a rare event, although recently it has become a more familiar topic. In October 1989 the Senate voted to convict Judge Alcee L. Hastings on eight of the seventeen charges brought in impeachment proceedings against him. The case against the judge was filed less than two years after this black Carter appointee assumed the bench. The matter began when a convicted felon with long-standing associations with organized crime walked into the U.S. attorney's office in Miami and asked for a plea bargain. If drug charges against him were reduced or dropped, he would be willing to provide information about a bribery scheme in Judge Hastings's court. An investigation followed, and criminal charges were brought against the judge, who was accused of soliciting and accepting a bribe and of "corruptly influencing and impeding the administration of justice." Ironically, the judge was found not guilty of the charges, but during the course of the trial he had inadvertently revealed information suggesting that he ran his courtroom in an unethical, though not criminal, manner. Less than one month after the trial, an investigation into Hastings's behavior was undertaken by the chief judge of the Eleventh Circuit, John Godbold. A circuit judicial council called more than 110 witnesses and examined more than twenty-eight hundred exhibits. The committee found against Hastings and then officially informed the House of Representatives that Hastings had engaged in conduct that "might constitute one or more grounds for impeachment." The House of Representatives conducted an inquiry through the use of a subcommittee and on its recommendation voted, 413–3, to impeach the judge. A trial was then held in the Senate. While some of the charges were thrown out, Judge Hastings was convicted on several counts and was promptly stripped of his judgeship.[53] Two weeks later the same fate befell Judge Walter L. Nixon, who was convicted on two of three impeachment charges. However, since 1789 the House has initiated such proceedings against only thirteen jurists—although about an equal number of judges resigned just before formal action was taken against them. Of these thirteen cases, only seven resulted in a conviction, which removed them from office. Considering all the men and women who have sat on the federal bench during the past two centuries, that is not a bad record. (In the past decade, four members of Congress were convicted of felonies in a single session.)

Although outright acts of criminality by those on the bench are few, a gray area of misconduct may put offending judges somewhere in the twilight zone between acceptable and impeachable behavior. What should be done with the federal jurist who hears a case despite an obvious conflict of interest, who consistently demonstrates biased behavior in the courtroom, who too often totters into court after a triple-martini lunch? A case in point is Judge Willis Ritter, who used to sit on the federal bench in Salt Lake City. One observer described Ritter as

ecumenically mean, which is to say he seems to dislike most persons who come into his court, be they defendant, government lawyer, private trial attorney, or ordinary citizen. Ritter is also selective about his fellow judges. He was once so estranged from another Utah federal judge that they wouldn't ride on the elevator together, much less speak; for a while the court clerk divided cases so that they didn't have to appear in the courthouse on the same day. . . . Ritter is one of the few federal judges in the nation who becomes so emotionally involved in his hearings that appeals courts often order him not to retry cases when they are reversed.[54]

One lawyer who had managed to fall from Judge Ritter's graces recalled an incident. As the lawyer was starting to present his case in open court, from out of the blue the judge began to hiss at him and continued to do so throughout the attorney's presentation. "Like a snake, he was going 'ssssss' all the time I was speaking," the astounded lawyer recounted later. "I never ever have been before a judge of this kind."[55]

Had Ritter committed impeachable offenses? He had not been guilty of "Treason, Bribery, or other high Crimes and Misdemeanors," although one could question whether he was serving "during good Behavior." Historically, little has been done in such cases other than issuance of a mild reprimand by colleagues (a useless gesture for a Judge Ritter) or impeachment (a recourse considered too drastic in most cases). In recent decades, however, actions have been taken to fill in the discipline gap. In 1966, for example, the Supreme Court upheld an action taken by the Tenth Circuit Judicial Council against U.S. District Judge Stephen S. Chandler of Oklahoma. The council had stripped him of his duties and authority (while permitting him to retain his salary and title) for a series of antics both on and off the bench that made Judge Ritter seem venerable by comparison.

In addition, on October 1, 1980, a new statute took effect, on which Congress had labored for several years. Titled the Judicial Councils Reform and Judicial

Conduct and Disability Act, the law has two distinct parts.[56] The first part authorizes the Judicial Council in each circuit, composed of both appeals and trial court judges and presided over by the chief judge of the circuit, to "make all necessary and appropriate orders for the effective and expeditious administration of justice within its circuit." The second part of the act establishes a statutory complaint procedure against judges. Basically, it permits an aggrieved party to file a written complaint with the clerk of the appellate court. The chief judge then reviews the charge and may dismiss it if it appears frivolous, or for a variety of other reasons. If the complaint seems valid, the chief judge must appoint an investigating committee consisting of himself or herself and an equal number of trial and circuit court judges. After an inquiry the committee reports to the council, which has several options: (1) the judge may be exonerated; (2) if the offender is a bankruptcy judge or magistrate, he or she may be removed; and (3) an Article III judge may be subject to private or public reprimand or censure, certification of disability, request for voluntary resignation, or prohibition against further case assignments. However, removal of an Article III judge is not permitted; impeachment is still the only recourse. If the council determines that the conduct "might constitute" grounds for impeachment, it will notify the Judicial Conference, which in turn may transmit the case to the U.S. House of Representatives for consideration.

Since the act went into effect, there has been no shortage of complaints. For example, in 2001, 766 ethical complaints were lodged against federal judges. However, only one resulted in a penalty—a private censure, and not even the judge's name was released.[57] Because of the confidential nature of this process, it is difficult to obtain a hard count of all the disciplinary actions. But there is evidence to indicate that between 1983 and 1990 at least eleven judges chose to retire after judicial conduct complaints were filed, and a number of others took senior status or reduced workloads because of deteriorating physical or mental health.[58] Thus the Judicial Conduct Act is apparently having some meaningful impact, although its effects cannot be measured with total precision.

Disability of Federal Judges

Perhaps the biggest problem has not been the removal of criminals and crackpots from the federal bench. Instead, it has been the question of what to do with jurists who have become too old and infirm to carry out their judicial responsibilities effectively. The problem is potentially a considerable one. In 2001 it was found that nearly 40 percent of the nation's more than twelve hundred working judges are on "senior status" and have thus opted not to retire.[59] As the former chief judge of the

Fifth Circuit Court of Appeals John Brown tersely put it, "Get rid of the aged judges, and you get rid of most of the problems of the federal judiciary: drunkenness, incompetence, senility, cantankerous behavior on the bench." [60] For example, Justice William O. Douglas suffered a stroke while on the Supreme Court but refused afterward to resign, even when it was clear to all that he should do so. In 1974 Chief Justice Burger "believed Douglas was developing the paranoid qualities of many stroke victims. Douglas complained that there were plots to kill him and to remove him from the bench. Once he was wheeled into the Chief's chambers and maintained it was his. Rumors circulated among the staff that Douglas thought he was the Chief Justice." But he stayed on. A year later he was still interpreting the Constitution for more than 200 million Americans, although he "was in constant pain and barely had the energy to make his voice audible. He was wheeled in and out of conference, never staying the entire session, leaving his votes with [William J.] Brennan [Jr.] to cast. [Louis F.] Powell [Jr.] counted the number of times Douglas fell asleep. Brennan woke him gently when it came time to vote." Eventually Douglas resigned, but he remained on the bench longer than he should have. On the Court at the same time as Douglas were Justices John Harlan and Hugo Black. The latter, at eighty-five, was in such poor health that Douglas was counseling him to resign. "But Black would not accept the advice." [61]

In contrast to Black, Harlan continued to run his chambers from his hospital bed. Nearly blind, he could not even see the ash from his own cigarette, but he doggedly prepared for the coming term. One day a clerk brought in an emergency petition. Harlan remained in bed as he discussed the case with the clerk. They agreed that the petition should be denied. Harlan bent down, his eyes virtually to the paper, wrote his name, and handed the paper to his clerk. The clerk saw no signature. He looked over at Harlan. "Justice Harlan, you just denied your sheet," the clerk said, gently pointing to the scrawl on the linen. Harlan smiled and tried again, signing the paper this time.[62]

Although the federal judiciary as a whole is not proportionally in the same state of ill health and advanced age as was the Supreme Court during the early 1970s, the problem of what to do with the aged or mentally disabled judge has not disappeared. Congress has tried with some success to tempt the more senior judges into retirement by making it financially more palatable to do so. Since 1984 federal judges have been permitted to retire with full pay and benefits under what is called the **rule of eighty,** that is, when the sum of a judge's age and number of years on the bench is eighty. Congress has also permitted judges to go on senior status instead of accepting full retirement. In exchange for a reduced caseload they are permitted to retain their office and staff and—equally important—the prestige and self-respect of being an active judge. Despite the congressional inducements to retire, "more vacancies occur as a result of death in harness, particularly at the higher levels, than in any other way." [63]

Some credible evidence suggests that judges often time their resignations to occur when their party controls the presidency so that they will be replaced by a jurist of similar political and judicial orientation. As one researcher concluded, "Among the Appeals and District judges there is a substantial contingent who bring to the bench political loyalties that encourage them, more often than not, to maneuver their departure in such a way that will maximize the chance for the appointment of a replacement by a president of their party." [64] This observation has been given even greater weight by a 1990 study that correlated federal trial judges' retirement patterns with a wide variety of variables. The study found, among other things, that especially since 1954, "judicial retirement/resignation rates have been strongly influenced by political/ideological considerations, and infused with partisanship." [65] Predicting electoral outcomes can sometimes be problematic, however, as indicated by this account of an Iowa district judge's decision about retirement:

By 1948 Iowa Southern District Federal Judge Charles A. Dewey had decided that the time had come for him to retire. The seventy-one-year-old jurist had served on the federal bench for two full decades, and he felt that he had earned the right to his government pension. As a good Republican, however, he felt that it would be best to withhold his resignation until after the November election when "President Thomas E. Dewey" would be in a position to fill the vacancy with another "right-minded" individual like himself. Much to Judge Dewey's chagrin, his namesake did not receive the popular mandate in the presidential election, and Judge Dewey did not believe that he could carry on for another four years until the American people finally "came to their senses" and put a Republican in the White House. Therefore, shortly after the November election, Judge Dewey tendered his resignation.[66]

A similar note is sounded by former chief justice William Howard Taft, who clung to his high court position lest he be replaced with someone whose policy values were more progressive than his own: "As long as things continue as they are, and I am able to answer in their place, I must stay in the Court in order to prevent the Bolsheviki [that is, American Communists] from gaining control." [67] More recently the liberal black Supreme Court justice Thurgood Marshall vowed not to "retire from the Court as long as Reagan remains in the White House." [68] (He kept his pledge throughout the Reagan years, but finally, in June 1991, a rather bitter and decrepit Thurgood Marshall yielded to Father Time and announced his resignation, saying, "I'm old and I'm coming apart." Republican George H. W. Bush was president.)

These illustrations provide further evidence that many jurists view themselves as part of a policy link between the people, the judicial appointment process, and the subsequent decisions of the judges and justices.

Summary

This chapter began with a collective portrait of the men and women who have served in the federal judiciary. We noted that despite the occasional maverick, the jurists have come from a narrow stratum within America's social and economic elite. The result is a core of judges who share similar values and who therefore strive, with minimal coercion, to keep the judicial system functioning in a relatively harmonious manner. Though formal qualifications for a seat on the bench are few, tradition has established several informal criteria, including a reasonable degree of professional competence, the right political affiliation and contacts, at least some desire for the job itself, and a bit of luck thrown in for good measure.

At the national level the judicial selection process includes a variety of participants, despite the constitutional mandate that the president shall do the appointing with the advice and consent of the Senate. If presidents are to dominate this process and appoint individuals having similar policy values, several conditions must be met: Chief executives must want to make ideologically based appointments; they must have an ample number of vacancies to fill; they must be adroit leaders with political clout; and the existing judiciary must be attuned to their policy goals. If most of these conditions are met, presidents tend to get the kind of judges they want. In other words, an identifiable policy link exists between the popular election of the president, the appointment of judges, and the substantive content of the judges' decisions.

Although much judicial socialization occurs before the judges don their black robes, a good deal of learning takes place after they assume the bench. Because both freshman socialization and occupational socialization are furthered by senior colleagues, the values and practices of one generation of judges are smoothly passed on to the next. Thus continuity in the system is maintained.

The disciplining and removal of corrupt or mentally unfit judges is still a problem, although at the national level it may be eased as a result of the Judicial Conduct Act of 1980, which seems to be having some effect. The fact that so many judges time their resignations to allow a president (or a governor) of similar party identification and values to appoint a replacement is further evidence that the jurists themselves see a substantive link between the appointment process and the content of many of their decisions.

Further Thought and Discussion Questions

1. At least half of President Bill Clinton's judicial appointees were women or minorities—a marked contrast with his predecessors and George W. Bush, who have appointed largely white males. Were Clinton's actions important for symbolic or political reasons only, or do women and minorities think and behave somewhat differently as judges?

2. In virtually all foreign countries a person cannot become a federal judge unless he or she has first attended a formal college for judges, has passed a rigid set of exams, or has had many years of specialized training. The United States, however, imposes no formal requirements whatsoever on a prospective federal judge; the presidential appointee need only be approved by the Senate. Would the United States benefit from emulating the model of other nations, or has its system served the citizenry well?

3. When senators are deciding whether or not to support a president's judicial nominations, should they consider only the nominees' qualifications or should they also consider how the nominees might vote in cases that are of interest to the senators?

NOTES

1. Richard A. Posner, *The Federal Courts: Challenge and Reform* (Cambridge, Mass.: Harvard University Press, 1996), 20.

2. For a more extensive study of this subject, particularly as it pertains to the U.S. appeals courts and the Supreme Court, see John R. Schmidhauser, *Judges and Justices: The Federal Appellate Judiciary* (Boston: Little, Brown, 1979), 55–58.

3. Debra Sharpe and Peggy Roberson, "Tower Backs Cobb for Federal Judge," *Beaumont Enterprise*, May 4, 1984, A1.

4. Henry J. Abraham, *The Judicial Process*, 7th ed. (New York: Oxford University Press, 1998), 34.

5. Schmidhauser, *Judges and Justices*, 49.

6. Jill Abramson, "Ruth Bader Ginsburg Has Spent Her Career Overcoming the Odds," *Wall Street Journal*, June 15, 1993, A6.

7. J. Woodford Howard Jr., *Courts of Appeals in the Federal Judicial System* (Princeton, N.J.: Princeton University Press, 1981), 121.

8. Howard Ball, *Courts and Politics: The Federal Judicial System* (Englewood Cliffs, N.J.: Prentice Hall, 1980), 201–202.

9. Peter McCormick, *Canada's Courts*, (Toronto: James Lorimer, 1994), 109.

10. As quoted in Joseph C. Goulden, *The Benchwarmers: The Private World of the Powerful Federal Judges* (New York: Weybright and Talley, 1974), 33.

11. Richard F. Schmitt, "Battle Erupts Over Federal Circuit Seat," *Wall Street Journal,* October 21, 1993, B8.

12. As quoted in Robert A. Carp and C. K. Rowland, *Policymaking and Politics in the Federal District Courts* (Knoxville: University of Tennessee Press, 1983), 55.

13. As a standard procedure, the Senate Judiciary Committee sends to the senator(s) of the state in which there is a district court vacancy a request, printed on a blue form, to approve or disapprove the nomination being considered by the committee. If approval is not forthcoming, the senator retains the slip; if there is no objection, the blue form is returned to the committee. For an excellent discussion of the history of the blue slip and its current status, see Brannon P. Denning, "The Judicial Confirmation Process and the Blue Slip," *Judicature* 85 (2002): 218–226.

14. As quoted in Ball, *Courts and Politics,* 176.

15. Cragg Hines, "Dispensing Legal Plums," *Houston Chronicle,* April 21, 1985, A1.

16. David Goldsmith, "Black Lawmakers Ask Clinton to Bypass Senate, Appoint 6," *Houston Chronicle,* November 13, 1999, A14.

17. Bennett Roth, "Bush Won't Use ABA to Evaluate His Judicial Picks," *Houston Chronicle,* March 23, 2001, A1.

18. Gregory A. Caldeira, Marie Hojnacki, and John R. Wright, "The Lobbying Activities of Organized Interests in Federal Judicial Nominations," *Journal of Politics* 62 (2000): 68.

19. Gregory A. Caldeira and John R. Wright, "Lobbying for Justice: Organized Interests, Supreme Court Nominations, and the United States Senate," *American Journal of Political Science* 42 (1998): 521.

20. "New NOW Leader to Put Heat on Bush," *Houston Chronicle,* July 2, 2001, A9.

21. "Bush's Pledge Fails to Appease NAACP," *Houston Chronicle,* July 10, 2001, A2.

22. Patty Reinert, "Environmental Groups to Look Closely at Future Federal Judges," *Houston Chronicle,* July 19, 2001, A8.

23. Julie Mason, "GOP Seeking Rules on Judicial Hearings," *Houston Chronicle,* June 7, 2001, A12.

24. The classic study of the role of the American Bar Association (ABA) is Joel B. Grossman, *Lawyers and Judges: The ABA and the Politics of Judicial Selection* (New York: Wiley, 1965).

25. For the humorous and interesting details of this controversy, see Goulden, *The Benchwarmers,* 61–62.

26. Susan Brodie Haire, "Rating the Ratings of the American Bar Association Standing Committee on the Federal Judiciary," *Justice System Journal* 22 (2001): 14–15.

27. Bennett Roth, "Bush Won't Use ABA to Evaluate His Judicial Picks," *Houston Chronicle,* March 23, 2001, A1.

28. Harold W. Chase, *Federal Judges: The Appointing Process* (Minneapolis: University of Minnesota Press, 1972), 21, 23.

29. As quoted in Donald Dale Jackson, *Judges* (New York: Atheneum, 1974), 122.

30. Sheldon Goldman and Elliot Slotnick, "Clinton's First Term Judiciary," *Judicature,* 80 (1997): 254–273.

31. Viveca Novak, "Empty-Bench Syndrome," *Time,* May 26, 1997, 37.

32. Greg McDonald, "Conservative Lawmakers Propose Impeachment of Activist Judges," *Houston Chronicle,* March 13, 1997, A6.

33. Sheldon Goldman and Elliot Slotnick, "Clinton's Second Term Judiciary: Picking Judges under Fire," *Judicature,* 82 (1999): 264–284.

34. Bennett Roth, "Bush Submits 11 Names for Federal Bench," *Houston Chronicle,* May 10, 2001, A1.

35. On September 4, 2003, Miguel Estrada withdrew his name from the appointment process, saying that he believed the time had come "to return my full attention to the practice of law and to regain the ability to make long-term plans for my family." Julie Mason, "2-Year Standoff Ends, as Estrada Drops Judge Bid," *Houston Chronicle,* September 5, 2003, A2.

36. As quoted in Ball, *Courts and Politics,* 167.

37. Wendy L. Martinek, Mark Kemper, and Steven R. Van Winkle, "To Advise and Consent: The Senate and Lower Federal Court Nominations, 1977–1998,"*Journal of Politics* 64 (2002): 358.

38. Charles M. Cameron, Albert D. Cover, and Jeffrey A. Segal, "Senate Voting on Supreme Court Nominees: A Neoinstitutional Model," *American Political Science Review* 84 (1990): 532. Also, see Jeffrey A. Segal, Charles M. Cameron, and Albert D. Cover, "A Spatial Model of Roll Call Voting: Senators, Constituents, Presidents, and Interest Groups in Supreme Court Confirmations," *American Journal of Political Science* 36 (1992): 96–121. For a more recent and equally sophisticated study of this phenomenon, see Sarah A. Binder and Forrest Maltzman, "Senatorial Delay in Confirming Federal Judges, 1947–1998," *American Journal of Political Science*46 (2002): 190–199.

39. This phenomenon also appears to occur among U.S. appeals court judges. See, for example, Stephen L. Wasby, " 'Into the Soup?': The Acclimation of Ninth Circuit Appellate Judges," *Judicature* 73 (1989): 13. This article is a good discussion of the socialization process of appeals court judges in general.

40. New federal district judges with prior state court experience have a somewhat easier time of it, particularly in terms of the psychological adjustment to the judgeship and dealing with some of the administrative problems. However, prior state court experience seems to be of little help in the jurist's efforts to become expert in federal law. See Robert A. Carp and Russell R. Wheeler, "Sink or Swim: The Socialization of a Federal District Judge," *Journal of Public Law* 21 (1972): 367–374.

41. "Easy OK Seen for Houston Judge," *Houston Chronicle*, April 6, 1989, A6.

42. All quoted in Howard, *Courts of Appeals in the Federal Judicial System*, 224.

43. Walter F. Murphy, *Elements of Judicial Strategy* (Chicago: University of Chicago Press, 1964), 50.

44. For a sophisticated study of this subject, see Timothy M. Hagle, "'Freshman Effects' for Supreme Court Justices," *American Journal of Political Science* 37 (1993): 1142–1157. See also Terry Bowen, "Consensual Norms and the Freshman Effect on the United States Supreme Court," *Social Science Quarterly* 76 (1995): 222–231; and Sandra L. Wood, Linda Camp Keith, Drew Noble Lanier, and Ayo Ogundele, " 'Acclimation Effects' for Supreme Court Justices: A Cross-Validation, 1888–1940," *American Journal of Political Science* 42 (1998): 690–697. Furthemore, a recent study found that "first-year associate justices were assigned less than half the opinions than can be expected by chance, . . . but that second-year associate justices . . . were not disadvantaged in opinion assignment in the salient cases." See, Saul Brenner, "Majority Opinion Assignment in Salient Cases on the U.S. Supreme Court: Are New Associate Justices Assigned Fewer Opinions?" *Justice System Journal* 22 (2001): 209–221.

45. Ruth Marcus, "Souter Draws Clear Bench Marks," *Houston Chronicle*, May 28, 1991, A4. Note, however, that not all Supreme Court appointees appear to manifest "the freshman effect." See, for example, Albert P. Melone, "Revisiting the Freshman Effect Hypothesis: The First Two Terms of Justice Anthony Kennedy," *Judicature* 74 (1990): 6–13.

46. "Souter: Slow Off the Mark," *Newsweek*, May 27, 1991, 4.

47. For the best discussion of this training, see Howard, *Courts of Appeals in the Federal Judicial System*, chap. 8.

48. Ty Clevenger, "Final Tribute Paid to Black," *Houston Chronicle*, July 28, 1997, A13.

49. Ibid., 229.

50. For examples of this, see Murphy, *Elements of Judicial Strategy*, 49–51.

51. Patty Reinert, "Colleagues Mourn Long-serving Justice," *Houston Chronicle*, April 16, 2002, A1.

52. For a good discussion of the impeachment process, including information on what the Founders had in mind regarding the terms "High Crimes and Misdemeanors," see "Impeaching Federal Judges: Where Are We and Where Are We Going?" *Judicature* 72 (1989): 359–365. (The article is an edited version of a panel discussion.) See also Mary L. Volcansek, *Judicial Impeachment* (Urbana: University of Illinois Press, 1993).

53. Information about the Hastings impeachment was taken from Volcansek, *Judicial Impeachment*, chaps. 4 and 5.

54. Goulden, *The Benchwarmers*, 298.

55. Philip Hager, "Legal Leaders Seek Way to Unseat Unfit Federal Judges," *Houston Chronicle*, October 2, 1977, A6.

56. For a good discussion of this subject, see Collins T. Fitzpatrick, "Misconduct and Disability of Federal Judges: The Unreported Informal Responses," *Judicature* 71 (1988): 282–283.

57. Gina Holland, "Judge Meddled in Affirmative Action Case, Review Finds," *Houston Chronicle*, June 6, 2003, A2.

58. All data in this paragraph derive from Volcansek, *Judicial Impeachment*, 13–14.

59. Jerry Markon, "Elderly Judges Handle 20% of U.S. Caseload," *Wall Street Journal*, October 8, 2001, A15. Yet it has to be said that many elderly judges are highly competent and alert. For example, in July 2003 Judge Milton Pollack, at age ninety-six (the third-oldest active federal judge), handed down a key opinion that dismissed a major class-action suit against the brokerage firm of Merrill Lynch & Co. Even critics of the decision did not challenge Judge Pollack's mental competence. See Ann Davis and Randall Smith, "Jurist Who Dismissed Merrill Suit Has a History of Bold Rulings; At 96, Continues to Wield Power," *Wall Street Journal*, July 3, 2003, C1.

60. As quoted in Goulden, *The Benchwarmers*, 292.

61. Bob Woodward and Scott Armstrong, *The Brethren* (New York: Simon and Schuster, 1979), 361, 392, 156.

62. Ibid., 157.

63. Henry J. Abraham, *The Judicial Process*, 7th ed. (New York: Oxford University Press, 1998), 44.

64. R. Lee Rainey, "The Decision to Remain a Judge: Deductive Models of Judicial Retirement," paper delivered at the annual meeting of the Southern Political Science Association, Atlanta, 1976, 16.

65. Deborah J. Barrow and Gary Zuk, "An Institutional Analysis of Turnover in the Lower Federal Courts, 1900–1987," *Journal of Politics* 52 (1990): 457.

66. Robert A. Carp, "The Function, Impact, and Political Relevance of the Federal District Courts: A Case Study," Ph.D. dissertation, University of Iowa, 1969, 76.

67. As quoted in C. Herman Pritchett, *The Roosevelt Court: A Study of Judicial Votes and Values, 1937–1947* (New York: Macmillan, 1948), 18.

68. "Grading the Presidents," *Newsweek*, September 21, 1987, 33.

SUGGESTED READINGS

Abraham, Henry J. *Justices, Presidents, and Senators: A History of the U.S. Supreme Court Appointments from Washington to Clinton*. Lanham, Md.: Rowman and Littlefield, 1999. A very well-researched and readable history of how presidents have attempted to influence the national political scene through their appointments to the nation's highest court.

Goldman, Sheldon. *Picking Federal Judges: Lower Court Selection from Roosevelt through Reagan*. New Haven, Conn.: Yale University Press, 1997. Based on thorough, careful scholarship, Goldman writes in easy-to-follow prose about the judicial selection process between 1933 and 1989.

Goldman, Sheldon, Elliot Slotnick, Gerard Gryski, Gary Zuk, and Sara Schiavoni. "W. Bush Remaking the Judiciary: Like Father Like Son?" *Judicature* 86 (2003): 282–309. This article discusses the judicial appointment strategy of George W. Bush's administration and profiles the men and whom he has appointed to the federal bench during his first two years in office.

Judicature 86 (2002). The entire issue is devoted to the selection process for federal judges.

Judicature 84 (2001). The entire issue focuses on President Bill Clinton and his impact on the federal judiciary.

Posner, Richard A. *The Federal Courts: Challenge and Reform.* Cambridge, Mass.: Harvard University Press, 1996. A perceptive account of how the federal courts function and the problems they face, written by a judge who is also a judicial scholar.

Ryan, John Paul, et al. *American Trial Judges: Their Work Styles and Performance.* New York: Free Press, 1980. A classic analysis of the role of American trial judges and the ways that their performance might be evaluated.

Twentieth Century Fund Task Force on Judicial Selection. *Judicial Roulette.* New York: Priority Press Publications, 1988. A concise, sophisticated review of the politics of federal judicial selection in recent decades.

Volcansek, Mary L. *Judicial Impeachment: None Called It Justice.* Urbana: University of Illinois Press, 1993. A comprehensive discussion of the removal of federal judges from office for misconduct.

CHAPTER 7

Policy Links between the Citizenry, the President, and the Federal Judiciary

President George W. Bush has appointed more women and minorities to the federal bench than any other Republican president. Many of his nominees, however, have been strongly opposed by liberals who argue that, despite their gender and skin color, these appointees are inordinately conservative on such key issues as abortion and affirmative action. In this photo the president welcomes Texas judge Priscilla Owen to the White House. Owen's nomination to the appellate bench has been thwarted by Democrats, who view her as too conservative.

B
ECAUSE THIS BOOK IS ABOUT policymaking, it is appropriate to examine the links between the policy values of the elected chief executive and the decisional propensities of federal judges. If in electing one presidential candidate rather than another, the citizenry expresses its policy choices, do such choices spill over into the kind of judges presidents appoint and the way those judges decide policy-relevant cases? For instance, if the people decide in an election that they want a president who will reduce the size and powers of the federal bureaucracy, does that president subsequently appoint judges who share that philosophy? And, equally important, when those judges hear cases that give them the opportunity either to expand or to reduce the extent of a bureaucrat's power, do they opt for the reduction of authority? Recent evidence, while incomplete, suggests the existence of some policy links.

This phenomenon will be examined by means of two questions. First, what critical factors must exist for presidents to be able to obtain a judiciary that reflects their own political philosophy? Second, what empirical evidence is there to suggest that judges' decisions to some degree carry the imprint of the presidents who selected them?

The President and the Composition of the Judiciary

Four general factors determine whether chief executives can obtain a federal judiciary that is sympathetic to their political values and attitudes.

Presidential Support for Ideologically Based Appointments

One key aspect of the success of chief executives in appointing a federal judiciary that mirrors their own political beliefs is the depth of their commitment to do so. Some presidents may be content merely to fill the federal bench with party loyalists and pay little attention to their nominees' specific ideologies. Some may consider ideological factors when appointing Supreme Court justices but may not regard them as important for trial and appellate judges. Other presidents may discount ideologically grounded appointments because they themselves tend to be nonideological. Still others may place factors such as past political loyalty ahead of ideology in selecting judges.

Bill Clinton was a chief executive in the first category—that is, he was a president without a clearly defined set of ideological positions. More than once he acknowledged that he would probably go down in history as the most conservative Democrat to occupy the White House during the twentieth century. Frequently referring to himself as a "new Democrat," Clinton tried to distance himself from the more liberal image that characterized the Democratic Party during most of the twentieth century. Throughout his administration Clinton sought to establish a judicial cohort that "looks like America"—a team reflective of the nation's diverse ethnicity and gender instead of a cohort characterized by any singular ideological perspective.

As a president, Harry Truman had strong political views, but when selecting judges he placed loyalty to himself ahead of the candidate's overall political orientation. Truman's premium on personal loyalty rather than ideology is generally reflected in the group of men he put on the bench. For example, scant linkage existed between Truman's personal liberal stance on civil rights and equal opportunity and his judicial selections. He appointed no blacks and no women, and at least three of his key southern district court appointees have been identified as being very unfriendly to the cause of civil rights.[1]

If Clinton and Truman exemplify presidents who eschewed ideological criteria, Ronald Reagan provides a good example of a chief executive who selected his judicial nominees with a clear eye toward their compatibility with his own conservative philosophy. During his two terms, Reagan appointed 368 judges to the district and appeals courts. Of these, 94 percent were Republicans, 93 percent were white, and 92 percent were males; the majority were well-off (46 percent had net worths of over $500,000, and more than one in five were millionaires); virtually all had established records as political conservatives and apostles of judicial self-restraint. As the Reagan administration's conservative programs began to bog down in the more liberal-minded Congress, the Reagan team looked more and more toward implementing their values through their judicial appointment strategy. As White House communications director Patrick J. Buchanan put it, "[Our conservative appointment strategy] . . . could do more to advance the social agenda—school prayer, anti-pornography, anti-busing, right-to-life and quotas in employment—than anything Congress can accomplish in 20 years."[2] President Reagan was not the only modern president to pack the bench with those who shared his political and legal philosophies. Presidents Johnson and Carter both successfully appointed activist liberal judges, and preliminary evidence suggests that President George W. Bush is having measurable success in filling the judiciary with committed ideological conservatives.

The Number of Vacancies to Be Filled

A second element affecting the capacity of chief executives to establish a policy link between themselves and the judiciary is the number of appointments available to them. The more judges a president can select, the greater the potential of the White House to put its stamp on the judicial branch. For example, George Washington's influence on the Supreme Court was significant because he was able to nominate ten individuals to the high court. Jimmy Carter's was nil because no vacancies occurred during his term as president.

The number of appointment opportunities depends on several factors: how many judicial vacancies are inherited from the previous administration (Clinton, for example, was left with a whopping one hundred district and trial court vacancies—14 percent of the total—by his predecessor, George H. W. Bush), how many judges and justices die or resign during the president's term, how long the president serves, and whether Congress passes legislation that significantly increases the number of judgeships. Historically, the last factor seems to have been the most important in influencing the number of judgeships available, and politics in its most basic form permeates this process. A study of proposals for new-judges bills in thirteen Congresses tested the following two hypotheses: (1) "proposals to add new federal judges are more likely to pass if the party controls the Presidency and Congress than if different parties are in power," and (2) "proposals to add new federal judges are more likely to pass during the first two years of the President's term than during the second two years." The author concluded that his "data support both hypotheses—proposals to add new judges are about 5 times more likely to pass if the same party controls the Presidency and Congress than if different parties control, and about 4 times more likely to pass during the first two years of the President's term than during the second two years." He then noted that these findings serve "to remind us that not only is judicial selection a political process, but so is the creation of judicial posts." [3] Thus the number of vacancies that a president can fill—a function of politics, fate, and the size of the judicial workloads—is another variable that helps determine a chief executive's impact on the composition of the federal judiciary.

The President's Political Clout

Another factor is the scope and degree of presidential skill in overcoming any political obstacles. One such stumbling block is the U.S. Senate. If the Senate is controlled by the president's political party, the White House will find it much easier to secure confirmation than if opposition forces are in control. Sometimes when the opposition is in power in the Senate, presidents are forced into a sort of political horse trading to get their nominees approved. For example, in the summer of 1999 President Clinton was obliged to make a deal with the conservative chairman of the Senate Judiciary Committee, Orrin Hatch. To obtain smooth sailing for at least ten of Clinton's judicial nominations that had been blockaded in the Senate, the president agreed to nominate for a federal judgeship a conservative Utah Republican, Ted Stewart, who was vigorously opposed by liberals and environmental groups. "Administration officials defended the deal, saying they would get more than an acceptable amount in return for nominating Stewart, whom they acknowledged would not be chosen for the Federal bench by a Democratic President under ordinary circumstances." [4]

The Senate Judiciary Committee is another roadblock preventing presidents who have the requisite will from placing their chosen men and women on the federal bench. Some presidents have been more adept than others at maneuvering their candidates through the jagged rocks of the Judiciary Committee rapids. Both Presidents Kennedy and Johnson, for example, had to deal with the formidable committee chairman James Eastland of Mississippi, but only Johnson seems to have had the political adroitness to get most of his liberal nominees approved. Kennedy lacked this skill. Under the Clinton administration, despite the president's considerable political acumen, he was never able to parlay those skills into much clout with the conservative and often hostile Senate Judiciary Committee.

The president's personal popularity is another element in the political power formula. Chief executives who are well liked by the public and command the respect of opinion makers in the news media, the rank and file of their political party, and the leaders of the nation's major interest groups are much more likely to prevail over any forces that seek to thwart their judicial nominees. Personal popularity is not a stable factor and is sometimes hard to gauge, but presidents' standing with the electorate clearly helps determine the success of their efforts to influence the composition of the American judiciary. For example, in 1930, President Herbert Hoover's choice for a seat on the Supreme Court, John J. Parker, was defeated in the Senate by a two-vote margin. If the nomination had been made a year or so earlier, before the onset of the Great Depression took Hoover's popularity by the throat, Parker might have gotten on the Supreme Court. Likewise, in 1968 President Johnson's low esteem among voters and the powers that be may have been partially responsible for Senate rejection of his candidate for chief justice, Abe Fortas, and also for the Senate's refusal to replace Fortas with Johnson's old pal Homer Thornberry. As one observer commented, "Johnson failed largely because most members of the Senate 'had had it' with the lame-duck President's nominations."[5] Conversely, President Dwight D. "Ike" Eisenhower's success in getting approval for an inordinately large number of nominees dubbed "not qualified" by the ABA (13.2 percent) may be attributed, at least in part, to his great popularity and prestige.

The Judicial Climate the New Judges Enter

A final matter affects the capacity of chief executives to secure a federal judiciary that reflects their own political values: the current philosophical orientations of the sitting district and appellate court judges with whom the new appointees would interact. Because federal judges have lifetime appointments during good behavior, presidents must accept the composition and value structure of the judiciary as it exists when they first take office. If the existing judiciary already reflects the president's political and legal orientation, the impact of new judicial appointees will be immediate and substantial. However, if the trial and appellate judiciary has values that are radically different from those of the new chief executive, the impact of subsequent judicial appointments will be weaker and slower to materialize. New judges must respect the controlling legal precedents and the constitutional interpretations that prevail in the judiciary at the time they enter it, or they risk having their decisions overturned by a higher court. Such a reality may limit the capacity of a new set of judges to get in there and do their own thing—at least in the short run.

When Franklin D. Roosevelt became president in 1933, he was confronted with a Supreme Court and a lower federal judiciary that had been solidly packed with conservative Republican jurists by his three GOP predecessors in the White House. A majority of the high court and most lower-court judges viewed most of Roosevelt's New Deal legislation as unconstitutional, and it was not until 1937 that the Supreme Court began to stop overturning virtually all of FDR's major legislative programs.

To make matters worse, his first opportunity to fill a Supreme Court vacancy did not come until the fall of 1937. Thus, despite the ideological screening that went into the selection of FDR's judges, it seems fair to assume that, at least between 1933 and 1938, Roosevelt's trial and appellate judges had to restrain their liberal propensities in the myriad of cases that came before them. This may explain in part why the voting record of the Roosevelt court appointees is not much more liberal than that of the conservative judges selected by Roosevelt's three Republican predecessors; the Roosevelt team just did not have much room to maneuver in a judiciary dominated by staunch conservatives.

The decisional patterns of the Eisenhower judges further serve to illustrate this phenomenon. Although the Eisenhower appointees were more conservative than those selected by Presidents Truman and Roosevelt, the differences in their rulings were small. One major reason was that the Eisenhower jurists entered a realm that was dominated from top to bottom by Roosevelt and Truman appointees, who were for the most part liberals. Ike's generally conservative judges were only marginally less constrained than were Roosevelt's liberal jurists in the face of a conservative-dominated judiciary.

President Reagan's impact on the judicial branch continues to be substantial. By the end of his second term, he had appointed an unprecedented 368 federal judges, 50 percent of those on the bench. When he entered the White House, the Supreme Court was already teetering to the right because of Nixon's and Gerald R. Ford's conservative appointments. Although Carter's liberal appointees still had places on the trial and appellate court benches, Reagan found a good many conservative Nixon and Ford judges on the bench when he took office. Thus he has played a major role in shaping the entire federal judiciary in his own conservative image, which will continue for some time to come. The judges appointed by George H. W. Bush had a much easier time making their impact felt because well over half of the judiciary already professed conservative, Republican values. However, President Clinton's impact on the judiciary has been slower to manifest itself because his judicial nominees entered an arena in which over 75 percent of the trial and appellate court seats were held by judges appointed by prior GOP presidents with very conservative orientations. When George W. Bush entered the White House, 51 percent of the federal judges had been appointed by Democratic presidents.

Presidents' Values and Their Appointees' Decisions

What evidence is there that presidents have been able to secure a judiciary in tune with their own policy values and goals? When the people elect a particular president, is there reason to believe that their choice will be expressed in the kinds of judges that are appointed and the kinds of decisions they render?

To answer these questions, we examined the liberal-conservative voting patterns of the teams of district court judges appointed by sixteen presidents during the twentieth century and the first three years of the twenty-first century. This comprehensive study is the only one that covers enough presidents, judges, and cases to allow for some meaningful generalizations. In essence, the focus is on whether liberal presidents appointed trial judges who decided cases in a more liberal manner and whether conservative chief executives were able to obtain district court jurists who followed their policy views.

In the realm of civil rights and civil liberties, liberal judges would generally take a broadening position, that is, their rulings would seek to extend these freedoms. Conservative jurists, by contrast, would prefer to limit such rights. For example, in a case in which a government agency wanted to prevent a controversial person from speaking in a public park or at a state university, a liberal judge would be more inclined than a conservative to uphold the right of the would-be speaker. Or in a case concerning affirmative action in public higher education, a liberal judge would be more likely to favor special admissions for minority petitioners. In the area of government regulation of the economy, liberal judges would probably uphold legislation that benefited working people or the economic underdog. Thus, if the secretary of labor sought an injunction against an employer for paying less than the minimum wage, a liberal judge would be more disposed to endorse the labor secretary's arguments, whereas a conservative judge would tend to side with business, especially big business. Another broad category of cases often studied by judicial scholars is criminal justice. Liberal judges are, in general, more sympathetic to the motions made by criminal defendants. For instance, in a case in which the accused claimed to have been coerced by the government to make an illegal confession, liberal judges would be more likely than their conservative counterparts to agree that the government had acted improperly.

FIGURE 7-1 Percentage of Liberal Decisions Rendered by District Court Appointees of Presidents Woodrow Wilson through George W. Bush

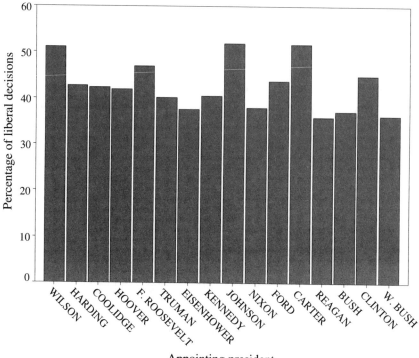

SOURCE: Data collected by Robert A. Carp, Kenneth L. Manning, and Ronald Stidham.

Figure 7-1 indicates the percentage of liberal decisions rendered by the district court appointees of Presidents Woodrow Wilson through George W. Bush. Fifty-one percent of the decisions of the Wilson judges are liberal, which puts these jurists almost on a par with those of Lyndon Johnson and Jimmy Carter for having the most liberal voting record. The liberal pattern of the Wilson judges is not surprising. Wilson was one of the staunchest liberal presidents of the twentieth century—particularly on economic issues. Moreover, he chose his judges on a highly partisan ideological basis: 98.6 percent of his appointments to the lower courts were Democrats—the record for any president in the twentieth century.

Succeeding Wilson in the White House were the three Republican chief executives of the 1920s: Warren G. Harding and his "return to normalcy" in 1921, followed by the equally conservative Calvin Coolidge and Herbert Hoover. The right-of-center policy values of these three presidents (and the undisputed Republican domination of the Senate during their incumbencies) are mirrored in the decisional patterns of the trial judges they selected. The liberalism score drops by 8 percentage points from Wilson to Harding, 51 to 43, and stays around that same level for the Coolidge and Hoover judicial teams.

Franklin Roosevelt's judges marked a shift back to left of center. At 47 percent liberal, the Roosevelt jurists are 5 percentage points more liberal than those of his immediate predecessor, Hoover. FDR used ideological criteria to pick his judges, and he put the full weight of his political skills behind that endeavor. He once instructed his dispenser of political patronage, James A. Farley, to use the judicial appointment power, in effect, as a weapon against senators and representatives who were balking at New Deal legislation: "First off, we must hold up judicial appointments in States where the [congressional] delegation is not going along [with our liberal economic proposals]. We must make appointments promptly where the delegation is with us. Second, this must apply to other appointments. I'll keep in close contact with the leaders." [6]

At first the comparatively conservative voting record of the Truman judges seems a bit strange in view of Truman's personal commitment to liberal economic and social policy goals. Only 40 percent of the Truman judges' decisions were liberal, a full 7 percentage points less than those of Roosevelt's jurists—and even 2 percentage points below those of the Hoover nominees. However, Truman counted personal loyalty much more heavily than ideological standards when selecting judges, and as a result many conservatives found their way into the ranks of Truman jurists.

Because of Truman's lack of interest in making policy-based appointments, coupled with strong opposition in the Senate and lack of popular support throughout much of his administration, his personal liberalism was generally not reflected in the policy values of his judges. Eisenhower's judges were more conservative than Truman's, as expected, but the difference is not great. This resulted in part because Eisenhower paid little attention to purely ideological criteria in making appointments and also because his judges had to work in the company of an overwhelming Democratic majority throughout the federal judiciary. These factors must have curbed many of the conservative inclinations of the Eisenhower jurists.

The 41 percent liberalism score of the judges appointed by John F. Kennedy represents a swing to the left. This is to be expected, and at first it may appear strange that Kennedy's team on the bench was not more left of center. However, Kennedy had problems in dealing with the conservative, southern-dominated Senate Judiciary Committee; he lacked political clout in the Senate, which often made him a pawn of senatorial courtesy; and he was unable to overcome the stranglehold of local

Democratic bosses, who often prized partisan loyalty over ideological purity—or even competence—when it came to appointing judges.

Johnson's judges moved impressively toward the left, and his judges were more liberal than Wilson's and much more so than Kennedy's. This can be accounted for on the basis of the four criteria that predict a correspondence between the values of chief executives and the orientation of their judges. Johnson knew how to bargain with individual senators and was second to none in his ability to manipulate and cajole those who were initially indifferent or hostile to the issues (or candidates) he supported. His impressive victories in Congress—for example, the antipoverty legislation and the civil rights acts—are monuments to his skill. Undoubtedly, too, he used his political prowess to secure a judicial team that reflected his liberal policy values. In addition, Johnson was able to fill a large number of vacancies on the bench, and his liberal appointees must have felt at home ideologically in a judiciary headed by the liberal chief justice Earl Warren.

If the leftward swing of the Johnson team is dramatic, it is no less so than the shift to the right made by the Nixon judges. Only 38 percent of the decisions of Nixon's jurists were liberal. Nixon placed enormous emphasis on getting conservatives nominated to judgeships at all levels. He possessed the political clout to secure Senate confirmation for most lower-court appointees—at least until Watergate, when the Nixon wine turned to vinegar—and the rightist policy values of the Nixon judges must have been prodded by a Supreme Court that was growing more and more conservative.

The 44 percent liberalism score of the Ford judges puts them right between the Johnson and Nixon jurists in terms of ideology. That Ford's jurists were less conservative than Nixon's is not hard to explain. First, Ford himself was much less of a political ideologue than his predecessor, as reflected in the way he screened his nominees and the type of individuals he chose. (Ford's appointment of the moderate John Paul Stevens to the Supreme Court, as compared with Nixon's selection of the highly conservative William H. Rehnquist, illustrates the point.) Also, because Ford's circuitous route to the presidency did not enhance his political effectiveness with the Senate, he would not have had the clout to force highly conservative Republican nominees through a liberal, Democratic Senate, even if he had wished to. (Recall that Ford was not elected to the presidency, having become chief executive upon the resignation of Richard Nixon.)

With a score of 52 percent, Jimmy Carter shares with Lyndon Johnson the record for having appointed judges with the most liberal voting records of the sixteen presidents under consideration. Despite Carter's call for an "independent" federal judiciary based on "merit selection," his judges were selected with a keen eye toward their potential liberal voting tendencies.[7] That a correspondence exists between the values of President Carter and the liberal decisional patterns of his judges should come as no surprise. Carter was clearly identified with liberal social and political values, and although his economic policies were perhaps more conservative than those of other recent Democratic presidents, Carter's commitment to liberal values in the areas of civil rights and liberties and of criminal justice was not in doubt. Carter, too, had ample opportunity to pack the bench. The Omnibus Judgeship Act of 1978, passed by a friendly Democratic Congress, created a record 152 new federal judicial openings for Carter to fill. He also possessed a fair degree of political clout with a Judiciary Committee and Senate controlled by Democrats. Finally, the Carter judicial team found many friendly liberals (appointed by Presidents Johnson and Kennedy) already sitting on the bench.

Reagan's judicial team has the distinction of having the most conservative voting record of all the judicial cohorts in our study. Only 36 percent of their decisions bear the liberal stamp. Reagan's conservative values and his commitment to reshaping the federal judiciary were well known. Early in his first presidential campaign Reagan had inveighed against left-leaning activist judges, and he promised a dramatic change. As did his predecessor, Reagan had the opportunity, through attrition and newly created judgeships, to fill the judiciary with persons reflecting his own inclinations. (At the end of his second term, about half the federal judiciary bore the Reagan label.) This phenomenon was aided by Reagan's great personal popularity throughout most of his administration and a Senate that his party controlled during six of his eight years in office. Finally, the Reagan cohort entered the judicial realm with conservative greetings from the sitting right-of-center Nixon and Ford judges.

The judicial cohort appointed by President George H. W. Bush continues in the conservative vein established by the Reagan administration. With a score of 37 percent, Bush's judges are only one percentage point higher than Reagan's jurists in rendering liberal decisions.

President Clinton and the Federal Judiciary

What kind of men and women did President Clinton select for service on the federal bench, and what has been the ideological direction of their decision making? The behavior of Clinton's judges has resulted in 45 percent liberal decision making. While this is certainly more progressive than the 36 and 37 percent figures for Presidents Reagan and George H. W. Bush, respectively, it is decidedly more conservative than the 52 percent liberal landmarks of Presidents Johnson and Carter. In a word, the Clinton judges are moderate. This comes as no surprise, given the explanatory model that we have set forth.

First, Clinton did not manifest any desire to make ideologically based judicial appointments. Instead, his goal was to put more women and minorities on the federal bench. As for ideology, one key member of the president's judicial selection team, who worked in both the Justice Department and the White House, put it this way: "Neither side is running an ideology shop. Neither of us consider ourselves to be the guardians of some kind of flame.... [T]his is not a do or die fight for American Culture. This is an attempt to get ... highly competent lawyers on the federal bench so they can resolve disputes."[8]

While Clinton did inherit a large number of unfilled judicial slots from the Bush administration, his Republican Congresses were loath to enact any type of omnibus judgeship bill that would have enhanced his capacity to pack the judiciary. Clinton also evinced little desire to expend political muscle in pushing through controversial candidates over Judiciary Committee and Senate objections. The woman primarily in charge of Clinton's judicial selections, Eleanor Dean Acheson, confirmed the administration's unwillingness to do major battle over judicial appointments: "There are a couple of cases in which we decided that even if we thought we had a shot at winning a fight ... that it was not worth the time and resources ... because these fights go for months and months, and during that period it is very difficult to concentrate."[9]

Finally, the Clinton judges entered a climate that was not conducive to liberal decision making. When they took their seats on the federal bench, about three-quarters of the sitting judges—including the supervisory appellate panels—were conservative Republicans appointed primarily by Presidents Reagan and Bush. Even if the Clinton judges had been closet liberals, they would have had little opportunity to express these values in a judiciary so dominated by those of a more conservative persuasion.

Given the moderate nature of the Clinton judges' decision making, it seems a bit strange that his jurists were so heavily criticized by Republican senators and representatives, some of whom even called for the impeachment of Clinton's so-called liberal-activist judges. To explore this topic in greater depth, we broke down the totality of decision making for the nine most recent presidencies into three categories of cases (see Table 7-1): criminal justice (such as motions made by criminal defendants), civil rights and liberties (such as freedom of speech, abortion, and racial discrimination), and labor and economic regulation (such as disputes between labor and management and governmental efforts to regulate the economy).

TABLE 7-1   Percentage of Liberal Decisions in Three Categories of Cases Rendered by District Court Appointees of Presidents John F. Kennedy through George W. Bush

Appointing president	Criminal justice	Civil rights and liberties	Labor and economic regulation
Kennedy	25.0	43.3	63.5
Johnson	36.4	58.1	63.1
Nixon	26.9	37.9	48.4
Ford	34.9	40.4	53.0
Carter	38.6	51.4	61.3
Reagan	25.2	32.4	48.8
George H. W. Bush	29.6	32.3	51.0
Clinton	40.1	42.1	54.3
George W. Bush	a	20.0	61.9

a. The numbers in this category are too small to report.

SOURCE: Unpublished data collected by Robert A. Carp, Kenneth L. Manning, and Ronald Stidham.

If the Clinton judges are inordinately liberal, some evidence should emerge as we turn our analytic microscope up this additional notch.

In the realm of criminal justice, 40 percent of the Clinton judges' decisions are liberal, which is greater than the 30 percent figure for the Bush judges, but is about on a par with Carter's judicial team, whose score was 39 percent. Still, in that realm his judges are indeed the most liberal of modern presidents. In the area of civil rights and liberties, 42 percent of Clinton's judges voted on the liberal side— certainly more liberal than the scores of 32 percent for both the Reagan and the Bush teams, but far below the scores of 51 and 58 percent for the appointees of President's Carter and Lyndon Johnson, respectively. Finally, in the realm of labor and economic regulations, Clinton's team, at 54 percent, again manifests moderation. This score is only three points higher than that of the jurists selected by President George H. W. Bush, and it is well below the scores in the low sixtieth percentile of the appointees of Presidents Kennedy, Johnson, and Carter. In sum, the data suggest that the Clinton judges are on the whole liberal in their decision making in the realm of criminal justice but quite ideologically moderate in the areas of civil rights and liberties as well as in labor and economic regulation.

President George W. Bush and the Federal Judiciary

What do we know about the current and potential ideological impact of George W. Bush's administration now that he has been in the White House for several years? To respond, we will refer to our four-part model, which addresses whether a chief executive can obtain a federal judiciary that is sympathetic to his political values and attitudes. First, is the president personally committed to making ideologically based appointments? The evidence suggests a qualified affirmation that President Bush is using ideology as a basis for his judicial nominations. Recall, for example, that just prior to the election of 2000, Bush publicly expressed admiration for Justice Antonin Scalia, who (with Justice Clarence Thomas) is the most conservative member of the Supreme Court.[10] Justice Scalia usually interprets the Constitution as restraining congressional power to regulate commerce and seeks to limit the expansion of many freedoms guaranteed by the Bill of Rights (generally conservative positions). In May 2001, after issuing his first batch of judicial nominees, President Bush made it clear that his judges will adhere to his conservative judicial philosophy. "Every judge I appoint will be a person who clearly understands the role of a judge is to interpret the law, not to legislate from the bench," he said.[11] And early in 2003 Bush's assistant attorney general, Viet Dinh, said in an interview that "we want to ensure that the President's mandate to us that the men and women who are nominated by him to be on the bench have his vision of the proper role of the judiciary. That is, a judiciary that will follow the law, not make the law."[12] To the extent that Bush's potential judges are being screened for their ideological purity, it appears to be mainly on social issues that touch upon abortion, gay rights, and affirmative action. There is no evidence that they are being tapped because they are opposed to organized labor or government regulation of the economy. Therefore, if we are to see any evidence of conservatism in the decision making of Bush appointees, it is likely to be in the category of civil rights and liberties—not in the realm of labor and economic regulation. (Nor is there much evidence that Bush appointees are being screened for having inordinately conservative views on the rights of criminal defendants.)

On a related matter, Bush appears to share to some degree Clinton's desire to increase the number of women and minorities on the bench. (As noted in Chapter 6, Bush has so far appointed a larger percentage of women and minorities to the bench than did either his father or Reagan, although still far fewer than did Clinton.) While none of these women and minority appointees appear to be particularly liberal, Bush, like Clinton, may be almost as interested in bringing a broader range of individuals to the bench as he is in appointing persons solely on the basis of pure conservative ideology.

The second element affecting a president's capacity to influence the ideological direction of the judiciary is the number of vacancies he can fill. This is, of course, influenced by the number of vacancies inherited from the president's predecessor, how long he serves in office, and whether or not Congress enacts legislation that significantly increases the number of judgeships. When George W. Bush assumed the presidency, he inherited eighty-two vacancies on the federal bench—quite a sizable number by historic standards. This was largely due to the bitter partisan politics that had occurred during the Clinton administration, which caused many of his judicial nominees to go without Senate confirmation. A second factor in this equation is that the number of judges who die or retire while on the bench is occurring at about the same rate under the Bush administration as it did for previous chief executives: during Bush's first two years in office seventy-one judges left the trial and appellate court benches. If this rate continues throughout Bush's four-year term, it would mean that he would be appointing about 17 percent of active federal judges just through the normal process of attrition.

What about the possibility of Congress passing a new omnibus judges bill that would give the president the opportunity to pack the judiciary with men and women of like-minded values—a phenomenon that greatly enhanced President Kennedy's and President Carter's ideological impact on the judiciary? Unfortunately for President Bush, he has had no such luck. It is true that in 2001 the Judicial Conference of the United States (the administrative arm of the federal judiciary) recommended to Congress that it create a total of fifty-four new district and appellate judgeships. It also called for "permanent authorization" of seven temporary district judgeships that had been previously established. However, the politically divided Congress was not too obliging. Congress refused to create any new appellate judgeships; it established only eight new district court judgeships and granted permanent authorization to only four temporary positions.[13]

So what is one to conclude about this second predictor of whether President Bush will potentially have a substantial impact on the ideological direction of the federal judiciary—the number of vacancies he can fill? The data suggest that in terms of pure numbers the president is being given about an average set of opportunities to have an ideological impact on the federal bench. The real question is whether he will be reelected in 2004. If he is, then approximately one-third or more of all active federal judges will bear the Bush stamp, and that would be a substantial impact. If his reelection bid is not successful, the effect of the Bush judges will be much more modest.

A third variable affecting the president's ideological impact is the extent of his political clout, that is, his power and skill in nudging a reluctant Senate and Senate Judiciary Committee to approve his nominees. Also included in this variable is the chief executive's personal popularity, which, if great, can enhance his capacity to attain confirmation of his nominees. Immediately after the 2000 election, the Senate was evenly divided between the two political parties, but because Vice President Richard Cheney could break any tie vote, the Republicans were technically in control of this chamber. In principle this would enhance President Bush's potential to obtain confirmation for judicial nominees of like-minded values. Soon after the election, however, a series of events occurred that greatly clouded this scenario. First, the Democrats obtained control of the Senate when Vermont Senator Jim Jeffords unexpectedly left the Republican Party caucus. All legislative action came to a halt for several weeks, as the struggle to reorganize the Senate became the major focus of attention. Equally important after Jeffords's defection, control of the Judiciary Committee went to the Democrats. The new committee chair, Senator Patrick Leahy, was in no frame of mind to become a rubber stamp for President Bush's judicial nominees. Then came the terrorist attacks on September 11, 2001, and public and legislative attention turned away from the work of the Judiciary Committee, becoming riveted on antiterrorism legislation and matters of national security. At the end of President Bush's first two years in office, his scorecard indicates mixed results. On the down side, two of his nominees (Priscilla Owen and Charles Pickering) received negative votes from the Judiciary Committee, and the names of twenty-eight other district and appellate court candidates were returned to the president without any action being taken by the committee. But the news was by no means all bad for the president. None of his judicial nominees were defeated on the floor of the Senate, and ninety-nine individuals, presumably all pro-lifers, were approved by the Judiciary Committee and by the Senate.

More recently, two chains of events have produced countervailing effects on the president's political clout in the Senate. On the positive side, the Republicans regained control of the Senate in the midterm elections of 2002, and along with it went control of the Judiciary Committee, now headed by Bush-friendly senator Orrin Hatch of Utah. But on the negative side, the president's approval ratings by the voters have slipped steadily between the spring and late fall of 2003. This is attributed to the public's perception that the nation may have been grossly misled on the reasons for going to war in Iraq and also to the belief of many Americans that the rebuilding of Iraq is becoming much too costly in terms of both dollars and military casualties. Furthermore, the American economy has continued to be very troubled, with soaring deficits and rising unemployment. Indeed by early October 2003, only 46 percent of the electorate said that the president should be reelected.[14] Although the decline in Bush's popular support has not translated into any marked decline in the rate at which his judicial nominees are being approved, neither is there any evidence that the Judiciary Committee and the Senate are rushing to do the president's bidding. As of September 1, 2003, there were fifty-four vacancies on the district and appellate courts[15]—no evidence that the president's judicial nominations are at a standstill, but neither does it suggest that the Senate and its Judiciary Committee are giving President Bush rapid action on his judicial nominations.

The final ingredient in the president's capacity to make his ideological mark on the federal judiciary is the judicial climate into which his new judges enter. If the climate is unfavorable because the judiciary is packed with jurists whose ideologies are opposed to that of the appointing president, the chief executive may have a long wait before his appointees can fully vent their judicial values. On the other hand, if the judiciary is evenly divided, or even somewhat disposed to the president's ideological values, the fruits of his appointments will be much more readily seen. This reality may be President Bush's primary ace in the hole. When he first took office, the ideological orientation of the judges was balanced with almost mathematical precision: 51 percent of the judges on the lower federal bench were appointed by Republican presidents, 49 percent by Democrats in the White House. In such a situation even a slight tilt in one direction can give one party a controlling edge in the judicial decision-making process and, perhaps more importantly, in the composition of the policy-making appeals court panels. Evidence of this phenomenon is already apparent at the end of President Bush's three years in office. By the summer of 2003, "of the 13 circuit courts in the country, Republican appointees control eight, Democratic appointees control three, and two are divided between the parties." [16] Assuming a normal attrition rate for judges leaving the bench, it is likely that by the end of his four-year term in office (and, if he is reelected, at the end of eight years), all of the thirteen circuits will have a majority of Republican judges. This will greatly enhance President Bush's potential to leave a significant ideological mark on the composition of the federal judiciary.

In sum, our model suggests that President Bush should be able to continue to move the federal judiciary in a more conservative direction. He has indicated a clear desire to appoint more conservative jurists (albeit this commitment is perhaps tempered by a desire to appoint more women and minorities to the courts). He is having an average number of new vacancies to fill, although his clout in getting his nominees through a highly divided Senate, combined with the president's declining popularity, is a negative factor. Finally, given the narrow balance of the judiciary at the beginning of the president's term between Republicans and Democrats,

President Bush continues to be in a critical position to tilt the ideological balance in a decidedly more conservative vein.

The Decision-Making Behavior of the George W. Bush Appointees

Figure 7-1 and Table 7-1 provide a first look at the decision-making patterns of President Bush's trial court appointees. Our numbers are still quite small, and therefore we must make our observations with great caution until the data base grows larger. (Indeed the number of Bush-judge decisions in the category of criminal justice was too small to report.) Still, the initial data are tantalizing. Figure 7-1 indicates that so far 36 percent of the Bush-judge decisions have been conservative. This puts him on a par with the appointees of Ronald Reagan and just one percentage point behind his slightly more liberal father, whose judges' liberalism score was 37 percent. Few observers will be surprised by these numbers, and they accord well with what most political commentators have predicted. What is intriguing, however, are the numbers in Table 7-1, which breaks down voting behavior into three general categories: criminal justice, civil rights and liberties, and labor and economic regulation. While the numbers in the first category are still too small too report, the data in the other two suggest a fascinating portrait. So far only 20 percent of the Bush-judge decisions in the area of civil rights and liberties have been liberal. If this trend continues as our data base enlarges, this would make the Bush team the most conservative of all modern presidents—and by an overwhelming margin. At 20 percent, this is some 22 percent behind the figure for Bill Clinton, but, just as interesting, it is 12 points behind the already conservative teams of judges appointed by Presidents George H. W. Bush and Ronald Reagan. As noted above, if the potential conservatism of President George W. Bush's judges is to manifest itself, it will be on issues such as abortion, gay rights, and rights of racial minorities, for those are the areas in which his potential judges appear to be screened. That his future jurists were not vetted for their conservative stands on labor unions or issues of government regulation is likewise clear from Table 7-1. Indeed, with a score of 62 percent in that category, the Bush jurists seem downright liberal compared with the scores of 49 and 51 percent, respectively, for Reagan and Bush's father. In sum, the early numbers seem to suggest that the Bush team is overall a conservative one, particularly in the realms where anecdotal evidence would largely predict it—social issues of civil rights and liberties.

Summary

At the national level the judicial selection process includes a variety of participants, despite the constitutional mandate that the president shall do the appointing with the advice and consent of the Senate. If presidents are to dominate this process and name to the bench individuals with similar policy values, several conditions must be met. Chief executives must want to make ideologically based appointments; they must have an ample number of vacancies to fill; they must be adroit leaders with political clout; and the existing judiciary must be attuned to their policy goals. If most of these conditions are met, presidents tend to get the kind of judges they want. In other words, an identifiable policy link exists between the popular election of the president, the appointment of judges, and the substantive content of the judges' decisions.

Further Thought and Discussion Questions

1. When presidents make judicial appointments, should they anticipate how their nominees are going to vote on important policy decisions, or should they consider only the quality of the nominee's formal credentials, such as the individual's ranking in his or her law school graduating class and the number of law review articles that the nominee has published?

2. Over time the judicial appointees of Republican presidents have had decidedly more conservative voting records on the bench than those of judges selected by Democratic chief executives. Is this evidence that our judicial system has been "tainted" by politics, or is it evidence that the democratic process prevails throughout our political system?

NOTES

1. "Judicial Performance in the Fifth Circuit," *Yale Law Review* 73 (1963): 90–133.

2. Jack Nelson, "Courts Main Hope for Reagan Social Stand," *Houston Chronicle,* March 18, 1986, A6.

3. Jon R. Bond, "The Politics of Court Structure: The Addition of New Federal Judges," *Law and Policy Quarterly* 2 (1980): 182, 183, 187.

4. Neil A. Lewis, "Clinton Critic Is Key to Deal to End Tie-up on Judgeships," *New York Times,* July 3, 1999, available online at http://www.nytimes.com

5. Henry J. Abraham, *The Judicial Process,* 3d ed. (New York: Oxford University Press, 1975), 77.

6. James A. Farley, "Why I Broke with Roosevelt," *Collier's,* June 21, 1947, 13.

7. See Jon Gottschall, "Carter's Judicial Appointments: The Influence of Affirmative Action and Merit Selection on Voting on the U.S. Courts of Appeals," *Judicature* 67 (1983): 165–173.

8. Sheldon Goldman and Elliot Slotnick, "Clinton's First Term Judiciary," *Judicature* 80 (1997): 256.

9. Ibid., 257.

10. Stuart Taylor Jr., "The Supreme Question," *Newsweek,* July 10, 2000, 20.

11. Bennett Roth, "Bush Submits 11 Names for Federal Bench," *Houston Chronicle,* May 10, 2001, A1.

12. Sheldon Goldman, Elliot Slotnick, Gerard Gryski, Gary Zuk, and Sara Schiavoni, "W. Bush Remaking the Judiciary: Like Father Like Son?" *Judicature* 86 (2003): 284.

13. Act of November 2, 2002; 116 Stat. 1786.

14. Howard Fineman and Tamara Lipper, "What, Me Worry?" *Newsweek,* October 6, 2003, 30.

15. "Judicial Boxscore," *The Third Branch* 35 (2003): 8.

16. Eleanor Clift, "The Courts: The Waiting Game," *Newsweek*, May 19, 2003, 9.

SUGGESTED READINGS

Abraham, Henry J. *Justices and Presidents: A Political History of Appointments to the Supreme Court*, 3d ed. New York: Oxford University Press, 1992. Offers an in-depth political history of appointments to the U.S. Supreme Court.

Goldman, Sheldon. *Picking Federal Judges: Lower Court Selection from Roosevelt through Reagan.* New Haven, Conn.: Yale University Press, 1997. Based on thorough, careful scholarship, Goldman writes in easy-to-follow prose about the judicial selection process between 1933 and 1989.

Goldman, Sheldon, Elliot Slotnick, Gerard Gryski, Gary Zuk, and Sara Schiavoni, "W. Bush Remaking the Judiciary: Like Father Like Son?" *Judicature* 86 (2003): 282–309. A discussion of the judicial appointment process and its dynamics for George W. Bush's first term in office.

Judicature 84 (2001). The entire issue is devoted to the impact of President Bill Clinton on the federal judiciary.

CHAPTER 8

Lawyers, Litigants, and Interest Groups in the Judicial Process

The Sixth Amendment provides that in all criminal prosecutions the accused shall have the assistance of counsel. Despite this guarantee, many argue that in the wake of 9/11, extraordinary steps must be taken to identify and prosecute those who would do harm to the United States. Others worry that the government will fail to protect the constitutional rights of the accused. Here, Nina Ginsberg, left, and Jonathan Shapiro, defense attorneys for convicted spy Brian Patrick Regan, appear outside the U.S. District Court in Alexandria, Virginia. Although Regan was found guilty of soliciting to sell intelligence information to Iraq and China, the jury denied the death penalty sought by the U.S. government.

I N THIS CHAPTER WE LAY the foundation for a detailed examination of the courts in action by focusing on three crucial actors in the judicial process: lawyers, litigants, and interest groups. Judges in the United States make decisions only in the context of cases brought to the courts by individuals or groups who have some sort of disagreement or dispute with each other. These adversaries, commonly called litigants, sometimes argue their own cases in such minor forums as small-claims courts, but they are almost always represented by lawyers in the more important judicial arenas.

Given the prominent role of lawyers in the U.S. system of justice, the first part of our discussion will be devoted to an examination of the legal profession. Next, the role of individual litigants and interest groups in the judicial process will be examined. Although our discussion applies generally to both the federal and state judicial systems, it will be necessary in some instances to distinguish between the two levels.

Lawyers and the Legal Profession

Our examination of lawyers focuses on the training and work of attorneys in the United States, first putting lawyers and the legal profession in a historical context.[1]

Development of the Legal Profession

The Colonial Period. Lawyers were not popular during the early colonial years, and there were few of them among the early settlers. Eventually, however, lawyers became necessary to a growing society facing problems that required their skills. Some who rendered legal services had been trained in England; others were laymen who had only a smattering of legal knowledge. In spite of constant complaints about those who practiced law, "there was a competent, professional bar, dominated by brilliant and successful lawyers . . . in all major communities by 1750."[2]

The colonies had no law schools during this period to train those interested in the legal profession. Some young men, especially those who lived in the South, which had no colleges, went to England for their education and attended the Inns of Court. The Inns were not formal law schools but were part of the English legal culture and allowed students to become familiar with English law.

Americans who aspired to the law during this period generally went through some form of clerkship or apprenticeship with an established lawyer. In other words, the student paid a fee to the lawyer, who promised to train him in the law. Some found this to be a fruitful experience, whereas others complained that it was of little or no value.

Each colony established its own standards for admission to the bar (the entire group of lawyers permitted to practice law in the courts of that colony). In some instances the colony's highest court was given control over licensing and admission to the bar. In Massachusetts each court admitted its own lawyers; in Rhode Island any court could admit lawyers, and admission by one court automatically conferred admission to all the courts in the colony.

The impact of lawyers on the American political system was evident during this early period. Of the fifty-six signers of the Declaration of Independence, twenty-five were lawyers, and thirty-one of the fifty-five delegates to the Constitutional Convention were lawyers.[3]

From the Revolution to the Mid-Nineteenth Century. After the Revolution, the number of lawyers increased rapidly because neither legal education nor admission to the bar was very strict. During the first half of the nineteenth century there were no large law firms. However, some lawyers garnered wealth by representing rich clients and prosperous merchants. Other lawyers simply eked out a living by handling petty claims in minor courts.

The right social background appears to have been as important then as it is today. As one American legal historian says:

> There is evidence, indeed, that the bar, after the first Revolutionary generation, drew even more heavily than before upon children of professionals, as compared to children of farmers or laborers. Between 1810 and 1840, it seems, more than half the lawyers, who were college graduates and were admitted to the bar in Massachusetts, were sons of lawyers and judges; before 1810 the figure was about 38 percent.[4]

The apprenticeship method continued to be the most popular way to receive legal training, but law schools were coming into existence. The first law schools grew out of law offices that had begun to specialize in training clerks or apprentices. The earliest such school was the Litchfield School, founded by Judge Tapping Reeve in 1784. This school, which used the lecture method, placed primary emphasis on commercial law.

Eventually, a few colleges began to teach law as part of their general curriculum. William and Mary College in Virginia was the first to establish a chair of law and appointed George Wythe to the professorship. Professorships were also established at the University of Virginia, the University of Pennsylvania, and the University of Maryland during the late eighteenth and early nineteenth centuries.

A chair of law was established at Harvard in 1816, and the first professor, Isaac Parker, worked to bring about a professional, independent law school. A major gift from Nathan Dane in 1826 helped to realize this goal. He gave Harvard $10,000 to support a professorship and suggested that Joseph Story be appointed the first Dane professor. Story was an associate justice of the U.S. Supreme Court when he accepted the position in 1829.[5] Harvard awarded an LL.B. (bachelor of laws) degree to students who completed the law school course. Harvard was to become the model for all the newer schools.

The Second Half of the Nineteenth Century. During this period the number of law schools increased dramatically. In 1850 only fifteen law schools were operating, but by 1900 there were 102.[6]

The law schools of that time and those of today have two major differences. First, law schools then did not usually require any previous college work. Second, in

1850 the standard law school curriculum could be completed in one year. Later in the 1800s many law schools instituted two-year programs.

In 1870 major changes were initiated at Harvard that were to have a lasting impact on legal training. In that year Christopher Columbus Langdell was appointed dean of the law school. As a start, he instituted stiffer entrance requirements. A student without a college degree was required to pass an entrance test. Langdell also made it more difficult to graduate. The law school course was increased to two years in 1871 and to three years in 1876. Another hurdle was the requirement that a student pass first-year final examinations before proceeding to the second-year courses.

Undoubtedly the most lasting change attributed to Langdell was the introduction of the case method of teaching. In place of lectures and textbooks, the method used casebooks (collections of actual case reports), which were designed to explain the principles of law, what they meant, and how they developed. Teachers then used the Socratic method to guide the students to a discovery of legal concepts found in the cases. Students initially resisted this new method of teaching law, but other schools eventually adopted the Harvard approach. It remains the accepted method in many law schools today.

As the demand for lawyers increased during the late 1800s, there was a corresponding acceleration in the creation of new law schools. Opening a law school was not expensive, and a number of night schools, using lawyers and judges as part-time faculty members, sprang into existence. Standards were often lax, and the curriculum tended to emphasize local practice. The major contribution of these schools was to make legal training more readily available to poor, immigrant, and working-class students.

Naturally, then, the legal profession itself changed dramatically during this time. Lawyers no longer came solely from the upper rungs of society. Bar associations became interested in legal education as a way of controlling entry into the profession. Around the turn of the century, the Association of American Law Schools was created and, along with the American Bar Association (ABA), became involved in the accreditation of law schools.

The Twentieth Century to the Present. The twentieth century saw some major changes in the legal profession. For one thing, the number of people wanting to study law dramatically increased. By the 1960s the number of applicants to law schools had grown so large that nearly all schools became more selective. The more prestigious schools accepted only the best students. In response to social pressure and litigation, many law schools began actively recruiting female and minority applicants.

During the first half of the twentieth century, the case method of instruction continued to dominate the legal education process. By the 1920s, however, the legal realist movement began to have an impact on the law school curriculum. Two new courses, administrative law and taxation, started to find their way into the curriculum. Some schools also began to add clinical training.

By the 1960s the curriculum in some law schools had been expanded to include social concerns such as civil rights law and law-and-poverty issues. Foreign law courses also became available. A more recent trend in law schools is an emphasis on the use of computers for everything from registration to classroom instruction, accessing court forms, and student services. In addition to common rankings of law schools on the basis of such things as quality of faculty, quality of special programs, and overall prestige, a listing of the "25 most wired law schools" recently appeared.[7] Also noteworthy is the increasing number of law schools that are offering courses or special programs in intellectual property law. That field of specialization has grown considerably in recent years and is one of the best-paying fields in the legal profession.

The twentieth century was an active period for the organized bar. In 1908 the ABA adopted a canon of ethics to guide the conduct of lawyers. Most states followed suit by adopting the ABA canon or one of their own.

Another twentieth-century development was the integrated bar. This simply means that all lawyers in the state belong to a single bar association, pay dues to it, and are disciplined by it. The move toward an integrated bar began about the middle of the century.

Finally, the increasing use of advertising by lawyers has had a profound impact on the legal profession. In a 1977 decision the U.S. Supreme Court struck down Arizona's ban on such advertising.[8] On television stations across the country one can now see lawyers making appeals to attract new clients. Furthermore, legal clinics, established to handle the business generated by the increased use of advertising, have spread rapidly.

Growth and Stratification

The number of lawyers in the United States has increased steadily over the past half century and exceeded one million by the turn of the twenty-first century.[9] Furthermore, American law schools annually produce far more attorneys than any other country does. According to one recent study, for instance, "Japan produces approximately 350 new lawyers each year, fewer than Harvard Law School alone."[10] The proportion of lawyers in the general population in the United States is also much higher than it is in other countries. In a comparison of five countries, Joseph Sanders found that

[i]n 1987 in the United States there was one attorney for every 350 inhabitants. In the United Kingdom the figure was 1 in 900, in West Germany, 1 in 1,300 and in France approximately 1 in 1,800. In Japan the ratio of Bengoshi to inhabitants was 1 in 9,200.[11]

Another scholar reported in 1986 that "there was one lawyer for 1,431 people in Belgium, one for 963 in Scotland, and one for 599 in Ontario Canada." [12]

Where do all the attorneys in the United States work? The Law School Admission Council provides some answers. Nearly 58 percent (57.8) of the class of 2001 were in private practice as of February 15, 2002, 11.8 percent worked for the government, 11.6 percent held a judicial clerkship, 11.3 percent were in the business field, 2.9 percent were employed in the public interest area, 1.5 percent were academics, and 1.3 percent were in the military.[13]

Some environments are obviously more profitable and prestigious than others. This situation has led to what is known as professional stratification. Because of the growing number of women and blacks entering the legal field and the increased specialization within the profession, America's lawyers have become a less homogeneous group. The result is a profession stratified into "two hemispheres divided by backgrounds, clients, functions, structures, rewards, and associations." [14]

One of the major factors influencing the prestige rating is the type of legal specialty and the type of clientele served. Lawyers with specialties who serve big business and large institutions occupy the top hemisphere; those who represent individual interests are in the bottom hemisphere.

At the top of the prestige ladder are the elite law firms. These are the Wall Street firms—the venerable law practices originally (or still) situated on New York City's Wall Street—and other large national firms.

The basic pattern followed by the large national firms was established early in the twentieth century by Paul D. Cravath, head of the Wall Street law firm Cravath, Swaine & Moore. The ideal candidate for the firm was a member of Phi Beta Kappa and editor of the law review at Harvard, Yale, or Columbia. Those recruited served a kind of internship during which they performed general work for a number of the firm's partners.[15] Later they moved into an area of specialization and by the tenth year were evaluated for a partnership with the firm. Some lawyers were rewarded with partnerships; others left for another job.

The Cravath approach was used by many other New York firms. Collectively the attorneys working for such firms became known as Wall Street lawyers. These attorneys are dedicated to the interests of their clients and work long, hard hours on their behalf. The Wall Street lawyers have traditionally been known less for court appearances than for the counseling they provide their clients. The clients must be able to pay for this high-powered legal talent, and thus they tend to be major corporations rather than individuals. However, many of these large national firms often provide pro bono (free) legal services to further civil rights, civil liberties, consumer interests, and environmental causes.

The large national firms consist of partners and associates. The associates are paid salaries and, in essence, work for the partners. According to a recent article, partner paychecks at large law firms went over the half-million-dollar mark during the past decade.[16] These firms compete for the best graduates from the nation's law schools, tempting first-year associates with large beginning salaries, annual salary increases, and, in some instances, opportunities for bonuses. The most prestigious firms have 250 or more lawyers and also employ hundreds of other people as paralegals (nonlawyers who are specifically trained to handle many of the routine aspects of legal work), administrators, librarians, and secretaries. In addition to New York City, prestigious firms are found in other major cities, such as Chicago, Houston, Los Angeles, San Francisco, and Washington, D.C. Many of these firms have branches in several U.S. cities and even abroad.

A notch below the attorneys working in large national firms are those employed by large corporations. Many corporations use national law firms as outside counsel, but increasingly they are hiring their own salaried attorneys as in-house counsel. The legal staffs of some corporations rival in size those of private firms. These corporations now compete with the major law firms for the best law school graduates.

The legal division of a typical large corporation is headed by a senior-level official known as the general counsel, who often also carries a title such as vice president or secretary. Instead of representing the corporation in court (a task usually handled by outside counsel when necessary), the legal division handles the multitude of legal problems faced by the modern corporation. For example, the legal division monitors the company's personnel practices to ensure compliance with federal and state regulations concerning hiring and removal procedures. The corporation's attorneys may offer assistance in strategic planning by advising the board of directors about such things as contractual agreements, mergers, stock sales, and other business practices. The company lawyers may also help educate other employees about the laws that apply to their specific jobs and make sure that they are in compliance with them. The legal division of a large company also serves as a liaison with outside counsel.

Most of the nation's lawyers toil in the bottom hemisphere, the lowest level of the legal profession in terms of prestige. One study aptly noted that "the Manhattan megafirm with scores of highly paid associates may command headlines for the moment, but the truth is that most lawyers ... work in firms of fewer than 20 lawyers." [17]

Whereas the attorneys in the upper hemisphere are primarily involved in representing corporate clients, the lawyers who work in the lower hemisphere are engaged in a wide range of activities. They are much more likely to be found, day in and day out, in the courtrooms of the United States. These are the attorneys who represent clients in personal injury suits, who prosecute and defend persons accused of crimes, who represent husbands and wives in divorce proceedings, who help people conduct real estate transactions, and who help people prepare wills, to name just a few activities.

Many attorneys, especially those in a solo practice, handle many types of cases instead of specializing in one or two areas. Some charge a flat hourly rate for their services; those representing plaintiffs in a personal injury suit often work under a contingency fee arrangement. Under this arrangement, the attorney receives no compensation in advance. Instead, if the suit is successful and the plaintiff is awarded monetary damages, the lawyer receives a certain percentage for his or her services.

Attorneys who work for the government are generally included in the lower hemisphere. Some, such as the U.S. attorney general and the solicitor general, occupy prestigious positions, but many toil in rather obscure and poorly paid positions. A number of attorneys opt for careers as judges at the federal or state level.

Another common distinction in terms of specialization in the legal profession is that between plaintiffs and defense attorneys. The former group initiates lawsuits, whereas the latter group defends those accused of wrongdoing in civil and criminal cases. Only rarely do they cross the line to assume the opposing role.

Because the remainder of this book focuses on the work of the courts, it seems appropriate to look more extensively at the lawyers who handle cases in these courts. In some instances the litigants are private individuals and are thus represented by attorneys who are engaged in private practice. In other cases one of the parties involved in the suit may be the state or federal government. When that occurs, a government attorney as well as a private lawyer may participate in the case.

Government Attorneys in the Judicial Process

Government attorneys work at all levels of the judicial process, from trial courts to the highest state and federal appellate courts. However, the bulk of the cases never move beyond the trial courts.

Federal Prosecutors. Although the exact origins of the public prosecutor are uncertain, the prosecution of criminal cases in colonial America became the responsibility of a district attorney (or a person with an equivalent title) who was appointed by the governor and assigned to a specific region. The practice persisted, and by the end of the American Revolution every state had passed legislation creating a public prosecutor. In most instances he was an elected county official. The Judiciary Act of 1789 also provided for a United States attorney to be appointed by the president for each federal district court. Since these beginnings, "the prosecutor has become the most powerful figure in the criminal justice system." [18]

Today each federal judicial district has a U.S. attorney and one or more assistant U.S. attorneys. The number of assistant U.S. attorneys varies from district to district, with larger urban areas having more than one hundred.

U.S. attorneys are appointed by the president and confirmed by the Senate. Nominees must reside in the district to which they are appointed and must be attorneys. They serve a formal term of four years but can be reappointed indefinitely or removed at the president's discretion.[19] The appointment of a U.S. attorney is often a political reward.[20] Overwhelmingly, only lawyers who belong to the president's party are considered; it has become customary for U.S. attorneys to resign their positions when the opposition party wins the presidency. Because each nominee must be confirmed by the Senate, the senator or senators who are of the president's party and represent the state where the vacancy exists become important actors in the appointment process. The assistant U.S. attorneys are formally appointed by the U.S. attorney general, although in practice they are chosen by the U.S. attorney, who forwards the selection to the attorney general for ratification. Assistant U.S. attorneys may be fired by the attorney general.

The basic tasks handled by U.S. attorneys and their assistants are to prosecute defendants in the federal district courts and to defend the United States when it is sued in a federal trial court. Primarily, then, they function as prosecutors for the federal government, with considerable discretion in deciding which criminal cases to prosecute. The U.S. attorneys have the authority to determine which civil cases to try to settle out of court and which ones to take to trial. The U.S. attorney is in a good position to influence the federal district court's docket. U.S. attorneys engage in more litigation in the federal district courts than anyone else.

Prosecutors at the State Level. Those who prosecute persons accused of violating state criminal statutes are commonly known as district attorneys. In most states they are elected county officials, but in a few states they are appointed. The district attorney's office usually employs a number of assistants who do most of the trial work. Most of these assistant district attorneys are recent graduates of law school and are using the position to gain trial experience. Many will later enter private practice, often as criminal defense attorneys. Others will seek to become district attorneys or perhaps judges after a few years.

The district attorney's office has a great deal of discretion in the handling of cases. Given budget and personnel constraints, not all cases can be afforded the same amount of time and attention. Therefore, some cases are dismissed, others are not prosecuted, and still others are prosecuted vigorously in court. Most cases, however, are subject to plea bargaining. This means that the district attorney's office agrees to accept the defendant's plea of guilty on a reduced charge or to drop some charges against the defendant in exchange for pleas of guilty on others.

District attorneys' offices are organized in different ways. Some use what is known as the horizontal, or zone, model. This model, often found in heavily populated areas, assigns assistants to different steps in the judicial process. Some will screen cases that enter the prosecutor's office. Others will be assigned to courts to deal with bond hearings, probable-cause hearings, misdemeanor cases, or felony cases. Still others will specialize in presenting cases to the grand jury. Those assigned to a particular courtroom become part of the **courtroom work group**, with whom they interact more than they do with the assistant prosecutors who have other assignments.[21]

A second organizational model, found frequently in smaller jurisdictions, is the vertical prosecution model, which gives each assistant full responsibility for an assigned caseload. This means that one person receives the case when it is filed and follows it through to a final disposition.

Finally, some jurisdictions use a mixed model, which attempts to combine the best features of the other two models. Routine cases are likely to be handled in a horizontal model, and certain types of cases call for the vertical model. For instance, the district attorney's office may establish bureaus to deal with organized crime, repeat offenders, drug trafficking, or other special problems. Such bureaus are staffed with persons having special training or experience in the particular areas.

Public Defenders. Often the person charged with violating a state or federal criminal statute is unable to pay for the services of a defense attorney. In some areas a government official known as a public defender bears the responsibility for representing indigent defendants. Thus the public defender is a counterpart of the prosecutor. Unlike the district attorney, however, the public defender is usually appointed rather than elected.

Some parts of the country have statewide public defender systems; in other regions the public defender is a local official, usually associated with a county government. In New York City an independent organization known as the Legal Aid Society represents all indigent criminal defendants except those charged with murder.[22] New York's Legal Aid Society also has a civil division.

Like the district attorney, the public defender employs assistants and investigative personnel. The organizational scheme used by public defenders has a great deal of similarity to that of the prosecutor's office. Some are organized horizontally, some vertically, and some in a mixed model.

Other Government Lawyers. At both the state and federal levels, some government attorneys are better known for their work in appellate courts than in trial courts. For example, each state has an attorney general who supervises a staff of attorneys charged with the responsibility of handling the legal affairs of the state. At the federal level, the Department of Justice has similar responsibilities on behalf of the United States.

The U.S. Department of Justice. Although the Justice Department is an agency of the executive branch of the government, it has a natural association with the judicial branch. Many of the cases heard in the federal courts involve the national government in one capacity or another. Sometimes the government is sued; in other instances the government initiates the lawsuit. In either case, an attorney must represent the government. Most of the litigation involving the federal government is handled by the Justice Department, although a number of other government agencies have attorneys on their payrolls.

The Justice Department has several key divisions. The Office of Solicitor General is extremely important in cases argued before the Supreme Court. The Justice Department also has seven legal divisions: Antitrust, Civil, Civil Rights, Criminal, Internal Security, Land and Natural Resources, and Tax. Each has a staff of specialized lawyers and is headed by an assistant attorney general. The seven legal divisions supervise the handling of litigation by the U.S. attorneys, take cases to the courts of appeals, and aid the solicitor general's office in cases argued before the Supreme Court.

U.S. Attorney General. The United States attorney general, a cabinet official, is the head of the Department of Justice. As such, some of his duties might be best described as bureaucratic or managerial in nature. Unlike the solicitor general, he does not regularly appear before the U.S. Supreme Court, or any other court for that matter. However, he does supervise the work of the U.S. attorneys in each district and may use that power to influence the scope of legal activity aimed at pursuing the administration's policy goals. The current attorney general, John D. Ashcroft, is no ordinary bureaucrat. In addition to his active role in fighting the war on terrorism and helping develop the Department of Homeland Security, he is perceived as taking seriously his role of reviewing the work of prosecutors in the federal trial courts, especially in death penalty cases. The *Washington Post* reports that Ashcroft has aggressively pursued the death penalty and has ordered federal prosecutors to seek the death penalty in a dozen or so cases where they did not recommend doing so.[23]

U.S. Solicitor General. The solicitor general of the United States, the third-ranking official in the Justice Department, is assisted by five deputies and about twenty assistant solicitors general. The solicitor general's primary function is to decide, on behalf of the United States, which cases will and will not be presented to the Supreme Court for review. Whenever an executive branch department or agency loses a case in one of the courts of appeals and wishes a Supreme Court review, that department or agency will formally request that the Justice Department seek certiorari. The solicitor general will determine whether to appeal the lower-court decision.

Many factors must be taken into account when making such a decision. Perhaps the most important consideration is that the Supreme Court is limited in the number of cases it can hear in a given term. Thus the solicitor general must determine whether a particular case is one of the ninety or so cases that deserve extensive consideration by the Court during that term. How successful have solicitors general been in this assessment? The most extensive study to date says that

the advantage that the solicitor general enjoys in his capacity as a petitioner is clear. The solicitor general sought certiorari in 1,294 cases between 1959 and 1989, and was successful in obtaining the Court's review 69.78 percent of the time. Certiorari requests were granted in only 4.9 percent of the private litigation.[24]

In addition to deciding whether to seek Supreme Court review of a particular lower-court decision, the solicitor general personally argues most of the government's cases heard by the high court. However, the solicitor general may feel that some kinds of cases are more appropriately argued by a person who holds a particular office in government. Former solicitor general Rex E. Lee pointed out that the "tradition has been that the hardest cases—the most important cases—usually are argued by the Solicitor General."[25]

Although the solicitor general works for the attorney general and serves at the pleasure of the president, it has traditionally been argued that this official "must have the independence to exercise his craft as a lawyer on behalf of the institution of government without being a mouthpiece for the President." [26] In recent years, however, some have suggested that the solicitor general's office has become more politicized and thus more likely to press for adoption of the president's agenda.[27]

Although the solicitor general has historically been best known for his work at the Supreme Court, there is evidence that the current solicitor general, Theodore B. Olson, has taken on additional duties related to the war on terrorism. It is reported that he has "taken charge of the Bush administration's aggressive assertion of executive authority in the war against terrorism" and helps prepare lower-court cases as well.[28]

State Attorneys General. Each state has an attorney general who serves as its chief legal official. In most states this official is elected on a partisan statewide ballot. The attorney general oversees a staff of attorneys who primarily handle civil cases involving the state. Although the prosecution of criminal defendants is generally handled by the local district attorneys, the attorney general's office often plays an important role in investigating statewide criminal activities. Thus the attorney general and his or her staff may work closely with the local district attorney in preparing a case against a particular defendant.

The state attorney general does not usually control appeals in the state courts, as the solicitor general does in the federal courts. Furthermore, the state attorney general normally argues cases before the state supreme court only when a state agency is involved in the case.

The state attorneys general also perform the important function of issuing advisory opinions to state and local agencies. Many of these agencies cannot afford their own legal staff. The attorney general's opinion will often interpret an aspect of state law not yet ruled on by the courts. Although the advisory opinion might eventually be overruled in a case brought before the courts, the attorney general's opinion is important in determining the behavior of state and local agencies.

Although state attorneys general are often seen simply as bureaucrats or managers of a state's Department of Justice, Mississippi attorney general Michael Moore has shown that they can also be innovative legal strategists. Moore became quite well known for the lawsuit he fashioned in 1994 against the tobacco industry. He focused on the cost to the state of treating smoking-related illnesses. Within a year, similar suits were filed by Minnesota, West Virginia, and Florida. By the end of 1998, forty-one state attorneys general had filed individual lawsuits against the tobacco industry. In the resulting settlement, the tobacco companies agreed to distribute $206 billion over twenty-five years to forty-six states, five commonwealths and territories, and the District of Columbia.[29]

Private Lawyers in the Judicial Process

In criminal cases in the United States the defendant has a constitutional right to be represented by an attorney. Some jurisdictions have established public defender's offices to represent indigent defendants. In other areas, there is some method of assigning a private attorney to represent a defendant who cannot afford to hire one. Those defendants who can afford to hire their own lawyers will do so.

Assigned Defense Counsel. In many jurisdictions throughout the country, especially rural areas, the standard procedure is to appoint a private lawyer to represent an indigent defendant. Usually the assignment is made by an individual judge on an ad hoc basis. Local bar associations or lawyers themselves often provide the courts with a list of attorneys who are willing to provide such services. Compensation for representing an indigent defendant is generally based on a flat rate for hours spent in and out of court. The fee varies from area to area and often according to the case's complexity. It is usually a good deal less than an attorney would earn for providing services to a private client.

Private Defense Counsel. Some attorneys in private practice specialize in criminal defense work. Such lawyers are more often found in solo practices or in small rather than large law firms. Although the private lives of criminal defense attorneys are depicted as glamorous on television, the average real-life criminal defense lawyer works long hours for low pay and low prestige.[30]

One of the major worries of the criminal defense attorney is getting paid. Because the clients are usually poor and often not trustworthy, the criminal defense lawyer generally requires advance payment of part of the fee. Often this is all the lawyer will collect. The average criminal defense attorney must therefore handle a large number of cases in order to survive. This heavy caseload means that the attorney must spend a great deal of time in court and in the office juggling cases. All told, the lawyer who specializes in criminal defense work typically leads a hectic life.

The Courtroom Work Group

Assistant district attorneys assigned to a specific courtroom become part of the courtroom work group. Instead of functioning as an occasional gathering of strangers who resolve a particular conflict and then go their separate ways, "courts are permanent organizations."[31]

The most visible members of the courtroom work group—judges, prosecutors, and defense attorneys—are commonly associated with specific functions. Prosecutors push for convictions of those accused of criminal offenses against the government;

defense attorneys seek acquittals for their clients; and judges serve as neutral arbiters to guarantee a fair trial. In reality, members of the courtroom work group share certain values and goals and are not the fierce adversaries that many Americans imagine. Cooperation among judges, prosecutors, and defense attorneys is the norm.

The most important goal of the courtroom work group is to handle cases expeditiously. Judges and prosecutors are interested in disposing of cases quickly to present a picture of accomplishment and efficiency. Because private defense attorneys need to handle a large volume of cases, resolving cases quickly works to their advantage. Public defenders seek quick dispositions simply because they lack adequate resources to handle their caseloads.

A second important goal of the courtroom work group is to maintain group cohesion. Conflict among the members makes work more difficult and interferes with the expeditious handling of cases. Therefore, the work group stresses cooperation and censures those who violate this norm.

Finally, the courtroom work group is interested in reducing or controlling uncertainty. In practice, this means that all members of the group strive to avoid trials. Trials, especially jury trials, produce a great deal of uncertainty, given that they require substantial investments of time and effort without any reasonable guarantee of a desirable outcome.

To attain the goals of handling cases expeditiously, maintaining group cohesion, and reducing uncertainty, work group members employ several techniques. Although unilateral decisions and adversarial proceedings occur, negotiation is the most commonly used technique in criminal courtrooms. The members negotiate on a variety of issues—continuances, hearing dates, and exchange of information, to mention just a few. Without a doubt, however, plea bargaining is the most heavily publicized subject of negotiation among members of the courtroom work group.

Legal Services for the Poor

Although criminal defendants are constitutionally entitled to be represented by a lawyer, those who are defendants in a civil case or who wish to initiate a civil case do not have the right to representation. This means that persons who do not have the funds to hire a lawyer may find it difficult to obtain justice.

To deal with this problem, legal aid services of one sort or another are now found in many areas. Legal aid societies were established in New York and Chicago as early as the late 1880s, and many other major cities followed suit in the twentieth century. Although some legal aid societies are sponsored by bar associations, most are supported by private contributions. Legal aid bureaus also are associated with charitable organizations in some areas. In addition, many law schools operate legal aid clinics to provide assistance for the poor as well as valuable training for law students.

In 1974 Congress created the Legal Services Corporation (LSC), which distributes money to a number of legal services agencies. By 1995 it had some twelve hundred offices dealing with such matters as family, consumer, housing, landlord-tenant, and welfare problems.[32]

Since the early 1980s the LSC has been unpopular among many conservatives, and Congress would like to phase it out. Critics contend that other agencies are available to provide legal aid to the needy.

One other source of legal help for indigents deserves mention. Many lawyers provide legal services **pro bono publico** (for the public good) because they consider this free assistance a professional obligation.

What about people who are not indigent but are still too poor to hire a competent private attorney? Two relatively low-cost methods are available: legal clinics and prepaid legal plans.[33]

A legal clinic is a high-volume, high-efficiency law firm. These clinics depend upon advertising and publicity to generate clients and keep costs down by relying on standard forms and delegating most of the routine work to paralegals. The clinics concentrate on such fairly common legal problems as divorces, traffic offenses, personal bankruptcies, and wills.

Prepaid legal plans, also referred to as legal insurance plans, may be financed in two ways. One method is to enroll a group of people, such as a labor union. Another method is simply to sign up individuals. Some plans make available a designated lawyer or group of lawyers from whom the client may choose. Other plans allow the client to choose any lawyer; however, a limit usually is placed on how much of the attorney's fee will be covered.

Litigants

In some cases taken before the courts, the litigants are individuals, whereas in other cases one or more of the litigants may be a government agency, corporation, union, interest group, or university. In short, almost any individual or group has the potential to become a litigant in the courts.

What motivates a person or group to take a grievance to court? In criminal cases the answer to this question is relatively simple. A state or federal criminal statute has allegedly been violated, and the government prosecutes the party charged with violating the statute. In civil cases the answer is not so easy. Although some persons readily take their grievances to court, many others avoid this route because of the time and expense involved. Still, enough cases are filed annually to cause concern about how the federal and state courts can manage their dockets.

In his study of the U.S. Supreme Court, Lawrence Baum concludes that the motives of litigants before that tribunal take two general forms: "ordinary" litigation and "political" litigation.[34] Baum's conclusions apply to other courts as well.

Political scientist Phillip Cooper points out that judges are called upon to resolve two kinds of disputes: private law cases and public law controversies. Private law disputes are those in which one private citizen or organization sues another. Public law controversies involve the government more directly. In these situations a citizen or organization contends that a government agency or official has violated a right established by a constitution or statute. Cooper goes on to state that "legal actions, whether public law or private law contests, may either be policy oriented or compensatory." [35]

A classic example of private, or ordinary, compensation-oriented litigation is when a person injured in an automobile accident sues the driver of the other car in an effort to win monetary damages to compensate for the medical bills he or she had to pay. This type of litigation is personal and is not aimed at changing governmental or business policies.

Some private law cases, however, are policy-oriented or political in nature. Personal injury suits and product liability suits may appear, on the surface, to be simply compensatory in nature but may also be used to change the manufacturing or business practices of the private firms being sued.

A case litigated by U.S. senator John Edwards of North Carolina, when he was a practicing lawyer in that state, provides a good example. The case began in 1993 after a five-year-old Raleigh, North Carolina, girl got stuck on the drain of a wading pool after another child had removed the drain cover. Such a powerful suction was created that, before she could be rescued, the drain had sucked out most of her large and small intestines. As a result, the girl will have to spend about eleven hours per day attached to intravenous feeding tubes for the rest of her life. In 1997 a jury awarded the girl's family $25 million in compensatory damages and, before the jury was to have considered punitive damages, the drain manufacturer and two other defendants settled for $30.9 million. Edwards said that the lawsuit revealed similar incidents in other areas of the country and presented a stark example of something industry insiders knew but others did not. Not only did the family win its lawsuit, but also the North Carolina legislature passed a law requiring multiple drains to prevent such injuries in the future.[36]

Most political or policy-oriented lawsuits, however, are public law controversies. That is, they are suits brought against the government primarily to stop allegedly illegal policies or practices. They may also seek damages or some other specific form of relief. A case decided a few years ago by the U.S. Supreme Court, *Lucas v. South Carolina Coastal Council,* provides a good example.[37] South Carolina's Beachfront Management Act forbade David H. Lucas to build single-family houses on two beachfront lots he owned. A South Carolina trial court ruled that Lucas was entitled to be compensated for his loss. The South Carolina Supreme Court reversed the trial court decision, however, and Lucas appealed to the U.S. Supreme Court. The high court ruled in Lucas's favor, saying that if a property owner is denied all economically viable use of his or her property, a taking has occurred and the Constitution requires compensation.

Political or policy-oriented litigation is more prevalent in the appellate courts than in the trial courts and is most common in the U.S. Supreme Court. Ordinary compensatory litigation is often terminated early in the judicial process because the litigants find it more profitable to settle their dispute or accept the verdict of a trial court. However, litigants in political cases generally do little to advance their policy goals by gaining victories at the lower levels of the judiciary. Instead, they prefer the more widespread publicity that is attached to a decision by an appellate tribunal. Pursuing cases in the appellate courts is expensive. Therefore, many lawsuits that reach this level are supported in one way or another by interest groups.

Interest Groups in the Judicial Process

Although interest groups are probably better known for their attempts to influence legislative and executive branch decisions, they also pursue their policy goals in the courts. Some groups have found the judicial branch to be far more receptive to their efforts than either of the other two branches of government. Interest groups that do not have the economic resources to mount an intensive lobbying effort in Congress or a state legislature may find it much easier to hire a lawyer and find some constitutional or statutory provision upon which to base a court case. Likewise, a small group with few registered voters among its members may lack the political clout to exert much influence on legislators and executive branch officials. Large memberships and political clout are not prerequisites for filing suits in the courts, however.

Interest groups may also turn to the courts because they find the judicial branch more sympathetic to their policy goals than the other two branches. The National Association for the Advancement of Colored People (NAACP) provides an excellent example. This group, which dates from the early twentieth century, soon realized that Congress and the executive branch generally were not sympathetic to the struggle for civil rights of black citizens. Seeing the courts as potentially more sympathetic, the NAACP started to focus its efforts on litigation as a means of achieving its goals. As the Supreme Court became more favorable to civil rights after 1937, the NAACP began to realize the value of the judiciary as a forum for its activities and eventually established the Legal Defense Fund, a separate organization composed of lawyers who represented them in litigation.

Following the pattern established by the NAACP, other minority group organizations began to use the courts. Cases dealing with the rights of Hispanics and women have been pursued vigorously by groups such as the Mexican-American Legal Defense and Education Fund and the National Organization for Women.

Throughout the 1960s interest groups with liberal policy goals fared especially well in the federal courts. In addition, the concept of the public interest law firm, attributed to consumer advocate Ralph Nader, gained prominence during this period. These law firms pursue cases that serve the public interest in general—including cases in the areas of consumer rights, employment discrimination, occupational safety, civil liberties, and environmental concerns.

In the 1970s, with the increasing conservatism of the federal courts stemming from President Richard M. Nixon's appointment strategy, some major changes began to take place in the interaction between interest groups and the judiciary. For one thing, conservative interest groups began to resort to the federal courts more frequently than they had in the 1950s and 1960s, thus resuming the trend of the late nineteenth and early twentieth centuries.[38] This was in part a reaction to the successes of liberal interest groups. Changes also resulted from the increasingly favorable forum that the federal courts provided for conservative viewpoints. The latter trend persisted throughout the 1980s because of President Ronald Reagan's success in placing judges on the federal bench who shared his conservative policy views.

The past three decades also saw predominantly liberal interest groups seeking forums other than the federal courts in which to pursue their policy goals. Some took their battles to the legislative branch, whereas others preferred to file their suits in state courts rather than in the federal courts.

Interest group involvement in the judicial process may take several different forms, depending upon the goals of the particular group. However, two principal tactics stand out: involvement in test cases and presentation of information before the courts through amicus curiae briefs.

Test Cases

Because the judiciary engages in policymaking only by rendering decisions in specific cases, one favorite tactic of interest groups is to make sure that a case appropriate for obtaining its policy goals is brought before the court. In some instances this means that the interest group will initiate and sponsor the case by providing all the necessary resources. Undoubtedly, the best-known example of this type of sponsorship is to be found in the *Brown v. Board of Education* case.[39] Although the suit against the Board of Education of Topeka, Kansas, was filed by the parents of Linda Brown, the NAACP supplied the legal help and money necessary to pursue the case all the way to the Supreme Court, where Thurgood Marshall (who later became a U.S. Supreme Court justice) argued the suit on behalf of the plaintiff and the NAACP. As a result, the NAACP gained a victory through the Supreme Court's decision that segregation in the public schools violates the Equal Protection Clause of the Fourteenth Amendment.

Interest groups may also provide assistance in a case initiated by someone else but that raises issues of importance to the group. A good example may be found in a freedom of religion case, *Wisconsin v. Yoder*.[40] In that case the state of Wisconsin filed criminal complaints charging Jonas Yoder and others with failure to send their children to school until the age of sixteen, as required by state law. Yoder and the others, members of the Amish sect, believed that education beyond the eighth grade led to the breakdown of the values they cherished and to "worldly" influences on their children.

An organization known as the National Committee for Amish Religious Freedom (NCARF), which had been formed in 1965 by non-Amish ministers, bankers, lawyers, and professors to defend the right of the Amish to pursue their way of life, came to the defense of Yoder and the others. The NCARF provided William R. Ball as defense attorney, as well as a number of expert witnesses who testified on behalf of the Amish.

Following a decision against the Amish in the trial court, the NCARF appealed to a Wisconsin circuit court, which upheld the trial court's decision. An appeal was made to the Wisconsin Supreme Court, which ruled in favor of the Amish, saying that the compulsory school attendance law violated the Free Exercise of Religion Clause of the First Amendment. Wisconsin then appealed to the U.S. Supreme Court, which on May 15, 1972, sustained the religious objection that the NCARF had raised to the compulsory school attendance laws.

Thus, even though the NCARF did not initiate the litigation, it found its test case and pursued it through four courts to obtain its objective. Without the actions of the NCARF, the religious freedom interests of the Amish might not have been adequately presented, especially at the appellate level, because the Amish generally refused to defend themselves in litigation.

How extensive is interest group sponsorship of cases? If one is referring to all cases where U.S. Supreme Court review is sought, the answer is that a very small proportion of them involve group sponsorship. However, group sponsorship is far more common in cases the Court hears.[41] One recent study found that half of the most important decisions of the 1986–1991 Supreme Court terms were made in cases sponsored by interest groups.[42]

The American Civil Liberties Union (ACLU), an organization dedicated to defending the Bill of Rights, is probably the interest group best known for sponsorship of cases in the nation's courts.[43] On the occasion of its seventieth anniversary in 1990, it was noted that "the ACLU had been involved in 80 percent of the post-1920 'landmark' cases regularly cited in constitutional law texts."[44]

The bulk of the literature on interest group involvement in litigation has focused on cases concerning major constitutional issues that have reached the Supreme Court. Because only a small percentage of cases ever reach the nation's highest court, however, much of the work of interest group lawyers deals with more routine work at the lower levels of the judiciary. Instead of fashioning major test cases for the appellate courts, these attorneys may simply be required to deal with the legal problems of their groups' clientele.

A study of the routine activities of three litigation-oriented civil rights groups active in Mississippi in the mid-1960s provides some interesting insights.[45] For one thing, the authors of this study found that although the attorneys associated with the Lawyers Committee for Civil Rights under Law, the Lawyers Constitutional Defense Committee, and the NAACP Legal Defense Fund evidently preferred to litigate in the federal courts, most of their work was done in the state and local tribunals. The activities of these attorneys covered a wide variety of needs. In addition to litigating major civil rights questions, they defended blacks and civil rights workers who ran into difficulties with the local authorities. These interest group attorneys, then, performed many of the functions of a specialized legal aid society.

Amicus Curiae Briefs

Submission of amicus curiae (friend of the court) briefs is the easiest method by which interest groups can become involved in cases. Consequently, it is also the most common form of group involvement. This method allows a group to get its message before the court even though it does not control the case. Provided it has the permission of the parties to the case or the permission of the court, an interest group may submit an amicus brief to supplement the arguments of the parties.

The frequency of amicus curiae participation has increased over the years. Two Supreme Court scholars recently noted that "on average, 75.5 percent of all full opinion cases decided between 1986 and 1996 contained at least one amicus curiae brief, and the average amicus case contained 4.4 briefs." [46]

Sometimes these briefs are aimed at strengthening the position of one of the parties in the case. When the *Wisconsin v. Yoder* case was argued before the U.S. Supreme Court, the cause of the Amish was supported by amicus curiae briefs filed by the General Conference of Seventh Day Adventists, the National Council of Churches of Christ in the United States, the Synagogue Council of America, the American Jewish Congress, the National Jewish Commission on Law and Public Affairs, and the Mennonite Central Committee. [47] All supported exemption of the Amish from the compulsory school attendance laws.

Some cases attract amicus briefs supporting both parties in the case. For example, approximately one hundred groups and individuals participated as amici curiae in *Lucas v. South Carolina Coastal Council.* A close examination reveals that "support-ers of Lucas and the state matched constituency for constituency, at least in the areas of government, environment/public interest, and land use." [48]

Sometimes friend-of-the-court briefs are used not to strengthen the arguments of one of the parties but to suggest to the court the group's own view of how the case should be resolved. A classic example occurred in *Mapp v. Ohio.* [49] When that case was presented to the Supreme Court, the argument by the parties focused (1) on the issue of whether someone should be convicted for "mere possession" of obscene material, and (2) on the "shocking" nature of the search that led to the discovery of the materi-al. However, the defendant's lawyer did not urge a change in the ruling that improp-erly seized evidence could still be used in the trial. Instead, the exclusionary issue was raised in the amicus curiae brief filed by the American Civil Liberties Union and the Ohio Civil Liberties Union. [50] The Supreme Court, without dealing with the obscenity issue, handed down a landmark constitutional decision excluding illegally seized evidence from trials in state courts (the exclusionary rule). Thus it was the interest group's argument that provided the policy view adopted by the Supreme Court.

Scholars have recently begun to pay more attention to the fact that amicus curi-ae briefs are often filed in an attempt to persuade an appellate court to either grant or deny review of a lower-court decision. A study of the U.S. Supreme Court found, for instance, that the presence of amicus briefs significantly increased the chances that the Court would give full treatment to the case and concluded that

interested parties can have a significant and positive impact on the Court's agenda by participating as amici curiae prior to the Court's decision on certiorari or jurisdiction.[51]

The government also can be a friend of the court. Unlike private interest groups, all levels of the government can submit amicus curiae briefs without obtaining permission. The solicitor general of the United States is especially important in this regard. One study of the solicitor general reports that this official was involved in 518 amicus cases decided by a full Supreme Court opinion between 1959 and 1986.[52]

The solicitor general is far more successful than private litigants in getting acceptance for certiorari petitions. In addition, the solicitor general's amicus briefs in support of others' appeals or petitions are largely successful. One study noted that

when the government filed an amicus brief on behalf of the appellant or petitioner, the Court granted review in 87.6 percent of the cases. Surprisingly, this success is even greater than when the government sought the Court's review of its own cases.[53]

The filing of amicus curiae briefs is a tactic used in appellate rather than trial courts. Although the literature on friend-of-the-court participation deals most extensively with federal courts, amicus briefs may be filed in state appellate courts as well. Such filings have become especially more noticeable with the advent of "new judicial federalism." An examination of litigation activity in sixteen state supreme courts indicates that there is not only a heightened presence of organized interests but also a wider range of groups participating as amici curiae.[54] Furthermore, findings indicate that "business groups, other organizational players, and even individual amici appear to be quite successful."[55] One specific way that amici curiae can be helpful in state supreme court cases is to intervene in support of a position advocated by an individual with a relatively low level of resources.[56]

Participation by amici curiae may also be found in courts of other countries. A recent study of the European Court of Justice says that

member states, institutions of the European Union, and in some cases, interested individuals may participate in cases to which they are not a party as a sort of amicus curiae.[57]

Summary

In this chapter we laid the groundwork for later chapters, which deal more extensively with the steps in the judicial process. Here our focus was on three important actors in the judicial process: lawyers, litigants, and interest groups.

We traced the development of the legal profession from its beginnings in colonial days to the contemporary practice of law. Our discussion focused on the stratification of the legal profession and the various types of lawyers who practice in the United States. Singled out for special emphasis were the government lawyers who are primarily involved in handling cases in the state and federal trial and appellate courts.

We next turned our attention to those who become litigants in U.S. courts. In some cases the adversaries are ordinary litigants who are primarily concerned with being compensated for their losses. At other times, the combatants are involved in political litigation and have as their major goal influencing public policy. Still other cases feature litigants who are interested in both personal compensation and exerting some influence over public policy.

We concluded with an examination of the role of interest groups in the judicial process. Following a brief look at the reasons groups become involved in litigation, we discussed the major strategies and tactics used by interest groups in the judicial arena: involvement in test cases and the use of amicus curiae briefs.

Further Thought and Discussion Questions

1. Given their importance in American society and government, why have lawyers, from the early colonial years to the present, been so unpopular?

2. What impact has stratification had on the delivery and quality of legal services in the United States?

3. How can a system that claims to be unbiased and impartial allow interest group participation in the judicial process?

NOTES

1. Our discussion draws heavily upon Lawrence M. Friedman, *A History of American Law*, 2d ed. (New York: Simon and Schuster, 1985).

2. Ibid., 97.

3. Ibid., 101.

4. Ibid., 306.

5. Ibid., 321.

6. Ibid., 607.

7. See Virginia Kirk, "Most Wired Law Schools," *National Jurist*, November/December 1998, 19.

8. *Bates v. State Bar*, 433 U.S. 350 (1977).

9. See Steven Vago, *Law and Society*, 7th ed. (Upper Saddle River, N.J.: Prentice Hall, 2003), 351.

10. Joseph Sanders, "Courts and Law in Japan," in *Courts, Law, and Politics in Comparative Perspective*, ed. Herbert Jacob, Erhard Blankenburg, Herbert M. Kritzer, Doris Marie Provine, and Joseph Sanders (New Haven, Conn.: Yale University Press, 1996), 320.

11. Ibid.

12. P. S. C. Lewis, "A Comparative Perspective on the Legal Profession in the 1980s," *Law and Society Review* 20 (1986): 82.

13. Law School Admission Council, *The Official Guide to ABA-Approved Law Schools, 2004 Edition* (Newtown, Pa.: Law School Admission Council, 2003), 44.

14. Richard Abel, "The Transformation of the American Legal Profession," *Law and Society Review* 20 (1986): 6.

15. See Erwin O. Smigel, *The Wall Street Lawyer: Professional Organization Man* (Glencoe, Ill.: Free Press, 1964).

16. William C. Smith, "Bailing from the Bench," *ABA Journal* 85 (May 1999): 22.

17. "Law Poll," *ABA Journal,* September 1, 1986, 44.

18. Howard Abadinsky, *Law and Justice,* 2d ed. (Chicago: Nelson-Hall, 1991), 187.

19. For a good case study of the firing of a U.S. attorney, see Howard Ball, *Courts and Politics: The Federal Judicial System* (Englewood Cliffs, N.J.: Prentice-Hall, 1980), 202–206.

20. For an in-depth analysis of the appointment process for U.S. attorneys, see James Eisenstein, *Counsel for the United States: U.S. Attorneys in the Political and Legal Systems* (Baltimore: Johns Hopkins University Press, 1978), chap. 3.

21. See James Eisenstein and Herbert Jacob, *Felony Justice* (Boston: Little, Brown, 1977).

22. Abadinsky, *Law and Justice,* 201.

23. See Dan Eggen, "Ashcroft Aggressively Pursues Death Penalty," *Washington Post,* July 1, 2002, A1.

24. Rebecca Mae Salokar, *The Solicitor General: The Politics of Law* (Philadelphia: Temple University Press, 1992), 25.

25. For a fuller discussion of this matter, see "Interview with Solicitor General Rex E. Lee," *The Third Branch* 14 (May 1982): 5.

26. Lincoln Caplan, "The Tenth Justice," pt. 1, *New Yorker,* August 10, 1987, 40.

27. See Caplan, "The Tenth Justice," pt. 1, 41–58; and Lincoln Caplan, "The Tenth Justice," pt. 2, *New Yorker,* August 17, 1987, 30–62. See also Stephen L. Wasby, *The Supreme Court in the Federal Judicial System,* 3d ed. (Chicago: Nelson-Hall, 1988), 146–147; and Salokar, *The Solicitor General,* 172–173.

28. See Charles Lane, "Olson's Role in War on Terror Matches His Uncommon Clout: Legal Strategy Seeks to Ensure Victory in Cases That Reach High Court," *Washington Post,* July 3, 2002, A21.

29. Our brief account is drawn from Rorie J. Spill, Michael J. Licari, and Leonard Ray, "Taking on Tobacco: Policy Entrepreneurship and the Tobacco Litigation," *Political Research Quarterly* 54 (September 2001): 605–622.

30. See Paul Wice, *Criminal Lawyers: An Endangered Species* (Beverly Hills, Calif.: Sage, 1978).

31. Eisenstein and Jacob, *Felony Justice,* 20. Our discussion of the concept of the courtroom work group relies heavily on Eisenstein and Jacob's discussion.

32. See Vago, *Law and Society,* 384.

33. Our discussion of legal clinics and prepaid legal plans is drawn from ibid., 385–386.

34. Lawrence Baum, *The Supreme Court,* 6th ed. (Washington, D.C.: CQ Press, 1998), 84–87.

35. Phillip J. Cooper, *Hard Judicial Choices* (New York: Oxford University Press, 1988), 13.

36. See Bob Van Voris, "The Torts of Summer," Law.com, http://www.law.com.

37. 505 U.S. 1003 (1992).

38. See Karen O'Connor and Lee Epstein, "The Rise of Conservative Interest Group Litigation," *Journal of Politics* 45 (May 1983): 479–489; and Lee Epstein, *Conservatives in Court* (Knoxville: University of Tennessee Press, 1985).

39. 347 U.S. 483 (1954).

40. 406 U.S. 205 (1972). See also the excellent discussion of this case in Richard C. Cortner, *The Supreme Court and Civil Liberties Policy* (Palo Alto, Calif.: Mayfield, 1975), 153–182. Our discussion is based on this study.

41. See Baum, *The Supreme Court*, 92.

42. See Lee Epstein, "Interest Group Litigation during the Rehnquist Court Era," *Journal of Law and Politics* 9 (Summer 1993): 715–717.

43. For a complete history of the American Civil Liberties Union, see Samuel Walker, *In Defense of American Liberties: A History of the ACLU* (New York: Oxford University Press, 1990).

44. Ibid., 371.

45. See Joseph Stewart Jr. and Edward V. Heck, "The Day-to-Day Activities of Interest Group Lawyers," *Social Science Quarterly* 64 (March 1983): 173–182.

46. Lee Epstein and Thomas G. Walker, *Constitutional Law for a Changing America: Rights, Liberties, and Justice*, 4th ed. (Washington, D.C.: CQ Press, 2001), 42.

47. See Cortner, *The Supreme Court and Civil Liberties Policy*, 169–170.

48. Lee Epstein and Thomas G. Walker, *Constitutional Law for a Changing America: Institutional Powers and Constraints*, 4th ed. (Washington, D.C.: CQ Press, 2001), 45.

49. 367 U.S. 643 (1961).

50. See Wasby, *The Supreme Court in the Federal Judicial System*, 151–152.

51. Gregory A. Caldeira and John R. Wright, "Organized Interests and Agenda Setting in the U.S. Supreme Court," *American Political Science Review* 82 (December 1988): 1122.

52. Salokar, *The Solicitor General*, 145.

53. Ibid., 27.

54. Lee Epstein, "Exploring the Participation of Organized Interests in State Court Litigation," *Political Research Quarterly* 47 (June 1994): 335–351.

55. Donald R. Songer and Ashlyn Kuersten, "The Success of Amici in State Supreme Courts," *Political Research Quarterly* 48 (March 1995): 40.

56. See Donald R. Songer, Ashlyn Kuersten, and Erin Kaheny, "Why the Haves Don't Always Come Out Ahead: Repeat Players Meet Amici Curiae for the Disadvantaged," *Political Research Quarterly* 53 (September 2000): 552.

57. Sally J. Kenney, "The European Court of Justice: Integrating Europe through Law," *Judicature* 81 (May–June 1998): 252.

SUGGESTED READINGS

Cortner, Richard C. *The Supreme Court and Civil Liberties Policy*. Palo Alto, Calif.: Mayfield, 1975. Case studies of several major Supreme Court decisions and how they evolved through the judicial system.

Eisenstein, James. *Counsel for the United States: U.S. Attorneys in the Political and Legal Systems*. Baltimore: Johns Hopkins University Press, 1978. A study of the selection, roles, and functions of U.S. attorneys.

Eisenstein, James, and Herbert Jacob. *Felony Justice*. Boston: Little, Brown, 1977. The authors describe the courtroom work group and its role in the processing of felony criminal cases.

Epstein, Lee. *Conservatives in Court*. Knoxville: University of Tennessee Press, 1985. A study of the tactics used by conservative interest groups to influence decisions of the U.S. Supreme Court.

Epstein, Lee, and Joseph F. Kobylka. *The Supreme Court and Legal Change: Abortion and the Death Penalty*. Chapel Hill: University of North Carolina Press, 1992. A study of the nature and tactics of interest groups involved in trying to influence decisions of the U.S. Supreme Court in abortion and death penalty cases.

Friedman, Lawrence M. *A History of American Law*, 2d ed. New York: Simon and Schuster, 1985. An excellent summary of the development of law in the United States.

Salokar, Rebecca Mae. *The Solicitor General: The Politics of Law*. Philadelphia: Temple University Press, 1992. An examination of the roles, functions, legal duties, and political activities of the U.S. solicitor general.

Walker, Samuel E. *In Defense of American Liberties: A History of the ACLU*. New York: Oxford University Press, 1991. A detailed historical analysis of one of the interest groups most frequently involved in the American judicial system.

CHAPTER 9

Crime and Procedures Prior to a Criminal Trial

Attorney General John Ashcroft insists that some of the procedural rights afforded criminal defendants in the United States—such as the right to a speedy and public trial and the right to confront one's accusers—should not be extended to terrorists or noncitizens accused of terrorist activities. Here, the attorney general holds an al Qaeda terrorist training manual while testifying before the Senate Judiciary Committee. Throughout its history, the United States has faced the challenge of preserving personal liberties during periods of armed conflict.

T HIS IS THE FIRST OF three chapters that examine U.S. courts from a judicial process perspective. This chapter analyzes the criminal process—from the stage when a law is first broken to subsequent stages such as arrest and indictment. Chapter 10 focuses on the criminal trial itself and its aftermath, such as sentencing and the appeals process. Finally, Chapter 11 examines the civil process in the same manner to provide a sense of how the system looks and feels to a litigant or observer. Keep in mind that there is no such thing as a single criminal or civil court process in the United States. Instead, the federal system has a court process at the national level, and each state and territory has its own set of rules and regulations that affect the judicial process. Norms and similarities do exist among all of these governmental entities, and our discussion will focus primarily on them, but we wish to emphasize that no two states have identical judicial process systems, and no state's system is identical to that of the national government.

The Nature and Substance of Crime

"The way you treat me is a crime," a mother scolds her headstrong teenager, who has been rude to her for the umpteenth time that day. Comments such as this are heard with some frequency in today's world. Although it is clear what the mother is getting at, in the literal sense no crime has been committed. Being discourteous to one's parents may be wrong and immoral, but in the United States, at least, it is not a crime because it does not violate any specific law. The nature of criminality can be understood by this example. An act is not automatically a crime because it is hurtful or sinful. (Only about half of the Ten Commandments are enforced by criminal law.) An action constitutes a true crime only if it specifically violates a criminal statute duly enacted by Congress, a state legislature, or some other public authority.

We must also keep in mind that the notion of what is considered a crime varies markedly from one nation and culture to another. For example, in May 2002 the world was shocked by the story of a woman in Pakistan who had been sentenced to death by stoning. Her crime was having sexual intercourse outside of marriage. But the reader may say: it is not a crime, but the offense is frowned upon in virtually all cultures. However, there is more to the story than that. The woman had been raped by her brother-in-law, but Pakistan's Koran-based law, known as *hudood*, makes little distinction between forced and consensual sex. When *hudood* was enacted twenty-four years ago, "all forms of adultery [were banned], whether the offense is committed with or without the consent of the parties." (By custom, however, it is almost always the women who are punished, whatever the facts.) [1]

A good working definition of a crime, then, is that it is an offense against the state punishable by fine, imprisonment, or death. A crime is a violation of obligations due the community as a whole and can be punished only by the state. The sanctions of imprisonment and death cannot be imposed by a civil court or in a civil action (although a fine may be either a civil or a criminal penalty).

In the United States crimes come in great variety. Most of them are sins of commission, such as aggravated assault and embezzlement; a few are sins of omission, such as failing to stop and render aid after a traffic accident or failing to file an income tax return. The state considers some crimes serious (such as murder and treason), and this seriousness is reflected in the corresponding punishments (such as life imprisonment or the death penalty). The state considers other crimes only mildly reprehensible (such as double parking or disturbing the peace), and punishments are akin to an official slap on the wrist (such as a light fine or a night in the local jail).

Some crimes constitute actions that virtually all citizens consider outside the sphere of acceptable human conduct (such as kidnapping or rape), whereas other crimes constitute actions about which opinion may be divided. Relevant laws include an 1897 Michigan statute (recently upheld and used) that can put someone in jail for up to ninety days and impose a fine of $100 for cursing in front of a child; a Nebraska statute that forbids bingo games at church suppers,[2] and a Virginia law that forbids unmarried couples to live under the same roof. (The laws of this and six other states regard such living arrangements as "lewd and lascivious.") Other criminal statutes are plain silly. In Wisconsin it is illegal to sing in a bar, and in Louisiana it is forbidden to appear drunk at a meeting of a literary society.

The most serious crimes in the United States are felonies. In a majority of the states a felony is any offense for which the penalty may be death or imprisonment in a penitentiary (a jail is not a penitentiary); all other offenses are misdemeanors or infractions. In other states (and under the U.S. Penal Code) a felony is an offense for which the penalty may be death or imprisonment for a year or more. Thus felonies are distinguished in some states according to the place where the punishment occurs. In some states and according to the federal government the length of the sentence is the key factor. Examples of common felonies include murder, forcible rape, and armed robbery.

Misdemeanors are regarded as petty crimes by the state, and their punishment usually consists of confinement in a city or county jail for less than a year. Public drunkenness, small-time gambling, and vagrancy are common examples of misdemeanors. Some states have a third category of offenses known as infractions. They often include minor traffic offenses (such as parking violations), and the penalty is usually a small fine. Fines may also be part of the penalty for misdemeanors and felonies.

Categories of Crime

A useful way to consider various types of crime is to sort them according to their public policy implications.[3] Five broad categories that constitute the primary offenses against the state in the United States today are conventional, economic, syndicated, political, and consensual.

Conventional Crimes

Property crimes make up the lion's share of the 24.2 million conventional crimes committed annually in the United States. In 2001 the U.S. Justice Department determined that 76 percent of all offenses (almost 18.3 million) were crimes against personal property, the largest number of these involving personal theft.[4] The government differentiates property crimes such as these from crimes of violence, although the two often go hand in glove. The thief who breaks into a house and inadvertently confronts a resistant owner is likely to be involved in more than just the property crime of burglary.

The less numerous, but more feared, conventional crimes are those against the person. These crimes of violence include murder and non-negligent manslaughter, forcible rape, robbery, and aggravated assault. In 2001, for every one thousand persons age twelve or older, there occurred one rape or sexual assault, two assaults with serious injury, and three robberies.[5] Murders were the least frequent violent victimization—about six victims per 100,000 persons.[6]

Despite these sobering statistics, and contrary to the popular myth about soaring crime rates, serious conventional crime has been declining over the past decade and a half, and even crimes of violence have started to recede. According to the Federal Bureau of Investigation, in 2001 the overall crime index rate continued its steady decline since 1994. Crimes against property declined 6 percent since 1994, and violent crime continued to drop since that year. (Indeed crimes of violence alone dropped some 10 percent from 2001).[7]

In our discussion of crime numbers and trends, it might be insightful to compare statistics in the United States with those of other nations that have similar traditions and keep good records. The conventional wisdom is that America is the most crime-infested nation among the modern industrial democracies. In actual fact, crime has been declining dramatically in the United States, and many Western democracies have crime rates much higher than that in the United States. France, for example, recorded 185 incidents of violent theft per 100,000 persons in 2000, while only 145 such incidents per 100,000 persons were recorded in the United States.[8] As for property crimes, the burglary rate in Australia is 40 percent higher than that in the United States, in Canada it is 12 percent greater, and in England and Wales it is 30 percent higher. Sweden and the Netherlands, countries that are said to be virtually crime-free, have burglary rates 35 and 84 percent, respectively, higher than in America. What about crimes of violence? Here the data present a mixed picture. In terms of victimization for minor crimes of violence, the risk is about the same in the United States as it is "in other common law countries (i.e., descendants of the British legal system). The glaring exception is the U.S. murder rate, which is about six times higher than that in other industrialized nations. But comparing a country with a diverse population such as the United States with other, somewhat more homogeneous populations ignores important demographic differences. Half the murderers and victims in the United States are African-Americans, whose victimization rate is seven times that of whites. The white homicide rate in the United States is about twice that in Europe, though the gap has been closing because the U.S. murder rate has been falling."[9]

Economic Crimes

Most thoughts about crime turn toward conventional criminal activity. Americans fear having someone break into their homes and hope that the kid who steals their hubcaps is "sent up for a long time." They want most of the nation's police resources devoted to combating these conventional, personally threatening crimes. Yet in dollars-and-cents terms, conventional crimes are not where the money is; the cost of economic crimes robs the nation blind. No two scholars can agree on the annual cost of such crimes because the vast majority of them remain undiscovered and unreported, but a conservative estimate would put the price tag at close to $200 billion.

What are economic crimes? It would be too narrow to call them merely white-collar crimes because such a definition does not take into consideration that many such crimes are committed by persons outside their occupations—for example, a person filing a grossly inflated insurance claim. Harold J. Vetter and Leonard Territo list four broad categories of economic crimes that plague the nation.

1. Personal crimes consist of nonviolent criminal activity that one person inflicts on another with the hope of monetary gain. Examples include intentionally writing a bad check, cheating on one's income tax, and committing welfare fraud.

2. Abuse of trust occurs when business or government employees violate their fidelity to their employer or clients and engage in practices such as commercial bribery, theft and embezzlement from the workplace, and filling out false expense accounts.

3. Business crimes are not part of the central purpose of the business enterprise but are incidental to (or in furtherance of) it. Misleading advertising, violations of the antitrust laws, and false depreciation figures computed for corporate income tax purposes are all business crimes. For example, in recent years the collapse of Enron and many other energy-related corporations can be traced to willfully deceptive accounting practices that resulted in the loss of tens of billions of dollars for the corporations' stockholders, employees, and subsidiaries. Likewise, insider trading and stock manipulation have dominated the headlines in cases involving Martha Stewart, WorldCom, and Global Crossing.

4. Con games are white-collar criminal activities committed under the guise of a business. The "magic electric belt" that you can send away for to improve your sex life, and the Ph.D. diploma that you can receive for only $100 and an essay on your life experiences both fall into this category.[10]

Not only are economic crimes extremely costly to the American people, but they also have two other characteristics that make them relevant to some of the broader themes of this chapter. First, economic crimes are harder to detect and prove in court than other conventional crimes. Convicting a thief who is caught red-handed running out of a jewelry store with a bag of watches and diamonds is a relatively easy and routine endeavor. Not so with most economic crimes. For example, a few years ago a Harris County (Houston), Texas, commissioner was accused of accepting an illegal gift from a contractor. The contractor had paved a mile-long driveway from the commissioner's home to a nearby highway. "It was just an anniversary gift to me and my wife," said the commissioner. It took two juries (one of them was hung), enduring weeks of testimony and deliberation, before the court could finally determine that a crime had been committed.

Because most citizens do not regard economic crimes as serious as burglary or assault, fewer law enforcement resources are earmarked for these illegalities. Also, sentencing judges and juries look much more kindly on the stockbroker whose "misjudgment" caused her to engage in a little illegal insider trading (after all, she didn't hurt anyone, did she?) than on the young pickpocket who was caught separating someone from his wallet.

Syndicated, or Organized, Crimes

Syndicated crime differs from others addressed here in that it is engaged in by groups of people and is often directed on some type of hierarchical basis. It represents an ongoing activity that is inexorably entwined with fear and corruption. Organized crime may manifest itself in a variety of ways, but it tends to focus on several areas that are particularly lucrative, namely, trafficking in illegal drugs (such as cocaine or marijuana), gambling, prostitution, and loan-sharking. The latter is moneylending at exorbitant interest rates as well as high repayment rates. (Failure to pay may net the borrower a broken thumb or worse.) Figures on the cost of organized crime are not readily available, but no one doubts that it totals many billions of dollars annually.

Political Crimes

The usual meaning of political crime has been that it constitutes an offense against the government: treason, armed rebellion, assassination of public officials, and sedition. However, in recent decades legal scholars have begun using the term to include crimes committed by the government against individual citizens, dissident groups, and foreign governments or nationals. Examples of this murky definition of political crime might include illegal wiretaps and bugging by the FBI of politically dissident groups or the refusal of the military to investigate incidents of sexual harassment.

Several factors complicate any analysis of political crimes and of how judges and juries ought to, and do, respond to them. One factor is that ordinary crimes can be committed to make a political point under the guise of what legal scholars call symbolic speech. When anti-abortion activists are jailed for blocking the entrance to an abortion clinic, are they being punished for an ordinary act of criminal trespass or for their religious beliefs? When a soldier publicly acknowledges that he is homosexual and is promptly booted out of the service, is he guilty of violating the code of military justice or is he being singled out for drawing attention to the military's discrimination against gays and lesbians? Questions such as these often bedevil the judges and juries who must address the would-be political criminal.

In this same vein, the demarcation between the political crime and its conventional counterpart is often blurred when the government chooses unpopular persons or dissidents for meticulous application of a law that would not be enforced against ordinary folk. An unpopular group of protesters may suddenly find themselves under arrest for parading without a permit or for disorderly conduct, whereas a loud and drunken band of revelers may have passed by an hour before without action by the authorities. A minority youth may be arrested for vagrancy or trespassing if he is found walking at night in an all-white neighborhood "where he clearly doesn't belong." The values and attitudes of American judges and juries are sorely tested when such cases appear before them in court.

Consensual Crimes

A final category is the so-called victimless crime, such as prostitution, gambling, illegal drug use, and unlawful sexual practices between consenting adults. Such crimes are called consensual because both perpetrator and client desire the forbidden activity, but to call them all "victimless" sticks in the throats of many. The children whose parents spend their money and time on drugs rather than on properly caring for them may well regard themselves as victims. And tidy homeowners whose streets suddenly become part of a prostitution circuit and whose shrubbery begins to serve as both bedroom and bathroom clearly would not agree that this activity is victimless. Nevertheless, because a great number of Americans question whether many of these consensual activities should be proscribed by the criminal code, difficult problems are created for law enforcement officials, judges, and juries.

A significant amount of discretion exists at all levels of the judicial process. The way in which decision makers exercise this discretion is a function of their values and attitudes. Because attitudes about consensual, or victimless, crimes vary significantly among police officers, the public at large (and the potential jurors they represent), and judges, studies not surprisingly reveal great differences in how the judicial system treats participants in consensual criminal activity.

Elements of a Crime

In theory, at least, every crime has several distinct elements. Furthermore, unless the state is able to demonstrate in court the existence of these essential elements, there can be no conviction. Although the judicial process in the courtroom may not focus separately and distinctly on each of these elements, they are at least implicit throughout the entire process of convicting someone of a criminal offense.

A Law Defining the Crime and the Punishment

If an act is to be prohibited or required by the law, a duly constituted authority (usually Congress or a state legislature) must properly spell out the matter so that the citizenry can know in advance what conduct is prohibited or required. The lawmakers must also set forth the penalties to be imposed upon the individual who engages in the harmful conduct. If no definition of the illegal act has been provided, and no penalty has been prescribed, there is no crime.

Several years ago one of the coauthors of this book served on a state grand jury, and on several occasions a sheriff's deputy presented evidence on a pyramid club scheme that he had been investigating. Persons, often elderly people living alone, were persuaded to buy membership shares in the club, and they were then asked to recruit other members. The original purchaser of the club membership would receive a percentage of the membership fees of all the new members, and so on. Some would make money from this scam, but ultimately most would be left holding the bag.

Before long, a majority of the grand jurors were persuaded that an indictment was in order, and the district attorney (D.A.) was so informed. After a day or so of delay, the D.A. appeared and said: "What this club is doing is wrong and shameful and people are being victimized, but in this state there is no law against pyramid schemes. You can do nothing." As the Latin maxim succinctly puts it, *nullum crimen sine lege*—no crime without law.

Several corollaries to this general principle also serve as grist for the criminal justice mill. One is that the U.S. Constitution forbids criminal laws that are **ex post facto,** that is, laws that declare certain conduct to be illegal after the conduct has taken place. Past harmful or undesirable actions may not be declared criminal under the U.S. legal system. Likewise, the state may not pass **bills of attainder,** which single out a particular person or group of persons and declare that something is criminal for them but legal for everyone else. In the United States, if an action (or inaction) is to be considered criminal, it must be so for all citizens.

A final corollary is that a law defining a crime must be precise, so that the average person can determine in advance what conduct is prohibited or required. As the U.S. Supreme Court has put it, a statute defining a crime must be "sufficiently explicit to inform those who are subject to it what conduct on their part will render them liable to penalties." [11] Imagine the ease (and, perhaps, fun) with which the Supreme Court struck down this Jacksonville, Florida, municipal vagrancy ordinance. Imagine, too, how many people could go very many days without running afoul of at least some of its all-encompassing proscriptions. Criminal penalties were levied against

rogues and vagabonds; dissolute persons who go about begging; common gamblers; persons who use juggling or unlawful games or plays; common drunkards; common night walkers, thieves, pilferers, or pickpockets; traders in stolen property; lewd, wanton, and lascivious persons; keepers of gambling places; common railers and brawlers; persons wandering or strolling around from place to place without any lawful purpose or object; habitual loafers; disorderly persons; persons neglecting all lawful business and habitually spending their time by frequenting houses of ill fame, gaming houses, or places where alcoholic beverages are sold or served; and persons able to work but habitually living on their wives or minor children.[12]

In addition to defining the crime, the law must have a formal penalty attached to it. Traditional jurisprudence has always held that the punishment is an integral part of the crime. A number of years ago the state of Wyoming sought to convict a man for practicing medicine without a license. The accused unquestionably was actively prescribing medicines and even performing operations. During his trial it was noticed that the law forbidding unlicensed medical practice said not a word about what would happen to someone who did it. The judge was forced to instruct the jury to bring in a verdict in favor of the accused. (The "doctor" promptly decided to leave town, and the Wyoming legislature soon added a penalty clause to the statute.)

The Actus Reus

Actus reus is the Latin phrase meaning the criminal action committed by the accused that gives rise to the legal prosecution. The actus reus is the material element of the crime and will vary from one offense to another. This element may be the commission of an action that is forbidden (for instance, assault and battery), or it may be the failure to perform an action that is required (for instance, a person's refusal to stop and render aid to the victim of a motor vehicle accident).

The Mens Rea

The **mens rea** is the essential mental element of the crime. An old legal axiom holds that "an act does not make the doer of it guilty, unless the mind be guilty; that is, unless the intention be criminal." The American legal system has always made a distinction between harm that was caused intentionally and harm that was caused by simple negligence or accident. "Even a dog," said Justice Oliver Wendell Holmes, "distinguishes between being stumbled over and being kicked." [13] Thus, if one person takes the life of another, the state does not always call it murder. If the killing was done with malice aforethought by a sane individual, it will likely be termed "murder in the first degree." But if the killing occurred in the passion of a barroom brawl, it would more likely be called "second-degree murder," which carries a lesser penalty. Reckless driving on the highway that results in the death of another would correspondingly be considered "negligent homicide"—a wrong, to be sure, but not as serious in the eyes of the state as the intentional killing of another.

Sometimes the judge or jury's determination of the mens rea defines the crime itself. Suppose that Police Officer Nelson comes upon Wino Willie lying inside a television warehouse on a cold winter's night. An arrest is made, but what should be the charge and the crime for eventual conviction: burglary or simple criminal trespass? Burglary is defined as "entering a building without the consent of the owner with the intent to commit theft," whereas trespass means "to enter a building or habitation without the effective consent of the owner." Did Willie break into that warehouse to steal televisions or to keep warm while he drank? The determination of the mens rea will influence whether Willie's time away from society is several years or a few months.

An Injury or Result

Except for regulatory crimes in which a definition of the injury is abstract (for example, an illegal merger of two large airlines), a crime consists of a specific injury or a wrong perpetrated by one person against another. The crime may harm society at large, such as selling military secrets to a foreign government, or the injury may be inflicted upon an individual and, because of its nature, is considered to offend society as a whole. The nature of the injury, as with the mens rea, often determines the nature of the crime itself. For example, consider two hotheads who have been cutting each other off in traffic. Finally they both stop their cars and come out fighting. Suppose one of them hits the other so hard that he dies. The crime may be murder (of some degree). If the man does not die but suffers serious bodily harm, the crime is aggravated assault. If the injury is minor, the charge may be simple assault. Because the nature of the injury often determines the offense, it is frequently asserted that the nature of the injury is the key legal element of the crime.

Some actions may be criminal even though no injury is inflicted. Most instances of criminal conspiracy fall into this category. For instance, if several persons were to plan to assassinate a judge or to bribe jurors in an attempt to keep a criminal from being convicted, the crime would be conspiracy to obstruct justice. This would be a crime even if the judge went unharmed and no money was ever passed to the jurors. All that is required is that the crime be planned and intended and that some specific, overt act be taken by one of the conspirators in furtherance of their plan (such as the purchase of a weapon or possession of a map of the route that the judge takes from his home to the courtroom).

A Causal Relationship between the Action and the Resultant Injury

Before there can be a conviction for a criminal offense, the state must prove that the accused's conduct constituted the proximate cause of the injury or result. This means that the defendant, acting in a natural and continuous sequence, produced the harmful situation. In other words, without the defendant's conduct, there clearly would have been no harm or injury. Proving a causal relationship is usually not difficult. If A stabs B with a knife and inflicts a minor wound, then A is guilty of assault with a deadly weapon. But what if B does not obtain proper medical care for the wound, develops an infection, and subsequently dies? Is A now guilty of manslaughter or murder? Or what if after being stabbed, B stumbles across a third party and causes injury to her? Is A to blame for this, too?

Resolution of questions such as these is often difficult for judges and juries. The law requires that all circumstances be taken into account. The accused can be convicted only if the state can prove that his or her conduct is the direct, immediate, or determining cause of the resultant harm to the victim. If other circumstances have come into play, the question becomes: Was the injury inflicted by the defendant sufficient to cause the result, had the intervening factor(s) not occurred? Only if the harmful consequences were beyond the control of the accused or were not a natural or probable consequence of his or her actions is the defendant free from criminal liability.

Procedures prior to a Criminal Trial

Before a criminal trial can be held, federal and state laws require a whole series of procedures and events. Some of these stages are mandated by the U.S. Constitution and state constitutions, some by court decisions, and others by legislative enactments. Custom and tradition often account for the rest. Although the exact nature of these procedural events varies from federal to state practice—and from one state to another—some basic similarities exist throughout the country. The focus here will be on the common patterns, but whenever possible, differences will be indicated. Furthermore, note that several procedures are not as automatic or routine as they might appear. The decision makers exercise at all stages ample discretion according to their values, attitudes, and views of the world.

The Arrest

About 900,000 law enforcement officers are at work in the United States today (not counting some 1.5 million private security guards). That is about one for every other person in jail and prison. Each year these officers make more than 14 million arrests (not counting traffic offenses).[14] Arrest is significant because it represents the first substantial contact between the state and the accused. The U.S. legal system provides for two basic types of arrest—those with a **warrant** and those without. A warrant is issued after a complaint, filed by one person against another, has been presented and reviewed by a magistrate who has found probable cause for the arrest. Arrests without a warrant occur when a crime is committed in the presence of a police officer or when an officer has probable cause to believe that someone has committed (or is about to commit) a crime. Such a belief must later be established in a sworn statement or testimony. In the United States up to 95 percent of all arrests are made without a warrant.

An officer's decision to make an arrest is far from simple or automatic. To be sure, the officer who witnesses a murder will make an arrest on the spot if possible. But most lawbreaking incidents are not that simple or clear-cut, and police officials possess—and exercise—wide discretion about whether to take someone into custody. Sufficient resources are simply not available to the police for them to proceed against all activities that Congress and the legislatures have forbidden. Consequently, discretion must be exercised in determining how to allocate the time and resources that do exist. To deny police discretion at the point of arrest, said political scientist Thurman Arnold, would be "like directing a general to attack the enemy on all fronts at once."

Criminal justice scholars have identified several areas in which police discretion is at a maximum: (1) minor or trivial offenses; (2) situations in which the victim will not seek prosecution; (3) cases in which the victim is also involved in misconduct; and (4) criminal conduct thought to reflect the mores of a community subgroup.

Trivial Offenses. Many police manuals advise officers that when minor violations of the law are concerned, a warning is a more appropriate response than a formal arrest. This not only makes common sense for borderline, trivial offenses but also reserves law enforcement resources for more serious conduct. Traffic violations, misconduct by juveniles, drunkenness, gambling, vagrancy, and use of the services of a prostitute all constitute less serious crimes and entail many close judgment calls by police.

The use of a warning instead of making an arrest or issuing a ticket is common for minor traffic violations. The officer's discretion in such situations is so well known to the motoring public that an errant driver's plea has almost become a cliché: "Couldn't you just give me a warning this time, officer?" The following interview with Adrian Speir, former state director of the Texas Department of Public Safety, is instructive about discretion vis-à-vis traffic violations and the allocation of police resources in general:

"We just don't have enough manpower to have as much law enforcement as it takes to bring about voluntary compliance [with the speed limit laws] on a statewide level," Speir said. "On a typical day, 578 highway patrol units are on duty, or an average of one for every 122 miles. Troopers have other things to do besides clock speeders—chase drunk drivers, appear in court, enforce criminal laws, answer accident calls, and the like. So, choices must be made, limits drawn," says Speir.

"Our people are instructed to enforce the law and to file a case in speeding when they are convinced there is a substantial violation of the law," he said. What is a "substantial violation"? "We mean a degree that would get a person above the arguments of nominal speedometer error, tire slippage, human error in reading the radar. We do not encourage our people to be too technical. We are trying to get above the argumentative stage," he said. So when do you pass the argumentative stage?

"I am not going to tell you that they have got a three-mile . . . tolerance or a five-mile tolerance. If I . . . [did], then people out in the state could drive that much above the limit," Speir said. He added that other factors might enter into a trooper's decision whether to write a speeding ticket, such as whether a driver was weaving in and out of traffic or using a car with defective equipment. Then, he said, "some counties are stricter about prosecution than others. If the county attorney feels five or six miles over the limit is not substantial, then that would indicate he would be batting his head against a brick wall if he filed cases under that limit." [15]

Another illustration of police discretion in the minor crime realm deals with gambling offenses. Although someone conducting a big-time, syndicated gambling operation might be arrested, the friendly little neighborhood poker game is often ignored by police officials. The former head of the Houston vice squad once told a group of prospective grand jurors that "if respectable groups are engaged in gambling, such as church groups, only a warning is issued—and even then only after a complaint had been received. . . . If Sister Rosita is running a church bingo game, I'm sure not going to arrest her. I just wasn't raised that way."

Whether to arrest the john who procures the intimate favors of a prostitute is also subject to police discretion, and officers are frequently under pressure to turn a blind eye. Houston's former vice squad head says, "It is not the policy of the police department to enforce the law which makes it illegal for a man to be in the company of a prostitute. Why, the man might be someone with a family or a bank president! Also, we have a lot of big conventions here in town, and when the men come here . . . they like to have a little fun. If you start arresting these people, they wouldn't hold their conventions here any more, and then we'd have the mayor and all the restaurant and hotel owners on our backs." (Tourism and conventions in Houston bring in $850 million annually and employ seventy-seven thousand people.) [16]

Finally, evidence exists that the demeanor of the accused may influence the decision of the officer. The following quotation from an interview between one of the coauthors of this book and an anonymous police officer is insightful, and its portrayal of reality is supported by much empirical evidence:

Q: In these minor sorts of cases how do you determine whether to make an arrest?

A: Well, lots of times it depends on whether the guy's got an attitude problem.

Q: A what?

A: An attitude problem. I mean if he's a smart ass and starts arguing with you and gets real lippy, we'll probably take him in. But if he's decent and admits he's wrong, we'll probably let him go. I mean, nobody enjoys filling out forms for hours on end that you got to do after you make an arrest.

Victim Will Not Seek Prosecution. Nonenforcement of the law is also the rule in situations where the victim of a crime will not expend his or her own time to help the state in the successful prosecution of a case. A crime victim may not cooperate with the police in making an arrest for a variety of reasons. In the instance of minor property crimes, the victim is often interested only in restitution; if that occurs, the victim may be satisfied. For example, when people are caught shoplifting, merchants frequently are unwilling to prosecute, asserting that they cannot afford the time away from the store to testify in court or they do not want to risk a loss of goodwill. Unless the police have already expended considerable resources in investigating a particular property crime, they are generally obliged to abide by the victim's wishes.

When the victim of a crime is in an ongoing relationship with the criminal, the police often decline to make an arrest. Such relationships include landlord and tenant, two neighbors (did X have a right to chop down Y's tree because its leaves continued to fall on X's yard?), and, until recently, husband and wife. In the latter case, however, heightened media coverage of domestic violence has had a significant impact on police procedures. An increasing number of studies by criminologists have indicated that arrests in domestic violence cases were effective in protecting the victim.[17] These and similar studies contributed to the passage of mandatory arrest laws now in effect in about a third of the states.[18]

Rape and child molestation constitute another major category of crimes for which there are often no arrests because the victims will not or cannot cooperate with the police. The victim is often personally acquainted with, or related to, the criminal, and the fear of reprisals or of ugly publicity is sufficient to inhibit pressing a complaint. For instance, less than half of all rapes and considerably less than half of all cases of child molestation are ever reported to the police. And in many cases that are reported, victims (or their parents) have second thoughts about prosecution, and the charges are subsequently dropped.

Victim Also Involved in Misconduct. When police officers perceive that the victim of a crime is also involved in some type of improper or questionable conduct, the officers frequently opt not to make an arrest. Suppose Mr. Macho engages and pays for the services of a lady of the evening, but she fails to show up at the appointed place. Mr. Macho knows his rights and complains to the local officer on the beat. In such circumstances the officer may possibly detain the prostitute long enough to obtain a return of the victim's money, or he may merely tease the complainant and suggest that he has learned his lesson. An arrest is unlikely to be made in any situation where the victim does not have clean hands, and officers know that, even if they do make an arrest, such cases are usually dropped by the prosecution.

Criminal Conduct Thought to Reflect the Mores of a Community Subgroup. A final area of maximum police discretion in making an arrest deals with lawbreaking that officers ignore because they regard it as normal and acceptable for members of racial minorities or the lower social classes. Studies have shown that police officers, usually white and from middle-class backgrounds, tend to regard the street violence, petty property crimes, and family altercations in minority and poor areas as just "normal for those kinds of people." However, such behavior in middle- and upper-middle-class neighborhoods is not seen as natural or acceptable, and officers are more likely to make an arrest.

For example, if Officer Jones is summoned to a million-dollar condominium on Chicago's exclusive Lake Shore Drive upon learning that a man has stabbed his socialite wife, he will likely make an arrest for assault with a deadly weapon. After all, people like that simply should not behave in such a fashion, and if they do, an arrest is in order. However, if Officer Jones had been called to a ghetto neighborhood across town for an identical incident, his diary of events would more likely read as follows: "Called to scene of family disturbance in minority area. Woman hurt. Took her to the emergency ward to get her sewed up. Everything quiet. No arrest."

A vivid real-life illustration of this phenomenon is contained in an excerpt from a computer transcript provided by the Los Angeles Police Department. A message transmitted from an officer's patrol car concerned a domestic dispute in a black household. One officer said it was "right out of 'Gorillas in the Mist.'" "Ha, ha, ha, ha," responded the unidentified correspondent, "let me guess who be the parties." [19] One suspects that the officers' account of this domestic dispute would have had a vastly different tone had the incident occurred in an upper-class, nonminority neighborhood. In sum, the decision to make an arrest when a crime has been committed is not always simple and automatic for the police officer. Although no one would seriously doubt that officers must be given leeway to exercise their common sense and good judgment in close-call situations, discretion clearly may be arbitrary and subject to abuse. At the very least, the decision making of police officers, to a substantial degree, is the product of their own attitudes and values, community pressures, the attitude of the accused, and organizational constraints—which is true as well for prosecutors, judges, and other court personnel.

Appearance before a Magistrate

After a suspect is arrested for a crime, he or she is booked at the police station, that is, the facts surrounding the arrest are recorded and the accused may be fingerprinted and photographed. The next major step is for the accused to appear before a lower-level judicial official whose title may be judge, magistrate, or commissioner. Such an appearance is supposed to occur "without unnecessary delay." Although the meaning of this phrase varies from state to state, the maximum delay permitted by law has traditionally been twenty-four hours. However, in 1991 the more conservative U.S. Supreme Court ruled, 5–4, that police may now detain an individual arrested without a warrant for up to forty-eight hours without a court hearing on whether the arrest was justified.[20]

This court appearance is the occasion of several important events in the criminal justice process. First, the accused must be informed of the precise charges and must be informed of all constitutional rights and guarantees. Among these rights is the now famous *Miranda v. Arizona* decision of the Warren Court handed down in 1966. The accused "must be warned prior to any questioning that he has the right to remain silent, that anything he says can be used against him in a court of law, that he has the right to the presence of an attorney, and that if he cannot afford an attorney one will be appointed for him prior to any questioning." [21] (Such warnings must also be given by the arresting officer if the officer questions the suspect about the crime.)[22] In some states the accused must be informed about other rights that are provided for in the state's Bill of Rights, such as the right to a speedy trial and the right to confront hostile witnesses.

In the aftermath of the September 11, 2001, terrorist attacks on America, part of the process described above does not always apply because those rights are not granted to U.S. citizens who are suspected terrorists. For example, Jose Padilla, a native New Yorker, has been held for months without being charged with a crime. (He is suspected of plotting a "dirty bomb" attack against his fellow Americans.) The U.S. government announced that Padilla has been declared an "enemy combatant," which means that he may be held indefinitely in a naval brig—without charges and without access to a lawyer. Lieutenant Colonel Rivers Johnson, a Pentagon spokesman, said Padilla "has not been charged with anything as of yet, and because he has not been charged, he has not been afforded the right to counsel. . . . Under the laws of war, the United States can detain him until the war ends. The legal authority to detain him exists whether or not he is charged with an offense." [23] At the same time, Yaser Hamdi, another American citizen, is currently being held without bail, criminal charges, access to attorneys, or the right to remain silent. These two men may soon have company. "Attorney General Ashcroft and the White House are considering creating military detention camps for all U.S. citizens deemed by the administration to be enemy combatants." [24] Many civil libertarians have challenged the government's position in this regard, but so far the Supreme Court has turned a deaf ear to these objections.[25]

Second, the magistrate will determine whether the accused is to be released on bail and, if so, will set the amount of bail. The only constitutional requirement for the amount is that it should not be "excessive." If the magistrate believes that the accused will appear for any future trial proceedings, no bail may be required and the accused may be released on his own recognizance. Bail is considered a privilege—not a right—and it may be denied altogether in capital punishment cases that indicate strong evidence of guilt, or if the magistrate believes that the accused will flee from prosecution no matter what the amount of bail.

The subject of bail has been riddled with controversy for a variety of reasons. It is often used as a form of preventive detention when a judge intentionally sets bail at a level that is impossible for the defendant to meet. A judge's decision to do this can be based on factors such as the defendant's prior criminal record, publicity the case may have generated, the recommendation of the prosecutor, and the defendant's previous conduct while out on bail. If a defendant cannot make bail (even $50 is prohibitive for those without means), he or she must remain in jail. This subjects legally innocent persons to punishment; it separates them from their family, friends, and jobs; it hinders their efforts to prepare for their defense in court; and it adds to the overcrowding that already bedevils most county jails. Each day in the United States some 500,000 persons are in jail awaiting trial, most of them unable to raise enough money to secure release on bail.[26]

An alternative to bail is to release the defendant on recognizance, basically on a pledge by the defendant to return to court on the appointed date for trial. Some jurisdictions have special programs designed to maximize the number of persons eligible for release on recognizance. Perhaps the best known and most often copied is the Manhattan Bail Project, which arranges for defendants to be interviewed by pretrial investigators according to a special point system that takes into consideration such factors as the defendant's prior record, ties to the local community, and employment.

In minor cases the accused may be asked to plead guilty or not guilty. If the plea is guilty, a sentence may be pronounced on the spot. If the defendant pleads not guilty, a trial date is scheduled. However, in the typical serious (felony) case the next primary duty of the magistrate is to determine whether the defendant requires a preliminary hearing. If such a hearing is appropriate, the matter is adjourned by the prosecution and a subsequent stage of the criminal justice process begins.

The Grand Jury Process or the Preliminary Hearing

At the federal level all persons accused of a crime are guaranteed by the Fifth Amendment to have their cases considered by a grand jury. However, the Supreme Court has refused to make this right binding on the states. Today only about half of the states use grand juries; in some states, they are used only for special types of cases. Those states that do not use grand juries employ a preliminary hearing or an examining trial. (A few states use both procedures.) Regardless of which method is used, the primary purpose of this stage in the criminal justice process is to determine whether there is probable cause for the accused to be subjected to a formal trial.

The Grand Jury. Grand juries consist of sixteen to twenty-three citizens, usually selected at random from the voter registration lists, who render decisions by a majority vote.[27] Their terms may last anywhere from one month to one year, and some may hear more than a thousand cases during their term. The prosecutor alone presents evidence to the grand jury. The accused and his or her attorney are not only absent from the proceedings but also usually have no idea which grand jury is hearing the case or when. If a majority believes probable cause exists, then an indictment, or true bill, is brought. Otherwise the result is a no bill.

Less than 5 percent of all grand jury decisions result in no bills, and contrary to popular belief, no bills do not necessarily serve as a measure of grand jury independence vis-à-vis the prosecutor. Often the district attorney will ask the grand jury to render a no bill for personal reasons. Here is a statement made by a prosecutor to a state grand jury on which one of the coauthors of this book served:

Now here's a case where I'd like a little help from you all. There's a guy that's been after me every day for the past month because he says his brother-in-law borrowed his TV and some money and won't give 'em back. He wants me to file theft charges, but I keep telling him we're not a bill collection agency. I told him I would take the case to the grand jury, and I'm sure hoping you'll vote a no bill, and as soon as you do, I'm going to get on the phone and tell that guy that those "bleeding hearts" on the grand jury [laughs] wouldn't bring an indictment. That would sure get me off the hook.

Historically, two arguments have been made in favor of grand juries. One is that grand juries serve as a check on a prosecutor who might be using the office to harass an innocent person for political or personal reasons. (Even though the innocent person might eventually be found not guilty at trial, the cost and embarrassment of being tried for a crime are clearly a significant form of harassment.) Ideally, an unbiased group of citizens would interpose themselves between an unethical prosecutor and the defendant.

A second justification for grand juries is to make sure that the D.A. has done some homework and has secured enough evidence to warrant the trouble and expense—for both the state and the accused—of a full-fledged trial. Sometimes in the haste and tedious routine of the criminal justice process, persons are brought to trial when insufficient evidence has been gathered to justify it. The following is a factual account of how a state grand jury served to prevent this from happening (albeit by accident):

We had one case where the prosecutor tells us that several witnesses claim they saw this guy driving a stolen vehicle. So we vote a true bill—no questions asked. Then later on in the day when we were eating our sandwiches during lunch, one lady [also on the grand jury] was leafing through the files just for something to do. She says to us: "Hey, you know that guy we indicted this morning for auto theft. He claims he was on National Guard duty at the time a thousand miles away."

Now we figured that that wasn't the sort of defense you'd lie about because it could be checked out so easily, so we called the D.A. back in. We asked him if he had called the guy's commanding officer on the WATS line to check out his story. The D.A. told us we weren't supposed to be trying this case and that there was probable cause because of the witnesses. But we made him call anyway, and sure enough there was a record that the guy was on guard duty the day the car was stolen. That day we did what a grand jury was supposed to be doing but, my God, it was only because that lady was bored with her baloney sandwich.

Substantial evidence is available that the prosecutor tends to dominate the grand jury process and that the jury's utility as a check on the motives and thoroughness of the district attorney is minimal.[28]

The Preliminary Hearing. In the majority of states that have abolished the grand jury system, a preliminary hearing is used to determine whether there is probable cause for the accused to be bound over for trial. At this hearing the prosecution presents its case, and the accused has the right to cross-examine witnesses and to produce favorable evidence. The defense usually elects not to fight at this stage of the criminal process; a preliminary hearing is waived by the defense in the vast majority of cases.

If the examining judge determines that there is probable cause for a trial or if the preliminary examination is waived, the prosecutor must file a **bill of information** with the court where the trial will be held. This serves to outline precisely the charges that will be adjudicated in the new legal setting. About two weeks are usually allowed for the process.

The Arraignment

Arraignment is the process in which the defendant is brought before the judge in the court where he or she is to be tried to respond to the grand jury indictment or the prosecutor's bill of information. The prosecutor or a clerk usually reads in open court the charges that have been brought against the accused. The defendant is informed that he or she has a constitutional right to be represented by an attorney and that one will be appointed without charge if necessary.

The defendant has several options about how to plead to the charges. The most common pleas are guilty and not guilty. But the accused may also plead not guilty by reason of insanity, former jeopardy (having been tried on the same charge at another time), or **nolo contendere** (no contest). Nolo contendere means, in effect, that the accused does not deny the facts of the case but claims that he or she has not committed any crime, or it may mean that the defendant does not understand the charges. The nolo contendere plea can be entered only with the consent of the judge (and sometimes the prosecutor as well). Such a plea has two advantages. It may help the accused save face vis-à-vis the public because he or she can later claim that technically no guilty verdict was reached even though a sentence or a fine may have been imposed. Also, the plea may spare the defendant from certain civil penalties that might follow a guilty plea (for example, a civil suit that might follow from conviction for fraud or embezzlement).

If the accused pleads not guilty, the judge will schedule a date for a trial. If the plea is guilty, the defendant may be sentenced on the spot or at a later date set by the judge. Before the court will accept a guilty plea, the judge must certify that the plea was made voluntarily and that the defendant was aware of the implications of the plea. A guilty plea is, to all intents and purposes, equivalent to a formal verdict of guilty.

The Possibility of a Plea Bargain

At both the state and federal levels at least 90 percent of all criminal cases never go to trial. That is because before the trial date a bargain has been struck between the prosecutor and the defendant's attorney concerning the official charges to be brought and the nature of the sentence that the state will recommend to the court. In effect, some form of leniency is promised in exchange for a guilty plea.

Under plea bargaining, the role of the judges in the criminal justice system is much smaller than is generally assumed. Most people believe that the courts operate under a pure adversary system in which the judge's role is to make a disinterested sentencing after hearing full arguments from both sides. But because plea bargaining virtually seals the fate of the defendant before trial, the role of the judge is simply to ensure that the proper legal and constitutional procedures have been followed.

Judicial scholars are not unanimous on why plea bargaining has become the norm instead of the exception, and some have argued that some form of plea bargaining has always existed. (That is, the state has always been more lenient to those who admit their guilt, are repentant, and cooperate with the government.) Nevertheless, evidence points out that the average felony trial is longer now than it was several decades ago and that defendants are now filing more pretrial pleas and postconviction motions than they did in the past. No doubt the changes stem at least in part from the Warren Court's many decisions favoring the rights of criminal defendants. But for whatever reasons the ever-increasing caseloads of the past several decades have made the judicial system more dependent on the quick and simple plea bargain. There are three (not mutually exclusive) basic types of such bargains.

Reduction of Charges. The most common form of agreement between a prosecutor and a defendant is a reduction of the charge to one less serious than that supported by the evidence. The defendant is thereby subject to a lower maximum sentence and is likely to receive a lighter sentence than would have been the case with a guilty verdict on the original charge. For example, a common plea bargain in many states for an individual accused of theft is to plead guilty to burglary with the intent to commit theft. This exposes the criminal to a substantially reduced range of sentence possibilities.

A second reason for a defendant to plead guilty to a reduced charge is to avoid a record of conviction for an offense that carries a social stigma. The "good family man" and "pillar of the church" caught in the act of "indecency with a child" might be willing to plead guilty to the reduced charge of disorderly conduct.

Another possibility is that the defendant may wish to avoid a felony record altogether. A college student who hopes to be a lawyer or a public school teacher might be eager to plead guilty to almost any misdemeanor offered by the prosecutor rather than face a felony charge and risk being excluded from the legal and teaching professions.

Deletion of Tangent Charges. A second form of plea bargain is the agreement of the district attorney to drop other charges pending against an individual. There are two variations on this theme. One is an agreement not to prosecute "vertically," that is, not to prosecute more serious charges filed against the individual. For example, it is common in many jurisdictions for individuals using credit cards illegally to be charged simultaneously with forgery and possession of a stolen credit card. A bargain may be made to drop the forgery indictment in exchange for a plea of guilty on the lesser charge. The second type of agreement is to dismiss "horizontal" charges, that is, to dismiss additional indictments for the same crime pending against the accused. It is not unusual for several counts of burglary to be dropped following a confession to one other burglary indictment. (For an indictment to be dropped, most jurisdictions require the prosecutor to file with the court a motion of **nolle prosequi**—"I refuse to prosecute"—but such motions are usually granted as a matter of course.)

Another variation of the type of plea bargaining concerned with dropping charges is the agreement in which a repeater clause is dropped from an indictment. At the federal level and in many states a person is considered a habitual criminal upon the third conviction for a violent felony anywhere in the United States. The mandatory sentence for the habitual criminal is life imprisonment. In state courts the habitual violent criminal charge is often dropped in exchange for a plea of guilty. For example, in Texas an individual convicted of theft as a habitual criminal must be sentenced to life imprisonment and will not be eligible for parole for at least twenty years. However, an individual who is offered the chance to plead guilty to "theft second offense" must be given a sentence of ten years in prison but will be eligible for parole after serving only one-third of that sentence. The difference between twenty years of working on the rock pile and three years and four months is a keen incentive for a "three-time loser" to admit to being a "two-time loser."

A final wrinkle of this type of plea bargaining is the agreement in which indictments in different courts are consolidated into one court so that the sentences may run concurrently. As indictments or preliminary hearing rulings are handed down in many jurisdictions, they are placed on a trial docket on a rotation system. (The first charge is placed on a docket of court 1, the second on court 2, and so on.) This means that a defendant charged with four counts of forgery and one charge of possession of a forged instrument might find himself or herself on the docket of five different courts. It is common practice in such multicourt districts to transfer all of a person's indictments to the first court listed. This gives the presiding judge the discretion of allowing all of the defendant's sentences to run concurrently. Although not often done, an individual who refuses to plead guilty to any charges may not have the other indictments transferred, creating the likelihood of stacked (consecutive) sentences.

A recent conspicuous example of a plea bargain that involved, among other things, the deletion of tangent charges occurred in the case of John Walker Lindh.

Lindh is an American citizen who spent five months as a Taliban soldier allegedly fighting against U.S. forces in Afghanistan. In a plea bargain that President George W. Bush himself took part in, Lindh agreed to serve twenty years in prison, and in turn prosecutors agreed to dismiss nine counts of the original indictment that accused Lindh of supporting the al Qaeda terrorist network and of conspiring to kill Americans. [29]

Sentence Bargaining. A third form of plea bargaining concerns a plea of guilty from the defendant in exchange for a prosecutor's agreement to ask the judge for a lighter sentence.[30] At first blush it might seem that this type of plea negotiation is a weak substitute for either the reduction-of-charge or the dropping-of-charge form. After all, under sentence bargaining the state can make only a nonbinding recommendation to the court regarding the sentence, whereas under the other two types the state's concessions are concrete and not subject to doubt.

The strength of the sentence negotiation, however, is based upon the realities of the limited resources of the judicial system. At the state level, at least, prosecutors are able to promise the defendant a fairly specific sentence with confidence that the judge will accept the recommendation. If the judge were not to do so, the prosecutor's credibility would quickly begin to wane, and many of the defendants who had been pleading guilty would begin to plead not guilty and take their chances in court. The result would be a gigantic increase in court dockets that would overwhelm the judicial system and bring it to a standstill. Prosecutors and judges understand this reality, and so do the defense attorneys.

Constitutional and Statutory Restrictions on Plea Bargaining. At both the state and federal levels, the requirements of due process of law dictate that plea bargains must be made voluntarily and with comprehension. This means that the defendant must be admonished by the court of the consequences of a guilty plea (for example, the defendant waives all opportunities to change his or her mind at a later date), that the accused must be sane, and that, as one typical state puts it, "It must plainly appear that the defendant is uninfluenced by any consideration of fear, or by any persuasion, or delusive hope of pardon, prompting him to confess his guilt." According to these requirements, the prosecutor's promise of a lighter sentence in exchange for a guilty plea seems to violate the letter, if not the spirit, of the Due Process Clause. Not so, the courts have ruled. As long as judges tell the defendants that, at least in principle, they are subject to any sentence that is pronounced and the accused acknowledge this, the requirement of due process has been met. Thus when a state court certifies that a guilty plea was "knowingly and understandingly made," a form of legal fiction has often been in the works.

For the first two types of plea bargains, some stricter standards govern the federal courts. One is that the judge may not participate in the process of plea bargaining; at the state level judges may play an active role in this process. Likewise, if a plea bargain has been made between the U.S. attorney and the defendant, the government may not renege on the agreement. If the federal government does so, the federal district judge must withdraw the guilty plea. Finally, the Federal Rules of Criminal Procedure require that "the court shall not enter a judgment upon a plea of guilty unless it is satisfied that there is a factual basis for the plea." This means that before a guilty plea may be accepted, the prosecution must present a summary of the evidence against the accused, and the judge must agree that there is strong evidence of the defendant's guilt.

Arguments For and Against Plea Bargaining. For the defendant the obvious advantage of the bargain is that he or she is treated less harshly than would be the case if convicted and sentenced under maximum conditions. Also, the absence of a trial often lessens publicity on the case, and because of personal interests or simple social pressures, the accused may wish to avoid the length and publicity of a formal trial. Finally, some penologists (professionals in the field of punishment and rehabilitation) argue that the first step toward rehabilitation is for a criminal to admit guilt and recognize his or her problem. The idea is that a guilty plea is at least nominally the first step toward a successful return to society.

Plea bargaining also offers some distinct advantages for the state and for society as a whole. The most obvious is the certainty of conviction, because no matter how strong the evidence may appear, an acquittal is always a possibility so long as a trial is pending. (Evidence may be stolen or lost; important witnesses may die or drop out of sight; the prosecutor may make a key error in court that results in a mistrial.) Also, the district attorney's office and judges are saved an enormous amount of time and effort by not having to prepare and preside over cases in which there is no real contention of innocence or that are not suited to the trial process. Finally, when police officers are not required to be in court testifying in criminal trials, they arguably have more time to devote to preventing and solving crimes.

In the case of John Walker Lindh, the government not only obtained the certainty of prison time in the plea deal but also derived other benefits. The plea bargain "relieves the government of a complicated criminal prosecution involving evidence from the battlefields of Afghanistan, testimony from intelligence officers and possibly even the appearance of Taliban and al Qaeda fighters brought from their prison at the U.S. Guantanamo Bay Naval Base in Cuba." [31]

Lest this all seem too good to be true, plea bargains do have a negative side. The most frequent objection to plea bargaining is that the defendant's sentence may be based on nonpenological grounds. With the large volume of cases making plea bargaining the rule, the sentence often bears no relation to the specific facts of the case, to the correctional needs of the criminal, or to society's legitimate interest in vigorous prosecution of the case. A second defect is that if plea bargaining becomes the norm of a particular system, undue pressure may be placed upon even innocent persons to plead guilty. Studies have shown that in some jurisdictions the less chance there is for conviction, the harder the bargaining may be, because the prosecutor wants to get at least some form of minimal confession out of the accused.

A third disadvantage of plea bargaining is the possibility of the abuse called **overcharging,** whereby the prosecutor brings charges against the accused that are more severe than the evidence warrants, with the hope that this will strengthen his or her hand in subsequent negotiations with the defense attorney. The coauthor of this book who served on a state grand jury had this exchange with a representative of the district attorney's office:

GRAND JUROR: In this case where one fellow killed another in that barroom fight, why do you want us to indict on a first-degree murder charge? There doesn't seem to be any premeditation here. You'll never get a conviction on that.

D.A.: Oh, I know. But it will strengthen our hand at the time when we talk with his attorney.

The grand jury in question chose to indict on a lesser and more appropriate charge.

Another flaw with the plea bargaining system is its very low level of visibility. This is the flip side of flexibility. Bargains between prosecutor and defense attorney are not made in open court presided over by a neutral jurist and for all to observe. Instead, they are more likely made over a cup of coffee in a basement courthouse cafeteria where the conscience of the two lawyers is the primary guide. When the defendant enters the guilty plea in open court and swears that no promise by the state has induced this plea, the prosecutor and defense counsel mutely corroborate the defendant's false statement. Meanwhile, the judge remains uninformed of the facts and is therefore unable to determine the fairness or validity of the agreement.

Finally, the system has the potential to circumvent key procedural and constitutional rules of evidence. Because the prosecutor need not present any evidence or witnesses in court, a bluff may result in a conviction, even though the case might not be able to pass muster with the Due Process Clause. The defense may be at a disadvantage because the rules of **discovery** (the laws that allow the defense to know in detail the evidence the prosecution will present) in some states limit the defense counsel's case preparation to the period after the plea bargain has occurred. Thus the plea bargain may deprive the accused of basic constitutional rights.

While the United States is unique in having the plea bargain serve as the norm at both state and federal levels, the procedure is not unknown in other countries. Germany, for example, uses a plea bargain between 20 to 30 percent of the time, but typically in cases where the penalty is a fine or no criminal sanction at all. It is rarely used in violent and other really serious cases. When it does occur, the state is still obliged to make an independent determination that the defendant is guilty. As one observer has noted: "Even if a bargain has been reached, and the defendant confesses during preliminary examination at the beginning of the trial, the prosecutor must be ready to offer such witnesses as the court deems necessary to support a finding of guilt. Thus, as Professor Joachim Herrmann observes, in Germany 'a confession does not replace a trial but rather causes a shorter trial.' This fact, plus section 153a of the German Code of Criminal Procedure, which allows the prosecutor to terminate the proceedings only when the defendant's guilt is 'minor,' keeps plea bargaining to a minimum in felony cases." [32]

The Adversarial Process as Contrasted with the Inquisitorial Method

The principles of the **adversarial process** as it exists in American criminal courts are largely true of civil trials as well. The adversarial model is based on the assumption that there are two sides to every case or controversy. In criminal cases the government claims a defendant is guilty while the defendant contends innocence; in civil cases the plaintiff asserts that the person he or she is suing has caused some injury while the respondent denies responsibility. In the courtroom each party vies against the other; each provides his or her side of the story as he or she sees it. The theory (or hope) underlying this model is that the truth will emerge if each party is given unbridled opportunity to present the full panoply of evidence, facts, and arguments before a neutral and attentive judge (and jury).

The lawyers representing each side are the major players in this courtroom drama. The judge acts more as a passive, disinterested referee whose primary role is to keep both sides within the accepted rules of legal procedure and courtroom decorum. The judge eventually determines which side has won in accordance with the rules of evidence, but only after both sides have had a full opportunity to fight it out.

While the adversarial process is the norm in the United States, it is not in most other countries, including almost all of the Western industrial democracies and Latin America. Most use a version of what legal scholars call the **inquisitorial method,** in which the judge (or judges) is the primary actor in the courtroom and the attorneys passively defend their clients' interests. Under this method the judge(s) actively and aggressively conducts an inquiry into the truth of the charges that the state or a plaintiff has lodged against a defendant. The French model is representative of that used in most countries employing the inquisitorial method. In a typical case, a panel of perhaps three judges would preside. These judges would be joined by several laypersons, ordinary citizens, who participate in overseeing the proceedings and help decide on innocence or guilt. But these ordinary citizens are not jurors in the American sense of the term. They merely sit with the professional judges on an elevated bench, and they all deliberate together. French courtrooms exhibit less drama because the lawyers for each side make many of their arguments in writing rather than orally, and so few verbal duels between the attorneys take place. Likewise, there are fewer skirmishes over evidence because virtually all evidence that the French judges deem relevant is allowed in. As the *Wall Street Journal* reported:

"There is much more of a bureaucratic climate—professionals doing their job[,]" [says George Bermann, a professor of international law at Columbia University]. The judges see their role as getting at the truth, rather than supervising an adversarial process, Prof. Bermann adds.

A critical difference is that the French criminal system—which is less civil-liberties oriented than the U.S. system—doesn't require proof beyond a reasonable doubt to convict a defendant. Instead, the French use a standard similar to that of the American civil system: Basically, the French judges—professional and lay—must be persuaded that guilt is more likely than innocence, a standard American lawyers call a "preponderance of the evidence."

Although French defendants begin with a presumption of innocence, "if the judges are convinced of guilt, that's it," says Prof. Bermann. The judicial panel's decision doesn't have to be unanimous, and individual judges' votes aren't generally made known. Verdicts with written opinions are issued on behalf of the court and don't reveal any dissent.[33]

Summary

We began this chapter with a discussion of the nature and substance of crime—at least as it is currently understood. We then reviewed the myriad procedures that constitute the judicial process at the federal and state levels. We analyzed the various aspects of crime that lead to an arrest, the subsequent appearance before a magistrate, and the activity of the grand jury or the preliminary hearing. We also observed how plea bargaining enormously tempers the criminal court process, and finally we outlined the key differences between the adversarial process used in the American courtroom and the inquisitorial methods that are the choice of most other nations. Throughout the chapter, we stressed that the backgrounds and attitudes of the criminal justice participants have as much to do with the nature and quality of justice as do the formal rules of the game.

Further Thought and Discussion Questions

1. Would the United States be better served to remove from the criminal statute books all laws that are not enforced, such as laws against small-time gambling and laws forbidding sexual activity between certain consenting adults? Does the refusal to enforce some laws while others are strictly enforced undermine respect for law in general?

2. The United States is on a par with Russia in having more persons per capita in prison than any other nation does. Is that a sign that the United States is a nation that enforces its laws, or is it an indication that something is inherently wrong with its criminal justice system?

3. Should America follow the example of many other countries when faced with terrorism or excessive domestic violence by simply suspending the constitutional rights of those accused of crimes? If so, who should make the decision to take this course of action, and how long should the suspension of rights be allowed to continue?

4. Should we abolish plea bargains entirely and instead have a full-blown trial for everyone accused of a crime? What if the defendant wanted to plead guilty and declined a trial? Should lower sentences be promised to defendants who acknowledge their guilt and cooperate with the police?

NOTES

1. Seth Mydans, "Pakistani Woman Faces Death for Being Raped, Keeping Child," *Houston Chronicle*, May 19, 2002, A28.

2. "Judge Upholds Cursing Law," *Houston Chronicle*, February 9, 1999, A5.

3. We wish to express our debt to Harold J. Vetter and Leonard Territo, from whom we borrowed this categorization. See Harold J. Vetter and Leonard Territo, *Crime and Justice in America* (St. Paul, Minn.: West, 1984), chap. 1.

4. These data were taken from the Web site of the U.S. Department of Justice, Bureau of Statistics, as downloaded June 25, 2003: http://www.ojp.usdoj.gov/bjs/cvict.htm.

5. Ibid.

6. Ibid. (These numbers are for 1999, the most recent year for which statistics were available.)

7. Ibid.

8. Keith B. Richburg, "French Face Rising Crime Reality," *Houston Chronicle*, September 1, 2001, A35.

9. Morgan O. Reynolds, "Europe Surpasses America—in Crime," *Wall Street Journal*, November 16, 1998, A14.

10. Vetter and Territo, *Crime and Justice in America*, 11.

11. *Whitney v. California*, 274 U.S. 357 (1927).

12. Ordinance unanimously declared invalid in *Patachristou v. City of Jacksonville*, 405 U.S. 156 (1972).

13. Quotation in David W. Neubauer, *America's Courts and the Criminal Justice System*, 2d ed. (Monterey, Calif.: Brooks/Cole, 1984), 64.

14. David W. Neubauer, *America's Courts and the Criminal Justice System*, 6th ed. (Belmont, Calif.: West/Wadsworth, 1999), 10, 12.

15. "Trying to Enforce Unpopular Law Is Plaguing the Highway Patrol," *Houston Chronicle*, September 25, 1977, 1:18.

16. News item, Houston, Texas, radio station KTRH, May 9, 2000, 8:50 a.m.

17. L. W. Sherman and R. A. Berk, "The Specific Deterrent Effects of Arrest for Domestic Assault," *American Sociological Review* 49 (1984): 261–272; and R. A. Berk and L. W. Sherman, "Police Responses to Domestic Violence Incidents: An Analysis of an Experimental Design with Incomplete Randomization," *Journal of the American Statistical Association* 83 (1988): 70–76.

18. For a more extensive discussion of this subject, see Gennaro F. Vito and Ronald M. Holmes, *Criminology* (Belmont, Calif.: Wadsworth, 1994), 83–85.

19. "Los Angeles Aftershocks," *Newsweek*, April 1, 1991, 18–19. (The exchange occurred the same night in March 1991 that a group of Los Angeles police officers beat up a black motorist, Rodney King. The incident was videotaped by a neighbor and was later shown extensively on national television.)

20. *County of Riverside v. McLaughlin*, 500 U.S. 44 (1991).

21. *Miranda v. Arizona*, 384 U.S. 436 (1966). This decision was undermined somewhat in 1991 when the U.S. Supreme Court ruled that under some circumstances confessions that are coerced from defendants by police can be used as evidence. *Arizona v. Fulminante*, 499 U.S. 279 (1991).

22. Two years after *Miranda* was decided, Congress attempted to subvert its effect by enacting 18 U.S.C., Sec. 3501, which in essence laid down a rule that the admissibility of a custodial suspect's statement should turn only on whether it was made voluntarily. This law was overturned by the Supreme Court in 2000 in the case of *Dickerson v. United States*, 530 U.S. 428 (2000). The Court said, in effect. that since *Miranda* was a constitutional decision of the Court, it could not be overturned by an act of Congress, and then the Court went on to reiterate its support of the essence of the 1966 ruling.

23. Patty Reinert, "Terror Suspect Can Be Held Long Term Without Charges," *Houston Chronicle*, June 11, 2002, A4.

24. Anita Ramasastry, "Do Hamdi and Padilla Need Company?" *Find Law's Legal Commentary*, as downloaded June 25, 2003: http://writ.news.findlaw.com/ramasastry/20020821.html.

25. For example, on April 29, 2003, the Supreme Court, in a 5–4 ruling, held that the "government may jail [without bail] legal immigrants who may have committed serious crimes to ensure they do not flee or commit new crimes while awaiting deportation hearings" (*Demore v. Kim*, 01-1491, 2003).

26. Neubauer, *America's Courts and the Criminal Justice System*, 13.

27. There are variations of this, however. In Texas, for example, grand juries consist of twelve persons chosen because they are friends or neighbors of judge-appointed jury commissioners. A vote of nine members is required for a decision.

28. See Robert A. Carp, "The Behavior of Grand Juries: Acquiescence or Justice?" *Social Science Quarterly* 55 (1975): 853–870. For some more current discussions of whether the grand jury is worth keeping and what steps might be taken to improve its work, see *Judicature* 81 (1998): 190–200.

29. Jess Bravin, "Lindh Agrees to Serve 20 Years in Plea Deal Backed by Bush," *Wall Street Journal*, July 16, 2002, A4.

30. Bargains on the sentence are primarily conducted at the state, not the federal, level because federal sentences are largely made within the bailiwick of the judge, with advice from the probation officer—with both acting under congressional sentencing guidelines that took effect November 1, 1987.

31. Bravin, "Lindh Agrees to Serve 20 Years In Plea Deal Backed by Bush."

32. Craig M. Bradley, "Reforming the Criminal Trial," in *Courts and Justice: A Reader*, 2d ed., ed. C. Larry Mays and Peter R. Gregware (Prospect Heights, Ill.: Waveland Press, 2000), 506–507.

33. Thomas Kamm and Paul M. Barrett, "How Would Paparazzi Who Stalked Diana Fare in French Court?" *Wall Street Journal*, September 2, 1997, A1.

SUGGESTED READINGS

Cole, George F. *The American System of Criminal Justice*, 7th ed. Belmont, Calif.: Wadsworth, 1995. A reader containing articles by America's top experts on topics such as police behavior and defense attorneys.

Messner, Steven F., and Richard Rosenfeld. *Crime and the American Dream*, 3d ed. Belmont, Calif.: Wadsworth, 2001. A short but well-written text that expands on the causes and social consequences of crime as outlined in this chapter.

Neubauer, David W. *America's Courts and the Criminal Justice System*, 6th ed. Belmont, Calif.: West/Wadsworth, 1999. A classic political science textbook on all the major stages present in the criminal justice process.

Reichel, Philip L. *Comparative Criminal Systems: A Topical Approach*, 3d ed. Upper Saddle River, N.J.: Prentice Hall, 2001. An excellent text that compares and contrasts pretrial criminal procedures in the United States and a number of other countries.

Walker, Samuel. *Sense and Nonsense about Crime and Drugs*, 5th ed. Belmont, Calif.: Wadsworth, 2000. A discussion of the pros and cons of both liberal and conservative approaches to preventing and punishing criminal behavior.

CHAPTER 10

The Criminal Trial and Its Aftermath

The right to an attorney is one of the most important rights guaranteed to the criminal defendant in the United States. Here, sniper suspect John Allen Muhammad delivers his opening arguments. In the initial phase of his trial, Mr. Muhammad waived his right to counsel and decided to represent himself. Soon, however, he rethought his decision, realizing that an untutored defendant without an attorney stood little chance of successfully navigating the legal complexities of the modern-day criminal trial.

THE PREVIOUS CHAPTER OUTLINED THE steps that lead up to a criminal trial in the United States, and this chapter focuses on the trial itself. We examine the rights of criminal defendants at trial, the process of selecting a jury, the role of the judge and the jury during the trial, the sentencing of criminal defendants, and lastly the possibility of an appeal. We also provide a discussion of the reasons given by penologists for punishing the convicted felon.

Procedures during a Criminal Trial

Assuming that no plea bargain has been struck and that the accused maintains his or her innocence, a formal trial will take place. This is a right that the Sixth Amendment guarantees to all Americans charged with federal crimes and a right guaranteed by the various state constitutions—and by the Fourteenth Amendment—to all persons charged with state offenses. The accused has many constitutional and statutory rights during the trial. The following are the primary rights that are binding on both the federal and state courts.

Basic Rights Guaranteed during the Trial Process

The Sixth Amendment says, "In all criminal prosecutions, the accused shall enjoy the right to a speedy and public trial." The Founders emphasized the word *speedy,* so that an accused would not languish in prison for a long time prior to the trial or have to wait an unduly long time before his or her fate is determined. But how soon is speedy? Although the Supreme Court has defined this word in various ways, Congress gave new meaning to the term when it passed the Speedy Trial Act of 1974.[1] The act mandated time limits, ultimately reaching one hundred days, within which criminal charges must be either brought to trial or dismissed. Most states have similar measures on the statute books, although the precise time period varies from one jurisdiction to another. By "public trial" the Founders meant to discourage the notion of secret proceedings whereby an accused could be tried without public knowledge and whisked off to some unknown detention camp—a state of affairs typical of totalitarian regimes today.

The Sixth Amendment also guarantees the right to an impartial jury. At the least this has meant that prospective jurors must not be prejudiced in any way before the trial begins. For example, a potential juror may not be a friend or relative of the prosecutor or the crime victim, nor may a person serve who believes that anyone of the defendant's race or ethnic ancestry is "probably the criminal type." What the concept of an impartial jury of one's peers has come to mean in practice is that jurors are to be selected randomly from voter registration lists—supplemented in an increasing number of jurisdictions by lists based on automobile registrations, driver's licenses, telephone books, welfare rolls, and so on.[2] Although this does not provide a perfect cross section of the community because not all persons are registered to vote, the Supreme Court has said that this method is good enough. The high court has also ruled that no class of persons (such as blacks or women) may be systematically excluded from jury service. This does not mean that a black defendant, for example, has a right to have other persons of the same racial background on a jury; it means only that no racial category may be intentionally kept from jury service.

Besides being guaranteed the right to be tried in the same locale where the crime was committed and to be informed of the charges, Americans have the right to be confronted with the witnesses against them. They have the right to know who their accusers are and what they are charging so that a proper defense may be formulated. The accused is also guaranteed the opportunity "to have the Assistance of Counsel for his defence." Prior to the 1960s, this meant that one had this right (at the state level) only for serious crimes and only if one could pay for an attorney. However, because of a series of Supreme Court decisions, the law of the land guarantees the accused an attorney if tried for any crime that may result in a prison term, and the government must pick up the tab for the legal defense for an indigent defendant. This is the rule at both the national and state levels.

With defense attorneys, as with many things in life, you usually get what you pay for. If money is no object, you can afford to hire an experienced and highly competent defense lawyer who will be a superb advocate on your behalf. This does not automatically mean that you will be acquitted if you are guilty, but it may mean that you will obtain a more advantageous plea bargain or a lighter sentence if convicted. If you are not wealthy or have no means at all, you may be forced to rely on the services of a public defender appointed on your behalf by the state. Most public defenders are relatively young and inexperienced, and although some have a reputation for putting on a vigorous defense (such as those in Cook County [Chicago], Illinois), most are not or will never be within the top ranks of the legal profession. [3]

Defense attorneys, whether paid by the defendant or the state, are often the subject of considerable criticism. They are accused of giving too little time and effort to their clients' cases because of the limited resources of most public defenders' offices and because private attorneys find it financially advantageous to turn over cases as rapidly as possible. Also, in many jurisdictions a public defender is given a fixed amount per case regardless of how much time a case requires. This may encourage a public defender to pressure a client to plead guilty so that his or her case will take less time. At the federal level the refusal of Congress to provide adequate funding for attorneys of indigent defendants has drawn the attention of the sitting chief justice of the United States, William H. Rehnquist. In 1999 he stated publicly that the lack of sufficient funds is "seriously hampering the ability of judges to recruit attorneys to provide effective representation." [4]

The Fifth Amendment to the U.S. Constitution declares that no person shall "be subject for the same offence to be twice put in jeopardy of life and limb." This is the famous Double Jeopardy Clause, which means in effect that no one may be tried twice for the same crime by any state government or by the federal government. It does not mean, however, that a person may not be tried twice for the same action if that action has violated both national and state laws. For example, someone who robs a federally chartered bank in New Jersey runs afoul of both federal and state laws. That person could legally be tried and acquitted for the offense in a New

Jersey court and subsequently be tried for that same action in federal court. Again, this clause means that the same level of government may not try a person twice for the same crime.

Another important right guaranteed to the accused at both the state and federal levels is not to "be compelled in any criminal case to be a witness against himself." This has been interpreted to mean that if the accused elects not to testify on his or her own behalf in court, this may not be used against the person by judge and jury. This guarantee serves to reinforce the principle that under the U.S. judicial system the burden of proof is on the state; the accused is presumed innocent until the government proves otherwise beyond a reasonable doubt.

Finally, the Supreme Court has interpreted the guarantee of due process of law to mean that evidence procured in an illegal search and seizure may not be used against the accused at trial. The source of this so-called exclusionary rule is the Fourth Amendment to the U.S. Constitution; the Supreme Court has made its strictures binding on the states as well. The Court's purpose was to eliminate any incentive the police might have to illegally obtain evidence against the accused. Many have argued that this right does not discourage improper police behavior and that it serves only as a technical loophole to free the guilty. Thus the more conservative Burger and Rehnquist Courts have taken steps to narrow the effect of the exclusionary rule. Civil libertarians have countered that this rule is a key element in the basic concepts of due process and fair play.

Selection of Jurors

If the accused elects not to have a bench trial—that is, not to be tried and sentenced by a judge alone—his or her fate will be determined by a jury. At the federal level twelve persons must render a unanimous verdict. At the state level such criteria apply only to the most serious offenses. In many states a jury may consist of fewer than twelve persons and render verdicts by other than unanimous decisions. (Acceptable votes might be eleven to one, ten to two, or five to one.)

A group of veniremen (sometimes known as an array) is summoned from a panel of potential jurors to appear in a given courtroom.[5] The veniremen are then questioned in open court about their general qualifications for jury service in a process known as **voir dire.** The prosecutor and the defense attorney ask general and specific questions of the potential jurors. Are they citizens of the state? Can they comprehend the English language? Have they or anyone in their family ever been tried for a criminal offense? Have they read about or formed any opinions about the case at hand?

In conducting the voir dire, the state and the defense have two general types of goals. The first is to eliminate all members of the panel who might have an obvious reason for not rendering an impartial decision in the case. Common examples might be someone who is excluded by law from serving on a jury (such as a person who is currently under indictment for a criminal offense); someone who is a friend or relative of a participant in the trial; and someone who openly admits a strong bias in the case. Objections to jurors in this category are known as challenges for cause, and the number of such challenges is unlimited. The judge determines whether these challenges are valid.

The second goal of the opposing attorneys in questioning the array of potential jurors is to eliminate those who they believe would be unfavorable to their side even though no overt reason for bias is apparent. This can be done because each side is given a number of **peremptory challenges**—requests to the court to exclude a prospective juror with no reason given. Most states customarily give the defense more peremptory challenges than the prosecution is given. At the federal level one to three challenges per juror are usually permitted each side, depending on the nature of the offense; as many as twenty are allowed in capital cases. The use of peremptory challenges is more of an art than a science and is usually based on the hunch of the attorneys. For example, in a case where a poor person stole groceries from a supermarket, a prosecutor might use available challenges to exclude jurors of low economic status, on the premise that they might be more sympathetic to the accused. Or in a case involving a sexual offender, a defense attorney might try to eliminate jurors who belong to fundamentalist religions, thinking that they would take a more judgmental stance in such matters than those with more broad-minded religious convictions.

In the past, attorneys were able to exclude potential jurors by using the peremptory challenge for virtually any reason whatsoever. However, in recent years the Supreme Court has interpreted the Fourteenth Amendment's Equal Protection Clause to restrict this unbridled discretion. In 1986 the high court ruled in the case of *Batson v. Kentucky* that prosecutors may not use their challenges to exclude blacks from serving on a criminal jury.[6] Out of this case came the *Batson* rule, which bars the discriminatory use of peremptory challenges. In 1994 the Court extended the rule to prohibit the exclusion of women.[7] Since then some courts have expanded the *Batson* rule to include other groups, for example, ethnic groups such as Italian-Americans and Jews and even barring exclusions based on sexual orientation.[8]

The process of questioning and challenging prospective jurors continues until all those duly challenged for cause are eliminated, the peremptory challenges are either used up or waived, and a jury of twelve (six in some states) has been created. In some states alternate jurors are also chosen. They attend the trial but participate in deliberations only if one of the original jurors is unable to continue in the proceedings. Once the panel has been selected, the jurors are sworn in by the judge or the clerk of the court.

In countries that use the inquisitorial method, if lay persons are used, their role is subordinate to that of the judges, and they are selected in a cursory process. In Brazil, for instance, jury selection in a typical case takes about ten minutes. A group of twenty-one potential jurors files into the courtroom. The judge spins a black device resembling a bingo mixer and pulls out seven names one by one, reading each name aloud. If no one objects, the chosen jurors climb into the jury box. "If there are objections, the judge looks stern, often overrules them and the trial . . . gets under way." [9]

Opening Statements

After the formal trial begins, both the prosecution and the defense make an opening statement (although in no state is the defense compelled to do so). Long and detailed statements are more likely to be made in jury trials than in bench trials. The purpose of opening statements is to provide members of the jury—who lack familiarity with the law and with procedures of criminal investigation—with an outline of the major objectives of each side's case, the evidence to be presented, the witnesses to be called, and what each side seeks to prove from the evidence of the witnesses. If the opening statements are well presented, the jurors will find it easier to grasp the meaning and significance of the evidence and testimony, and ideally they will be less likely to get confused and bogged down in the complexities and technicalities of the case. The usual procedure is for the state to make its opening statement first and for the defense to follow with a statement about how it will refute that case.

The Prosecution's Case

After the opening statements, the prosecutor presents the evidence amassed by the state against the accused. Evidence is generally of two types—physical evidence and the testimony of witnesses. The physical evidence may include such things as bullets, ballistics tests, fingerprints, handwriting samples, blood and urine tests, and other documents or items that serve as physical aids. The defense may object to the admission of any of these tangible items and, if successful, will have the item excluded from consideration. If unsuccessful, the physical evidence is labeled by one of the courtroom personnel and becomes part of the official record.

Most evidence at criminal trials takes the form of testimony of witnesses. The format is a question-and-answer procedure that may appear a bit stilted, but its purpose is to elicit specific information in an orderly fashion. The goal is to present only evidence that is relevant to the case at hand and not to give confusing or irrelevant information or illegal evidence that might result in a mistrial (for example, evidence that the accused had a prior conviction for an identical offense). The following hypothetical question and answer between a district attorney and a police officer is typical:

D.A.: Please state your name and occupation.

OFFICER: My name is Justen Muchow. I am employed as a police officer by the city of Elgin, Illinois.

D.A.: Did you have reason to be at or near the corner of Dundee Avenue and North Liberty Street about seven o'clock on the evening of March 5?

OFFICER: Yes, I was summoned to a liquor store near that address after a witness phoned the department and said she saw someone breaking into the building.

D.A.: What did you observe after you arrived on the scene?

OFFICER: I observed a white male with what appeared to be a crate of liquor under his arm.

D.A.: What was he doing at the time?

OFFICER: He was running away from the building.

D.A.: What did you do at that time?

OFFICER: I subdued the man and placed him under arrest.

D.A.: Is the person whom you saw running from the building and arrested sitting in this courtroom today?

OFFICER: Yes, sir.

D.A.: Would you point out that man?

OFFICER: He is sitting to the left of the defense attorney.

D.A.: Your Honor, may the record show that the officer pointed to the defendant in this case?

After each witness, the defense attorney has the right to cross-examine. The goal of the defense will be to impeach the testimony of the prosecution witness, that is, to discredit it. The attorney may attempt to confuse, fluster, or anger the witness, causing him or her to lose self-control and begin providing confusing or conflicting testimony. The testimony of the witness for the prosecution may also be impeached if defense witnesses who contradict the version of events suggested by the state are subsequently presented. Upon completion of the **cross-examination,** the prosecutor may conduct a redirect examination, which serves to clarify or correct some telling point made during the cross-examination. After the state has presented all its evidence and witnesses, it rests its case.

The Case for the Defense

The presentation of the case for the defense is similar in style and format to that of the prosecution. Tangible evidence is less common in the defense's case, and most of the evidence will be that of witnesses who are prepared to rebut or contradict the prosecution's arguments. The witnesses are questioned by the defense attorney in the same style as those in the prosecution case. Each defense witness may in turn be cross-examined by the district attorney, and then a redirect examination is in order.

The real difference between the case for the prosecution and the case for the defense lies in their obligation before the law. The defense is not required by law to present any new or additional evidence or any witnesses at all. The defense may consist merely of challenging the credibility or the legality of the state's evidence and witnesses. The defense is not obligated to prove the innocence of the accused; it need show only that the state's case is not beyond a reasonable doubt. The defendant need not even take the stand. (However, if he or she elects to do so, the accused faces the same risks of cross-examination as any other witness.)

After the defense has rested its case, the prosecution has the right to go back on the attack and present rebuttal evidence. In turn, the defense may offer a rejoinder known as a surrebuttal. After that, each side is ready for the closing arguments. This is often one of the more dramatic episodes in the trial because each side seeks to sum up its case, condense its strongest arguments, and make one last appeal to the jury. New evidence may not be presented at this stage, and the arguments of both sides tend to ring with emotion and appeals to values that transcend the immediate case. The prosecutor may talk about the crime problem in general, about the need for law and order, and about the need not to let compassion for the accused get in the way of empathy for the crime victim. The defense attorney may remind the jurors "how we have all made mistakes in this life" or argue that in a free, democratic society any doubt they have should be resolved in favor of the accused. The prosecution probably avoids emotionalism more than the defense attorney does, however, because many jury verdicts have been reversed on appeal after the district attorney injected prejudicial statements into the closing statements.

Role of the Judge during the Trial

The judge's role in the trial, although important, is a relatively passive one. He or she does not present any evidence or take an active part in the examination of the witnesses. The judge is called upon to rule on the many motions of the prosecutor and of the defense attorney regarding the types of evidence that may be presented and the kinds of questions that may be asked of the witnesses. In some jurisdictions the judge is permitted to ask substantive questions of the witnesses and also to comment to the jury about the credibility of the evidence that is presented; in other states the judge is constrained from such activity. Still, the American legal tradition has room for a variety of judicial styles that depend on the personality, training, and wisdom of individual judges. This was vividly demonstrated in the O. J. Simpson trial, presided over by California state judge Lance Ito, and the Zacarias Moussaoui trial, presided over by U.S. district judge Leonie Brinkema. The comparatively inexperienced Ito never appeared to be in control of the courtroom proceedings, which lasted for eight long months. He allowed an inordinately large number of peremptory challenges, which greatly delayed jury selection; he permitted the attorneys to bicker endlessly, both in and outside of the courtroom; and he refused to restrict lengthy excursions on the witness stand (for example, allowing nine days of testimony by police criminalist Dennis Fung). Brinkema, by contrast, kept tight reins on Moussaoui, and this was clear even from the time of his arraignment. Seasoned court watchers noted that "the veteran trial judge . . . [moved] to prevent Moussaoui from transforming his trial into a politically charged show trial to vent anti-American views." [10] She ordered two U.S. marshals to restrain Moussaoui every time he attempted to speak out of turn; she designated court-appointed stand-by attorneys to pick up Moussaoui's self-defense "in the event that he ignores judicial admonitions or breaches courtroom etiquette; and she significantly limited the scope of Moussaoui's eleven hand-written pre-trial motions, holding that she would hear the motions only "if oral argument will assist the court." [11] While judicial styles vary from one courtroom to another, all American jurists are expected to manifest some similar traits.

First and foremost, the judge is expected to play the part of a disinterested party whose primary job is to ensure that both sides are allowed to present their cases as fully as possible within the confines of the law. If judges depart from the appearance or practice of being fair and neutral parties, they run counter to fundamental tenets of American jurisprudence and risk having their decisions overturned by an appellate court. For example, in June 2001 the federal district judge who presided over the famous Microsoft antitrust case was singled out for unusually severe criticism for his handling of the case. During the trial Judge Thomas Penfield Jackson told reporters outside the courtroom that "Microsoft Corp. Chairman Bill Gates had a Napoleon complex, that the software giant deserved to be smacked with a

2-by-4, and that the company ought to follow the example of Imperial Japan when it surrendered unconditionally to the victorious forces of the U.S. government." [12] Because the judge made those comments to reporters when court was not in session, Jackson denied Microsoft "an opportunity to object, perhaps even to persuade him"otherwise, an angry, unanimous Court of Appeals ruled. The appellate court further held that the judge's conduct was "deliberate, repeated, egregious and flagrant," and it "destroyed the appearance of impartiality" that judges are supposed to maintain. The appeals court went on to disqualify Judge Jackson from any future contact with the case. [13] Thus American judges must be, or at least appear to be, objective, disinterested decision makers.

Although judges do, for the most part, play such a role, their backgrounds and values affect their decisions in close calls—when they have to rule on a motion for which the arguments are equally strong or on a point of law that is open to a variety of interpretations. Evidence of this discretion and the way it is influenced by the values of the judges come from a variety of sources.

Role of the Jury during the Trial

Passive is the word that characterizes the jurors' role during the trial. Their job is to listen attentively to the cases presented by the two opposing attorneys and then come to a decision based solely on the evidence that is set forth. They are ordinarily not permitted to ask questions either of the witnesses or of the judge, nor are they even allowed to take notes during the proceedings. This is not because of constitutional or statutory prohibitions but primarily because it has been the traditional practice of courts in America. The adversarial form of justice requires lawyers to play the primary role during the trial; the judge and jury are to behave as dispassionate observers.

Not all trial courts in the United States strictly follow this norm, however, and in recent years many judges have allowed jurors to become more involved in the judicial arena. For over a decade, Chicago's chief U.S. district court judge, John F. Grady, has permitted jurors in his courtroom to take notes. Grady contends that asking juries to absorb passively all the testimony they hear "is like asking a college student to take a course without any notes and then take a final exam by memory." He further comments, "Judges who try cases without a jury sure don't sit there and do nothing—they take notes and ask questions." Many practicing attorneys and judicial scholars do not agree. Some lawyers fear that interruptions from the jury box will upset their carefully planned trial strategies, ride roughshod over time-honored rules of evidence, or change jurors from neutral observers to advocates of one side or the other. As one prominent Kansas City, Missouri, attorney put it, "When you're scoring a baseball game, you're prone to miss something on the field."

In some states a few trial judges have allowed jurors to take fairly active roles in the trial. For instance, Wisconsin circuit court judge Mark Frankel likes to recall a trial in which one of his jurors elicited "the smoking gun." The case concerned a stabbing in which the defendant claimed that he acted in self-defense. The district attorney held the victim's blood-stained jacket and sweater in front of the jurors and pointed to the slits where the knife had entered. Then one juror, acting on a re-markable hunch, passed Judge Frankel a note asking him to order the victim to put on the garments in question and then twist around in a variety of positions. Frankel agreed. To the astonishment of many in the courtroom, the slits in the garments lined up perfectly only when the victim curled up into a self-protective crouch—thus casting real doubt on the defendant's argument that he had stabbed the victim in self-defense. The jury subsequently convicted the defendant. Frankel concluded that the juror's suggestion "changed the whole picture of the case."[14]

Likewise, at the federal level jurors in recent years have been allowed greater par-ticipation in the questioning of witnesses. At least four U.S. appellate courts have given tacit approval to the practice so long as jurors are not permitted to blurt out queries in the midst of the trial and attorneys are given a chance to object to specific questions before they are posed to witnesses.[15] Still, at both state and federal levels the role of the jury remains basically passive, and the jury liberation movement remains in the experimental stage.

Instructions to the Jury

An important function of the judge during the trial is to charge the jury after the prosecution and defense have rested their cases. Although the jury's job is to weigh and assess the facts of the case, the judge must instruct the jurors about the mean-ing of the law and how the law is to be applied. The judge's instructions can be drafted in a way that favors one side or another. For example, if someone were ac-cused of embezzlement and the judge favored acquittal, it might be possible to give the jury such a narrow legal definition of the word *embezzlement* that it would be dif-ficult to bring in a guilty verdict. Likewise, if the judge were disposed toward conviction, a broader discussion of the laws on embezzlement might facilitate a conviction.

Both the prosecutor and the defense attorney know that the nature of the instructions can nudge the jury in one direction or another. Consequently, each side in the case often submits its own set of instructions to the judge, asking that its version be the official one read to the jury. The judge may then select one of the two sets of instructions or, as often as not, develop one of his or her own (perhaps based on selected parts of those offered or on a previously used set of instructions).

Because many cases are overturned on appeal as a result of faulty jury instructions, judges tend to take great care that the wording be technically and legally correct. The problem with this, however, is that although highly technical legal instructions may please an appellate court, they are often incomprehensible to individual jurors. Some studies indicate that jurors spend up to 25 percent of their deliberation time simply trying to decipher what the instructions mean.[16] A 1992 study of jurors in Cook County (Chicago), Illinois, revealed that as many as 75 percent did not understand parts of the instructions given to them in death penalty cases.[17] Judges tend to decline the jury's subsequent pleas to clarify instructions or to put them into everyday language because doing so would risk saying something that could move one side or the other to appeal the instructions.

Whatever the thrust or bias of the instructions, they must all have some basic elements. One is to define for the jurors the crime with which the accused is charged. This may involve giving the jurors a variety of options about what kind of verdict to bring. For example, if one person has taken the life of another, the state may be trying the accused for first-degree murder. Nevertheless, the judge may be obliged to acquaint the jury with the legal definition of second-degree murder or manslaughter if it should determine that the defendant was the killer but did not act with malice aforethought. Or if the accused is pleading not guilty for reason of insanity, the judge must offer in the instructions the proper legal definition of insanity.

The judge also must remind the jury that the burden of proof is on the state and that the accused is presumed to be innocent. If, after considering all the evidence, the jury still has a reasonable doubt as to the guilt of the accused, it must bring in a verdict of not guilty. Jurors are often troubled by what this means. "How sure do we have to be," they often ask themselves, "75 percent, 90 percent, 99 percent?" What is reasonable, and how strong may the doubt be? One judge defined the matter as follows:

It is such a doubt as would cause a juror, after careful and candid and impartial consideration of all the evidence, to be so undecided, that he cannot say that he has an abiding conviction of the defendant's guilt. It is such a doubt as would cause a reasonable person to hesitate or pause in the graver or more important transactions of life. However, it is not a fanciful doubt nor a whimsical doubt, nor a doubt based on conjecture.[18]

Despite this and other guidelines that the juror may be given to help determine reasonable doubt, in the final analysis each person has to decide alone at the moment when he or she votes to acquit or convict.

Finally, the judge usually acquaints the jurors with a variety of procedural matters: how to contact the judge if they have questions, the order in which they must consider the charges if there are more than one, and who must sign the official documents that express the verdict of the jury. After the instructions are read to the jury (and the attorneys for each side have been given an opportunity to offer objections), the jurors retreat to a deliberation room to decide the fate of the accused.

The Jury's Decisions

The jury deliberates in complete privacy; no outsiders observe or participate in its debate. During their deliberation jurors may request clarification of legal questions from the judge, and they may look at items of evidence or selected segments of the case transcript, but they may consult nothing else—no law dictionaries, no legal writings, no opinions from experts. When a decision has been reached by a vote of its members, the jury returns to the courtroom to announce its verdict. If a decision has not been reached by nightfall, the jurors are sent home with firm instructions to neither discuss the case with others nor read about it in the newspapers. In very important or notorious cases, the judge might order **sequestration** of the jury, which means that its members will spend the night in a local hotel away from the public eye. For example, in a highly publicized case in Houston in March 2002 Andrea Pia Yates was on trial for drowning her five young children in the bathtub of their home. To protect the jurors from the massive media coverage of the trial, they were sequestered at a local hotel for almost a month—"the longest anyone can remember in . . . [the] County." [19]

If the jury becomes deadlocked and cannot reach a verdict, it may report that fact to the judge. In such an event the judge may insist that the jury continue its effort to reach a verdict, saying something like the following: "The state and the accused have spent a lot of time and money on this case, and if you can't agree, then another jury just like you folks is going to have to go through this whole thing again." (There is nothing like instilling a little guilt to motivate human behavior.) Or, if the judge is convinced that the jury is hopelessly deadlocked, he or she may dismiss the jury and call for a new trial.

Research studies indicate that most juries dealing with criminal cases make their decisions fairly quickly. Almost all juries take a vote soon after retiring to their chambers ("just a nonbinding straw vote to see where we are"). In 30 percent of the cases it takes only one vote to reach a unanimous decision. (As the foreman of the jury that convicted Oklahoma City bomber Timothy McVeigh put it, "It was unanimous from the get-go.")[20] In 90 percent of the remainder, the majority on the first ballot eventually wins out. Hung juries—those in which no verdict can be reached—tend to occur only when a large minority existed on the first ballot.

Scholars have also learned that juries often reach the same verdict that the judge would have, had he or she been solely responsible for the decision. One large jury study asked judges to state how they would have decided jury cases over which they presided. The judge and jury agreed in 81 percent of the criminal cases (about the same as in civil cases). In 19 percent of the criminal cases the judge and jury disagreed, with the judge showing a marked tendency to convict where the juries had acquitted. Most disagreement occurred over drunk-driving and rape cases.[21]

In drunk-driving cases many jurors apparently envisioned themselves in similar situations and had sympathy for the accused. In forcible rape cases the jury was likely to believe that the woman had encouraged the attack because of the way she was dressed or the place where the rape occurred—for instance, in the back room of a bar. This phenomenon was vividly called to the nation's attention when a state jury in Fort Lauderdale, Florida, acquitted the defendant in a rape case despite clear and overwhelming evidence that he had sexually assaulted the victim. When juror Roy Diamond was asked by a reporter why his jury had opted for acquittal in the face of such clear-cut evidence, he replied: "She asked for it. The way she was dressed with that skirt you could see everything she had. She was advertising for sex." (The twenty-two-year-old victim had been wearing a tank top, lace skirt, and no undergarments at the time of the assault.)[22]

In recent years studies have documented another phenomenon characterizing jurors' behavior. As citizens, they may denounce crime and call for greater measures to curtail and punish it, but as jurors they seek to understand the criminal act and link punishment to their explanation of the behavior. In a 1995 study one scholar asked experimental jurors to sentence a man for writing a $100 check drawn on an imaginary bank account.[23] As the study continued, additional facts about the defendant were revealed to the jurors. When they were told that he had a long criminal record, the sentence jumped from ten months to thirty years. However, when the jurors heard a defense psychiatrist explain the defendant's behavior, the penalty dropped from thirty to five years. (When psychiatrists testified for both sides, the sentence evened out at fifteen years.)[24] In a parallel experimental study jurors decided a case about a battered woman who killed her abusive husband under three different situations: the woman was a good wife and mother; she was incompetent in those roles; and, lastly, she was a bad wife and mother. As the battered woman went from good to bad, the percentage of guilty verdicts rose dramatically—even though, legally, her fitness as a wife and mother had nothing to do with the probability of her guilt.[25]

Jurors, like police officers, prosecutors, grand jurors, and judges, reflect their personal values and backgrounds in their decision-making process. Studies have shown that men speak up more than women in the jury deliberation process and have more influence on the final outcome. Not surprisingly, well-educated people play a more significant role than those with weak educational backgrounds. Some evidence also suggests that ethnic or racial minorities carry some of their under-dog values into the jury deliberation rooms and are more likely to favor the accused.

When the members of the jury do finally reach a decision, they return to the courtroom and their verdict is announced in open court, often by the jury foreman. At this time either the prosecutor or the defense attorney often asks that the jury be polled, that is, that each juror is asked individually if the verdict reflects his or her own opinion. The purpose is to determine whether each juror supports the overall verdict or whether he or she has caved in to group pressure. If the polling procedure reveals that the jury is not of one mind, it may be sent back to the jury room to continue deliberations; in some jurisdictions a mistrial may be declared. If a mistrial is declared, the case may be tried again before another jury. There is no double jeopardy because the original jury did not agree on a verdict. If the jury's verdict is not guilty, the defendant is discharged on the spot and is free to leave the courtroom (unless other charges are pending).

Conviction Rates and the Likelihood of Being Sent to Prison

About 89 percent of all persons charged with felonies in the United States are convicted. This may seem high, but in a country such as Japan—not known for having an unduly draconian criminal justice system—a full 99 percent of all criminal defendants are convicted.[26] At the federal level in the United States 74 percent of those convicted were sent to prison in fiscal 2001, up from 60 percent in 1990. Federal convicts were likely to serve 87 percent of their sentence (before parole) in 2001, up from 65 percent in 1990.[27] At the state level, 68 percent of all convicted felons in 1998 were sentenced to confinement behind bars, but of this number, the typical defendant served only 47 percent of his or her term, a figure that has remained fairly constant over the years.[28]

Procedures after a Criminal Trial

At the close of the criminal trial, two stages generally remain for the defendant if he or she has been found guilty: sentencing and an appeal.

Sentencing

Sentencing is the court's formal pronouncement of judgment upon the defendant, at which time the punishment or penalty is set forth.

Penologists have traditionally given four justifications for punishing those who break the laws of society: retribution, incapacitation, deterrence, and rehabilitation. Each one contains separate, though not mutually exclusive, philosophies about why the state should punish offenders. Some emphasize past actions, while others focus on the future behavior of the criminal. Some place their primary focus on the rights and needs of society, while others are more oriented toward the criminal as a human being.

Retribution in its most basic sense stems from the ancient principle of revenge—the moral right of society to punish those who have inflicted harm on a member of that society, or as the book of Leviticus succinctly puts it: "An eye for an eye, a tooth for a tooth." Although there is harshness in this principle, it carries the modulating notion that the state should punish according to some form of due process of law—as opposed to private citizens carrying out a rampage of revenge. In addition, once the punishment is exacted, that is the end of the matter. The state and the victim do not have the right to commence a vendetta against the criminal or his family. Nonetheless, this philosophy of punishment has underlying weaknesses. First, if taken literally it would force the state into untold acts of brutality. For example, if by intent or by accident Mr. X causes the blindness of another person, do citizens want the state to put out both of Mr. X's eyes as retribution? Likewise, while the concept of inflicting injury for injury is comprehensible in terms of crimes of violence, it is not a useful tool for crimes against property. For instance, if Ms. Y were found to have engaged in a willful and unlawful misuse of a computer software program, what would be the appropriate punishment in terms of "an eye for an eye"?

A second justification for punishment is incapacitation. Its underlying assumption is that if offenders are removed from society by putting them in prison (or by executing them), they will no longer be a threat to society. This proposition clearly has some truth, however simplistic, especially because increasing evidence shows that a small number of criminals are responsible for a large number of crimes: "Lock the crooks up and we'll all be better off for it." Nevertheless, this philosophy does not address some key questions. For example, for how long should the criminal be put in prison? What about evidence suggesting that prison time makes criminals harder and meaner and thus even a greater threat to society when their incarceration ends? Finally, does the state have any responsibility to reform or rehabilitate the offender?

Deterrence is a third reason to justify the state's handing down a punishment. The focus is not so much on punishing the wrongdoer (although it does that), but rather on trying to prevent others from breaking the law. If the state severely punishes a criminal, this will serve as a warning to others that the same will happen to them if they break the law. This philosophy is partly based on the notion that people obey the law not just because they are good but also because they do not want to be caught and punished. The more immediate and severe the punishment, the greater the likelihood that people will adhere to the law. While this argument is persuasive, in the real world it does not always work this way. America is second only to Russia in the percentage of its population in prison, yet the United States still has a huge amount of crime. Likewise, much crime, particularly crimes of violence, is committed on the spur of the moment or under the influence of drugs or alcohol, when the wrongdoers are in no state of mind to calculate the odds of getting caught or the severity of their possible punishment.

Finally, rehabilitation is a more modern justification for punishing the lawbreaker. Its thesis is that people commit crimes because society has failed to provide them with a proper home environment when they were young, a good education, or a job. It also acknowledges that a criminal may be ill physically or mentally or possibly a victim of substance abuse. Thus the purpose of the sentence is not to punish but to treat the individual needs of the lawbreaker. ("Teach him a trade and get him off the bottle, and he won't have to steal for a living.") While rehabilitation works in some cases, this philosophy has begun to sink under the weight of current evidence. For example, more than 67 percent of former inmates released from state prisons in 1994 were arrested again within three years—up from more than 62 percent in 1983.[29] Furthermore, in recent decades data have shown that former inmates are likely to engage in criminal activity regardless of whether they were treated harshly in prison or offered a gentle rehabilitating hand. Likewise, evidence shows that prisoners are often motivated to enroll in prison-offered counseling, education, and religious programs, not because they wish to change their behavior but because this good behavior can be used to gain an early release from prison.

In sum, while all four philosophies of sentencing have some compelling elements, each contains some inconsistencies and shortcomings, and none seem to address all the complex aspects of this important but very complicated societal issue.[30]

At the federal level and in most states, only judges impose sentences.[31] However, in several states the defendant may elect to be sentenced by either a judge or a jury, and in capital cases states generally require that no death sentence be imposed unless it is the unanimous decision of twelve jurors. Some states have a bifurcated procedure for determining innocence or guilt and then imposing a sentence for the guilty: After reaching a guilty verdict, the jury deliberates a second time to determine the sentence. In several states a new jury is impaneled expressly for sentencing. At this time the rules of evidence are more relaxed, and the jury may be permitted to hear evidence that was excluded during the trial (for example, the previous criminal record of the accused).

After the judge pronounces the sentence, several weeks customarily elapse between the time the defendant is found guilty and the time the penalty is imposed. This interval permits the judge to hear and consider any post-trial motions that the defense attorney might make (such as a motion for a new trial) and to allow a probation officer to conduct a pre-sentence investigation. The probation officer is a professional with a background in criminology, psychology, or social work who makes a recommendation to the judge about the length of the sentence to be imposed. The probation officer customarily examines factors such as the background of the criminal, the seriousness of the crime committed, and the likelihood that the criminal will continue to engage in illegal activity. Judges are not required to follow the probation officer's recommendation, but it is a major factor in the judge's determination of what the sentence should be. Judges are presented with a variety of alternatives and a range of sentences. Many of these alternatives involve the concept of rehabilitation and call for the assistance of professionals in the fields of criminology and social science.

The lightest punishment that a judge can hand down is probation. This is often the penalty if the crime is regarded as minor or if the judge believes that the guilty person is not likely to engage in future criminal activity. (For example, a woman with no prior criminal record who kills her husband after being beaten and maltreated for twenty years is unlikely to go on a rampage of bank robberies or additional killings.) If a probated sentence is handed down, the criminal may not spend any time in prison, provided that the conditions of the probation are met. These might include staying away from bars or convicted criminals, not committing other crimes, or, with increasing frequency, performing some type of community service. For example, figure skater Tonya Harding was ordered to serve food to senior citizens as her community service after she was found guilty of taking part in an attack on her Olympic rival Nancy Kerrigan. These alternative sentencing programs have been prompted by tight budgets and overcrowded prisons and have been on the rise in recent years. (Ten years ago there were about twenty formal alternative sentencing programs nationwide; in 1994 there were more than three hundred.)[32] If a criminal serves out his or her probation or alternative sentence without incident, the criminal record is usually wiped clean, and in the eyes of the law it is as if no crime had ever been committed.

If the judge is not disposed toward probation and feels that hard time is in order, he or she must impose a prison sentence that is within a range prescribed by law. For example, in a certain state the penalty for aggravated assault may be a prison term of "no less than five but no more than fifteen years in the state penitentiary." The reason for a range of years instead of an automatically assigned number is that the law recognizes that not all crimes and criminals are alike and that, in principle, the punishment should fit the crime. Thus a criminal with a prior record who held up a liquor store might be given a longer sentence than the person with no record who embezzled some money to pay for his child's life-or-death surgery.

In an effort to eliminate gross disparities in sentencing for basically the same set of circumstances, the federal government and many states have attempted to develop precise guidelines to ensure greater consistency among judges. At the national level this effort led to the Sentencing Reform Act of 1987, which established a set of guidelines to structure the sentencing process.

The guidelines contain a Sentencing Table with 43 offense levels on the vertical axis and six categories of criminal history on the horizontal axis. Offenders in criminal history category 1 would likely have little or no criminal record, while those in category 6 would likely have extensive criminal histories.

The judge would find the applicable guideline sentencing range, which the table expresses in months of imprisonment, by determining the offense level and then reading across the axis to the proper criminal history category. Offense level 4, for example, which could apply to an offender convicted of theft of $100 or less, prescribes a sentencing range of 0 to 4 months for an offender in criminal history category 1, and 6 to 12 months for an offender in criminal history category 6. Offense level 38, which could apply to an offender convicted of aircraft hijacking, prescribes a sentencing range of 235–293 months for offenders in criminal history category 1, and 360 months to life for offenders in both the 5th and 6th criminal history categories.[33]

Congress provided that judges may depart from the guidelines only if they find an aggravating or mitigating circumstance that the commission did not adequately consider. Although the congressional guidelines do not specify the kinds of factors that could constitute grounds for disregarding the sentencing guidelines, Congress did state that the grounds could not include race, gender, national origin, creed, religion, socioeconomic status, drug dependence, or alcohol abuse.[34]

What have been the effects of the Sentencing Reform Act? Besides stirring up a storm of controversy among U.S. judges who resent restrictions on their traditionally broad sentencing authority, two observations now appear warranted. First, the majority of federal judges do seem to be adhering to the guidelines, and thus aggregate disparities among judges have declined. Second, evidence is mounting that "many judges are devising ways to get around the rules in their own cases." A number of recent studies have found that judges, prosecutors, and defense lawyers may cooperate to circumvent the guidelines when they believe the projected sentence is too harsh. They do this by fudging the facts of a crime. Examples include classifying guns found on drug dealers as being used for sport and therefore not covered by the guidelines, or reducing the weight of marijuana based on the drying that would occur between the time of arrest and the trial date. For example, in the summer of 2003, Ed Rosenthal, the self-proclaimed "Guru of Ganja," was convicted for cultivating more than one hundred marijuana plants, a crime that could potentially have landed him behind bars for sixty years. (Federal prosecutors had asked for a six-and-a-half-year prison term.) But U.S. district judge Charles Breyer felt that Rosenthal genuinely believed that what he was doing was not against the law because he was acting as an agent for the medical marijuana program in Oakland, California, which allowed sick people to obtain marijuana if they had a letter from a doctor. Said Judge Breyer: [Rosenthal] "was unaware his conduct was not immunized from federal prosecution." The sentence: one day in jail.[35] So much for the mandated federal guidelines. It is true that sentences may be appealed if it appears that the judge has departed from the congressional guidelines, but this does not happen often. (For instance, of the more than 230,000 sentences handed down by federal judges from 1999 through 2002, prosecutors appealed only 282 of them, including 138 where the defendants also appealed.)[36]

The states, too, have a variety of programs for avoiding vast disparities in judges' sentences. By 1995 twenty-two states had created commissions to establish sentencing guidelines, and as of late 1997, such guidelines were in effect in seventeen states.[37] Likewise, almost all of the states have enacted **mandatory sentencing laws** that require an automatic specific sentence upon conviction of certain crimes—particularly violent crimes, crimes in which a gun was used, or crimes perpetrated by habitual offenders. How successful have these reforms been a decade or so after they were put in place? One recent study concluded that "state guidelines reforms have clearly succeeded in their goal of encouraging more informed and rational sentencing policy decisions. Published evaluations also suggest that state guidelines have generally succeeded in achieving their goals of reducing sentencing disparity, lessening the impact of short-term political pressures on sentencing policy, and linking sentencing severity to available correctional resources."[38]

Despite their enormous impact on the sentence, judges do not necessarily have the final say on the matter. Whenever a judge sets a prison term, it is still subject to the parole laws of the federal government and the states. Thus parole boards (and sometimes the president and governors, who may grant pardons or commute sentences) have the final say about how long an inmate stays in prison. Evidence collected by the Justice Department for the state level suggests that parole boards and governors have not been hesitant about exercising their prerogatives. The average prisoner at the state level serves only 47 percent of his or her sentence, although at the federal level this has gone up to 87 percent. Pressure to increase these median time periods has grown because of the numerous mandatory minimum-time sentencing laws that have been enacted in recent years by Congress and the various state legislatures. (For example, in 1990 the typical federal prisoner served only 65 percent of his or her sentence.)[39]

An Appeal

At both the state and federal levels everyone has the right to at least one appeal after being convicted of a felony, but in reality few criminals avail themselves of this privilege. An appeal is based on the contention that an error of law was made during the trial process. Such an error must be reversible, as opposed to harmless. An error is considered harmless if it had no effect on the outcome of the trial. A **reversible error,** however, is a serious one that might have affected the verdict of the judge or jury. For example, a successful appeal might be based on the argument that evidence was improperly admitted at trial, that the judge's instructions to the jury were flawed, or that a guilty plea was not voluntarily made. However, appeals must be based on questions of procedure and legal interpretations, not on factual determinations of the defendant's guilt or innocence. Furthermore, under most circumstances one cannot appeal the length of one's sentence in the United States (as long as it was in the range prescribed by law). This is unlike the practice in most other Western democracies, which routinely permit criminals to contest in the appeals courts the length of their prison terms.

Criminal defendants do have some degree of success on appeal about 20 percent of the time, but this does not mean that the defendant goes free. The usual practice is for the appellate court to remand the case (send it back down) to the lower court for a new trial. At that point the prosecution must determine whether the procedural errors in the original trial can be overcome in a second trial and whether it is worth the time and effort to do so. A second trial is not considered double jeopardy because the defendant has chosen to appeal the original conviction.

In 1991 the Supreme Court made it harder for convicted criminals, especially those on death row, to repeatedly challenge the constitutionality of their convictions. The high court ruled that when a prisoner files a second habeas corpus petition in federal court, the prosecutor must specify which claims are being made for the first time.[40] The prisoner is then obliged to provide compelling reasons as to why these new issues, such as the unavailability of factual or legal information, were not raised in the initial petition. The prisoner must demonstrate that his or her case was prejudiced by the alleged constitutional violations.[41]

The Supreme Court's tightening of the screw for death penalty appeals has not been without effect. To illustrate, in 1976 fewer than five hundred persons were awaiting execution, but by the beginning of 2002, some 3,581 persons were on death row either at the federal penitentiary in Terre Haute, Indiana, or in its counterparts in the thirty-eight states that have capital punishment. In 2002, seventy-one inmates were executed—five more than in 2001. The state of Texas topped the list with some thirty-three executions.[42] The increased use of capital punishment is, in fact, part of a worldwide phenomenon. For example, between 2000 and 2001 the number of known executions around the world doubled. In 2001 some 3,048 persons were executed in thirty-one countries; 90 percent of these executions were in China, Iran, Saudi Arabia, and the United States.[43]

Despite the willingness of Congress and state legislature to enact death sentence statutes and the equal willingness of judges and juries to hand down the ultimate penalty, America still seems to be troubled about the fairness of the laws and by the increasing evidence that innocent persons have been, and are being, executed. In terms of the fairness issue, it has long been known that minorities are more likely than whites to receive a death sentence. For example, of persons executed in 2001, 26 percent were black and 5 percent were Hispanic.[44] Another issue is that innocent persons, often represented by attorneys of questionable ability, are being sentenced to death. "In the last decade DNA tests have provided stone-cold proof that sixty-nine people were sent to prison and death row in North America for crimes they did not commit," and the "number has been rising at a rate of more than one a month."[45] Perhaps the most visible manifestation of this phenomenon was the decision of Illinois's conservative Republican governor, George Ryan, in January 2003, to commute the death sentences of all 167 inmates on death row. The governor noted that thirteen death row inmates had been exonerated since 1987 through appeals and DNA evidence (as well as in several cases as the result of persistent investigations by college journalism students).[46] Indeed the attorney general of Maryland noted recently that "102 people on death rows around the country have been exonerated since the U.S. Supreme Court allowed states to reinstate capital punishment in 1976." [47] Even the moderately conservative Supreme Court Justice Sandra Day O'Connor stated publicly that "after 20 years on the high court, I have to acknowledge that serious questions are being raised about whether the death penalty is being fairly administered in this country.... Perhaps most alarming ... is the fact that if statistics are any indication, the system may well be allowing some innocent defendants to be executed." [48] Increasing evidence shows that appellate courts, at both federal and state levels, are giving more careful scrutiny to death penalty appeals that are lawfully made, and there appears to be an increasing willingness to require DNA testing when such tests are feasible. [49]

Further evidence of the Supreme Court's growing disenchantment with the death penalty can be found in its 2002 decision in *Atkins v. Virginia*, 536 U.S. 304, which ruled that mentally retarded persons could not be legally executed in the United States.

One final observation about the appellate process in general is appropriate. The media and champions of law and order often make much of appellate courts that turn loose obviously guilty criminals and reverse convictions on technicalities. Surely this does happen, and one might argue that it is inevitable in a democratic country whose legal system is based on fair play and the presumption of the innocence of the accused. But a few basic facts and figures must be kept in mind. First, about 90 percent of all defendants plead guilty, and this plea virtually excludes the possibility of an appeal. Of the remaining group, two-thirds are found guilty at trial, and only a small percentage of these appeal. Of those who do appeal, only about 20 percent have any measurable degree of success. Of those whose convictions are reversed, many are found guilty at a subsequent trial. (For example, in the famous case of *Miranda v. Arizona*, which spearheaded the criminal rights emphasis of the Warren Court, Ernesto Miranda's conviction was overturned by the high court because tainted evidence had been used to convict him. Nevertheless, at a subsequent trial—minus the tainted evidence—he was again convicted for the same crime.) [50] In fact, well under 1 percent of persons convicted of crimes are subsequently freed because of reversible court errors. Most people would consider that an acceptable risk in a free society.

Summary

We began this chapter by outlining the basic rights of the accused in a criminal trial and looked at the vagaries of the jury selection process. We then examined the key players at the trial—the prosecutor, the defense attorney, and the judge—and

contrasted the roles of these individuals (as well as jurors) with those in other countries that employ the inquisitorial method. After discussing the work of the jury, we
examined the post-trial procedures of sentencing and appeal. Throughout the
chapter, we stressed that the backgrounds and attitudes of the criminal justice participants have as much to do with the nature and quality of justice as do the formal
rules of the game. Whether the subject is police officers, prosecutors, judges, or juries,
the criminal justice system is greatly influenced by the role perceptions, mores, and
values of the men and women who dispense justice in America.

Further Thought and Discussion Questions

1. In America judges and juries sit passively while attorneys have the main
responsibility for conducting the trial and presenting the evidence. In most European
and South American counties, which use the inquisitorial method, the judges and
jurors sitting together actively conduct the trial and seek to learn the truth while
the attorneys take a passive role. What method does a better job at getting at the
truth and serving justice?

2. In recent years eighty-seven convicted murderers on death row were freed at
the last minute because DNA (deoxyribonucleic acid) evidence proved that they
had not committed the crime. Does this prove that justice does work in the American criminal justice system, or is it a sign of pathology in the way criminal trials are
conducted in the first place?

3. In the United States the length of a prison sentence cannot be appealed if it is
within the range prescribed by law. That is not the case in many countries, such
as the United Kingdom, where convicted persons may appeal the length of their
sentence if they believe it to be unjust. Would it be a good idea if convicted felons in
this country could appeal the severity of their prison terms?

4. Studies show that the recidivism rate is about the same whether prisoners are
treated humanely during their time in prison or whether they are subjected to
harsh treatment with few amenities. If so, wouldn't it be a good idea to significantly
cut prison budgets that allow expenditures for the few amenities of prison life
(e.g., a library, exercise facilities, educational opportunities)? Or are there humane
reasons for treating those behind bars with a modicum of decency and respect?

NOTES

1. In the case of *Barker v. Wingo*, 407 U.S. 514 (1972), the Supreme Court permitted a delay of as much
as five years because it felt the various trial date postponements were justified.

2. Also, in many jurisdictions laws exempt persons in specific occupations (for example, doctors, members of the clergy, police officers) and in specific situations (for example, full-time students, persons over sixty-five years of age, mothers with young children at home).

3. However, a recent study indicates that when all other relevant variables are held constant, there is virtually no difference in the outcome whether the defendant used a public defender or retained counsel. Marian R. Williams, "A Comparison of Sentencing Outcomes for Defendants with Public Defenders Versus Retained Counsel in a Florida Circuit Court," *Justice System Journal* 23/2 (2002): 249–257.

4. Aaron Epstein, "Rehnquist Faults Congress for Serious Court Problems," *Houston Chronicle*, January 1, 1999, A1.

5. Little systematic evidence exists of how many potential jurors show up when called for jury duty, but fragmentary data are alarming. For example, in Harris County (Houston), Texas, of nearly 600,000 residents who were summoned for possible jury service between November 1994 and November 1995, only 57 percent showed up. Joe Stinebaker, "Many Called, Few Serve," *Houston Chronicle*, July 22, 1996, A14.

6. *Batson v. Kentucky*, 476 U.S. 79 (1986).

7. *J.E.B. v. Alabama*, 511 U.S. 127 (1994).

8. Daniel Wise, " 'Batson' Protection Extended to Jews," *National Law Journal*, April 28, 1997, A10; and Victoria Slind-Flor, "Illegal to Exclude Gays from Jury," *National Law Journal*, August 26, 1996, A11.

9. Laurie Goering, "In the Spirit of the Spanish Inquisition, Intimidation Thrives in Brazil Courts," *Houston Chronicle*, May 10, 1996, A34.

10. Stewart M. Powell, "Moussaoui's Judge Is Asserting Control," *Houston Chronicle*, June 30, 2002, A4.

11. Ibid.

12. Jess Bravin, "Opinion Slams Judge's Talking Out of Court," *Wall Street Journal*, June 29, 2001, B1.

13. Ibid.

14. Tamar Jacoby with Tim Padgett, "Waking Up the Jury Box," *Newsweek*, August 7, 1989, 51.

15. "Jurors May Question Witnesses during Trial, Appeals Court Rules," *Wall Street Journal*, August 6, 1992, B3. For an excellent study of this general subject matter, see Larry Heuer and Steven Penrod, "Juror Notetaking and Question Asking During Trials," *Law and Human Behavior* 18 (1994): 121–150; and Larry Heuer and Steven Penrod, "Increasing Juror Participation in Trials through Note Taking and Question Asking," *Judicature* 79 (1996): 256–263.

16. See Shari Seidman Diamond and Judith N. Levi, "Improving Decisions on Death by Revising and Testing Jury Instructions," *Judicature* 79 (1996): 224–233; and Peter Annin and Tom Morganthau, "The Verdict: Death," *Newsweek*, June 23, 1997, 41.

17. Helene Cooper, "Death Sentence Vacated Because Study Reveals Juror Misunderstanding," *Wall Street Journal*, September 28, 1992, B6.

18. *Moore v. U.S.*, 345 F.2d 97 (D.C. Cir. 1965).

19. Lisa Teachey, "Tight Rein Placed on Jury for Yates," *Houston Chronicle*, March 10, 2002, A12.

20. Annin and Morganthau, "The Verdict," 41.

21. For an excellent classic study of jury behavior, see Harry Kalven Jr. and Hans Zeisel, *The American Jury* (Boston: Little, Brown, 1966).

22. "Overheard," *Newsweek*, October 16, 1989, 23.

23. Experimental jurors are citizens who were asked to participate in some type of jury simulation exercise. They sit as jurors for a hypothetical case (or a series of cases) designed by an academic experimenter and render a verdict. They usually are then debriefed by the experimenter conducting the study.

24. Norman J. Finkel, *Commonsense Justice: Jurors' Notions of the Law* (Cambridge, Mass.: Harvard University Press, 1995), 146–150.

25. James Q. Wilson, *Moral Judgment* (New York: HarperCollins, 1997), 91.

26. J. Mark Ramseyer and Eric B. Rasmusen, "Skewed Incentives: Paying for Politics as a Japanese Judge," *Judicature* 83 (2000): 195.

27. These numbers were taken from the Web site of the U.S. Department of Justice, Office of Justice Programs, downloaded June 11, 2003: http://www.ojp.usdoj.gov/bjs/fed.html.

28. These numbers were taken from the Web site of the U.S. Department of Justice, Office of Justice Programs, downloaded June 19, 2003: http://www.ojp.usdoj.gov/bjs/sent.html.

29. Genaro C. Armas, "Number of Rearrested Former Inmates Rising," *Houston Chronicle*, June 3, 2002, A6.

30. In discussing the justification for sentences, we have borrowed from David W. Neubauer, *America's Courts and the Criminal Justice System*, 5th ed. (Belmont, Calif.: Wadsworth, 1996), 269–274.

31. However, according to a 1994 law passed by Congress (18 USC Sec. 3593 and 3594), in capital cases only a jury can hand down a death sentence.

32. David Mulholland, "Judges Finding Creative Ways of Punishment," *Wall Street Journal*, May 24, 1994, B1.

33. "News from the Sentencing Commission," *The Third Branch* 19 (May 1987): 3–4.

34. Ibid., 5.

35. "Grower Gets 1 Day in Jail over Medical Marijuana," *Houston Chronicle*, June 5, 2003, A20.

36. Jess Bravin and Gary Fields, "House Panel to Prove U.S. Judge," *Wall Street Journal*, March 12, 2003, A2.

37. Michael Tonry, "Twenty Years of Sentencing Reform: Steps Forward, Steps Backward," *Judicature* 78 (1995): 171.

38. Richard S. Frase, "State Sentencing Guidelines: Still Going Strong," *Judicature* 78 (1995): 177.

39. These data were taken from the following two Web sites: http://www.ojp.usdoj.gov/bjs/sent /html, downloaded June 19, 2003, and http://www.ojp.usdoj.gov/bjs/fed/html, downloaded June 11, 2003.

40. A petition for habeas corpus is a civil petition by either a state or a federal prisoner, usually filed after he or she has been convicted and has had that conviction upheld by an appellate court. The petition does not focus on whether the evidence supported a conviction but instead challenges the constitutionality of various police, lawyer, or judicial practices that supposedly violated the rights of the defendant.

41. *McCleskey v. Zant*, 499 U.S. 467 (1991).

42. U.S. Department of Justice, Office of Justice Programs. These data were taken from the following Web site, downloaded June 20, 2003: http://www.ojp.usdoj.gov/bjs/cp.html.

43. "Report: Executions Doubled in 2001," *Houston Chronicle*, April 10, 2002, A20.

44. "Capital Punishment 2001," U.S. Department of Justice, Office of Justice Programs (December 2002), 1.

45. Jim Dwyer, Peter Neufeld, and Barry Scheck, "When Justice Lets Us Down," *Newsweek*, February 14, 2000, 59.

46. Don Babwin, "Advocate Becomes Opponent: Governor Could No Longer 'Play God,' " *Houston Chronicle*, January 14, 2003, A8.

47. "Official Urges Maryland to Abolish Death Penalty," *Houston Chronicle*, January 31, 2003, A16.

48. "O'Connor Rethinks Death Penalty Justice," *Houston Chronicle*, July 5, 2001, A7.

49. The June 12, 2000, issue of *Newsweek* carried a series of articles about the current status of the death penalty, DNA testing, and the response of the public and the courts to these phenomena. See also Jonathan Atler and Mark Miller, "A Life or Death Gamble," *Newsweek*, May 29, 2000, 23–27.

50. *Miranda v. Arizona*, 384 U.S. 436 (1966).

SUGGESTED READINGS

Ebbe, Obi N. Ignatius, ed. *Comparative and International Criminal Justice Systems: Policing, Judiciary and Corrections.* Boston: Butterworth-Heinemann, 1996. An excellent introduction to the judicial and corrections systems in both Western and developing nations.

Eisenstein, James, and Herbert Jacob. *Felony Justice: An Organizational Analysis of Criminal Courts.* Boston: Little, Brown, 1977. A discussion of how judges, prosecutors, defense attorneys, and others in the criminal court system interact as members of work groups that serve to reinforce each other's roles.

Hastie, Reid, Steven D. Penrod, and Nancy Pennington. *Inside the Jury.* Cambridge, Mass.: Harvard University Press, 1983. An excellent discussion of the history of and legal constraints on jury behavior, with a sophisticated, data-containing behavioral model of how a jury functions.

Judicature 78 (January–February 1995). The entire issue of this journal examines the current status of sentencing and efforts at reform.

Judicature 83 (May–June 2000). The entire issue of this journal is dedicated to an examination of the twenty-first century American jury.

Levine, James P. *Juries and Politics.* Pacific Grove, Calif.: Brooks/Cole, 1992. A concise review of the legal and social science literature on juries.

Neubauer, David W. *America's Courts and the Criminal Justice System,* 6th ed. Belmont, Calif.: West/Wadsworth, 1999. A classic political science textbook on all the major stages present in the criminal justice process.

CHAPTER 11

The Civil Court Process

Courts are increasingly encouraging or requiring litigants in civil cases to attempt to resolve their disputes by means other than a trial—an approach known as alternative dispute resolution, or ADR. As ADR has become more prevalent, law schools have added classes on mediation and established clinics that provide practical experience in mediating disputes. Shown here, C. J. Larkin, a law professor at Washington University, conducts a mock mediation. Professor Larkin also helps manage a project designed to mediate disputes between neighbors.

T HIS CHAPTER CONTINUES OUR EXAMINATION of courts from a judicial process perspective, focusing on the civil courts. After discussing how civil law differs from criminal law and describing the most important categories of civil law, we will consider alternatives to trials and then proceed step by step through the civil trial process.

The Nature and Substance of Civil Law

The American legal system observes several important distinctions between criminal and civil law. Criminal law is concerned with conduct that is offensive to society as a whole. Civil law pertains primarily to the duties of private citizens to each other. In civil cases the disputes are usually between private individuals, although the government may sometimes be a party in a civil suit. Criminal cases always involve government prosecution of an individual for an alleged offense against society.

Civil actions are separate and distinct from criminal proceedings. In a civil case the court attempts to settle a particular dispute between the parties by determining their legal rights. The court then decides upon an appropriate remedy, such as awarding monetary damages to the injured party or issuing an order that directs one party to perform or refrain from a specific act. In a criminal case the court decides whether the defendant is innocent or guilty. A guilty defendant may be punished by a fine, imprisonment, or both.

In some instances the same act may give rise to both a criminal proceeding and a civil suit. Suppose that Joe and Pete, two political scientists attending a convention in Atlanta, are sharing a taxi from the airport to their downtown hotel. During the ride they become involved in a heated discussion over President George W. Bush's appointees to the federal courts. By the time the taxi stops at their hotel, the discussion has become so heated that Joe suggests they settle their differences right then and there. If Pete strikes Joe in the ribs with his briefcase as he gets out of the taxi, Pete may be charged with criminal assault. In addition, Joe might file a civil suit against Pete in an effort to obtain a monetary award sufficient to cover his medical expenses.

Civil cases far outnumber criminal cases in both the federal and state courts, although they generally attract less media attention. Nonetheless, they often raise important policy questions and cover a broad range of disagreements in society. One leading judicial scholar summarizes the breadth of the civil law field as follows:

Every broken agreement, every sale that leaves a dissatisfied customer, every uncollected debt, every dispute with a government agency, every libel and slander, every accidental injury, every marital breakup, and every death may give rise to a civil proceeding.[1]

As virtually any dispute between two or more persons may provide the basis for a civil suit, the number of suits is huge. However, most of them fall into one of five basic categories.[2]

The Main Categories of Civil Law

The five main categories are contract law, tort law, property law, the law of succession, and family law.

Contract Law

Contract law is primarily concerned with voluntary agreements between two or more people. Some common examples include agreements to perform a certain type of work, to buy or sell goods, and to construct or repair homes or businesses. Basic to these agreements are a promise by one party and a counterpromise by the other party, usually a promise by one party to pay money for the other party's services or goods. For example, assume that Mr. Burns and Ms. Colder enter into an agreement whereby Colder agrees to pay Burns $125 if he will cut and deliver a cord of oak firewood to her home on December 10. If Burns does not deliver the wood on that date, he has breached the contract and Colder may sue him for damages.

Although many contracts are relatively simple and straightforward, some complex fields build on contract law or contract ideas. One such field is commercial law, which focuses primarily on sales involving credit or the installment plan. Commercial law also deals with checks, promissory notes, and other negotiable instruments.

Another closely related field—one that has become especially prominent in recent years—is bankruptcy and creditors' rights. Bankrupt individuals or businesses may go through a process that essentially wipes the slate clean and allows the person filing for bankruptcy to begin again. The bankruptcy process is also designed to ensure fairness to creditors. Bankruptcy law has been a major concern of legislators for several years, and a large number of special bankruptcy judges are now attached to the U.S. district courts.

The final area is the insurance contract, which is important because it applies to so many people. The insurance industry is regulated by government agencies and subject to its own distinct rules.

Tort Law

Tort law may generally be described as the law of civil wrongs. It concerns conduct that causes injury and fails to measure up to some standard set by society.

Actions for personal injury or bodily injury claims are at the heart of tort law, and automobile accidents have traditionally been responsible for a large number of these claims. One of the most rapidly growing subfields of tort law is product liability. This category has become an increasingly effective way to hold corporations accountable for injuries caused by defective foods, toys, appliances, automobiles, drugs, and a host of other products. This type of case is what many have in mind when they complain about a "litigation explosion" in the United States or describe America as a "litigious society."

Perhaps one reason for the tremendous growth in product liability cases is a change in the standard of proof. Traditionally, negligence (generally defined as carelessness or the failure to use ordinary care, under the particular circumstances revealed by the evidence in the lawsuit) must be proved before one person is able to collect damages for injuries caused by someone else. However, some have argued that for many years reliance on the negligence concept has been declining, especially in product liability cases. In its place, the courts often use a strict liability standard, which means that a victim can collect damages even if there was no negligence and even if the manufacturer was careful.

Another reason commonly suggested for the growing number of product liability cases is the size of jury awards when the decision favors the plaintiff. Jury awards for damages may be of two types: compensatory and punitive. Compensatory damages are intended to cover the plaintiff's actual loss. Examples include repair costs, doctor bills, and hospital expenses. Punitive (or exemplary) damages are designed to punish the defendant or serve as a warning to refrain from such behavior in the future. The use of punitive damages is not universal, however. The French judicial system does not allow such damages to punish the defendant for what a jury considers to be outrageous behavior.[3]

Data from a major study by the National Center for State Courts put the problem in perspective.[4] In product liability cases in the nation's seventy-five largest counties in 1996 the plaintiff won in 37.2 percent of the cases. That figure alone may not sound too impressive when compared with other types of cases. For example, in cases involving automobiles, plaintiffs won 57.5 percent of the time; plaintiffs in asbestos cases won 55.6 percent of the time. However, the size of jury awards in product liability cases makes people sit up and take notice. The $379,000 median jury award in these cases tops the list of the National Center for State Courts. In contrast, automobile and asbestos cases received median jury awards of $18,000 and $227,000, respectively.

Some have argued that the potential for large awards in tort cases encourages plaintiffs to file suits that are not strong or lack merit altogether. This is not so in all countries, however. The British courts, with the exception of libel cases, do not offer plaintiffs the opportunity to win the large jackpot verdicts that are handed down in the United States.[5] In addition to potentially large jury verdicts, some lay the blame on plaintiffs' attorneys who are willing to pursue cases on a contingency fee basis.

As a result of concern over large jury awards and the increasing number of so-called frivolous cases, government officials, corporate executives, interest groups, and members of the legal community have called for legislation aimed at tort reform. Throughout the 1990s a number of states enacted a variety of tort reform measures. The American Tort Reform Association, which serves as an advocate of such reform, reports that states have limited awards for noneconomic damages, modified their laws governing punitive damages, and enacted statutes penalizing plaintiffs who file frivolous lawsuits.[6] In a case decided on April 7, 2003, the U.S. Supreme Court weighed in on the question of awards for punitive damages. The Court ruled that an award of $145 million, in which full compensatory damages are $1 million, is excessive and violates the Due Process Clause of the Fourteenth Amendment.[7]

One method of discouraging frivolous lawsuits that has captured the attention of many Americans is the "loser pays" concept, whereby a losing plaintiff would pay his or her legal expenses as well as those of the defendant. Although this is a novel idea in the United States, it is not unknown in other countries. According to Herbert Kritzer, "Britain relies on the principle that the loser should pay the legal fees of both sides." [8] German courts also follow the loser-pays-all-costs concept.[9]

In short, American courts have increasingly been called upon to protect consumers against defective products. Although it has long been argued that consumers should have freedom of choice in the marketplace, they now have less freedom to make an unsafe choice.[10]

Still another rapidly growing subfield of tort law is medical malpractice. Ironically, the number of medical malpractice claims has increased even as great advances in medicine have been made. Yet two ongoing problems in contemporary medicine are the increased risks imposed by new treatments and the impersonal character of specialists and hospitals.[11] Patients today have high expectations, and when a doctor fails them, their anger may lead to a malpractice suit.[12]

Courts generally use the traditional negligence standard rather than the strict liability doctrine in resolving medical malpractice suits. This means that the law does not attempt to make doctors guarantee successful treatment, but instead tries to make the doctor liable if the patient can prove that the physician failed to perform in a manner consistent with accepted methods of medical practice. This means that to prevail against the doctor in court, the injured patient needs at least the testimony of one or more expert witnesses stating that the doctor's conduct was not reasonable.[13]

Property Law

A distinction traditionally has existed between real property and personal property. The former normally refers to real estate—land, houses, and buildings—and has included growing crops. Basically, everything else is considered personal property, including money, jewelry, automobiles, furniture, and bank deposits.

Most adults in America have some involvement with both real estate and personal property. Most are renters or homeowners, or they live with someone who is. However, for most Americans, personal property—their possessions—means more to them than real estate. But "as far as the law is concerned, the word *property* means primarily real property; personal property is of minor importance." [14] No special field of law is devoted to personal property. Instead, it is generally considered under the rubric of contract law, commercial law, and bankruptcy law.

Property rights have always been important in the United States. Some have argued, for instance, that the protection of property rights was the major motivation of the Framers of the U.S. Constitution. [15] Another pertinent example is that in the early days of America only male landowners were eligible to vote.

Today property rights have reached the point of being far more complex than mere ownership of something. The notion of property now includes, among other things, the right to use that property. [16]

One important branch of property law today deals with land use controls. Zoning is the most familiar type of land use restriction. Zoning ordinances divide a municipality into districts designated for different uses. For instance, one neighborhood may be designated as residential, another as commercial, and yet another as industrial.

Early zoning laws were challenged on the grounds that restrictions on land use amounted to taking the land in violation of the Fifth and Fourteenth Amendments. A provision of the Fifth Amendment, made applicable to the states by the Fourteenth Amendment, says: "Nor shall private property be taken for public use without just compensation." In a sense, zoning laws do take from the owners of land the right to use their property in any way they see fit. Nonetheless, courts have generally ruled that zoning laws are not regarded as a taking in violation of the Constitution. [17]

Although the courts have given zoning authorities broad powers, they do not have unlimited powers. According to the Supreme Court, the regulations must "bear a substantial relation to the public health, safety, morals, or general welfare." [18]

Today zoning is a fact of life in cities and towns of all sizes throughout the United States. City planners and other city officials regard zoning ordinances as necessary for the planned and orderly growth of urban areas. It is a constant source of amazement to many that Houston, one of the nation's largest cities, developed without a comprehensive zoning ordinance.

The Law of Succession

The law of succession considers how property is passed along from one generation to another. The American legal system recognizes a property owner's right to dispose of it as he or she wishes. One common way to do this is to execute a will. If a valid will exists, the courts enforce it. However, if no will was written (or if it was improperly drawn up), the person has died intestate, and the state must dispose of the property.

The state's disposition of the property is carried out according to the fixed procedure set forth in its statutes. By law, intestate property passes to the deceased person's heirs, that is, to the nearest relatives. Occasionally a person who dies intestate has no living relatives. In that situation, the property escheats, or passes, to the state in which the deceased resided. State laws often prohibit the more remote relatives, such as second cousins and great-uncles and aunts, from inheriting.[19]

Increasingly, Americans are preparing wills to ensure that their property is disposed of according to their wishes, not according to a scheme determined by the state. A will is a formal document. It must be carefully drafted, and in most states it must be witnessed by at least two persons. In some jurisdictions a will can be executed without witnesses. Such a document is known as a holographic will, and it must be handwritten by the testator, the person whose will it is.

Family Law

Family law clearly touches the lives of a great many Americans each year. It concerns such things as marriage, divorce, child custody, and children's rights.

The conditions necessary for entering into a marriage are spelled out by state law. These laws traditionally cover the minimum age of the parties, required blood tests or physical examinations, mental condition of the parties, license and fee requirements, and waiting periods.

The termination of a marriage was once rare. In the early nineteenth century some states granted divorces only through special acts of the legislature. South Carolina simply did not allow divorce. In the other states, divorces were granted only when one party proved some grounds for divorce. In other words, divorces were available only to innocent parties whose spouses were guilty of such actions as adultery, desertion, or cruelty.

The twentieth century saw an enormous change in divorce laws, moving away from restrictive laws and toward a concept known as no-fault divorce. This trend was the result of two factors. First, for many years there was an increasing demand for divorces. Second, the stigma once attached to divorced persons all but disappeared.

The no-fault divorce system means that the traditional grounds for divorce have been eliminated. Basically, the parties simply explain that irreconcilable differences exist between them and that the marriage is no longer viable. In some states the defendant is not even required to appear in court. In short, the no-fault divorce system has put an end to the adversarial nature of divorce proceedings.

Not so easily solved are some of the other problems that may result from an ended marriage. Child custody battles, disputes over child support payments, and disagreements over visitation rights still find their way into court on a regular basis. Custody disputes are probably more common and contentious today than they were before the no-fault divorce. The child's needs come first, and courts no longer automatically assume that this means granting custody to the mother. Fathers are increasingly being granted custody, and it is also now common for courts to grant joint custody to the divorced parents.

The Courts and Other Institutions Concerned with Civil Law

Disagreements are common in the daily lives of Americans. These disagreements can usually be settled outside the legal system. Sometimes they are so serious, however, that one of the parties sees no alternative but to file a lawsuit.

Deciding Whether to Go to Court

Every year thousands of potential civil cases are resolved without a trial because the would-be litigants settle their problems in another way or the prospective plaintiff decides not to file suit. When faced with a decision to call upon the courts, to try to settle differences, or to simply forget the problem, many people resort to a simple cost-benefit analysis. That is, they weigh the costs associated with a trial against the benefits they are likely to gain if they win. Should a quick calculation indicate that the tangible and intangible costs in terms of such things as time, money, publicity, stress, and anxiety outweigh the benefits, most people will opt for an alternative to a trial. However, if the prospective plaintiff perceives the costs to be low enough, then he or she might file suit against the defendant.

One classic study of civil litigation patterns relied upon a telephone survey of approximately one thousand households selected at random in each of five federal judicial districts: South Carolina, eastern Pennsylvania, eastern Wisconsin, New Mexico, and central California.[20] The authors of the study found that about 40 percent of the households reported a grievance totaling $1,000 or more during the previous three years, and approximately 20 percent reported two or more such grievances.

Figure 11-1 presents a dispute pyramid that indicates what happens to one thousand typical grievances. Although many grievances are never pursued any further, some result in the plaintiff's initiating a claim. A claim may be accepted, partially accepted, or rejected. A recent study, based on comparisons of American and British data on personal injuries, concluded that "Britons are more likely to 'grin and bear it.' " [21] Attributing fault to someone else is an important variable, and it appears that in Britain the key principle is "when in doubt, don't claim," while in America it is "when in doubt, consider claiming." [22]

Claims that are met with a partial or total rejection move on to become disputes. The odds are high that a claim will become a dispute. In the survey under discussion, approximately 63 percent of the claims became disputes (met with partial or total rejection).

The authors of the study next focused on the extent to which disputants hired attorneys and took their cases to court. Overall, they found that attorneys were hired in less than one-fourth of the disputes and that only about 11 percent of the disputants reported taking their dispute to court. This finding should not be seen as minimizing the importance of lawyers and judges, however. Each party's understanding of everyone's legal position is based on the lawyer's advice, which is in turn based on an understanding of previous court decisions.

FIGURE 11-1   Typical Dispute Pyramid for 1,000 Grievances

Court filings   50

Lawyers consulted   103

Disputes   449

Claims   718

Grievances   1,000

SOURCE: Richard E. Miller and Austin Sarat, "Grievances, Claims, and Disputes: Assessing the Adversary Culture," *Law and Society Review* 15 (1980–1981): 544.

Alternative Dispute Resolution

In practice, few persons make use of the entire judicial process. Instead, most cases are settled without resort to a full-fledged trial. In civil cases a trial may be both slow and expensive. As the statistics on judicial workload indicate, most courts are hard-pressed to keep up with their dockets. In many areas the backlogs are so enormous that it takes three to five years for a case to come to trial. Also, civil trials may be exceedingly complex.

The expense of a trial is often enough to discourage potential plaintiffs. The possibility of losing always exists. Even if the plaintiff wins, there may be a long wait before the judgment is satisfied, that is, if it is ever completely satisfied. In other words, a trial may simply create a new set of problems for the parties concerned. For all these reasons, alternative methods of resolving disputes have increasingly been discussed.

The alternative dispute resolution (ADR) movement is now well established in the United States. From major corporations to attorneys to individuals, support for alternative methods has been growing. Corporate America is interested in avoiding prolonged and costly court battles as the only way to settle complex business disputes. In addition, attorneys are more frequently considering alternatives such as mediation and arbitration when there is a need for faster resolution of cases or confidential treatment of certain matters. And individual citizens are increasingly turning to local mediation services for help in resolving family disputes, neighborhood quarrels, and consumer complaints.

Alternative dispute resolution processes are carried out under a variety of models. These models are commonly classified as "private, court-referred, and court-annexed, but the latter two often are called court-connected."[23] In other words, some private ADR processes are independent of the courts. A court-referred ADR process operates outside the court but still has some relationship to it. In some instances the relationship is formal. For example, the court may contract for ADR services, with the stipulation that they be provided according to rules and procedures specified by the court. In another jurisdiction the relationship may be less formal. The court might simply refer parties to an ADR provider without monitoring the progress of the case. The court administers the ADR process in a court-annexed program. In this scenario, the authority flows from statute or court rules. Case progress is supervised by the court, and the individuals providing the ADR service are directly responsible to the court. Depending on the model and the issue, "ADR processes may be voluntary or mandatory; they may be binding or allow appeals from decisions rendered; and they may be consensual, adjudicatory, or some hybrid of the two."[24]

Proponents point to several generally recognized goals that may be accomplished by alternative dispute resolution procedures. Among these are

to provide readily accessible, fair, and appropriate means to resolve disputes; to increase the parties' participation in the dispute resolution process; to reduce litigant costs; to relieve congestion and demands on court resources; and to avoid delay in resolving disputes.[25]

Some commonly used ADR processes are mediation, arbitration, neutral fact-finding, mini-trial, summary jury trial, and private judging.

Mediation. Mediation is a private, confidential process in which an impartial person helps the disputing parties identify and clarify issues of concern and reach their own agreement. The mediator does not act as a judge. Instead, the parties themselves maintain control of the final settlement.

Although almost any type of dispute may be resolved through mediation, it is especially appropriate for situations in which the disputants have an ongoing relationship. Examples include disputes between family members, neighbors, employers and employees, and landlords and tenants. Mediation is also useful in divorce cases because it changes the procedure from one of confrontation to one of cooperation. Child custody and visitation rights are frequently resolved through mediation as well. And in many areas, personal injury and property claims involving insurance companies are settled through mediation. In short, a wide variety of disputes that once found their way into courts are now being settled through mediation.

Arbitration. The arbitration process is similar to going to court. After listening to both parties in a dispute, an impartial person, called an arbitrator, decides how the controversy should be resolved. There is no judge or jury. Instead, the arbitrator, selected by both parties, makes the final decision. Arbitrators are drawn from all different types of professional backgrounds and frequently volunteer their time to help people resolve their problems.

Disputants choose arbitration because it saves time and money and is more informal than a court hearing. Most arbitrations are completed in four months or less, as compared with six months to several years for court decisions.

Arbitration is used privately to resolve a variety of consumer complaints. Examples include disputes over poor automobile repairs, problems with the return of faulty merchandise, and overcharging for services. Arbitration is also being used in court-referred and court-annexed processes to resolve several types of disputes. Business, commercial, and employment disputes are examples of issues that courts are now trying to resolve by arbitration.

Neutral Fact-Finding. Neutral fact-finding is an informal process whereby an agreed-upon party is asked to investigate a dispute. The dispute usually involves complex or technical issues. The neutral third party analyzes the disputed facts and issues his or her findings in a nonbinding report or recommendation.

This process can be particularly useful in handling allegations of racial or gender discrimination within a company because such cases often provoke strong emotions and internal dissension. If both parties are employees of the same company, conflicts of interest could interfere with a supervisor or manager's ability to conduct an impartial investigation of alleged discrimination. To avoid the appearance of unfairness, a company may turn to a neutral third party in hopes of reaching a settlement all the employees can respect.

A variation of neutral fact-finding is Early Neutral Evaluation (ENE). Parties using ENE have their attorney present the basic core of the dispute to a neutral evaluator in the presence of the parties. This takes place after the case has been filed in court but before discovery of facts is conducted. The neutral evaluator provides a candid assessment of the strengths and weaknesses of the case. Then, if the parties cannot reach a settlement, the neutral evaluator helps narrow the dispute and suggests guidelines for managing the discovery process.

Mini-Trial. In a mini-trial each party presents its position in a trial-like fashion before a panel composed of selected representatives for both parties and neutral third parties. Every panel has one neutral adviser. Mini-trials are designed to help define the issues and develop a basis for realistic settlement negotiations. The representatives of the two sides present an overview of their positions and arguments to the panel. As a result, each party becomes more knowledgeable about the other party's position. Having heard each side's presentation, the panel, including the adviser, meets to develop a compromise solution. The neutral adviser may also issue an advisory opinion regarding the merits of the case. This advisory opinion is nonbinding unless the parties have previously agreed in writing to be bound by it.

The primary benefit of a mini-trial is that both parties have an opportunity to develop solutions. This is enhanced by the fact that each has representation and access to detailed information.

Summary Jury Trial. A summary jury trial involves a court-managed process that takes place after a case has been filed but before it reaches trial. Each party presents its arguments to a jury (normally six persons). An overview of each side's argument and abbreviated opening and closing arguments are presented. Attorneys are typically given a short amount of time (an hour or less) for their presentations. They are limited to presenting information that would be admissible at trial. No testimony is taken from sworn witnesses, and proceedings are generally not recorded. Because the proceedings are nonbinding, rules of procedure and evidence are more flexible than in a normal trial.

The jury hands down an advisory, nonbinding decision based on the arguments presented. In this setting the verdict is designed to give the attorneys and their clients insight into their cases. It may also suggest a basis for settlement of the dispute. If the dispute is not resolved during or immediately following the summary jury trial proceeding, a pretrial conference is held before the court to discuss settlement.

One of the major advantages of a summary jury trial is the brief amount of time involved. A summary jury trial is typically concluded in less than a day compared with several days or weeks for full-fledged trials.

Private Judging. This version of alternative dispute resolution makes use of retired judges who offer their services in a variety of ADR processes. In California, for example, a number of retired superior court judges offer their services for a fee. Advocates claim that using a private judge instead of a sitting court judge has several advantages. First, the parties are able to select a person with the right qualifications and experience to handle the matter. Second, the parties can be assured that the matter will be handled when first scheduled and not be continued because the court's calendar is too crowded. Finally, the cost can be less than that incurred in full litigation.

Private judging is not without its problems, however. Some critics point to the high fees charged by the retired judges as an area of concern. In a recent California appellate court decision criticizing "rent-a-judge" rulings, it was noted that some of the retired judges may charge $500 or more per hour.[26] The appellate court pointed out that some sitting judges were leaving the bench for greener pastures.

Specialized Courts

The state court systems frequently include a number of specialized courts that are set up to handle particular types of civil cases. Domestic relations courts are often established to deal with such matters as divorce, child custody, and child support. In many jurisdictions probate courts handle the settlement of estates and the contesting of wills.

Perhaps the best known of the specialized courts are the small-claims courts. These courts have jurisdiction to handle cases in which the money being sued for is not above a certain amount. The amount varies by jurisdiction, but the maximum is usually $500 or $1,000. The first small-claims court, established in Cleveland in 1913, had a simplified process, a nominal filing fee, and no requirement that the parties be represented by a lawyer. By 1920 other major cities, including Chicago, Minneapolis, New York, and Philadelphia, as well as the state of Massachusetts, had set up small-claims courts based on the Cleveland model.[27]

Today small-claims courts allow less complex cases to be resolved more informally than in most other trial courts. Filing fees are low, and the summons to the other party to appear in court can often be served by certified mail. Pleadings are often not required, and the use of attorneys is often discouraged.

These courts are not without their problems, however. One complaint prevalent in a number of large cities is that collection agencies use these courts as a relatively cheap and efficient way to collect small debts. New York has enacted legislation to prohibit this use of small-claims courts.[28] And because lawyers are often not used in small-claims court, persons who are not familiar with their legal rights and do not know much about preparing their cases may be at a disadvantage, especially when the other party is experienced in such courts.

Administrative Bodies

A number of government agencies have also established administrative bodies with quasi-judicial authority to handle certain types of cases. At the federal level, for example, agencies such as the Federal Trade Commission and the Federal Communications Commission carry out an adjudication of sorts within their respective spheres of authority. An appeal of the ruling of one of these agencies may be taken to a federal court of appeals.

At the state level, a common example of an administrative body that aids in the resolution of civil claims is a workers' compensation board. This board determines whether an employee's injury is job-related and thus whether the person is entitled to workers' compensation. Many state motor vehicle departments have hearing boards to make determinations about revoking driver's licenses. Another type of administrative board commonly found in the states rules on civil rights matters and cases of alleged discrimination.

The Civil Trial Process

Although many disputes are resolved through some method of alternative dispute resolution, in a specialized court, or by an administrative body, a large number of cases each year still find their way into one of the nation's civil courts.

Generally speaking, the adversarial process used in criminal trials is also used in civil trials, with just a few important differences. First, a litigant must have standing.

This concept means simply that the person initiating the suit must have a personal stake in the outcome of the controversy. Otherwise, there is no real controversy between the parties and thus no actual case for the court to decide.

A second major difference is that the standard of proof used in civil cases is a preponderance of evidence, not the more stringent beyond-a-reasonable-doubt standard used in criminal cases. A preponderance of evidence is generally taken to mean that the evidence is sufficient to overcome doubt or speculation. It clearly means that less proof is required in civil cases than in criminal cases.

A third major difference is that many of the extensive due process guarantees that a defendant has in a criminal trial do not apply in a civil proceeding. For example, neither party is constitutionally entitled to counsel. The Seventh Amendment does guarantee the right to a jury trial in lawsuits "where the value in controversy shall exceed twenty dollars." Although this amendment has not been made applicable to the states, most states have similar constitutional guarantees.[29] The right to a jury trial is commonly assumed in the United States, but it is not universal. In France, for example, there are no juries in civil cases.[30]

Figure 11-2 indicates the basic steps involved in the progression of a civil suit from the filing of a complaint to the termination of the case.

FIGURE 11-2   Trial Progression of Civil Actions

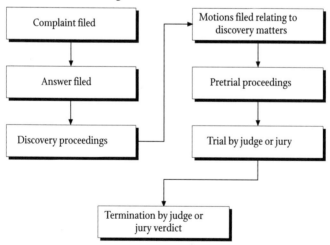

SOURCE: The Federal Judiciary home page, maintained by the Administrative Office of the U.S. Courts, http://www.uscourts.gov/understanding_courts/gifs/figure3.gif.

Filing a Civil Suit

The person initiating the civil suit is known as the plaintiff, and the person being sued is the defendant or the respondent. A civil action is known by the names of the plaintiff and the defendant, such as *Jones v. Miller.* The plaintiff's name appears first. In a typical situation, the plaintiff's attorney pays a fee and files a complaint or petition with the clerk of the proper court. The complaint states the facts on which the action is based, the damages alleged, and the judgment or relief being sought.

It is useful to understand how a decision is made as to which court should hear the case. The decision involves the concepts of jurisdiction and **venue.** Jurisdiction deals with a court's authority to exercise judicial power, and venue means the place where that power should be exercised.

Jurisdictional requirements are satisfied when the court has legal authority over both the subject matter and the person of the defendant. This means that several courts can have jurisdiction over the same case. Suppose, for example, that you are a resident of Dayton, Ohio, and are seriously injured in an automobile accident in Tennessee when the car you are driving is struck from the rear by a car driven by a resident of Kingsport, Tennessee. Total damages to you and your car run about $80,000. A state trial court in Ohio has subject matter jurisdiction, and Ohio can in all likelihood obtain jurisdiction over the defendant. In addition, the state courts of Tennessee probably have jurisdiction. Federal district courts in both Ohio and Tennessee also have jurisdiction because diversity of citizenship exists and the amount in controversy is over $75,000. Assuming that jurisdiction is your only concern, you, as plaintiff, can sue in any of these courts.

Other questions are raised by this hypothetical example: Which of these courts is the proper one to handle the case? Which is the best place for this case to be tried? These questions bring up the problem of venue.

Venue is often a matter of convenience, given that improper venue can be waived. In other words, if a court has proper jurisdiction, and the parties do not object to venue, the court can render a valid judgment.

The determination of proper venue may be prescribed by statute, based on avoiding possible prejudice, or it may simply be a matter of convenience. The federal law states that proper venue is the district in which either the plaintiff or the defendant resides, or the district where the injury occurred. State venue statutes vary somewhat, but they usually stipulate that when land is involved, proper venue is the county where the land is located. In most other instances venue is the county where the defendant resides.

Venue questions may also be related to the perceived or feared prejudice of either the judge or the prospective jury. For this reason, attorneys sometimes object to holding the trial in a particular area and may move for a change of venue. Although this type of objection is perhaps more commonly associated with highly publicized criminal trials, it also occurs in civil trials.

Once the appropriate court has been determined and the complaint has been filed, the court clerk will attach a copy of the complaint to a summons, which is then issued to the defendant. The summons may be served by personnel from the sheriff's office, a U.S. marshal, or a private process-service agency.

The summons directs the defendant to file a response, known as a pleading, within a certain period of time (usually thirty days). If the defendant does not do so, he or she may be subject to a default judgment.

These simple actions by the plaintiff, the clerk of the court, and a process server set the civil case in motion. What happens next is a flurry of activities that precede a trial and may last for several months. Approximately 75 percent of cases are resolved without a trial during this time.[31]

Pretrial Activities

Motions. Once the summons has been served on the defendant, a number of motions can be made by the defense attorney. A motion to quash requests that the court void the summons on the grounds that it was not properly served. For example, a defendant might contend that the summons was never personally delivered to him or her, as required by state law.

Two types of motions are meant to clarify or to object to the plaintiff's petition. A motion to strike requests that the court excise, or strike, certain parts of the petition because they are prejudicial, improper, or irrelevant. Sometimes the defense attorney will file a motion asking the court to require the plaintiff to be more specific about the complaint. For instance, the defendant's attorney may ask that the alleged injuries be described in greater detail.

A fourth type of motion often filed in a civil case is a motion to dismiss, which may argue, for example, that the court lacks jurisdiction. Or it may insist that the plaintiff has not presented a legally sound basis for action against the defendant, even if the allegations are true. This action is called a demurrer in many state courts.

The Answer. If the complaint survives the judge's rulings on the motions, the defendant then submits an **answer** to the complaint. The response may contain admissions, denials, defenses, and counterclaims. When an admission is contained in an answer, there is no need to prove that fact during the trial. A denial, however, brings up a factual issue to be proved during the trial. A defense says that certain facts set forth in the answer may bar the plaintiff from recovery.

The defendant may also create a separate action by seeking relief against the plaintiff. This is known as a counterclaim. In other words, if the defendant thinks that a cause of action against the plaintiff arises from the same set of events, he or she must present the claim to the court in response to the plaintiff's claim. The plaintiff may want to file a reply to the defendant's answer. In that reply, the plaintiff may admit, deny, or defend against the allegations of fact contained in the answer.

Discovery. Although surprise was once a legitimate trial tactic, the present legal system provides discovery procedures that "take the sporting aspect out of litigation and make certain that legal results are based on the true facts of the case—not on the skill of the attorneys." [32] In other words, to prevent surprise at the trial and to encourage settlement, each party is entitled to information in the possession of the other. The term *discovery* "encompasses the methods by which a party or potential party to a lawsuit obtains and preserves information regarding the action." [33]

There are several tools of discovery. A **deposition** is the testimony of a witness taken under oath outside the court. As in the courtroom, the question-and-answer format is used. All parties to the case must be notified that the deposition is to be taken, so that their attorneys may be present to cross-examine the witness.

A second tool of discovery is known as **interrogatories**—written questions that must be answered under oath. Interrogatories can be submitted only to the parties in the case, not to witnesses. They are useful in obtaining descriptions of evidence held by the opposing parties in the suit.

The production of documents is a third tool. One of the parties often requests an inspection of documents, writings, drawings, graphs, charts, maps, photographs, or other items held by the other party.

Finally, when the physical or mental condition of one of the parties is at issue, the court may order that person to submit to an examination by a physician.

What happens if a party refuses to comply with discovery requests? The judge may compel compliance, deem the facts of the case established, dismiss the cause of action, or enter judgment by default.

The Pretrial Conference. As a result of the discovery phase, surprise is no longer a major factor in civil cases. Therefore, a large number of cases are settled without going to trial.[34] In the event the parties do not reach a settlement of their own accord, the judge may try to facilitate such an agreement during a pretrial conference.

Judges call such conferences to discuss the issues in the case informally with the opposing attorneys. The general practice is to allow only the judge and the lawyers to attend the conference, which is normally held in the judge's chambers.

The judge and the attorneys use the conference in an effort to come to some agreement on uncontested factual issues, which are known as stipulations. The purpose of stipulations is to make the trial more efficient. The attorneys also share with each other a list of witnesses and documents that are a part of each case. In the words of Judge J. Skelly Wright, "We make each side disgorge completely and absolutely everything about its case. There can't possibly be surprise, if the lawyers know what they are doing." [35]

Lawyers and judges may also use the pretrial conference to try to settle the case. Some judges actively work to bring about a settlement to avoid going to trial.

The Civil Trial

Selection of Jury. The right to a jury trial in a civil suit in a federal court is guaranteed by the Seventh Amendment. State constitutions likewise provide for this right. A jury trial may be waived, in which case the judge decides the matter. Although the jury traditionally consists of twelve persons, today the number varies. Most of the federal district courts now use juries of fewer than twelve persons in civil cases. A majority of states also authorize smaller juries in some or all civil trials.

Jurors must be selected in a random manner from a cross section of the community. A large panel of jurors is called to the courthouse, and when a case is assigned to a court for trial, a smaller group of prospective jurors is sent to a particular courtroom.

Following the voir dire examination, which may include challenges to certain jurors by the attorneys, a jury to hear the particular case will be seated. Lawyers may challenge a prospective juror for cause, in which case the judge must determine whether the person challenged is impartial. Each side may also exercise a certain number of peremptory challenges—excusing a juror without stating any reason. However, the U.S. Supreme Court has recently ruled that the equal protection guarantee of the Fourteenth Amendment prohibits the use of such challenges to disqualify jurors from civil trials because of their race or gender. [36] Peremptory challenges are fixed by statute or court rule and normally range from two to six.

Opening Statements. After the jury has been chosen, the attorneys present their opening statements. The plaintiff's attorney begins, explaining to the jury what the case is about and what the plaintiff's side expects to prove. The defendant's lawyer can usually choose either to make an opening statement immediately after the plaintiff's attorney finishes or to wait until the plaintiff's case has been completely presented. If the defendant's attorney waits, he or she will present the entire case for the defendant continuously, from opening statement onward. Opening statements are valuable because they outline the case and make it easier for the jury to follow the evidence as it is presented.

Presentation of the Plaintiff's Case. In the average civil case, the plaintiff's side is first to present and attempt to prove its case to the jury and last to make closing arguments. In presenting the case, the plaintiff's lawyer will normally call witnesses to testify and produce documents or other exhibits.

Upon being called, the witness will undergo direct examination by the plaintiff's attorney. Then the defendant's attorney will have the opportunity to ask questions or cross-examine the witness. The Arizona Supreme Court recently took steps to help jurors do a better job of making decisions in civil cases. Among other things, the state's highest court voted to allow jurors to pose written questions to witnesses via the judge.[37] Other states are considering implementing Arizona's practice. Following the cross-examination, the plaintiff's lawyer may conduct a redirect examination, which may be followed by a second cross-examination by the defendant's lawyer.

Generally speaking, witnesses may testify only about matters they have observed; they may not express their opinions. An important exception to this general rule is that expert witnesses are specifically called upon to give their opinions in matters within their areas of expertise.

To qualify as an expert witness, a person must possess substantial knowledge about a particular field. Furthermore, this knowledge must normally be established in open court. Both sides often present experts whose opinions are contradictory. When this happens, the jury must ultimately decide which opinion is the correct one.

When the plaintiff's side has presented all its evidence, the attorney rests the case. It is now the defendant's turn.

Motion for Directed Verdict. After the plaintiff's case has been rested, the defendant will often make a motion for a directed verdict. With the filing of this motion, the defendant is saying that the plaintiff has not proved his or her case and thus should lose. The judge must then decide whether the plaintiff could win at this point if court proceedings were to cease. Should the judge determine that the plaintiff has not presented convincing enough evidence, he or she will sustain the motion and direct the verdict for the defendant. Thus the plaintiff will lose the case.

The motion for a directed verdict is similar to the pretrial motion to dismiss, or demurrer. Essentially, each says "So what?" to the plaintiff—the former in court and the latter before trial.

Presentation of the Defendant's Case. Assuming that the motion for a directed verdict is overruled, the defendant then presents evidence. The defendant's case is presented in the same way as the plaintiff's case—that is, employing direct examination of witnesses and presentation of documents and other exhibits. The plaintiff has the right to cross-examine witnesses. Redirect and recross questions may follow.

Rebuttals. After the presentation of the defendant's case, the plaintiff may bring forth rebuttal evidence, which is aimed at refuting the defendant's evidence. Next, the defendant's lawyer may present evidence to counter the rebuttal evidence. This rebuttal-and-answer pattern may continue until the evidence has been exhausted.

Closing Arguments. After all the evidence has been presented, the lawyers make closing arguments, or summations, to the jury. The plaintiff's attorney speaks both first and last. That is, he or she both opens the argument and closes it, and the defendant's lawyer argues in between. At this stage each attorney attacks the opponent's evidence for its unreliability and may also attempt to discredit the opponent's witnesses. In doing so, the lawyers often wax eloquent or deliver an emotional appeal to the jury. However, the arguments must be based upon facts supported by the evidence and introduced at the trial. In other words, they must stay within the record.

Instructions to the Jury. Assuming that a jury trial has not been waived, the instructions to the jury follow the conclusion of the closing arguments. The judge informs the jury that the verdict must be based on the evidence presented at the trial. The judge's instructions also inform the jurors about the rules, principles, and standards of the particular legal concept involved. In civil cases a finding for the plaintiff is based on a preponderance of the evidence. This means that the jurors must weigh the evidence presented during the trial and be convinced that the greater weight of the evidence, in merit, favors the plaintiff.

The Verdict. The jury retires to the seclusion of the jury room to conduct its deliberations. The members must reach a verdict with no outside contact. In some instances the deliberations are so long and detailed that the jurors must be provided with meals and sleeping accommodations until they can reach a verdict. The verdict, then, represents the jurors' agreement after detailed discussions and analyses of the evidence. Sometimes the jury deliberates in all good faith but cannot reach a verdict. When this occurs, the judge may declare a mistrial, which means that a new trial may have to be conducted.

After the verdict is reached, the jury returns to open court and delivers its verdict to the judge. The parties are informed of the verdict. It is then customary for the jury to be polled by the judge—the jurors are individually asked whether they agree with the verdict.

Post-trial Motions. Once the verdict has been reached, a dissatisfied party may pursue a variety of tactics. The losing party may file a motion for judgment notwithstanding the verdict. This type of motion is granted when the judge decides that reasonable persons would not have rendered the verdict the jury reached. Put another way, this decision says that the verdict is unreasonable in light of the facts presented at the trial and the legal standards to be applied to the case.

The losing party may also file a motion for a new trial. The usual basis for this motion is that the verdict goes against the weight of the evidence. The judge will grant the motion on this ground if he or she agrees that the evidence presented simply does not support the verdict reached by the jury. A new trial may also be granted for a number of other reasons: excessive damages, grossly inadequate damages, the discovery of new evidence, and errors in the production of evidence, to name a few.

In some cases the losing party also files a motion for relief from judgment. This type of motion may be granted if the judge finds a clerical error in the judgment, discovers some new evidence, or determines that the judgment was induced by fraud.

Judgment and Execution. A verdict in favor of the defendant ends the trial. However, a verdict for the plaintiff requires yet another stage in the process. There is no sentence in a civil case, but a determination of the remedy or damages to be assessed must be made. This determination is called the judgment.

In situations where the judgment is for monetary damages and the defendant does not voluntarily pay the set amount, the plaintiff can ask to have the court clerk issue an order to execute the judgment. The execution is issued to the sheriff and orders the sheriff to seize the defendant's property and sell it at auction to satisfy the judgment. An alternative is to order a lien, which is the legal right to hold property that may be used for payment of the judgment.

Appeal. If one party feels that an error of law was made during the trial, and if the judge refuses to grant a post-trial motion for a new trial, the dissatisfied party may appeal to a higher court. Probably the most common grounds for appeal are that the judge allegedly admitted evidence that should have been excluded, refused to admit evidence that should have been introduced, or failed to give proper instructions to the jury.

An attorney lays the groundwork for an appeal by objecting to the alleged error during the trial. This objection goes into the trial record and becomes part of the trial transcript, which may be reviewed by an appellate court. The appellate court decision may call for the lower court to enforce its earlier verdict or to hold a new trial.

Summary

In this chapter we focused on the handling of civil cases. We began by looking at some of the important categories of civil law: contracts, torts, property, the law of succession, and family law.

We then discussed the alternative dispute resolution movement, which has been in existence for some time but has only recently captured significant attention from the courts. We described several ADR techniques being used by federal and state courts to solve the problems of increasing caseloads and troublesome backlogs.

Finally, we examined the procedure followed in resolving civil cases. Once a complaint has been filed in a civil case, a number of pretrial motions may narrow the scope of the dispute or lead to a settlement of the case. As in criminal cases, most civil cases never go to trial. The discovery process is also useful in narrowing the scope of the case and preventing surprises should the case proceed to trial.

The cases that are not settled prior to trial become part of a fairly standard process, which was discussed step by step. Where appropriate, we pointed out the differences between a civil trial and a criminal trial.

Further Thought and Discussion Questions

1. Do the high amounts often awarded by juries as punitive damages in product liability cases indicate that juries are out of control or that manufacturers are producing an inordinate number of defective or unsafe products?

2. Are jurors qualified to determine the amount of compensatory and punitive damages that should be awarded to a successful plaintiff? Or should that task be handled only by a judge?

3. Does the increased use of various methods of alternative dispute resolution conflict with the often-heard view that every person is entitled to his or her day in court?

NOTES

1. Herbert Jacob, *Justice in America*, 4th ed. (Boston: Little, Brown, 1984), 210.

2. We are indebted to Lawrence M. Friedman, from whom we borrowed the classifications and on whose work our discussion is based. See Lawrence M. Friedman, *American Law* (New York: W. W. Norton, 1984), 141–153.

3. See Doris Marie Provine, "Courts in the Political Process in France," in *Courts, Law, and Politics in Comparative Perspective*, ed. Herbert Jacob, Herbert M. Kritzer, Doris Marie Provine, Erhard Blankenburg, and Joseph Sanders (New Haven, Conn.: Yale University Press, 1996), 237.

4. All figures were obtained from Brian J. Ostrom and Neal B. Kauder, *Examining the Work of State Courts 1998: A National Perspective from the Court Statistics Project* (Williamsburg, Va.: National Center for State Courts, 1999), 34–35.

5. See Herbert Kritzer, "Courts, Justice, and Politics in England," in *Courts, Law, and Politics in Comparative Perspective*, ed. Jacob, Kritzer, Provine, Blankenburg, and Sanders, 145.

6. See American Tort Reform Association Web site available online at http://www.atra.org/.

7. *State Farm Mutual Automobile Insurance Co. v. Campbell et al.* (2003), available online at http://supct.law.cornell.edu/supct/html/01-1289.ZS.html.

8. Kritzer, "Courts, Justice, and Politics in England," 140.

9. See Erhard Blankenburg, "Changes in Political Regimes and Continuity of the Rule of Law in Germany," in *Courts, Law, and Politics in Comparative Perspective*, ed. Jacob, Kritzer, Provine, Blankenburg, and Sanders, 303.

10. William T. Schantz, *The American Legal Environment* (St. Paul, Minn.: West, 1976), 565.

11. See L. Lander, *Defective Medicine* (New York: Farrar, Straus and Giroux, 1978), chap. 1.

12. Mitchell S. G. Klein, *Law, Courts, and Policy* (Englewood Cliffs, N.J.: Prentice Hall, 1984), 196.

13. See S. Law and S. Polan, *Pain and Profit: The Politics of Malpractice* (New York: Harper and Row, 1978), 7, 8.

14. Friedman, *American Law*, 146.

15. See Charles A. Beard, *An Economic Interpretation of the Constitution of the United States* (New York: Macmillan, 1913).

16. Klein, *Law, Courts, and Policy*, 183.

17. See *Village of Euclid v. Ambler Realty Co.*, 272 U.S. 365 (1926).

18. See *Nectow v. City of Cambridge*, 277 U.S. 188 (1928).

19. See Schantz, *The American Legal Environment*, 291.

20. Richard E. Miller and Austin Sarat, "Grievances, Claims, and Disputes: Assessing the Adversary Culture," *Law and Society Review* 15 (1980–1981): 525–566.

21. Kritzer, "Courts, Justice, and Politics in England," 126.

22. Ibid.

23. Susan L. Keilitz, "Alternative Dispute Resolution in the Courts," in *Handbook of Court Administration and Management*, ed. Steven W. Hays and Cole Blease Graham Jr. (New York: Marcel Dekker, 1993), 384.

24. Ibid.

25. Ibid.

26. "Judge Slams Rent-a-Judge Rulings," *National Law Journal*, November 11, 1996, A8. The case is *McMillan v. Superior Court*, B105356 (1996).

27. See Howard Abadinsky, *Law and Justice*, 2d ed. (Chicago: Nelson-Hall, 1991), 273; and Christine B. Harrington, *Shadow Justice: The Ideology and Institutionalization of Alternatives to Court* (Westport, Conn.: Greenwood, 1985).

28. See Abadinsky, *Law and Justice*, 273.

29. See Jack H. Friedenthal, Mary Kay Kane, and Arthur R. Miller, *Civil Procedure* (St. Paul, Minn.: West, 1985).

30. Provine, "Courts in the Political Process in France," 238.

31. See Abadinsky, *Law and Justice*, 268.

32. Schantz, *The American Legal Environment*, 169.

33. Friedenthal, Kane, and Miller, *Civil Procedure*, 380.

34. See Kenneth M. Holland, "The Federal Rules of Civil Procedure," *Law and Policy Quarterly* 3 (1981): 212.

35. J. Skelly Wright, "The Pretrial Conference," in *American Court Systems: Readings in Judicial Process and Behavior*, ed. Sheldon Goldman and Austin Sarat (San Francisco: Freeman, 1978), 120.

36. See *Edmondson v. Leesville Concrete Co.*, 500 U.S. 614 (1991) and *J.E.B. v. Alabama Ex Rel. T.B.*, 511 U.S. 127 (1994), respectively. The Supreme Court declined to hear a case from Minnesota that raised the question of whether the same principle should be extended to religion. See Linda Greenhouse, "Fierce Combat on Fewer Battlefields," *New York Times*, July 3, 1994, E4.

37. See Margaret A. Jacobs, "Arizona High Court Alters Jury Practices," *Wall Street Journal*, November 2, 1995, B4.

SUGGESTED READINGS

Alfini, James J. "Alternative Dispute Resolution and the Courts: An Introduction." *Judicature* (1986): 252. A good introduction to arbitration and mediation.

Carter, Lief, Austin Sarat, Mark Silverstein, and William Weaver. *New Perspectives on American Law.* Durham, N.C.: Carolina Academic Press, 1997. An excellent discussion of contracts, property, and torts, as well as a good overview of civil procedure.

Friedenthal, Jack H., Mary Kay Kane, and Arthur R. Miller. *Civil Procedure.* St. Paul, Minn.: West, 1985. A discussion of the rules relating to civil procedures in the courts.

Friedman, Lawrence. *American Law.* New York: W. W. Norton, 1984. A good introduction to the nature and substance of civil law in the United States.

Hames, Joanne Banker, and Yvonne Ekern. *Introduction to Law,* 2d ed. Upper Saddle River, N.J.: Pearson Education, Inc., 2002. A good introduction to law in the United States, with good discussions of family law, wills, trusts, probate, and alternative dispute resolution.

Harrington, Christine B. *Shadow Justice: The Ideology and Institutionalization of Alternatives to Court.* Westport, Conn.: Greenwood, 1985. The book focuses on the various alternatives available to people in resolving disputes.

Jacob, Herbert. *Silent Revolution: The Transformation of Divorce Law in the United States.* Chicago: University of Chicago Press, 1988. A detailed account of reforms in divorce law in the United States.

Jacob, Herbert, Herbert M. Kritzer, Doris Marie Provine, Erhard Blankenburg, and Joseph Sanders. *Courts, Law, and Politics in Comparative Perspective.* New Haven, Conn.: Yale University Press, 1996. An excellent comparative study of the processing of civil cases (as well as criminal cases). The countries included in the book are the United Kingdom, France, Germany, Japan, and the United States.

Kritzer, Herbert M. *The Justice Broker: Lawyers and Ordinary Litigation.* New York: Oxford University Press, 1990. The book focuses on civil proceedings in the United States.

Melone, Albert P., and Allan Karnes. *The American Legal System.* Los Angeles: Roxbury Publishing Company, 2003. An excellent discussion of all major aspects of civil law, civil case processing, and alternative dispute resolution.

Miller, Richard E., and Austin Sarat. "Grievances, Claims, and Disputes: Assessing the Adversary Culture." *Law and Society Review* 15 (1980–1981): 525–566. A study of the evolution of civil cases from grievances to court cases.

CHAPTER 12

Decision Making by Trial Court Judges

Most criminal court cases in the United States are never appealed. Of those that are, an overwhelming majority are simply affirmed by the appellate courts. Such facts underscore the importance of the intelligence, honesty, and competence of the trial court judge in assuring the fairness and integrity of the U.S. judicial process. In this photo, Judge Larry Fidler makes a point during a sentencing hearing for former Symbionese Liberation Army fugitive Sara Jane Olson. Olson received 20-years-to-life for conspiring to blow up police cars in 1975.

O N WHAT BASIS AND FOR what reasons do judges in the United States rule the way they do on the motions, petitions, and judicial policy questions that require their attention? We will respond to this query by summarizing the theories and research findings of a large number of judicial scholars who have tried to find out what makes judges tick. (Chapter 13 will examine the special case of decision making on the collegial appellate courts at the state and federal levels.) In this chapter we will examine federal and state jurists as a group because, to a large extent, the variables that influence judicial decision making are the same for judges at both levels. For instance, both types of judges tend to be strongly governed by court precedents, and virtually all judges reflect to some degree their political party affiliation. Where differences between federal and state judges can be anticipated, we will take note of this. For example, one would expect public opinion to have less effect on federal judges, who are appointed for life, than it has on those state judges who must regularly stand for reelection.

It is useful to begin with a brief discussion of the decision-making environment in which trial judges and their appellate colleagues operate. Because of the differing purposes and organizational frameworks of trial and appellate courts, judges of each type face particular kinds of pressure and expectations. However, all jurists are subject to two major kinds of influence, as described by Richard J. Richardson and

Kenneth N. Vines: the legal subculture and the democratic subculture.[1] In any given case, it is often difficult to determine the relative impact of a specific influence on a judge. Studies have suggested that when judges, especially trial judges, find no significant precedent to guide them—that is, when the legal subculture cupboard is bare—they tend to turn to the democratic subculture, an amalgam of determinants that includes their own political inclinations.

At the base of the federal and state judicial hierarchies are the trial court judges, who preside over the judicial process and corporately make hundreds of millions of decisions each year. Some decisions pertain to legal points and procedures raised by litigants even before a trial begins, such as a motion by a criminal defendant's lawyer to exclude from trial a piece of illegally obtained evidence. During the trial a judge must rule on scores of motions made by the attorneys in the case—for example, an objection to a particular question asked of a witness or a request to strike contested testimony from the record. Even after a verdict has been rendered, a trial judge may be confronted with demands for decisions—for instance, a litigant's request to reduce a monetary award made by a civil jury.

Trial judges can and occasionally do take ample time to reflect on the more important decisions and may consult with their staff or other judges about how to handle a particular legal problem. Nevertheless, a significant portion of their decision making must be done on the spur of the moment, without the luxury of lengthy reflection or discussion with staff or colleagues. As one trial judge told us, "We're where the action is. We often have to 'shoot from the hip' and hope you're doing the right thing. You can't ruminate forever every time you have to make a ruling. We'd be spending months on each case if we ever did that." (Virtually all of the judges interviewed for this study were promised anonymity.)

Decision making by the appeals courts and the supreme courts is different in several important respects. By the time a case reaches the appellate level, the record and facts have already been established. The jurists' job is to review dispassionately the transcript of a trial that has already occurred, to search for legal errors that may have been committed by others. Few snap judgments are required. And although the appeals courts and a supreme court may occasionally hear oral arguments by attorneys, they do not examine witnesses and they are removed from the drama and confrontations of the trial courtroom. Another difference in the decision-making process is that the trial level is largely individualistic, whereas the appellate level is to some degree the product of group deliberation.

Despite the acknowledged differences between trial and appellate judge decision making, all American jurists have many values in common. We will examine several studies that have sought to explain why judges, in general, think and act as they do, using Richardson and Vines's basic analytic framework. The thrust of these scholarly efforts has differed. Some view judges as judicial computers who take in a volume of facts, law, and legal doctrines and spew out "correct" rulings—determinations that are virtually independent of the judges' values and characteristics as human beings. Other researchers tend to explain judicial decision making in terms of the personal orientations of the judges. A decision is seen not so much as the product of some unbiased, exacting thought process that judges learn in law school but rather as having been affected by the judge's life experiences, prejudices, and overall social values. As with most theories of human behavior, each of these approaches has its fair share of the truth, but none provide the whole story.

The Legal Subculture

It is useful in examining the legal subculture as a source of trial judge decision making to focus on a number of specific questions. What are the basic rules, practices, and norms of this subculture? Where do judges learn these principles, and what groups or institutions keep judges from departing from them? How often and under what circumstances do judges respond to stimuli other than those from the traditional legal realm?

The Nature of Legal Reasoning

In a popular television series of the 1970s, *The Paper Chase*, the formidable Professor Kingsfield promises his budding law students that if they work hard and entrust their mush-filled brains to him, he will instill in them the ability "to think like a lawyer." How do lawyers and judges think when they deliberate in their professional capacities? One classic answer to this question is that "the basic pattern of legal reasoning is reasoning by example. It is a three-step process described by the doctrine of precedent as follows: (1) similarity is seen between cases; (2) the rule of law inherent in the first case is announced; and (3) the rule of law is made applicable to the second case." [2]

For example, the cases of *Lane v. Wilson* and *Gomillion v. Lightfoot* had similar arguments and factual situations.[3] In the former case, a black citizen of Oklahoma brought suit in federal court, alleging that he had been deprived of the right to vote. In 1916 the legislature of that state had passed a law, ostensibly designed to give formerly disenfranchised black citizens the right to vote, that required them to register—but the registration period lasted only twelve days. (White voters were for all practical purposes exempted from this scheme through the use of a "grandfather clause.") If blacks did not sign up within that short interval, never again would they have the right to vote. The Oklahoma legislature clearly realized that a twelve-day period was wholly inadequate for blacks to mount a voter registration drive and that the vast majority would not acquire the franchise. The plaintiff in this case did not get on the registration rolls in 1916. When he was thereafter forbidden to vote, he brought suit, claiming that the Oklahoma registration scheme was unconstitutional. The Supreme Court agreed with the plaintiff. In striking down the statute, it set forth this principle, or rule of law: "The Fifteenth Amendment nullifies sophisticated as well as simple-minded modes of discrimination." [4]

Two decades later another black citizen, Charles Gomillion, brought suit in the federal courts, alleging a denial of his right to vote as secured by the Fifteenth Amendment. Here an Alabama statute altered the Tuskegee city boundaries from a square to a twenty-eight-sided figure, allegedly removing "all save only four or five of its 400 Negro voters while not removing a single white voter or resident." Although not denying a legislature's right to alter city boundaries "under normal circumstances," the Court saw through the Alabama legislature's thinly disguised attempt to deny suffrage to the black citizens of Tuskegee. Reasoning that the situation in *Gomillion* was analogous to that in the Oklahoma case, the Court used the precedent of *Lane v. Wilson* to strike down the Alabama law: "It is difficult to appreciate what stands in the way of adjudging a statute having this inevitable effect invalid in light of the principles of which this Court must judge, and uniformly has judged, statutes that, howsoever speciously defined, obviously discriminate against colored citizens. 'The Fifteenth Amendment nullifies sophisticated as well as simple-minded modes of discrimination.' *Lane v. Wilson*." This is one example of the judicial reasoning process—of thinking like Professor Kingsfield's lawyer. Two cases are compared because the facts or principles are similar; a rule of law gleaned from the first case is applied to the second. This step-by-step process is the essence of proper and traditional legal reasoning.

Adherence to Precedent

A related value held by trial and appellate judges is a commitment to follow precedents— decisions rendered on similar subjects by judges in the past. The sacred doctrine of stare decisis ("stand by what has been decided") is a cardinal principle of the common law tradition. In a series of interviews, William Kitchin asked federal district judges to rate the importance of "clear and directly relevant" precedents in their decision-making process. Precedent attained a score of 90.44 on a

100-point scale, whereas the judge's "personal, abstract view of justice in the case" was ranked only 60.69.[5] As for appellate court judges, one study of appeals courts in the Second, Fifth, and District of Columbia Circuits concluded that "adherence to precedent remains the everyday, working rule of American law, enabling appellate judges to control the premises of decision of subordinates who apply general rules to particular cases."[6] The U.S. Supreme Court, although technically free to depart from its own precedents, does so rarely, for when "the Court reverses itself or makes new law out of whole cloth—reveals its policy-making role for all to see—the holy rite of judges consulting a higher law loses some of its mysterious power."[7] Indeed a recent study of the Supreme Court found that "in any given decade, the Court overturns less than .002 percent of its previous decisions."[8]

Ideally, adherence to past rulings endows the law with predictability and continuity and reduces the dangerous possibility that judges will decide cases on a momentary whim or with an individualistic sense of right and wrong. Not all legal systems have placed such emphasis on stare decisis. In early Greek times, for example, the judge-kings decided each case on the basis of what appeared fair and just to them at the moment. When a judge-king resolved a dispute, the judgment was assumed to be the result of direct divine inspiration.[9] The early Greek model is thus the antithesis of the common law tradition. However, strict adherence to past precedent may be something of a legal fiction. Judges can and do distinguish among various precedents in creating new law. This helps to keep the law flexible and reflective of changing societal values and practices. Many scholars have argued that the readiness of common law judges to occasionally discard or ignore precedents that no longer serve the public has contributed to the survival of the common law tradition.

Constraints on Trial Judge Decision Making

Another significant element of the legal subculture is found under the heading of what one prominent scholar has called the "great maxims of judicial self-restraint."[10] These maxims derive from a variety of sources—the common law, statutory law, legal tradition—but each serves to limit and channel the decision making of state and federal judges. Because these various principles have already been discussed in detail, we will merely reiterate here a few of the major themes of judicial self-restraint.

Before a judge will agree to consider a lawsuit, a definite case or controversy at law or in equity must exist between bona fide adversaries under the Constitution. The case must concern the protection or enforcement of valuable legal rights or the punishment, prevention, or redress of wrongs directly related to the litigants. Allied with this maxim is the principle that U.S. judges may not render advisory opinions, that is, rulings on abstract, hypothetical questions. (This rule is not followed as strictly in many state systems.) Also, all parties to a lawsuit must have standing, or a substantial personal interest infringed by the statute or action in question.

The rules of the game also forbid jurists to hear a case unless all other legal remedies have been exhausted. In addition, the legal culture discourages the judiciary from deciding political questions or matters that ought to be resolved by one of the other branches of government, by another level of government, or by the voters. Judges are also obliged to give the benefit of the doubt to statutes and official actions when their constitutionality is being questioned. A law or an executive action is presumed to be constitutional until proven otherwise. (Some judges adhere to this principle on economic issues but not on matters of civil rights and civil liberties, believing that in these matters the burden of proof is on the government.) In this same realm, judges feel bound by the norm that if a law must be invalidated, they will do so on as narrow a ground as possible or will void only that portion of the statute that is unconstitutional.

Finally, American jurists may not throw out a law or an official action simply because they personally believe it is unfair, stupid, or undemocratic. For a statute or an official deed to be invalidated, it must clearly be unconstitutional. Judges do not always agree about what is a clearly unconstitutional act, but most acknowledge that broad matters of public policy should be determined by the people through their elected representatives—not by the judiciary.

The Impact of the Legal Subculture: An Example

Because the principles that make up the legal subculture—reasoning, precedent, and restraint—tend to be abstract, it is useful to illustrate them with a real-life example. *Evers v. Jackson Municipal Separate School District* was an uncomplicated 1964 school integration case in which a group of black children and their parents sought to enjoin the "district and its officials from operating a compulsory biracial school system." [11] The facts and controlling precedents were clear: (1) Jackson, Mississippi, was overtly maintaining a segregated public school system; (2) the U.S. Supreme Court had ruled a decade earlier, in *Brown v. Board of Education*, that such segregation was unconstitutional; and (3) the U.S. Court of Appeals for the Fifth Circuit, which has jurisdiction over Mississippi, had handed down a string of rulings ordering the integration process to go forward.

The federal trial judge in *Evers,* Sidney Mize, did not like the commands he heard from the legal subculture. Appointed to the federal bench in 1937, Mize was an unabashed segregationist, as his written opinion in this case clearly shows. After discussing a score of alleged physical and mental differences between blacks and whites, Mize argued further that

in the case of Caucasians and Negroes, such differences may be directly confirmed by comparative anatomical and encephalographic measurements of the correlative physical structure of the brain and of the neural and endocrine systems of the body. The evidence was conclusive to the effect that the cranial capacity and brain size of the average Negro is approximately ten per cent less than that of the average white person of similar age and size, and that brain size is correlated with intelligence.[12]

On an ostensibly more positive and benign note, Judge Mize also argued, "From the evidence I find that separate classes allow greater adaptation to the differing educational traits of Negro and white pupils, and actually result in greater scholastic accomplishments for both." [13]

It seems clear where this decision was headed. But wait: Enter the legal subculture. After fourteen single-spaced printed pages of argument against the integration of the Jackson schools, Mize yielded to the requirements of legal reasoning, respect for precedent, and judicial self-restraint. Almost sheepishly he concluded his decision with these unexpected words:

Nevertheless, this Court feels that it is bound by what appears to be the obvious holding of the United States Court of Appeals for the Fifth Circuit that if disparities and differences such as that reflected in this record are to constitute a proper basis for the maintenance of separate schools for the white and Negro races it is the function of the United States Supreme Court to make such a decision and no inferior federal court can do so.[14]

Mize then quietly enjoined the school district and its officials from operating a compulsory biracial school system. The legal subculture tiptoed to victory.

Wellsprings of the Legal Subculture

The institutions that instill and maintain the legal values in the United States are "the law schools, the bar associations, the judicial councils, and other groups that spring from the institutionalization of the 'bench and the bar.' " [15]

"The purpose of law school," a scholar wrote, "is to change people; to turn them into novice lawyers; and to instill in them a nascent self-concept as a professional, a commitment to the value of the calling, and a claim to that elusive and esoteric style of reasoning called 'thinking like a lawyer.' " [16] The world just does not look the same to someone on whom law school has worked its indoctrinating magic. Facts and relationships in the human arena that formerly went unnoticed suddenly become "compelling" and "controlling" to the fledgling advocate. Likewise, other facets of reality that previously had been important in one's world view are now dismissed as "irrelevant and immaterial."

Besides the indoctrination that occurs in law school, the values of the legal sub-culture are maintained by the state and national bar associations and by a variety of professional-social groups whose members are from both bench and bar—for example, the honorary Order of the Coif.[17] The values and practices of jurists are handed down from one generation to another. Thus the traditions and tenets of the American legal subculture are well tended by powerful support groups. They are rightly accorded ample deference if one is to understand judicial decision making in America.

The Limits of the Legal Subculture

Despite the taut nature of judicial reasoning and the importance of stare decisis and judicial self-restraint, the legal subculture does not totally explain the behavior of American jurists. If objective facts and obvious controlling precedents were the only stimuli to which jurists responded, the judicial decision-making process would be largely mechanical, and all judicial outcomes would be predictable. Yet even the legal subculture's most loyal apologists would concede that judges often distinguish between precedents and that some judges are more inclined than others toward self-restraint.

To understand the thinking of judicial decision makers and the evolution of the law, it is necessary to consider more than law school curricula and the canons of the bar associations. One of the first great minds to realize this was Justice Oliver Wendell Holmes Jr., who over a century ago wrote that

the life of the law has not been logic; it has been experience. The felt necessities of the time, the prevalent moral and political theories, intuitions of public policy, avowed or uncon-scious, even the prejudices which judges share with their fellow-men have had a good deal more to do than syllogism in determining the rules by which men should be governed. The law embodies the story of a nation's development through many centuries, and it cannot be dealt with as if it contained only the axioms and corollaries of a book of mathematics. In or-der to know what it is, we must know what it has been, and what it tends to become. . . . The very considerations which judges most rarely mention, and always with an apology, are the secret root from which the law draws all the juices of life. I mean, of course, considerations of what is expedient for the community concerned.[18]

By about the 1920s a whole school of thought had developed that argued that ju-dicial decision making is as much the product of human, extralegal stimuli as it is of some sort of mechanical legal thought process. Adherents of this view, who were known as **judicial realists,** insisted that judges, like other human beings, are influenced by the values and attitudes learned in childhood. As one of these realists put it, a judge's background "may have created plus or minus reactions to women, or blonde women, or men with beards, or Southerners, or Italians, or Englishmen, or plumbers, or ministers, or college graduates, or Democrats. A certain facial twitch or cough or gesture may start up memories, painful or pleasant." [19]

Since the late 1940s, the study of the personal, extralegal influences on decision making has become more rigorous. Often calling themselves judicial behavioralists, modern-day advocates of the realist approach have improved on it in two ways. First, they have tried to test empirically many of the theories and propositions advanced by the realist school. Second, they have attempted to relate their findings to more scientifically grounded theories of human behavior. Thus, whereas a realist might have asserted that a Democratic judge would probably be more supportive of labor unions than a Republican jurist would be, a judicial behavioralist might go a step further by taking a generous random sample of labor-union-versus-management decisions and statistically determining whether Democratic judges are significantly more likely than their GOP counterparts to back the union. It is one thing to intuitively ascribe a cause for human behavior; it is another to subject an assertion to careful empirical analysis.

The Democratic Subculture

The legal subculture has an impact on American jurists. Evidence shows that popular democratic values—manifested in a variety of ways through many different mediums—have an influence as well. Some scholars have argued that the only reason courts have maintained their significant role in the American political system is that they have learned to bend when the democratic winds have blown. That is, judges have tempered rigid legalisms with commonsense popular values and have maintained "extensive linkages with the democratic subculture."

Very often, legal elites such as bar associations and judicial councils are more noticeable spokesmen for the federal judiciary than are the spokesmen of the democratic subculture. However, representatives of the democratic subculture, such as members of political parties, members of social and economic groups, and local state political elites, can also be observed commenting on controversial questions. In matters like staffing the courts, determining their structure and organization, and fixing federal jurisdiction, democratic representatives have access through Congress and other institutions that are influential in establishing judicial policy. Although Congress provides a main channel to the federal courts, access for democratic values is also obtained through the President, the attorney general, and nonlegal officials who deal with the judiciary. In addition, the location of federal courts throughout the states and regions renders them unusually susceptible to local and regional democratic forces.[20]

In discussing the democratic subculture, we will focus on the influences most often observed by students of the American court system—political party identification, localism, public opinion, and the legislative and executive branches of government.

The Influence of Political Party Affiliation

Do the political party affiliations of judges affect the way they decide certain cases? The question is straightforward enough, but the responses are by no means in unanimous agreement. To most attorneys, judges, and court watchers among the general public, the question rings with outright impertinence, and their answer is usually something like this: After taking the judicial oath and donning the black robe, a judge is no longer a Republican or a Democrat. Former affiliations are (or at least certainly should be) put aside as the judge enters a realm in which decisions are the product of evidence, sound judicial reasoning, and precedent, as opposed to such a base factor as political identification. Or, as Donald Dale Jackson quipped in his perceptive book *Judges*, "Most judges would sooner admit to grand larceny than confess a political interest or motivation."[21]

Despite the cries of indignation from those who contend that the legal subculture explains virtually all judicial decision making, a mounting body of evidence strongly suggests that judges' political identification does affect their behavior on the bench.[22] Studies have shown that other personal factors—such as religion, gender, race, pre-judicial career, and the level of prestige of their law school education—may also play a role. However, only political party affiliation seems to have any significant and consistent capacity to explain and predict the outcome of judicial decisions.[23] One prominent student of American politics explains why there may be a cause-and-effect relationship between judges' party allegiance and their decisional patterns:

If judges are party identifiers before reaching the bench, there would be a basis for believing that they—like legislators—are affected in their issue orientations by party. . . . Furthermore, judges are generally well educated and the vote studies show that the more educated tend to be stronger party identifiers, to cast policy preferences in ideological terms, to have clearer perceptions of issues and of party positions on those issues, to have issue attitudes consistent with the positions of the party with which they identify, and to be more interested and involved in politics. For judges, even more than for the general population, party may therefore be a significant reference group on issues.[24]

Federal District Court Judges. Given the relationship between party affiliation and court decision making, the following observation should come as no surprise: As a whole, Democratic trial judges on the U.S. district courts are more liberal than their Republican colleagues. In a study of more than sixty-six thousand published district court decisions reached between 1932 and 2002, Democratic judges took the liberal position 47 percent of the time, whereas Republican jurists did so in only 38 percent of the cases.[25] Thus, for our seventy-year time frame, the Democrats' ratio of liberal-to-conservative opinions has been 1.45 times greater (more liberal) than the Republican ratio.[26] Although the overall differences cannot be called overwhelming, neither can they be dismissed as inconsequential.

As the data in Table 12-1 suggest, differences between Republican and Democratic judges depend considerably on the type of case. An analysis of partisan voting patterns in twenty-five separate case categories indicates that differences between judges from the two parties were greatest for cases concerning the right to privacy (for example, abortion, gay and lesbian rights), race discrimination controversies, disputes about state and local government efforts to regulate the economic lives of their citizens, and support for affirmative action programs involving race and gender. Partisan differences were modest in cases involving rent controls and excess profits, in disputes between union members and their union hierarchy, and in suits brought by the secretary of labor (or the National Labor Relations Board) against a labor union.

All these facts and figures would become more meaningful if one could enter into the minds of typical Republican and Democratic judges and view the world from their perspectives. Barring that, however, excerpts of interviews with two jurists who are lifelong members of each of the two parties are revealing. Sitting in the same city and on the same day, they discussed a subject that in recent decades has divided Republican and Democratic judges—their philosophy of criminal justice and, more specifically, their views about sentencing convicted felons. The rank-and-file Democrat (appointed by Lyndon B. Johnson) said in part:

Most of the people who appear before me for sentencing come from the poorer classes and have had few of the advantages of life. They've had an uphill fight all the way and life has constantly stepped on them. . . . I come from a pretty humble background myself, and I know what it's like. I think I take all this into consideration when I have to sentence someone, and it inclines me towards handing down lighter sentences, I think.

One hour later a lifelong Republican (appointed by Richard M. Nixon) addressed the same issue, but with a different twist at the end:

TABLE 12-1 Liberal Decisions of Federal District Court Judges in Order of Magnitude of Partisan Differences for Twenty-five Types of Cases, 1932–2003

	Overall	Democrat	Republican	Partisan difference	Odds ratio[a]
Right to privacy	47%	66%	34%	32%	3.75
Race discrimination	45	55	33	22	2.42
Local economic regulation	66	76	57	19	2.37
Affirmative action programs (race and gender)	56	68	49	19	2.23
Women's rights	49	57	42	15	1.78
Freedom of religion	50	56	43	13	1.74
Criminal convictions	37	43	31	12	1.69
Freedom of expression	57	63	51	12	1.68
Fourteenth Amendment	36	42	30	12	1.67
Age discrimination	34	41	30	11	1.62
Rights of the disabled	41	48	37	11	1.60
U.S. habeas corpus pleas	27	30	22	8	1.56
Voting rights	48	53	44	9	1.45
Environmental protection	62	67	58	9	1.44
Criminal court motions	30	34	27	7	1.42
Secretary of Labor or NLRB v. employer	61	65	57	8	1.41
U.S. commercial regulation	69	73	65	8	1.40
Alien petitions	40	43	35	8	1.39
Union v. company	51	54	48	6	1.27
Employee v. employer	37	40	35	5	1.26
Native American rights and law	50	53	47	6	1.25
State habeas corpus pleas	25	27	23	4	1.22
Secretary of Labor or NLRB v. union	63	67	62	5	1.18
Rent control, excess profits	60	62	58	4	1.14
Union member v. union	42	44	41	3	1.14

SOURCE: Data collected by Robert A. Carp, Kenneth L. Manning, and Ronald Stidham.

NOTE: NLRB stands for the National Labor Relations Board.

[a] The odds ratio, also called the cross-product ratio, is a measure of the relationship between two dichotomous variables. Specifically, it is a measure of the relative odds of respondents from each independent variable category being placed in a single dependent variable category.

When I was first appointed, I was one of those big law-and-order types. You know—just put all those crooks and hippies in jail and all will be right with the world. But I've changed a lot. I never realized what poor, pathetic people there are who come before us for sentencing. My God, the terrible childhoods and horrendous backgrounds that some of them come from! Mistreated when they were kids and kicked around by everybody in the world for most of their lives. Society has clearly failed them. As a judge there's only one thing you can do: send them to prison for as long as the law allows because when they're in that bad a state there's nothing anyone can do with them. All you can do is protect society from these poor souls for as long as you can.

Although we would not contend that all Republican and all Democratic trial judges think precisely in these terms, we believe that something of the spirit of partisan differences is captured in these two quotations.

Federal Appeals Court Judges. As for partisan variations in the voting patterns of U.S. appeals court judges, here, too, evidence shows that their (prior) party affiliation tempers their decision making to some degree.[27] Studies conducted during the 1960s by Sheldon Goldman and others concluded that "on balance, the findings underscore the absence of a sharp ideological party cleavage in the United States but also give support to the contention that the center of gravity of the Democratic party is more 'liberal' than that of the Republican party." [28] These early studies indicated that partisan differences tended to be greatest on economic issues. GOP jurists were more likely than their Democratic counterparts to oppose government efforts to regulate the economy and to support business in its judicial tussles with labor. More recently, however, the field of battle has switched from the economic realm to that of the rights of criminal defendants and civil rights and liberties. Studies show that Democratic judges on the whole tend to be more supportive of the rights of criminal defendants and of those seeking to expand First and Fourteenth Amendment freedoms.[29]

For example, a 1990 study of voting patterns among appellate court judges was conducted for decisions made en banc—by all or a specified number of the judges in a circuit court of appeals instead of by the usual three-judge panels. This study focused primarily on partisan differences in cases dealing with criminal justice and civil liberties issues. The researchers found that support for criminal appellants by the Democrats (in effect, the Jimmy Carter appointees) was 58.9 percent, whereas for Republican appointees the figures were significantly lower—19.9 percent for Nixon's judicial team and 22.3 percent for Ronald Reagan's. Likewise, the Carter Democrats supported the civil liberties petitioners 67.1 percent of the time, whereas Nixon's cohort did so 38.5 percent of the time and Reagan's team took the stance in only 29.8 percent of the cases.[30]

U.S. Supreme Court Justices. Does political party affiliation affect the way members of the U.S. Supreme Court decide some of their cases? Although scholars have found this to be a difficult subject to investigate, the evidence suggests a mild but positive yes. The research hurdle stems, in part, from the fact that the Court has nine justices, and generalizing about the behavior of groups this small is virtually impossible. Moreover, numerous political parties have been represented on the

Court in its more than two-century history, and the definitions of Federalist, Democrat, Whig, Republican, liberal, and conservative have varied so much over time that generalizations become difficult. For example, prior to the 1920s, most mainstream Democrats opposed civil rights for blacks. Since that era most champions of the civil rights movement have been Democrats. In the jargon of the trade, the variables are so numerous and the n's (number of justices) are so small that statistically significant observations are extremely difficult to make.

Despite the methodological problems involved, some judicial scholars have sought to explore this subject. In a comprehensive study of the relationship between party affiliation and the liberal-conservative voting patterns of the justices in the twentieth century, one scholar found that between 1903 and 1939 party identification was "clearly a good cue for selecting judicial decision-makers with the proper values." That is, on matters of support for the economic underdog, Democratic justices were more liberal than their Republican colleagues. Since 1940 the greater liberalism of Democratic Court members has also extended to matters of civil rights and liberties, thereby reaffirming "the concept that judges are not random samples of their group." But even this scholar concedes, as did those who studied partisan voting by the appeals court and trial court judges, that the relationships are weak.

The inability to predict at high rates of probability is not surprising when one considers the assumptions that must be made and the variety of other influences on the Court, such as political and environmental pressures, social change, precedent, reasoned argument, intracourt social influences and idiosyncrasy.[31]

A major study of partisan voting patterns on the Supreme Court focused on criminal justice cases. Among other things, the researchers concluded, "Democratic control of the Court and the White House, coupled with a high proportion of the Court's docket devoted to criminal issues, results in significantly higher support levels for criminal defendants than under the condition of the Republicans occupying the presidency and a majority of the Supreme Court seats with a relatively low priority placed on criminal justice appeals."[32] Nonetheless, some scholars urge caution before making a flat-out pronouncement about the relationship between the justices' backgrounds and their subsequent voting patterns. For example, one prominent researcher has argued that previous studies may be time-bound—that is, during some time periods decisional differences among the justices might be explained by background characteristics, whereas during others background is only a modest predictor of behavior.[33] When one is faced with such conflicting and tentative studies, it is clear that the final chapter of a book on this subject is yet to be written.

Partisanship in State Courts. The federal courts are not the only arena in which Republican and Democratic jurists sometimes square off against one another. Partisan voting patterns often occur as well among the men and women who sit on the trial and appellate court benches. However, the evidence at the state level is weaker, for three general reasons. First, the state courts have not been studied as extensively and systematically as have the federal courts. This may be because some political scientists have held the (mistaken) view that state judiciaries are less important than their federal counterparts or because many state court decisions are unpublished and therefore much more difficult to obtain and study. Second, partisanship among state jurists is not strongly uniform across the country. In some states, for instance, judicial selection is truly bipartisan (or nonpartisan), and both political parties may support the same candidates. Also, many state judges do not have extensive relationships with a political party. Though they may have partisan identifications, they may not view judicial questions as being reflective of their party's ideology. Finally, America still has a number of one-party states in which virtually all judges bear the same party label. Thus it would make little sense to study partisan differences among judges in states such as Mississippi or West Virginia, where almost all the jurists are Democrats, or to study partisan variations among appellate justices in Texas, where virtually all are now Republicans. Nonetheless, keen levels of partisanship have been documented in some jurisdictions—particularly in the states with big cities.

Michigan is a state in which partisan voting patterns among the judges, especially on the state supreme court, have been noteworthy. Studies have shown that on labor-management issues, for example, Democrats on the bench were significantly more likely to support the side of the worker in unemployment compensation cases and in issues dealing with workers' compensation (on-the-job injuries). Democratic judges are also more likely to support criminal defendants seeking a new trial, to favor government efforts to regulate business, and to side with persons who sue business enterprises—all consistent with the voting behavior of Democrats on the federal bench.[34]

In a study of partisan conflict on a California intermediate court of appeals, significant differences were found between Democrats and Republicans in both criminal and civil cases.[35] Studying issues such as votes in criminal justice cases, labor-management disputes, debtor/creditor disagreements, and consumerism, the author concluded that "as previous research . . . would have predicted, the results are in the expected direction, with Republican panels significantly more likely to reach conservative outcomes than Democratic panels."[36]

Illinois, Iowa, Maryland, New York, and Pennsylvania are examples of other states where researchers have found meaningful partisan differences between Republican and Democratic judges.[37]

A Note on Partisan Voting in Foreign Courts. Partisan voting behavior of jurists in other nations is not unknown, but it is more difficult to pinpoint for several reasons. First, in virtually all other countries judges do not run for elective office in an openly partisan manner, as they do in those American states that elect judges. Also, in these foreign nations potential judicial candidates are more likely to eschew active partisan politics prior to their appointment to the bench. Identifying a judge's party affiliation and correlating it with a particular substantive voting pattern is therefore more difficult. Nevertheless, many studies suggest that a judge's background, which is highly correlated with his or her political orientation, does meaningfully affect the jurist's decisions on the bench.[38] Likewise, other studies have identified the existence of clear ideological voting patterns of appellate court judges on foreign courts, and these ideological values can usually be traced to a political party within that country.[39]

An Appraisal. The political party affiliation of the judges and justices can make a difference in the way they decide cases. Of all the background variables studied, it seems to be the most compelling and consistent. But a word of caution is in order. Although evidence of partisan influence on judicial behavior is convincing, it by no means suggests that Democrats always take the liberal position on all issues, whereas Republicans always opt for the conservative side. Rather, it's a matter of tendencies, that is, when the decision is a close call, a Democrat on the bench tends to be more liberal than a Republican judge. When controlling precedents are absent or ambiguous or when the evidence in the case is about evenly divided, Democrats are more inclined than Republicans to be supportive of civil rights and liberties, to support government regulation that favors the worker or the economic underdog, and to turn a sympathetic ear toward the pleas of criminal defendants.

The Impact of Localism

A wide range of influences are included in the term *localism,* and we will regard it as a broad second category of factors that affect federal and state judicial decision making. A growing body of literature suggests that federal judges are influenced by the traditions and mores of the region in which their courts are located or, in the case of Supreme Court justices, by the geographic area in which they were reared. For trial and appeals court judges, geographic differences define both the legal and the democratic subcultures as well as the nature of the questions they must decide.

Historically, such judges have had strong ties to the state and the circuit in which their courts are situated, and on many issues judicial decision making reflects the parochial values and attitudes of the region. As two leading students of the subject have noted:

A persistent factor in the molding of lower court organization has been the preservation of state and regional boundaries. The feeling that the judiciary should reflect the local features of the federal system has often been expressed by state officials most explicitly. Mississippi Congressman John Sharp Williams declared that he was "frankly opposed to a perambulatory judiciary, to carpetbagging Nebraska with a Louisianian, certainly to carpetbagging Mississippi or Louisiana with somebody north of Mason and Dixon's line." [40]

Why should judges in one district or circuit decide cases differently from their colleagues in other localities? Why should a Supreme Court justice make decisions differently from colleagues who hail from other parts of the United States?[41] Richardson and Vines have put the matter succinctly:

Since both district and appeals judges frequently receive legal training in the state or circuit they serve, the significance of legal education is important. If a federal judge is trained at a state university, he is exposed to and may assimilate state and sectional political viewpoints, especially since state law schools are training grounds for local political elites.... Other than education, different local environments provide different reactions to policy issues, such as civil rights or labor relations. Indeed, throughout the history of the lower court judiciary there is evidence that various persons involved in judicial organization and selection have perceived that local, state, or regional factors make a difference and have behaved accordingly.[42]

Moreover, trial and appellate judges tend to come from the district or state in which their courts are located, and the vast majority were educated in law schools of the state or circuit they work in. (For example, two-thirds of all district judges in one study were born in the state where their court is located, and 86 percent of all circuit judges attended a law school in their respective circuits.)[43] Also, the strong local ties of many judges tend to develop and mature even after their appointment to the bench.[44]

In identifying with their regional base, judges are similar to other political decision makers. Public attitudes and voting patterns on a wide range of issues vary from one section of America to another.[45] As for national political officials, there is evidence that regionalism affects the voting patterns of members of Congress on many important issues—for example, civil rights, conservation, price controls for farmers, and labor legislation.[46] Furthermore, sectional considerations have their impact within each political party—for instance, northern Democrats are more liberal than their southern counterparts on many significant issues.

Regionalism at the Three Judicial Levels. When President George Washington appointed the first Supreme Court, half of its members were northerners and half were southerners. Washington's choices were surely more than just a symbolic gesture to give a superficial balance to the Court. Having successfully led a group of squabbling former colonies during the Revolutionary War, Washington understood that the attitudes and mores of his fellow citizens differed widely from one locale to another and that justices would not be immune to these parochial influences. Studies of the early history of the high court reveal that sectionalism did creep into its decision-making patterns—particularly along North-South lines. For example, a study of Supreme Court voting patterns in the sectional crisis that preceded the Civil War noted that the four justices who were most supportive of southern regional interests were all from the South, whereas jurists from the northern states usually favored the litigants from that region.[47]

In the twentieth century, evidence also supports the belief that where the justices came from tempered their decision making to some degree.[48] A fairly dramatic manifestation of this principle is found in President Nixon's famous "southern strategy." After the appointment of Warren E. Burger as chief justice in 1969,

pressure had been building on Nixon to name a southerner to the Court. Though he had never publicly promised a southern nominee, Nixon's intentions were never seriously doubted. Aware that a judge in the South enjoyed a prestige unrivaled in any other section of the country, Nixon advisors believed that he could do southerners no higher favor than to appoint one of their own to the highest court in the land. Even before Nixon assumed office, he had successfully identified with the southern cause. "The one battle most white southerners feel they are fighting is with the Court and Nixon has effectively identified himself with that cause," wrote election analyst Samuel Lubell. "Only Nixon can change the makeup of the Court to satisfy southern aspirations." [49]

Nixon then nominated Clement Haynsworth Jr. of South Carolina, who was rejected by the Senate. Next he submitted the name of G. Harrold Carswell of Florida, but this nomination met the same fate as Haynsworth's. An angry Nixon then stated, "As long as the Senate is constituted the way it is today, I will not nominate another southerner." [50]

Although political leaders and much of the general public believe that a relationship exists between the justices' regional backgrounds and their judicial decisions, scholars have had difficulty in documenting this phenomenon. First, links between the justices' regional heritage and their subsequent voting behavior are very difficult to pinpoint, and they exist at most for probably a few regionally sensitive issues. Also, after Supreme Court justices are appointed and move to Washington, they may over time take on a more national perspective, loosening to a significant degree the attitudes and narrow purview of the regions in which they were reared and educated. For example, in his early days in Alabama, Hugo Black had been a member of the Ku Klux Klan, but after his judicial appointment in 1937, he became one of the most articulate advocates of civil rights ever to sit on the Supreme Court.

Some evidence indicates that regionalism pervades the federal judicial system at the appeals court level as well. A 1981 study noted regional differences on such important questions as rights of the consumer, pleas by criminal defendants, petitions by workers and by blacks, public rights in patent cases, and immigration litigation. The author of this study concluded that "regionalism is an inescapable adjunct of adjudicating appeals in one of the oldest regional operations of federal power in existence." He observed that although the appeals courts may adhere to national standards, such norms are nevertheless "regionally enforced. In the crosswinds of office and constituencies, Courts of Appeals may mediate cultural values—national and local, professional and political—in federal appeals." [51] In a study of regional variations in the voting of court of appeals judges, Susan Haire noted, for example, that "in search and seizure cases, Western judges were more liberal than their counterparts in the East (including the South) whereas in race-based employment discrimination cases Western judges adopted positions that were more conservative than their colleagues in the East." [52]

In studies of federal district judges, East-West differences were never very great. However, significant variations have traditionally existed between judges living in nonsouthern states and those holding court in the South. Between 1932 and 1979, only 39 percent of the southern judges' decisions were liberal, whereas the figure was 45 percent for jurists in the nonsouthern states. However, Table 12-2 indicates that in the past two decades these differences have declined to a mere 2 percent, although on some specific issues southern jurists still manifest strongly conservative sentiments. For example, a 1990 study showed that federal district judges in the more conservative South were almost 70 percent more likely to take an anti-abortion stance than their colleagues in the North. This was found to be consistent with the values of the region as measured by public opinion polls and other data.[53]

Regional influences on judges' voting behavior are by no means a uniquely American phenomenon. For example, even in a small country such as Norway, the way judges vote in certain types of cases is often influenced by the regions they come from. One early study found that for violations of the conscientious objector laws, the likelihood of being convicted varied from a low of 3 percent if the judge

TABLE 12-2   Liberal and Conservative Decisions by Southern and Nonsouthern Judges in Two Time Periods

| | | Nonsoutherners | | Southerners | |
		%	n	%	n
1932–1979	Liberal	45.3	9,647	38.9	4,220
	Conservative	54.7	11,639	61.1	6,623
	Odds ratio (α) = 1.30				
1980–2002	Liberal	43.1	11,089	41.0	4,247
	Conservative	56.9	14,649	58.9	6,100
	Odds ratio (α) = 1.09				

SOURCE: Unpublished data collected by Robert A. Carp, Kenneth Manning, and Ronald Stidham.

was located in the Western Military District (Vestlandet) to a high of 54 percent if the jurist was from the Northern District (Nordland).[54]

Variances in Judicial Behavior among the Circuits. Not only does judicial decision making vary from one region of the country to another, but each of the circuits, according to studies, has its own particular way of administering the law and making decisions. One reason is that circuits tend to follow sectional lines that mark off historical, social, and political differences. Another reason is that the circuit courts of appeals tend to be idiosyncratic, and thus the standards and guidelines they provide to the trial judges will reflect their own approach.[55] In a recent study of variations in the behavior of appellate judges from one circuit to another, the "findings . . . strongly suggest judges' decisional tendencies are shaped by the circuit." In her analysis Haire found "meaningful policy differences" in such fields as search and seizure cases, obscenity rulings, and employment discrimination lawsuits.[56] Likewise, a study published in 2002 indicates that there were significant circuit-by-circuit variations in the degree to which these entities adhered to Supreme Court precedents.[57] Similarly, the behavior of U.S. trial judges has been observed to vary on a circuit-by-circuit basis. Between 1980 and 2002, for example, in the Washington, D.C., district court, 53 percent of the judges' decisions were liberal; and this is followed closely by the U.S. Ninth Circuit, whose district court judges handed down liberal decisions 51 percent of the time. (The Ninth Circuit covers many of the western states, including the traditionally liberal states of California, Hawaii, Washington, and Oregon.) At the other end of the scale is the Fourth Circuit (Maryland, North and South Carolina, Virginia, and West Virginia), whose trial jurists rendered liberal decisions only 37 percent of the time.[58]

Variances in Trial Judge Behavior among the States. At first blush it may appear strange to argue that U.S. judicial decisions vary significantly from one state to another, because the state is not an official level of the federal judicial hierarchy, which advances from district to circuit to nationwide system. Nonetheless, direct and indirect evidence suggests that each state is unique in the way its federal judges administer justice. There are several explanations for this. First, a state, like a circuit or a region, is often synonymous with a particular set of policy-relevant values, attitudes, and orientations. One would automatically expect, for instance, that on some issues U.S. trial and appellate judges in Texas would act differently from Massachusetts jurists, not so much because they are from different states but because they are from different political, economic, legal, and cultural milieus. Second, many judges regard their states as meaningful boundaries and behave accordingly. For example, a U.S. trial judge in Louisiana told us: "One thing I frequently discuss with the other judges here is sentencing matters. Judge X has been a big help with this. I wouldn't want to hand down a sentence which is way out of line with what the other judges are doing here in this state for the same crime."[59]

Another example occurred in the fall of 2002, when all of South Carolina's active federal trial judges voted "to ban secret legal settlements, stating that such agreements have made the courts complicit in hiding the truth about hazardous products, inept doctors and sexually abusive priests.... Mary Squiers, who tracks individual federal courts' rules for the U.S. Judicial Conference, said only Michigan had a similar rule, which unseals secret settlements after two years."[60]

Third, note the impact upon federal judicial behavior of diversity of citizenship cases—suits that constitute almost a quarter of the district courts' civil business and about one in ten civil appeals to circuit courts. Because the Supreme Court requires the lower courts to apply state instead of federal law in such cases, it behooves U.S. trial judges to keep abreast of and be sensitive to the latest developments in state law. The effect may be the same for circuit judges. For example, when three-judge appellate panels are appointed for diversity of citizenship cases, the tendency is to name circuit judges from states whose law governs. As one scholar observed, "A 'slight local tinge' thus colored diversity opinions as part of a general tendency of members to defer to colleagues most knowledgeable about the subject."[61]

Quantitative studies of federal trial judges' voting behavior substantiate the proposition that meaningful differences are evident on a state-by-state basis. Such differences have been increasing since the late 1960s. Also, both circuits that cross North-South boundaries (the Sixth and the Eighth) and the district courts in the border and southern states are markedly more conservative than those in the other states.[62] This suggests that local and regional values—as personified by the state—have a greater influence on trial judge decision making than do those of the circuit as a whole.

Localism and the Behavior of State Judges. If regional factors leaven the bread of federal judicial decisions, this phenomenon is even more pervasive for state jurists. State judges, even more than their federal counterparts, tend to be local folks—born, bred, educated, and socialized in the locale in which they preside. Whether they have been elected directly by the people or appointed as a result of their political connections with the governor or the local political machine, state judges are likely to mirror the values and attitudes of their environment. A study by Martin A. Levin, who compared and contrasted judges and justices in Minneapolis and Pittsburgh, provides a fitting example.[63]

In Minneapolis the state trial judges are elected on a nonpartisan ballot, and in practice the political parties have almost no role in the selection of judges. "The socialization and recruitment of [the] . . . judges reflect this pattern of selection. Most of these judges [as the majority of the local population] have Northern European-Protestant and middle-class backgrounds, and their pre-judicial careers have been predominantly in private legal practice. . . . Such career experiences seem to have stimulated these judges to be interested more in 'society' than in the defendant." Minneapolis's conservative, middle-class environment, from which its judges come, is reflected in the law-and-order, no-nonsense grist of the judicial mill.

This pre-judicial experience, reinforced by their lack of party or policy-oriented experiences and their middle-class backgrounds, seems to have contributed to the legalistic and universalistic character of their decision-making and their eschewal of policy and personal considerations. In their milieu, rules were generally emphasized, especially legal ones, and these rules had been used to maintain and protect societal institutions. Learning to "get around" involved skill in operating in a context of rules. The judges' success seems to have depended more on their objective achievements and skills than on personal relationships.[64]

The environment of the Pittsburgh jurists is in stark contrast. The highly partisan (Democratic) judges reflect the working-class, ethnic group-based values of the political machine that put them on the bench. They were likely to have held public office before becoming judges and, as a result, were much more people-oriented than their counterparts in Minneapolis. They often felt that their own "minority ethnic and lower-income backgrounds and these government and party experiences had developed their general attachment to the problems of the 'underdog' and the 'oppressed.' " Levin concludes this about the impact of the local environment and recruitment process on judicial behavior:

> Their political experiences and lack of much legalistic experience apparently contributed to the highly particularistic and nonlegalistic character of their decision-making, their emphasis on policy considerations, and their use of pragmatic criteria. . . . Personal relationships, especially with constituents, were emphasized, and focused on particular and tangible entities. Success depended largely on the ability to operate within personal relationships. It depended on *whom* one knew, rather than on *what* one knew. Abstractions such as "the good of society as a whole" seem to have been of little concern.[65]

Although social science still needs to develop more systematic empirical evidence for the relationship between the local environment and the output of state courts, these two brief case studies are indicative of the kind of phenomena we are describing.

The Impact of Public Opinion

If one were to approach a typical judge or justice and ask whether public opinion affected the decisions made from the bench, the jurist might respond with a fair measure of indignation. The answer might be something like this: "Look, as a judge with a lifetime appointment, I'm expected to be free from the pressures of public opinion. That's part of what we mean when we say that we're a 'government of laws—not of men.' When I decide a case, I look at the law and the facts. I don't go out into the streets and take some sort of public opinion poll to tell me what to do."

Yet to some degree and on certain issues, American judges do seem to temper their decision making with public opinion. There are several intuitive reasons for this. First, judges, as human beings, as parents, as consumers, and as residents of the community, are themselves part of public opinion. Putting on a black robe may stimulate a greater concern for responsible, objective decision making, but it does not void a judge's membership in the human race. As one judicial scholar has noted, "Since judges, both appointed and elected, usually have been born and reared locally and recruited from a local political system, it seems likely that public opinion would have an effect, especially in issues that are locally visible and controversial. In addition . . . many judges seem to consider themselves independent judicial officials who represent local populations in the courts. Consequently, judges may feel that they ought to take local values into account."[66] Even a conservative and strict constructionist such as Supreme Court Chief Justice William Rehnquist has acknowledged this in a revealing statement:

> Judges, so long as they are relatively normal human beings, can no more escape being influenced by public opinion in the long run than can people working at other jobs. And, if a

judge on coming to the bench were to decide to hermetically seal himself off from all manifestations of public opinion, he would accomplish very little; he would not be influenced by current public opinion, but instead would be influenced by the state of public opinion at the time he came to the bench.[67]

Likewise, in June 2003, when the Supreme Court handed down its bombshell decision that overturned the Texas sodomy law, a majority of the Court indicated that it wished to keep in step with *world* public opinion. In a televised interview on the ABC show *This Week,* Justices Sandra Day O'Connor and Stephen Breyer recalled that in deciding the case the justices discussed "whether the court should take into account the legal opinions of other world courts, such as the European Court of Human Rights. Breyer agreed with Kennedy's view that the foreign court's views that gays and lesbians had a right to privacy in their sexual behavior showed that the U.S. Supreme Court's prior decision to the contrary was not in keeping with Western tradition. . . . 'We see this all the time, Justice O'Connor and I, and the others, how the world really—it's trite but it's true—is growing together,' Breyer said." [68]

The following is a further example of judges' keen sensitivity to *local* public opinion. It was previously noted that the federal district judges in South Carolina unanimously voted to abolish the use of secret settlements in their state. Why? The justification for this decision, as stated by Chief Judge Joseph F. Anderson Jr., clearly reveals that he and the other trial judges were responding to the public mood: "Here is a rare opportunity for our court to do the right thing and take the lead nationally in a time when the Arthur Andersen/Enron/Catholic priest controversies are undermining public confidence in our institutions and causing a growing suspicion of things that are kept secret by public bodies." [69]

Second, in many instances public opinion is supposed to be an official factor in the decision-making process. For example, in the implementation of the famous *Brown v. Board of Education* school desegregation ruling, the Supreme Court refused to set strict national guidelines for how its decision was to be carried out. Instead, individual federal district judges were to implement the high court decision, based on the judges' determination of local moods, conditions, and traditions.[70] Likewise, when the Supreme Court ruled that federal courts could hear cases concerning malapportionment of state legislatures, it refused to indicate how its decision was to be carried out. It was, in effect, left to the lower federal courts to implement the ruling in accordance with the way they viewed local needs, conditions, and the state political climate.[71] Another example may be found in the obscenity rulings of the Burger Court, in which the justices determined that the courts should use community values and attitudes in determining what materials are obscene.[72]

Thus, not only is it impossible for judges to rid themselves of the influence of public opinion, but in many important types of cases they are obliged to consider the attitudes and values of the public. This does not mean that judges go out and take opinion polls whenever they face a tough decision, but public opinion is often one ingredient in the decision-making calculus.

Third, both federal and state judges are aware that ultimately their decisions cannot be carried out unless there is a reasonable degree of public support. As Lawrence Baum has noted, "Justices care about public regard for the Court, because high regard can help the Court in conflicts with the other branches of government and increase people's willingness to carry out its decisions." [73] It has been an open secret for a long time that when the Court is about to hand down a bombshell decision likely to be unpopular among many groups of Americans, the author of the majority opinion takes great pains to word the decision so as to generate popular support for it—or at least to salve the wounds of those potentially offended by it. Examples of high court decisions in which the author is thought to have written as much for the public at large as for the usual narrow audience of lawyers and lower-court judges include the following: *Marbury v. Madison,* in which the Court claimed for itself the right to declare acts of Congress unconstitutional; *Brown v. Board of Education,* which called for an end to racial segregation in the public schools; *Roe v. Wade,* in which the Court upheld a woman's right to an abortion; and *United States v. Nixon*—the Watergate case—in which the justices ordered the president of the United States to yield to the authority of the courts.[74]

The empirical evidence for the impact of public opinion is suggestive but hardly conclusive, in part because relatively few comprehensive studies of the phenomenon have been conducted and the proposition is difficult to prove. While many of the earliest studies of this subject produced conflicting conclusions, more recent and exhaustive investigations have begun to map a real, albeit imperfect, relationship between public opinion and jurists' decisional patterns.[75] In 1993 two Supreme Court researchers concluded that popular sentiment "exercises important influence on the decisions of the Court even in the absence of changes in the composition of the Court or in the partisan and ideological make up of Congress and the presidency." [76] However, they qualified their findings by noting that there was a fairly lengthy interval—three to seven years—between a change in the public mood and a corresponding alteration in justices' voting behavior.[77] Moreover, these voting changes tended to be concentrated among only a handful of justices.[78]

The most recent team of researchers to address this matter came up with a set of conclusions that are more emphatic and contain fewer qualifications about the link between public mood changes and Supreme Court decisional patterns. Roy B. Flemming and B. Dan Wood discovered that "public opinion *directly* affects decisions by individual members of the Court" and that "the result holds across various issue areas, is not restricted to only a few justices, and that the justices' responses are relatively quick with a lag of only one term." [79] Equally interesting and significant, however, are studies indicating that at the lower federal court levels (that is, the appeals and trial courts) no systematic evidence whatever could be found to connect the voting patterns of the judges to public mood—either the national mood or even public opinion shifts in the judges' own states. These studies suggest that the Supreme Court may be singular and unique and that its decision-making environment makes the justices particularly susceptible to shifts in the public mood—conditions that do not apply to lower appellate and trial court judges.[80] Further studies will have to resolve this apparent enigma about why lower federal court jurists appear to be immune to shifts in the public mood while U.S. Supreme Court justices are not. Research is now under way to determine whether shifts in public opinion affect the decision making of federal appeals court judges as well as U.S. trial jurists.

Researchers have also explored this phenomenon at the state level. For example, a study of California state courts found that the severity of sentencing in marijuana cases often changed soon after a popular referendum was held on reducing criminal penalties for personal use of the drug. For example, judges who had given light sentences prior to the referendum sometimes gave harsher sentences if the local vote was in favor of maintaining criminal penalties. Conversely, harsh-sentencing jurists sometimes became more lenient when the vote indicated that the public favored reducing the penalties.[81]

Given that in a majority of states judges must periodically run for election, they probably are more attuned to public opinion than are federal judges, who have lifetime tenure. One study of elected state supreme court justices found that "to appease their constituencies, justices who have views contrary to those of the voters and the court majority, and who face competitive electoral conditions will vote with the court majority instead of casting unpopular dissents on politically volatile issues." [82] Likewise, a more recent study involving state supreme court justices' voting behavior in death penalty cases found a clear link between their voting patterns and voter sentiment about capital punishment. The authors noted that "while Democrats and Republicans generally exhibit behavior patterns that are quite distinct, these distinctions are blurred by variables related to retaining office. Having to face voters more frequently, thereby risking the chance of being removed from office, encourages justices in state supreme courts, who otherwise might vote consistently to overturn death sentences instead, to manifest conservative voting patterns in these cases." [83]

The following more down-to-earth example illustrates a state judge's stronger grass-roots political awareness and also the greater degree to which elected jurists interact with the local environment. On November 28, 1988, Jack Hampton, a state district court judge in Dallas, gave a thirty-year prison sentence to a defendant who had been convicted of murdering two gay men. The killer, Richard Bednarski, had testified in court that he and some friends went to a central Dallas park to "pester homosexuals" and ended up killing two of them in what authorities called an execution-style slaying. (Bednarski placed a gun in one victim's mouth and pulled the trigger; he then shot the other man several times.) Because of the heinous and unprovoked nature of the crime and because Hampton is known as a "hanging judge" who usually gives life sentences for murder, the *Dallas Times Herald* decided to interview the judge about his lighter-than-usual sentence. During the interview Judge Hampton said that the murder victims more or less got what they asked for, because they were "queers" who "wouldn't have been killed if they hadn't been cruising the streets picking up teenage boys." [84]

Immediately after the interview was published, public protests were staged by human rights groups, local church leaders, and various gay rights organizations. Protest rallies were held, including one attended by five hundred people at the City Hall Plaza, where letters of support were read from Sen. Edward M. Kennedy of Massachusetts and Texas state treasurer Ann Richards. Also, formal complaints were filed with the Texas Commission on Judicial Conduct, calling for Hampton to be disciplined. In reply, this elected judicial official issued a four-paragraph letter to a group of eight Methodist ministers. Judge Hampton said he wished "to apologize" for his "poor choice of words that appeared in a recent newspaper story." He promised that in his court "everyone is entitled to and will receive equal protection."

Was the judge's public apology a response, at least in part, to his perception of public opinion and its possible effect on his bid for reelection? This might be surmised from the judge's later statement, responding to a question about the possible political fallout from the incident: "If it makes anybody mad, they'll forget it by 1990" (when Judge Hampton was up for reelection).[85]

This particular incident is not typical of the behavior of state judges, but it demonstrates the degree to which locally elected judicial officials respond to the tides of public opinion. Very rarely do lifetime judicial appointees, such as federal judges, feel the need to justify their sentencing behavior in interviews with the local press or to issue public apologies when public opinion turns critical of their behavior. For better or worse, public opinion does affect judicial behavior, and this is particularly true when judges must be accountable directly to the electorate.

Thus, despite the traditional notion of the blindfolded justice weighing only the facts in a case and the relevant law, common sense and statistical evidence support the assertion that jurists do keep their eyes (and ears) open to public opinion.

The Influence of the Legislative and Executive Branches

The executive and legislative branches are the final set of stimuli that the democratic subculture may bring to bear on the behavior of American judges.

Congress and the President. Perhaps the most obvious link between the values of the democratic subculture and the output of the federal courts is that the people elect the president and members of the Senate, and the president appoints judges and justices, with the advice and consent of the Senate. The chief executive and certain key senators greatly influence what kind of men and women will sit on the bench, but even after judges have been appointed, the president and Congress may have an impact on the content and direction of judicial decision making.

First, to a large degree the jurisdiction of the federal trial and appellate courts is determined by the Congress of the United States, which has the authority to determine the types of issues that may become appropriate matters for judges to resolve. For example, when Congress passed the Civil Rights Acts of 1964, Title VII and its subsequent amendments greatly expanded the rights of women to be free from gender discrimination in the workplace. In doing so, Congress, in effect, expanded the jurisdiction of the federal courts to hear a large number of disputes that previously had been outside the purview of the federal judiciary. And the evidence suggests that the courts have not been idle in expanding the power Congress gave them.[86] Conversely, Congress may restrict the jurisdiction of the federal courts. In response to popular dissatisfaction with many court rulings on busing, abortion, school prayer, and so on, Congress has considered passage of a number of bills designed to restrict the right of the courts to render decisions on these subjects.[87] Even if Congress does not pass such legislation, the threat to do so may cause the federal courts to pull in their horns when it comes to deciding cases in ways that are not in accord with the will of the president or Congress.

Second, judicial decision making is likely to be bolder and more effective if it has the active support of at least one other branch of the federal government, and ideally of both of them.[88] School integration is a case in point. When the federal courts began to order desegregation of the public schools after 1954, they met with considerable opposition—primarily from those parts of the country most affected by the Supreme Court ruling in the *Brown* case. It is doubtful whether the federal courts could have overcome this resistance without the support given them (sometimes reluctantly) by the president and Congress. For example, in 1957 Arkansas governor Orville Faubus sought to obstruct a district judge's order to integrate Little Rock's Central High School. President Dwight D. Eisenhower then mobilized the National Guard and, in effect, used federal bayonets to implement the judge's ruling. President John F. Kennedy likewise used federal might to support a judge's decision to admit a black student to the University of Mississippi in the face of massive local resistance. Congress also lent its hand to federal desegregation rulings. For instance, it voted to withhold federal aid to school districts that refused to comply with district court desegregation decisions. Surely White House and congressional support emboldened the Supreme Court and the lower judiciary to carry on with their efforts to end segregation in the public schools.

Presidential and congressional actions may sometimes lead rather than just implement judicial decision making. One study analyzed the impact on trial judge behavior of the 1937 Supreme Court decisions that permitted much greater government regulation of the economy.[89] As expected, federal district judges' support for government regulation increased markedly after the Supreme Court gave its official blessing to the government's new powers. However, it was also learned that district court backing for labor and economic regulation had been building before the Supreme Court's decisions: Pro-regulation decisions by U.S. trial judges increased from 44 percent in 1936 to 67 percent in 1937—a change of 23 percentage points. The authors attributed this at least in part to the fact that prior to 1937 the president and Congress, in response to public opinion, were strongly pushing legislation that favored an expanded federal role in labor and economic regulation.[90]

Thus the Supreme Court and the lower courts are not, and cannot be, immune to the will of Congress and the chief executive as they go about their judicial business. Not only does the president, with the advice and consent of the Senate, select all members of the federal judiciary, but to a large degree Congress also prescribes the jurisdiction of the federal courts and often the qualifications of those who have standing to sue in these tribunals. Moreover, many court decisions cannot be meaningfully implemented without the support of the other two branches of government—a fact not lost on the judges and justices themselves. Sometimes, too, the courts appear to follow the lead of the president and Congress on various public policy matters. Whichever set of circumstances is the case, the legislative and executive branches of government clearly constitute an important source of nonjudicial influence on court behavior.

The State Legislature and the Governor. Just as the legislative and executive branches affect judicial decision making at the national level, their counterparts at the state and local levels also have great influence. In almost half of the jurisdictions the popularly elected governor (or the state legislature) selects the state judges, and a policy link is likely to exist among the value sets of the voters, the appointing officials, and the judges who render subsequent decisions. More specifically, the authors of one study found three major ways that the political branches affect the role of the state courts.[91]

First, legislation sponsored by the governor or passed by the legislature regulates the types of claims that can be adjudicated in state courts and also brought to the state appellate courts. For example, class action suits may be easily brought in state judicial tribunals. (Such suits facilitate access to the courts by allowing large numbers of potential litigants with small individual claims to band together, thereby reducing or eliminating entirely the financial costs of seeking redress.) Actions by the legislature determine who may bring such suits and under what circumstances. The evidence suggests that the states vary greatly in this area. Some states make it very easy to initiate such suits, whereas in others access to the courts is very difficult.[92]

Second, actions by the legislature (which may or may not be part of the governor's political agenda) determine the authority of the state supreme court to regulate its workload and focus on important cases. For example, it is generally accepted that for most cases litigants should have the right to appeal trial court decisions. In states that have an ample number of intermediate appellate courts this right to appeal is readily available. However, in states without a sufficient number of intermediate appeals courts or in states where the supreme court is forced by law to deal with a succession of relatively minor disputes, the chances are slim that litigants will have their cases heard by the supreme court. This fact is significant in terms of the distribution of justice, but it is also important for another reason. In states where the legislature forces the supreme court to overwork on judicial trivia, the court does not have time to devote much attention to cases that raise important policy questions. For instance, after the legislature in North Carolina created intermediate courts of appeals, a study concluded that this action enabled the state high court to assume "a position of true leadership in the legal development of the state." [93] Thus actions by the legislature (supported or opposed by the governor) may determine whether the supreme court plays a major or a minor role in policy questions important to the state.

Finally, because a prime function of courts is to enforce existing legal norms, the sorts of issues that state courts address depend to a large degree on the substantive law of the state. For instance, seventeen state constitutions contain "little ERAs" (equal rights amendments); ten states specifically protect the right to privacy; and some states guarantee a right to quality of the environment.[94] Thus a judge in a state where good air quality is guaranteed will have a much greater opportunity and right to issue an injunction against a polluter than will the judge in a state where such a right is not legally provided. An example of a legislature's taking an issue out of the hands of its state judges occurred in Hawaii after its supreme court ruled in 1993 that same-sex couples could marry. Shortly after the court's decision, the legislature began a process to modify the state constitution to deny marriage licenses to same-sex couples, thereby overruling the state supreme court and taking the matter out of its jurisdiction.[95] The point here is that judges render decisions within the existing constitutional and legal environment of their respective states. Such an environment is largely the product of political decisions made by the governor and the legislature as representatives of the electorate.

In sum, the output of the state courts, like that of federal tribunals, is to a significant degree the result of the political values and policy goals of the chief executive and the legislative branch of government.

The Subcultures as Predictors

Scholarly opinion differs on whether judicial decision making is essentially the product of facts, laws, and precedent (the legal subculture model) or whether the various extralegal factors carry more weight (the realist-behavioralist view). In other words, are court decisions better explained by understanding the facts and law that impinge upon a given case or by knowing which newspaper the judge reads in the morning or how the judge voted in the last election?

The clue to answering the question lies in knowing what kind of case the judge is being asked to decide. The vast majority of federal trial judges' cases and much appellate judicial business involve routine norm enforcement decisions. In cases in which the law and the controlling precedents are clear, the victor will be the side that is able to marshal better evidence to show that its factual case is stronger. In other words, in the lion's share of cases, the legal subculture model best explains and predicts judicial decision making. When traditional legal cues are ambiguous or absent, however, judges are obliged to look to the democratic subculture for guidance in their decision making.

When the Legal Evidence Is Contradictory

It is probably fair to say that in a majority of cases the facts, evidence, and controlling precedents distinctly favor one side. In such instances the judge is clearly obliged to decide for the party with the stronger case. Not to do so would violate the judge's legal training and mores; subject a trial or appeals court judge to reversal by a higher court, an event most jurists find embarrassing; and render the Supreme Court vulnerable to the charge that it was making up the law as it went along—an impression not flattering to the high court justices. However, judges often find themselves in situations in which the facts and evidence are about equally compelling on both sides, or in which a roughly equal number of precedents sustain a finding for either party. As one U.S. trial judge in Houston told us:

> There are days when you want to say to the litigants, "I wish you guys would've settled this out of court because I don't know what to do with you." If I grant the petition's request, I can often modify the relief requested [in an attempt to even out the decision], but still one side has got to win and one side has got to lose. I could cite good precedents on either side, and it's no good worrying about the appeals court because there's no telling what they would do with it should the judge's decision be appealed.

The following is an example in which a U.S. trial judge was forced to decide a case by his own lights (that is, using his democratic subculture values) because the cues from the legal subculture were clearly contradictory or nonexistent. Judge Robert E. Coyle, who holds court in the Eastern District of California (Fresno), was presented with a case that stemmed from an employment discrimination complaint filed with the Equal Employment Opportunity Commission (EEOC). Alicia Castrejon had been employed by the Tortilleria La Mejor of Farmersville, California, and claimed in her suit that she had been dismissed from her job because of previous complaints filed with the EEOC against her employer.

The legal issue was whether Castrejon had the right to file a suit in the first place because she was an undocumented immigrant. When Congress passed the Immigration Reform and Control Act of 1986, which prohibits employment of undocumented workers, it did not specify whether immigrants who have applied for amnesty are protected during the period when their applications are being processed. Castrejon had filed for amnesty, but her application had not been acted on at the time she filed her employment discrimination complaint.

The judge looked to the Department of Labor and to the EEOC for some legal guidance on the matter of the interim rights of undocumented residents. Both of these federal agencies maintained that workers are covered by federal labor and antidiscrimination laws even if they are here illegally. But the judge learned that many employers had been interpreting the Immigration Reform and Control Act to mean that illegal immigrants are not protected, and they were able to point to a 1987 ruling by a federal district judge in Alabama. That decision dismissed an undocumented immigrant's claim for minimum wages and overtime because, the judge said, that would conflict with the congressional act of 1986. The legal subculture was giving Judge Coyle few cues as to the "right" answer, and the existing cues were contradictory. Furthermore, in deciding this case, the judge had to tap attitudes and values derived from his democratic subculture and to put much of his legal subculture orientation on hold.

After sitting on the case for more than two years, the judge finally issued a ruling in February 1991 that had a significant immediate impact on hundreds of thousands of immigrants. For reasons known fully only to Judge Coyle, he ruled that undocumented workers do have the right to pursue discrimination suits against an employer—regardless of legal residency status. In his decision the judge acknowledged the seeming incongruity of discouraging illegal immigration while at the same time allowing undocumented workers to seek legal recourse against discrimination on the job: "We doubt, however, that many illegal aliens come to this country to gain the protection of our labor laws. Rather it is the hope of getting a job—at any wage—that prompts most illegal aliens to cross our borders." [96]

In situations such as this, judges have little choice but to turn to their personal value sets to determine how to resolve the cases. Decision making is affected by local attitudes and traditions or by the judge's perception of the public mood or the will of the current Congress or state legislature or administration.

Since the advent of the Burger Court in 1969, and continuing throughout the Rehnquist Court, an inordinate number of the Supreme Court's decisions have been regarded as "ideologically imprecise and inconsistent," often sustained by weak 5–4 majorities. This has increased the likelihood that trial and appellate judges will respond to stimuli from the democratic rather than the legal subculture. That is, the confusion created by the Court in setting forth ambiguous or contradictory guidelines has meant that judges in the lower federal and state courts—and perhaps even members of the Supreme Court—have been forced to rely on (or have felt free to give vent to) their personal ideas about how the law should read. As one study concluded, "With the decline of the fact-law congruence after 1968 the . . . [lower courts] became more free to take their decision-making cues from personal-partisan values rather than from guidelines set forth by the Higher Court." [97]

When a Case Concerns New Areas of the Law

Researchers also set aside the legal subculture model and turn to the democratic subculture approach when jurists are asked to resolve new types of policy questions for which statutory law and appellate court guidelines are virtually absent. Since about 1937 most new and uncharted areas of the law (at least at the federal level) have been in the realms of civil liberties and criminal justice rather than in the area of labor and economic regulation. Since 1937 the federal courts have leaned toward self-restraint and deference to the elected branches when it comes to ordering the economic lives of the American people.[98] Moreover, in recent decades Congress has legislated, often with precision, in the areas of economic regulation and labor relations, and this has further restricted the discretion of judges in these fields. As a result, the noose of the legal subculture has been drawn tightly around trial judges' necks, and little room is left for creative decision making or for responding to the tug of the heart instead of the clear command of the law. Since New Deal days the legal subculture, not the democratic subculture, has been the better predictor of trial and appellate judge decision making in labor and economic regulation cases.

Since the 1930s the opposite trend has been observable for issues of criminal justice and civil rights and liberties:

The "great" and controversial decisions of the Stone, Vinson, Warren, and Burger Courts [as well as the Rehnquist Court] focused primarily on issues of civil liberties and of the rights of criminal defendants, and it is precisely those sorts of issues which evoked the greatest partisan schisms among the justices. Research has shown that . . . [the lower courts] were by no means immune to the debates and divisions which racked the nation's High Court; they, too, seem to have split along "political" lines more often on criminal justice and on civil rights matters than they did with other sorts of cases.[99]

The ambiguity (or perhaps the constant state of flux) of the law on such matters as the rights of criminal defendants, First Amendment freedoms, and equal protection of the law has given the federal jurists greater opportunity to respond than they have had in the labor and economic realms, where their freedom of action has been more circumscribed. Put another way, since the 1930s the democratic subculture model has become increasingly important as a predictor of judicial behavior on issues pertaining to the Bill of Rights.[100]

A series of interviews with a wide range of district and appellate court judges lends further credence to this notion. In William Kitchin's study, the trial judges were asked about their willingness to "innovate," that is, their inclination to make new law in areas where appellate court or congressional guidelines were ambiguous or nonexistent. After asking why judges create new law through judicial innovation, Kitchin noted:

One answer is that the courts innovate because other branches of government ignore certain significant problems which, to individual judges, cry out for attention. Accordingly, the individual district judge innovates in an attempt to fill a legal vacuum, as one judge commented, "The theory is that judges should not be legal innovators, but there are some areas in which they have to innovate because legislatures won't do the job. Race relations is one of these areas. . . ." Other areas mentioned as needing judicial innovation because of legislative inaction were housing, equal accommodations, and criminal law (especially habeas corpus).[101]

Another study of decisional patterns and variations in U.S. district judge decision making showed that "the subjects that . . . [the Kitchin study] found to represent the greatest areas of freedom in judicial decision making are the very same subjects that we find to maximize partisan voting differences among the district judges. In situations where judges are more free to take their decision-making cues from sources other than appellate court decisions and statutes, they are more likely to rely on their personal-partisan orientations."[102]

A relatively new area of the law is the definition of obscenity, for which there are few appellate court and congressional guidelines, and thus lower-court judges must fend for themselves. Prior to 1957 no Supreme Court decisions of note had been handed down on the matter of obscenity. In that year the nation's high court ruled that obscenity was not protected by the First Amendment and said that it could be defined as material that dealt with sex "in a manner appealing to prurient interest."[103] Seven years later the Supreme Court said that hypothetical "national standards" should be used in determining what appealed to the prurient interest of the average person.[104] However, nine years after that the Court changed its mind and ruled that "state community standards" could be employed.[105] But what is obscenity? No one seems to know with any greater certainty today than Justice Potter Stewart did in 1964 when he confessed that he could not intelligibly define obscenity, but "I do know it when I see it."[106] As U.S. District Judge José Gonzalez wrote in 1990 in determining that an album by the controversial Miami-based rap group 2 Live Crew was obscene, "It is an appeal to 'dirty' thoughts and the loins, not to the intellect and mind." (The 2 Live Crew's attorney defended the album as "art" and said, "Put in its historical context, it is a novel and creative use of sound and lyrics.")[107] Given the reluctance or the inability of Congress and the Supreme Court to define obscenity, America's trial and appellate judges have little choice but to look to their personal values and perceptions of the local public need to determine what kinds of books, films, art, and plays the First Amendment protects in their respective jurisdictions.

Another lively new area of the law that is currently bedeviling federal judges is the subject of sexual harassment. Ever since Congress added sexual harassment to the list of items prohibited in the workplace by Title VII of the Civil Rights Act of 1964, federal jurists have had a difficult time defining what sexual harassment means. Obvious examples are clear enough (a boss explicitly telling a female employee that sexual favors are required for a pay raise), but the gray areas are taxing judges' minds. For example, a U.S. trial judge in Los Angeles was recently asked to rule that there was sexual harassment in an office because the breasts of female workers were being compared and sexual toys were being given as presents. The judge ruled that, according to his lights, while the office in question had been turned into a "bawdy sorority," federal law did not provide a "cause of action for embarrassment." [108]

But confusion in this new realm by no means ends with trying to define traditional forms of sexual harassment. The federal courts are now trying to determine whether same-sex harassment can be understood to mean a violation of one's civil rights. For instance, in May 1997 a U.S. appeals court in Atlanta considered a case involving a waiter at a hotel restaurant whose maître d' had made sexual advances to him. This court said that such activity did come within the strictures of the 1964 Civil Rights Act, although other courts have clearly ruled to the contrary.[109] Even here the confusion and uncertainty do not end. What about sexually oriented horseplay among straight men? A recent suit in a federal court in Denver was brought against the United Parcel Service of America by Michael Garcia, a heterosexual maintenance mechanic. Garcia claimed that his boss "tried to unnerve him by prodding him from behind with a radio antenna and touching him in front of co-workers." The company claimed in similar cases that this amounted to no more than "locker-room" antics—not harassment—to which Garcia responded that "I've played many sports in my time and I've never seen that kind of action in any locker rooms I've been in." [110] How was the judge to address the issues in this case? With the legal subculture virtually silent in this realm, the jurist was certainly obliged to look to the democratic subculture to find an answer.

Judicial innovation in new legal realms or in the absence of appellate court or legislative guidelines is by no means confined to federal jurists; it is just as significant an occurrence at the state court level. For example, in late 2001 the New Jersey Supreme Court was asked to decide a novel question: Can a man have the frozen embryos he and his ex-wife created implanted in the body of the man's new wife?

The case involved Mr. "M.B." and Mrs. "J.B.," who created seven embryos during the course of their marriage and had them frozen by a company specializing in that activity. (The couple had struggled with infertility, and in vitro fertilization had been used to allow them to have children.) The couple was divorced in 1998, but the divorce settlement left open the question of custody of the embryos. Mr. "M.B." remarried and wished to have the frozen embryos implanted in his new wife, but the first wife objected, stating that she "did not want to become a parent against her will." The New Jersey Supreme Court ruled that Mr. "M.B." could retain the embryos or have them destroyed, but he could not have them implanted in his new wife. As one Atlanta attorney who has handled several cases involving disputed embryos said of this case: "There is really no guiding principle nationwide in these cases. There are very few states that have looked at the issue." [111] This case is a vivid reminder that judicial policymaking in new legal realms is by no means the exclusive activity of the federal courts.

The Judge's Role Conception

In the discussion of which better explains judicial decision making—the rules of the legal subculture or stimuli from the democratic subculture—one additional factor must be considered: how judges conceive of their judicial role. Judicial scholars often talk about three basic decision-making categories regarding whether judges should make law when they decide cases. Lawmakers are those who take a broad view of the judicial role. Often referred to as activists or innovators, these jurists contend that they can and must make law in their decisions, because the statutory law and appellate or Supreme Court guidelines are often ambiguous or do not cover all situations and because legislative intent is frequently impossible to determine. In Kitchin's study of federal district judges, 14 percent were classified in this category, whereas in an investigation of appeals court judges, 15 percent were associated with this role.[112]

At the other end of the continuum are the law interpreters, who take a narrow, traditional view of the judicial function. Sometimes called strict constructionists, they do not believe that judges should substitute judicial wisdom for the rightful power of the elected branches of government to make policy. They tend to eschew making innovative decisions that may depart from the literal meaning of controlling precedents. In the Kitchin study, 52 percent of the U.S. trial judges were found to be law interpreters, whereas only 26 percent of the appeals court judges were so designated.[113] This finding is consistent with the fact that federal district judges are more concerned with routine norm enforcement, whereas the appellate judges' involvement—and their perception of it—is with broader questions of judicial policy.

Midway between the law interpreters and the lawmakers are judges known as pragmatists or realists, who believe that on occasion they are obliged to make law, but that for most cases a decision can be made by consulting the controlling law or appellate court precedents. Studies have indicated that a third of federal district judges assume this moderate role, whereas a full 59 percent of their appellate court colleagues do so.[114] Comparing federal jurists with state judges, one scholar has noted, "A slightly greater number of federal than state judges take the pragmatist or realist views, possibly because they have more opportunities to make innovative decisions."[115]

Thus, whether judicial decisions are better explained by the legal model or by the democratic model depends not only on the nature of the cases and the state of the controlling law and precedents, but also to some degree on how the individual judges evaluate these factors. In virtually every case that comes before them, judges have to determine how much discretion they have and how they wish to exercise it. This is a subjective process, and, as one research team put it, "activist judges will find more discretion in a given fact situation than will their more restrained colleagues."[116]

Summary

Federal and state judges make hundreds of millions of decisions each year, and scholars have sought to explain the thinking behind these decisions. Two schools of thought provide explanations. One theory is based on the rules and procedures of the legal subculture. Judges' decisions, according to this model, are the product of traditional legal reasoning and adherence to precedent and judicial self-restraint. Another school of thought, the realist-behavioralist approach, argues that judges are influenced in their decision making by such factors as party affiliation, local values and attitudes, public opinion, and pressures from the legislative and executive branches. In the vast majority of cases, the legal subculture model is the more accurate predictor of judicial decision making. However, stimuli from the democratic subculture often become useful in accounting for judges' decisions (1) when the legal evidence is contradictory or equally compelling on both sides; (2) if the situation concerns new areas of the law and significant precedents are absent; and (3) when judges are inclined to view themselves more as activist lawmakers than as law interpreters.

Further Thought and Discussion Questions

1. Should a judge's political party affiliation affect the way he or she makes decisions on the bench? Most Americans would say "no," although they prefer to elect their judges and do this on a party basis. Is there an inherent inconsistency in these preferences?

2. Should judges' decisions reflect public opinion? Most Americans would find that offensive. However, no less an authority than Chief Justice William H. Rehnquist says it is inevitable and unavoidable that judges reflect public opinion. Sometimes, for example, trial judges are encouraged by the appellate courts to reflect the public mood in their decision making.

3. Judges are much more likely in some situations to hand down decisions that reflect their personal values. What are the circumstances that allow one to predict whether a judge will render a decision "in accordance with the law" or in accordance with his or her personal attitudes?

NOTES

1. Richard J. Richardson and Kenneth N. Vines, *The Politics of Federal Courts* (Boston: Little, Brown, 1970). Although Richardson and Vines developed their model primarily for federal courts, we believe that their hypotheses and conclusions are equally true for state judges.

2. Edward H. Levi, *An Introduction to Legal Reasoning* (Chicago: University of Chicago Press, 1948), 1–2.

3. *Lane v. Wilson,* 307 U.S. 268 (1939); and *Gomillion v. Lightfoot,* 364 U.S. 339 (1960).

4. *Lane v. Wilson,* 307 U.S. 275 (1939).

5. William Kitchin, *Federal District Judges* (Baltimore: College Press, 1978), 71.

6. J. Woodford Howard Jr., *Courts of Appeals in the Federal Judicial System: A Study of the Second, Fifth, and District of Columbia Circuits* (Princeton, N.J.: Princeton University Press, 1981), 187.

7. Walter F. Murphy, *Elements of Judicial Strategy* (Chicago: University of Chicago Press, 1964), 204.

8. Jeffrey A. Segal and Robert M. Howard, "How Supreme Court Justices Respond to Litigant Requests to Overturn Precedents," *Judicature* 85 (2001): 151.

9. Henry Sumner Maine, *Ancient Law* (Boston: Beacon Press, 1963), 3–19.

10. Henry J. Abraham, *The Judicial Process,* 7th ed. (New York: Oxford University Press, 1998), chap. 9.

11. *Evers v. Jackson Municipal Separate School District,* 232 F. Supp. 241 (1964).

12. Ibid., 247.

13. Ibid., 249.

14. Ibid., 255.

15. Richardson and Vines, *The Politics of Federal Courts,* 8–9.

16. Steven Vago, *Law and Society,* 5th ed. (Englewood Cliffs, N.J.: Prentice-Hall, 1997), 354.

17. Steven Vago, *Law and Society,* 6th ed. (Upper Saddle River, N.J.: Prentice Hall, 2000), chap 9.

18. Oliver Wendell Holmes Jr., *The Common Law* (Boston: Little, Brown, 1881), 1–2.

19. Jerome Frank, *Courts on Trial: Myth and Reality in American Justice* (Princeton, N.J.: Princeton University Press, 1950), 151.

20. Richardson and Vines, *The Politics of Federal Courts*, 10.

21. Donald Dale Jackson, *Judges* (New York: Atheneum, 1974), 18.

22. One recent study noted that, between 1959 and 1998, 140 books, articles, dissertations, and conference papers reported empirical data showing a link between judges' political party affiliation and their judicial behavior. Daniel R. Pinello, "Linking Party to Judicial Ideology in American Courts: A Meta-Analysis," *Justice System Journal* 20 (1999): 219–254.

23. Some studies suggest that age, socioeconomic status, and religion may influence some judges in some of their cases, but the associations are weak. See, for example, Sheldon Goldman, "Voting Behavior on the United States Courts of Appeals Revisited," *American Political Science Review* 69 (1975): 491–506; John R. Schmidhauser, "The Justices of the Supreme Court: A Collective Portrait," *Midwest Journal of Political Science* 3 (1959): 1–57; and Donald Leavitt, "Political Party and Class Influences on the Attitudes of Justices of the Supreme Court in the Twentieth Century," paper delivered at the annual meeting of the Midwest Political Science Association, Chicago, 1972. Other studies suggest that these background factors have virtually no explanatory power—for example, Howard, *Courts of Appeals in the Federal Judicial System*, chap. 6. For a more detailed discussion of this subject and a literature review, see C. K. Rowland and Robert A. Carp, *Politics and Judgment in Federal District Courts* (Lawrence: University Press of Kansas, 1996), chap. 2.

24. David W. Adamany, "The Party Variable in Judges' Voting: Conceptual Notes and a Case Study," *American Political Science Review* 63 (1969): 59.

25. These figures are based on unpublished data collected by Robert A. Carp, Ronald Stidham, and Kenneth Manning.

26. For a more extensive discussion of the odds ratio and methodology used in this study, see Rowland and Carp, *Politics and Judgment in Federal District Courts*, 180–181.

27. For a good review of the early literature on this subject, see Goldman, "Voting Behavior on the United States Courts of Appeals Revisited," 491, note 2. See also Howard, *Courts of Appeals in the Federal Judicial System*, chap. 6.

28. Sheldon Goldman, "Voting Behavior on the United States Courts of Appeals, 1961–1964," *American Political Science Review* 60 (1966): 384.

29. See, for example, Donald Songer, "Consensual and Nonconsensual Decisions in Unanimous Opinions of the United States Courts of Appeals," *American Journal of Political Science* 26 (1982): 225–239; Donald Songer and Sue Davis, "The Impact of Party and Region on Voting Decisions in the United States Courts of Appeals, 1955–1986," *Western Political Quarterly* 43 (1990): 317–334; and Ronald Stidham, Robert A. Carp, and Donald R. Songer, "The Voting Behavior of President Clinton's Judicial Appointees," *Judicature* 80 (1996): 16–21.

30. Christopher E. Smith, "Polarization and Change in the Federal Courts: *En Banc* Decisions in the U.S. Courts of Appeals," *Judicature* 74 (1990): 137.

31. Leavitt, "Political Party and Class Influences on the Attitudes of Justices of the Supreme Court in the Twentieth Century," 18–19.

32. Lee Epstein, Thomas G. Walker, and William J. Dixon, "The Supreme Court and Criminal Justice Disputes: A Neo-Institutional Perspective," *American Journal of Political Science* 33 (1989): 838.

33. S. Sidney Ulmer, "Are Background Models Time-Bound?" *American Political Science Review* 80 (1986): 957–967.

34. S. Sidney Ulmer, "The Political Party Variable in the Michigan Supreme Court," *Journal of Public Law* 11 (1962): 352–362; and Malcolm M. Feeley, "Another Look at the 'Party Variable' in Judicial Decision-Making: An Analysis of the Michigan Supreme Court," *Polity* 4 (1971): 91–104.

35. Philip L. Dubois, "The Illusion of Judicial Consensus Revisited: Partisan Conflict on an Intermediate State Court of Appeals," *American Journal of Political Science* 32 (1988): 946–967.

36. Ibid., 953–954.

37. For a good bibliography of the literature on partisan voting patterns among state judges, see ibid., 965–967. Also, see the literature review in this article: Paul R. Brace and Melinda Gann Hall, "Studying Courts Comparatively: The View from the American States," *Political Research Quarterly* 48 (1995): 5–29.

38. Donald P. Kommers, "The Federal Constitutional Court in the West German Political System," in *Frontiers of Judicial Research*, ed. Joel B. Grossman and Joseph Tanenhaus (New York: John Wiley, 1969), 73–132; Fred L. Morrison, "The Swiss Federal Court: Judicial Decision Making and Recruitment," in *Frontiers of Judicial Research*, ed. Grossman and Tanenhaus, 133–162; and Glendon Schubert, "The Dimensions of Decisional Response: Opinion and Voting Behavior of the Australian High Court," in *Frontiers of Judicial Research*, ed. Grossman and Tanenhaus, 163–195.

39. See, for example, Glendon Schubert and David J. Danelski, eds., *Comparative Judicial Behavior: Cross-Cultural Studies of Political Decision-Making in the East and West* (New York: Oxford University Press, 1969); Matthew E. Wetstein and C. L. Ostberg, "Search and Seizure Cases in the Supreme Court of Canada: Extending an American Model of Judicial Decision Making across Countries," *Social Science Quarterly* 80 (1999): 757–774; and J. Mark Ramseyer and Eric B. Rasmusen, "Skewed Incentives: Paying for Politics as a Japanese Judge," *Judicature* 83 (2000): 190–195.

40. Richardson and Vines, *The Politics of Federal Courts*, 71.

41. For a more elaborate discussion of this phenomenon, see Robert A. Carp and C. K. Rowland, *Policymaking and Politics in the Federal District Courts* (Knoxville: University of Tennessee Press, 1983), chap. 4.

42. Richardson and Vines, *The Politics of Federal Courts*, 73.

43. Ibid., 72.

44. For example, see Robert A. Carp and Russell Wheeler, "Sink or Swim: The Socialization of a Federal District Judge," *Journal of Public Law* 21 (1972): 359–393. See also Robert A. Carp, "The Influence of Local Needs and Conditions on the Administration of Federal Justice," paper delivered at the annual meeting of the Southwestern Political Science Association, Dallas, 1971.

45. See, for example, Angus Campbell, Philip E. Converse, Warren E. Miller, and Donald E. Stokes, *The American Voter* (New York: Wiley, 1960); Everett Carll Ladd Jr. and Charles D. Hadley, *Transformations of the American Party System*, 2d ed. (New York: W. W. Norton, 1978); V. O. Key Jr., *Public Opinion and American Democracy* (New York: Knopf, 1967); and Robert S. Erikson and Kent L. Tedin, *American Public Opinion: Its Origins, Content, and Impact*, 7th ed. (Boston: Allyn Bacon, 2003).

46. Barbara Hinckley, *Stability and Change in Congress* (New York: Harper and Row, 1978); Randall B. Ripley, *Congress: Process and Policy*, 2d ed. (New York: W. W. Norton, 1978); V. O. Key Jr., *Politics, Parties, and Pressure Groups*, 5th ed. (New York: Crowell, 1964), especially chaps. 9 and 24; and J. H. Fenton, "Liberal-Conservative Divisions by Sections of the United States," *Annals* 344 (1962): 122–127.

47. John R. Schmidhauser, "Judicial Behavior and the Sectional Crisis of 1837–1860," *Journal of Politics* 23 (1961): 615–640. To be more precise, Schmidhauser found that justices' party affiliations and their geographic orientations were highly interrelated. Because the four justices who were most supportive of southern regional interests were all southern Democrats, and because the two justices with the strongest pro-northern voting patterns were northern Whigs, Schmidhauser concluded that the effects of party and region were virtually inseparable.

48. Leavitt, "Political Party and Class Influences on the Attitudes of Justices of the Supreme Court in the Twentieth Century."

49. James F. Simon, *In His Own Image* (New York: David McKay, 1973), 103–104.

50. Ibid., 123.

51. Howard, *Courts of Appeals in the Federal Judicial System*, 55, 79, 156.

52. Susan Brodie Haire, "Judges' Decisions in the United States Courts of Appeals: A Reassessment of Geographic Patterns in Judicial Behavior," Ph.D. dissertation, University of South Carolina, 1993, 160.

53. Steve Alumbaugh and C. K. Rowland, "The Links Between Platform-Based Appointment Criteria and Trial Judges' Abortion Judgments," *Judicature* 74 (1990): 161.

54. Vilhelm Aubert, "Conscientious Objectors before Norwegian Military Courts," in *Judicial Decision-Making*, ed. Glendon Schubert (New York: Free Press of Glencoe, 1963), 206–207.

55. For example, see Goldman, "Voting Behavior on the United States Courts of Appeals, 1961–1964," 370–385.

56. Haire, "Judges' Decisions in the United States Courts of Appeals," 163 and chap. 5.

57. Sara C. Benesh and Malia Reddick, "Overruled: An Event History of Lower Court Reaction to Supreme Court Alteration of Precedent," *Journal of Politics* 64 (2002): 534–550.

58. Based on unpublished data collected by Robert A. Carp, Kenneth Manning, and Ronald Stidham.

59. Carp and Wheeler, "Sink or Swim," 376.

60. Adam Liptak, "A Lid on Secret Settlements," *Houston Chronicle*, September 2, 2002, A12.

61. Howard, *Courts of Appeals in the Federal Judicial System*, 234.

62. For example, see Carp and Rowland, *Policymaking and Politics in the Federal District Courts*, 106–116.

63. This discussion is based on material taken from Martin A. Levin, *Urban Politics and the Criminal Courts* (Chicago: University of Chicago Press, 1977).

64. Ibid., 136–142.

65. Ibid., 142–147.

66. Henry R. Glick, *Courts, Politics, and Justice*, 3d ed. (New York: McGraw-Hill, 1993), 321.

67. As quoted in William Mishler and Reginald S. Sheehan, "The Supreme Court as a Countermajoritarian Institution? The Impact of Public Opinion on Supreme Court Decisions," *American Political Science Review* 87 (1993): 89.

68. "John H. Cushman Jr., "O'Connor Not Retiring," *Houston Chronicle*, July 7, 2003, A1.

69. Adam Liptak, "A Lid on Secret Settlements," *Houston Chronicle*, September 2, 2002, A12.

70. *Brown v. Board of Education*, 349 U.S. 294 (1955).

71. *Baker v. Carr*, 369 U.S. 186 (1962).

72. *Miller v. California*, 413 U.S. 15 (1973).

73. Lawrence Baum, *The Supreme Court*, 5th ed. (Washington, D.C.: CQ Press, 1995), 151. For a good discussion of this subject, see David G. Barnum, "Supreme Court and Public Opinion: Judicial Decision Making in the Post–New Deal Period," *Journal of Politics* 47 (1985): 652–666.

74. The full citations are as follows: *Marbury v. Madison*, 1 Cranch 137 (1803); *Brown v. Board of Education*, 347 U.S. 483 (1954); *Roe v. Wade*, 410 U.S. 113 (1973); and *United States v. Nixon*, 418 U.S. 683 (1974).

75. For examples of these earlier studies, see Glen T. Broach et al., "State Political Culture and Sentence Severity in Federal District Courts," *Criminology* 16 (1978): 373–382; and Ronald Stidham and Robert A. Carp, "Trial Courts' Responses to Supreme Court Policy Changes: Three Case Studies," *Law and Policy Quarterly* 4 (1982): 215–235.

76. Mishler and Sheehan, "The Supreme Court as a Countermajoritarian Institution?" 96.

77. Ibid., 87–101; and Mishler and Sheehan, "Popular Influence on Supreme Court Decisions: A Response to Helmut Norpoth and Jeffrey A. Segal," *American Political Science Review* 88 (1994): 716–724.

78. Mishler and Sheehan, "The Supreme Court as a Countermajoritarian Institution?" 87–101.

79. Roy B. Flemming and B. Dan Wood, "The Public and the Supreme Court: Individual Justice Responsiveness to American Policy Moods," *American Journal of Political Science* 41 (1997): 468–498.

80. See, for example, Ashlyn Kuersten, Kenneth L. Manning, and Robert A. Carp, "The Political Context of Lower Court Decision Making," paper delivered at the annual meeting of the Southern Political

Science Association, Savannah, Georgia, 1999; and Kenneth L. Manning, Ashlyn K. Kuersten, and Robert A. Carp, "Public Opinion and the Political Context of Lower Court Decision Making," paper delivered at the annual meeting of the American Political Science Association, Washington, D.C., 2000.

81. James H. Kuklinski and John E. Stanga, "Political Participation and Government Responsiveness: The Behavior of California Superior Courts," *American Political Science Review* 73 (1979): 1090–1099.

82. Melinda Gann Hall, "Electoral Politics and Strategic Voting in State Supreme Courts," *Journal of Politics* 54 (1992): 427.

83. Paul R. Brace and Melinda Gann Hall, "The Interplay of Preferences, Case Facts, Context, and Rules in the Politics of Judicial Choice," *Journal of Politics* 59 (1997): 1223.

84. "Dallas Judge Apologizes for 'Poor Choice of Words,'" *Montrose Voice*, December 23, 1988, 5.

85. "Overheard," *Newsweek*, January 2, 1989, 13.

86. For example, in 2003 the Supreme Court ruled that in employment discrimination suits authorized by Congress, employees do not need direct evidence of bias in order to bring a lawsuit against an employer; indirect evidence is sufficient. *Desert Palace, Inc. v. Costa*; available online at http://supct.law.cornell.edu/supct/html/02-679.

87. However, many constitutional scholars argue that the right of the federal courts to hear such cases stems directly from Article III of the Constitution and that therefore Congress could not legally curtail court jurisdiction over these subjects except by initiating an amendment to the Constitution.

88. See, for example, Stephen L. Wasby, *The Impact of the United States Supreme Court* (Homewood, Ill.: Dorsey Press, 1970), especially 255–256; and Harrell R. Rodgers Jr. and Charles S. Bullock III, *Coercion to Compliance* (Lexington, Mass.: Heath, 1976).

89. *National Labor Relations Board v. Jones and Laughlin Steel Corp.*, 301 U.S. 1 (1937); and *West Coast Hotel Co. v. Parrish*, 300 U.S. 379 (1937).

90. Stidham and Carp, "Trial Courts' Responses to Supreme Court Policy Changes," 218–222.

91. G. Alan Tarr and Mary Cornelia Aldis Porter, *State Supreme Courts in State and Nation* (New Haven, Conn.: Yale University Press, 1988), chap. 2.

92. Ibid., 45.

93. Roger D. Groot, "The Effects of an Intermediate Appellate Court on the Supreme Court Product: The North Carolina Experience," *Wake Forest Law Review* 7 (1971): 548–572.

94. Tarr and Porter, *State Supreme Courts in State and Nation*, 51.

95. Meki Cox, "Hawaii Starts Benefits to Gay Couples," *Houston Chronicle*, July 9, 1997, A5.

96. This example is based on Jim Carlton and Amy Dockser Marcus, "Undocumented Worker's Suit Is Upheld," *Wall Street Journal*, February 25, 1991, B5. The case citation is *E.E.O.C. v. Tortilleria La Mejor*, 758 F. Supp. 585 (E.D. Cal. 1991).

97. Carp and Rowland, *Policymaking and Politics in the Federal District Courts*, 37.

98. However, on matters of local economic regulation, voting differences among judges are still sharp (see Table 12-1). Only at the national level have federal judges tended to refrain from substituting their own views for those of elected officials.

99. Carp and Rowland, *Policymaking and Politics in the Federal District Courts*, 39.

100. At the state level, whether high court ambiguity is thought to be greater on civil rights and liberties issues or in the labor and economic realm varies from one jurisdiction to another. Note the several areas discussed in Chapter 3, under the heading "Norm Enforcement and Policymaking in the State Courts," in which state courts have taken the lead in bringing about policy-making innovations.

101. Kitchin, *Federal District Judges*, 104.

102. Carp and Rowland, *Policymaking and Politics in the Federal District Courts*, 40.

103. *Roth v. United States* and *Alberts v. California*, 354 U.S. 476 (1957).

104. *Jacobellis v. Ohio*, 378 U.S. 184 (1964).

105. *Miller v. California*, 413 U.S. 15 (1973).

106. *Jacobellis v. Ohio*, 378 U.S. 184 (1964) at 197.

107. Laura Parker, "Federal Judge in Florida Rules 2 Live Crew Album Is Obscene," *Houston Chronicle*, June 7, 1990, A11.

108. Ann Davis, "When Ribaldry among Men Is Sex Harassment," *Wall Street Journal*, June 5, 1997, B1.

109. "Same-Sex Harassment: Is It Illegal and Under What Circumstances?" *Wall Street Journal*, June 3, 1997, A1.

110. Davis, "When Ribaldry among Men Is Sex Harassment."

111. John P. McAlpin, "Father Not Allowed to Donate Embryos," *Houston Chronicle*, August 15, 2001, A4.

112. Kitchin, *Federal District Judges*, 107.

113. Ibid.

114. Ibid.

115. Glick, *Courts, Politics, and Justice*, 335.

116. Carp and Rowland, *Policymaking and Politics in the Federal District Courts*, 14.

SUGGESTED READINGS

Burton, Steven J. *An Introduction to Law and Legal Reasoning*, 2d ed. New York: Aspen Publishers, 1995. Explains what it has traditionally meant to "think like a judge"; explores the judicial reasoning process.

Carter, Lief H., and Thomas F. Burke. *Reason in Law*, 6th ed. New York: Pearson Education, 2001. A short, excellent discussion of how judges think and reason and a good explication of the legal subculture.

Goldman, Sheldon, and Austin Sarat, eds. *American Court Systems: Readings in Judicial Process and Behavior*, 2d ed. White Plains, N.Y.: Longman, 1989. A reader containing contemporary approaches to explaining why judges think and act the way they do.

Murphy, Walter F., C. Herman Pritchett, and Lee Epstein. *Courts, Judges, & Politics*, 5th ed., Part Four. New York: McGraw-Hill, 2002. An excellent collection of edited essays on both traditional and modern ways of explaining how judges make decisions.

Richardson, Richard J., and Kenneth N. Vines. *The Politics of Federal Courts: Lower Courts in the United States*. Boston: Little, Brown, 1970. A classic discussion of the influences of both the legal subculture and the democratic subculture on judicial decision making.

Rowland, C. K., and Robert A. Carp. *Politics and Judgment in Federal District Courts*. Lawrence: University Press of Kansas, 1996. A comprehensive study of decision making at the federal district court level, based on a large data sample.

Schubert, Glendon. *Judicial Behavior: A Reader in Theory and Research*. Chicago: Rand McNally, 1964. A classic reader in judicial decision making; excellent essays introduce each chapter.

Tanenhaus, Joseph, and Walter F. Murphy. *The Study of Public Law*. New York: Random House, 1972. Systematically discusses the history of public law and examines the various approaches to its study.

CHAPTER 13

Decision Making in Collegial Courts

For years the Supreme Court has been closely divided between conservatives and moderates, with an unprece-dented number of cases decided by votes of five-to-four. Several justices are currently on the verge of retirement. In anticipation of one or more vacancies, court watchers are contemplating whether the president's next Supreme Court appointments will solidify a conservative majority or whether they will move the Court in a more liberal direction. In all likelihood, the matter will be resolved by the results of the 2004 presidential election.

U NTIL NOW WE HAVE TREATED decision making by American judges at all levels as if it were essentially the product of the same two influences—the legal and the democratic subcultures. To a substantial degree, this is a valid approach. Jurists on multijudge appellate courts adhere to the same legal reasoning process as do their colleagues on the trial court bench. Lower-court judges may be influenced in close cases by their political party affiliation, just as members of the appeals courts are. But before an analysis of judicial decision making can be complete, one vital difference between trial courts and the state and federal appellate courts must be recognized. The former render decisions that are largely the product of a single individual, whereas the latter, as **collegial courts,** make decisions through group interaction. As one former trial judge, now a member of an appellate court, said:

The transition between a district judge and circuit judge is not an easy one, primarily because of, shall I say, the autocratic position occupied by the district court judge. He is the sole decider. He decides as he sees fit, and files the decision in a form as he sees fit. A Court of Appeals decides by committee. One of the first traumas I had was when opinions were sent back by the other judges asking me to add this sentence, change that, etc., to get concurrence. I admit at the beginning I resisted that. It was pride. I learned it was a joint project, but it was a very difficult thing. I see the same in others.[1]

What are the extra ingredients that go into a decision made by the nine-member Supreme Court or by a three-judge state appellate panel? What is the essence of the dynamics of multijudge decision making that distinguishes it from a judgment made by a single jurist? We will discuss several theoretical approaches that have attempted to get a handle on this slippery subject. Although we will continue to address these phenomena as they affect both state and federal judges, the several judicial systems will not be treated as separate entities. There is no reason to believe that the variables and forces being explored here affect state jurists and federal judges in different ways. For example, when we contend that the corporate decision of a collegial court is often the product of personal interaction, there is no reason to believe that such interpersonal variables would be significantly different for the U.S. Supreme Court or the highest tribunal of a given state.[2] An increasing amount of comparative data about appellate jurists in other countries reveals that some patterns of collegial court behavior may be international in nature.

Cue Theory

As long as trial and appeals courts have jurisdiction over a case, the judges must render some type of decision on the merits. They have little discretion about the composition of their dockets. If the judges view a particular case as presenting a trivial question, they will not spend time agonizing over it, but they are still obliged to provide some kind of formal ruling on the substance of the matter. Not so with the Supreme Court. Of the approximately eight thousand petitions presented to the Court each year, the justices agree to hear only a few hundred on the merits—and in recent years fewer than a hundred of these carry with them full-blown written opinions. Since the enactment of Public Law 100–352 in 1988, the Supreme Court has had almost complete control over its own docket. That is, the justices decide which issues they want to tackle in a given term and which ones are not ripe for adjudication or must be summarily dismissed for "want of a substantial federal question." This has importance because what the Supreme Court decides not to rule on is often as significant as the cases it does choose to scrutinize. (The state supreme courts vary greatly in the amount of control they have over their dockets.)[3]

In other countries few courts have as much control over their dockets as that possessed by the U.S. Supreme Court. For example, the highly important and prestigious European Court of Justice is required to hear all cases referred to it, however unimportant. To avoid dealing with what would otherwise be a crushing and impossible workload, the court has developed a number of mechanisms. For example, the court (like most foreign judicial tribunals and lower U.S. federal courts) is divided into chambers. Panels of three or five judges sit together to hear a particular case. When the law requires that the full court hear a case, the court may sit with a quorum of eleven judges instead of all fifteen.[4]

Judicial scholars have sought to identify the reasons for giving special attention to some petitions, while the rest never receive those important four votes needed for the Supreme Court to grant certiorari and decide the case. A pioneering study of this question was conducted by a research team during the early 1960s.[5] Analysts began by examining the Court's official reasons for granting certiorari, as set forth in Rule 17, which specifies that the Court may hear a case if (1) an appeals court has decided a point of local law in conflict with local decisions, (2) a court of appeals has departed from "the usual course of judicial proceedings," (3) a conflict is perceived between a lower-court decision and a Supreme Court precedent, (4) a conflict exists on a point of law among the various federal circuits, or (5) the Court feels it must have the final word on a particularly important question.

The research team tested these official reasons by comparing the cases for which certiorari was granted with those in which review was denied. The official reasons did not prove to be an accurate or useful guide to the Court's decision making. For example, in over 50 percent of the cases selected for review, the Court's official reason for its actions was that the cases were "important"—however that was defined. The researchers thought they could do better. They set out to identify certain key characteristics of the cases granted review as well as those denied it. They hoped to develop some predictive statements that were more precise and reliable than Rule 17. The result was **cue theory**.

Cue theory is based on the assumption that the Supreme Court justices have neither the time nor the desire to wade through myriad pages in the thousands of petitions presented to them each year. Therefore, they presumably must have developed some sort of shortcut to help them select the petitions. The researchers hypothesized that the justices must look for cues in each petition—readily identifiable characteristics that trigger a positive response as they skim through the cumbersome piles of legal documents. After all, people have their own particular cue theories as they go about their daily lives. Someone would not read through a four-page circular on a local store's white sale, for instance, if he or she already had an ample supply of bedding. Just as people look for cues in sorting through their daily mail, justices on the Supreme Court do likewise as they sort through the petitions for certiorari that arrive daily. At least this is what the research team reasoned.

The results of the team's hypotheses and investigations were encouraging. Of the several possible cues they tested for, three were found to be highly relevant. In order of importance they were: (1) whether the U.S. government was a party to a case and was asking for Court review, (2) whether a civil rights or civil liberties issue was debated, and (3) whether there was dissension among the judges in the court that had previously heard the case (or disagreement between two or more courts and government agencies). If a case contained all three cues, there was an 80 percent chance that certiorari would be granted; if none were present, the chance dropped to a mere 7 percent. Clearly, the researchers had developed a useful model to explain this one aspect of Supreme Court behavior.

During the past three decades judicial scholars have further tested, elaborated on, and revised cue theory. Some studies have found a relationship between the way the justices voted on a grant of certiorari and their eventual vote on the merits of the case at conference.[6] Additional studies have suggested that a fourth cue has considerable weight—the ideological direction of the lower-court decision.[7] In comparing selected periods of the Warren Court (1967–1968 and 1968–1969 terms) and the Burger Court (1976–1977 and 1977–1978 terms) on certiorari voting, the analysts reached several conclusions. First, during the liberal Warren Court era, the justices were more likely to review economic cases that had been decided in a conservative manner by the lower court—especially when the U.S. government was seeking Court review.[8] Second, and conversely, the more conservative Burger Court tended to review liberal lower-court economic decisions. Third, the Burger Court was more disposed to scrutinize a civil libertarian position taken by a lower court than it was a lower-court decision limiting civil liberties.

A study of the first three terms of the Rehnquist Court reveals the presence of a new hybrid strategy for granting certiorari. Unlike the Warren and Burger Courts, the Rehnquist Court has not engaged in much "error correction" activity, that is, overturning lower-court decisions with which it disagrees. Instead, it has chosen to affirm a tremendous percentage of conservative lower-court decisions with which it is in ideological harmony, thereby underscoring the values inherent in these cases. It is also more likely to accept cases that concern issues on which lower-court judges had rendered conflicting decisions. The researchers conceded that they could only speculate as to why the Rehnquist Court had switched gears in this decision-making area.[9]

Cue theory, then, is one predictor of high court voting behavior. One contemporary judicial scholar has summarized the certiorari behavior of the Court during the past several decades:

When the civil rights movement was building in importance (1950s), the Supreme Court, under the leadership of Chief Justice Earl Warren, paid special attention to cases involving civil liberties violations, and during the 1960s various underdog appellants, such as aliens, minorities, criminal defendants, laborers, and other have-nots, were more successful than others in getting *certiorari*. However, as the Supreme Court has shifted toward the conservatives, upperdogs such as governments at all levels and businesses have received more attention by the Supreme Court.[10]

Small-Group Analysis

As applied to the judiciary, most **small-group analysis** is based on the thesis that judges want to influence the judgments of their colleagues and to be on the winning side as often as possible. This school of thought assumes that judges' positions are not written in stone from the start but are susceptible to moderation or even to a 180-degree turn on occasion. More specifically, scholars believe that a good deal of interaction takes place among justices from the time a case is first discussed in conference to the moment the final decision is rendered in open court some weeks or months later. One researcher has referred to the appellate judges' openness to change as **"fluidity."** [11]

The way judges relate to one another affects their behavior on the court. Examination of the personal papers of members of the Supreme Court, interviews with appellate court jurists, and reminiscences of former law clerks all reveal the impact of group dynamics on voting behavior and the content of written opinions.[12] Two characteristics in particular seem to carry weight when justices seek to influence their colleagues—personality and intellect. Judges who are viewed as warm, good-hearted, fair-minded, and so on seem able to put together winning coalitions and hammer out compromises a bit more effectively than colleagues with a reputation for condescension, self-righteousness, hostility, or vindictiveness.[13] As one researcher put it after interviewing supreme court justices in Louisiana, Massachusetts, New Jersey, and Pennsylvania:

Generally, the judges believed it is important for court members to moderate their own personal idiosyncrasies in order to maintain as much harmony in the group as possible. Such things as arrogance, pride, sense of superiority, and loss of temper were condemned. . . . A pleasing personality . . . can be particularly important on collegial courts because the judges interact on a continuous basis: they operate as a small, permanent committee.[14]

This reflection on human nature should come as no surprise. A student who had served on his university's multimember student court provided an illustration of this phenomenon, and although a student tribunal is certainly not a state or federal appellate court, the dynamics are similar:

We had this guy on the court . . . who was one of these people that you just kind of naturally take to. I mean, he had a good sense of humor and was real decent and outgoing. I don't think he was that much of a "brain" or anything, but you always felt that he honestly wanted to do the right thing. Well, when we were split on some case— especially on matters of what punishment to hand down—and he suggested a way out, I think we all listened pretty carefully to what he thought was fair. He was just that sort of person.

The other personal attribute that is part of small-group dynamics is the knowledge and intellectual capacity of the individual judge.[15] A justice with a superior intellect or wide experience in a particular area of the law has a good deal more clout than a jurist who is seen as an intellectual lightweight. As one appeals court judge observed:

Personality doesn't amount to so much as opinion-writing ability. Some judges are simply better than others. Some know more, think better. It would be strange if among nine men all had the same ability. Some simply have more respect than others. . . . That's bound to be so in any group. The first thing, is the judge particularly broad and experienced in the field? A couple of judges are acknowledged masters in admiralty. What they think carries more weight. I don't have much trouble being heard on criminal law or state government. I've been there. Ex-district judges on Courts of Appeals certainly carry more weight in discussion of trial procedures, instructions to juries, etc. Every judge is recognized for a particular proficiency obtained before or after his appointment. It saves enormous spadework and drudgery [to assign opinions accordingly]. No one could develop an expertise in all these fields.[16]

The techniques or strategies that justices use in their conscious (or even unconscious) efforts to maximize their impact on multijudge courts can be grouped in three general categories: persuasion on the merits, bargaining, and threat of sanctions. Although the tactics overlap and are inherently interrelated, each has a different central focus.

Persuasion on the Merits

This strategy means that, because of their training and values, judges are open to persuasion based on sound legal reasoning bolstered by legal precedents. Unless judges have taken a hard and fast position from the start, most can be swayed by an articulate and well-reasoned argument from a colleague with a differing opinion.

One study of the Supreme Court concluded that the justices

can be persuaded to change their minds about specific cases as well as about broad public policies, and intellectual persuasion can play an important role in such shifts. . . . Time and time again positions first taken at conference are changed as other Justices bring up new arguments. Perhaps most convincing in demonstrating the impact of intellectual factors are the numerous instances on record in which the Justice assigned the opinion of the Court has reported back to the conference that additional study had convinced him that he and the rest of the majority had been in error.[17]

For example, Justice Robert Jackson, hardly a wilting violet when it came to holding fast to a judicial point of view, once commented: "I myself have changed my opinion after reading the opinions of the other members of this Court. And I am as stubborn as most. But I sometimes wind up not voting the way I voted in conference because the reasons of the majority didn't satisfy me."[18]

Judges on state appellate courts appear to be just as willing to have their positions altered by arguments seasoned by precedent and sound judicial reasoning. After interviews with supreme court justices in four states, one scholar observed:

When differences become evident, members of the court may attempt to persuade other judges to adopt their view by vigorously presenting their position or arguing the merits of their way of analyzing the case. Because of different amounts of influence exerted by the chief justice or by judges who have special personal status on the court, certain members of the court may be "persuaded" to abandon their own position and adopt the views of others.[19]

The persuasion on merits strategy cannot be pushed too far, however. If the facts and legal arguments are straightforward, a justice may not be open to change. And judges who are deeply committed to a specific point of view or whose egos are sufficiently great will probably be impervious to legal arguments inconsistent with their own views. For instance, Thurgood Marshall and (later in his career) Harry A. Blackmun were profoundly and morally opposed to the principle of capital punishment and often said so in their opinions. It is doubtful that any amount of legal reasoning or any calling up of "sacred precedents" could have altered their belief that executions constitute "cruel and unusual punishment" by contemporary standards.

Bargaining

Bargaining may be a strange word to use in talking about the personal interaction of judges on collegial courts. When students first hear the term, they often think of the vote-trading technique called logrolling that legislators sometimes use. For example, one lawmaker might say to another, "If you vote for a new federal dam in my district, I'll vote to build a couple of new post offices in yours." Is this what happens with judges, too? Is there evidence that they sometimes say to one another, "If you vote for me in this case, I'll decide with you in one of your 'pet cases' "? No, there is virtually no such evidence. Bargaining does take place, but it is more subtle and does not involve vote swapping. Although some bargaining occurs in the give-and-take that goes on in conference, when the initial votes are taken, most attention is focused on the scope and contents of the majority (or even the dissenting) opinion. A recent study of the phenomenon concluded that "in 58.8% of [the cases studied] members of the majority conference coalition bargained with the opinion author" and that, in the authors' opinion, "our results therefore suggest that justices are indeed rational actors—systematically making judgments about the most efficacious tactic to secure favored outcomes." [20]

To understand how the bargaining process works, it is important to realize that usually much more is at stake in the outcome of a decision than merely whether party A or party B wins. Judges also have to discuss such questions as these: How broad should the decision be? Should they suggest in their written opinion that this case is unique, or should they open the gates and encourage other suits of this nature? Should they overturn what appears to be the controlling precedent or should they "distinguish around" it and let the precedent stand? Should they base their decision on constitutional grounds or should they allow the victor to win on more technical and restrictive grounds? In other words, most decisions at the appellate level are not zero-sum games in which the winner automatically takes all. Important supplementary issues almost always have to be discussed or bargained for.

Two landmark cases of the 1970s provide a good example. In 1973 the Supreme Court handed down a joint decision on the matter of abortion.[21] To most citizens the only issue the Court had to decide was whether abortion is legal. Although that may have been the bottom-line issue, many others were at stake, and the bargaining over them among the majority justices was intense.[22] What is human life and when does it begin? Should the decision rest on the Ninth Amendment or should it be based on the Due Process Clause of the Fourteenth Amendment? Does a fetus have any constitutional rights? Does a woman face a greater health risk in having an abortion than in delivering a child after carrying it to full term? Can a woman decide to have an abortion on her own or does a physician have to concur? If the latter, how many doctors must concur? And this by no means completes the list.

The justices spent over a year trying to hammer out a decision on the abortion cases that would be acceptable to a majority. Draft opinions were sent around, altered, and changed again, as the official opinion writer, Justice Harry Blackmun, tried to accommodate all views—or at least not offend someone in the majority so strongly that he would join the dissenters. Bob Woodward and Scott Armstrong noted in their book *The Brethren: Inside the Supreme Court* that the law clerks "in most chambers were surprised to see the Justices, particularly Blackmun, so openly brokering their decision like a group of legislators." [23] But the law clerks themselves were not immune to the bargaining process. In the Supreme Court's cafeteria, law library, and gymnasium the clerks asked one another whether "your Justice" could go along with this or that compromise or related that "my Justice" would never support an opinion containing such and such an offensive clause.

Bargaining of this nature is just as common on state collegial courts as it is at the national level. This statement by one state supreme court justice is quoted by a scholar who regards it as typical:

> You might say to another judge that if you take this line out, I'll go along with your opinion. You engage in a degree of compromise and if it doesn't hurt the point you're trying to make in an opinion, you ought to agree to take it out.... The men will write an opinion and circulate it. And then the other judges will write a letter or say at conference, can you change this or that, adjust the language here, etc.... Your object is to get a unanimous court. That's always best. [24]

In a significant portion of appellate court cases, then, bargaining is the name of the game; it is one way in which a group of jurists, in a unanimous or majority opinion, is able to present a united front. The author of one classic study focusing on the Supreme Court has observed:

> For Justices, bargaining is a simple fact of life. Despite conflicting views on literary style, relevant precedents, procedural rules, and substantive policy, cases have to be settled and opinions written; and no opinion may carry the institutional label of the court unless five Justices agree to sign it. In the process of judicial decision-making, much bargaining may be tacit, but the pattern is still one of negotiation and accommodation to secure consensus. Thus how to bargain wisely—not necessarily sharply—is a prime consideration for a Justice who is anxious to see his policy adopted by the Court. A Justice must learn not only how to put pressure on his colleagues but how to gauge what amounts of pressure are sufficient to be "effective" and what amounts will overshoot the mark and alienate another judge. In many situations a Justice has to be willing to settle for less than he wants if he is to get anything at all. As [Louis] Brandeis once remarked, the "great difficulty of all group action, of course, is when and what concession to make." [25]

Appellate judges do most of their face-to-face bargaining at the three-judge conferences and then iron out the details of the opinion later, using the telephone and short memos. As with Supreme Court decision making, a threat to dissent can often result in changes in the way the majority opinion is drafted.

When a conservative minority sought to amend a middle-of-the-road compromise by which the 5th circuit achieved unanimity in the Mississippi school case, for example, a former legislator reportedly threatened to bolt to the left. "They came back into the fold in a hurry," a colleague remarked. "So you see, the judicial process is like legislation. All decisions are compromises." [26]

Threat of Sanctions

In addition to persuasion on the merits and bargaining, there is one other tactic that jurists use in their efforts to maximize their impact on multimember appellate tribunals—the threat of sanctions. Basically, three sanctions against colleagues can be invoked: the vote, the willingness to write a strong dissenting opinion, and the threat to "go public."

The Judge's Vote. The threat to take away one's vote from the majority, and thus dissent, may cause the majority to alter its views. For example, in 1889 Justice Horace Gray sent this message to Justice Samuel Miller:

After a careful reading of your opinion in *Shotwell v. Moore,* I am very sorry to be compelled to say that the first part of it . . . is so contrary to my conviction, that I fear, unless it can be a good deal tempered, I shall have to deliver a separate opinion on the lines of the enclosed memorandum. I am particularly troubled about this, because, if my scruples are not removed, and Justices [Stephen J.] Field, [Joseph P.] Bradley and [Lucius Q. C.] Lamar adhere to their dissent, your opinion will represent only four judges, half of those who took part in the case.[27]

His back against the wall because of the narrow majority, Justice Miller was obliged to yield to his colleague's costly "scruples."

For the most part, the potential effect of a threat to dissent from the majority depends on how small that majority is. If the initial vote of a three-judge appellate panel was 3–0, one member's threat to dissent would not be all that serious; there would still be a 2–1 majority. Conversely, if at a preliminary Supreme Court conference the vote was 5–4, the threat to defect by one of those five would be of concern to the remaining four. By the end of the 1993–1994 term, Justice Anthony M. Kennedy had voted with the majority in thirteen of the Court's fourteen cases decided by a 5–4 vote. His support in close cases was likely much sought after.

The newly acquired judicial papers of Thurgood Marshall provide a colorful example of how pivotal one justice's vote can be. In January 1989 the Court decided to take the case of *Webster v. Reproductive Health Services,* which dealt with the constitutionality of Missouri's law severely restricting abortions.[28] Many Court observers believed that a viable conservative majority on the Court could strike down the 1973 *Roe v. Wade* and *Doe v. Bolton* decisions that established the constitutional right to an abortion. Justice Marshall's informal tally sheet dated April 28 indicated five tentative initial votes to uphold the Missouri law: Justices William H. Rehnquist, Byron R. White, Antonin Scalia, Anthony M. Kennedy, and Sandra Day O'Connor. Rehnquist assigned the majority opinion to himself, and Justice Harry Blackmun penned a bitter dissent in which he said, in part, that the right to abortion "no longer survives."

"Over the course of two months, in flurries of court memos, the justices traded views and language. Throughout, O'Connor remained the pivotal swing vote. But she couldn't bring herself to join Rehnquist. Within days of the end of the term, O'Connor changed her mind. She signaled her switch when she wrote that *Roe* was 'problematic,' rather than 'outmoded,' as she had said in an earlier draft." [29]

Nonetheless, "on June 27, Rehnquist circulated his fourth draft. The document still said, 'Chief Justice Rehnquist delivered the opinion of the Court,' traditional wording indicating that he had not given up his hopes of getting O'Connor's support. Then something definitive happened to the Rehnquist majority. On June 28, O'Connor and Blackmun submitted drafts referring to the Rehnquist opinion as a 'plurality,' rather than a majority." [30] The next day Rehnquist circulated his final draft, in which, for the first time, he called his opinion the "judgment" of the Court instead of the majority opinion, meaning, in effect, that the Missouri law would be upheld but there would be no reversal of *Roe v. Wade*. This illustration shows vividly how important a single justice's vote can be when the Court is split evenly between two ideological camps.

Sometimes, however, the impact of one's vote is not merely a function of how divided the court is. On occasion the perceived need for unanimity may be so strong that any justice's threat to vote against the prevailing view may have a disproportionate effect. For example, prior to the 1954 *Brown v. Board of Education* decision, a majority on the Supreme Court opposed segregation in the schools. Chief Justice Earl Warren and the other liberals believed, however, that a simple majority was not enough to confront the backlash expected if segregation were struck down. Only a unanimous Court, they felt, would have any chance of seeing its will prevail throughout the nation. Therefore, the liberal majority bided its time during the early 1950s until the moment came when all nine justices were willing to take on the malignant giant of racial segregation.

A more recent example occurred when President Bill Clinton, the former governor of Arkansas, wished to postpone the sexual harassment suit brought against him by former Arkansas state employee Paula Jones. He argued that the president should be immune to such troublesome and time-consuming litigation during his tenure in the White House. Otherwise, he and his attorneys argued, the chief executive would be plagued by scores of such suits brought by publicity-seeking troublemakers, who would prevent him from devoting his full time and energies to the task of governance. A district court judge rejected the president's motion to dismiss the case entirely but did agree to postpone the case until the end of Clinton's presidency. Both parties were unhappy with the trial court's rulings and both appealed. A panel of the Eighth Circuit Court of Appeals ruled against the president in a split vote, and Clinton appealed to the U.S. Supreme Court.

The high court's decision was unanimous, and it went against the president. Speaking for the majority, Justice John Paul Stevens said in part: "We think the District Court may have given undue weight to the concern that a trial might generate unrelated civil actions that could conceivably hamper the President in conducting the duties of his office. If and when that should occur, the court's discretion would permit it to manage those actions in such fashion (including deferral of trial) that interference with the President's duties would not occur. But no such impingement upon the President's conduct of his office was shown here." [31] The decision was important not only for the opinion it expressed but also because the vote was unanimous; even the president's two Supreme Court appointees (Ruth Bader Ginsburg and Stephen G. Breyer) voted against him. A unanimous vote coming from the deeply divided Rehnquist Court underscored the legal principle involved in the case, and it quashed any notion that partisan politics was a variable in the decision. The defection of just a single vote, while not changing the outcome, would have detracted from the decisive impact of a totally unified court.

State judges, too, may feel the need for unanimity in certain types of cases. For example, one New Jersey Supreme Court justice told a researcher: "We did have a case where we felt a unanimous opinion was necessary. No one felt strongly about a dissent, so no dissents were made. . . . A religious case, for example, needs a unanimous decision. Courts don't try to be divisive on this." [32]

Although the impact of the threat to abandon the majority is usually in direct proportion to the closeness of the vote, occasions arise when a majority will pay top dollar to keep any judge or justice from breaking ranks. That is, the majority may accommodate the contents and scope of its majority opinion to suit the demands of the minority justices in order to get them to join the final opinion and make it unanimous.

The Willingness to Write a Strong Dissent. There are dissents and there are dissents. Appellate court jurists who intend to vote against the majority must decide whether to write a lengthy, assertive dissenting opinion or merely dissent without opinion. If jurists are not regarded by other justices—or by the public at large—as being prestigious or articulate, their threat to write a dissenting opinion may be taken with the proverbial grain of salt. If, however, potential dissenters are respected jurists with a reputation for a keen intellect or for often being right in the long run, the situation is different. The other judges may be willing to alter their views to accommodate potential dissenters' positions or at least dissuade them from attacking the majority position. As one Court observer has noted:

> There are factors which push the majority Justices, especially the opinion writer, to accept accommodation. An eloquent, tightly-reasoned dissent can be an upsetting force. [Harlan F.] Stone's separate opinions during the thirties pointed up more sharply the folly of the conservative Justices than did any of the attacks on the Court by elected politicians. The majority may thus find it profitable to mute criticism from within the Court by giving in on some issues.[33]

Thus the second sanction—the threat to write a dissenting opinion—depends on the circumstances for its effectiveness. Sometimes it may be regarded as no more than a nuisance or the fruit of judicial egomania. On other occasions it may be viewed as likely to weaken the impact of the majority opinion.

In state courts the threat to author a strong dissent has a smaller impact simply because dissents are more infrequent at that level. Consensus and unanimity are the norms in most of the state appellate tribunals, whereas this is clearly not the case at the federal level. Since the 1943 term at least 50 percent of Supreme Court decisions have produced dissents. However, using data from the early to mid-1960s, researchers have found that fewer than ten state supreme courts produced dissents in 20 percent or more of their cases, and only the high courts in Michigan, New York, and Pennsylvania produced dissents at or above the 40 percent mark.[34]

Not all countries value the concept of dissenting opinions, which some regard as a threat to the concepts of legal clarity and national harmony. In these nations dissents are not published. Italy and Switzerland provide historical examples, although anyone interested in how the Swiss judges voted would be free to attend the conferences and listen to what the judges said and watch how they voted. In Germany and Japan dissenting and concurring opinions by constitutional court judges were at one time strictly forbidden, although by the early 1970s both nations began to adopt the American practice of publishing such opinions.[35]

The Threat to "Go Public." On rare occasions an appellate judge may use the ultimate weapon against colleagues—public exposure. Such strong medicine is usually administered only when a jurist believes a colleague (or a group of judges) has violated the basic rules of the game. The judge then threatens to hang out the dirty linen for all to see. For example, one appeals court judge told how, as a newcomer to the bench, he had threatened public exposure to force a senior colleague to withdraw an opinion filed without obtaining the permission of the new judge to include him in the opinion—a possibility he had been warned of by another judge on the court: "It was my first sitting as a circuit judge," he recalled. "It was not a major case. But there was strong give and take!" [36]

In 1967 Judges John Danaher and Warren E. Burger (soon to be Chief Justice Burger) accused three of their appellate court colleagues of consciously attempting to foist on the Washington, D.C., Circuit a minority position on criminal procedures.[37] Ironically, some four years later it was Burger who was threatened with public exposure by a Supreme Court colleague who felt that Burger was trying to turn his minority status on a case into a majority position.

When the vote was taken at conference on the abortion cases (*Roe v. Wade*, considered jointly with *Doe v. Bolton*), Chief Justice Burger was in the minority. According to Supreme Court practice, this meant that the senior member of the majority—in this case William O. Douglas—would have been assigned to speak for the Court. Ignoring Court protocol, Burger assigned the official opinion writing to his alter ego, Harry Blackmun. This enraged Douglas. But the pot did not boil over until several months later, when Burger lobbied from his minority status to have the case postponed until the next term. (Douglas wanted the decision to be handed down immediately.) These extracts from *The Brethren* capture something of the drama of the confrontation:

This time Douglas threatened to play his ace. If the conference insisted on putting the cases over for reargument, he would dissent from such an order, and he would publish the full text of his dissent. Douglas reiterated the protest he had made in December about the Chief's assigning the case to Blackmun, Burger's response and his subsequent intransigence.... Douglas ... continued: "When, however, the minority seeks to control the assignment, there is a destructive force at work in the Court. When a Chief Justice tries to bend the Court to his will by manipulating assignments, the integrity of the institution is imperiled."

Douglas's pen then became more acid:

Borrowing a line from a speech he had given in September in Portland, Douglas then made it clear that, despite what he had said earlier, he did in fact view the Chief and Blackmun as Nixon's Minnesota Twins. "Russia once gave its Chief Justice two votes; but that was too strong even for the Russians." [38]

Douglas was ultimately prevailed upon to refrain from publishing this petulant opinion.

The threat to go public is probably a less potent weapon at the state level than it is for federal judges—particularly Supreme Court justices—because state appellate courts are generally much less visible to the general public except in the most unusual and controversial cases. If a judge on a typical state appellate court were to threaten to go public and reveal some irregularity to which he or she had been subjected, the jurist might be told, "So who cares?"

Despite the availability of several sanctions, they are usually invoked with varying degrees of hesitation, lest a judge or justice acquire a reputation for intransigence. For example, with regard to a justice's willingness to write a dissenting opinion, one perceptive scholar has noted:

Although dissent is a cherished part of the common law tradition, a Justice who persistently refuses to accommodate his views to those of his colleagues may come to be regarded as an obstructionist. A Justice whose dissents become levers for legislative or administrative action reversing judicial policies may come to be regarded as disloyal to the bench.[39]

Putting it in more human terms, one appeals court judge observed that "you have to keep on living with each other. In the next case the situations may be reversed."[40]

The Special Role of the U.S. Chief Justice, the U.S. Chief Judges, and State Supreme Court Chief Justices

The heads of the multijudge federal and state appellate tribunals have a number of special duties and responsibilities. Their respective roles constitute one more ingredient in the recipe for small-group interaction.

The Chief Justice of the United States. The Constitution makes only passing reference to this official, whose stature has come to loom so large in the eyes of the American people. Despite the constitutional slight, the chief justice can have considerable impact on the decision-making process. The key seems to be whether the chief justice possesses the capacity and the will to use the formal and informal powers that have accrued to the office during the past two centuries.

The chief justice's greatest potential for leadership is at the conference, where the cases are discussed and the justices' initial votes are taken. Because the chief has the primary responsibility for setting the agenda of the conference and traditionally is the first to offer an opinion about each case, the potential for influencing both the format and the tone of the deliberation is significant. David J. Danelski has identified two roles for justices at conference: **social leader** and **task leader.** The social leader "attends to the emotional needs of his associates by affirming their values as individuals and as Court members, especially when their views are rejected by the majority. Ordinarily he is the best liked member of the Court. . . . In terms of personality, he is apt to be warm, receptive and responsive." The task leader, however, is the intellectual force behind the conference deliberations, focusing on the final decision and trying to keep the Court consistent with itself. Danelski describes how the two roles complement each other:

As presiding officer of the conference, the Chief Justice is in a favorable position to assert task and social leadership. His presentation of cases is an important task function. His control of the conference's process makes it easy for him to invite suggestions and opinions, seek compromises, and cut off debate that appears to be getting out of hand, all important social functions.[41]

One observer, commenting on the transition from the Burger to the Rehnquist Court, has noted these differences in leadership style:

Differences are already apparent during oral arguments. Rehnquist is sharper, more thoughtful, more commanding and wittier than his predecessor in the center chair. And from the far right of the bench, Scalia almost bubbles over with energy and questions for counsel. No less revealing is that in the week before the start of the 1986–87 term on the first Monday in October, Rehnquist managed to get the justices to dispose of over 1,000 cases (granting 22 and denying or otherwise disposing of the rest). He did so in only two days, whereas it usually took Burger more than twice as long to get through about the same number.[42]

Not only does Rehnquist seem to possess the task leadership skills that provide the intellectual stimulus of his chief justiceship, but evidence shows his social leadership skills as well. One study noted that

Mr. Rehnquist's consensus-building is aided by the more friendly and informal style he has imposed at the court, which is for many a stark and pleasing contrast with the stiff and formal manner of former Chief Justice Warren Burger. Observers say this comfortable style, along with a powerful intellect, has made Mr. Rehnquist far more influential at the high court than Mr. Burger ever was. "The fact that he is agreeable, affable, well-liked, low-keyed, has made him a more effective leader as the court begins to emerge with what looks to be a conservative working majority," says A. E. Dick Howard, a University of Virginia Law School professor.[43]

In the past the chief justice also had a key role in setting up what is called the *discuss list*—special petitions selected out of the many to which the Court will give full consideration. The chief's law clerks helped with this task, but the chief guided their judgment. In the Burger and Rehnquist Courts the chief justice has played a much smaller role in establishing the discuss list. At the present time a majority of the justices pool their law clerks and give a single clerk the authority to summarize a particular petition for all the justices participating in the pool. However, not all members of the Court participate in this practice—for example, the moderately liberal Justice Stevens has his clerks screen all petitions and write memos only on those they deem important enough for him to consider. Whether the chief justice chooses to play a major or minor role in this process, the activity is important because it determines which cases the Court will consider as a group and which are to be summarily dismissed.[44]

The final power of the chief justice is the assignment of opinions, that is, designation of who will write the official decision of the Court.[45] This task falls to the chief justice only if he is in the majority when the vote on a case is taken at conference; otherwise, the most senior justice in the majority selects the opinion writer. The chief justice has the greatest control over an opinion when he assigns it to himself, and traditionally he has retained many important cases for that reason.[46] In such cases as *Marbury v. Madison, Brown v. Board of Education,* and *United States v. Nixon,* the chief justice used his option to speak as the official voice of the Court.

The chief justice who chooses not to write the opinion may assign it to that member of the majority whose views are closest to the dissenters', with the hope that some of the minority may subsequently switch their votes to the majority view.[47] Or, as has most often been the case in recent decades, the chief justice will assign the opinion to an ideological alter ego so that the grounds for the decision will be favorable to his own. A 1996 study of opinion assignments made by Chief Justice Rehnquist indicated that he has utilized this power for institutional rather than policy reasons. For example, he has had an eye for evenly distributing the workload and assigning opinions to justices who have expertise in the subject matter of the case. He has not been as keenly motivated as other chief justices to assign opinions to those whose ideologies are closest to his own. The authors of this study concluded: "Our model suggests that each justice's efficiency, expertise, and the number of majority opinion assignments by other justices—and not ideological compatibility—are the factors that shape Rehnquist's decisions. The only instance where Rehnquist demonstrates a bias related to ideology is when the initial majority coalition cannot afford to lose a single vote."[48]

Determining who will speak for the court has policymaking implications in other countries as well. For example, in a comprehensive study of the Supreme Court in India, one author noted that the person chosen to write the Court's opinion has an inordinate capacity to influence public policy. He then adds: "This is especially true if the chief justice subscribes to that particular philosophy, and continues to appoint the same justice(s) to hear a certain type of case."[49]

Despite the considerable influence a chief justice may have on the Court's small group, the crucial factor seems to be whether the chief has both the capacity and the desire to exert such potential authority. For example, the great first chief justice, John Marshall, possessed both these traits, which helped fill the intellectual vacuum on the Court during the early 1800s:

Marshall, like the majority of justices in the court's history, was an experienced politician. . . . He guided the Court in a series of sweeping decisions . . . through force of personality and a talent for negotiation. Justice William Johnson, a Jefferson appointee, grumbled to his patron about Marshall's dominance. Wondering why Marshall invariably wrote the Court's opinions, Johnson reported to Jefferson that he had "found out the real cause. [William] Cushing was incompetent. [Samuel] Chase could not be got to think or write. [William] Paterson was a slow man and willingly declined trouble, and the other two judges [Marshall and Bushrod Washington] you know are commonly estimated as one judge." [50]

Although John Marshall had the skill and the desire to influence the Court, not all of his successors possessed these traits. For example, the nation's chief justice between 1941 and 1946, Harlan Fiske Stone, had neither the talent nor the will for either task leadership or social leadership. As his biographer sadly wrote of him, "He was totally unprepared to cope with the petty bickering and personal conflict in which his court became engulfed." [51]

The Chief Judges of the U.S. Appeals Courts. As with the chief justice, the leadership potential of the administrative circuit heads is determined, in part, by their intellectual and negotiating skills and their desire to put them to use. [52] In reality, however, their potential effect on their respective circuits is probably smaller than is the potential impact of the chief justice of the Supreme Court. First, because most appellate court decisions are made by three-judge panels on a rotating basis, the chief judge is not likely to be part of most circuit decision making. Second, the circuits are more decentralized than the Supreme Court. Finally, the chief judge is not nearly so prominent a figure in the eyes of the public or of other government decision makers. As one former chief judge said about the job: "The only advantage is that the title sounds more imposing if you are speaking in public or writing an article. Otherwise it's a pain in the ass." [53]

Much of a chief judge's work is administrative (such as docketing cases, keeping financial records, adjusting caseloads), but administration and policymaking are not mutually exclusive endeavors. The chief judge of the former U.S. Fifth Circuit once acknowledged: "So many times judicial problems slop over into administrative problems and vice versa" that the real questions are when and where this effect occurs. Commenting on the influence of the chief judges, one observer has said:

As with strong presidents [or strong chief justices, he might have added] . . . the spillover depends on the personality of the chief and the countervailing force of experienced colleagues. The impact of chief judges was most noticeable on freshmen and the composition of three-judge district courts. ("If all the judges are new, he'll pack a wallop out of proportion to one vote.") Southern judges made no bones about packing three-judge district courts in race relations cases. ([The liberal] "[Elbert P.] Tuttle was not about to set up a three-judge court with [segregationists such as Benjamin F.] Cameron and [William H.] Cox on it; this occurs no more.") Of all administrative powers, plainly the most potent instruments of policy leadership involve the assignment of work.[54]

The State Supreme Court Chief Justices. To some extent, the powers and leadership potential of state chief justices mirror those of the U.S. chief justice, but significant differences exist, not only between the federal and state levels but also from one state to another. At the national level, the chief justice is appointed by the president with the advice and consent of the Senate. In some states—Michigan, for example—the chief justice is chosen by fellow associate justices; in Texas and Ohio the chief justices are elected directly by the people.[55]

The states also differ in regard to whether the chief justice has the most power in the assignment of opinions. Only four states, including Hawaii, follow closely the practice of the U.S. Supreme Court in assigning opinions. In more than a quarter of the states the chief justice assigns opinions in all cases, whether or not he or she is in the majority.[56] Well over half of the states use an automatic method of opinion assignment, whereby a justice either draws cases by lot or, more often, receives them by rotation. In less than half of the twenty states that use the rotation system, the assignments hold only if the justice to whom the case is assigned is in the majority.

On the effectiveness of the chief justice under the different methods of opinion assignment, one scholar has concluded:

A chief justice who is an extraordinary leader can make the court perform more effectively and efficiently by using selective opinion assignment. A court without an extraordinary leader may be better served by a rotational method of assignment. . . . Nondiscretionary methods best maintain social cohesion, but the chief justice's discretion in assigning opinions can best accomplish the efficient disposition of the workload.[57]

As with the U.S. chief justice, however, nothing inherent in the office guarantees that a state supreme court chief justice will be an active and effective leader. Intellect, personality, political skills, and a fair degree of happenstance still interact and blend in mysterious ways to create chief justices whom court watchers term either "great" or "ineffectual." On the positive side, there have been people such as Arthur Vanderbilt, who became chief justice of the New Jersey Supreme Court in 1948. As one scholar observed of him:

Once installed as chief justice . . . he had to contend with a set of judges who had served under the old constitution and did not fully share either his vision or his aims. Nevertheless, Vanderbilt provided impetus and direction to the movement for judicial reform in the state, and, as chief justice, he secured the gains of the reform movement, gave the court stature, and ensured it the independence it needed to play a major role in the governance of the state. Despite the obvious differences, the comparison that springs to mind is with John Marshall, who—like Vanderbilt—assumed the leadership of a relatively moribund court and transformed it.[58]

One can also point to Howell Heflin, chief justice of the Alabama Supreme Court, whose dynamic leadership and political skills during the 1970s brought about much-needed judicial reforms in the state and effective leadership on the court.[59]

On the negative side, many examples can be cited of persons who came to the state high court bench with great potential but lacked the ability or the political savvy (and perhaps the luck) to provide leadership when confronted with opposition or political lethargy. For instance, when Frank D. Celebrezze headed the Ohio Supreme Court during the early 1980s, he blatantly politicized the court until he was driven from office by the voters in the 1986 election. One observer summarized the unhappy period of his chief justiceship:

Squabbles on the Celebrezze court were important because, owing to the Celebrezze agenda, the court was important. The irony of Celebrezze's stewardship is that as his court attained prominence, his actions, so visible on so many fronts, brought the court as an institution into disrepute. During [Celebrezze's term as chief justice] Ohioans perceived their court as a "circus." [60]

Evidence of Small-Group Interaction

We have argued that small-group dynamics include persuasion on the merits between individual judges, bargaining among the appellate jurists, and the threat of sanctions—a judge changing his or her vote, a willingness to write a strong dissent, and (at least for federal judges) the threat to go public. We have also contended that supreme court chief justices and chief judges of the appeals courts can potentially affect the decision making of their respective small judicial groups. The evidence for this cited thus far has largely been anecdotal or subjective, but more rigorous empirical data are available to back up our arguments.

One study compared U.S. Supreme Court justices' initial votes at conference with the final votes as they appeared in the published reports for the years 1946 to 1956.[61] Any change in the two sets of votes was attributed to small-group interaction. The findings reveal several things. First, there were vote changes in about 60 percent of all cases. Most of these changes occurred when a justice who had not participated in the first vote or who had been a dissenter opted to join the majority position.

But when one considers all votes for all cases, the justices changed positions only 9 percent of the time. In such instances of vote change, the initial majority position lost out in only 14 percent of the cases. A study of conference and final votes underestimates the extent of small-group interaction, because plenty of such interaction takes place prior to the initial conference vote.[62] The most recent study of fluidity on the Supreme Court not only confirms that it is an ongoing phenomenon but also reveals that most of the vote changes stem from justices who move from the minority to the majority positions rather than vice versa. The authors of the study suggested that "the majority opinion author has little incentive to be responsive to the suggestions of a dissenter. Since the majority opinion becomes the law of the land, justices who wish to shape the law have an incentive to be part of the majority. Consistent with this theory is the fact that justices who initially voted with the majority switched only 4.6% of the time, and justices who initially dissented switched 18.1% of the time."[63]

Many other empirical studies dealing with the federal appeals courts and state supreme courts likewise suggest the importance of small-group dynamics as a factor in judicial decision making.[64]

Although it is unclear how many final outcomes are determined by small-group dynamics, it is a major factor in the drawing up of the majority opinion and in setting forth its perimeters and corollaries. Scholars still lack a precise measure of the impact of small-group interaction, but it seems fair to say that it is considerable. Attempts to be more precise—both theoretically and empirically—about the output of appellate court decision making have resulted in the development of several analytic approaches that seek to explain and analyze this phenomenon with greater and more quantifiable precision. The first and primary of these approaches is **attitude theory**; the others are variations of what is called the rational choice model.

Attitude Theory

Many judicial scholars have been dissatisfied with small-group analysis, arguing that the fruits of such exploration are barely worth their efforts. Although not denying that personal interactions make a difference in some cases and perhaps play a key role in a handful of decisions, they contend that the richest ore for explaining judicial behavior can be found in other mines. A decision-making model that claims greater explanatory power deals with discovery of the justices' basic, judicially relevant attitudes and with the coalitions, or blocs, formed by jurists who share similar attitudes.[65] This approach rests on the assumption that judges—particularly appellate jurists—view cases primarily in terms of the broad political and socioeconomic issues they raise and that they generally respond to these issues in accordance with their personal values and attitudes. The justices' official reasons for their decisions (found in their published opinions) are regarded as mere rationalizations. For example, suppose that Judge X strongly believes that the government should never tamper with freedom of the press. If a case comes before the court in which censorship is the central issue, Judge X will follow his convictions and vote on the side of the news media. His written opinion may be full of impressive legal citations, quotations from eminent law reviews, or lofty discussions of the importance of maximum freedom of expression in a democracy. But all of this, the scholars of attitude theory contend, is only a rationalization after the fact. The real reason for Judge X's vote was his strong dislike for the concept of government censorship.

The attitude theorists do not claim that their decision-making models explain everything, and they do not deny that judges must often decide cases against the grain of their personal values. For instance, a justice may be a strong environmentalist, but if a pro-environment petitioner has absolutely no standing to sue, the justice is unlikely to yield to the tug of the heart. Nevertheless, supporters of the judicial attitude approach contend that it can explain a significant portion of judicial behavior and is well worth the research time and effort that such studies require.

Specific questions about this approach arise: Where do judicial attitudes originate? How does one learn about a judge's attitudes? What are some of the limitations of the attitudinal model?

First, appellate jurists acquire their relevant attitudes from the same sources that people in general do—from parents and friends, educational institutions, the media, political activities, and so on. Thus attitude theorists and those who study judicial background characteristics clearly have overlapping interests. The difference is that the latter want to know from what sources the justices acquire their values, whereas the former concentrate on measuring the effects of judges' values—regardless of their origin—on collegial decision making. The attitude scholars acknowledge that some beliefs change during a jurist's tenure on the bench, but they postulate "that attitudes are 'relatively enduring.'"[66]

Second, judges unfortunately have shown no willingness to answer the sort of in-depth questionnaires that might reveal judicially significant attitudes—particularly on matters that relate to issues that may come before them in court. Likewise, judges are reluctant to give speeches, grant interviews, or write articles that bare their judicial souls. They consider such behavior inappropriate, and many resist making it easy for reporters and social scientists to suggest a link between their personal values and the way they decide cases.

Third, one criticism of this approach has focused on the source of the attitude theorists' data: the contents of the written opinions that are used to categorize judges' primary values. A justice who writes a strong opinion attacking government interference with the free operation of the marketplace is said to have a conservative economic attitude. This sort of approach has opened researchers to the charge that they have created a tautology: A justice writes several conservative economic opinions, is classified as an economic conservative, and, lo and behold, aggregate analysis of his or her voting patterns concludes that the judge is a conservative on economic issues. Such theorists respond that this criticism is unfair because the patterns they have uncovered have proved to be consistent over time and susceptible to duplication by other researchers using similar methodologies. Furthermore, the best and most recent study based on attitude theory successfully formulated and applied three separate and independent ways to eliminate the circular reasoning problem: using facts derived from lower-court records of cases decided by the U.S. Supreme Court, conducting content analysis of editorials appearing in publications prior to a justice's confirmation, and employing the justices' prior voting behavior as a predictor of votes in subsequent cases.[67]

Another shortcoming is that the attitudinal model has not been used successfully to explain and predict lower-court behavior, and some scholars have even argued that the model is inherently not applicable to trial judge decision making.[68] As the dean of the attitudinal model, Professor Harold Spaeth, acknowledges,

Lower courts do operate in an environment distinctly different from that of the Supreme Court. These differences may cause lower-court judges to decide on bases other than their personal policy preferences. They may be electorally accountable and as a result render decisions that enhance their reelection. Others may seek higher positions—either inside or outside the judiciary—and color their decisions accordingly. Most courts are subject to appellate review. Judges thereon may decide according to their superiors' dictates rather than their own preferences. And with the exception of some state supreme courts, judges do not have control of their dockets as the justices do. Hence, their decision making may involve run-of-the-mill litigation in which policy matters are either absent or not amenable to discretion because a jury decides or because matters are open and shut.[69]

The fact that attitude theory may be time-bound is another criticism that its supporters concede. Virtually all research has focused on recent decades instead of the past, and during many periods in the Supreme Court's history the vast majority of decisions were unanimous, and thus there would be no variance to measure or explain. Finally, critics of attitude theory note that it has been applied only to the justice's final vote—the one specified in the reports of the Court's decisions. Its thrust thus misses the important matters of coalition formation and opinion writing.

Despite these limitations, attitude theory is still regarded by most judicial behavioralists as the most elegant and persuasive model for predicting appellate judge behavior. Students of foreign collegial court systems have used it effectively to explain decision making on these tribunals. For example, a recent study of voting on search and seizure cases by justices on the Canadian Supreme Court found that the attitudinal model "correctly predicts 77 percent of the judicial decisions, providing a 25 percent improvement . . . over the null model. More important, many of the same factual variables that prove significant in the U.S. cases are significant in Canada as well." The researchers further concluded that Canadian "justices [like their American counterparts] rely on the predisposed attitudes they have toward particular factual circumstances to guide their decisions." [70] Earlier studies using the attitudinal model found it highly instructive in explaining the voting patterns of justices in countries as diverse as Australia, Canada, India, Japan, and the Philippines.[71]

Rational Choice Theory

The **rational choice theory** by no means rejects the basic assumptions of attitude theory. Rational choice theorists generally agree that appellate court jurists are primarily motivated by their personal, deeply felt attitudes about public policy and vote accordingly in their judicial decisions. But the rational choice school contends that there is more to it than that, and that the attitudinal position is somewhat simplistic and shortsighted. They contend that goal-directed justices operate in what they term "strategic" or "inter-dependent decision-making contexts." The justices realize that the fate of their policy goals often depends on the values of other decision makers, such as their colleagues on the bench, the president, and members of Congress. The justices must often include in their calculus not only what they personally want as a case outcome but also how such an outcome might be affected by the decisions of these other actors. As two key scholars associated with the rational choice approach put it:

If justices are "single-minded seekers of legal policy" [as the attitude theorists contend], would those justices not care about the ultimate state of that policy? To rephrase the question, why would justices who are policy maximizers take a position they know Congress would overturn? To argue that justices would do this—merely vote their attitudes—is to argue that the Court is full of myopic thinkers, who consider only the shape of policy in the short term. It is also to argue that justices do not consider the preferences of other political actors and the actions they expect others to take when they make their decisions and simply respond to stimuli before them. Such a picture does not square with much important writing about the Court . . . or with the way many social scientists now believe that political actors make decisions.[72]

These and other scholars have found empirical evidence to support the basic tenets of the rational choice approach.[73] Indeed, studies of supreme courts outside the United States suggest that this approach may provide a good model for understanding the court's behavior. For example, in a recent study of the Indian Supreme Court during the 1990s, the author concluded, "By directly confronting issues pertaining to the independence and well being of the judicial branch, the Indian Supreme Court attempted to gain greater control over the administration of the judiciary and restructure its relations with other political actors."[74]

As with all explanatory models, there are variations on a theme, and rational choice is no exception. Some exponents of this model argue, for example, that when it comes to congressional responses to Supreme Court decisions, the justices do more than merely act to minimize the possibility of a conflict with Congress (which might result in a congressional override of the Court's decision). These theorists note that the Court often calls for and invites congressional action to help secure the policy goals that the justices desire. One study found clear evidence of this phenomenon and concluded:

Our most striking finding concerned the ideological position of the justices who joined in the Court's majority opinion. The strong statistical impact of this variable suggests that one motivation for invitations to override is a concern with achieving both good law and good policy. More specifically, one response to a perceived conflict between the two is for justices to follow the law as they see it while asking Congress to supplant their choice with good policy as they see it.[75]

Rational choice theory, then, is not a rejection of the attitudinal model but argues that attitude theorists are too narrow in their approach. The rational choice school suggests that justices often consider in their decision making the possible responses of other political actors—sometimes even going so far as to invite some of these other actors to modify or supplement the high court's decisions.

Practical Applications of These Four Approaches

Sometimes these theoretical approaches are a bit difficult to appreciate in the abstract. This can be remedied by providing an example that explores how theorists in each of these four categories might examine and evaluate particular judicial phenomena. In the following section we look at the 2003 Supreme Court decisions on affirmative action (*Grutter v. Bollinger*[76] and *Gratz v. Bollinger*[77]) as vehicles to demonstrate the approaches of theorists in all four categories.

The *Grutter* and *Gratz* cases were a direct challenge to affirmative action in the United States and arose from class action suits filed in 1997 that questioned the constitutionality of affirmative action programs used in the admissions process at the University of Michigan. *Gratz* challenged the validity of a scoring system used in undergraduate admissions at the university. The program assigned points to applicants for a variety of factors, including, among others, student grades, test scores, geographic origin, and race. Under the University's point system, only those students who reached a certain number of points were eligible for admission to the university. In the *Grutter* case, Michigan's law school admission process was questioned. This was a highly individualized process and did not utilize a quantitative methodology in deciding which students to admit. However, race was one factor in the admissions process in an effort to achieve a diverse student body. Affirmative action foes were backed by the George W. Bush administration, which filed briefs with the Court urging the justices to overturn the Michigan programs. They argued that both Michigan programs involved racial quotas, which the Court had previously rejected as violating the Fourteenth Amendment's equal protection guarantee.[78] Ultimately, these cases offer insight on how scholars might utilize a variety of models to develop a better understanding of decision making in multimember courts.

Cue Theory

A number of factors suggest that cue theory may have provided some predictive ability in the 2003 Michigan affirmative action cases. Unquestionably, affirmative action has been one of the most salient issues that federal courts have addressed over the past thirty years. This fact alone might have given the justices reason to pay especially close attention to the *Grutter* and *Gratz* appeals. Yet a review of the amicus curiae briefs filed at the appellate level may also have indicated to the justices the importance of the Michigan cases. An unusually large number of amicus briefs were filed in the Michigan cases, and those who filed briefs were notable for their prominence, including U.S. Solicitor General Theodore Olson, the American Bar Association, a group of over thirty Fortune 500 corporations, and the deans of the nation's top law schools. Also distinguishing the Michigan affirmative action cases was the fact that the Sixth Circuit had granted rare en banc reviews of the two cases prior to their appeal to the Supreme Court. In sum, the legal history of these cases leading up to the high court provided ample cues to the justices that the cases were exceptional, and hence worthy of particular attention.

Small-Group Analysis

Judges who work together in small groups typically cultivate a sense of professional collegiality as a means of maintaining an effective working environment. Supreme Court Justice Sandra Day O'Connor recently noted, "When you work in a small group of that size, you have to get along, and so you're not going to let some harsh language, some dissenting opinion, affect a personal relationship. You can't do that." Her colleague Justice Stephen Breyer concurred: "I have never heard one member of the court say something insulting about another, even as a kind of joke. It's professional. We conduct our discussions in what I would call a very civilized way." [79]

However, while jurists who work in small groups often maintain a certain level of civility in their interactions, this does not mean that sharp differences do not emerge or that justices do not find themselves bridging differences within a small cohort. Perhaps no current jurist better exemplifies the importance of such small-group interaction than O'Connor. The Reagan appointee has been widely viewed as a critical swing vote on the Court. Analysis of the voting patterns of the current Court reveals a rather consistent trend. On the right, Justices Antonin Scalia, Clarence Thomas, William Rehnquist, and, to a slightly lesser extent, Anthony Kennedy, are generally considered reliable conservatives. Justices John Paul Stevens, Ruth Bader Ginsburg, David Souter, and Stephen Breyer frequently cast liberal votes. This has often left Justice O'Connor as the deciding vote in a number of key cases. Indeed, legal experts widely predicted that the Michigan cases would be decided in a 5–4 vote, and eyes were focused upon O'Connor as the deciding vote. "It is very likely that it will be 5–4," predicted one law professor. "The question is, 5–4 which way?" [80] The experts' 5–4 forecast was correct; O'Connor ultimately voted in *Grutter* to hand a key victory to affirmative action supporters. But her position in the majority in this case was hardly unusual; in fact, O'Connor was in the majority in all thirteen of the 5–4 decisions handed down by the Court in the 2002–2003 term, not once issuing a dissenting opinion when the Court was so closely divided. It is clear that the Court splits in predictable coalitions, with O'Connor often being the key swing vote.

Attitudinal Model

One can readily hypothesize that the attitudinal model may have been applicable in the 2003 affirmative action cases. As previously mentioned, the ideological preferences of the justices on both the left and the right were very powerful in predicting the jurists' votes in the *Grutter* and *Gratz* decisions, and most legal observers accurately predicted how most of the justices would vote in these cases. Yet the cases also provided at least two instances in which the justices may have drawn upon their own personal experiences in guiding their decisions.

Justice Clarence Thomas, the court's only African American, issued a sharp and impassioned dissent in *Grutter*. He began his opinion with a quote from the noted African American abolitionist Frederick Douglass, who, in response to questions about how America should treat blacks, urged, "Do nothing with us! Your doing with us has already played mischief with us." Thomas continued:

Like Douglass, I believe blacks can achieve in every avenue of American life without the meddling of university administrators. Because I wish to see all students succeed whatever their color, I share, in some respect, the sympathies of those who sponsor the type of discrimination advanced by the University of Michigan Law School. The Constitution does not, however, tolerate institutional devotion to the status quo in admissions policies when such devotion ripens into racial discrimination.[81]

Thomas bitterly accused "cognoscenti" of seeking "racial aesthetics," intoning that "the [Michigan] Law School wants to have a certain appearance, from the shape of the desks and tables in its classrooms to the color of the students sitting at them." [82] One observer expressed a widely held view that Thomas reached his conclusions "by drawing on the benefit of his life experience with racism and discrimination. . . . [Thomas] drew most of his ammunition from his life experience. Instead of dwelling on legal briefs and case law, as did many of his colleagues, Thomas wrote from the heart about the stigma imposed on beneficiaries of affirmative action, those who he called 'test subjects' who were 'tarred as undeserving.'" [83] This issue may have been especially salient for Thomas, as it has been noted that he is sensitive to the perception that it was his race— rather than his ability or credentials— that opened professional doors for him. Thomas once stated that as a black student at Yale Law School, he felt that a "monkey was on my back" because he perceived that classmates believed he was granted admission to the prestigious Ivy League school primarily because of his race.[84] Similarly, some have suggested that it was Thomas's skin color that landed him a seat on the nation's highest court.[85] It is not difficult, therefore, to read Thomas's opinion in *Grutter* as, according to one observer, "the angry exclamation of a black man who feels personally patronized and demeaned by what he sees as racial gerrymandering." [86]

Justice O'Connor's vote in *Grutter* also may have been influenced by personal attitudes. One former Supreme Court law clerk suggested that the reason for O'Connor's decision in the case "may be traceable to her own experiences with gender discrimination and the difficulties of juggling a career and family. O'Connor was famously near the top of her Stanford Law School class, yet received no offers to work as a lawyer. The mother of three sons, she worked part-time early in her career, as many women do. On the Court, she is famous for her special concern for the welfare of women and children." [87] Indeed, it has been noted that "three of the justices—Ruth Bader Ginsburg, Sandra Day O'Connor, and Clarence Thomas—have personally experienced the barriers of discrimination and racism that affirmative action is intended to help break down." [88] Though these jurists may have drawn sharply different conclusions from their experiences, it is nonetheless noteworthy that personal attitudes may have framed the opinions they handed down in the Michigan affirmative action cases.

Rational Choice

One may also identify shades of strategic decision making in the Michigan cases. Indeed, it may be argued that the Court struck the optimal strategic position in its decisions in both cases.

Like so many other profound debates in American political life, the affirmative action debate has given rise to two opposing ideological positions, with a large swath of opinion falling somewhere in the middle. On the left, the most energetic supporters of affirmative action have generally advocated the use of quantifiable targets as a means of aggressively achieving racial diversity and remedying the effects of past and ongoing discrimination. However, programs that call for rigid quotas have been struck down by the courts. Though unpopular among many liberal civil rights activists, such rulings have enjoyed wide public support.[89] On the conservative side, conversely, there has been long-standing opposition to all forms of affirmative action and any attempt to consider race in employment and educational matters. Yet public opinion surveys have shown that although Americans may oppose such things as race-based university admissions, they recognize the value of racial and ethnic diversity and the need to expand opportunity in the United States. These mixed public views have led one scholar to note that "the American public is somewhat conflicted on this issue." [90]

It was against this political backdrop that the Michigan cases were debated. Liberals hoped that the Court would uphold the undergraduate and law school affirmation action programs, while conservatives sought just the opposite— the elimination of *any* consideration of race in university admissions. Ultimately, the Court's decisions in *Gratz v. Bollinger* and *Grutter v. Bollinger* constituted an approach that left neither side entirely satisfied, yet it is arguably optimal for the Court from a strategic perspective.

In striking down the undergraduate admissions program in *Gratz*, the Court handed a clear victory to affirmative action foes who argued that Michigan's point system was a de facto quota. However, the Court gave a key victory to liberal supporters of affirmative action in *Grutter* by upholding the narrow use of race as one of a number of factors to be considered in the admissions process and recognizing a compelling state interest in ensuring racial diversity in the educational process.[91] Although the Michigan decisions were a measured victory for backers of affirmative action, the Court also left the door open to future legal challenges from opponents when the majority wrote that "we expect that 25 years from now the use of racial preferences will no longer be necessary." [92] It was, in sum, a decision in which the Court brought some resolution to a contentious issue while cautiously avoiding the adoption of a position that might damage its popularity— hence, its legitimacy— among large segments of the population. Furthermore, it was a ruling that corresponded closely to the views held by significant numbers of political and economic elites in America.[93] Rational choice scholars examining the *Gratz* and *Grutter* rulings could easily conclude that the Court engaged in strategic behavior and, given the political circumstances, handed down the optimal decision.

Summary

We began this chapter with the observation that decision making by judges on collegial appellate courts is in some key ways different from decision making by judges acting alone on trial benches. Because of these differences, scholars have devised theories and research techniques to capture the special reality of decision making by jurists on federal and state multijudge appellate courts. We took a close look at the discretionary review process of the Supreme Court and noted that the issues it decides not to rule on are often as substantively important as those cases it selects for full review. In this context we discussed the importance of cue theory—the attempt by scholars to learn the characteristics of those few cases chosen from the many for Supreme Court consideration.

We then focused on several separate theoretical approaches to explain the decision making of multijudge courts: small-group analysis, attitude theory, and the rational choice model. (In our discussion we often noted the similarity of patterns in United States courts and those of other countries and also those instances in which the American experiences seem to be unique.) Each of these theoretical models has its own working assumptions and research techniques that are used to glean the explanatory data. Although it is tempting to speculate on which of these several approaches provides the best insights into appellate court behavior, it is probably fairest to say that the jury of judicial scholars is still out. An increasing belief in recent years is that models representing a combination of these and other approaches provide much greater explanatory power than any of them taken alone.[94] Finally, using the example of the Supreme Court's 2003 affirmative actions decisions, we indicated how theorists in all four categories might select and evaluate relevant data.

Further Thought and Discussion Questions

1. In the past, Congress largely mandated which cases would be heard by the U.S. Supreme Court, but today the high court justices have almost complete control over their own docket. Is it a good idea for the Supreme Court to control its own agenda—without even being required to offer an explanation for refusing to hear almost 99 percent of the cases appealed to it?

2. When appellate court justices get together to discuss a case and decide its outcome, are their deliberations on a high and lofty plane, or are their motivations and actions no different from those of any group of ordinary citizens acting as an organized committee?

3. Using the two University of Michigan affirmative action cases as a point of reference, do you think any of the four theories—cue, small-group analysis, attitude, and rational choice—yield more, or better, insight into collegial courts' decision making? Or is each approach equally helpful in its own way? Might one particular theory be more, or less, relevant to different cases?

4. Are patterns of appellate judge behavior similar throughout the world, or are the decision-making patterns of America's collegial court jurists unique?

NOTES

1. From an interview with an appeals court judge, as quoted in J. Woodford Howard Jr., *Courts of Appeals in the Federal Judicial System* (Princeton, N.J.: Princeton University Press, 1981), 135.

2. However, for a discussion of the causes of dissent in state supreme courts and how such causes may differ from those at the federal level, see Paul Brace and Melinda Gann Hall, "Neo-Institutionalism and Dissent in State Supreme Courts," *Journal of Politics* 52 (1990): 54–70.

3. Alabama, for example, imposes a burdensome original jurisdiction on its supreme court, and Arizona requires its high court to hear appeals in a wide variety of cases. However, Florida has given its supreme court broad discretion in case selection. See G. Alan Tarr and Mary Cornelia Aldis Porter, *State Supreme Courts in State and Nation* (New Haven, Conn.: Yale University Press, 1988), 49.

4. For a good discussion of the working of the European Court of Justice, see Sally J. Kenney, "The European Court of Justice: Integrating Europe through Law," *Judicature* 81 (1998): 250–255. Also, for the first sophisticated multivariate study of agenda setting by the Canadian Supreme Court, see Roy B. Flemming and Glen S. Kurtz, "Selecting Appeals for Judicial Review in Canada: A Replication and Multivariate Test of American Hypotheses," *Journal of Politics* 64 (2002): 232–248.

5. Joseph Tanenhaus, Marvin Schick, Matthew Muraskin, and Daniel Rosen, "The Supreme Court's Certiorari Jurisdiction: Cue Theory," in *Judicial Decision-Making*, ed. Glendon Schubert (New York: Free Press, 1963), 111–132.

6. See, for example, S. Sidney Ulmer, "The Decision to Grant Certiorari as an Indicator to Decision 'On the Merits,' " *Polity* 4 (1972): 429–447. Nevertheless, in a later study Ulmer found that despite the inordinate willingness of the high court to hear cases brought by the U.S. government, such willingness did not translate into subsequent support for the government's position, at least in civil liberties cases. See S. Sidney Ulmer, "Governmental Litigants, Underdogs, and Civil Liberties in the Supreme Court: 1903–1968 Terms," *Journal of Politics* 47 (1985): 899–909.

7. See, for example, Donald R. Songer, "Concern for Policy Outputs as a Cue for Supreme Court Decisions on Certiorari," *Journal of Politics* 41 (1979): 1185–1194; and S. Sidney Ulmer, "Selecting Cases for Supreme Court Review: An Underdog Model," *American Political Science Review* 72 (1978): 902–910.

8. Virginia C. Armstrong and Charles A. Johnson, "Certiorari Decisions by the Warren and Burger Courts: Is Cue Theory Time Bound?" *Polity* 15 (1982): 141–150.

9. Jeffrey A. Segal and Harold J. Spaeth, "Rehnquist Court Disposition of Lower Court Decisions: Affirmation Not Reversal," *Judicature* 74 (1990): 84–88.

10. Henry R. Glick, *Courts, Politics, and Justice*, 3d ed. (New York: McGraw-Hill, 1993), 280.

11. J. Woodford Howard Jr., "On the Fluidity of Judicial Choice," *American Political Science Review* 62 (1968): 43–57.

12. See, for example, Walter F. Murphy, *Elements of Judicial Strategy* (Chicago: University of Chicago Press, 1964); Bob Woodward and Scott Armstrong, *The Brethren: Inside the Supreme Court* (New York: Simon and Schuster, 1979); Howard, *Courts of Appeals in the Federal Judicial System*, and Alpheus T. Mason, *Harlan Fiske Stone: Pillar of the Law* (New York: Viking, 1956).

13. In the parlance of judicial scholars, this is referred to as the social leadership function. See David J. Danelski, "The Influence of the Chief Justice in the Decisional Process," in *Courts, Judges, and Politics*, 3d ed., ed. Walter F. Murphy and C. Herman Pritchett (New York: Random House, 1979), 695–703. For an empirical analysis of the phenomena discussed by Danelski, see Stacia L. Haynie, "Leadership and Consensus on the U.S. Supreme Court," *Journal of Politics* 54 (1992): 1158–1169.

14. Henry Robert Glick, *Supreme Courts in State Politics* (New York: Basic Books, 1971), 59.

15. This is termed the task leadership function. See Danelski, "The Influence of the Chief Justice in the Decisional Process."

16. Howard, *Courts of Appeals in the Federal Judicial System*, 230–231.

17. Murphy, *Elements of Judicial Strategy*, 44.

18. As quoted in ibid.

19. Glick, *Supreme Courts in State Politics*, 89.

20. James F. Spriggs II, Forrest Maltzman, and Paul J. Wahlbeck, "Bargaining on the U.S. Supreme Court: Justices' Responses to Majority Opinion Drafts," *Journal of Politics* 61 (1999): 503.

21. *Roe v. Wade*, 410 U.S. 113 (1973); and *Doe v. Bolton*, 410 U.S. 179 (1973).

22. Woodward and Armstrong, *The Brethren*, chaps. entitled "1971 Term" and "1972 Term."

23. Ibid., 233.

24. Glick, *Supreme Courts in State Politics*, 66.

25. Murphy, *Elements of Judicial Strategy*, 57.

26. Howard, *Courts of Appeals in the Federal Judicial System*, 209.

27. As quoted in Charles Fairman, *Mr. Justice Miller and the Supreme Court, 1862–1890* (Cambridge, Mass.: Harvard University Press, 1939), 320.

28. *Webster v. Reproductive Health Services*, 492 U.S. 490 (1989).

29. David A. Kaplan, "A Legacy of Strife: Marshall's Papers Shed Light on the Court—and the Library of Congress," *Newsweek*, June 7, 1993, 69.

30. Benjamin Weiser and Bob Woodward, "Roe Decision Nearly Overturned 4 Years Ago, Justice's Files Show," *Houston Chronicle*, May 24, 1993, A2.

31. *Clinton v. Jones*, 520 U.S. 681 (1997).

32. Henry Robert Glick and Kenneth N. Vines, *State Court Systems* (Englewood Cliffs, N.J.: Prentice-Hall, 1973), 79.

33. Murphy, *Elements of Judicial Strategy*, 63–64.

34. Henry R. Glick and George W. Pruet Jr., "Dissent in State Supreme Courts: Patterns and Correlates of Conflict," in *Judicial Conflict and Consensus: Behavioral Studies of American Appellate Courts*, ed. Sheldon Goldman and Charles M. Lamb (Lexington: University Press of Kentucky, 1986), 200.

35. Walter F. Murphy and Joseph Tanenhaus, *The Study of Public Law* (New York: Random House, 1972), 152–153.

36. As quoted in Howard, *Courts of Appeals in the Federal Judicial System*, 209.

37. *Ross v. Sirica*, 380 F.2d 557 (D.C. Cir. 1967).

38. Woodward and Armstrong, *The Brethren*, 187, 188.

39. Murphy, *Elements of Judicial Strategy*, 61.

40. As quoted in Howard, *Courts of Appeals in the Federal Judicial System*, 209.

41. Danelski, "The Influence of the Chief Justice in the Decisional Process," 696.

42. David M. O'Brien, "The Supreme Court: From Warren to Burger to Rehnquist," *PS* 20 (1987): 12.

43. Stephen Wermiel, "Consensus Builder: Rehnquist Emerges as a Skillful Leader of the Court's Majority," *Wall Street Journal*, June 29, 1989, A1.

44. For an excellent discussion of research findings about the discuss list and the U.S. Supreme Court, see Gregory A. Caldeira and John R. Wright, "The Discuss List: Agenda Building in the Supreme Court," *Law and Society Review* 24 (1990): 809–836.

45. For an excellent discussion of this subject, see David W. Rohde and Harold J. Spaeth, *Supreme Court Decision Making* (San Francisco: Freeman, 1976), chap. 8.

46. Lee Epstein and Jeffrey A. Segal, "Measuring Issue Salience," *American Journal of Political Science* 44 (2000): 66–83.

47. However, some research has challenged the "conventional wisdom . . . that assignment of the majority opinion to the marginal member of the minimum winning original coalition might ensure its survival." In a study of the Warren Court the researchers found that "although the marginal justice is

substantially advantaged in opinion assignment, coalition maintenance is not thereby enhanced." Saul Brenner and Harold J. Spaeth, "Majority Opinion Assignments and the Maintenance of the Original Coalition on the Warren Court," *American Journal of Political Science* 32 (1988): 72–81. See also Saul Brenner, "Reassigning the Majority Opinion on the United States Supreme Court," *Justice System Journal* 11 (1986): 186–195.

48. Forrest Maltzman and Paul J. Wahlbeck, "May It Please the Chief? Opinion Assignments in the Rehnquist Court," *American Journal of Political Science* 40 (1996): 438.

49. Robert Moog, "Activism on the Indian Supreme Court," *Judicature* 82 (1998): 128.

50. Donald Dale Jackson, *Judges* (New York: Atheneum, 1974), 329.

51. As quoted in Danelski, "The Influence of the Chief Justice in the Decisional Process," 698. For a good discussion of the importance of Harlan F. Stone's leadership style as it affected future chief justiceships, see Thomas G. Walker, Lee Epstein, and William J. Dixon, "On the Mysterious Demise of Consensual Norms in the United States Supreme Court," *Journal of Politics* 50 (1988): 361–389.

52. For two excellent recent studies of the role and work of the chief judge of the U.S. appeals courts, see Stephen L. Wasby, "The Work of a Circuit's Chief Judges," *Justice System Journal* 24 (2003): 63–90; and Virginia A. Hettinger, Stefanie A. Lindquist, and Wendy L. Martinek, "The Role and Impact of Chief Judges on the United States Courts of Appeals," *Justice System Journal* 24 (2003): 91–117.

53. As quoted in Howard, *Courts of Appeals in the Federal Judicial System*, 228.

54. Ibid., 229. In a few instances the chief judges have been accused of stacking the three-judge panels, which are supposed to operate on a more or less random, rotational basis. For example, see *Armstrong v. Bd. of Educ. of Birmingham*, 323 F.2d 333, 352–361 (5th Cir. 1963); 48 F.R.D. 141, 182 (1969). See also Burton M. Atkins and William Zavoina, "Judicial Leadership on the Court of Appeals: A Probability Analysis of Panel Assignment in Race Relations Cases on the Fifth Circuit," *American Journal of Political Science* 18 (1974): 701–711.

55. For an excellent recent study of the recruitment process for state supreme court chief justices, see Laura Langer, Jody McMullen, Nicholas P. Ray, and Daniel D. Stratton, "Recruitment of Chief Justices on State Supreme Courts: A Choice between Institutional and Personal Goals," *Journal of Politics* 65 (2003): 656–675.

56. Victor E. Flango, Craig R. Ducat, and R. Neal McKnight, "Measuring Leadership through Opinion Assignments in Two State Supreme Courts," in *Judicial Conflict and Consensus*, ed. Goldman and Lamb, 217.

57. Ibid., 218–219.

58. Tarr and Porter, *State Supreme Courts in State and Nation*, 186.

59. Ibid., chap. 3.

60. Ibid., 148.

61. Saul Brenner, "Fluidity on the United States Supreme Court: A Reexamination,"*American Journal of Political Science* 24 (1980): 526–535.

62. For a more recent article on this subject, and one that addresses some aspects not included in Brenner's earlier article, see Robert H. Dorff and Saul Brenner, "Conformity Voting on the United States Supreme Court," *Journal of Politics* 54 (1992): 762–775.

63. Forrest Maltzman and Paul J. Wahlbeck, "Strategic Policy Considerations and Voting Fluidity on the Burger Court," *American Political Science Review* 90 (1996): 590–591.

64. For example, see Goldman and Lamb, *Judicial Conflict and Consensus*, pts. 2 and 3; and Glick, *Supreme Courts in State Politics*.

65. For the best statement of attitude theory, along with an excellent summary of the relevant literature, see Jeffrey A. Segal and Harold J. Spaeth, *The Supreme Court and the Attitudinal Model* (New York: Cambridge University Press, 1993). For a sophisticated and up-to-date debate among judicial scholars

about the utility of various forms of attitudinal models, see the first six articles in *American Journal of Political Science* 40 (1996): 971–1083.

66. Rohde and Spaeth, *Supreme Court Decision Making*, 75.

67. Segal and Spaeth, *The Supreme Court and the Attitudinal Model*.

68. C. K. Rowland and Robert A. Carp, *Politics & Judgment in Federal District Courts* (Lawrence: University Press of Kansas, 1996), especially chaps. 6 and 7.

69. Harold J. Spaeth, "The Attitudinal Model," in *Contemplating Courts*, ed. Lee Epstein (Washington, D.C.: CQ Press, 1995), 313.

70. Matthew E. Wetstein and C. L. Ostberg, "Search and Seizure Cases in the Supreme Court of Canada: Extending an American Model of Judicial Decision Making across Countries," *Social Science Quarterly* 80 (1999): 757, 770.

71. Glendon Schubert and David J. Danelski, eds., *Comparative Judicial Behavior: Cross-Cultural Studies of Political Decision-Making in the East and West* (New York: Oxford University Press, 1969).

72. Lee Epstein and Thomas G. Walker, "The Role of the Supreme Court in American Society: Playing the Reconstruction Game," in *Contemplating Courts*, ed. Epstein, 322.

73. For example, see Lee Epstein and Jack Knight, *The Choices Judges Make* (Washington, D.C.: CQ Press, 1998).

74. Robert Moog, "The Indian Supreme Court in the 1990s," *Judicature* 85 (2002): 268–276.

75. Lori Hausegger and Lawrence Baum, "Inviting Congressional Action: A Study of Supreme Court Motivations in Statutory Interpretation," *American Journal of Political Science* 43 (1999): 182.

76. Available online at http://supct.law.cornell.edu/supct/html/02-241.ZS.html.

77. Available online at http://supct.law.cornell.edu/supct/html/02-516.ZS.html.

78. See *University of California Regents v. Bakke*, 438 U.S. 265 (1978).

79. The justices shared these thoughts during an unusual television interview broadcast by ABC News on July 7, 2003. See *Dallas Morning News*, "Two High Court Justices Grant Rare TV Interview," July 7, 2003 (http://www.dallasnews.com/sharedcontent/dallas/politics/national/stories/070703dnnatjustices.53019.html).

80. See Anne Gearan, "Affirmative Action Has Day Before High Court Today," *Fort Worth Star-Telegram*, April 1, 2003 (http://www.dfw.com/mld/dfw/news/nation/5531148.html).

81. Thomas dissent, *Grutter v. Bollinger* (2003).

82. Ibid.

83. Ruben Navarrette, "Thomas' Views Came From the Heart," *Dallas Morning News*, June 28, 2003, A33.

84. Juan Williams, "A Question of Fairness," *Atlantic Monthly*, February, 1987, 73.

85. See Maureen Dowd, "Justice Clarence Thomas Denies His Past," *New York Times*, June 25, 2003, A25.

86. Bill Keller, "Mr. Diversity," *New York Times*, June 28, 2003, A15.

87. Edward Lazarus, "The Ghost of Justice Powell," July 10, 2003: http://writ.newsfindlaw.com/lazarus/20030710.html.

88. James M. O'Neill, "Justices' Pasts Factor Into College Debate," *Philadelphia Inquirer*, June 16, 2003, A1.

89. "Survey: Most Against Race-Based Admissions," June 9, 2003: http://us.cnn.com/2003/EDUCATION/06/09/race.admissions.reut/.

90. Ibid.

91. Charles Lane, "Affirmative Action for Diversity Is Upheld," *Washington Post*, June 24, 2003, A1.

92. *Grutter v. Bollinger* (2003). Available online at http://supct.law.cornell.edu/supct/html/02-241.ZS.html.

93. Lane, "Affirmative Action for Diversity Is Upheld," 2003.

94. For examples of these combined or integrated approaches, see Donald R. Songer and Susan Haire, "Integrating Alternative Approaches to the Study of Judicial Voting: Obscenity Cases in the U.S. Courts of Appeals," *American Journal of Political Science* 36 (1992): 963–982; Paul Brace and Melinda Gann Hall, "Integrated Models of Judicial Dissent," *Journal of Politics* 55 (1993): 914–935; and Carol Ann Traut and Craig F. Emmert, "Expanding the Integrated Model of Judicial Decision Making: The California Justices and Capital Punishment," *Journal of Politics* 60 (1998): 1166–1180.

SUGGESTED READINGS

Cannon, Mark W., and David M. O'Brien, eds. *Views from the Bench: The Judiciary and Constitutional Politics*. Chatham, N.J.: Chatham House, 1985. A collection of essays, mainly by appellate judges, about how such jurists ought to carry out their functions and duties.

Epstein, Lee, and Jack Knight. *The Choices Justices Make*. Washington, D.C.: CQ Press, 1998. This book presents an excellent summary of the several current theoretical approaches to the study of appellate court decision making.

Goldman, Sheldon, and Charles M. Lamb, eds. *Judicial Conflict and Consensus: Behavioral Studies of American Appellate Courts*. Lexington: University Press of Kentucky, 1986. An excellent collection of empirical studies on how appellate courts operate and how they are influenced by both internal and external factors.

Howard, J. Woodford Jr. *Courts of Appeals in the Federal Judicial System*. Princeton, N.J.: Princeton University Press, 1981. A well-written study of decision making at the level of the U.S. appellate courts; contains both quantitative and anecdotal information.

Judicature 83 (2000). The entire issue focuses on "Social Science, the Courts, and the Law." There are, for example, articles on the U.S. Supreme Court Judicial Data Base, use of the U.S. Courts of Appeals Data Base, and a comparison of courts, using data from different American states.

Justice System Journal 22 (2001). The entire issue is devoted to current research on state courts; some of the articles contain useful data that could be used to perform studies of state appellate judge behavior.

Justice System Journal 24 (2003). This issue contains two long articles that provide interesting and up-to-date information about the role of a federal circuit's chief judge: "The Work of a Circuit's Chief Judge," by Stephen L. Wasby, and "The Role and Impact of Chief Judges on the United States Courts of Appeals," by Virginia A. Hettinger, Stefanie A. Lindquist, and Wendy L. Martinek.

Murphy, Walter F. *Elements of Judicial Strategy*. Chicago: University of Chicago Press, 1964. Emphasizes the importance of interpersonal interactions on the outcome of collegial court decision making.

O'Brien, David M. *Storm Center*, 6th ed. New York: Norton, 2003. A historical overview and contemporary discussion of the dynamics of decision making by the U.S. Supreme Court.

Perry, H. W., Jr. *Deciding to Decide: Agenda Setting in the United States Supreme Court*. Cambridge, Mass.: Harvard University Press, 1991. Emphasizes the importance of the Supreme Court's decisions with respect to the types of cases it agrees or declines to hear;

the author argues that these decisions are as important as the ultimate disposition of the cases the Court does consider.

Segal, Jeffrey A., and Harold J. Spaeth. *The Supreme Court and the Attitudinal Model Revisited.* New York: Cambridge University Press: 2002. Two of the best scholars in the field provide an excellent analysis of the predominant model for analyzing the decision making of the Supreme Court.

Tarr, G. Alan, and Mary Cornelia Aldis Porter. *State Supreme Courts in State and Nation.* New Haven, Conn.: Yale University Press, 1988. Analyzes decision making at the state supreme court level, with specific analyses of three selected state courts.

Woodward, Bob, and Scott Armstrong. *The Brethren: Inside the Supreme Court.* New York: Simon and Schuster, 1979. A journalistic account of behind-the-scenes interpersonal interactions on the Burger Court.

CHAPTER 14

Implementation and Impact of Judicial Policies

The lofty pronouncements of the Supreme Court often spring from the circumstances of people far removed from the justice's Washington, D.C., courtroom. For instance, the Tecumseh, Oklahoma, school district required middle and high school students to consent to urine testing for drugs in order to participate in any extracurricular activity. High schooler Lindsay Earls, pictured here at Dartmouth College in November 2001, and others challenged the policy. The Court ruled, however, that the policy was a reasonable means of furthering the interest of preventing and deterring drug use and did not violate the Fourth Amendment.

I N THE PREVIOUS TWO CHAPTERS we focused on decision making by judges. In this chapter we extend the discussion to examine what happens after a decision has been reached. Decisions made by judges are not self-executing, and a wide variety of individuals—other judges, public officials, even private citizens—may be called upon to implement a court's decisions. We will look at the various actors involved in the implementation process, their reactions to judicial policies, and the methods they may use to respond to a court's decision.

Depending upon the nature of the court's decision, the judicial policy may have a narrow or a broad impact. A suit for damages incurred in an automobile accident would directly affect only the persons involved and perhaps their immediate families. But the famous *Gideon v. Wainwright* decision has directly affected millions of people in one way or another.[1] In *Gideon* the Supreme Court held that states must provide an attorney for indigent defendants in felony trials. Scores of people—defendants, judges, lawyers, taxpayers—have felt the effects of that judicial policy. As we discuss the implementation process, we will also look at the impact of judicial policymaking on society.

The Impact of Higher-Court Decisions on Lower Courts

Americans often view the appellate courts, notably the U.S. Supreme Court, as most likely to be involved in policymaking. The trial courts are frequently seen as norm enforcers rather than policymakers. Given this traditional view, the picture that often emerges portrays the Supreme Court as making a decision that is then implemented by a lower court. In short, some envision a judicial bureaucracy with a hierarchy of courts much like superiors and subordinates.[2] More recent studies have cast doubt on the bureaucracy theory, arguing that "most of the work of the lower courts seems less dependent on the Supreme Court than . . . bureaucracy [theory] would indicate."[3] In other words, lower-court judges have a great deal of independence from the appellate courts and may be viewed as "independent actors . . . who will not follow the lead of higher courts unless conditions are favorable for their doing so."[4] For example, not all federal district judges immediately enforced the Supreme Court's public school desegregation decision.[5] Some judges allowed school districts to engage in a variety of tactics ranging from evasion to postponement of the Supreme Court mandate.[6]

Lower-Court Discretion

Why do the lower-court judges have so much discretion when implementing a higher court's policy? In part, the answer may be found in the structure of the U.S. judicial system. The judiciary has always been characterized by independence, decentralization, and individualism. Federal judges are protected by life tenure and traditionally have been able to run their courts as they see fit. Disciplinary measures are not at all common, and federal judges have historically had little fear of impeachment. To retain their positions, the state trial court judges do not have to worry about the appellate courts in their system. They simply have to keep the electorate satisfied. In short, lower-court judges have a good deal of freedom to make their own decisions and respond to upper-court rulings in their own way.

The discretion exercised by a lower-court judge may also be a product of the higher court's decision itself. For example, following the famous school desegregation decision in 1954, the Supreme Court heard further arguments on the best way to implement its new policy. In 1955 it handed down its decision in *Brown v. Board of Education of Topeka II.*[7] In that case the Court was faced with two major questions: (1) How soon are the public schools to start desegregating? (2) How much time should they be given to complete the process? Federal district judges given the task of enforcing the high court's ruling were told that the public schools should make a prompt and reasonable start and then proceed with all deliberate speed to bring about desegregation. What constitutes a prompt and reasonable start? How rapidly must a school district proceed to be moving with all deliberate speed? Because the Supreme Court justices did not provide specific answers to these questions, many lower-court judges were faced with school districts that continued to drag their feet while at the same time claiming they were acting within the high court's guidelines.

A second example concerns the Supreme Court's decision in the 1962 reapportionment case *Baker v. Carr.*[8] The Court held that allegations of malapportioned state legislative districts in Tennessee presented a justiciable, not a political, question—that is, apportionment cases could properly be litigated in the courts. The case was remanded (sent back down) to the federal court for the middle district of Tennessee in Nashville for implementation. Justice William J. Brennan Jr.'s opinion for the Court concluded with the statement, "The cause is remanded for further proceedings consistent with this opinion." No guidelines were provided; the federal district judge was not told how rapidly to proceed or what methods to use. Justice Thomas C. Clark, in a concurring opinion, pointed out that the Court "fails to give the District any guidance whatever."[9]

Therefore, federal district judges implementing either of the policies described above could exercise a high degree of freedom and still legitimately say that they were in compliance with the Supreme Court's mandate. Although not all high court decisions allow such discretion, a good number of them do. Opinions that are ambiguous or poorly written are almost certain to encounter problems during the implementation process.

A court's decision may be unclear for several reasons. Sometimes the issue or subject matter may be so complex that it is difficult to fashion a clear policy. In obscenity cases, for instance, the Supreme Court has had little difficulty in deciding that pornographic material is not entitled to constitutional protection. Defining obscenity has proved to be another matter. Phrases such as "prurient interest," "patently offensive," "contemporary community standards," and "lacks serious literary, artistic, political, or scientific value" have become commonplace in obscenity opinions. These terms leave considerable room for subjective interpretation. It is little wonder that one Supreme Court justice admitted that he could not define obscenity but added that "I know it when I see it." [10]

Policies established by collegial courts are often ambiguous because the majority opinion is written to accommodate several judges. At times such opinions read more like committee reports than forceful, decisive statements. The majority opinion may also be accompanied by several concurring opinions. When this happens, lower-court judges lack a clear-cut precedent to follow. Death penalty cases serve as an example. In 1972 the Supreme Court struck down the death penalty in several states, but for a variety of reasons. Some justices opposed the death penalty per se, on the ground that it constitutes cruel and unusual punishment in violation of the Eighth Amendment to the Constitution. Others voted to strike down the state laws because they were applied in a discriminatory manner. [11] The uncertainty created by the 1972 decision affected not only lower-court judges but also state legislatures. The states passed a rash of widely divergent death penalty statutes and caused a considerable amount of new litigation.

A lower-court judge's discretion in the implementation process may also be affected by the manner in which a higher court's policy is communicated. The first step in implementing a judicial policy is to learn of the new appellate court ruling. Presumably, lower-court judges automatically are made aware of a higher court's decision, but that is not always so. The court from which a case has been appealed will certainly be informed of the decision. The federal district court for the middle district of Tennessee was told of the Supreme Court's decision in *Baker v. Carr* because its earlier decision was reversed, and the case was remanded to it for further action. However, systematic formal efforts are not made to inform other courts of the decision or to see that lower-court judges have access to a copy of the opinion. The decisions that contain the new judicial policy are simply made available to the public in printed form or on the Internet, and judges are expected to read them if they have the time and inclination.

Opinions of the Supreme Court, lower federal courts, and state appellate courts are available in a large number of courthouse, law school, and university libraries and are also increasingly available on the Internet. Some court opinions can now be read on the same day they are handed down or within just a few days. However, this widespread availability does not guarantee that they will be read and clearly understood. One complication is that many lower-level state judges, such as justices of the peace and juvenile court judges, are nonlawyers with little interest or skill in reading complex judicial decisions. [12] Finally, even those judges who have an interest in higher-court decisions and the ability to understand them do not have adequate time to keep abreast of all the new opinions.

Given these problems, how do judges become aware of upper-court decisions? One way is to hear of them from lawyers presenting cases in the lower courts. It is generally assumed that the opposing attorneys will present relevant precedents in their arguments before the judge. Those judges who are fortunate enough to have law clerks may also rely upon them to search out recent decisions from higher courts.

Thus some higher-court policies are not quickly and strictly enforced because lower-court judges are not aware of them. Even those of which they are aware may not be as clear as a lower-court judge might like. Either reason contributes to the discretion exercised by lower-court judges placed in the position of having to implement judicial policies.

Interpretation by Lower Courts

One study noted that "important policy announcements almost always require interpretation by someone other than the policy maker." [13] This is certainly true in the case of judicial policies established by appellate courts. The first exercise of a lower-court judge's discretion may be to interpret what the higher court's decision means.

Consider an example from a famous Supreme Court decision concerning the types of speech that are protected by the Constitution. In that 1919 case the Court announced that "the question in every case is whether the words used are used in such circumstances and are of such a nature as to create a clear and present danger that they will bring about the substantive evils that Congress has a right to prevent." [14] With that statement the Court announced what is known as the clear-and-present-danger doctrine. Although it may seem simple in the abstract to say that a person's right to speak is protected unless the words create a clear and present danger, lower-court judges do not decide cases in the abstract. They must accommodate higher-court policy decisions to the concrete facts of an actual case. Place yourself in the position of a lower-court judge deciding a case shortly after the announcement of the clear-and-present-danger policy. Assume that you were presiding over the trial of an individual who, in the course of a speech to a group of people on a busy street corner in a large city, advocated the violent overthrow of the U.S. government. As the judge, you might well have had to answer in your own mind one or more of the following questions as you tried to interpret the clear-and-present-danger doctrine: (1) How well defined must the danger be for it to be clear? (2) How imminent must the danger be for it to be present? (3) Is the danger in question one the government has a right to prevent? (4) Did the speech cause any danger? (5) At what point is the government allowed to intervene or stop the speech? Interpreting what is meant by the clear-and-present-danger policy is no simple task. Modern courts grapple with the free-speech question just as the courts in 1919 did.

The manner in which a lower-court judge interprets a policy established by a higher court depends upon a number of factors. Many policies are not clearly stated. Thus reasonable people may disagree over the proper interpretation. Even policy pronouncements that do not suffer from ambiguity are sometimes interpreted differently by different judges.

A judge's personal policy preferences will also affect the interpretation he or she gives to a higher-court policy. Judges come to the courts with their own unique background characteristics. Some are Republicans, others are Democrats; one judge may be liberal, another conservative. They come from different regions of the country. Some have been prosecutors; others have been primarily defense or corporate lawyers. A policy enthusiastically embraced by some judges may be totally rejected by others.

Strategies Employed by Lower Courts

Appellate court policies are open to different interpretations. Those who favor and accept a higher court's policy will naturally try to enforce it and perhaps even expand upon it. Those who dislike a higher court's policy decision may implement it sparingly or only under duress.

A judge who basically disagrees with a policy established by a higher court can employ a number of strategies. One rarely used strategy is defiance, whereby a judge simply does not apply the higher court's policy in a case before a lower court. One study of judicial implementation offers this example:

Desegregation brought out considerable trial court defiance; in one extreme case, a Birmingham, Alabama, municipal judge not only refused to follow Supreme Court decisions desegregating municipal facilities but also declared the Fourteenth Amendment unconstitutional.[15]

Such outright defiance is highly unusual. Other strategies are less extreme. A study of the libel decisions of the U.S. courts of appeals between 1964 and 1974 did not find a single case of noncompliance with Supreme Court mandates.[16] Another study, focusing on compliance with the Supreme Court's *Miranda v. Arizona* decision, found only one instance of possible noncompliance and twelve decisions that could be classified as narrow compliance among the 250 cases studied.[17]

Another strategy often employed by judges not favorably inclined toward a higher-court policy is to avoid having to apply the policy. Sometimes a case may be disposed of on technical or procedural grounds so that the judge does not have to rule on the merits of the case. It may be determined, for example, that the plaintiff does not have standing to sue or that the case has become moot because the issue was resolved before the trial commenced. Lower-court judges sometimes avoid accepting a policy by declaring a portion of the higher-court decision to be dicta. Dicta refers to the part of the opinion that does not contribute to the central logic of the decision. It may be useful as guidance but is not seen as binding. What constitutes dicta is open to varying interpretations.

Yet another strategy often employed is to apply the policy as narrowly as possible. One method is for the lower-court judge to rule that a precedent is not controlling because of factual differences in the higher-court case and the one before the lower courts. Therefore precedent does not have to be followed. Two good examples are the lower-court applications of the Supreme Court's decisions in *Escobedo v. Illinois* and *Miranda v. Arizona*.

The *Escobedo* decision held that a suspect being interrogated has to be allowed access to his or her lawyer. *Miranda* went a step further, declaring that suspects taken into custody must be advised of their constitutional rights and that any confession made by a suspect who had not been so advised is invalid. A leading judicial scholar explains how these two landmark decisions were treated by some lower-court judges:

Lower court judges who did not like the *Escobedo* ruling . . . refused to apply *Escobedo* to anyone who did not already have a lawyer. Similarly, judges who did not like the *Miranda* ruling did not require warnings to be given to those not in custody, and then defined "in custody" as narrowly as possible.[18]

As noted in Chapter 3, state court judges faced with interpreting or implementing policies on civil liberties often rely on what is termed "new judicial federalism," an idea that originated in the early 1970s, primarily as a result of Warren E. Burger's appointment as chief justice of the U.S. Supreme Court. Many civil libertarians, fearful that the new Burger Court would erode or overturn major Warren Court decisions, began to look to state bills of rights as alternative bases for their court claims. The Burger Court encouraged a return to state constitutions by pointing out that the states could offer greater protection under their own bills of rights than was available under the federal Bill of Rights.

Initially, courts used this approach to circumvent specific Burger Court decisions. However, over the past twenty-five years "state courts have undertaken major initiatives involving school finance, exclusionary zoning, the rights of defendants, and the right to privacy." [19]

Recent studies have cautioned against too much optimism among those who advocate reliance on state constitutions as a way to avoid conservative precedents espoused by the Burger and Rehnquist Courts. In separate examinations of criminal justice decisions from all fifty state high courts, Barry Latzer and Michael Esler concluded that state supreme courts continue to rely on federal law in the vast majority of their decisions.[20]

Not all lower-court judges are opposed to a policy announced by a higher court. Some judges have risked social ostracism and various kinds of harassment to implement policies they believed in even though these policies were not popular in their communities.[21]

A judge who is in basic agreement with a higher-court policy is likely to give that policy as broad an application as possible. The precedent might be expanded to apply to other areas.

For example, in *Griswold v. Connecticut* the Supreme Court held that a Connecticut statute forbidding the use of birth control devices was unconstitutional because it infringed upon a married couple's constitutional right to privacy.[22] In other words, the Court said that the use of birth control devices is a personal decision to be made without interference from the state. Five years later, a three-judge federal district court expanded the *Griswold* precedent to justify its finding that the Texas abortion statute was unconstitutional.[23] The court ruled that the law infringed upon an unmarried woman's right of privacy to decide, at least during the first trimester of pregnancy, whether to obtain an abortion. Thus the lower court went further than the Supreme Court in striking down state involvement in such matters.

Influences on Lower-Court Judges

Lower courts are not slaves of the higher courts when implementing judicial policies. They have a high degree of independence and discretion. At times the lower courts must decide cases for which the higher courts have not provided precise standards. Whenever this occurs, lower-court judges must turn elsewhere for guidance in deciding a case before them.

One study notes that in such a position lower-court judges "may take their cues on how to decide a particular case from a wide variety of factors including their party affiliation, their ideology, or their regional norms." [24] Several analyses point out that differences between Democratic and Republican lower-court judges are especially pronounced when Supreme Court rulings are ambiguous, when there is a transition from one Supreme Court period to another, or when the issue area is so new and controversial that more definite standards have not yet been formulated.[25]

Regional norms have also been mentioned prominently in the literature as having an influence on lower-court judges when they interpret and apply higher-court decisions.[26] One study found, for example, that "federal judges tend to be more vigilant in enforcing national desegregation standards in remote areas than when similar issues arise within the judge's immediate work/residence locale." The prevailing local norms may mean that "when faced with desegregating his own community a judge may be more concerned with public reaction than when dealing with an outlying area."[27]

Congressional Influences on the Implementation Process

Once a federal judicial decision is made, Congress can offer a variety of responses. It may aid or hinder the implementation of a decision and can also alter a court's interpretation of the law. Finally, Congress can mount an attack on individual judges. Naturally, the actions of individual members of Congress will be influenced by their partisan and ideological leanings.

In the course of deciding cases, the courts are often called upon to interpret federal statutes. On occasion the judicial interpretation may differ from what a majority in Congress intended. When that situation occurs, the statute can be changed by new legislation that, in effect, overrules the court's initial interpretation.[28] A good example of this occurred in March 1988, when Congress effectively overruled the Supreme Court's decision in *Grove City College v. Bell*.[29] At issue in the case was the scope of Title IX of the 1972 Education Act amendments, which forbids sex discrimination in education programs. In the *Grove City* case, which involved a small Pennsylvania college, the Court ruled that only the specific "program or activity" receiving federal aid was covered by Title IX. According to that interpretation, only Grove City College's financial aid office was affected by the law. Many in Congress interpreted Title IX to mean that the entire college was subject to the act's prohibitions.

To overturn the Court's decision and restore the interpretation favored by many legislators, Congress passed the Civil Rights Restoration Act. President Ronald Reagan vetoed the bill, but on March 22, 1988, the House and Senate mustered the necessary two-thirds vote to override the president's veto. In this way Congress established its view that if one part of an entity receives federal funds, the entire entity is covered by Title IX of the Education Act.[30] This example notwithstanding, the vast majority of the federal judiciary's statutory decisions are not touched by Congress.

In addition to ruling on statutes, the federal courts interpret the Constitution. Congress has two methods to reverse or alter the effects of a constitutional interpretation it does not like. First, it can respond with another statute. On June 21, 1989, in *Texas v. Johnson*, the Supreme Court overturned a Texas flag desecration statute that made it illegal to "cast contempt" on the flag by "publicly mutilating, defacing, burning, or trampling" it. Gregory Lee Johnson had been found guilty of violating the law when he burned an American flag at the 1984 Republican National Convention in Dallas.[31] Although President George H. W. Bush and some legislators argued in favor of a constitutional amendment to overturn the Court's decision, others preferred not to tinker with the Constitution. Instead, Congress enacted a statute designed to avoid the constitutional problems of the Texas law by eliminating any reference to the motives of a person who damages an American flag. The Flag Protection Act of 1989 was passed by Congress on October 12, 1989, and became effective on October 28 after President Bush allowed it to become law without his signature.[32] The new law was immediately challenged in several flag-burning demonstrations that were held in various parts of the country on October 28–30. In one of these exhibitions, held on the steps of the Capitol on October 30, Gregory Lee Johnson joined several others in igniting an American flag. However, he was not among those charged with violating the new federal statute. In 1990 the Supreme Court declared the Flag Protection Act unconstitutional.[33]

Second, a constitutional decision can be overturned directly by an amendment to the U.S. Constitution. Although many such amendments have been introduced over the years, it is not easy to obtain the necessary two-thirds vote in each house of Congress to propose the amendment and then achieve ratification by three-fourths of the states. The attempt to overturn the Supreme Court's 1989 flag-burning decision by a constitutional amendment provides an excellent example of this difficulty. Although the amendment was strongly supported by President Bush, it was rejected in the Senate on October 19, 1989, by a 51–48 vote, fifteen votes short of the required two-thirds of those present and voting.[34]

Only four Supreme Court decisions in the history of the Court have been overturned by constitutional amendments. The Eleventh Amendment overturned *Chisholm v. Georgia* (dealing with suits against a state in federal court); the Thirteenth Amendment overturned *Scott v. Sandford* (dealing with the legality of slavery); the Sixteenth Amendment overturned *Pollock v. Farmers' Loan and Trust Co.*

(pertaining to the constitutionality of the income tax); and the Twenty-sixth Amendment overturned *Oregon v. Mitchell* (giving eighteen-year-olds the right to vote in state elections).[35]

Congressional attacks on the federal courts in general and on certain judges in particular are another method of responding to judicial decisions. These attacks are sometimes in the form of verbal denouncements that allow a member of Congress to let off steam over a decision or series of decisions. A good recent example involved an unpopular decision by U.S. district judge Harold Baer of the Southern District of New York. In January 1996, he ruled in *U.S. v. Bayless*[36] that incriminating evidence in a drug case should be excluded because police officers violated the defendant's Fourth Amendment protection against unlawful search and seizure.[37] The outcry in Congress was immediate and generally harsh. Former speaker of the House Newt Gingrich said of the decision, "This is the kind of pro-drug-dealer, pro-crime, anti-police and anti-law enforcement attitude that makes it so hard for us to win the war on drugs." [38] As 1996 was a presidential election year, politicians of both parties expanded their discussions to a more general debate about the types of judges each candidate would try to place on the federal bench. Judge Baer later vacated his previous ruling and denied the defendant's motion to suppress the evidence.[39]

Federal judges may be impeached and removed from office by Congress. Although the congressional bark may be worse than its bite in the use of this weapon, it is still part of its overall arsenal, and the impeachment of several federal judges in recent years serves as a reminder of that fact.

Finally, the confirmation process offers a chance for an attack on the courts. As a new federal judicial appointee goes through hearings in the Senate, individual senators sometimes use the opportunity to denounce individual judges or specific decisions. Without doubt, the best example was President Reagan's nomination of Judge Robert H. Bork (of the D.C. Circuit Court of Appeals) as an associate justice of the Supreme Court. A number of senators on the Judiciary Committee took Judge Bork to task for opinions he had written in specific cases, his writings while serving as a law professor at Yale University, and his views on several controversial Supreme Court decisions (notably *Roe v. Wade*).[40]

However, Congress and the federal courts are not natural adversaries, even though it occasionally may appear that way. Retaliations against the federal judiciary are fairly rare, and often the two branches work in harmony toward similar policy goals. For example, Congress played a key role in implementing the Supreme Court's school desegregation policy by enacting the Civil Rights Act of 1964, which empowered the Justice Department to initiate suits against school districts. Title VI of the act also provided a potent weapon in the desegregation struggle by threatening the denial of federal funds to schools guilty of segregation. In 1965 Congress further solidified its support for a policy of desegregated public schools by passing the Elementary and Secondary Education Act. This act gave the federal government a much larger role in financing public education and thus made the threat to cut off federal funds a most serious problem for many segregated school districts.[41] Such support from Congress was significant because the likelihood of compliance with a policy is increased when unity prevails among the branches of government.[42]

Executive Branch Influences on the Implementation Process

At times the president may be called upon directly to implement a judicial decision. An example is the famous Nixon tapes case.[43] The Senate committee investigation into the cover-up of the 1973 break-in at the Democratic Party headquarters in the Watergate Hotel in Washington, D.C., led directly to high government officials working close to the president. It was also revealed during the investigation that President Richard M. Nixon had installed an automatic taping system in the Oval Office. Leon Jaworski, who had been appointed special prosecutor to investigate the Watergate affair, subpoenaed certain tapes that he felt might provide evidence needed in his prosecutions of high-ranking officials. Nixon refused to turn over the tapes on the grounds of executive privilege and the need for confidentiality. The Supreme Court's decision—which, ironically, was announced on the same day that the Judiciary Committee of the House of Representatives launched hearings on whether to impeach Nixon—instructed the president to surrender the subpoenaed tapes to Judge John J. Sirica, who was handling the trials of the government officials. Nixon eventually did comply with the high court's directive, thereby implementing a decision that led to his downfall. Within two weeks, in August 1974, he resigned from the presidency.

Even when not directly involved in the enforcement of a judicial policy, the president may still be able to influence its impact. Because of the status and visibility of the position, a president, simply by words and actions, may encourage support for, or resistance to, a new judicial policy. For instance, it has been argued that President Dwight D. Eisenhower's lack of enthusiasm for the *Brown v. Board of Education* decision and "his unwillingness to support it in more than a pro forma fashion encouraged southern resistance." [44] As a consequence, Eisenhower later had to send federal troops to Little Rock, Arkansas, to enforce the district court's integration order. Sending in troops made President Eisenhower's participation in the implementation process more direct.

A president can propose legislation aimed at retaliating against the courts. President Franklin D. Roosevelt, for instance, urged Congress to increase the size of the Supreme Court so he could "pack" it with justices who supported New Deal legislation. President Reagan used this tactic in another way. He was a consistently strong supporter of constitutional amendments to overturn the Supreme Court's decisions on school prayer and abortion.

The appointment power also gives the president an opportunity to influence federal judicial policies. Although senatorial courtesy is important in the appointment of federal district judges, evidence points to the fact that the president dominates the process at the Supreme Court and courts of appeals levels.

During his campaign for the presidency in 1968, Nixon made the Supreme Court an issue by criticizing the Warren Court for its liberal decisions and activist approach. He promised that, if elected, he would appoint "strict constructionists" to the Supreme Court and lower federal courts. In his first year in office, Nixon appointed Warren Burger as chief justice and Harry A. Blackmun as an associate justice. Two years later, Nixon was able to appoint another pair of justices—Lewis F. Powell Jr. and William H. Rehnquist.

How successful was President Nixon in accomplishing his goal of altering the policy direction of the Supreme Court? One student of the transition from the Warren Court to the Burger Court said that

on the whole the Court's decisions demonstrated considerable withdrawal from and undercutting of Warren Court policies affecting the entire range of civil liberties policies.[45]

Thus Nixon was generally able to accomplish his goal for the Supreme Court. Also, the uncertainty and ambiguity in Court precedents caused by the transition from the Warren to the Burger Court left the lower federal courts with more discretion.[46]

Presidents have long realized that lower federal judges are important in the judicial policy-making process. For this reason, many chief executives have shown an interest in appointing lower-court judges who share their basic ideologies and values.[47]

A president can also influence judicial policymaking through the activities of the Justice Department. The attorney general and staff subordinates can emphasize specific issues according to the overall policy goals of the president. For example, the 1964 Civil Rights Act authorized the Justice Department to file school desegregation suits. This allowed the executive branch to become more actively involved in implementing the policy goal of racial equality. The other side of the coin, however, is that the Justice Department may, at its discretion, deemphasize specific policies by not pursuing them vigorously in the courts.

Another official who is in a position to influence judicial policymaking is the solicitor general. Historically, this person has been seen as having dual responsibility, to both the judicial and the executive branches. Because of the solicitor general's close relationship with the Supreme Court, he or she is sometimes referred to as the "tenth justice." [48] The solicitor general is often viewed as a counselor who advises the Court about the meaning of federal statutes and the Constitution. The solicitor general also determines which of the cases involving the federal government as a party will be appealed to the Supreme Court. Furthermore, he or she may file an amicus curiae brief urging the Court to grant or deny another litigant's certiorari petition or supporting or opposing a particular policy being urged upon the high court. The solicitor general thus reacts to the policy decisions of the Supreme Court.

Many judicial decisions are implemented by the various departments, agencies, bureaus, and commissions that abound in the executive branch. The Supreme Court decision in *Frontiero v. Richardson* called upon the U.S. Air Force to implement a policy it had originally opposed.[49] The *Frontiero* case called into question congressional statutes that provided benefits for married male members of the Air Force but did not provide similar benefits for married female members. Under the laws, a married Air Force serviceman residing off the base was entitled to an allowance for living quarters regardless of whether his wife was employed or how much she earned. Married female members of the Air Force, however, were not entitled to such an allowance unless their husbands were physically or mentally incapable of self-support and dependent on their wives for more than half their support. Lieutenant Sharron Frontiero challenged the policy on the ground that it constituted sexual discrimination in violation of the Fifth Amendment. Her suit was filed in a federal district court in Alabama on December 23, 1970. It was not until April 5, 1972, that the three-judge district court announced its decision upholding the Air Force policy. Lieutenant Frontiero appealed to the Supreme Court, which overturned the lower-court decision on May 14, 1973. The Air Force was then required to implement a policy it had fought for nearly three years.

Other Implementers

In addition to lower-court judges, Congress, the president, and others in the executive branch, many other actors are involved in the interpretation and implementation of judicial policies.[50]

Although the focus thus far has been primarily on various federal officials, implementation of judicial policies is often performed by state officials. Many of the Supreme Court's criminal due process decisions, such as *Gideon v. Wainwright* and *Miranda v. Arizona,* have been enforced by state court judges and other state officials. State and local police officers, for instance, have played a major role in implementing the *Miranda* requirement that criminal suspects must be advised of their rights. The *Gideon* ruling that an attorney must be provided at state expense for indigent defendants in felony trials has been implemented by public defenders, local bar associations, and individual court-appointed lawyers.

State legislators and executives are also frequently drawn into the implementation process, often as unwilling participants. A judge who determines that a wrong has been committed may use the power to issue an equitable decree as a way of remedying the wrong. The range of remedies available is broad because cases vary in the issues they raise and the types of relief sought. Among the more common options from which a judge may choose are process remedies, performance standards, and specified remedial actions.[51] Process remedies provide for such things as advisory committees, citizen participation, educational programs, evaluation committees, dispute resolution procedures, and special masters. The remedies do not specify a particular form of action. Performance standards call for specific remedies—a certain number of housing units or schools or a certain level of staffing in a prison or mental health facility. The specific means of attaining these goals are left to the discretion of the officials named in the suit. Examples of specified remedial actions are school busing, altered school attendance zones, and changes in the size and condition of prison cells or hospital rooms. This type of remedy gives the defendant no flexibility concerning the specific remedy or the means of attaining it.

Implementation of these remedial decrees often devolves, at least partially, to the state legislatures. An order calling for a certain number of prison cells or a certain number of guards in the prison system might require new state expenditures, which the legislature would have to fund. Similarly, an order to construct more modern mental health facilities or provide more modern equipment would mean an increase in state expenditures. Governors would also naturally be involved in carrying out these types of remedial decrees because they typically are heavily involved in state budgeting procedures. Also, they may sign or veto laws. Some even have an item veto power, which permits them to veto certain budget items while approving others.

Sometimes judges appoint certain individuals to assist in carrying out the remedial decree. Special masters are usually given some decision-making authority.

Court-appointed monitors are also used in some situations, but they do not relieve the judge of decision-making responsibilities. Instead, the monitor is an information gatherer who reports on the defendant's progress in complying with the remedial decree. When orders are not implemented or when barriers of one kind or another block progress in providing a remedy, a judge may name someone as a receiver. A good example occurred in the 1970s when the fights within Alabama's mental health agencies and facilities made it virtually impossible to obtain the action Judge Frank Johnson wanted. Finally, Judge Johnson ordered the governor to take over as receiver and empowered him to disregard normal organizational barriers.[52]

Space does not permit discussion of every state and local public official in the implementation process, but one group of individuals has been so deeply involved in implementing judicial policies that we feel compelled to deal with them here, if only briefly. These implementers are the thousands of men and women who constitute school boards throughout the country.

Two major policy areas stand out as having embroiled school board members in considerable controversy as they faced the inevitable task of trying to carry out Supreme Court policy. First, when the high court ruled in 1954 that segregation has no place in the public schools, school boards and school superintendents, along with federal district judges, bore the brunt of implementing that decision.[53] Their role in this process has affected the lives of millions of schoolchildren, parents, and taxpayers all over America.

The second area that has involved school boards is the Supreme Court's policies on religion in the public schools. In *Engel v. Vitale* (1962), the Court held unconstitutional a New York requirement that a state-written prayer be recited daily in the public schools.[54] Some school districts responded to the decision by requiring instead the recitation of a Bible verse or the Lord's Prayer. Their reasoning was that the state did not write the Lord's Prayer or the Bible, so they were not violating the Court's policy. A year later, the Supreme Court struck down these new practices, pointing out that the constitutional violation lay in endorsing the religious activity and its determination did not depend on whether the state had written the prayer.[55] Some school districts continued to seek ways to provide religious activities for students. *Santa Fe Independent School District v. Doe*, decided by the U.S. Supreme Court in 2000, serves as a good example.[56] In that case the school district implemented a policy allowing two student elections: one to determine whether "invocations" should be delivered over the public address system at varsity football games and a second to select the person to deliver the "invocation." By a 6–3 vote the high court held that this policy also violates the Constitution's Establishment Clause.

Both of these policy areas involve basically private citizens—school board officials—in implementing controversial, emotion-charged policies. Furthermore, the school board officials may neither understand nor agree with the policies they are directed to enforce.

The Impact of Judicial Policies

Thus far, the focus has primarily been on the implementation of judicial policies by various government officials, which is entirely appropriate because court decisions are often specifically directed at other public policymakers. However, as one judicial scholar notes, "Supreme Court decisions can and do have significant effects on society." [57] Some argue that American courts may be too heavily engaged in making decisions that affect society and too involved in policymaking. This is not the case in all countries. For example, a recent study of Canadian judges concluded:

Clearly, judicial activism is more common and more accepted among American judges. Although the level of judicial activism may be increasing in Canada, Canadian judges still seem uncomfortable with the concept of judicial policy making.[58]

A few of the policies developed by the courts have had significant effects on society as a whole, notably on the issues of racial equality, criminal due process, and abortion.

Racial Equality

Many point to the Supreme Court's *Brown* decision as the impetus for the drive for racial equality in the United States. Congress and the executive branch were also involved in the process of ensuring implementation of the decision's desegregation policy, but the courts took the lead in pursuing a national policy of racial equality. Thus one of the most important ways the federal judiciary can influence policy is to place issues on the national political agenda.

In the beginning, the court decisions were often vague, leading to evasion of the new policy. The Supreme Court justices and many lower federal judges were persistent in decisions following *Brown* and, in this way, kept the policy of racial equality on the national political agenda. Their persistence paid off with passage of the 1964 Civil Rights Act, ten years after *Brown*. That act, which had the strong support of Presidents John F. Kennedy and Lyndon B. Johnson, squarely placed Congress and the president on record as advocating racial equality in America.

One other aspect of the federal judiciary's importance in the policy-making process is illustrated by *Brown* and the cases that followed it. Although the courts stood virtually alone in the quest for racial equality for several years, their decisions did not go unnoticed. The *Brown* decision, as one team of scholars of judicial impact states,

was a highly visible Court decision, a judicial attempt to generate one of the greatest social reforms in American history. And certainly in the years that followed, African Americans and their allies brought considerable pressures on other governmental bodies to desegregate the schools. Indeed, the pressures soon went far beyond schools to demand integration of all aspects of American life.[59]

Some debate has arisen, however, over whether *Brown* was a major cause of this mobilization of effort. One scholar empirically examined the causal link between *Brown* and civil rights mobilization by studying the coverage of civil rights in periodicals dating from 1940 to 1965.[60] He concluded that no evidence exists that *Brown*'s "influence was widespread or of much importance to the battle for civil rights."[61] Other scholars, however, attribute much greater influence to *Brown* in the mobilization process.[62]

Although gains have been made, the battle over racial equality and equal opportunity for racial minorities is far from over, as indicated by two important Supreme Court decisions handed down on June 23, 2003. As discussed more fully in Chapter 13, these two cases—*Gratz v. Bollinger*[63] and *Grutter v. Bollinger*[64]—addressed the University of Michigan's use of race in its freshman and law school admissions policies.

Criminal Due Process

Judicial policymaking in the area of criminal due process is most closely associated with the era of the Warren Court. As a former solicitor general said, "Never has there been such a thorough-going reform of criminal procedure within so short a time."[65] The Warren Court decisions were aimed primarily at changing the procedures followed by the states in dealing with criminal defendants. By the time Chief Justice Earl Warren left the Supreme Court, new policies had been established to deal with a wide range of activities. Among the most far-reaching decisions of the Warren Court were *Mapp v. Ohio, Gideon v. Wainwright,* and *Miranda v. Arizona.*[66]

The *Mapp* decision extended to the states the exclusionary rule, which had applied to the national government for a number of years. This rule required state courts to exclude from trial evidence that had been illegally seized by the police. Although some police departments, especially in major urban areas, have tried to establish specific guidelines for their officers to follow in obtaining evidence, such efforts have not been universal. Because of variations in police practices and differing lower-court interpretations of what constitutes a valid search and seizure, implementation of *Mapp* has not been consistent throughout the country.

Perhaps even more important in reducing the originally perceived impact of *Mapp* has been the lack of solid support for the exclusionary rule among the Supreme Court justices. The decision was not a unanimous one to begin with, and over the years some of the justices, notably Chief Justice Warren Burger, have been openly critical of the exclusionary rule. Not surprisingly, some decisions of the Burger and Rehnquist Courts have somewhat curtailed application of the exclusionary rule. In 1984 the Burger Court adopted a limited good-faith exception to the exclusionary rule, which allows officers to seize evidence in good faith, relying on search warrants that may later prove to be defective.[67] The Rehnquist Court reaffirmed the good-faith exception in 1995 in *Arizona v. Evans*.[68] Decisions of the Burger and Rehnquist Courts have broadened the scope of legal searches, thus limiting the applicability of the rule.[69]

The *Gideon v. Wainwright* decision held that attorneys must be provided for indigent defendants when they go to trial in a felony case in state courts. Many states routinely provided attorneys in such trials even before the Court's decision. The other states began to comply in a variety of ways. Public defender programs were established in many regions. In other areas, local bar associations cooperated with judges to implement some method of complying with the Supreme Court's new policy.

The impact of *Gideon* is clearer and more consistent than that of *Mapp*. One reason, no doubt, is that many states had already implemented the policy called for by *Gideon*. It was simply more widely accepted than the policy established by *Mapp*. The policy announced in *Gideon* was also more sharply defined than the one in *Mapp*. Although the Court did not specify whether a public defender or a court-appointed lawyer must be provided, it is still clear that the indigent defendant must have the help of an attorney. The Burger Court did not retreat from the Warren Court's policy of providing an attorney for indigent defendants, as it did on the search-and-seizure issue addressed by *Mapp*. All of these factors add up to a more recognizable impact for the policy announced in *Gideon*.

In *Miranda v. Arizona* the Supreme Court went a step further, ruling that police officers must advise suspects taken into custody of their constitutional rights, one of which is to have an attorney present during questioning. These rights are so clearly stated that police departments have had the ruling printed on cards for officers to carry in their shirt pockets; when suspects are taken into custody, the officers read the suspects their rights.

If measured simply in terms of police officers reading the *Miranda* rights to persons they arrest, then compliance with the Supreme Court policy reaches a high level. Some researchers, however, have questioned the impact of *Miranda* because of the method used to advise suspects of their rights. It is one thing to read to a person from a card; it is another to explain what is meant by the high court's requirements and then try to make the suspect understand them. Viewed from this standpoint, the impact of the policy announced in *Miranda* is not as clear.

Two years after the decision, Congress reacted to *Miranda* by enacting a statute that, in essence, made the admissibility of a suspect's statements turn solely on whether they were made voluntarily. The statute received little attention until 1999, when the U.S. Court of Appeals for the Fourth Circuit ruled on a case involving an alleged bank robber who moved to suppress a statement made to the FBI on the ground that he had not received "*Miranda* warnings" before being interrogated. The court of appeals held that the statute was satisfied because his statement was voluntary. The decision raised the question of whether the congressional act or the high court's *Miranda* decision should be followed. On June 26, 2000, the U.S. Supreme Court held that *Miranda,* being a constitutional decision of the Court, could not, in effect, be overruled by an act of Congress.[70] In other words, *Miranda* still governs the admissibility of statements made during custodial interrogation in state and federal courts.

In sum, the impact of the Supreme Court's criminal justice policies has been mixed, for several reasons. In some instances ambiguity is a problem. In other cases less than solid support for the policy may be evident among justices, or support erodes when some members of the Court are replaced by others. All of these variables translate into greater discretion for the implementers.

Abortion

In *Roe v. Wade* the Supreme Court ruled (1) that a woman has an absolute right to an abortion during the first trimester of pregnancy; (2) that a state may regulate the abortion procedure during the second trimester to protect the mother's health; and (3) that, during the third trimester, the state may regulate or even prohibit abortions, except where the life or health of the mother is endangered.[71]

The reaction to this decision was immediate, and primarily negative.[72] It came in the form of letters to individual justices, public speeches, the introduction of resolutions in Congress, and the advocacy of "right to life" amendments in Congress. As might be expected, given the controversial nature of the Court's decision, hospitals did not wholeheartedly offer to support the decision by changing their abortion policies.

Reaction to the Court's abortion policy has not only continued but also has moved into new areas. In recent presidential elections the two major party platforms and candidates have taken opposing stands on this issue. Democratic platforms and nominees have generally expressed support for *Roe v. Wade*, whereas the Republican platforms and contenders have noted opposition to the Supreme Court's decision.

Congress has also been a hotbed of activity in response to the Court's policy. Unable to secure passage of a constitutional amendment to overturn *Roe v. Wade*, anti-abortion forces have used another approach. For several years they successfully obtained amendments to appropriations bills preventing the expenditure of federal funds for elective abortions. In 1980 the Supreme Court upheld the constitutionality of such a prohibition.[73]

Most of the legislation in the aftermath of *Roe* has been at the state level. One study reports that within two years of the decision thirty-two states had passed sixty-two laws relating to abortion, most aimed at limiting access to abortions, regulating abortion procedures, or prohibiting abortions under certain conditions.[74]

Interest-group activity increased dramatically after the *Roe* decision. Groups opposing the decision often organized public demonstrations against the decision and later began to picket clinics. Interest groups that support the *Roe v. Wade* decision have been more likely to focus their efforts on the courts.

The difference in strategies was clearly evident when the Supreme Court heard *Webster v. Reproductive Health Services* in 1989.[75] This case attracted widespread attention because the U.S. Department of Justice explicitly asked the Court to overturn *Roe v. Wade* (only four justices went on record as favoring this). A record seventy-eight amicus curiae briefs, supported by more than three hundred organizations, were filed in the case; filings or signings by pro-choice groups outnumbered those of pro-life groups by a 5–1 margin.[76]

During the 1999–2000 term the Supreme Court had another opportunity to overrule *Roe v. Wade* when it decided *Stenberg v. Carhart*.[77] By one vote, the Court reaffirmed the *Roe* decision and struck down a Nebraska law criminalizing dilation and extraction (termed "partial birth abortion" by opponents) because the law placed an undue burden on the woman seeking an abortion by limiting her options to less safe procedures.[78]

While battles over the abortion issue were being fought in the courts, political campaigns, and legislative arenas, others preferred a more direct approach, blockading and holding demonstrations at abortion centers. The Supreme Court has ruled, however, that reasonable time, place, and manner restrictions may be placed on such demonstrations.[79]

Conclusion

Some judicial policies have a more significant impact on society than others. The judiciary plays a greater role in developing the nation's policies than the Framers of the Constitution envisioned. However,

American courts are not all-powerful institutions. They were designed with severe limitations and placed in a political system of divided powers. To ask them to produce significant social reforms is to forget their history and ignore their constraints.[80]

Within this complex framework of competing political and social demands and expectations is a policy-making role for the courts. Because the other two branches of government are sometimes not receptive to the demands of certain segments of society, their only alternative is to turn to the courts. Civil rights organizations, for example, made no real headway until they found the Supreme Court to be a supportive forum for their school desegregation efforts. They were then able to use *Brown* and other decisions as a springboard to attack a variety of areas of discrimination. Thus a champion at a high government level may offer hope to individuals and interest groups.

As civil rights groups attained some success in the federal courts, others were encouraged to employ litigation as a strategy. For example, as several scholars have found, supporters of women's rights followed a pattern established by minority groups when they began taking their grievances to the courts.[81] What began as a more narrow pursuit for racial equality was broadened to a quest for equality for other disadvantaged groups in society.

Clearly, the courts can announce policy decisions that attract national attention and perhaps emphasize that other policymakers have failed to act. In this way the judiciary may invite the other branches to exercise their policy-making powers. Follow-up decisions indicate the judiciary's determination to pursue a particular policy and help keep alive the invitation for other policymakers to participate in the endeavor.

All things considered, the courts seem best equipped to develop and implement narrow policies that are less controversial in nature. The policy established in the *Gideon* case provides a good example. The decision that indigent defendants in state criminal trials must be provided with an attorney did not meet any strong protests. Furthermore, it was a policy that primarily required the support of judges and lawyers; action by Congress and the president was not necessary. A policy of equality for all segments of society, however, is so broad and laden with controversy that it must move beyond the judiciary. As it does so, the courts become simply one part, albeit an important part, of the policy-making process.

Summary

We began this chapter by pointing out that judicial decisions are not self-executing. The courts depend upon a variety of individuals, both inside and outside the judicial branch, to carry out their rulings.

Lower-court judges are prominent in the implementation process. Our discussion of their role in carrying out decisions of higher courts emphasized the discretion they exercise. Factors that account for the flexibility that rests with the lower-court judge include the decentralization of the judicial system and the ambiguity of higher-court rulings. We also examined the strategies that lower-court judges may employ in resisting appellate court decisions they dislike.

Congress and the president may also be involved in the implementation process. Each of these branches can react either positively or negatively to a court decision. As described in some detail, they may exert a wide range of influences in enforcing a judicial decision.

We also noted that some policies call upon state officials to take part in the implementation process. State court judges, for example, played the major role in enforcing the Warren Court's decisions on criminal due process. Local school boards have also been called upon to carry out Supreme Court policies.

We concluded the chapter with a discussion of the impact on society of several important federal court policies. Explanations were offered as to why some policies have a greater impact on society than others. Most important, perhaps, is that if a ruling faces strong opposition—such as the Supreme Court's original decision on abortion—Congress and other implementers are likely to drag their feet. The final section of the chapter offered some thoughts on the role of courts in bringing about changes in society. It was noted that the judiciary can act as a kind of beacon for traditionally underrepresented groups seeking to achieve their goals.

Further Thought and Discussion Questions

1. What arguments can you make for the level of discretion lower-court judges should have when implementing decisions of appellate courts? How does this level of individual discretion affect the application of justice in society?

2. Should the judicial branch have the ability to develop and implement public policy, or should that power belong exclusively to the executive and legislative branches? One of our assumptions in this book is that judges routinely engage in

policymaking, but what would judicial decisions look like if they were completely divorced from the context of public policy?

3. What are the major strengths and weaknesses of the U.S. Supreme Court in influencing social policies in the United States?

NOTES

1. *Gideon v. Wainwright*, 372 U.S. 335 (1963).

2. For a good description of the bureaucratic theory, see Walter F. Murphy, "Chief Justice Taft and the Lower Court Bureaucracy: A Study in Judicial Administration," *Journal of Politics* 24 (1962): 453–476.

3. Richard J. Richardson and Kenneth N. Vines, *The Politics of Federal Courts* (Boston: Little, Brown, 1970), 144.

4. Lawrence Baum, "Implementation of Judicial Decisions: An Organizational Analysis," *American Politics Quarterly* 4 (1976): 91.

5. The desegregation policy was announced in *Brown v. Board of Education of Topeka*, 347 U.S. 483 (1954). For a study of the lower federal courts involved in implementing *Brown*, see Jack W. Peltason, *Fifty-Eight Lonely Men* (New York: Harcourt, Brace and World, 1961).

6. For an excellent account of the school desegregation struggle in Georgia, see Harrell R. Rodgers Jr. and Charles S. Bullock III, *Coercion to Compliance* (Lexington, Mass.: Lexington Books, 1976).

7. *Brown v. Board of Education of Topeka II*, 349 U.S. 294 (1955).

8. *Baker v. Carr*, 369 U.S. 186 (1962).

9. Ibid., 237, 251.

10. The statement was made by Justice Potter Stewart in *Jacobellis v. Ohio*, 378 U.S. 184 (1964).

11. *Furman v. Georgia*, 408 U.S. 238 (1972). A good account of the various views held by the justices, as well as the behind-the-scenes events leading to the final decision, may be found in Bob Woodward and Scott Armstrong, *The Brethren: Inside the Supreme Court* (New York: Simon and Schuster, 1979), 205–220.

12. For a good discussion of this point with pertinent examples, see Bradley C. Canon and Charles A. Johnson, *Judicial Policies: Implementation and Impact*, 2d ed. (Washington, D.C.: CQ Press, 1999), 49–50.

13. Ibid., 29.

14. *Schenck v. United States*, 249 U.S. 47 (1919).

15. Canon and Johnson, *Judicial Policies*, 38.

16. See John Gruhl, "The Supreme Court's Impact on the Law of Libel: Compliance by Lower Federal Courts," *Western Political Quarterly* 33 (1980): 517.

17. See Donald R. Songer and Reginald S. Sheehan, "Supreme Court Impact on Compliance and Outcomes: *Miranda* and *New York Times* in the United States Courts of Appeals," *Western Political Quarterly* 43 (1990): 307.

18. Stephen L. Wasby, *The Supreme Court in the Federal Judicial System*, 4th ed. (Chicago: Nelson-Hall, 1993), 376.

19. See G. Alan Tarr, *Understanding State Constitutions* (Princeton, N.J.: Princeton University Press, 1998), 166.

20. See Barry Latzer, "The Hidden Conservatism of the State Court Revolution," *Judicature* 74 (1991): 190–197; and Michael Esler, "State Supreme Court Commitment to State Law," *Judicature* 78 (1994): 25–32.

21. See Peltason, *Fifty-Eight Lonely Men*; and Richardson and Vines, *The Politics of Federal Courts*, 98–99.

22. *Griswold v. Connecticut*, 381 U.S. 479 (1965).

23. *Roe v. Wade*, 314 F. Supp. 1217 (1970).

24. Ronald Stidham and Robert A. Carp, "U.S. Trial Court Reactions to Changes in Civil Rights and Civil Liberties Policies," *Southeastern Political Review* 12 (1984): 7.

25. See, for example, Kathleen L. Barber, "Partisan Values in the Lower Courts: Reapportionment in Ohio and Michigan," *Case Western Reserve Law Review* 20 (1969): 406–407; Robert A. Carp and C. K. Rowland, *Policymaking and Politics in the Federal District Courts* (Knoxville: University of Tennessee Press, 1983), chap. 2; C. K. Rowland and Robert A. Carp, "A Longitudinal Study of Party Effects on Federal District Court Policy Propensities," *American Journal of Political Science* 24 (1980): 301; and Ronald Stidham, Robert A. Carp, and C. K. Rowland, "Women's Rights before the Federal District Courts, 1971–1977," *American Politics Quarterly* 11 (1983): 214.

26. See, for example, Peltason, *Fifty-Eight Lonely Men*; Kenneth N. Vines, "Federal District Judges and Race Relations Cases in the South," *Journal of Politics* 26 (1964): 338–357; Richardson and Vines, *The Politics of Federal Courts*, 93–100; and Michael W. Giles and Thomas G. Walker, "Judicial Policy-Making and Southern School Segregation," *Journal of Politics* 37 (1975): 917–936.

27. Giles and Walker, "Judicial Policy-Making and Southern School Segregation," 931.

28. For a good discussion of this practice, with pertinent recent examples, see Leon Friedman, "Overruling the Court," *Hofstra Law Report* 11 (Spring 2002): 16–19.

29. 465 U.S. 555 (1984).

30. For accounts of the hearings, see Nadine Cohodas, "Echoes from the Past Punctuate *Grove City* Debate," *Congressional Quarterly Weekly Report*, March 12, 1988, 677; and Mark Willen, "Congress Overrides Reagan's *Grove City* Veto," *Congressional Quarterly Weekly Report*, March 26, 1988, 774.

31. *Texas v. Johnson*, 491 U.S. 397 (1989).

32. "D.C. Flag Burning Tests New Law," *Congressional Quarterly Weekly Report*, November 4, 1989, 2952.

33. *United States v. Eichman*, 496 U.S. 310 (1990).

34. Joan Biskupic, "Anti-Flag Burning Amendment Falls Far Short in Senate," *Congressional Quarterly Weekly Report*, October 21, 1989, 2803.

35. 2 Dallas 419 (1793); 19 Howard 393 (1857); 158 U.S. 601 (1896); and 400 U.S. 112 (1970), respectively.

36. 913 F. Supp. 232.

37. Our discussion of the political criticism of Judge Baer is drawn from Jennifer A. Segal, "Judicial Decision Making and the Impact of Election Year Rhetoric," *Judicature* 84 (2000): 26–33.

38. Quoted in ibid., 30.

39. *U.S. v. Bayless*, 921 F. supp 211 (1996).

40. See Nadine Cohodas, "For Robert Bork, The Real Test Begins Now," *Congressional Quarterly Weekly Report*, September 12, 1987, 2159–2163; Nadine Cohodas and Mark Willen, "Who Is Bork?" *Congressional Quarterly Weekly Report*, September 12, 1987, 2164–2168; Ronald V. Elving, "The Supreme Court: How Much Difference Would Justice Bork Make?" *Congressional Quarterly Weekly Report*, September 12, 1987, 2169–2171; and Nadine Cohodas, "Reagan's Judiciary," *Congressional Quarterly Weekly Report*, September 12, 1987, 2176–2177.

41. See James E. Anderson, David W. Brady, and Charles S. Bullock III, *Public Policy and Politics in America* (North Scituate, Mass.: Duxbury Press, 1978), 291–292; and Charles S. Bullock III, "Equal Education Opportunity," in *Implementation of Civil Rights Policy*, ed. Charles S. Bullock III and Charles M. Lamb (Monterey, Calif.: Brooks/Cole, 1984), 57–58.

42. Wasby, *The Supreme Court in the Federal Judicial System*, 256.

43. *United States v. Nixon*, 418 U.S. 683 (1974).

44. Canon and Johnson, *Judicial Policies*, 129.

45. Wasby, *The Supreme Court in the Federal Judicial System*, 16.

46. See Carp and Rowland, *Policymaking and Politics in the Federal District Courts*, 43.

47. For a discussion of this point, see Ronald Stidham, Robert A. Carp, and C. K. Rowland, "Patterns of Presidential Influence on the Federal District Courts: An Analysis of the Appointment Process," *Presidential Studies Quarterly* 14 (1984): 548–560.

48. See Lincoln Caplan, "Annals of Law: The Tenth Justice," pt. 1, *The New Yorker*, August 10, 1987, 32. Also see Lincoln Caplan, *The Tenth Justice: The Solicitor General and the Rule of Law* (New York: Knopf, 1988).

49. *Frontiero v. Richardson*, 411 U.S. 677 (1973).

50. One study, for example, analyzed judicial implementation and impact from the standpoint of the roles of four populations: an interpreting population, an implementing population, a consumer population, and a secondary population. See Canon and Johnson, *Judicial Policies*.

51. Our discussion of the use of powers to provide equitable remedial decrees is largely drawn from Phillip J. Cooper, *Hard Judicial Choices* (New York: Oxford University Press, 1988), 12–14, 342, 348–349.

52. Ibid., 348–349.

53. See Rodgers and Bullock, *Coercion to Compliance*; and Giles and Walker, "Judicial Policy-Making and Southern School Segregation."

54. *Engel v. Vitale*, 370 U.S. 421 (1962).

55. See *Abington School District v. Schempp*, 374 U.S. 203 (1963).

56. 530 U.S. 290.

57. Lawrence Baum, *The Supreme Court*, 7th ed. (Washington, D.C.: CQ Press, 2001), 259.

58. Mark C. Miller, "Judicial Activism in Canada and the United States," *Judicature* 81 (1998): 265.

59. Canon and Johnson, *Judicial Policies*, 206.

60. See Gerald N. Rosenberg, *The Hollow Hope: Can Courts Bring About Social Change?* (Chicago: University of Chicago Press, 1991).

61. Ibid., 156.

62. See, for example, Canon and Johnson, *Judicial Policies*; Doug McAdam, *Political Process and the Development of Black Insurgency* (Chicago: University of Chicago Press, 1982); and Aldon Morris, *The Origins of the Civil Rights Movement* (New York: Free Press, 1984).

63. Available online at http://supct.law.cornell.edu/supct/html/02-516.ZS.html.

64. Available online at http://supct.law.cornell.edu/supct/html/02-241.ZS.html.

65. Archibald Cox, *The Warren Court* (Cambridge, Mass.: Harvard University Press, 1968), 74.

66. *Mapp v. Ohio*, 367 U.S. 643 (1961); *Gideon v. Wainwright*, 372 U.S. 335 (1963); and *Miranda v. Arizona*, 384 U.S. 436 (1966).

67. See *United States v. Leon*, 468 U.S. 897 (1984); and *Massachusetts v. Sheppard*, 488 U.S. 981 (1984).

68. 514 U.S. 1 (1995).

69. See the discussion of search and seizure in Otis H. Stephens Jr. and John M. Scheb II, *American Constitutional Law*, 2d ed. (Belmont, Calif.: West/Wadsworth, 1999), 587–594.

70. *Dickerson v. United States*, 530 U.S. 428.

71. *Roe v. Wade*, 410 U.S. 113 (1973).

72. For a good case study of the impact of *Roe v. Wade*, including reactions to the decision, see Canon and Johnson, *Judicial Policies*, 5–16. Our discussion is drawn largely from this study.

73. See *Harris v. McRae*, 448 U.S. 297 (1980).

74. See Eva Rubin, *Abortion, Politics, and the Courts: Roe v. Wade and Its Aftermath* (New York: Greenwood Press, 1987), 127.

75. 492 U.S. 490.

76. See Canon and Johnson, *Judicial Policies*, 14; and Barbara H. Craig and David O'Brien, *Abortion and American Politics* (Chatham, N.J.: Chatham House, 1988), 204 and 214–218.

77. 530 U.S. 914.

78. See "Highlights of the Supreme Court's 1999–2000 Term," http://supct.law.cornell.edu/supct/oohighlts.html.

79. See *Hill v. Colorado*, 530 U.S. 703 (2000).

80. Rosenberg, *Hollow Hope*, 343.

81. See Richard C. Cortner, "Strategies and Tactics of Litigants in Constitutional Cases," *Journal of Public Law* 17 (1968): 287–307; Jo Freeman, *The Politics of Women's Liberation* (New York: David McKay, 1975); Leslie Friedman Goldstein, "Sex and the Burger Court: Recent Judicial Policy Making toward Women," in *Race, Sex, and Policy Problems*, ed. Marian Lief Palley and Michael B. Preston (Lexington, Mass.: Lexington Books, 1979), 103–113; and Karen O'Connor, *Women's Organizations' Use of the Courts* (Lexington, Mass.: Heath, 1980).

SUGGESTED READINGS

Bullock, Charles S. III, and Charles M. Lamb, eds. *Implementation of Civil Rights Policy.* Monterey, Calif.: Brooks/Cole, 1984. A collection of articles that focus on how civil rights policies are carried out.

Canon, Bradley C., and Charles A. Johnson. *Judicial Policies: Implementation and Impact,* 2d ed. Washington, D.C.: CQ Press, 1999. A good study of the process and actors involved in carrying out and enforcing judicial decisions.

Cooper, Phillip J. *Hard Judicial Choices.* New York: Oxford University Press, 1988. The book focuses on the use of remedial decrees in carrying out judicial decisions.

Craig, Barbara H., and David M. O'Brien. *Abortion and American Politics.* Chatham, N.J.: Chatham House, 1993. A good study of the response to the Supreme Court's abortion decisions.

Legal Information Institute's Supreme Court Collection. Available online at: http://supct.law.cornell.edu/supct/. An excellent source of information about the U.S. Supreme Court's history, justices, and opinions.

Peltason, Jack W. *Fifty-Eight Lonely Men.* New York: Harcourt, Brace and World, 1961. An excellent study of the southern federal judges who were given the task of implementing the U.S. Supreme Court's *Brown v. Board of Education* decision.

Rodgers, Harrell R., Jr., and Charles S. Bullock III. *Coercion to Compliance.* Lexington, Mass.: Lexington Books, 1976. A good study of the implementation of school desegregation policies in Georgia.

Rosenberg, Gerald N. *Hollow Hope: Can Courts Bring About Social Change?* Chicago: University of Chicago Press, 1991. The book focuses on the ability of courts to effect social change.

Wasby, Stephen L. *The Impact of the United States Supreme Court: Some Perspectives.* Homewood, Ill.: Dorsey, 1970. The author discusses the various actors involved in the process of implementing decisions of the U.S. Supreme Court.

CHAPTER 15

Policymaking by American Judges: A Synthesis

Justices Sandra Day O'Connor and Stephen Breyer have predicted that future Supreme Court decisions will be influenced by the rulings of foreign and international tribunals. This revelation was first made in the aftermath of the recent Supreme Court decision in Lawrence v. Texas, *which paved the way for legal equality for gays and lesbians. Here, inside The Hague's Peace Palace, the World Court hears a case on genocide. In the years to come, the decisions of this body and other foreign courts may affect the decision-making process of America's highest judicial tribunal.*

"A N EDUCATION," THE SAYING GOES, "is what you have left after you've forgotten what you've learned." This text has presented many facts, theories, statistics, and examples about the federal and state court systems. But as time goes on and the myriad details are largely forgotten, what knowledge should you retain about the operation and policymaking of American courts? It is the purpose of this chapter to extract from the preceding fourteen chapters certain key ideas and significant themes that we would like you to remember long after most of the factual tidbits have faded from memory.

The decisions of federal and state judges and justices affect the lives of all Americans. Whether one is referring to the norm enforcement rulings or to broader policy-making decisions, the output of federal and state courts permeates the warp and woof of the body politic in the United States. To have a full and accurate understanding of the American political system, it is necessary to be cognizant of the work of the men and women who wear the black robe. In examining decision making by the judiciary, we must consider two basic questions. First, what are the conditions that cause judges to engage in policymaking and to do so boldly? Second, does the literature give any clues as to the substantive direction of this policymaking—that is, will it be conservative or liberal, supportive of or antagonistic toward the status quo? In seeking answers to these two basic questions, we have synthesized four sets of variables that shed some light in this area: (1) the nature of the case or issue presented to the court, (2) the values and orientations of the judges, (3) the nature of the judicial decision-making process, and (4) extraneous influences that serve to implement and sustain judicial decisions.

The Nature of the Case or Issue

One critical variable that clearly affects the degree to which (and sometimes the direction in which) American jurists influence citizens' lives is the type of controversy that might serve as grist for the judicial mills. If it is the sort of issue that judges can resolve with room for significant maneuvering, the impact of the case on public policy may be impressive. Conversely, if American jurists are forbidden to enter a certain decision-making realm or enter with only limited options, the policy impact will be nil. This general proposition has several aspects.

Jurisdiction

In Chapter 4 we outlined the jurisdiction of the three levels of the federal and state judiciaries. A knowledge of this topic is inherently important, but it takes on a second meaning in the context of this discussion—namely, that judges may not make policy in subject areas over which they have no legal authority. The controversy between the United States and its traditional European allies (such as France and Germany) over whether military action was necessary to topple former Iraqi leader Saddam Hussein was of great significance to the American people—and our national security may have been greatly affected by it. However, U.S. judges did not affect that controversy because they have no jurisdiction over foreign and defense policy disputes between the United States and other nations. Conversely, the courts will have considerable policy impact in matters concerning racial segregation and the prosecution of corporate executives accused of accounting irregularities, because such disputes fall squarely within the legal jurisdiction of the U.S. judiciary.

Although the courts do have some leeway in determining whether they have jurisdiction over a particular subject, for the most part jurisdictional boundaries are set forth in the U.S. and state constitutions and by acts of Congress and the state legislatures. In the same context, a legislative body's power to create and restrict the courts' jurisdiction can often greatly affect the direction of judicial decision making. For example, Congress, by virtue of the Voting Rights Act, has granted citizens the right to sue local governments in federal courts if those governments alter the boundaries of electoral districts in order to significantly dilute the voting strength of minorities. By giving courts jurisdiction in this area and telling judges, in effect, how to decide the cases (by establishing the decision-making goals), Congress has had a major impact on judicial policymaking. Likewise, the threat several years ago by some members of Congress to remove certain matters from federal court jurisdiction, such as the power to use busing as a tool for desegregation, has policy-making potential of equal magnitude.

Judicial Self-Restraint

The nature-of-the-case variable is also related to whether a controversy falls into one of those forbidden realms where the "good judge" should not set foot. One judge might like to rule on a particular matter that is crying for adjudication, but if the litigant has not yet exhausted all legal or administrative remedies, the jurist will have to stay his hand. Another judge might want to overturn a particular presidential action because she thinks it "smacks of fascism," but if no specific part of the Constitution has been violated, she will have to express her displeasure in the voting booth, not in the courtroom. The enormous emphasis that the judicial system places on respecting past precedents (the doctrine of stare decisis) further deters jurists from impulsive decision making. The various maxims of judicial self-restraint come from a variety of sources, including the Constitution, tradition, and acts of Congress and state legislatures; some have been imposed by the judges themselves. But whatever the source, they serve to channel the potential areas of judicial policymaking. Judges would have little success in attempting to adjudicate matters if doing so would soon bring reversal, censure, or organized opposition from those in a position to "correct" a judge who has strayed from the accepted pathway of judicial behavior.

Norm Enforcement versus Policymaking

Throughout this book we have discussed judicial behavior as including both norm enforcement and significant policymaking. Most cases fall into the former category, particularly for the lower judiciary. That is, in the majority of cases, judges routinely cite the applicable precedents, yield to the side with the weightiest evidence, and apply the statutes that clearly control the given situation. Discretion is at a minimum. In these routine cases, judges are not so much making policy as they are applying and enforcing existing norms and policy. In addition to norm enforcement, however, judges are presented with cases in which the room to maneuver—the potential to make policy—is much greater. Such opportunities exist at all levels of the judiciary, but appellate judges and justices probably have more options for significant policymaking than do their colleagues on the trial court bench. Since the late 1930s, Bill of Rights issues, not labor and economic questions, have provided judges with the greatest opportunities for significant policymaking.

In exploring this subject, we identified several situations (or case characteristics) that greatly enhance the judge's capacity to make policy rather than merely enforce existing policy. One such opportunity occurs when the legal evidence is contradictory or is equally strong on both sides. It is not uncommon for judges to preside over a case in which the facts and evidence for both sides are about equally compelling, or there are a fairly equal number of precedents that would sustain a finding for either party. Being pulled in several directions at once may not be an entirely comfortable position, but it does allow the jurists freer rein to strike out on their own than they could if prevailing facts and law impelled them toward one position.

Likewise, judicial policymaking can flower when jurists are asked to resolve new types of controversies for which statutory law and past judicial precedents are virtually absent. For example, when the federal courts were asked whether artificially created life forms could be patented, they could not avoid making policy. (Even the refusal to decide is a decision, as the existentialists have long argued.) Thus some cases by their very nature invite judicial policymaking, whereas others carry with them no such invitation. Judges differ in their perceptions of whether a given case offers an opportunity for creative, innovative decision making. To some extent such differences are a function of the judges themselves. But our contention here is that the nature of the controversy itself determines to a large extent whether a case calls for garden-variety norm enforcement or invites major judicial policymaking.

Summary

In considering whether and in what direction judges' decisions will significantly affect people's lives, we can say this: The nature of the case is a vital component in this line of inquiry. Judges can make policy only in those areas over which the U.S. and state constitutions and the legislative branches have granted them jurisdiction, and only in a manner consistent with the norms of judicial self-restraint. Also, if the controversies presented to the judges provide some room to maneuver—as do many current civil rights and liberties issues—more policymaking is likely to occur than it would if the cases were circumscribed by clearly controlling precedents and law.

The Values and Orientations of the Judges

A second set of variables to be considered in reaching an understanding of judicial policymaking and the direction it will take concerns the judges themselves. What are their background characteristics? How were they appointed (or elected) and by whom? How do they conceive of their judicial role? By learning something about the values and orientations of the men and women who are tapped for judicial service, people are better able to explain and predict what they will do on the bench. (Also recall from Chapters 8, 9, 10, and 11 that the attitudes and values of other actors in the judicial process—for example, police officers, prosecutors, and the solicitor general—affect the content and direction of their important duties.)

We have looked at judicial background characteristics in a variety of contexts in this book. Here we will examine several that have particular relevance vis-à-vis judicial policymaking and its direction.

Judges as a Socioeconomic Elite

In Chapters 5 and 6, we pointed out that America's jurists come from a narrow segment of the social and economic strata. To an overwhelming degree they are offspring of upper- and upper-middle-class parents and come from families with a tradition of political, and often judicial, service. They are the men and women to whom the U.S. system has been good, who fit in, and who have succeeded. The mavericks, malcontents, and ideological extremists are discreetly weeded out by the judicial recruitment process.

What does all this suggest about judicial policymaking and its direction? Given the striking similarity of the jurists and the backgrounds from which they come, their overall policymaking is generally going to be fairly modest, conventional, and ideologically moderate. Although many judges have a commitment to reform and will use their policy-making opportunities to achieve this end, it is to adjust and enhance a way of life that they basically believe in. Seldom bitten is the hand of the socioeconomic system that feeds them. Although an occasional maverick may slip in or develop within the judicial ranks, most judges are basically conservative, in that they hold dear the traditional institutions and rules of the game that have brought success to them and their families. America's elite has its fair share of both liberals and conservatives, but it does not have many who would use their discretionary opportunities to alter radically the basic social and political system.

Judges as Representatives of Their Political Parties

Although the nature of the judicial recruitment process gives virtually all U.S. judges a similar and fairly conventional cast, there are differences. The prior political party affiliation of jurists does alter the way they exercise their policy-making discretion when the circumstances of a case offer room to maneuver. Judges and justices who come from the ranks of the Democratic Party have been somewhat more liberal than their colleagues from Republican ranks. This has meant, for one thing, that Democrats on the bench are more likely to favor government regulation of the economy—particularly when such regulation appears to benefit the underdog or the worker in disputes with management. In criminal justice matters, Democratic jurists are more disposed toward the motions made by defendants. Finally, in questions concerning civil rights and liberties, the Democrat on the bench tends to establish policies that favor a broadening position.

In the same context, we stress the important policy link between the partisan choice made by voters in a presidential election, the judges whom the chief executive appoints, and the subsequent policy decisions of these jurists. When voters make a policy choice in electing a conservative or a liberal to the presidency, they have a discernible impact upon the judiciary as well. We have noted that this phenomenon occurs not only in the United States but also in many other nations, including Canada, Germany, and Japan. Despite the many participants in the judicial selection process and the variety of forces that would thwart policy-oriented presidents (and governors) from getting "their kind of people" on the bench, it is still fair to say that, to an impressive degree, chief executives tend to get the type of men and women they want in the judiciary.

In a speech made just prior to the 1984 presidential election, conservative Supreme Court justice William H. Rehnquist discussed this phenomenon with unusual candor. Although he was speaking primarily about the Supreme Court, his remarks pertain to the entire U.S. judiciary. There is "no reason in the world," said Rehnquist, why President Ronald Reagan should not attempt to "pack" the federal courts. The institution has been constructed in such a way that the public will, in the person of the president, have something to say about the membership of the Court and thereby indirectly about its decisions. Thus, Rehnquist felt, presidents may seek to appoint people who are sympathetic to their political and philosophical principles. After calling new judicial appointments "indirect infusions of the popular will," Rehnquist added that it "should come as no surprise" that presidents attempt to pack the courts with people of similar policy values, but "like murder suspects in a detective novel, they must have motive and opportunity."[1]

Judges as Manifestations of Localism

Another aspect of the values and orientations of judges has an impact on their policy-making process: the attributes and mores they carry with them from the region where they grew up or hold court. We have documented a wide variety of geographic variations in the way both trial and appellate jurists view the world and react to its demands. For example, we noted that on many policy issues northern jurists have been more liberal than their colleagues in the South. We also noted that regional variations in judicial decision making are not unique to the United States. For example, conscientious objector cases in Norway were decided differently depending on the region of the country in which the case was heard (see Chapter 12).

Not only does judicial policymaking vary from one region to another, but studies reveal that each of the circuits tends to be unique in the way its appellate and trial court judges administer the law and make decisions. The presence of significant state-by-state differences in the behavior of U.S. trial judges is further evidence that judges bring to the bench certain local values and orientations that subsequently affect their policy-making patterns.

Judges' Conceptions of Their Role

We noted three basic ways in which judges conceive of their role vis-à-vis the policy-making process. At one end of the spectrum are the lawmakers, who take a broad view of the judicial role. These jurists, often referred to as activists or innovators, contend that they can and sometimes must make significant public policy when rendering many of their decisions. At the other end of the spectrum are the law interpreters, who take a narrow view of the judicial function. Sometimes called strict constructionists, they believe that norm enforcement is the only proper role of the judge. In between are the pragmatists, or realists, who contend that judging is primarily a matter of enforcing norms, but that on occasion they can and must formulate new judicial policy.

Understanding the conception of the role that a judge brings to the bench (or develops on the bench) will not reveal much about the substantive direction of his or her policymaking. It is possible to be an activist either as a conservative or as a liberal. One can go out on a judicial limb and give the benefit of the doubt to the economic giant or to the underdog, to the criminal defendant claiming police brutality, or to the police officer urging renewed emphasis on law and order. But a knowledge of the way judges conceive of their role will provide a good indication of whether they are more inclined to defer to the norms and policies set by others or to strike out occasionally and make policy on their own.

Summary

In attempting to learn about judicial policymaking and its substantive direction, we have set forth a second factor that helps channel our thinking—the values and orientations that the judges bring with them to the bench. Four factors are particularly relevant: (1) America's judges come from the establishment's elite, which serves to discourage radical policymaking; (2) judges' policymaking is reflective of their partisan orientations and of the executive who nominated them; (3) policy decisions manifest the local values and attitudes that judges possess when they first put on the black robe; and (4) judges will engage in more policymaking if they bring to the bench a belief that it is right and proper for judges to act in this manner.

The Nature of the Judicial Decision-Making Process

Knowing how judges think and reason, how they are influenced in their decision making, provides a good clue about judicial policymaking. Although this factor is inexorably intertwined with the first two outlined here, it is distinct enough to warrant a separate discussion. In the section about the legal subculture in Chapter 12, we examined the nature of the legal reasoning process that is at the heart of the system of jurisprudence in America. We noted that this is essentially a three-step process described by the doctrine of stare decisis, as follows: (1) similarity is seen between cases; (2) the rule of law inherent in the first case is announced; and (3) the rule of law is made applicable to the second case. Adherence to past precedents is also part and parcel of the legal reasoning process. Skillfully shaping and crafting the wisdom of the past, as found in previous court rulings, and applying it to contemporary problems are what this time-honored process is all about.

Decision making by collegial courts has some dimensions not inherent in the behavior of trial judges sitting alone. In Chapter 13 we examined several approaches used by judicial scholars to get a theoretical handle on the way appellate court judges and justices think and act. One of these approaches is small-group dynamics, which views the output of the appellate judiciary as being strongly influenced by three general phenomena: persuasion on the merits, bargaining, and the threat of sanctions.

Persuasion lies at the heart of small-group dynamics. It means that judges, because of their training and values, are receptive to arguments based on sound legal reasoning, often seasoned with relevant legal precedents. Both hard and anecdotal evidence indicates that judicial policies are influenced in the refining furnace of the judicial conference room.

Bargaining, too, molds the content and direction of judicial policy outputs. The compromises made among jurists—during the decision-making conference and while an opinion is being drafted—to satisfy the majority judges are almost always the product of bargaining. It is not that judges say to one another: "If you vote for my favorite judicial policy position, I'll vote for yours." Instead, a justice might phrase a bargaining offer—say, in a case dealing with the right of students to appeal to the federal court adverse disciplinary rulings from a state university—more like this: "I don't agree with your opinion as it now stands permitting students to appeal all adverse disciplinary decisions to the local federal district court. That's just too liberal for me, and I don't approve of interfering in university affairs to that degree. However, I could go along with a majority opinion that permitted appeals in really serious disciplinary matters that might result in the permanent suspension of a student." The first justice must then decide how badly the colleague's vote is needed—badly enough to water down the opinion to include only cases dealing with permanent suspension instead of all cases, as in the original opinion? This is how judicial policies are generated through bargaining.

The sanctions previously discussed include a variety of items in the genteel arsenal of judicial weaponry. A judge's threat to take a vote away from the majority and to dissent may cause the majority judges to alter the content of a policy decision. A judge's willingness to write a strong, biting dissent is another sanction that occasionally causes a unity-conscious majority to consider policy changes in an opinion. The threat to "go public" is a third tactic used by judges in collegial courts to alter the policy course of other jurists. Public exposure of an objectionable internal court practice or stance is probably the least pleasant of the sanctions. Finally, we noted that chief justices of the U.S. and state supreme courts and their counterparts at the appellate and trial court levels all have singular opportunities to guide and shape the policy decisions of the courts. The status and options that are part of their unique leadership positions offer an opportunity to craft court policy if they have the desire and innate ability to make the most of it.

In addition to small-group dynamics, we looked at an approach to appellate court decision making known as attitude theory. This school of thought views judges as possessing a stable set of attitudes that guide their policy choices. Such attitudes exist on issues involving civil rights and liberties, social matters (such as voting and ethnic status), and economic questions dealing with the equal distribution of wealth. Justices with similar attitudes on these matters tend to vote on cases in a similar manner and thus form voting blocs. Research has impressively demonstrated that members of the appellate judiciary do decide cases in accordance with consistent underlying values and that voting blocs do behave according to predictable patterns. Attitude theory has been used successfully to explain and predict the voting patterns of appellate court jurists in many other nations, such as Australia, Canada, India, Japan, and the Philippines.

An approach that has been gaining many new adherents in recent years is rational choice theory. This model does not reject the assumptions of attitude theory, but it contends that the attitudinal model is simplistic and shortsighted. Rational choice theorists argue that goal-directed justices operate in what they call strategic or interdependent decision-making contexts. The justices understand that the outcome of their policy goals depends on the values of other decision makers, such as Congress, the president, and other justices on the Court. When making decisions, the justices must consider not only how they want the case to be decided but also how such an outcome might be affected by the decisions of these other actors. Rational choice theorists have been able to marshal some impressive data to sustain their theoretical contentions.

What does this third general factor—the nature of the judicial decision-making process—say about judicial policymaking and its substantive direction? We offer two observations. First, most policymaking by judges is likely to be slow and incremental. This is exactly what one would expect from a reasoning process that relies so heavily on respecting precedents and places such emphasis on stability and continuity. The decision-making process of American judges does not lend itself to radical and abrupt departures from precedents and past behavior. Yet change does occur and new policies are made. But legal history suggests that American jurists have often "reformed to preserve," and that is a principle often associated with conservatism.

Second, an understanding of the judicial thought process and of the small-group dynamics of collegial courts does not in itself reveal anything about the substantive direction of a court's policymaking. However, knowing which judges and justices are masters at persuasion, bargaining, and the use of sanctions does provide some insight into explaining and predicting the content of judicial policy decisions. If, on a given court, the conservatives have developed a mastery of these tactics, the bettor would do well to wager a few dollars on more conservative judicial decisions.

The Impact of Extraneous Influences

The making and implementation of judicial policy decisions undoubtedly are influenced by a variety of actors and forces outside the courtroom. It is not just judges and law clerks with leather-bound casebooks and arguments by silver-tongued lawyers that affect the shaping and carrying out of judicial decisions. Into the calculus must also go such unwieldy variables as the values and ability of the chief executive, the will of Congress or the legislature, the temper of public opinion, the strength and ideological orientation of key interest groups, and the attitudes and goodwill of those called on to implement judicial decisions in the real world.

The chief executive's input into the making and implementation of key judicial decisions is considerable. As the policy choice of the citizenry in the past election, the chief executive has the opportunity to fill the courts with men and women who share the basic political and judicial philosophies of the administration. Once on the court, judges may be encouraged or discouraged in their policymaking by the words and deeds emanating from the White House or the governor's mansion. For instance, the willingness of Presidents Dwight D. Eisenhower and John F. Kennedy to use federal troops to help enforce judicial integration orders must have encouraged subsequent policy decisions regarding presidents' use of armed force to achieve this goal. Conversely, President George H. W. Bush's vocal opposition to the use of racial or gender quotas in employers' hiring practices or in the awarding of government contracts may have caused many federal judges to think at least twice before ordering or condoning the use of such quotas. The overall role of the chief executive in implementing judicial policy decisions was examined in Chapter 14.

Congress has an impact on the creation and nurturing of judicial policy decisions, just as the legislature does at the state level. In its power to establish most of the original and appellate jurisdiction of the federal judiciary, Congress has the capacity to determine the subject matter arenas where judicial policy battles are fought. In its capacity to establish the number of courts and determine the financial support they will have, Congress can show its approval or displeasure regarding the third branch of government. By accepting or rejecting presidential nominees to the courts, the Senate helps to determine who the judicial decision makers will be and hence their value orientations. Finally, the implementation of many key judicial policy decisions is dependent on legislation that Congress must pass to make the ruling a meaningful reality for those affected by it. Had Congress not passed several key bills to implement the courts' desegregation orders (discussed in Chapter 14), integration of the public schools would be little more than a nice idea for those whom the rulings were intended to benefit.

Public opinion also has a role to play in this policy-making process—not an outrageous prospect for a nation that calls itself a democracy. In rendering key policy decisions, judges can hardly be oblivious to the mood and values of the citizenry of which they themselves are a part. In many policy areas (such as obscenity, desegregation, and legislative apportionment), the Supreme Court has ordered judges to take the local political and social climate into consideration when tendering their rulings. The support or opposition of the public is often a key variable in determining whether a judge's orders are carried out in the spirit as well as the letter of the law.

Interest-group activity is another thread in the tapestry of judicial policymaking. Such organizations often provide the president (or a state governor) with the names of individuals whom they support for judicial office, and they lobby against those whose judicial values they consider suspect. They often provide the vehicle for key judicial decisions by instigating legislation, sponsoring test cases, and giving legal and financial aid to those litigants whose cases they favor. They can thwart implementation of judicial decisions or help carry them out more effectively (see Chapter 14).

The final group of extraneous forces consists of those individuals and organizations that are expected to implement the judicial policy decision on a daily basis out on the street: the police officer who is asked to be sure that the accused understand their legal rights; the physician who must certify that a requested abortion is truly in the interest of a pregnant woman's mental health; the personnel officer at a state institution who could readily find some technicality for refusing to hire a minority applicant; or the censor on the town's movie review board who is told that nudity and obscenity are not synonymous but who does not want to believe it. The values, motivations, and actions of such individuals must be considered to fully understand the judicial policy-making process. Their good-faith support of a judicial policy decision is vital to making it work; their indifference or opposition may cause the judge's ruling to die aborning.

Our intention in this chapter is to get a grip on the slippery handle of policymaking by American judges. Although many more questions have been raised than answered, perhaps this discussion has provided a little better understanding of where to search for some of the answers. To learn the conditions that allow for bold policymaking, and to predict the direction that policymaking will take, attention must be focused on the nature of the case or controversy that can properly be brought into court; on the values and orientations of the jurists who preside over these courts; on the precise nature of the decision-making process of American judges; and, finally, on a variety of extraneous actors and forces whose values and effects filter into the American judicial process from beginning to end.

NOTES

1. "Rehnquist Says It's OK for a President to Pack High Court," *Houston Chronicle,* October 19, 1984, A3.

Glossary

Activism (judicial). The willingness of a judge to inject into a case his or her own personal values about what is good and bad public policy.

Actus reus. The material element of the crime, which may be the commission of a forbidden action (for example, robbery) or the failure to perform a required action (for example, to stop and render aid to a motor vehicle accident victim).

Adversarial process. The process used in American courtrooms where the trial is seen as a battle between two opposing sides, and the role of the judge is to act as a sort of passive referee. See also *inquisitorial method.*

Advisory opinions. Rendering a decision on an abstract or hypothetical question (something that American courts are not supposed to do).

Alternative dispute resolution (ADR). Methods of resolving disputes (often with the help of neutral third parties) without a trial. Mediation and arbitration are two well-known ADR techniques.

Amicus curiae. ("Friend of the court.") A person (or group), not a party to a case, who submits views (usually in the form of written briefs) about how the case should be decided.

Answer. The formal written statement by a defendant responding to a civil complaint and setting forth the grounds for his or her defense.

Appellate jurisdiction. The authority of a higher court to review the decision of a lower court.

Arraignment. The process in which the defendant is brought before the judge in the court where he or she is to be tried to respond to the grand jury indictment or the prosecutor's bill of information.

Attitude theory. The theory of appellate judge behavior that holds that once the researcher learns the judges' basic set of attitudes, he or she can explain and predict how those judges will vote in the cases that come before them.

Bail. A sum of money put up with the court by the defendant to ensure that he or she will appear at the time of trial.

Bench trial. Trial without a jury in which the judge decides which party prevails.

Bill of attainder. A law, forbidden by the U.S. Constitution, that makes conduct illegal for one person (or class of persons) but not for the population in general.

Bill of information. A statement of the charges against the accused prepared by the prosecutor, which, if approved by a judge, will require the accused to stand trial for the alleged crimes. This is used in states that do not employ a grand jury.

Blue slip. The device that senators use to invoke the practice of senatorial courtesy when they are objecting to a president's nomination to a district judgeship.

Certification. The procedure by which one of the U.S. appeals courts asks the U.S. Supreme Court for instructions or clarification about a particular legal matter. Either the justices may choose to honor this request or not, or they may request that the entire record of the case be sent to the Supreme Court for review and final judgment.

Civil law. The law that pertains to the relationship between one private citizen and another, and between a private citizen and a corporation, or between one corporation and another.

Class action. A suit brought by persons having similar grievances against a common entity; for example, a group of smokers with lung cancer suing a tobacco company.

Collegial courts. Courts having more than one judge, which are almost always appellate courts.

Common law. A system of law inherited from England based on legal precedents or tradition instead of statutory law or systematic legal codes.

Complaint. A written statement filed by the plaintiff that initiates a civil case. It states the wrongs allegedly committed by the defendant and requests relief from the court.

Concurrent jurisdiction. A situation in which two courts have a legal right to hear the same case. For example, both the U.S. Supreme Court and U.S. trial courts have concurrent jurisdiction in certain cases brought by or against ambassadors or counsels.

Concurring opinion. An opinion by a member of a court that agrees with the result reached in the case but offers its own rationale for the decision.

Conservative. For judges this means support for the prosecution in criminal cases, support for the government in its attempts to restrict freedom of expression, and support for the individual (or corporation) that is being regulated by the government

Corpus juris. The entire body of law for a particular legal entity.

Court of appeals. A court that is higher than an ordinary trial court and has the function of reviewing or correcting the decisions of trial judges.

Courtroom work group. The regular participants in the day-to-day activities of a particular courtroom. The most visible members of this group are judges, prosecutors, and defense attorneys.

Crime. An offense against the state punishable by fine, imprisonment, or death.

Criminal law. The law that pertains to offenses against the state itself, actions that may be directed against a person but that are deemed to be offensive to society as a whole—for example, armed robbery or rape.

Cross-examination. During a trial, the questions posed to a witness who has been called to the stand by the opposing attorney.

Cue theory. The theory that Supreme Court justices do not have the time to carefully review all cases that are appealed to them, so they develop short-hand methods of seeking out easy-to-find cues to help them determine whether they want to review a particular case.

Damages. Money paid by defendants to successful plaintiffs in civil cases to compensate the plaintiffs for their injuries. Compensatory damages are designed to cover the plaintiff's actual loss; punitive damages are designed to punish the defendant.

Declaratory judgment. When a court outlines the rights of the parties under a statute, a will, or a contract.

Defendant. In a civil case, the person or organization against whom the plaintiff brings suit; in a criminal case, the person accused of the crime.

Deposition. An oral statement made before an officer authorized by law to administer oaths. Such statements are often taken to examine potential witnesses in the discovery process.

Discovery. The process by which lawyers learn about their opponent's case in preparation for trial. Typical tools of discovery include depositions, interrogatories, and requests for documents.

Dissenting opinion. An opinion by a member of a court that disagrees with the result reached in the case by the court.

Diversity of citizenship suit. A civil legal proceeding brought by a citizen of one state against a citizen of another state.

En banc. ("In the bench" or "as a full bench.") Court sessions with the entire membership of a court participating, not just a smaller panel of judges.

Equity. That realm of the law in which the judge is able to issue a remedy that will either prevent or cure the wrong that is about to happen; for example, an injunction against an illegal strike by a union.

Ex post facto law. Forbidden by the U.S. Constitution, this law declares conduct to be illegal after the conduct takes place.

Federal question. If a court case centers around the interpretation of a federal law, the U.S. Constitution, or a treaty, then it contains a federal question and the case may be heard by a U.S. court.

Felony. Any offense for which the penalty may be death or imprisonment in a penitentiary.

Fluidity. The degree that appellate court judges change their opinions between the time a conference vote is taken and the vote is announced in open court.

Grand jury. A body of sixteen to twenty-three citizens who listen to evidence of criminal allegations, which is presented by the prosecutors, and determine whether probable cause exists to believe an individual committed an offense. See also *indictment*.

Habeas corpus. A writ (court order) that is usually used to bring a prisoner before the court to determine the legality of his or her imprisonment.

Impeachment. The only way in which a federal judge may be removed from office. The House of Representatives brings the charge(s), and the Senate, following trial, convicts by a two-thirds vote of the membership.

Indictment. The decision of a grand jury to order a defendant to stand trial because the jury believes that probable cause exists to warrant a trial.

Inquisitorial method. The procedure used in most European and Latin American courtrooms in which the judge and jury take an active role in the trial and the attorneys act only to aid and supplement the judicial inquiry. See also *adversarial process.*

Interrogatories. Written questions sent by one party in a lawsuit to an opposing party as part of pretrial discovery in civil cases. The party receiving the interrogatories is required to answer them in writing under oath.

Judgment. The official decision of a court finally resolving the dispute between the parties to the lawsuit.

Judicial realist. One who believes that judges, like other human beings, are influenced by the values and attitudes learned in childhood.

Judicial review. The power of the judicial branch to declare acts of the executive and legislative branches unconstitutional.

Jurisdiction. The authority of a court to hear and decide legal disputes and to enforce its rulings.

Justiciability. Whether a judge ought to hear or refrain from hearing certain types of cases. It differs from jurisdiction, which pertains to the technical right of a judge to hear a case. For example, lawsuits dealing with political questions are considered nonjusticiable.

Law. A social norm that is sanctioned in threat or in fact by the application of physical force. The party that exercises such physical force is recognized by society as legitimately having this kind of authority, such as a police officer.

Liberal. For judges this means support for the defendant in criminal cases, support for a broadening position for freedom of expression, and support for the government in its attempt to economically regulate individuals and corporations.

Magistrate. A lower level judicial official to whom the accused is brought after the arrest. A magistrate has the obligation of informing the accused of the charges against him or her and of his or her legal rights.

Mandatory sentencing laws. Statutes that require automatic jail time for a convicted criminal, usually for a minimum period of time. This is often for violent crimes in which a gun was used and for habitual offenders.

Mens rea. The mental element of the crime; that is, what was intended by the perpetrator of the crime. Usually the more intentional and willful the mental state, the more serious the crime.

Merit selection. A method of selecting state judges that requires the governor to make the appointment from a short list of names submitted by a special commission established for that purpose. After serving for a short period of time, the judge must run in a retention election. Voters thus determine whether the judge should be retained for a full term.

Misdemeanor. A petty crime. Punishment usually is confinement in a city or county jail for less than a year.

Moot. Describes a case when the basic facts or the status of the parties have significantly changed in the interim between when the suit was filed and when it comes before the judge.

Nolle prosequi. ("I refuse to prosecute.") A motion filed by a prosecutor before a judge in which the prosecutor sets forth specific and justifiable reasons that he or she does not wish to press charges against a criminal defendant.

Nolo contendere. ("No contest.") A plea by a criminal defendant in which he or she does not deny the facts of the case but claims that he or she has not committed any crime, or it may mean that the defendant does not understand the charges.

Opinion of the court. A judge's written explanation of the court's decision. Because the case may be heard by a panel of judges in an appellate court, the opinion can take two forms. If all the judges completely agree with the result, one judge will write the opinion for all. If all the judges do not agree, the formal decision will be based on the view of the majority, and one member of the majority will write the decision.

Oral argument. An opportunity for lawyers to summarize their position before the court and to answer the judges' questions.

Ordinance-making power. The power of state governors to fill in the details of legislation passed by state legislatures.

Original jurisdiction. The court that by law must be the first to hear a particular type of case. For example, in suits with at least $75,000 at stake between citizens from different states, the federal district courts are the courts of original jurisdiction.

Overcharging. The process whereby a prosecutor charges a criminal defendant with crimes more serious than the facts warrant to obtain a more favorable plea bargain from the defendant's attorney.

Per curiam. ("By the court.") An unsigned opinion of the court, often brief.

Peremptory challenge. An objection that an attorney might have to a prospective juror. The juror may be eliminated from the array without the attorney having to give a public reason for the objection. The number of such challenges is limited by law.

Petit jury (or trial jury). A group of citizens who hear the evidence presented by both sides at trial and determine the facts in dispute.

Plaintiff. The person who files the complaint in a civil lawsuit.

Plea bargain. A bargain or deal that has been struck between the prosecutor and the defendant's attorney whereby some form of leniency is promised in exchange for a guilty plea.

Political question. When the courts refuse to rule because they believe that under the U.S. Constitution the founders meant that the matter at hand should be dealt with by Congress or the president, the courts are refusing to rule on a political question.

Private law. This deals with the rights and obligations that private individuals and institutions have when they relate to one another.

Probation. Punishment for a crime that allows the offender to remain in the community and out of jail so long as he or she follows court-ordered guidelines about his or her behavior.

Pro bono publico. ("For the public good.") Usually refers to legal representation undertaken without fee for some charitable or public purpose.

Public law. The relationships that individuals have with the state as a sovereign entity; for example, the tax code, criminal laws, and Social Security legislation.

Rational choice theory. The theory that appellate judges' votes may be explained by knowing more than just their basic attitudes. Judges realize that the fate of their policy goals often depends on the values of other decision makers, such as their colleagues on the bench, the president, and members of Congress.

Recess appointment. An appointment made by the president when Congress is in recess. Persons appointed in this manner may hold office only until Congress reconvenes.

Reversible error. An error committed at the trial court level that is so serious that it requires the appellate court to reverse the decision of the trial judge.

Role (judicial). How judges view themselves as jurists and the degree to which they believe in judicial activism or judicial self-restraint.

Rule of eighty. When the sum of a judge's age and number of years on the bench is eighty, Congress permits the individual to retire with full pay and benefits.

Rule of four. On the Supreme Court at least four justices must agree to take a case before the Court as a whole will consider it.

Self-restraint (judicial). The reluctance of a judge to inject into a case his or her own personal ideas of what is good or bad public policy.

Senatorial courtesy. Under this practice senators of the president's political party who object to a candidate that the president wishes to appoint to a district judgeship in their home state have a virtual veto over the nomination.

Sequestration (of jury). In very important or notorious cases the jury may be kept away from the public eye by the judge, and this usually means that the jury is housed and fed as a group at taxpayers' expense.

Small-group analysis. The theory that appellate court behavior may be explained in part from what social scientists know generally about the decision-making process of small groups of any kind.

Social leadership (on appellate courts). A judge performing this role attends to the emotional needs of his or her associates by affirming their values as individuals and as court members, especially when their views are rejected by the majority.

Socialization (judicial). The process by which a new judge is formally and informally trained to perform the specific tasks of the judgeship.

Standing. The status of someone who wishes to bring a lawsuit. To have standing the person must have suffered (or be immediately about to suffer) a direct and significant injury.

Stare decisis, the doctrine of. ("Stand by what has been decided.") In effect, the tradition of honoring and following previous decisions of the courts and established points of law.

Statutory law. The type of law enacted by a legislative body, such as Congress, a state legislature, or a city council.

Task leadership (on appellate courts). A judge performing this role is the intellectual force behind the conference deliberations, focusing on the actual decision and trying to keep the court consistent with itself.

Three-judge district courts. With some types of important cases Congress has mandated that the case cannot be heard by a U.S. trial judge acting alone but has to be decided by a panel of three judges, one of whom must be an appeals court judge.

Three-judge panels (of appellate courts). Most decisions of the U.S. courts of appeals are not made by the entire court sitting together but by three judges, often selected at random, to hear any given case.

Tort. A civil wrong or breach of duty to another person.

Trial de novo. A new trial in which the entire case is retried as if no prior trial had occurred.

Venue. The geographical location in which a case is tried.

Voir dire. The procedure by which opposing attorneys question potential jurors to determine whether the jurors might be prejudicial to their individual cases.

Warrant. Issued after a complaint, filed by one person against another, has been presented and reviewed by a magistrate who has found probable cause for the arrest.

Writ of certiorari. An order issued by the U.S. Supreme Court directing the lower court to transfer records for a case that it will hear on appeal.

Writ of mandamus. A court order compelling a public official to perform his or her duty.

Annotated Constitution

THE CONSTITUTION OF THE UNITED STATES OF AMERICA

[Preamble]

The preamble does not confer any governmental power, but the Supreme Court has referred to it as a source of legal direction. See McCulloch v. Maryland, 17 U.S. 316 (1819); Martin v. Hunter's Lessee, 14 U.S. 304 (1816).

We, the People of the United States, in Order to form a more perfect Union, establish Justice, insure domestic Tranquillity, provide for the common defence, promote the general Welfare, and secure the Blessings of Liberty to ourselves and our Posterity, do ordain and establish this Constitution for the United States of America.

ARTICLE I

Section 1

The recognition of "legislative powers" implies that there are separate and distinct governmental powers: legislative, executive, and judicial.

All legislative Powers herein granted shall be vested in a Congress of the United States, which shall consist of a Senate and House of Representatives.

Section 2

The Constitution sets the qualifications for federal elective office. The Supreme Court has ruled that states may not impose their own restrictions, such as term limits. See U.S. Term Limits, Inc. v. Thornton, 514 U.S. 779 (1995).

The House of Representatives shall be composed of Members chosen every second Year by the People of the several States, and the Electors in each State shall have the Qualifications requisite for Electors of the most numerous Branch of the State Legislature.

No Person shall be a Representative who shall not have attained to the age of twenty five Years, and been seven Years a Citizen of the United States, and who shall not, when elected, be an Inhabitant of that State in which he shall be chosen.

States must apportion congressional districts in such a manner that each district contains an approximately equal number of residents in order to ensure that each person's vote carries equal political weight—"one person, one vote." See Reynolds v. Sims, *377 U.S. 533 (1964).*

Representatives and direct Taxes shall be apportioned among the several States which may be included within this Union, according to their respective Numbers, which shall be determined by adding to the whole Number of free Persons, including those bound to Service for a Term of Years, and excluding Indians not taxed, three fifths of all other Persons. The actual Enumeration shall be made within three Years after the first Meeting of the Congress of the United States, and within every subsequent Term of ten Years, in such Manner as they shall by Law direct. The Number of Representatives shall not exceed one for every thirty Thousand, but each State shall have at Least one Representative; and until such enumeration shall be made, the State of New Hampshire shall be entitled to chuse three, Massachusetts eight, Rhode-Island and Providence Plantations one, Connecticut five, New-York six, New Jersey four, Pennsylvania eight, Delaware one, Maryland six, Virginia ten, North Carolina five, South Carolina five, and Georgia three.

When vacancies happen in the Representation from any State, the Executive Authority thereof shall issue Writs of Election to fill such Vacancies.

Only thirteen judges and two presidents have been impeached in U.S. history. Neither president was convicted, but seven of the thirteen jurists were removed.

The House of Representatives shall chuse their Speaker and other Officers; and shall have the sole Power of Impeachment.

The Seventeenth Amendment supersedes this provision and allows for the popular election of senators.

Section 3

The Senate of the United States shall be composed of two Senators from each State, chosen by the Legislature thereof, for six Years; and each Senator shall have one Vote.

Immediately after they shall be assembled in Consequence of the first Election, they shall be divided as equally as may be into three Classes. The Seats of the Senators of the first Class shall be vacated at the Expiration of the second Year, of the second Class at the Expiration of the fourth Year, and of the third Class at the Expiration of the sixth Year, so that one third may be chosen every second Year; and if Vacancies happen by Resignation, or otherwise, during the Recess of the Legislature of any State, the Executive thereof may make temporary Appointments until the next Meeting of the Legislature, which shall then fill such Vacancies.

No Person shall be a Senator who shall not have attained to the Age of thirty Years, and been nine Years a Citizen of the United States, and who shall not, when elected, be an Inhabitant of that State for which he shall be chosen.

Recent discussions have proposed using the vice president's power as the presiding officer of the Senate to change Senate rules in order to achieve confirmation of some controversial judicial nominees. The strategy is to have the vice president declare that the cloture rule—which requires that sixty senators must agree to end a filibuster—does not apply to judicial nominations. The elimination of the rule would pave the way for a simple majority to end a filibuster and for a vote to be held on the

The Vice President of the United States shall be President of the Senate but shall have no Vote, unless they be equally divided.

disputed judicial candidates. However, such a move would constitute an aggressive power play by the president at the expense of senatorial powers and institutional comity. See Stuart Taylor Jr., "The Judicial Selection Wars," Atlantic Monthly, May 27, 2003, available online at http://www.theatlantic.com/politics/nj/taylor2003-05-27.htm

The Senate shall chuse their other Officers, and also a President pro tempore, in the Absence of the Vice President, or when he shall exercise the Office of President of the United States.

The Senate shall have the sole Power to try all Impeachments. When sitting for that Purpose, they shall be on Oath or Affirmation. When the President of the United States is tried the Chief Justice shall preside: And no Person shall be convicted without the Concurrence of two thirds of the Members present.

The Senate may establish its own rules and procedures for handling impeachment cases. See Nixon v. U.S., 506 U.S. 224 (1993).

Judgment in Cases of Impeachment shall not extend further than to removal from Office, and disqualification to hold and enjoy any Office of honor, Trust or Profit under the United States: but the Party convicted shall nevertheless be liable and subject to Indictment, Trial, Judgment and Punishment, according to Law.

The Constitution vests in Congress, not the courts, the power to determine the legitimacy of congressional elections—an inherently political question.

Section 4
The Times, Places and Manner of holding Elections for Senators and Representatives, shall be prescribed in each State by the Legislature thereof; but the Congress may at any time by Law make or alter such Regulations, except as to the Places of chusing Senators.

The Twentieth Amendment changed the date of congressional assembly to January 3 and set January 20 as the beginning and ending date of a presidential term.

The Congress shall assemble at least once in every Year, and such Meeting shall be on the first Monday in December, unless they shall by Law appoint a different Day.

Section 5

Each House shall be the Judge of the Elections, Returns and Qualifications of its own Members, and a Majority of each shall constitute a Quorum to do Business; but a smaller Number may adjourn from day to day, and may be authorized to compel the Attendance of absent Members, in such Manner, and under such Penalties as each House may provide.

Each House may determine the Rules of its Proceedings, punish its Members for disorderly Behaviour, and, with the Concurrence of two thirds, expel a Member.

The Congressional Record is the official journal of the proceedings of Congress. It is available online at http://www.gpoaccess. gov/crecord.

Each House shall keep a Journal of its Proceedings, and from time to time publish the same, excepting such Parts as may in their Judgment require Secrecy; and the Yeas and Nays of the Members of either House on any question shall, at the Desire of one fifth of those Present, be entered on the Journal.

Neither House, during the Session of Congress, shall, without the Consent of the other, adjourn for more than three days, nor to any other Place than that in which the two Houses shall be sitting.

By federal law, judicial salaries are linked to congressional salaries— federal judges receive

Section 6

The Senators and Representatives shall receive a Compensation for their Services, to be ascertained *pay increases only when members of Congress do.*

by Law, and paid out of the Treasury of the United States. They shall in all Cases, except Treason, Felony and Breach of the Peace, be privileged from Arrest during their Attendance at the Session of their respective Houses, and in going to and returning from the same; and for any Speech or Debate in either House, they shall not be questioned in any other Place.

This provision, which is one of many that separate governmental powers, prohibits members of Congress from simultaneously serving in the judicial branch.

No Senator or Representative shall, during the Time for which he was elected, be appointed to any civil Office under the Authority of the United States, which shall have been created, or the Emoluments whereof shall have been encreased during such time; and no Person holding any Office under the United States, shall be a Member of either House during his Continuance in Office.

Section 7

All Bills for raising Revenue shall originate in the House of Representatives; but the Senate may propose or concur with amendments as on other Bills.

Bills must be approved or rejected in their entirety. The line-item veto, which allows executives to veto specific provisions of a spending bill while leaving the remainder of the legislation intact, was ruled unconstitutional. See Clinton v. City of New York, 524 U.S. 417 (1998).

Every Bill which shall have passed the House of Representatives and the Senate, shall, before it become a law, be presented to the President of the United States: If he approve he shall sign it, but if not he shall return it, with his Objections to that House in which it shall have originated, who shall enter the Objections at large on their Journal, and proceed to reconsider it. If after such Reconsideration two thirds of that House shall agree to pass the Bill, it shall be sent, together with the Objections, to the other House, by which it shall likewise be reconsidered, and if approved by two thirds of that House, it shall become a Law. But in all such Cases the Votes of both Houses shall be determined by Yeas and Nays, and the Names of the Persons voting for and against the Bill shall be entered on the Journal of each House respectively. If any Bill shall not be returned by the President within ten Days (Sundays excepted) after it shall have been presented to him, the Same shall be a Law, in like Manner as if he had signed it, unless the Congress by their Adjournment prevent its Return, in which Case it shall not be a Law.

Every Order, Resolution, or Vote to which the Concurrence of the Senate and House of Representatives may be necessary (except on a question of Adjournment) shall be presented to the President of the United States; and before the Same shall take Effect, shall be approved by him, or being disapproved by him, shall be repassed by two thirds of the Senate and House of Representatives, according to the Rules and Limitations prescribed in the Case of a Bill.

Section 8

Courts have ruled that the federal power to tax is broad and that judges should generally defer to the legislative branch on the question of what constitutes proper taxation. See McCray v. U.S., 195 U.S. 27 (1904).

The Congress shall have Power To lay and collect Taxes, Duties, Imposts and Excises, to pay the Debts and provide for the common Defence and general Welfare of the United States; but all Duties, Imposts and Excises shall be uniform throughout the United States;

To borrow Money on the credit of the United States;

The ability to regulate interstate economic activity is a major source of congressional authority. The Commerce Clause has been at the center of a large number of important

To regulate Commerce with foreign Nations, and among the several States, and with the Indian Tribes;

Supreme Court cases, and courts have generally allowed Congress to exercise broad regulatory power (Gibbons v. Ogden, 22 U.S. 1 [1824]; U.S. v. Darby, 312 U.S. 100 [1941]), exercise federal police powers (Champion v. Ames, 188 U.S. 321 [1903]), even promote civil rights (Heart of Atlanta Motel v. U.S., 379 U.S. 241 [1964]). However, recent years have witnessed instances of the Court's reluctance to defer to Congress's use of the Commerce Clause. See U.S. v. Morrison, 529 U.S. 598 (2000); U.S. v. Lopez, 514 U.S. 549 (1995).

To establish an uniform Rule of Naturalization, and uniform Laws on the subject of Bankruptcies throughout the United States;

To coin Money, regulate the Value thereof, and of foreign Coin, and fix the Standard of Weights and Measures;

To provide for the Punishment of counterfeiting the Securities and current Coin of the United States;

To establish Post Offices and post Roads;

To promote the Progress of Science and useful Arts, by securing for limited Times to Authors and Inventors the exclusive Right to their respective Writings and Discoveries;

The Constitution leaves the structure of the lower federal courts up to Congress. This is an oft-overlooked power balance between the legislative and judicial branches.

To constitute Tribunals inferior to the supreme Court;

To define and punish Piracies and Felonies committed on the high Seas, and Offences against the Law of Nations;

To declare War, grant Letters of Marque and Reprisal, and make Rules concerning Captures on Land and Water;

To raise and support Armies, but no Appropriation of Money to that Use shall be for a longer Term than two Years;

To provide and maintain a Navy;

To make Rules for the Government and Regulation of the land and naval Forces;

To provide for calling forth the Militia to execute the Laws of the Union, suppress Insurrections and repeal Invasions;

To provide for organizing, arming, and disciplining, the Militia, and for governing such Part of them as may be employed in the Service of the United States, reserving to the States respectively, the Appointment of the Officers, and the Authority of training the Militia according to the discipline prescribed by Congress;

To exercise exclusive Legislation in all Cases whatsoever, over such District (not exceeding ten Miles square) as may, by Cession of Particular States, and the Acceptance of Congress, become the Seat of the Government of the United States, and to exercise like Authority over all Places purchased by the Consent of the Legislature of the State in which the Same shall be, for the Erection of Forts, Magazines,

A "letter of marque" is a document from a government that grants a private person the power to seize the subjects of a foreign state. A "letter of reprisal" provides for an act of retaliation against someone for injuries received.

Arsenals, dock-Yards and other needful Buildings;—And

The Necessary and Proper Clause—also known as the Elastic Clause—is the source of the "implied powers" doctrine. Implied powers expand Congress's authority beyond the enumerated powers listed in Art. I, Sec. 8, to include the goals and objectives associated with such powers. See McCulloch v. Maryland, 17 U.S. 316 (1819).

To make all Laws which shall be necessary and proper for carrying into Execution the foregoing Powers and all other Powers vested by this Constitution in the Government of the United States, or in any Department or Officer thereof.

Section 9

The Migration or Importation of such Persons as any of the States now existing shall think proper to admit, shall not be prohibited by the Congress prior to the Year one thousand eight hundred and eight, but a Tax or duty may be imposed on such Importation, not exceeding ten dollars for each Person.

Habeas corpus is the procedure by which a court inquires into the legality of a person's detention. Should the detention be found improper, the court may issue an order directing authorities to release the petitioner.

The Privilege of the Writ of Habeas Corpus shall not be suspended, unless when in Cases or Rebellion or Invasion the public Safety may require it.

There are three types of ex post facto laws: those "which punish as a crime an act previously committed, which was innocent when done; which make more burdensome the punishment for a crime, after its commission; or which deprive one charged with crime of any defense available according to law at the time when the act was committed." See Collins v. Youngblood, *497 U.S. 37 (1990).*

No Bill of Attainder or ex post facto Law shall be passed.

No Capitation, or other direct, Tax shall be laid, unless in Proportion to the Census of Enumeration herein before directed to be taken.

No Tax or Duty shall be laid on Articles exported from any State.

No Preference shall be given by any Regulation of Commerce or Revenue to the Ports of one State over those of another: nor shall Vessels bound to, or from, one State, be obliged to enter, clear or pay Duties in another.

No Money shall be drawn from the Treasury, but in Consequence of Appropriations made by Law; and a regular Statement and Account of the Receipts and Expenditures of all public Money shall be published from time to time.

No Title of Nobility shall be granted by the United States: And no Person holding any Office of Profit or Trust under them, shall, without the Consent of the Congress, accept of any present, Emolument, Office, or Title, of any kind whatever, from any King, Prince or foreign State.

Section 10

No State shall enter into any Treaty, Alliance, or Confederation; grant Letters of Marque and Reprisal; coin Money; emit Bills of Credit; make any Thing but gold and silver Coin a Tender in Payment of Debts; pass any Bill of Attainder, ex post facto Law, or Law impairing the Obligation of Contracts, or grant any Title of Nobility.

No State shall, without the Consent of the Congress, lay any Imposts or Duties on Imports or Exports, except what may be absolutely necessary for executing its inspection Laws: and the net Produce of all Duties and Imposts, laid by any State on Imports or Exports, shall be for the Use of the Treasury of the United States; and all such Laws shall be subject to the Revision and Controul of the Congress.

No State shall, without the Consent of Congress, lay any Duty of Tonnage, keep Troops, or Ships of War in time of Peace, enter into any Agreement or Compact with another State, or with a foreign Power, or engage in War, unless actually invaded, or in such imminent Danger as will not admit of delay.

ARTICLE II

Compare the language of Art. 1, Sec. 1 ("All legislative Powers herein granted...."), to Art. 2, Sec. 1 ("The executive Power shall be

Section 1

The executive Power shall be vested in a President of the United States of America. He shall hold his Office during the Term of four Years, and, together with the Vice President, chosen for the same Term, be elected, as follows:

vested...."). The Constitution is quite specific about legislative powers, but it is less clear about what constitutes executive power.

The presidential election methodology and term of office have been the most revisited issues in the Constitution. They are the subject of five amendments: the Twelfth (changes to the election of the president via the electoral college); the Twentieth (changes to the commencement of the terms of the president, vice president, and members of Congress); the Twenty-second (imposing a limit of two terms for a president); the Twenty-third (provision for presidential electors from the District of Columbia); and the Twenty-fifth (provisions for instances of presidential and vice-presidential vacancy of office and disability).

Each State shall appoint, in such Manner as the Legislature thereof may direct, a Number of Electors, equal to the whole Number of Senators and Representatives to which the State may be entitled in the Congress: but no Senator or Representative, or Person holding an Office of Trust or Profit under the United States, shall be appointed an Elector.

The Electors shall meet in their respective States, and vote by Ballot for two Persons, of whom one at least shall not be an Inhabitant of the same State with themselves. And they shall make a List of all the Persons voted for, and of the Number of Votes for each; which List they shall sign and certify, and transmit sealed to the Seat of the Government of the United States, directed to the President of the Senate. The President of the Senate shall, in the Presence of the Senate and House of Representatives, open all the Certificates, and the Votes shall then be counted. The Person having the greatest Number of Votes shall be the President, if such Number be a Majority of the whole Number of Electors appointed; and if there be more than one who have such Majority, and have an equal Number of Votes, then the House of Representatives shall immediately chuse by Ballot one of them for President; and if no Person have a Majority, then from the five highest on the List the said House shall in like Manner chuse the President. But in chusing the President, the Votes shall be taken by States, the Representatives from each State having one Vote; a quorum for this Purpose shall consist of a Member or Members from two thirds of the States, and a Majority of all the States shall be necessary to a Choice. In every Case, after the Choice of the President, the Person having the greatest Number of Votes of the Electors shall be the Vice President. But if there should remain two or more who have equal Votes, the Senate shall chuse from them by Ballot the Vice President.

The Congress may determine the Time of chusing the Electors, and the Day on which they shall give their Votes; which Day shall be the same throughout the United States.

No Person except a natural born Citizen, or a Citizen of the United States, at the time of the Adoption of this Constitution, shall be eligible to the Office of President; neither shall any person be eligible to that Office who shall not have attained to the Age of thirty five Years, and been fourteen Years a Resident within the United States.

In Case of the Removal of the President from Office, or of his Death, Resignation, or Inability to discharge the Powers and Duties of the said Office, the Same shall devolve on the Vice President, and the Congress may by Law provide for the Case of Removal, Death, Resignation or Inability, both of the President and Vice President, declaring what Officer shall then act as President, and such Officer shall act accordingly, until the Disability be removed, or a President shall be elected.

The current annual salary for the president is $400,000.

The President shall, at stated Times, receive for his Services, a Compensation, which shall neither be encreased nor diminished during the Period for which he shall have been elected, and he shall not receive within that Period any other Emolument from the United States, or any of them.

With regard to the presidential oath of office, the Constitution does not require the words "so help me God," which are customarily uttered after the mandated language. Recent tradition has the chief justice administering the oath of office, although the Constitution does not mandate this practice.

Before he enter on the Execution of his Office, he shall take the following Oath or Affirmation:—"I do solemnly swear (or affirm) that I will faithfully execute the Office of President of the United States, and will to the best of my Ability, preserve, protect and defend the Constitution of the United States."

Section 2

The President shall be Commander in Chief of the Army and Navy of the United States, and of the Militia of the several States, when called into the actual Service of the United States; he may require the Opinion, in writing, of the principal Officer in each of the executive Departments, upon any Subject relating to the Duties of their respective Offices, and he shall have Power to Grant Reprieves and Pardons for Offences against the United States, except in Cases of Impeachment.

The president has especially broad powers in the area of foreign affairs: "the President alone has the power to speak or listen as a representative of the nation." See U.S. v. Curtiss-Wright, 299 U.S. 304 (1936).

The president's authority to "hire" also includes

He shall have Power, by and with the Advice and Consent of the Senate, to make Treaties, provided two thirds of the Senators present concur; and he shall nominate, and by and with the Advice and Consent of the Senate, shall appoint Ambassadors, other public Ministers and Consuls, Judges of the supreme Court, and all other Officers of the United States, whose Appointments are not herein otherwise provided for, and which shall be established by Law: but the Congress may by Law vest the Appointment of such inferior Officers, as they think proper, in the President alone, in the Courts of Law, or in the Heads of Departments.

the power to "fire," except in instances where the Constitution or statute specifically limits the president's removal authority. See Myers v. U.S., 272 U.S. 52 (1926).

Presidents may appoint federal judges through the recess appointment process, but their commissions are not permanent unless they are approved by the Senate after it reconvenes.

The President shall have Power to fill up all Vacancies that may happen during the Recess of the Senate, by granting Commissions which shall expire at the End of their next Session.

The president is chief law enforcement officer, and "Congress [cannot] transfer from the President to the courts the Chief Executive's most important constitutional duty, to 'take Care that the Laws be faithfully executed.'" See Lujan v. Defenders of Wildlife, 504 U.S. 555 (1992).

Section 3

He shall from time to time give to the Congress Information on the State of the Union, and recommend to their Consideration such Measures as he shall judge necessary and expedient; he may, on extraordinary Occasions, convene both Houses, or either of them, and in Case of Disagreement between them, with Respect to the Time of Adjournment, he may adjourn them to such Time as he shall think proper; he shall receive Ambassadors and other public Ministers; he shall take Care that the Laws be faithfully executed, and shall Commission all the Officers of the United States.

Section 4

The President, Vice President and all Civil Officers of the United States, shall be removed from Office on Impeachment for and Conviction of, Treason, Bribery, or other high Crimes and Misdemeanors.

ARTICLE III

Section 1

The judicial Power of the United States, shall be vested in one supreme Court, and in such inferior Courts as the Congress may from time to time ordain and establish. The Judges, both of the supreme and inferior Courts, shall hold their Offices during good Behaviour, and shall, at stated Times, receive for their Services, a Compensation, which shall not be diminished during their Continuance in Office.

The Supreme Court is the only court specifically mentioned in the Constitution, which leaves the structure of the federal court system entirely up to Congress. "During good behavior" is understood to mean lifetime tenure, with removal only in cases of impeachment for improper professional conduct. The current annual salary for a U.S. district court judge is $154,700; appellate court jurists are paid $164,000; and Supreme Court justices earn $198,600.

Section 2

The judicial Power shall extend to all Cases, in Law and Equity, arising under this Constitution, the Laws of the United States, and Treaties made, or which shall be made, under their Authority;—to all Cases affecting Ambassadors, other public ministers and Consuls;—to all Cases of admiralty and maritime Jurisdiction;—to Controversies to which the United States shall be a Party;—to Controversies between two or more States;—between a State and Citizens of another State;—between Citizens of different States;—between Citizens of the same State claiming Lands under Grants of different States, and between a State, or the Citizens thereof, and foreign States, Citizens or Subjects.

Judicial power is "the right to determine actual controversies arising between diverse litigants, duly instituted in courts of proper jurisdiction." See Muskrat v. U.S., 219 U.S. 346 (1911). As an extension of their power to decide cases, courts have the authority to do such things as punish those in contempt of their authority (Michaelson v. U.S., 266 U.S. 42 [1924]); issue writs and orders (McIntire v.

Wood, *11 U.S. 504 [1813]*), (Ex parte Boll-man, *8 U.S. 75 [1807]*); and admit and disbar attorneys (Ex parte Garland, *71 U.S. 333 [1867]*).

The power of judicial review is not specifically enumerated in the Constitution, but it is implicit in the Supreme Court's appellate authority. See Marbury v. Madison, *5 U.S. 137 (1803).*

In all Cases affecting Ambassadors, other public Ministers and Consuls, and those in which a State shall be Party, the supreme Court shall have original Jurisdiction. In all the other Cases before mentioned, the supreme Court shall have appellate Jurisdiction, both as to Law and Fact, with such Exceptions, and under such Regulations as the Congress shall make.

The Constitution guarantees the right to a trial by jury in two places: here and in the Sixth Amendment.

The Trial of all Crimes, except in Cases of Impeachment, shall be by Jury; and such Trial shall be held in the State where the said Crimes shall have been committed; but when not committed within any State, the Trial shall be at such Place or Places as the Congress may by Law have directed.

The Founders were fearful that the charge of treason might be used to punish political enemies, as this had been done in England. Therefore, they restricted the definition of the charge and limited the means by which someone might be convicted of treason to instances involving multiple witnesses or outright confession.

Section 3

Treason against the United States, shall consist only in levying War against them, or in adhering to their Enemies, giving them Aid and Comfort. No Person shall be convicted of Treason unless on the Testimony of two Witnesses to the same overt Act, or on Confession in open Court.

The Congress shall have Power to declare the Punishment of Treason, but no Attainder of Treason shall work Corruption of Blood, or Forfeiture except during the Life of the Person attainted.

This section of the Constitution generally deals with the principle of "comity." This consists of a body of rules and practices that essentially establish that the courts in one jurisdiction will extend recognition and enforcement of rights claimed by individuals by virtue of the laws of another jurisdiction. This is why, for example, one may be married under the laws of Minnesota, move to Florida, and still be lawfully married.

ARTICLE IV

Section 1

Full Faith and Credit shall be given in each State to the public Acts, Records, and judicial Proceedings of every other State. And the Congress may by general Laws prescribe the Manner in which such Acts, Records and Proceedings shall be proved, and the Effect thereof.

Section 2

The Citizens of each State shall be entitled to all Privileges and Immunities of Citizens in the several States.

A Person charged in any State with Treason, Felony, or other Crime, who shall flee from Justice, and be found in another State, shall on Demand of the executive Authority of the State from which he fled, be delivered up, to be removed to the State having Jurisdiction of the Crime.

This clause was a pillar of the tragedy of slavery. It enabled slave owners to seize and return to slavery those who fled to free states while also prohibiting free states from granting release to those who escaped from bondage.

No Person held to Service or Labour in one State, under the Laws thereof, escaping into another, shall, in Consequence of any Law or Regulation therein, be discharged from such Service or Labour, but shall be delivered up on Claim of the Party to whom such Service or Labour may be due.

The Supreme Court has held that states enjoy "equal footing" and that "equality of constitutional right and power is the condition of all the States of the Union, old and new." See Escanaba Co. v. Chicago, 107 U.S. 678 (1883).

Section 3

New States may be admitted by the Congress into this Union; but no new State shall be formed or erected within the Jurisdiction of any other State; nor any State be formed by the Junction of two or more States, or Parts of States, without the Consent of the Legislatures of the States concerned as well as of the Congress.

The Congress shall have Power to dispose of and make all needful Rules and Regulations respecting the Territory or other Property belonging to the United States; and nothing in this Constitution shall be so construed as to Prejudice any Claims of the United States, or of any particular State.

What constitutes "a Republican Form of Government" is a political question, according to the Supreme Court: "[I]t rests with Congress to decide what government is the established one in a State . . . as well as its republican character." See Luther v. Borden, 48 U.S. 1 (1849).

Section 4

The United States shall guarantee to every State in this Union a Republican Form of Government, and shall protect each of them against Invasion; and on Application of the Legislature, or of the Executive (when the Legislature cannot be convened) against domestic Violence.

The amendment process is the means by which the Constitution may be formally modified. However, the most common way the document has been effectively changed is through evolving judicial interpretation.

ARTICLE V

The Congress, whenever two thirds of both Houses shall deem it necessary, shall propose Amendments to this Constitution, or, on the Application of the Legislatures of two thirds of the several States, shall call a Convention for proposing Amendments, which, in either Case, shall be valid to all Intents and Purposes, as Part of this Constitution, when ratified by the Legislatures of three fourths of the several States, or by Conventions in three fourths thereof, as the one or the other Mode of Ratification may be proposed by the Congress; Provided that no Amendment which may be made prior to the Year One thousand eight hundred and eight shall in any Manner affect the first and fourth Clauses in the Ninth Section of the first Article; and that no State, without its Consent, shall be deprived of its equal Suffrage in the Senate.

ARTICLE VI

All Debts contracted and Engagements entered into, before the Adoption of this Constitution, shall be as valid against the United States under this Constitution, as under the Confederation.

The Supremacy Clause asserts that "the States have no power, by taxation or otherwise, to retard, impede, burden, or in any manner control, the operations of the constitutional laws enacted by Congress." See McCulloch v. Maryland, 17 U.S. 316 (1819).

This Constitution, and the Laws of the United States which shall be made in Pursuance thereof; and all Treaties made, or which shall be made, under the Authority of the United States, shall be the supreme Law of the Land; and the Judges in every State shall be bound thereby, any Thing in the Constitution or Laws of any state to the Contrary notwithstanding.

The Senators and Representatives before mentioned, and the Members of the several State Legislatures, and all executive and judicial Officers, both of the United States and of the several States, shall be bound by Oath or Affirmation, to support this Constitution; but no religious Test shall ever be required as a Qualification to any Office or public Trust under the United States.

The Constitution was ultimately ratified by all thirteen colonies. The document did not provide for a means to address any potential political crises that might have resulted had one or more states refused to join the Union.

ARTICLE VII

The Ratification of the Conventions of nine States, shall be sufficient for the Establishment of this Constitution between the States so ratifying the same.

AMENDMENTS TO THE CONSTITUTION OF THE UNITED STATES OF AMERICA

At its base, the First Amendment guarantees spiritual and intellectual liberty. As such, it affords what are arguably the most important protections in the Constitution. Justice Harlan F. Stone suggested that First Amendment freedoms should be accorded a "preferred position" in interpreting the Constitution. See U.S. v. Carolene Products Co., 304 U.S. 144 (1938).

Amendment I (*The first ten amendments were ratified December 15, 1791*)

Congress shall make no law respecting an establishment of religion, or prohibiting the free exercise thereof; or abridging the freedom of speech, or of the press; or the right of the people peaceably to assemble, and to petition the Government for a redress of grievances.

Despite the heated political debate surrounding gun control, the Second Amendment has been the source of remarkably little Supreme Court litigation. In the most notable case, the Court

Amendment II

A well regulated Militia, being necessary to the security of a free State, the right of the people to keep and bear Arms, shall not be infringed.

upheld restrictions on sawed-off shotguns. The justices suggested that the key purpose of the amendment is to protect states' authority to maintain a militia. See U.S. v. Miller, 307 U.S. 174 (1939).

There has never been a Supreme Court case that directly addressed the Third Amendment. However, the Supreme Court referred to this amendment as part of the constitutional underpinning of the right to privacy. See Griswold v. Connecticut, 381 U.S. 479 (1965).

Amendment III

No Soldier shall, in time of peace be quartered in any house, without the consent of the Owner, nor in time of war, but in a manner to be prescribed by law.

The Fourth Amendment does not prohibit governmental searches—only "unreasonable" ones. The amendment's protections would be virtually meaningless without the exclusionary rule, which prohibits prosecutorial use of evidence obtained via improper searches. See Mapp v. Ohio, 367 U.S. 643 (1961).

Amendment IV

The right of the people to be secure in their persons, houses, papers, and effects, against unreasonable searches and seizures, shall not be violated, and no Warrants shall issue, but upon probable cause, supported by Oath or affirmation, and particularly describing the place to be searched, and the persons or things to be seized.

The Fifth Amendment
deals primarily with
criminal justice rights,
one of the most impor-
tant of which is the
guarantee of due
process—the principle
that legal procedure
must not conflict with
the Constitution or the
law, and that the law
must be equally applied.
Note that the Fifth
Amendment allows the
government, if it follows
due process, to deprive a
person of life. This is a
clear indication that
executions are permitted
under the Constitution.
The Takings Clause,
found at the end of the
Fifth, is generally not a
criminal justice matter.
However, it protects
individuals from arbi-
trary property seizures.
Note that government is
allowed to take property
(a power known as "em-
inent domain") if it
meets two requirements:
the owner must receive
"just compensation" for
the property and the
action must be for some
"public use."

Amendment V

No person shall be held to answer for a capital, or otherwise infamous crime, unless on a presentment or indictment of a Grand Jury, except in cases arising in the land or naval forces, or in the Militia, when in actual service in time of War or public danger; nor shall any person be subject for the same offence to be twice put in jeopardy of life or limb; nor shall be compelled in any criminal case to be a witness against himself, nor be deprived of life, liberty, or property, without due process of law; nor shall private property be taken for public use, without just compensation.

The Sixth Amendment is
another amendment
that confers criminal
justice guarantees. This

Amendment VI

In all criminal prosecutions, the accused shall enjoy the right to a speedy and public trial, by an impartial jury of the State and district wherein the crime shall is the second place in the Constitution where one finds the guarantee of a right to a jury trial (the first is in Art. III, Sec. 2). The right to a lawyer is also guaranteed in the Sixth Amendment. The right to retain an attorney is, in essence, the right to protect one's rights. See Gideon v. Wainwright, 372 U.S. 335 (1963). This is why, as some have noted, "probably no other right guaranteed to the criminally accused is more important than the right to counsel." See Lee Epstein and Thomas Walker, Constitutional Law for a Changing America (Washington, D.C.: CQ Press, 2001), 556.

Although the Seventh Amendment guarantees the right to a jury trial in federal civil cases, such a right has not been held to apply to state courts. See Alexander v. Virginia, 413 U.S. 836 (1973).

The Supreme Court has resisted giving an exact definition of what constitutes "cruel and unusual": "Difficulty

have been committed, which district shall have been previously ascertained by law, and to be informed of the nature and cause of the accusation; to be confronted with the witnesses against him; to have compulsory process for obtaining witnesses in his favor, and to have the Assistance of Counsel for his defence.

Amendment VII

In Suits at common law, where the value in controversy shall exceed twenty dollars, the right of trial by jury shall be preserved, and no fact tried by a jury, shall be otherwise re-examined in any Court of the United States, than according to the rules of the common law.

Amendment VIII

Excessive bail shall not be required, nor excessive fines imposed, nor cruel and unusual punishments inflicted.

would attend the effort to define with exactness the extent of the constitutional provision...."
See Wilkerson v. Utah, *99 U.S. 130 (1878).*

Federalists such as James Madison were concerned that a bill of rights could be interpreted as listing all of the rights of citizens, and thus deny more liberties than it protected (see The Federalist, No. 84*). To guard against such an interpretation, the Ninth Amendment was adopted.*

Amendment IX
The enumeration in the Constitution, of certain rights, shall not be construed to deny or disparage others retained by the people.

The Tenth Amendment has become a popular rallying point for those who seek to limit federal legislative authority and expand states' rights.

Amendment X
The powers not delegated to the United States by the Constitution, nor prohibited by it to the States, are reserved to the States respectively, or to the people.

The Eleventh Amendment was adopted in order to overturn the unpopular Supreme Court decision Chisholm v. Georgia *(2 U.S. 419 [1793]). The justices ruled in* Chisholm *that citizens of another state could*

Amendment XI *(Ratified February 7, 1795)*
The Judicial power of the United States shall not be construed to extend to any suit in law or equity, commenced or prosecuted against one of the United States by Citizens of another State, or by Citizens or Subjects of any Foreign State.

sue states in federal court. At that time many people feared that allowing such suits would interfere with states' rights.

The Twelfth Amendment modifies Art. II, Sec. 1, and was adopted to prevent the recurrence of a tie vote, as occurred in the election of 1800, when Thomas Jefferson and Aaron Burr received an equal number of votes in the electoral college. Exposing flaws of the electoral college, the close election was ultimately decided in the House of Representatives, despite the fact that the electors had intended Jefferson to be president and Burr to be vice president.

Amendment XII *(Ratified June 15, 1804)*

The Electors shall meet in their respective states and vote by ballot for President and Vice-President, one of whom, at least, shall not be an inhabitant of the same state with themselves; they shall name in their ballots the person voted for as President, and in distinct ballots the person voted for as Vice-President, and they shall make distinct lists of all persons voted for as President, and of all persons voted for as Vice-President, and of the number of votes for each, which lists they shall sign and certify, and transmit sealed to the seat of the government of the United States, directed to the President of the Senate;—The President of the Senate shall, in the presence of the Senate and House of Representatives, open all the certificates and the votes shall then be counted;—The person having the greatest Number of votes for President, shall be the President, if such number be a majority of the whole number of Electors appointed; and if no person have such majority, then from the persons having the highest numbers not exceeding three on the list of those voted for as President, the House of Representatives shall choose immediately, by ballot, the President. But in choosing the President, the votes shall be taken by states, the representation from each state having one vote; a quorum for this purpose shall consist of a member or members from two-thirds of the states, and a majority of all the states shall be necessary to a choice. And if the House of Representatives shall not choose a President whenever the right of choice shall devolve upon them, before the fourth day of March next following, then the Vice-President shall act as President, as in the case of the death or other constitutional disability of the President—The person having the greatest number of votes as Vice-President, shall be the Vice-President, if such number be a majority of the whole number of Electors appointed, and if no person have a majority, then from the two highest numbers on the list, the Senate shall choose the Vice-President; a quorum for the purpose shall consist of two-thirds of the whole number of Senators, and a majority of the whole number shall be necessary to a choice. But no person constitutionally ineligible to the office of President shall be eligible to that of Vice-President of the United States.

The first of the three Civil War amendments, the Thirteenth effectively codified President Abraham Lincoln's 1863 proclamation freeing the slaves.

Amendment XIII *(Ratified December 6, 1865)*
Section 1. Neither slavery nor involuntary servitude, except as a punishment for crime whereof the party shall have been duly convicted, shall exist within the United States, or any place subject to their jurisdiction.

Section 2. Congress shall have power to enforce this article by appropriate legislation.

The Fourteenth Amendment is profoundly important on a number of fronts. The Citizenship Clause overturned the Supreme Court's decision in Dred Scott v. Sanford *(60 U.S. 393 [1857]) and conferred citizenship—and thus legal rights—upon former slaves. This amendment enshrines the citizenship principle of* jus solis, *in which*

Amendment XIV *(Ratified July 9, 1868)*
Section 1. All persons born or naturalized in the United States and subject to the jurisdiction thereof, are citizens of the United States and of the State wherein they reside. No State shall make or enforce any law which shall abridge the privileges or immunities of citizens of the United States; nor shall any State deprive any person of life, liberty, or property, without due process of law; nor deny to any person within its jurisdiction the equal protection of the laws.

Section 2. Representatives shall be apportioned among the several States according to their respective numbers, counting the whole number of persons in *citizenship is determined by place of birth. The Privileges and Immunities Clause was effectively undermined in the Slaughter House Cases (83 U.S. 36 [1873]). However, the Fourteenth's Equal Protection and Due Process Clauses have been the means by which the Supreme Court has applied to the states most of the provisions of the Bill of Rights, and the clauses are frequently the basis for legal challenges to laws that are alleged to be discriminatory.*

each State, excluding Indians not taxed. But when the right to vote at any election for the choice of electors for President and Vice President of the United States, Representatives in Congress, the Executive and Judicial officers of a State, or the members of the Legislature thereof, is denied to any of the male inhabitants of such State, being twenty-one years of age, and citizens of the United States, or in any way abridged, except for participation in rebellion, or other crime, the basis of representation therein shall be reduced in the proportion which the number of such male citizens shall bear to the whole number of male citizens twenty-one years of age in such State.

Section 3. No person shall be a Senator or Representative in Congress, or elector of President and Vice President, or hold any office, civil or military, under the United States, or under any State, who, having previously taken an oath, as a member of Congress, or as an officer of the United States, or as a member of any State legislature, or as an executive or judicial officer of any State, to support the Constitution of the United States, shall have engaged in insurrection or rebellion against the same, or given aid or comfort to the enemies thereof. But Congress may by a vote of two-thirds of each House, remove such disability.

Section 4. The validity of the public debt of the United States, authorized by law, including debts incurred for payment of pensions and bounties for services in suppressing insurrection or rebellion, shall not be questioned. But neither the United States nor any State shall assume or pay any debt or obligation incurred in aid of insurrection or rebellion against the United States, or any claim for the loss or emancipation of any slave; but all such debts, obligations and claims shall be held illegal and void.

Section 5. The Congress shall have power to enforce, by appropriate legislation, the provisions of this article.

Although the Fifteenth Amendment has prohibited racial discrimination in voting since its ratification in 1870, in the period after its approval states adopted a number of voting hurdles. Among these were poll taxes, white primaries (intraparty elections in which only whites could vote), literacy tests, racial gerrymanders (the drawing of electoral district boundaries to maximize the advantage of whites), and grandfather clauses. These impediments had profoundly discriminatory effects and ran directly counter to the spirit of the Fifteenth Amendment.

Amendment XV *(Ratified February 3, 1870)*
Section 1. The right of citizens of the United States to vote shall not be denied or abridged by the United States or by any State on account of race, color, or previous condition of servitude.

Section 2. The Congress shall have power to enforce this article by appropriate legislation.

The Sixteenth Amendment is another amendment that negated a Supreme Court decision. The Court initially overturned the federal income tax in its ruling in Pollock v. Farmers' Loan & Trust Co. *(157 U.S. 429 [1895]; 158 U.S. 601 [1895]).*

Amendment XVI *(Ratified February 3, 1913)*
The Congress shall have power to lay and collect taxes on incomes, from whatever source derived, without apportionment among the several States, and without regard to any census or enumeration.

Amendment XVII *(Ratified April 8, 1913)*
The Senate of the United States shall be composed of two Senators from each State, elected by the people thereof, for six years; and each Senator shall have one vote. The electors in each State shall have the qualifications requisite for electors of the most numerous branch of the State legislatures.

When vacancies happen in the representation of any State in the Senate, the executive authority of such State shall issue writs of election to fill such vacancies: Provided, That the legislature of any State may empower the executive thereof to make temporary appointments until the people fill the vacancies by election as the legislature may direct.

This amendment shall not be so construed as to affect the election or term of any Senator chosen before it becomes valid as part of the Constitution.

Amendment XVIII *(Ratified January 16, 1919)*
Section 1. After one year from the ratification of this article the manufacture, sale, or transportation of intoxicating liquors within, the importation thereof into, or the exportation thereof from the United States and all territory subject to the jurisdiction thereof for beverage purposes is hereby prohibited.

Section 2. The Congress and the several States shall have concurrent power to enforce this article by appropriate legislation.

Section 3. This article shall be inoperative unless it shall have been ratified as an amendment to the Constitution by the legislatures of the several States, as provided in the Constitution, within seven years from the date of the submission hereof to the States by the Congress.

The Eighteenth Amendment, the nation's disastrous experiment with writing public policy into the Constitution, was later overturned by the Twenty-first Amendment.

In 1914, women in only eleven states enjoyed some voting rights, although Wyoming had famously accorded universal suffrage to women as early as 1869.

Amendment XIX *(Ratified August 18, 1920)*

The right of citizens of the United States to vote shall not be denied or abridged by the United States or by any State on account of sex. Congress shall have power to enforce this article by appropriate legislation.

Amendment XX *(Ratified January 23, 1933)*

Section 1. The terms of the President and Vice President shall end at noon on the 20th day of January, and the terms of Senators and Representatives at noon on the 3d day of January, of the years in which such terms would have ended if this article had not been ratified; and the terms of their successors shall then begin.

Section 2. The Congress shall assemble at least once in every year, and such meeting shall begin at noon on the 3d day of January, unless they shall by law appoint a different day.

Section 3. If, at the time fixed for the beginning of the term of the President, the President elect shall have died, the Vice President elect shall become President. If a President shall not have been chosen before the time fixed for the beginning of his term, or if the President elect shall have failed to qualify, then the Vice President elect shall act as President until a President shall have qualified; and the Congress may by law provide for the case wherein neither a President elect nor a Vice President elect shall have qualified, declaring who shall then act as President, or the manner in which one who is to act shall be selected, and such person shall act accordingly until a President or Vice President shall have qualified.

Section 4. The Congress may by law provide for the case of the death of any of the persons from whom the

House of Representatives may choose a President whenever the right of choice shall have devolved upon them, and for the case of the death of any of the persons from whom the Senate may choose a Vice President whenever the right of choice shall have devolved upon them.

Section 5. Sections 1 and 2 shall take effect on the 15th day of October following the ratification of this article.

Section 6. This article shall be inoperative unless it shall have been ratified as an amendment to the Constitution by the legislatures of three-fourths of the several States within seven years from the date of its submission.

Amendment XXI *(Ratified December 5, 1933)*

Section 1. The eighteenth article of amendment to the Constitution of the United States is hereby repealed.

Section 2. The transportation or importation into any State, Territory, or possession of the United States for delivery or use therein of intoxicating liquors, in violation of the laws thereof, is hereby prohibited.

Section 3. This article shall be inoperative unless it shall have been ratified as an amendment to the Constitution by conventions in the several States, as provided in the Constitution, within seven years from the date of the submission hereof to the States by the Congress.

Amendment XXII *(Ratified February 27, 1951)*

Section 1. No person shall be elected to the office of the President more than twice, and no person who has held the office of President, or acted as President, for more than two years of a term to which some other person was elected President shall be elected to the office of the President more than once.

The Twenty-first is the only amendment adopted by ratifying conventions in three-fourths of the states. All other amendments have been approved by state legislatures.

Presidents prior to Franklin D. Roosevelt followed a long-standing tradition, established by George Washington, of serving for no more than two terms. Breaking the unwritten rule, FDR was elected four times. The Twenty-second Amendment was adopted to formalize the two-term tradition.

But this Article shall not apply to any person holding the office of President, when this Article was proposed by the Congress, and shall not prevent any person who may be holding the office of President, or acting as President, during the term within which this Article becomes operative from holding the office of President or acting as President during the remainder of such term.

Section 2. This article shall be inoperative unless it shall have been ratified as an amendment to the Constitution by the legislatures of three-fourths of the several States within seven years from the date of its submission to the States by the Congress.

Over the past forty years, numerous proposals have been made to pass a constitutional amendment that would remove the District of Columbia from the control of Congress and grant it status as a state. However, the issue of D.C. statehood gets entangled with party politics, and the idea has gained little traction. Because the District of Columbia is a bastion of Democratic Party support, Republicans have generally resisted the idea of establishing it as the fifty-first state.

Amendment XXIII *(Ratified March 29, 1961)*
Section 1. The District constituting the seat of Government of the United States shall appoint in such manner as the Congress may direct: A number of electors of President and Vice President equal to the whole number of Senators and Representatives in Congress to which the District would be entitled if it were a State, but in no event more than the least populous State; they shall be in addition to those appointed by the States, but they shall be considered, for the purposes of the election of President and Vice President, to be electors appointed by a State; and they shall meet in the District and perform such duties as provided by the twelfth article of amendment.

Section 2. The Congress shall have power to enforce this article by appropriate legislation.

The poll tax was adopted by a number of southern states as a means of

Amendment XXIV *(Ratified January 23, 1964)*
Section 1. The right of citizens of the United States to vote in any primary or other election for President or Vice President, for electors for President or Vice

discouraging the poor—and especially African Americans—from voting. The Twenty-fourth Amendment was ratified in 1964 to force these states to end the discriminatory policy.

President, or for Senator or Representative in Congress, shall not be denied or abridged by the United States or any State by reason of failure to pay any poll tax or other tax.

Section 2. The Congress shall have power to enforce this article by appropriate legislation.

Amendment XXV *(Ratified February 10, 1967)*
Section 1. In case of the removal of the President from office or of his death or resignation, the Vice President shall become President.

Section 2. Whenever there is a vacancy in the office of the Vice President, the President shall nominate a Vice President who shall take office upon confirmation by a majority vote of both Houses of Congress.

Section 3. Whenever the President transmits to the President pro tempore of the Senate and the Speaker of the House of Representatives has written declaration that he is unable to discharge the powers and duties of his office, and until he transmits to them a written declaration to the contrary, such powers and duties shall be discharged by the Vice President as Acting President.

Section 4. Whenever the Vice President and a majority of either the principal officers of the executive departments or of such other body as Congress may by law provide, transmit to the President pro tempore of the Senate and the Speaker of the House of Representatives their written declaration that the President is unable to discharge the powers and duties of his office, the Vice President shall immediately assume the powers and duties of the office as Acting President.

Thereafter, when the President transmits to the President pro tempore of the Senate and the Speaker of the House of Representatives has written declaration that no inability exists, he shall resume the powers and duties of his office unless the Vice President and a majority of either the principal officers of the executive department or of such other body as Congress may by law provide, transmit within four days to the President pro tempore of the Senate and the Speaker of the House of Representatives their written declaration that the President is unable to discharge the powers and duties of his office. Thereupon Congress shall decide the issue, assembling within forty-eight hours for that purpose if not in session. If the Congress, within twenty-one days after receipt of the latter written declaration, or, if Congress is not in session, within twenty-one days after Congress is required to assemble, determines by two-thirds vote of both Houses that the President is unable to discharge the powers and duties of his office, the Vice President shall continue to discharge the same as Acting President; otherwise, the President shall resume the powers and duties of his office.

The Voting Rights Act of 1965 extended the right to vote in federal, state, and local elections to those aged eighteen and older. However, in Oregon v. Mitchell (400 U.S. 112 [1970]) the Supreme Court determined that Congress did not have the authority to set age requirements for state and local elections. The Twenty-sixth Amendment was quickly passed, circumventing the Court's ruling.

Amendment XXVI *(Ratified July 1, 1971)*

Section 1. The right of citizens of the United States, who are eighteen years of age or older, to vote shall not be denied or abridged by the United States or by any State on account of age.

Section 2. The Congress shall have power to enforce this article by appropriate legislation.

This amendment was initially proposed in 1789 but received scant support at the time. It was approved eighty-four years later, in 1873, by the Ohio legislature, and, following research by an enterprising legislative staff person in Texas, was revisited and finally approved in 1992. Thus 203 years elapsed between the initial proposal and final ratification. See Richard Bernstein, "The Sleeper Wakes: The History and Legacy of the Twenty-seventh Amendment," Fordham Law Review 61 (1992):497.

Amendment XXVII *(Ratified May 7, 1992)*

No law varying the compensation for the services of the Senators and Representatives shall take effect, until an election of Representatives shall have intervened.

Subject Index

Case Index